CLASS
STATE
IDEOLOGY
AND
CHANGE

CLASS
STATE
IDEOLOGY
—AND—
CHANGE

J. PAUL GRAYSON

Department of Sociology
Atkinson College, York University

MARXIST PERSPECTIVES ON CANADA

Canadian Cataloguing in Publication Data
Main entry under title:
Class, state, ideology and change
ISBN 0-03-920127-9

1. Socialism and society - Addresses, essays, lectures. 2. Canada -
Economic conditions - Addresses, essays, lectures. 3. Canada - Social
conditions - Addresses, essays, lectures. 4. Labor and laboring classes
- Canada - Addresses, essays, lectures. I. Grayson, John Paul, 1944-

HX542.C53   330.971'06   C80-094066-0

31, 992

Printed in Canada

1 2 3 4 5   84 83 82 81 80

PREFACE

Class, State, Ideology and Change: Marxist Perspectives on Canada, is a collection of articles on Canada written in a way consistent with some of the fundamental concerns of Marxism. The contributions are from individuals who, according to conventional classifications, can be described as anthropologists, historians, political economists, and sociologists. It is clear, however, that their scholarly interests cut across conventional disciplinary boundaries. To put the matter another way, the collection has an inter-disciplinary orientation. Hopefully, it therefore will be of interest to students in more than one field.

Although the articles are grouped under the headings class, state, ideology and change, the concerns of many span more than one of these categories. In addition, the articles deal with matters of fundamental concern to Canadians: the question of unequal exchanges among regions, Canadian and Quebec nationalism, the ideological mechanisms that support unequal treatment of women, deindustrialization, and so on. A final section of the book focuses on the indigenous Canadian political economy tradition and Marxism.

The *General Introduction* that precedes the readings is intended to provide those new to Marxism with a very broad idea of the ways in which the concepts class, state, ideology and change are used by some well known theorists. There has been no attempt made to introduce the reader to the complex debates currently under way in Marxist circles. (Marxist journals themselves provide a better vehicle for such discussions.) In turn, each of the major sections of the book is preceded by a brief introduction. These link relevant dimensions of the articles that follow them to matters raised in the *General Introduction*.

The collection as it stands can easily be used as the major text in lower level courses dealing with Canada. In upper level courses it might be supplemented by other collections such as Leo Panitch (ed.), *The Canadian State*. Other relevant materials can be found in the bibliography by Clement et al. described in the *Postscript* to this volume.

ACKNOWLEDGEMENTS

I would like to thank Carl Cuneo, Linda Grayson and Jerry Hunnius for helpful comments on the organization and content of this book. I would also like to thank Joe McKeon for expediting publication.

J. Paul Grayson

R.T. Naylor. "Dominion of Capital: Canada and International Investment". Reprinted from *Domination*, edited by Alkis Kontos, by permission of University of Toronto Press.© University of Toronto Press 1975.

Steven Langdon. "The Emergence of the Canadian Working Class Movement, 1845-75". Reprinted from *The Journal of Canadian Studies,* Volume 8:2 by permission of the author.

Craig Heron and Bryan D. Palmer. "Through the Prism of the Strike: Industrial Conflict in Southern Ontario, 1901-14". Reprinted from *Canadian Historical Review,* Volume 58, by permission of the authors and University of Toronto Press.

Bernard Bernier. "The Penetration of Capitalism in Quebec Agriculture". Reprinted from *The Canadian Review of Sociology and Anthropology,* Volume 13:4, by permission of the author and the publisher.

Carl J. Cuneo. "Class Contradictions in Canada's International Setting". Reprinted from The Canadian Review of Sociology and Anthropology, Volume 16:1, by permission of the author and the publisher.

K. Mellos. "Developments in Advanced Capitalist Ideology". Reprinted from *Canadian Journal of Political Science,* Volume 11:4, December, 1978, by permission of the author and the publisher.

Carl J. Cuneo. "State, Class and Reserve Labour: The Case of the 1941 Canadian Unemployment Insurance Act". Reprinted from *The Canadian Review of Sociology and Anthropology,* Volume 16:2, by permission of the author and the publisher.

Rianne Mahon. "Regulatory Agencies: Captive Agents or Hegemonic Apparatuses". Reprinted from *Studies in Political Economy,* Volume 1:1, Spring 1979, by permission.

Christopher Huxley. "The State, Collective Bargaining and the Shape of Strikes in Canada." Reprinted from *Canadian Journal of Sociology: Le Journal de Sociologie Canadien,* Spring 1979, by permission of the author and the publisher.

Allan Smith. "The Myth of the Self-Made Man in English Canada, 1850-1914". Reprinted from *Canadian Historical Review,* Volume 59:2, by permission of the author and University of Toronto Press.

Marcel Rioux. "The Development of Ideologies in Quebec". Reprinted from *Communities and Change in French Canada,* 1973 by permission of Holt, Rinehart and Winston of Canada, Limited.

Jack Layton. "Nationalism and the Canadian Bourgeoisie: Contradictions of Dependence". Reprinted from *Canadian Review of Studies in Nationalism*, Volume 3:2, by permission of University of Prince Edward Island, Charlottetown.

J. Paul Grayson and L.M. Grayson. "Class and Ideologies of Class in the English-Canadian Novel". Reprinted from *The Canadian Review of Sociology and Anthropology*, Volume 15:3, by permission of the author and the publisher.

D. Smith. "An Analysis of Ideological Structures and How Women are Excluded: Considerations for Academic Women". Reprinted from *The Canadian Review of Sociology and Anthropology*, Volume 12:4 (1), by permission of the author and the publisher.

H. Veltmeyer. "Dependency and Underdevelopment: Some Questions and Problems". Reprinted from *Canadian Journal of Political and Social Theory*, Volume Two, No. Two, Spring/Summer 1978, pp. 55-71, by permission.

David Frank. "The Cape Breton Coal Industry and the Rise and Fall of the British Empire Steel Corporation". Reprinted from *Acadiensis*, VII (Autumn 1977) pp. 3-34, by permission of the author and the publisher.

J.F. Conway. "Populism in the United States, Russia and Canada: Explaining the roots of Canada's Third Parties". Reprinted from *Canadian Journal of Political Science*, Volume 11:1, March, 1978, by permission of the author and the publisher.

Paul Bélanger and Céline Saint-Pierre. "Economic Dependence, Political Subordination and National Oppression". Reprinted from *Sociologie et sociétés, Volume 10:2, October, 1978, by permission of les Presses de l'Université de Montréal, Montréal.*

J. Paul Grayson and L.M. Grayson. "Unequal Cultural Exchange: A Study of Regionalism and Canadian Writers". Reprinted from brief presented to the Annual Meetings of the Canadian Sociology and Anthropology Association, June, 1979, by permission of the authors.

Paul Lamy. "The Globalization of American Sociology: Excellence or Imperialism". Reprinted from *The American Sociologist*, Volume 11, May 1976, pp. 104-114, by permission of the author and The American Sociological Association.

Ian Parker. "Harold Innis, Karl Marx and Canadian Political Economy". Reprinted from *Queen's Quarterly*, Volume 84:4, Winter 1977, by permission of the author and the publisher.

Mel Watkins. "The Staple Theory Revisited". Reprinted from *Journal of Canadian Studies*, Volume 12:5, Winter 1977, by permission of the author and the publisher.

Photograph on front cover: courtesy of Miller Services, Inc.

CONTENTS

Change

Marxism and Canadian Political Economy

ERRATA

Errors corrected below were identified after pages in which they appear were printed. They are the responsibility of the publisher and not the editor, J. Paul Grayson.

p. 44,   left column, line 7, should read: "aid had been given by the IMU Central Fund"

p. 99,   right column, lines 27-30 should read: "capitalism has brought about an intensification and diversification in class contradictions. Since the growth of US monopoly capitalism in Canada has been mainly in the sphere"

p. 163,   right column, last line, should read: "increased from $520 million in 1971 to $553"

p. 169:   The reference to Lipset in the third sentence of the section "The Shape of Strikes in Canada" should read page 204. The sixth sentence in the same paragraph should state that Shorter and Tilly use the measure of "man-days lost per striker" to make international comparisons of average strike duration. The accompanying footnote 3 explains why Shorter and Tilly use the median to measure the average duration of strikes, but this applies to their study of strikes in France and not to the discussion of international differences in strike activity. Footnote 7 should give 1927 as the year of publication for Selekman's book. Lastly, the year of publication for Woods' Labour Policy in Canada should be listed in the "References" as 1973.

p. 183,   left column, line 31, should read: "than the American state has. While the policy"

p. 208,   left column, line 10, should read: "The national element would be merged in"

p. 214,   left column, lines 46-7, should read: "knew each other and the prince granted his largesse to the good (those who voted for him)"

p. 215,   right column, lines 42-43, should read: "We would like now to characterize this third ideology, which *Cité Libre* set itself"

p. 219:   Note 5 should give the title of Wade's book as *The French Canadians 1760 - 1967.*

p. 235,   right column, last line, should read: "are manifested. As a consequence we decided to"

In the article by Marcel Rioux, "The Development of Ideologies in Quebec," (pp. 205-220) IDEOLOGUE has been misspelled.

GENERAL
INTRODUCTION

Introduction

A decade ago, Canadian undergraduates would have been hard pressed to identify any works on Canada written from a Marxist perspective. Faculty would not have fared much better. Some would have been able to mention Marcel Rioux's, *Quebec in Question* (English edition, 1971). Others might have known C.B. Macpherson's, *Democracy in Alberta* (1953), or Stanley Ryerson's, *Unequal Union* (1968). The well-informed would have been able to add at least one of Pentland's articles (1959) to the list. But, by and large, most would have been unaware of these works.

The same may be true today. In 1980, however, no one can hide behind the excuse, somewhat legitimate a decade ago, that few Marxist analyses of Canadian society are readily available. Although Marxism is not the dominant perspective from which Canadian society is usually analysed, over the last ten years, scholars in a variety of disciplines have contributed some first-rate works from this perspective.

A number of these appeared in Ian Lumsden's, *Close the 49th Parellel* (1970). This volume was followed by, among others, Gary Teeple's, *Capitalism and the National Question in Canada* (1972). In 1977, Leo Panitch edited a collection of original articles on the Canadian state under the title, *The Canadian State: Political Economy and Political Power*. The collection, *Underdevelopment and Social Movements in Atlantic Canada* (1979), edited by Brym and Sacouman, is in the same tradition.

Collections of readings are not the only form in which Marxist studies have appeared. (Nor are those mentioned the only ones available). Marxist notions clearly underlay some aspects of the examination of continental elites undertaken by Wallace Clement in, *Continental Corporate Power* (1977). The same holds true for R.T. Naylor's two volume *The History of Canadian Business, 1867-1914* (1975). Indeed, if the number of acrimonious reviews generated by a work is any measure of its importance, Naylor's work is among the most significant of the decade.

Less read, but equally insightful, is Philip Resnick's, *The Land of Cain: Class and Nationalism in English Canada, 1945-1975* (1977), that offers an excellent analysis of the class base of Post-War Canadian nationalism.

At a more popular level, for some time, *Canadian Dimension* has provided a number of Marxist critiques and interpretations of Canadian developments. In English Canada, *This Magazine, Our Generation* and *The Last Post* have participated in similar activities. In Quebec, certain magazines have also supplied popular interpretations of social and political developments. An indication of Quebec's receptivity to popular expressions of Marxism is provided by the tens of thousands of copies of Léandre Bergeron's, *History of Quebec* (English edition, 1971) that have been sold. Countless thousands of Quebecois have also been reached by the comic book version of this particular work.

It is not possible to list all the important works from a Marxist perspective that have emerged over the last ten years. Nor, for that matter, is it necessary. It is important to stress that the unavailability of materials can no longer be viewed as a legitimate excuse for excluding Marxist materials from courses in Canadian history, political science, economics, anthropology, and sociology.

Given the number of available works, it is also questionable that a comprehensive course on Canada can be offered without reference to Marxist materials. Clearly, it is now possible to point to a nascent Marxist school of thought in most academic disciplines dealing with Canada. The point is brought home by the fact that in addition to the sources cited, many of the major Canadian academic journals, have, over the past decade, published articles written from a Marxist viewpoint. It was partially in an attempt to make some of these materials more accessible to undergraduate students and instructors, and to provide a general collection of Marxist oriented reading for courses on Canada, that the present volume was put together.

It must be stressed at the outset, that there is no consensus concerning the nature of good

Marxist analysis. It is likely, therefore, that some readers will disagree with the inclusion of some of the articles in this volume. *The criterion used in making the selection was that the readings could answer questions that might be raised within a general Marxist framework.*

Some writings, such as those by Cuneo and Mellos, are explicit in their use of Marxist terms and ideas. Others, like those by Naylor and Langdon, are less explicit: they may not use as much Marxist terminology; but their overall analysis is consistent with fundamental Marxist propositions. In at least one case—the article by Lamy—important questions are asked. But they are not then answered in a clear Marxist fashion. The article nonetheless effectively sets the stage for following ones that take up, and attempt to deal with, from a Marxist perspective, some of the implications of Lamy's analysis. Of other inclusions, it might be said that while the articles deal with matters in a way that is consistent with basic Marxist tenets, *we cannot necessarily assume that their authors consider themselves Marxist scholars.* While the distinction is a fine one, it is nonetheless important. It is unlikely, however, that there are many cases in which the perspective revealed by the particular work is not indicative of a general acceptance by the author of Marxist theory, or aspects of it.

A close reading of the following articles should enable those unfamiliar with Marxist thought to grasp some of its fundamentals. It should also provide a general idea of the ways in which works from a Marxist framework can enhance our understanding of Canadian history and society. Although many of the main points of Marxist thought and the most important features of Canadian society can be grasped in this manner, it might prove useful, at this juncture, to mention, briefly, some of the important ideas that will reappear throughout the text.

Some of the most important concepts include class, state, ideology and change. Others could also be added to the list. In any one analysis, it is often difficult to tell which of these concepts is central. One of the strengths of the works included in this book, however, is that, in general, they do not attempt to restrict themselves to the elaboration of a particular concept. Rather, they attempt to analyse Canadian social phenomena utilizing whatever concepts are necessary. In addition, these analyses are not restricted by narrow and artificial disciplinary boundaries. Both of these points help account for the ability of the Marxist perspective to inspire totalistic and integrated analyses of social phenomena.

Despite these caveats, for the sake of convenience, the readings are organized in terms of the four basic concepts previously noted: class, state, ideology and change. In addition, an attempt is made, in a final section, to demonstrate some of the linkages that exist between what can be described as Canadian political economy and Marxism. More than one student of Canadian society has viewed Marxism, as revealed in articles such as the following, as in many ways the heir to the indigenous Canadian political economy tradition that suffered a near fatal blow as a consequence of the wholesale Americanization of academia that has occurred over the past fifteen or so years.

Before embarking on a general discussion of some important concepts, it is imperative to note the current range of work that can be placed under a general Marxist rubric. Debates centring on the nature of the state that have appeared in the *New Left Review* are one indication of a broad diversity of opinion. Other discussions have focused on the nature of the 'white collar', 'middle', or 'new petty bourgeois' class that is found in advanced capitalist societies. Rather than reproduce these debates, an outline will be given of some basic concepts and the ways in which they have been used by some Marxist scholars. This practice implicitly favours some usages over others and, in essence, downplays some important current debates that are taking place in Marxist circles. At the same time, this tactic may enable readers unfamiliar with Marxist ideas to more adequately grasp the implications of the following articles.

Class

Within the Marxist perspective, class is defined in terms of the relations of individuals to the means of production. The *means of production* include such things as, "on the one hand useful materials from natural sources: minerals, coal, petroleum, wood, water, etc; and on the other hand the instruments of production: tools, machinery, and . . . advanced equipment . . . " (Jalée, 1977:10). In some cases, those who extract resources, produce commodities, grow things, and so on, own the means of production. Such was the case with the independent artisan in the Middle Ages or the independent prairie farmer in twentieth-century Canada. In other cases, those who extract resources, produce commodities, or grow things do not own their means of production. Rather, they work for those who do. In return for their labour, they are paid wages. This situation typifies workers in Canadian mines, factories, and employees on large company farms. In very broad and simplified terms, then, we can initially identify, in Canadian society, a *bourgeoisie*, who own the means of production, and a *proletariat*, or *working class*, who work for wages.

In addition, there are two further general classes that require identification. First, there are those who, in a sense, like many farmers and small businessmen, own their means of production, yet do not hire people. Or, if they do hire, it is a very small number. Such individuals do not compare to corporate giants like General Motors or IBM. They are therefore placed in a separate category usually called the *petty bourgeoisie*. Second, in advanced capitalist societies like Canada, there are large numbers of individuals who neither own their own means of production nor engage in production, extraction or agriculture. Teachers, state functionaries, some professionals, technocrats, etc. can be placed in this class. Such individuals clearly expedite certain operations essential to the smooth functioning of capitalist society. For the time being, they can be termed the *new petty bourgeoisie* (Poulantzas, 1978). It should be pointed out, however, that some analysts simply view these groups as extensions of the proletariat, or working class (Miliband, 1977).

It might also be noted that the *means of production* as defined here, in conjunction with: 1) the actual *labour power* of individuals carrying out their activities; and 2) the skills, techniques, etc., that form part of the common stock of social knowledge (these things are frequently referred to as *general labour*), constitute the *productive forces* of society. In combination, the relations to the means of production and the productive

forces are referred to as the *mode of production* that typifies society. The dominant mode in Canada is capitalist.

According to Mandel (1976), the capitalist mode of production, in general, has three features. At least two of these have been mentioned in connection with the specific description of classes in Canada. The first characteristic is the "separation of the producer from his means of production" (1976:31). A second is "the concentration of the means of production in monolopy form and in the hands of a single social class, the bourgeoisie" (1976:33). The third feature involves the existence "of a social class which has no possessions save its own hands and no means of subsistence other than the sale of its labour power" (1976:34).

Once again, a caveat is in order. Some theorists, when defining the mode of production, also include the entire ideological apparatus of a society as part of the mode of production (Laclau, 1977; Williams, 1977). For the time being, however, we will accept the minimal definition advanced here. Modifications can be made when the necessity arises. It will be clear later that an understanding of the concept of mode of production is essential to a number of articles included in the volume.

What does require further elaboration at this juncture is the division that can frequently occur within one class. This possibility, it will be seen later, goes a long way toward explaining the weakness of the Canadian industrial bourgeoisie and the consequent Americanization of the economy. In general, Poulantzas argues that, "The Marxist theory of social classes . . . distinguishes *fractions* and strata of a class . . . on the basis of differentiation in the economic sphere, and of the role . . . of political and ideological relations. The theory," he continues, "also distinguishes *social categories*, defined principally by their place in the political and ideological relations" (1978:23). Thus, while in broadest terms, classes can be defined initially in terms of relations to the means of production, it is clear that political and ideological matters help distinguish different groups within classes.

Also important are discriminations that can be made between *class origin*, *class determination*, and *class position* (Poulantzas,

1978). The first, quite simply, refers to the class into which an individual is born. Many elite studies that have been carried out on Canadian society (e.g. Porter, 1965; Clement, 1975) have made the discovery of the class origins of elite members one of their primary objectives. But more important, in any class analysis, is an examination of class determination and class position. The former refers to the structural position–proletarian, new petty bourgeois, etc.–occupied by an individual or group. The latter can loosely be viewed as the political and/or ideological stance taken by a particular class. For example, if members of the new petty bourgeoisie help advance the interests of the working class, their class position is proletarian. Their class determination remains petty bourgeois; their class origins may be quite varied. Designations such as these enable the researcher to distinguish between class as an analytical category and class as an empirical referent.

In any society, the number and nature of classes are variable. So are the relations between them. Some historical periods or societies are characterized by wholesale conflict between classes. Such overt struggles are currently underway in France and Italy. In other periods or societies, the struggle between classes is more muted, usually because one class has the upper hand, not only in the economic, but in the political and ideological realms as well. Although there have been periodical fluctuations, it is clear that in Canada the bourgeoisie have enjoyed a *hegemony* in all three realms. The consequence has been an absence in Canada of the more dramatic symptoms–like revolutions–of class struggle experienced in some European societies.

Class struggle is nonetheless ubiquitous. It is built into the antagonistic relations between labour and capital in capitalist societies like Canada. The wealth and power of the bourgeoisie are contingent upon their continuing ability to extract *surplus value* from the working class. In essence, part of the labour carried out by the worker is needed to sustain himself/herself and his/her family. The value of such labour is received by the worker in the form of wages. A second component of the worker's labour eventually accrues to the bourgeoisie in the form of profits.

Although this is a crude digest of a complicated theoretical matter, it is clear, from the Marxist perspective, that the only way in which the working class can receive the full product of its labour is through the elimination of the class responsible for its exploitation. The bourgeoisie can only exist as a class so long as it continues to appropriate a portion of the labour of the proletariat. Consequently, the potential for overt class conflict is ever present.

State

There is no agreement among Marxists concerning the nature and functions of the state (Gold et al., 1975). In his controversial, *The State in Capitalist Society*, Miliband (1969) distinguishes between the 'state system' and the 'political system.' The former is composed of "the government, the administration, the military and the police, the judicial branch, sub-central government and parliamentary assemblies" (1969:54). The latter "includes many institutions, for example parties and pressure groups, which are of major importance in the political process" (1969:54). These bodies, like giant corporations, wield power. But not state power.

Taking a different tact, some Marxists focus on the state in terms of its repressive and ideological components (Althusser, 1971b). Although there is disagreement over the extent to which various social institutions can be included in what are referred to as the apparatuses of state, many accept the existence of an *ideological state apparatus* and a *repressive state apparatus*. The former, which *can* include the educational system, the mass media, and even the family, ensures the dissemination of ideas and beliefs that are consistent with the continued rule of the bourgeoisie. The latter, that embraces the judiciary, the police, the military, etc., can be used to repress the activities of those who step out of line. Although the divisions between the apparatuses are not always easily seen–some institutions may have roles in both apparatuses–both are responsible for the production and reproduction of capitalist social relations. In addition, in advanced capitalist societies, the role of the ideological state apparatus is more and more important in the maintenance of the status quo (Miliband, 1977). For it is in these societies that, in a sense, the economic conditions are most antithetical to a perpetuation of the capitalist system.

Independent of how they define the state, for most Marxists, class and state are closely related. Yet once again there are differences of opinion. On one side, although their numbers are dwindling, are those who view the state as the exclusive agent of the bourgeoisie. The state, through its agencies, acts in a way that is always consistent with the interests of the owners of the means of production. In a sense, state policies and activities merely reflect the aspirations of one class.

A more acceptable position centres on the notion that the state has a certain amount of autonomy vis à vis the various classes found in a capitalist society. As a consequence, it can enact measures that ostensibly are in keeping with the interests of, for example, the working class. The enactment in various capitalist societies of unemployment insurance schemes is a case in point. Despite policies such as these, it is argued that all activities of the state, in the long run, can be viewed as attempts to further the interests of the dominant class or class fraction. If unemployment insurance is to the advantage of the working class, it also contributes to labour stability and consequent increased profits for the bourgeoisie.

It is important to note, however, that the state can miscalculate. The introduction of measures intended to further the long-term interests of specific classes or fractions can backfire. The behaviour of some states prior to revolutionary overthrows is proof of this contention.

Definitions of the state and its relations to classes are not the only matters over which theorists disagree. Opinion is also divided on the means whereby class interests are channelled into state activities. For some (Miliband, 1969), the state behaves in a fashion consistent with predominantly bourgeois class interests because of the formal and informal ties that exist between members of the bourgeoisie and a state elite. Frequently, this is referred to as the *instrumentalist* position. That these ties exist in Canada has been demonstrated by a number of researchers (Clement, 1975, 1977; Fournier, 1976; Newman, 1975; Olsen, 1977; Porter, 1965). Closely related is a second interpretation: independent of personal connections, the capitalist class, because of superior resources, organization through pressure groups, etc., is capable of wielding a disproportionate amount of influence on the various agencies of state. The activities of companies engaged in the exploitation of the Athabasca tar sands (Pratt, 1976) lends credence to this interpretation. A final position, the *structuralist* one, embodies the notion that certain activities are incumbent upon the state as a consequence of the logic of the system—in our case, capitalist—in which it operates. Independent of the class of policy makers, or their formal or informal connections to the bourgeoisie, they behave in a way consistent with the preservation of the system of which the state is an important component. Some of the analyses included in this volume adopt this perspective. While some Marxists might argue to the contrary, it is likely that at different times and under different circumstances, each of these propositions has validity.

Independent of how the state's relation to classes is viewed, there is somewhat of a consensus that state activities have important implications for the perpetuation of the capitalist system. For some, the primary functions of the capitalist state are those of *accumulation, legitimization,* (O'Connor, 1973) and *coercion* (Panitch, 1977). The accumulation function refers to the activities of state that contribute to the process of capital accumulation by the bourgeoisie. The provision of roads, waterways, etc. is one example of how, in Canada and elsewhere, the state meets its obligations in this area. Other measures, such as the enactment of social welfare policies, are designed to maintain social harmony or legitimize existing social relations. When this legitimizing function is insufficient to maintain the amount of docility required to ensure the smooth functioning of the capitalist system, the coercive function, through the police, military, etc., can be exercised.

While the functions of the state recently identified by Miliband differ somewhat from those advanced here, they cover similar terrain. According to Miliband, it is possible to identify four state functions in capitalist society:

(a) the maintenance of 'law and order' in the territorial area over which the state is formally invested with sovereignty—the repressive function; (b) the fostering of consensus in regard to the existing social order, which also involves the discouragement of 'dissensus'–the ideological cultural function; (c) the economic function in the broad sense of the term; (d) the advancement, so far as possible, of what is held to be the 'national interest' in relation to external affairs–the international function (1977:90).

The explicit inclusion of (d) is particularly important given the current potential for nuclear destruction.

Despite differences–and many more than those cited exist–Marxist theorists of the state have at least one thing in common. They share a " . . . categorical rejection of [the] view of the state as the trustee, instrument or agent of 'society as a whole.' " Liberal theorists, who view the state "as standing above particular and necessarily partial groups, interests, and classes" (Miliband, 1977:66) are merely mystifying the real power relations in capitalist society. Moreover, they contribute to the continued dominance of the bourgeoisie.

Ideology

There are, according to Williams (1977:55), three ways in which Marxists have used the concept of *ideology*:

1) a system of beliefs characteristic of a particular class or group;
2) a system of illusory beliefs–false ideas or false consciousness–which can be contrasted with true or scientific knowledge;
3) the general process of the production of meaning and ideas.

It might be stressed that not all Marxists include all three elements in their analyses of ideology. More importantly, Marx and Engels were themselves inconsistent in their usage of the term. These ambiguities notwithstanding, for the purposes of this volume, we can paraphrase usages 1) and 2). Ideology, that is, will be viewed as a system of beliefs that legitimizes the ruling positions of particular classes–in the case of Canada, the bourgeoisie. It will also be viewed as a backdrop of ideas against which the individual interprets his/her everyday experiences. To the degree that this backdrop is connected to particular

class interests, it follows that most social situations and encounters are charged with political consequences. In Canada, for example, the individual is usually believed to be responsible for his/her employment status. Despite major structural problems with the economy, then Prime Minister Trudeau, in 1979, therefore exhorted the jobless to look a little harder. As people accept this type of remedy for unemployment, those in positions of control over the economy escape blame for the situation–one in which there are too few jobs to go around. In short, the ideology protects the class interests of those in power by individualizing failure. At the same time, of those unfortunate enough to be unemployed, many interpret their own failure as resulting from their not having what it takes to function in the labour market. In essence, they interpret their own experience in terms of the dominant ideology.

A concept closely related to ideology is that of *superstructure*. Moreover, its usages have been equally varied. To quote Williams (1977:76-77) once more, there are three meanings for superstructure that emerge from the texts of Marx and Engels. These are: "(a) legal and political forms which express existing real relations of production; (b) forms of consciousness which express a particular class view of the world; (c) a process in which, over a whole range of activities, men become conscious of a fundamental economic conflict and fight it out."

If these usages are accepted, if follows that superstructure is comprised of institutions–like the legal system–forms of consciousness–like liberalism–and political and cultural practices–like the engagement of the working class in some societies in battles against the bourgeoisie. If it seems as though there is a great deal of overlap between some of the ways in which superstructure and ideology might be used, it is because many Marxists have been less than clear in their delineation of the terms.

Equally important to these two concepts is the primitive notion that both ideology and superstructure are in some way secondary to the *economic base* of society, and, in essence, necessarily reflect the relations of production found in any particular society. While selective quotations could be drawn from the works of Marx and Engels to support this interpretation, it is equally possible, in certain

6

instances, to view ideology and various elements of the superstructure of society developing in accordance with their own impetus. At certain junctures in history, these may *articulate* with the economic base in varying fashions (Althusser, 1971a). Therefore, it is possible, for example, for art and literature to develop in accordance with the possibilities inherent in particular literary and/or artistic traditions with little input from developments occurring in the base. It is equally possible, that at a certain juncture, the developments in the base will have an immediate impact on a tradition that has otherwise remained undisturbed over several generations. These possibilities are difficult to comprehend and often present problems for Marxist scholars.

Independent of the connections between ideology, superstructure and base, it is a fair comment that in most contemporary capitalistic societies, both ideology and superstructure work to the advantage of the bourgeoisie. In other words, the fundamental belief systems, legal structures, educational institutions, etc. function in a way consistent with the material interests of the dominant group. As noted in the previous section, several Marxists are therefore willing to look at the state in terms of its ideological and repressive functions (Althusser, 1971b).

The last point that must be dealt with before leaving the discussion of ideology, is the idea that Laclau (1977) has defined as *class reductionism*. Until recently, he believes that it was most common for Marxists to stress that all ideologies derived from particular classes in society. More importantly, all ideologies served the interests of distinct classes. In essence, this type of analysis was another example of a way in which ideology was simply seen as a reflection of economic interests or the base of society.

In contrast to class reductionism, Laclau suggests three important points. First, not all ideologies necessarily serve the interests only of the class that may have generated them. For example, Latin American landowners in many instances embraced liberalism, despite its European bourgeois origins. The explanation for their acceptance is simple: it served their interests. Second, similar ideologies may be embraced by different classes. But each class is capable of emphasizing separate elements of the ideology that are most in keeping with its own interests. Thus, a general ideology that may include nationalism as one of its elements is fascism. (The class base of this movement has been primarily petty bourgeois.) Another is socialism, based on the peasantry, as found in many third-world countries. The difference between the two cases is the way in which a fairly important emphasis on nationalism combines with other elements of the ideology. In fascism, it is clear that nationalism and racial superiority were closely related. But nationalism, as in the case of peasant based socialism, can also be clearly connected to other ideological elements. Third–and closely related–Laclau makes reference to *popular democratic struggles*. Such activities may involve the participation of many different classes found in society. The basis of co-operation in these cases are historical traditions that transcend class lines. The possibility of this type of activity helps explain the united struggles that have developed in colonial societies to throw off the yoke of foreign oppressors. It also helps explain the united efforts of Iranians to finally, in 1979, overthrow the regime of the Shah. From one vantage point, it may even assist in an understanding of some of the events occurring in contemporary Quebec.

Change

In an often quoted passage from the Preface to *A Contribution to the Critique of Political Economy*, Marx reveals some of his fundamental ideas regarding change in society. To fully appreciate the implications of his words, the introductory reader might take a second look at the definitions previously provided for *forces of production* and *relations to the means of production*. The advanced reader will already be familiar with the propositions stated by Marx in this passage:

At a certain stage of their development, the material forces of production in society come in conflict with the existing relations of production, or–what is but a legal expression for the same thing–with the property relations within which they had been at work before. From forms of development of the forces of production these relations turn into their fetters. Then occurs a

7

period of social revolution. (Marx, 1859/1964: 51-52)

In short, for a while, the class relations of a society facilitate the development of the available forces of production. In Canada, for example, although it is difficult to pinpoint a date, we might think that capitalist relations of production permitted the maximum utilization of available forces of production up to a certain point in our history. After, however, the class relations were no longer compatible with the maximum utilization of the productive forces. Rather, they impeded a more efficient organization of the forces of production. When this juncture was reached, as Marx states, the relations of production–particularly in their legal form–put a brake on further developments of the productive forces. Under certain conditions *contradictions* such as these result in revolutions and the development of new relations to the means of production that are conducive to further developments of the forces of production.

In Canada, of course, we have had no revolutions resulting from contradictions such as these (unless the 1837 rebellions are considered a revolution). The explanation can be found in the strength of the state apparatuses referred to in a former section and their ability to promote the interests of the bourgeoisie. Despite the objective contradictions between productive forces and relations to the means of production that might have developed in Canada, the working class continues to think in ways that have led to inaction on its part. These ways of thinking are disseminated through various religious organizations, educational systems, media, political parties, etc.–the ideological state apparatus. In saying this there is no implication of a global conspiracy on the part of those who stand to lose most from change. It is suggested that because of their objective position in society, such classes have both: 1) views that are consistent with the maintenance of their position; and 2) sufficient power to impose these views on others. When others are not prepared to accept the dominant ideology that underlays these views, the repressive state apparatus can be activated to ensure conformity. Although it will not be discussed here, such activations have been

frequent over the course of Canadian history.

Although in the passage dealt with, Marx concentrated on indigenous social developments leading to change, later Marxists have spent a great deal of time analysing exogenous factors that result in change. In one form or another, the focus of these scholars has been on *imperialism*. As with many Marxist ideas, there is no consensus regarding the way in which imperialism should be used. Nor is there agreement over the ways it relates to other commonly used ideas (Foster-Carter, 1978).

Despite these difficulties, in different periods, imperialism can be viewed as a result of the need of major capitalistic powers to seek such things as foreign areas of investment, raw materials, and markets. The exact reason for imperialism, and the forms it has taken, have varied from country to country and from time to time.

In the late nineteenth century, for example, one compelling reason for forced entry of European powers into weak states was the opportunity such entry provided for investment purposes. In other periods, the need for markets and raw materials have been more important in explaining the imperialism of various states. Also in the nineteenth century, the common form taken by imperialism in large areas of Africa was direct military and political control by European powers. In contemporary Africa, direct military and political control are less obvious. But important economic relations between some African states and European powers seriously curtail the autonomy of the former and perpetuate the imperialistic relationship.

Independent of the reasons for imperialism, or the forms it has taken, one way of analysing its consequences that has particular validity focuses on an examination of the forces and relations of production as found in the subordinated society. Logically, there are a number of scenarios that can result from foreign intrusion. First, it is possible that an imperialist power may disrupt the existing forces of production through, for example, the introduction of new productive techniques. Such activities may or may not have consequences for the relations of production. Second, the imperialist power may leave the forces of production largely undisturbed but may, primarily through force, attempt to change the productive relations extant in society. Third, it may attempt to change both the forces and relations of production. Fourth, it may change neither.

All of these possibilities, it must be emphasized, are consistent with the extraction of economic surplus from the subordinated society—the form of extraction, though, may vary. It must also be appreciated that it is quite possible to integrate a society that maintains a 'pre-capitalistic' mode of production into a broader capitalistic framework or *world system*. Indeed, as long as they can continue to expropriate, through various means such as trade, tribute, etc., the economic surplus of other societies, it is often to the advantage of imperialist powers to leave pre-capitalistic modes of production relatively intact. Whether or not this or the other options noted will prevail depends upon a number of historically and geographically specific factors.

In Canada, to begin discussion, it can be noted that the entry of European powers resulted in the eventual destruction of the pre-capitalistic mode of production of native peoples. In addition, at various points in its history, Canada has served as a source of raw materials, as an area of investment, and as a market for imperialist societies, like France, Britain, and the United States. These also can be referred to as *metropolitan* societies. Because of its subordination to other societies, Canada, like Australia, New Zealand, etc., can be defined as a *hinterland* society. One of the characteristics of hinterland societies is the outflow of *economic surplus*, in a number of forms, to metropolitan societies.

Relations between the two types of society are also characterized by a power imbalance that favours the metropolis. Consequently, as numerous observers point out, many of the changes that occur within the hinterland result from developments in the metropolitan societies. In Canada, for example, much structural unemployment is related to the decisions of multinational corporations to undertake their research and development operations south of the border. As will be demonstrated later in the volume, it is also possible, within a society, to identify regions that dominate over others (Mandel, 1973). Within societies, one frequently finds a modified replication of the dynamic that occurs between metropolitan and hinterland societies. In Canada, this possibility has had im-

portant implications for the study of change.

Although the metropolis-hinterland relationship is common in world history, it is worth pointing out that compared to citizens of most hinterland societies, Canadians have had a relatively high standard of living. In addition, some fractions of the Canadian bourgeoisie engage in activities that lead to a drain of economic surpluses from other societies into Canada (Clement, 1977). In essence, despite the ubiquity of outside influence, Canada is not typical of most hinterlands.

These discussions of class, state, ideology and change should in no way be regarded as complete. They were not intended to be. They were designed to provide some idea of the principles around which the following selections are organized. It must be added that there are many more excellent Marxist analyses available than, because of space limitations, it was possible to include in this book.

Despite the fact that readings have been organized around four basic concepts, it will be apparent that, *in many senses, each reading deals with class, state, ideology and change*, as well as with numerous other ideas. In many cases, it will be evident that articles could have been assigned to more than one section. As stated earlier, one of the strengths of Marxist analysis is that it provides the tools that facilitate a total and integrated analysis of society. Given the potential break-up of the country, regional disparities, increasing rates of unemployment, inflation, foreign ownership and resulting 'deindustrialization' of the economy, such examinations are sorely needed.

9

CLASS

Introduction

The articles in this section were chosen with one basic thought in mind: to illustrate the number and nature of classes in Canadian society and to examine the relations that have existed between them. The main contemporary classes, it will be remembered, are four in number. The first of these, a bourgeoisie, is defined in terms of its ownership and control of the means of production. Its polar opposite is a working class or proletariat who are engaged in the productive process, yet do not own their means of production. A third group can be identified as those engaged in administration, professionals, and so on. Frequently, such groups are termed new petty bourgeois. Last of all are a number of small businessmen and farmers who, while they may not employ labour, at least exercise a certain amount of ownership and/or control over their enterprises, i.e. a petty bourgeoisie. Despite the general applicability of these distinctions, the relative size, importance and relations between these classes vary from period to period.

In Canada, for example, using a certain amount of simplification, it is possible to divide, as Naylor does in the following article, the bourgeoisie into at least two major fractions, who, in view of recent scholarship, can be thought to have had important consequences for Canadian development. The first, and most important of these, is a mercantile fraction whose major interests, historically, can be located in finance, commerce, transportation and utilities. According to Naylor (1975), the importance of this group in accounting for Canadian industrial *underdevelopment* cannot be overemphasized. Deriving their profits primarily from financing and facilitating the exploitation and shipment of staple commodities—fish, fur, wheat, etc.—from Canada to first Britain and then the United States, this group, more or less since the 'conquest', actively—and successfully—engaged in promoting state policies conducive to their interest. The canal building schemes of the early nineteenth century, later railway construction, the implementation of various tariffs, and so on, to the degree that they facilitated the production and shipment of staple products, worked, in the first instance, to the interests of this fraction. In the twentieth century, as it could profit in terms of advancing loans, and in the shipment of staple and end products, the mercantile fraction, which eventually took on the characteristics of a corporate capitalist class, (in this case corporate capitalism is marked by the subordination of industry to finance capital) has, in many ways, promoted the foreign control of Canadian primary and secondary industry. Investments in foreign ventures, in Canada, it would appear, are less risky than investments in Canadian industrial endeavours.

Contrasted to this group is an industrial fraction of the bourgeoisie. Unlike the mercantile fraction, and its corporate capitalist successor, its profits derive solely from the

11

manufacture of commodities. Unlike the experience of both Britain and the United States, this fraction has, in Canada, remained weak. In fact, some indicators point to its increasing ineffectiveness.

The reasons for its weak position can be found in the strength of the mercantile fraction and its ability to influence state policy in accordance with its own interests, the fact that large scale industry in Canada developed after the mercantile fraction had consolidated its grip on the state, a continued reliance on Britain for "economic favours," and so on. Whatever the reasons, the result is clear. In the late twentieth century, the inability of this fraction to compete successfully with American technology and organization has led to their virtual extinction, at least in large scale, high technology enterprises. Multinationals have moved in to fill the void. The particular pattern of development represented by these events is referred to by Naylor as "industrialization by invitation."

It must be stressed that the Naylor thesis has not gone unchallenged. Various scholars believe that they have found holes in the argument (MacDonald, 1975; Bliss, 1976; Drummond, 1978). But, despite its weaknesses, others have upheld the basic validity of his central thesis regarding the historic dominance of mercantile over industrial capital (Watkins, 1977; Drache, 1978). Future research will no doubt help to clarify some of the questions resulting from Naylor's analysis.

Further analytical divisions in the bourgeoisie are made by Clement. Once again, however, he bases his categories on the roles played by certain classes in the productive process. Also, some of his divisions cut across those already referred to by Naylor.

The first fraction Clement refers to are termed the dominant indigenous. Such individuals, who are predominantly Canadian, are "very active in finance, transportation, and utilities, to a lesser extent in trade, and much less in manufacturing and resources." A second fraction, the middle-range indigenous, are in "relatively small scale manufacturing." The dominant comprador fraction, in turn, "is active in manufacturing and resources, . . . and is located in branch plants of foreign-controlled multinationals" (1977a:25). Clearly, one of the major differences between Clement and Naylor is the

elaboration of the nature of the compradors—largely a product of the twentieth-century United States multinationals—by the former.

According to at least one source (Pentland, 1959), beginnings of a class of individuals who derived their livelihood from providing wage labour can be identified in seventeenth-century New France. A larger group, the predominantly Irish immigrants who provided labour for the completion of the canal systems in the early nineteenth century, also qualify as wage labourers. By the end of the nineteenth century, and with the development of large scale urban industry, it was clear that the working man was here to stay (Clark, 1948).

There have been changes, however, in the nature of this class. Although he does not strictly adhere to the characterization of class advanced here, Johnson (1972: 164) records that in 1901 those classified as primary workers comprised 7.8 percent of the non-agricultural work force. In 1961 they comprised 3.4 percent. During the same period, the proportion of manual workers slid from 47.6 percent to 35.0 percent of the total. At the same time, those he defines as white-collar workers increased from 29.0 percent of the 1901 total to 45.7 percent in 1961.

Given the definitions used here, however, this latter group, which includes those Johnson defines as propriety and managerial, professional, clerical, commercial, and financial, belong in the ranks of the working class and new petty bourgeoisie. An accurate statement of long term trends for each class is therefore difficult on the basis of these data. Nonetheless, although the absolute figures are small, all of those Johnson puts in the white-collar category, as noted above, have experienced a percentage increase since 1901. When farmers are examined, however, the reverse is true. They have declined from 40.3 percent of the labour force to 10.2 percent (1972:163). Although his data on small businessmen does not cover as great a time span, it is clear that their numbers have declined from 6.6 percent of the labour force in 1948 to 4.1 percent in 1968 (1972:152). These trends noted by Johnson have been substantiated by more recent data (Statistics Canada, 1974:125).

Overall, then, on the basis of figures presented above by Johnson, and elsewhere by Resnick (1977), it is clear that during the present century there has been a decline in the number of individuals that have been called blue-collar working class. The petty bourgeoisie—farmers and small businessmen—have also declined in numbers. The new petty bourgeoisie, however, have experienced an increase in their ranks. So have white-collar workers. Although Resnick (1977:44) estimates the current size of the bourgeoisie at approximately 10 000, it is not possible to determine whether or not this figure represents an increase or a decline—the comparative figures are unavailable. However, given the concentration that has occurred in the economy over the past eighty years, it can be hypothesized that the bourgeoisie would have been relatively larger in 1900 than today.

What the figures on the relative size of classes do not reflect is the overt class conflict that has frequently marked the relations between classes. Such conflicts are focused on in the following readings. Class conflict per se, it will be remembered, is endemic in the structure of capitalist society.

If we examine Canada over the past century or so, it seems clear from the evidence presented by scholars such as Langdon in a following article, that *overt* class conflict between the bourgeoisie and the working class—manifested, in this case, through the formation of trade unions and strikes—began with the establishment of fair-sized industrial enterprises and an impersonal labour market in the last century. It was only through the institution of the trade union and the mechanism of the strike that the working class could hope to preserve its standard of living, dignity, and working conditions. As Herron and Palmer point out in their article, the second of these concerns was particularly important around the turn of the century. In efforts to increase the amount of surplus value that accrued to the owners of factories— or, to use a term borrowed from conventional economics, to increase "productivity"—the principles of "scientific management" were imported from the United States. The consequence of these measures was to further integrate the workers into the rhythm of the machine rather than vice versa. Naturally, many workers resisted. In many instances, they were temporarily successful. Over the long haul, though, in many circumstances, they were defeated. One of the most dramatic

defeats occurred in Winnipeg in 1919 (Bercuson, 1978).

The industrial worker is not the only one who has engaged in conflict with the bourgeoisie. The emergence of many farm movements, particularly in the twenties and thirties, can be taken as an index of struggle between opposing classes (Macpherson, 1953; Conway, 1978). The activities of some of these movements will be taken up in the section on change. For the time being, it is sufficient to note that the farmer has been fighting a losing battle. As Bernier points out in his article, the number of independent commodity producers in Quebec decreases by the day. It is not possible to generalize these findings to all of Canada, but other evidence suggests that similar patterns are operative elsewhere (Hedley, 1976). Where farmers are able to remain on the land they must often supplement farm incomes by wage labour in urban factories. In other instances they may enter into "sharing" arrangements with large companies: the farmer supplies the land and labour; the company provides the capital equipment and livestock. In both cases, the farmer undergoes proletarianization.

The many changes that have occurred in capitalist society over the past century lead Cuneo, in the final article in this section, to argue for a more differentiated notion of class and class conflict than is commonly used. In addition to the familiar form of oppression that is associated with the bourgeoisie's extraction of surplus value from an industrial proletariat, Cuneo suggests that oppression also occurs in the realms of "circulation," "consumption," and "finance." An application of those categories to Canadian society will result in a greater understanding of the class dynamic than currently exists.

While the following articles provide a general introduction to the class dimension of Canadian society, they by no means provide a complete picture. (For example, there is no article that analyses the activities of the new petty bourgeois; however, part of this gap will be filled in the articles by Rioux, and Bélanger and Saint-Pierre, in later sections.) Moreover, there remains a great deal of research yet to be completed before a complete picture becomes possible. In carrying out this research scholars will be required to cross the rigid boundaries that in many minds still exist between the subject matters of the various disciplines.

DOMINION OF CAPITAL: CANADA AND INTERNATIONAL INVESTMENT

R. T. Naylor

Over the past decade the world economy has witnessed a multilateral movement of capital on a scale unprecedented since the great era of international investment prior to the First World War. Britain was then the chief metropolis from which finance capital spread to the far reaches of an ever-expanding empire, formal and informal, while lesser powers struggled in emulation. Since the Second World War, American international economic power based on the global operations of the multinational corporation has dominated the Western economy, although over the past ten years other, less potent, industrial states have striven with increasing success to challenge American hegemony by their own corporate expansion. In both eras the international flow of capital has been the instrument of economic and political domination par excellence. And in both periods Canada has been the leading example of a 'borrowing' country, a recipient on the greatest scale of the flows of economic power crossing national borders in the form of international investment. The contours of Canadian economic evolution under the aegis of capital invested from abroad provide an illuminating view of the structure of dependence inherent in the international capitalist order, past and present. They show well the patterns of dynamic development and underdevelopment experienced by a hinterland economy, given that a substantial degree of critically important economic decision-making originates from outside its borders.

Economic domination by itself clearly does not preclude economic development in the sense of the growth of national income, population, and even per capita income. It need not even exclude the possibility of innovation and changes in technology and industrial structure. But what domination does imply is that the direction of economic development—that is, which sectors of the economy flourish and which stagnate—is dictated by the needs of the metropolitan economy. Economic

domination minimizes autonomous growth and change. Furthermore, it necessarily implies a net outflow of surplus from the hinterland to the metropolitan economy either through repatriated earnings from investment or through adverse terms of trade—a surplus which otherwise could have been captured by the economy to generate local capital formation.

The crux of the problem of domination inheres in the relation between metropolitan capital and local capital in the hinterland. Acrimonious debate has turned upon the question as to which of two antagonistic positions best describes the hinterland-metropolitan capitalist linkage. Does domination from abroad by virtue of the greater economic power of the metropolis admit of or lead to the creation of a national capitalist class whose long-term interests are inherently at variance with those of the metropole? Does it on the contrary produce only a local capitalist class that is either totally subordinate to or completely integrated with that of the metropole, whose *raison d'être* is at one with that of the metropole, and who can never be expected to challenge its relative position? In brief, does capital have an address and a nationality, or is it truer to say that it has no country, that any complication produced by the coexistence of big and small is simply a sideshow in its universal game of despoiling the globe's resources? The Canadian experience sheds a great deal of light on these questions. But to understand the Canadian experience, one must first make explicit reference to the metropolitan economies out of whose process of economic expansion the Canadian economy and society sprang into being.

The Expansion of the Metropoles

The evolution of the contemporary international capitalist order proceeded in discernible stages from its birth in sixteenth-

15

century Europe, where the old feudal order had decayed, the population was growing again after the ravages of wars and plagues, and the pace of commerce had accelerated. Prices rose with the economic expansion of the late fifteenth and early sixteenth centuries, and the resulting quest for gold and silver assumed an awesomely destructive dimension as entire civilizations were sacrificed in the scramble. Gold and silver took on a new significance in this era because the expansion of trade and rising prices necessitated a greater quantity of circulating medium. The rise of the nation-state in the wake of economic resurgence led to the assertion of national political power and to demands for currency unification and national capital markets for government finance, as well as to the breakup of the old cosmopolitan medieval credit system on the shoals of antagonistic sovereignties. The spread of commerce beyond the old European trading system to new and distant peripheries demanded a greater supply of cash, and the growth of multilateral trade also made cash payments necessary. Finally the change in the foundation of social power from the ownership of land, whose more or less fixed rent yields at a time of rising prices threatened and often destroyed feudal nobles, to new, more portable forms of wealth was predicated on an expanded supply of bullion.

The first stage of European capitalist expansion was that of overt theft, of the plunder and enslavement of Amerindians for work in the mines. It was the great era of publicly sponsored piracy as other nations who lacked Iberia's direct access to New World gold and silver sought their share of the spoils in other ways. The cod fisheries and the exchange of fish for Spanish gold became an early source of imperialist rivalries in the North Atlantic. Actual European settlement, apart from that strictly required for looting or supervising the mining of gold or the drying of fish on a seasonal basis, was minimal in the early years.

In stage two, piracy or overt theft gradually evolved into trade or covert theft. For example, Queen Elizabeth's share of the booty brought back by Sir Francis Drake in the Golden Hind sufficed not only to pay off her entire foreign debt but left enough to establish the Levant Company with a monopoly of the Mediterranean trade. The profits of the Levant Company in turn spawned the East India Company. The age of the great chartered companies, state sanctioned monopolies charged with military and governmental powers as well as economic privilege, had begun. And although these companies were the instrument of mercantile expansion of all Western powers, the English in particular perfected their use. These conglomerations of capital, the first historical instances of economic organizations with bona fide modern corporate characteristics, signaled a change in European attitudes to the colonies. Companies with commitments to colonize and governmental powers replaced the casual gift of New World territory as fiefdoms to court favourites. Agricultural settlement and the more intensive exploitation of the colonies for their staple products proceeded, and the demand for manpower increased. Chartered companies, such as England's Royal African Company, flourished when slaves replaced gold as the most lucrative traffic of the Atlantic adventures. In the British West Indies early tobacco farms based on small holdings and indentured labour were eclipsed by the rise of the sugar plantation based on Black slavery. In the Spanish islands where sugar was a lucrative crop, the Indian population was nearly extinct within fifty years of the Spanish arrival and was replaced by Black slaves. Black slaves also spread across the mainland of the Americas, south, central and north, wherever the plantation mode of staple production became feasible. New products, foodstuffs, and basic raw materials for mass consumption or industrial use now flowed in trade from the colonies to the metropolis—in contrast to the spices, jewels, and specie for luxury consumption that had been the backbone of pre-capitalist trade between Europe and the East.

Stage three saw the Industrial Revolution begin in late eighteenth-century Britain and spread throughout western Europe. Until the 1870s British industrial hegemony, based first on cotton and later on iron and steel, saw few serious challenges. It was a period when the character of British investments abroad underwent substantial change. Until the end of the Napoleonic wars, British capital flowed abroad chiefly in the form of mercantile credit in conjunction with international commodity flows, or the operating of chartered companies, or in the form of British government loans and subsidies to allied states for military and related purposes. Thereafter the earnings of British shipping, insurance, and other services abroad more than offset a fairly steady balance of trade deficit and provided the funds for a sizeable expansion in the flow of private long-term capital abroad. Capital flowed through the 'merchant banks' like the Baring Brothers or Glyn, Mills and Company to government finance, canal, railway, and other infrastructural investment guaranteed by or closely linked to government, and only to a much lesser degree industrial or mining funds, which remained overwhelmingly the product of private subscription, rather than the work of the British capital market. Capital, of course, continued to move abroad on a private basis to the British planters and entrepreneurs who controlled and directed staple extraction abroad. But the great mercantile monopolies, apart from the Hudson's Bay Company which still had a lease on life, were defunct institutions in terms of aiding and abetting British overseas expansion.

Stage four began with a crash—that of 1873 and the ensuing Great Depression. The era of a free flow of commodities typical of the age of the Industrial Revolution ended in a wave of tariff building by the industrializing nations in an attempt to prevent the worldwide deflation from undermining their industrial hopes. Britain, with its enormous stake in international commodity flows, was the major abstainer.

As the free flow of finished commodities was increasingly inhibited by tariff and other barriers to trade, the international economy underwent some major structural changes. Countries began to seek their own spheres of market influence for the export of finished goods and their own assured supplies of raw materials. At the same time international capital flows in the form of financial capital accelerated as did the international migration of labour to populate the white settler states of the peripheral areas.

Britain was the world leader in these transformations. By as early as 1893 some 15 per cent of her natural wealth was invested abroad. And her domestic savings available for foreign investments were supplemented from abroad by the workings of the key currency system built around the pound. Since the tenure of Sir Isaac Newton as Master of the Mint, the gold standards he had created ensured that the world of commerce and finance would revolve about the City of London. Instead of sterile gold, countries began holding their foreign exchange reserves in the form of short-term, interest yielding balances in London, which could be channelled off by British financial institutions along with Britain's own savings into long-term investments overseas.

The need for markets, the search for raw materials, the defence of invested capital, all dictated a scramble for colonies not only by Britain but, especially after 1896 when world prices began to rise again, by other Western powers. Between the partial economic recovery of 1878 and the end of the war for the seizure of the Boer republic's gold resources, Britain alone added 5 million square miles and 88 million people to an already vast empire. Especially desirable were the white settlers' states whose output of cheap raw materials led to a secular improvement in the British terms of trade and, of course, a deterioration in their own. Australia provided wheat and wool, New Zealand dairy and meat products, South Africa gold, diamonds, and a wide range of agricultural produce. Grains and livestock from the Argentine and Canada supplemented the traditional staples of the old Empire. These white settlers' states functioned not only as raw material hinterlands but also as important markets for British industrial products.

But major transformations in the world order were already taking shape, changes of such a radical nature that the old metropolis would be swept aside in a maelstrom of wars and depressions. The world expansion after 1896 saw the birth of the age of electricity, the internal combustion engine, and a vast increase in the chemical industries. The centre of industrial activity shifted irrevocably from the old metropolis to the new. From 1914 to 1939 came twenty-five years of cataclysmic change, the death of the British empire, and the end of the world hegemony of finance capital.

Finance-capital represented the portfolio investments of financial institutions or rich individuals. Such capital moved easily into government finance in the colonies, into mortgages, into railroad finance, into public utility finance, and sometimes—but much less so—into mining. British loans went abroad seeking an assured rate of return in investment outlets with safe collateral, with the implicit or explicit guarantee of governments, or into utility and similar investments that generally had an assured monopoly to guarantee a return. British direct investments abroad were much rarer, and industrial investments were particularly scarce. The new age of automobiles, electricity, and chemicals was outside the purview of the British investors. It was quite otherwise for the new behemoth.

Stage five had its origins well back into the nineteenth-century development patterns of the United States, and in particular of the American firm. American industrial growth began effectively in the great era of individual enterprise following the War of 1812, when the old colonial commercial oligarchy was displaced from the seat of economic power by the nascent industrial and agribusiness class. With the expansion of the 1850s and the Civil War, the railroads spanned the continent, creating a national market and with it a national firm reaching to integrate horizontally across the country. As the Civil War expansion gave way to the depression of the 1870s and 1880s, the new corporate giants began in earnest the process of integrating vertically to control their raw material resources. And as the world economic revival of the 1890s dawned, the American firm began its international expansion in the form of the multidivisional corporation, integrated vertically and horizontally over a multitude of product lines and challenging the old European powers in their traditional export markets abroad. The years before the First World War saw the modest beginnings of the instrument of metropolitan expansion that would in a few decades come to dominate the world stage, the multinational corporation. Initially, the movement abroad by direct investment of these American firms was small and was restricted primarily to Mexico and Canada, a natural spillover of the internal growth of the American firms. Prior to the war the US remained a net debtor to Britain, and the number and scale of the US industrial firms ready to make the quantum leap to modern multinational status was limited. The world remained essentially a preserve of European, especially British, finance capital until the war and the economic chaos of the postwar recession weakened the British system, and the ensuing depression fractured

it completely.

The post-Second-World-War era began with American industrial hegemony over the Western world unchallenged. Marshall Plan 'aid' dollars replaced the pound sterling as the medium of international exchange. Beginning with the search for new raw material sources the American multinational firms recommenced their global spread. Initially Canada was the forefront of the new class of borrowing country, but by the mid 1950s European reconstruction made the European market especially desirable. American investment, while continuing to flow into Canadian resources and manufacturing, in relative terms shifted increasingly to European final product markets. By 1963 the shift in emphasis became pronounced, but at the same time the symptoms of the incipient decline of the American system were evident.

European economic recovery especially after the mid-1950s was rapid and broad based. Economic resurgence behind common market tariff walls was accompanied by a government-assisted cartelization movement. Together with the even more pheonomenal economic rebirth of Japan these developments spawned a system of competing corporate empires on a world scale as direct investment flowed from Europe and Japan into various resource hinterlands and even into the United States itself. For the US the sixties were increasingly bleak. Balance of payments problems resulting from the growth of competition abroad and the increase in military expenses to maintain global hegemony precipitated a series of currency crises. Each successive crisis was followed by an increasingly severe effort to impose the costs of empire on the captive satellite economies by stepping up the rate of repatriation of earnings and other devices to maintain or increase the American hold on foreign industrial structures while reducing the outflow of capital necessitated by such a hold. Finally in 1972 came virtual economic abdication as the US ceased to try to maintain the exchange value of the dollar. This abdication, coupled with a vast expansion of petrodollars in 1974, helped to shift the centre of the world monetary system increasingly towards Europe, while at the same time it became no longer amenable to control by any one power.

In very broad outline these are the major structural transformations of the world capi-

18

talist order of late. A much debated question has been Canada's position in these contemporary structures—whether it is best regarded as a small economy of the developed metropolitan type or a remarkably large and wealthy one of the colonial variant. Is it an industrial economy whose exports happen to be almost entirely primary products, or is it a staple-extracting hinterland that just happened to achieve large-scale industrialization? Its national income, industrial structure, and the foreign investments its own capitalists have undertaken on their own account point in the first direction, while the importance of the export of staples in generating national income, the derivative and dependent nature of its industrial structure, the overwhelming volume of foreign, especially American, investment in that industrial structure, and its assiduous cultivation of bilateral agreements with the US point in the second. The nature of the present structure can perhaps best be understood with reference to those of the past.

The Development of the Hinterland

New France and Newfoundland

Dependence on an external metropole is and has been a fundamental fact of Canadian economic and social life from the earliest days of white conquest and settlement. An accidental and largely unwelcome offshoot of the sixteenth-century scramble for New World gold, Canada grew very slowly in the seventeenth and eighteenth centuries as a fishing base and elaborate fur-trading post. These early staples of fish and fur fitted well into the logic of European overseas expansion in its primary phase. The fisheries, cultivated by the English in particular to provide a trade to drain Spanish bullion, for a considerable time contributed nothing to the development of the hinterland areas, Newfoundland in particular, apart from providing a pretext for the extermination of the island's indigenous population. What little settlement emerged in Newfoundland in the early centuries of the fishery was a casual and energetically discouraged byproduct of the fisheries. Genuine development, as opposed to the simple and seasonal looting of the immediate resource base, was absent. And of course the motivation behind the fisheries was inseparable from that of Iberian expansion in phase one,

the quest for precious metals. Not until after the mid-seventeenth century, with the steadily growing displacement of the annual English fleet by a rising resident fishery, did the industry spawn stable settlement, and even then for another 150 years indigenous growth was harried and hampered by the efforts of the English fishing interests to maintain control. Moreover the growth of a resident fishery implied settlement on the periphery of the island and little more. Capital requirements were still furnished by British merchants who extended credit in advance of the catch, and the island's resident fishing industry remained inextricably tied to the metropolitan capitalists by the chain of debt that the system engendered.

This chain of debt-bondage was the first instance in Canadian history of what became the normal pattern. The staple-producer relies on markets in the metropole to pursue the process of staple extraction. Commercial credit extended in the fisheries was the original form of that investment. Because the producer was indebted to the merchant, and thus the hinterland economy to the metropole, production patterns remained set. More production of the staple was required to settle the debt, and current receipts almost never sufficed to settle past debts. The debt grew, and so did the need for yet more staple production to try to pay it off.

The French fur trade, especially in its early years, also fits into the phase one pattern. A luxury-commodity trade which discouraged large-scale settlement and any genuine self-sustaining development, it did however induce some more concrete results than the early fisheries. The early fur trade was the preserve of French mercantile monopoly corporations, charged with governmental and colonizing as well as trading functions and sponsored purely by private capital. While a class of indigenous fur merchants did slowly emerge and at one point played a substantial role in the prosecution of the trade, the control of distribution of furs and the importation of merchandise and credit by the metropolitan monopoly largely nullified any significance such a development could have on local progress. And with the destruction of the Huron Indian trading and agricultural system by the English allies, the Iroquois, the character of the fur trade was changed and metropolitan domination reinforced.

The new wave of French expansion into the Americas after the 1660s saw a much more active role of the state both in the direct establishment of bona fide governmental institutions to replace those exercized formerly by privately owned corporations, and in the state subsidization of commerce, industry, and government abroad. As the French fur trade was forced to reach ever deeper into the continent, great fixed-capital outlays in the form of military posts and garrisons were required to protect commercial routes and suppress competition. A new agricultural settlement policy to replace the Huron supply system followed. Some short-lived industrialization efforts which might have helped the development of a local bourgeoisie were also made; but these waned quickly in the face of metropolitan disapproval, and the colony relapsed to the status of fur-trapping hinterland, albeit with a considerably augmented population.

The France-New France colonial relation brought capital imports to the hinterland that were of greater relative importance than at any subsequent point in Canadian history. And the link between capital flow and the commerce in furs was nearly absolute both in the private and the public sectors. Commercial credit extended by La Rochelle, Bordeaux, and other merchant companies involved an unbreakable chain of debt and dependence. The merchant houses of the metropole established branch houses or local commission merchants in the colony to negotiate the movement of furs to France. The same companies in turn were intermediaries for the return flow of manufactured goods to the colony at fixed terms of trade. The high profits, if somewhat erratic, of the fur trade helped discourage capital from entering other pursuits. Furthermore, half of the profits went back to the metropole directly as the share of the French partners; while of the profits that accrued to local agents, those not reinvested in the trade were spent in France on commodities to be imported to the colony. The very success of the fur trade and the resultant tie-up of capital therein ensured that such commodities would never be produced in New France itself. The chain of short-term debt guaranteed, just as in the fisheries, the simple reproduction of past production patterns.

The resulting balance-of-trade deficit of New France, the direct consequence of the inflow of commercial credit and the reinforcement of the fur-extracting bias of the economy, had to be covered on capital account in three ways. The least significant was the private investments in the colonial resources and industries, other than commercial credit in the fur trade, undertaken by French capitalists. Apart from a couple of timber establishments and the early ventures of French entrepreneurs in the 1660s (industrialization efforts which were subsidized by the government), these private investments were negligible. Second were the fairly sizeable imports of capital by clerical establishments. Much of the clerical expenditures were linked directly to the fur trade—while the clergy may not actually have traded in furs with the Indians as some accused them of doing, they certainly recognized the critical link between the fur traffic and their Christianizing mission and, apart from disputes over the debauchment of Indians with brandy, actively encouraged the trade. Furthermore, the clerical establishments exported considerable sums from their colonial revenues for investment in France, which would at least partly offset the favourable capital-account effects of their import of funds. And, finally, a substantial amount, as much as one-third, of clerical expenditure on public goods in the form of hospitals and educational establishments came from government subsidies.

The inflow of capital in government account was by far the most important offset to the trade deficit. Much of this capital was also inextricably linked to the fur trade. Military expenditures, the largest item, were prompted directly by the extension of the trade into the interior. Much of the funds for civil administration were so directed as well, as the colony for all of its history was ruled by speculators who robbed the public purse with impunity to divert funds into their fur-trade interests or related commercial pursuits. The colony thus became a haven for either the upstart bourgeois or the bankrupt aristocrat to make or repair his fortunes in the commerce in pelts.

Part of the state subsidies, it is true, found their way into industrial development. But the only large-scale industrial ventures of the French period were the forest and ship-building industries and iron-mining and smelting. None of these ventures had bona fide roots in the colony to permit any spurt of development. In both cases the industries relied on American technique, French government subsidies, and a military market supported by the French Crown, which market was in turn linked to the fur trade. Relying upon external capital and American technique, derivative from and dependent on the staple trade, these industries in a real sense were the prototype for future Canadian industrial history.

In New France even the circulating medium depended on the fur trade. The specie sent in on government account in the early years flowed out again, often on the same ship. To counteract the adverse effects of the balance-of-trade deficit draining circulating medium out, the colony used fiat issues of currency of various sorts by the military authorities or the civil administrators, or both, with no coordination between them. To further complicate the monetary situation, merchants' bills of exchange and fur-trade company certificates with a value fixed in terms of fur were also circulated. All of the currencies were derivative from the fur trade, directly in the case of fur certificates, and indirectly in the case of military 'ordonnances' to finance the building of infrastructure in the interior to protect trade routes, merchants' bills issued by the wholesale houses who dominated the import of merchandise and export of furs, and the issue of civil authorities to cover the deficit left by the shortage of French appropriation for the colony or the yield of its tax on fur exports. The government issues were theoretically restricted to the amount of the annual subsidy from the French Ministry of Marine, and were required to be redeemed annually in bills of exchange in France, which bills in turn were redeemable in specie in France. In fact escalating expenditures in the colony, coupled with a reduction in appropriations for the colony in France when financial difficulties caused by war beset the metropolitan government, threw the colonial finances into chaos. A steadily growing supply of irredeemable paper fed the wartime inflationary process in the dying days of New France. The result was a unique state of international indebtedness for Canada. For the only period of its history an enormous paper debt was owed to the colony from the metropolis. The subsequent repudiation of this debt added to the already enormous economic problems of the wartime economy. Commercial dislocation and conquest by the British destroyed the already weak Canadian commercial class and led directly to the hegemony of a group of newly arrived British merchants.

There was little or nothing inherent in the structure of the colonial relation between France and New France to permit sustained local capital formation and the development of a vigorous local capitalist class. Domination by metropolitan merchants inhibited accumulation, and the profits of the fur trade kept the attention of local merchants restricted to short-term investments within that trade. While France after the mid-seventeenth century undertook a program of colonial expansion based on the search for industrial and other raw materials and the creation of a system of sugar plantations, Canada remained confined to the pattern of development typical of the earliest phase of European expansion – looting the surface for luxury commodities with little or no intensive, even if dependent, local development.

British North America, 1763-1867

Phase two of European expansion, albeit with many retrograde elements deriving from an early dependence on furs, was ushered into Canadian development by the British Conquest. With the active collaboration of the British military authorities, Anglo-American and British commercial capital quickly supplanted French and Canadian capital in the still dominant fur trade. French and Canadian capital had been weakened by the ravages of inflation and plundering by officials during the war, by the flight of French capital after the war, and by the obviously superior commercial and financial connections the British merchants had with the new metropolis.

Initially little seemed to have changed, apart from the different nationality of the commercial élite. Capital entered the colony in the form of commercial credit accompanying commodity flows – furs out and general manufactured merchandise in. Substantial amounts of British government funds moved in on military account and to subsidize the establishment of Loyalist settlers after the American Revolution. Industry was almost totally lacking, capital accumulation on any significant scale was restricted to the fur trade, and specie coming into the colony flowed out almost immediately to cover the balance-of-trade deficit.

However the effects of the shift of metropole from France to the more dynamic industrial metropolis of Britain were not long in manifesting themselves. While the American Revolution led to a northward migration of the fur-trading capital formerly strong in New York, a migration that would have tended to confirm the colony's traditional role, other forces were at work to transform it role. As Britain industrialized, its demand for imported foodstuffs rose. Rising world grain prices led to an expansion of Canada's wheat exports. During the declining years of French rule a sporadic export trade in grain had begun; with the dawn of the British era wheat-growing for external markets became generalized throughout Quebec, and Ontario (Upper Canada) witnessed the opening of its agrarian frontier for grain cultivation. As well, after the American Revolution the locus of the British West Indies trade moved north to Nova Scotia. Halifax especially grew as an imperial entrepôt and British export-import firms set up branches there. New Brunswick became the new centre of the imperial mast trade, with other types of timber exports showing a rising importance. In fact, near famines often resulted in the province as the existing manpower began servicing the British demand for colonial timber. British timber-dealing houses moved directly into the province, providing capital and direction for the exploitation of the forests. The fishing industry underwent a great expansion, responding to both the eclipse of the French fisheries and the blocking of American competition.

For several decades the inflow of external capital retained essentially the same pattern as during the French régime. Commercial companies in the import-export trade accounted for a sizeable sum in the form of commercial credit to finance the inflow of manufactures and outflow of staples. Rather than establishing branches, metropolitan houses generally extended such credit to Canadian factors or agents, but branch houses were certainly not unknown. On government account came funds for public works, subsidies for administration of the colony, and military subventions. After the initial Loyalist influx, subsidies to immigrants by government ceased and were partly replaced by capital carried in by Loyalists themselves. While the bulk of the inflow of settlers from the US was made up of impoverished families attracted by free land, some of the Loyalists carried considerable wealth with them.

In Nova Scotia the flow of funds on military account was the foundation of early development. War meant prosperity, a prosperity which terminated in crisis whenever peace broke out. During times of peace the cream of Halifax's mercantile community would gather in a local coffee house and denounce the government, calling for 'loud war by land and sea.' In addition to military account, piracy ensured a steady influx of specie, again inextricably linked to a state of war. Nova Scotia was also remarkable for providing the first instance in British North America of government debt privately held abroad. The colonial government had begun to issue 'bounty certificates,' promises to pay subsidies to certain people who undertook specified agricultural or other improvements. These certificates were usually obtained by fraud, voted by the Halifax merchants who controlled the Assembly to individuals who owed them money, and then re-acquired by these same Halifax merchants at heavy discounts. Eventually yielding par value, most found their way into the hands of the leading merchant-financier of Halifax who retired to England to direct colonial affairs from there, still retaining in his hands the bulk of the province's public debt.

In New Brunswick, which received apart from government a much smaller military account, the inflow of British money largely took the form of commercial credit for the timber trade that grew during the Napoleonic wars. Prince Edward Island was completely in the hands of a few absentee proprietors whose quit rents were supposed to have formed the basis of government finance. In fact little flowed in for this purpose and no money for improvements came in until 1825.

After the War of 1812, the patterns of Canadian development shifted. Prior to the war, British North America's existence independent of the US was always tenuous; after the war there was little doubt as to where its short-term and indeed medium-term future lay. The border with the US was sealed and the colonies' dependence on Britain confirmed. At the same time the nature of the British metropolis underwent a radical change. The old mercantile-colony system quickly dissolved in the face of a rising tide of industrial expansion which burst asunder the commercial restrictions of the old empire to search for worldwide hegemony. New raw materials came in demand: cheap food to nourish the quickly growing industrial proletariat and timber as a construction material, ship-building material, and industrial fuel. British capital flowing abroad belonged not only to governments or commercial houses; private long-term capital exports became an established and steadily growing phenomenon. The human waste created by the factory system and by the deliberate destruction of Irish and Scottish peasant farms to create capitalist agriculture to feed the metropolis flowed to the overseas colonies along with capital. Some of the early emigrants carried their not inconsiderable personal wealth, but most of the well-to-do moved on to the US. At the same time three British controlled and financed land companies developed, and these did funnel some funds into the province [of Canada] for improvements. But the companies' expenditures were small, and their existence in two cases was very brief.

For British North America the new international order implied two contradictory tendencies. On one hand, British demand for colonial staples, wheat and wood in particular, continued to escalate, carrying with it a precarious prosperity in some of the resource-rich areas and a reinforcement of dependence on the metropolitan market. On the other hand, their protected position within the empire was sacrificed by Britain's rush to multilateralism in trade and by the rapid development of other resource hinterlands within the British nexus.

To develop the new export staples, major works of commercial infrastructure were required in Canada for the first time. British long-term capital in the form of purchases of public debt, effected through the intermediary of British private banks, came to the province of Canada to finance such works, especially canals in the era before 1840.

The year 1835 was a watershed in the history of external investment in Canada. That year the government of Upper Canada converted its debt from one denominated in currency to one denominated in sterling with the express purpose of conducting its future borrowings in Britain, on the premise that such a move would free Canadian funds from long-term investments and make them available for other undertakings, notably commercial investments. Along with the British funds came American investment on a significant scale for the first time in Canadian history. Major works of infrastructure like the Welland Canal, other navigation companies, and even a couple of short-lived banks, were the outgrowth of American direct investments, while some American money even entered the field of commerce with the establishment of import-export firms in Montreal. These ventures however were minor in comparison to the growth of other commercial establishments.

While British commercial houses were still active and prominent, as the process of commercial capital accumulation proceeded in Canada, the British houses' commission merchants and agents gradually ceded place to Canadian wholesale houses who dealt with British firms on a more equitable footing. With the evolution of a Canadian capitalist structure geared to the provision of short-term commercial credit came the development of an indigenous banking system. These banks would stand behind local merchants, from whose capital they generally grew, discounting their bills and issuing notes, thus rectifying the old problem of specie shortage resulting from persistent trade-balance deficits. For the first time a paper currency existed backed by the general worth of Canadian wholesale merchants rather than by periodic subventions from imperial treasuries. The development of banking and the growth of Canadian commercial capitalism were inseparable, and both were ultimately linked to the imperial trade system. The banks' chief role was the short-term financing of the movement of staples to Britain and the flow of manufactures back to Canada. They played virtually no role in financing agricultural development or in public or industrial finance.

By the late 1830s and early 1840s the contradictions inherent in the diverging tendencies of the period—the growing dependence on the British industrial system for marketing colonial staples on the one hand, and the abolition of formal imperial ties on the other—

became absolute. The British financial stake in the colony, especially in light of the fact that the British government had financed directly most of the construction of the canal system, was very large and very precarious. The rebellion of 1837 led to near bankruptcy of the province of Upper Canada and an inability to float further loans in Britain, while the essential waterways system was still incomplete. The financial condition of the province caused near panic among the private banks in Britain who had marketed the province's public debt and caused a lot of anxiety in British government circles. The solution was quite simple–by joining the bankrupt upper province to the solvent lower one, and spreading the burden of debt repayment over both, Canadian credit could be restored. And the new united province of Canada had no trouble raising the necessary funds to complete the canal system: it was a precedent noted well for the future.

The end of the old system of colonial preferences precipitated economic collapse for the Montreal commercial community, and their reaction to the crisis is worth noting, for it set the pattern for much to follow. In the course of three days in 1849 over 1000 people, the cream of the Montreal commercial and financial community, signed a manifesto calling for annexation to the United States. The rationale behind such a policy was stated clearly in the manifesto: 'The proposed union would render Canada a field for American capital into which it would enter as freely for the prosecution of public works and private enterprise as into any of the present states.' The manifesto called explicitly for Canadian development to be predicated on the spillover of the industrialization process then in train in the northeastern United States. It stressed the necessity of the US market for engendering investment to effect a recovery, which American investment would then alleviate the high rate of unemployment. American capital would flow in for railway building as well. Political stability would be enhanced by the effects of the union, and hence provide a more suitable climate for the investment of foreign and domestic capital. The return of prosperity would inflate the value of the land in which much of Canada's elite measured their 'wealth,' and it would help induce more migration and stem the outflow of population. While annexation never occurred,

most of the desired results came about in one form or another.

As the old colonial system disintegrated, the North American colonies were forced to assume certain governmental functions themselves. Fiscal independence and the ability to regulate financial institutions, until then inhering in the Colonial Secretariat in London, were soon ceded to the colonies. Fiscal 'responsibility' meant simply that the colonial government became responsible for its own debts. It is thus scarcely surprising that 'responsible' government was foisted on the colonies by Britain over the vehement objections of the leading colonial businessmen who saw in 'responsible' government a diminution in borrowing power in Britain and the threat of being made to account for already existing debts. And inside Canada pressure began to mount for closer commercial ties with the US to find an industrial metropolis whose demand for Canadian raw materials would offset the loss of the formerly protected British market. The transfer of the commercial nexus from an almost exclusively British orientation in favour of increasing the flow of raw produce to the US manifested itself in both of the key staples of the era. While Canadian grain generally continued to find British markets, it increasingly moved via New York rather than Montreal. At the same time the British demand for Canadian timber fell as the Age of Steam and Steel dawned in Britain, while American demand for Canadian lumber as a building material in the opening of its western agricultural frontier and the industrialization of the east grew apace. The result of the shift in the orientation of the forest industry was to replace British commercial capital invested in the Canadian industry with American direct investment in saw mills and timber limits, shifting the relations of production from merchant-independent proprietor to capital-wage labour.

However, the shift in commercial orientation of the economy did not engender any diminution in British capital invested in Canada. Quite the contrary. Under the aegis of the Act of Union and especially at the time of the negotiation of a reciprocal lowering of raw material tariffs with the US, British capital poured into the province to support the dawn of the railway age. Railway promoters seized control of the government apparatus to use state revenues to support railway-building, both directly through subsidies and 'loans' and indirectly via the guarantee of securities sold by the promoters in Britain. While commercially the colony moved further from the British nexus, financially the power of the British investment houses, especially the Barings and Glyn, Mills, had never been so great.

Nor was the investment of British capital restricted to government or corporate debt earmarked for railway purposes. As the Canadian economy slowly matured from the exceedingly primitive pioneer structure typical of the very early decades of the nineteenth century, efforts to develop a local financial system proceeded apace. In the evolution of these institutions the response of the British financier was the all-important consideration. The first trust and mortgage loan company in Canada, established by the mercantile community of Kingston in 1843, stated in its charter that a crucial objective of its formation was to facilitate the influx of British money. Exactly the same consideration underlay both the formation of the Toronto Stock Exchange in 1853 and the passage of the first Canadian companies act introducing the general principle of limited liability in 1850. British capital was invested in the shares of some of the early commercial banks of the province in addition to the British commercial long credit that was essential to the early banks discounting activities. An experiment with 'free banking,' that is, small banks of deposit and issue, was abandoned in 1855 precisely because British capital was afraid to invest in such a presumably unstable banking structure.

Nonetheless railway finance was and remained the single most important link between British finance and the Canadian economy. The railway projects tied the Barings in particular more closely to the province than to any of their other clients, such that the Canadian political apparatus became little more than an overseas administrative arm of the private bank. The power ceded by the Colonial Office in Whitehall got no further than Lombard Street, there to stay for the rest of the century. The power of the bankers' was enormous and frequently exercised. In 1851, at the bankers' request, the province passed an act agreeing that the public debt would not be increased without prior consultation with the Barings and Glyn, Mills. To aid the democratic decision-making process, the Barings prevented Canadian securities from being quoted on the British Stock Exchange lists until the act was passed.

The Barings and Glyn were financial agents to the government of New Brunswick and Nova Scotia as well, though so much of their resources were tied up in Canada they could lend but little to the other provinces. Nonetheless some debts did exist. In fact debts to the Barings were about the only thing the British North American colonies had in common before Confederation. These debts in the Maritimes were largely the result of railway finance (and frauds as well), and provoked the same kind of direct interference by the British financiers in the political process there as was typical in Canada.

There were other major external sources of capital for the Atlantic region. Newfoundland remained the direct fiefdom of the London fish peddling interests. After 1825, for the first time the group of noble and ersatz nobel proprietors who ruled Prince Edward Island from afar allowed a few coins to make their way into land improvement–a paltry investment repaid many times over in rising rents. New Brunswick timber stands remained the happy hunting ground of British commercial houses: the American influx in the province was not as dramatic as in Canada–in large measure because the British government had simply ceded a substantial piece of New Brunswick timber lands directly to the New England lumber barons. In Nova Scotia the external investments were diverse. The great British commercial houses retained substantial agencies there even after the repeal of the Navigation Laws eliminated a large measure of Halifax's special position in the British West Indies trade. Halifax banks took a place in the long credit system in moving the imperial trade. The flow of funds on military account to Halifax remained substantial, and the natural resources of the province attracted the interest of overseas investors. The Nova Scotia gold rush of the 1850s drew in British and American funds; and the great Cape Breton coal fields were firmly in the grasp of the British-controlled General Mining Association, with a monopoly to 1857 granted by the British Crown.

The interior of British North America submitted to an exceedingly archaic mode of control. The power of the great chartered trading monopolies was a history-book phenomenon in the mid nineteenth century. Yet the western regions were controlled absolutely by the Hudsons's Bay Company, an absolute government with military and fiscal as well as monopolistic commercial powers. The gold rush of the 1850s in British Columbia tore that part of the Hudson's Bay Company fiefdom from it as a wave of individual American prospectors plus a battery of American gold dealers and assorted commercial and transportation interests swept the area. Still British finance and investment, in the form of Hudson's Bay Company subsidiaries in the transportation and commercial spheres and the sale of government bonds in London to finance the building of infrastructure, continued to dominate the economic structure.

Canada was by far the most important colony from the point of view of British investment. Fiscal policy in the province was inseparable from railway finance. In 1858 and 1859 an economic crisis struck the province, and the response set a crucial precedent for the future. The crisis was met in part by concessions to foreign capital whose vagaries by this time had a powerful effect on the state of prosperity of the Canadian economy. With the British-controlled railway system teetering on the verge of bankruptcy, tariffs were raised to augment government revenues. The minister of finance stated baldly that the purpose of the fiscal changes was 'to protect those parties in England who have invested in our Railway and Municipal bonds.'

Canadian interest in the importation of industrial capital began to manifest itself in this era. Businessmen's organizations with a number of objectives had begun to manifest themselves. Some were protectionist; all were in favour of rapid development. In Upper Canada the leader of the principal 'protectionist' bloc saw industrial development as synonymous with the importation of foreign manufacturing capital. While some business organizations called for the raising of tariff walls to stimulate local capital formation, he called for lowering of the tariff between Canada and the US to force British manufacturing firms to migrate to Canada, from which they would be better able to export to the United States. In 1866 tariff reductions were decided upon, one purpose of which was to encourage an influx of foreign indus-trial investments by reducing production costs in the province.

The American Civil War led to an economic boom in the province of Canada, and its close precipitated a commercial and financial crisis from 1864 to 1866. In Britain investors, already worried about the threat of American invasion of Canada, which would in all likelihood be followed by a repudiation of the Canadian public debt, saw railway earnings plummet and the lines facing bankruptcy once more. A financial crisis broke out in Britain early in 1867 complicating even further the delicate problem of colonial finance. The Barings and the Glyns were called upon for more interim financing for the province and fretted openly about the possibility of repayment.

Railway security issues were impossible, and even a government issue in 1866 was only partly saleable at a very substantial discount. A time of grave crisis when the traditional economic structures were proven untenable required imaginative leadership and political acumen to find a solution that would augur well for the future; both of these qualities were conspicuously absent from the ranks of those who found an expedient to temporarily salvage the provincial credit.

Dominion of Canada 1867-1914

Confederation followed logically from the 1840 union of the two Canadian provinces, which widened the tax base and thus assured the repayment of colonial debt. The result was to attach the revenues of the Maritime provinces to the empty treasury of the province of Canada. Both the British private banks and the Canadian financial élite and railroad promoters pushed avidly for the scheme as the sole means at hand for restoring the province's sagging credit. London finance was quick to give its assent to the new system of public credit. Less than six months after Confederation the new dominion placed a major loan in Britain without difficulty; six months previously dominion bonds had been only partly saleable at heavy discounts.

Railway finance proceeded apace. A few scattered instances of British direct investments in branch factories also occurred. Some British capital flowed into natural resources, especially petroleum in southern Ontario, and in general the inflow of capital revived somewhat. However these movements ground to a halt with the crisis of 1873 and the ensuing Depression. To reactivate the flow some other policy was required. Like a conditioned reflex Canadian governments responded to crises by efforts to cultivate the approval of foreign investors. What was new however was the type, the scale, and the role of the new investments in the Canadian development process.

There are two principal routes, with some minor variants, that an economy can follow on the road to industrialization. Manufacturing industry can grow up 'naturally' from a small scale, even artisanal mode of production when capital accumulation is a largely internal pheonomenon based on the reinvestment of the firm's own profits. A second path implies direct development to large-scale oligopolistic enterprise where outside capital is invested to facilitate its expansion and where the state takes an active, direct role in its growth. The outside capital required could come from commercial capital accumulation, from the state, or from foreign investment. The first path, if successfully followed, would lead to the emergence of a flourishing and independent national entrepreneurial class. The second may or may not; it may simply reproduce the conservatism of commercial capitalism in a new guise, the development of inefficient non-innovative, and backward industrial structures with a penchant for dependence on foreign technology, foreign capital, and state assistance.

In Canada during the formative years of the Confederation era, both paths of development were available. A string of small industrial establishments, catering to local markets, growing through reinvested earnings without outside capital, dominated a number of manufacturing fields—agricultural implements, meat-packing, much of secondary iron and steel, wool, boots and shoes, among others. These industries were largely, though certainly not exclusively, located in small urban centres and linked to the prosperity of surrounding agricultural areas.

On the other hand, the chief metropolitan centres of Canada witnessed another pattern of evolution as the wholesale merchants who grew to prominence in the staple trades began to reach back to control production. Iron and steel, cotton, and sugar-refining in particular

came under their control. There also emerged large-scale textile and woolen factories which quickly eclipsed the artisanal ones, and industries like railroad rolling stock with obvious links to the commercial sector of the economy grew up in this era. These industries had several salient characteristics. Their scale of production had to be large from the outset by virtue of the technology they utilised, their markets had to be widespread to cover their heavy fixed costs, and they relied on outside capital and assistance, from accumulated merchants' capital, from foreign investment and technology, and from the state.

Apart from the Patent Act of 1872 (which stipulated that for a foreign patentee to maintain his rights he had to ensure that manufacture of the patent took place in Canada within two years of the patent being granted, an act whose importance became evident at a later period), the chief forms of state intervention were the National Policy tariff of 1878-9 and a subsequent set of iron and steel subsidies and further upward tariff revisions. While the tariff of 1878-9 was a fiscal instrument designed specifically to deal with the crises of the 1870s its long-term effects were far-reaching.

A number of capitalist interests pressured for the high-tariff policy. Among domestic interests the wholesale merchants in the iron and steel, textile, and West Indies trades used the tariff wall to invest in primary iron and steel, cotton and woolen mills, and sugar refineries, often with British partners. The petroleum industry of southern Ontario, in a state of crisis and overloaded with British creditors and investors demanding a return, joined the pro-tariff ranks. The British capitalists and their Canadian junior partners in the Cape Breton coal fields did likewise.

Among small-scale industrialists in Ontario a split emerged. A very wide range of small-scale manufacturing interests fought the tariff, seeing in it an impetus to monopoly, which would quickly squeeze out the small producer, and a tax on a wide range of crucial industrial raw materials, especially primary iron products and coal. At the same time a large group who had benefitted from the artificial protection to Canadian industry that the American Civil War engendered, faced with renewed competition at the end of that war—a competition made more serious by depreciation of the American exchange rate and the beginnings of a long-term downward movement of prices which squeezed profit margins–responded by opting for protection. The split in the ranks of small-scale producers, with one group allying temporarily with Montreal commerce, and the British investors in other key sectors on the tariff issue carried the National Policy.

The objectives of the tariff were much more than the protection of existing industries, guaranteeing returns on already existing British industrial investments, or the provision of a climate for commercial capital to shift to industrial investments. Many industries in fact opposed and were crippled by the high duties. The tariff was explicitly intended to attract American and British industrial investments into Canada. During the tariff debates, a Conservative Senator declared, 'To secure the success of manufacturers we must endeavour to encourage the manufacturers and capitalists of Great Britain and the United States to establish workshops in the Dominion.' Yet perhaps the most important objective was the most traditional of all–to raise revenue especially in light of the major railroad projects being contemplated. The tariff revenue could be poured into promoters' pockets as a subsidy to construction. The minister of finance declared that if the tariff surplus were as much as anticipated, 'We will not from the day to the finishing of the Canadian Pacific Railway require to go the the English market except to replace those liabilities which matured.' Indirectly the tariff revenues guaranteed the repayment of government debts contracted earlier for railroad purposes. The immediate effect of the tariff was that Canadian public securities in London immediately rose to the top of the colonial list.

While a brief boom coincided with the new fiscal policy, by 1883 recession hit again, and the new large-scale industrial capacity, especially sugar-refining, iron and steel, and cotton faced collapse. Apart from new tariff increases, an iron and steel subsidy system, and a spate of new borrowings in London, there was little scope for government action. The period from 1873 to 1896, except for the 1879-83 revival, was one of very slow growth: the population was not growing, the western areas were largely empty, and few foreign branch plants were responding to the high tariff wall. But the world revival of 1869 brought a secular boom to Canada as well.

The transformation of the world economic order after that date had four main characteristics: 1/ it gave a new importance to raw material hinterlands with rising staple prices and industrial demand; 2/ it witnessed the renewed flow of financial capital from Europe, especially Britain, to the new and old raw material hinterlands of the empire, formal and informal; 3/ it also witnessed the transformation of the industrial base of the Western world with the old age of steam and steel giving way to the era of electricity, the chemical industry, and the internal combustion engine; 4/ the importance of the new industries meant a shift in the locus of world industrial power. Despite Britain's continued commercial and financial dominance, it was in the US above all where the new industrial system matured.

In Canada these trends manifested themselves dramatically. The staple frontier expanded rapidly in the West; the industrial base did likewise in the East; and a flood of immigrants provided both farmers and workers whose falling real incomes built the new prosperity for the Canadian commercial and financial élite. British portfolio investment was an essential building block for the new structures, and there was little the Canadian business and political élite would not do to encourage its influx to sustain the enormous program of railway development, to finance land settlement, to fund all levels of government, to float public utilities, and even for a brief atypical period to purchase industrial bonds to support a merger wave. In the name of maintaining the confidence of British finance, strikes were broken, provincial statutes threatened with disallowance and sometimes even actually disallowed, and the social efficacy of liberal democracy itself was publicly challenged by at least one eminent banker. The dominion government showed an unseemly haste to undermine and subvert the small amount of financial independence it had been ceded at Confederation by agreeing to disallow or repeal all laws that would impede or inhibit the British coupon-clipper from receiving the just reward of his great labour on behalf of Canadian economic development. The Dominion further pledged to the imperial financial élite Canadian troops for the war of colonial annexation in South Africa. In exchange for Canada's pledging financial fealty and despatching the troops, federal government securities were admitted in London to the much coveted Trustee List, whereby English trust funds could for the first time be invested in them. The Liberal finance minister who negotiated the arrangement could not restrain himself from crowing in the House of Commons that 'this action of the British government in coming to the assistance of Canada will be worth in actual cash every cent that it costs to send Canadian troops to South Africa.'

The results of the influx of British capital were several. The transportation system, public utilities, and financial institutions that were built up with the aid of British capital were confirmed in both their dominant position in the economy and in their Canadian ownership, private while solvent and public after bankruptcy; the impact of British finance capital reinforced the propensity to staple extraction for imperial markets; and the Canadian economy was bequeathed a huge burden of fixed-interest debt that had to be met out of the proceeds of rapid resource extraction for export to earn the foreign exchange required to repay the British loans.

Capital formation under Canadian control reinforced these patterns. Canadian banks drained funds out of the industrial centres of the eastern provinces and the agricultural (mixed-farming) areas of Ontario, formerly the staple frontier, and shifted the funds to the Canadian West. Both Maritime industrialism and the Quebec industrial entrepreneurs who had built up local industries in small urban centres underwent secular decline. The Ontario mixed-farming areas were depopulated and food production there underwent a relative decline. On the other hand the new staple-extracting areas flourished as a single cash crop frontier as the Canadian banks poured funds into financing grain movements for export, and Canadian insurance, mortgage, and trust companies drew funds out of the east or from abroad to channel into mortgage lending on the prairies. The result of the movement of capital into staples was to create a vacuum in the financing of industry, government, and other long-term investments that foreign capital had to fill.

The Canadian banking and monetary system of the period reflected well the structure of dependence on external finance. The reserves of the banking system, instead of being held in specie or in government of Canada notes, were held largely in the form of call loans in New York on the supposed rationale that the money there could be liquidated on demand for use in Canada when required. In fact the call loans in New York rose steadily and in times of crisis or need for more liquid funds it was the call loan business in Canada that contracted. As to government notes, these were scrupulously limited in issue to avoid provoking the ire of the Canadian chartered banking cartel. The result was to block off another potential source of finance for the government and force it to rely ever more heavily on external borrowings to finance the infrastructure it was building. As to those notes that were issued they were backed by a reserve of gold or British government securities, while the chartered banks had no reserve ratio at all.

A booming agricultural frontier should aid the industrialization process in several ways. It should provide cheap food under conditions of rising productivity for the industrial proletariat. It should generate surplus income for investment in industrial capital formation. And it should provide a market for the products of the industrial sector. In fact in Canada the new agricultural hinterland produced grain for export to imperial markets primarily, at the same time draining off funds and helping to underdevelop the mixed-farming areas producing foodstuffs for local consumption. Bread prices in Canada during the 'wheat boom' were higher than bread prices in Britain made from Canadian grain. Even flour was imported into the prairies from other parts of Canada or abroad. As to surplus income, the flow in fact moved the other way—from the industrial East to the agrarian West. The only aid to industry provided by the agricultural frontier was a market, a protected market for Eastern industry, while farmers sold their goods on international markets subject to the depredations of Canadian financial and commercial intermediaries as well as the vagaries of world grain prices. And much of the impetus to industrialization benefitted the American industrial system that was dominating an ever larger proportion of the Canadian industrial process.

American industrial capitalism entered Canada in four principal forms. In the pre-Confederation era came a flow of American technology via the theft of patents: American patterns and industrial designs were blatantly copied, often from imports which had an already established market. At the same time there came a migration of American industrial entrepreneurs who shifted bodily north of the border. The distilleries of Ontario, the sewing machine factories, foundries, and other parts of the secondary iron and steel industry, and especially the agricultural implements industry, were largely the products of one or both of these movements. After the Patent Act of 1872 which forced the American inventor to find a Canadian agent or establish a branch factory to retain his patent, and after the National Policy tariff of 1879 which cut American firms off from the Canadian market, the pattern changed. Instead of a flow of entrepreneurs and unattached technology which could be easily integrated into the Canadian economy, there came a movement of licensed affiliates dependent on a parent firm and controlled by an American parent, or joint ventures of American and Canadian capital around American product lines. There came as well a movement of direct investment in the form of full-fledged industrial branch plants. The new pattern carried with it a structure of industrial dependence that grew over time, a dependence that clearly could not be measured by any calculations of the value of foreign direct investment alone, there often being no flow of capital accompanying dependence by patent affiliation.

At first the licensed ventures existed in and returned royalties to their American parents in a number of scattered fields. But after the new prosperity following the 1896 recovery, a distinct pattern emerged. The new industries of the second industrial revolution—chemicals, automobiles, electrical apparatus, mining machinery, etc.—almost to the last firm entered Canada in the form of licensed ventures of American parents. These new industries were the growth industries of the future. And although there was often little if any direct American investment in them the patent relationship ensured their dependence and that innovation in technique and product line would be contingent upon decisions taken in the US. Canadian financial and commercial capitalists often invested in the industries based on American technology. During the National Policy boom of 1879 to 1883 the Canadian commercial and financial élite had allied with British capital and technique to make large scale investmets in sugar refining, cotton, primary iron and steel and other industries of the earlier epoch of industrialization. With the coming of the second industrial revolution they did the same with American capital and technique.

American direct investment grew steadily with the boom of the 1896-1914 period. Initially branch plants were established to regain markets lost behind the high tariff. Subsequently new forces came into play. The growth of the American national firm spilled over into Canada; tariff rates in Canada rose; the expansion of the Canadian market attracted new entrants; and the growth of the British Empire itself during this period made a Canadian location for an American firm all the more attractive. With Canada's growing exports of staples, further incentives to the migration of American capital existed. The American giant cereal mills moved in to process Canadian grains for export, and, secondarily only for the domestic market, increasingly displaced small local mills. Meat-packing too felt the effects of the expansion with American refrigeration techniques entering Canada in the form of branches of the giant American firms. A range of sophisticated metal products followed.

In resources industries the steady inflow of American capital into forests and mines accelerated. In part this increase in the rate of investment simply reflected the growing shortage of cheap, easily accessible resources in the US. In part it reflected the tendency of Canadian commercial capitalism, especially the banks and railways, to foster rapid extraction of primary products for export rather than encourage secondary processing. And in part it was a result of the actions of the provincial governments, starved for revenue, who responded to their rising expenditure liabilities by encouraging the rapid exploitation of royalty-yielding natural resources. In a few cases some effort was made to force some initial processing of the resources in Canada, with pulpwood export duties, threatened but not effected nickel duties, lead bounties, and a renewed iron and steel bounty system. The result, when the policies were effective, was to substitute some American direct investment in processing industries for American direct investment in resource industries.

The one major exception was the primary iron and steel industry whose foundations went back to the mid-nineteenth century but whose early financial career had been precarious. The old industry had been British-controlled, but its obsolete equipment and plant were idle when the boom began at the end of the century. The industry revived under specific conditions. The railway-building orgy that led to the opening of the western staple frontier guaranteed a home market, and Canadian commercial capital responded. American techniques were adopted. A sea of government largesse, federal, provincial, and municipal, was heaped upon the precocious infant. And the industry was built up and directed by American entrepreneurs in conjunction with Canadian commercial capitalists and British portfolio investment. These Americans were refugees from [sic] the big squeeze J.P. Morgan was then imposing on the American industry, which eliminated many of the small entrepreneurs who migrated north without any corporate strings attached. Like the agricultural implements and distilling industries in an earlier period, this industry, although totally derivative, had no corporate linkages and therefore grew to independence. From the time of the Forges of St. Maurice during the French régime to the true foundation of the industry in the early twentieth century, the pattern of development of primary iron and steel showed a remarkable persistence. External capital, state subsidies, American technique, and commercial demand–either derivative from the fur trade and the military posts required to defend it as in the French régime or derivative from the wheat trade and the railways needed to move it as during the late years of the British régime–these factors in conjunction with local commercial capitalists built and maintained the industry.

The Canadian economy since the First World War

The years 1912 and 1913 saw the spectre of chronic recession hanging over the Canadian economy: world wheat prices plummetted, the overextended railroads faced bankruptcy, and a merger movement of industry, financed by British capital, came to a sudden halt with a drastic liquidation threatening. The war, however, brought respite. An enormous industrial expansion in the East occurred based predominantly on imperial munitions requirements; the western grain frontier revived again as high wheat prices encouraged inefficient and overextended farming, and for a while the railroads looked solvent. War however only delayed the crash that was inevitable after the rush of development of the preceding decade. The railways began to collapse as early as 1917; the postwar recession forced nationalization of two of the systems. The banking system was salvaged only by a postwar continuation of the wartime manna of government fiat issues. The merger wave fell apart, and grain prices fell catastrophically.

The war and its aftermath also eroded considerably the ability of Canada to raise loans in Britain. The British economy entered a long era of crisis, and investors who had already felt the bite from the postwar crash were reluctant to re-enter the Canadian loan business. More and more portfolio capital had to be raised in the US, and the flow of American direct investment continued to grow with a wave of takeovers of industries, especially automobiles, electricty, and the like, that had formerly operated as joint ventures and licensed ventures affiliated to American oligopolies. By as early as 1921 the structure of ownership that has continued to prevail to the present day was firmly in place. Canadian capital controlled the competitive, low level of technology sector, especially consumer non-durable goods. Canadian capital was solidly in control of the primary iron and steel industry whose capacity had been augmented enormously by its role in the massive blood bath in Europe during the war. The agricultural implements industry, while most of it was Canadian-controlled, nonetheless had a substantial American interest, as did the agri-business sector, milling, and meat-packing. In the smelting and refining of non-ferrous metals, especially where new electrical techniques were required, in petroleum-refining, in automobile, electrical apparatus, and chemical manufacturing American capital was solidly entrenched. Yet Canadian policy remained predicated on the need for even more foreign investment, especially American direct investment, to sustain the process of economic growth.

One enigma immediately emerges from the posture struck by the Canadian ruling clique in the postwar period–why they chose to pursue the policy of industrialization by invitation vis-à-vis the American corporate system. The experiences of the war had pointed in another direction. War had cut Canada off from external capital. The war had been financed internally by a massive redistribution of income from the poor to the rich. A flood of paper currency caused rapid inflation of incomes of the rich while wages and farm incomes were held down. The redistribution thus built up enough great fortunes to provide an internal market for bond issues to aid the process of war finance, the burden of repayment of which could be spread over the population at large by the steep tariff and excise duties on consumer goods. Domestic financing was not only adequate for the massive internal economic expansion of the war but also for Canadian exports of capital to finance the war effort abroad. At the same time in the postwar period no great commitments to build infrastructure on the level of the prewar investments were necessary.

The decision to continue to foster the inflow of foreign capital, especially direct investment, was the result of several factors. The chronic postwar recession caused panic in financial circles in Canada, and the conditioned response to recession was to try to alleviate the short-run problem by increasing the long-run problem, by importing more foreign capital to offset the crises caused by an over-reliance on foreign capital in the prewar period. Furthermore an organized and militant labour force in Canada entered the political scene for the first time as a factor of immense importance, and the possibility of continuing to finance expansion by a squeeze on working-class incomes was considerably circumscribed. The Canadian capital market before the war had been thoroughly integrated with that of New York, especially via the activities of the Canadian banks in Wall Street; the war had meant a temporary interruption and when it ended the normal flow of funds was renewed as quickly as possible. A Canadian entrepreneurial class, small and weak though it had been, no longer existed to all intents and purposes—the least-cost, least-risk pattern of industrial development by a junior partnership role had already been well rehearsed. The pending collapse of the British Empire was obvious to all, and the need for a new metropole to replace Britain was widely appreciated. All of these factors, coupled with the 'natural' expansion of American big

business typical of the era, determined the development pattern that was followed. American investment thus grew steady during the decade of the twenties while British investment fell absolutely and relatively. The inflow continued into the Great Depression as the proven device of high tariff walls was used once more. The success of the new tariff of 1932 was registered immediately in an increase in the number of American branch plants in Canada, an influx encouraged in the hope that, at least in part, it would offset the virtual cessation of domestic private net investment during the Depression. It would further provide the foreign exchange earnings to help settle the staggering burden of fixed interest payments due to Britain as a result of past borrowings: interest and dividend payments during the Depression combined with falling prices of staple exports to absorb 25 per cent of total foreign exchange earnings.

During the Second World War, as in the First, the private inflow of capial was replaced by a massive outflow in loans and grants to allied economies to finance their war effort; at the same time output surged ahead. However, with the return of peace, the traditional patterns were quickly resumed. The 1950s saw the dawn of a long boom, fed by American investment, primarily in Canadian natural resources, though the flow of investment into manufacturing plant also accelerated. The investments in the resource industries were encouraged by a number of factors. By the mid 1950s the American government deemed twenty-nine industrial raw materials as likely to be in short supply in the US in the near future, if not already. For twelve of them Canada was regarded as the major source of supply, not only by virtue of availability but also security. In one other case Canada was classified as the major supplementary source should the leading producer fail to fill US political or economic needs. And the list of commodities discussed did not include forest products or energy where US reliance on Canadian products was accelerating rapidly. The boom in resources in the 1950s was led by investment in Alberta oil and gas. US capital poured into forest products on an unprecedented scale. And in the 1960s American interest in hydro-electric power production and fresh water supplies in Canada led to the emergence of a number of grandiose schemes for their development. The flow of investment also reflected Canadian policy. Tax concessions to foster rapid resource depletion were built into the fiscal structures of all levels of government. As to manufacturing, the structure of foreign, especially American, investment began to change. Instead of investments in branch plants for the production of American product lines, simple horizontal extensions of the American firm, or vertical integration via investments in the production of raw and semiprocessed materials to meet the needs of the American parent, the conglomerate merger phenomenon began to dominate the movement of American capital across the border. A growing number of Canadian businesses were absorbed by American firms intent on diversifying their interests to spread risks and profit-taking over a large number of product lines and enterprises.

The consequences of the assiduously cultivated tightening of the American hold have been several and far-reaching. Commodity trade patterns have been increasingly twisted into a north-south basis with a substantial part of it taking the form of intracompany transfers. Of this trade, the Canadian subsidiaries and even the independent sectors export raw and semifinished products, while Canada imports finished products from the US. The only significant manufactures exported from Canada are automobiles and parts, exported to the US by completely American-controlled Canadian branch plants of the large automobile producers, and armaments exported under the Defence Production Sharing Agreement. Both these exports represent efforts to transfer the locus of part of the production of American firms to their Canadian subsidiaries. Both were a modern variant of the old game of inducing a northward flow of American industrial capacity by commercial policy. With tariff increases contrary to international law and with preferential tariffs anathema under the new postwar American rules of the game, the bilateral discriminatory arrangement necessary to induce the movement had to take these other forms. Both also had the effect of making two of the largest sources of employment in Canada directly dependent on the whims of the American State Department and thus involved, much as had the resource-alienation policy, an implicit guarantee of good political behaviour on the part of the Canadian government.

The industrial structure that exists in Canada today, apart from exhibiting the greatest degree of dependence of any in the world, for the same reasons is notoriously inefficient and non-innovative. The pay-off from the Patent Act of 1872 and all its successor legislation had been very powerful. After the Patent Act and again after the National Policy tariff of 1879 patents granted to Canadian residents fell absolutely. As a percentage of total patents issued, those granted to Canadian residents for the next hundred years exhibited a secular decline. And the current Canadian record of patents granted to its own residents is one of the worst in the world. Technological backwardness and lack of industrial research in Canada are self-reinforcing.

While the industrial structure has been increasingly pulled into the American orbit, even to the extent that American anti-trust legislation bears a powerful influence on its organization, the capital market has done likewise. As the American balance of payments crisis deepened in the 1960s with a deterioration of the balance of trade and an increased outflow on capital account to maintain the military infrastructure around the world, the American government responded by a series of measures to try to improve the capital account by twisting the patterns of private investment. In 1963 a 15 per cent interest equalization tax was imposed to cut back on the amount of portfolio borrowing being done in the US by foreign governments and firms. Canada begged for exceptional status and it was granted, almost automatically. The intent of the tax was to cut back the long-term portfolio capital outflow while, it was hoped, leaving intact the flow of direct investment abroad. At that time there could be no question of curtailing the outflow of funds on military account. Two years later more drastic measures were tried—the 'voluntary' guidelines which pressured American multinational firms to cut back on their export of capital, to do a larger share of their long-term borrowings abroad, to repatriate short-term assets held abroad, and to step up the rate at which they repatriated earnings from their foreign affiliates. With its own balance of payments crisis looming as an immediate consequence of the American action, the Canadian government again begged exemption. It was granted, but for a price. In return for its privileged access to the American capital market, giving it unrestricted ability to pawn its natural and industrial resources, Canada had to peg the level of its foreign exchange reserves and relend any surplus above an agreed figure to the US. The agreement to peg the reserves was bad enough, effectively precluding as it did any independent monetary policy in Canada; to the extent that any was possible before, it vanished thereafter. But, more important, the guidelines gave the American government the power to dictate the investment policies of a large part of the manufacturing and resources sector of the economy. In 1968, in exchange for further exemptions from the new mandatory guidelines, the Canadian government made what was, even for it, a catastrophic concession. It froze the already perverse pattern of international capital flows into the status of an officially sanctioned and enforced pattern. US funds flow into Canada on long term to take control of resources and businesses, while the foreign exchange is automatically relent to the US on short term. Canada thus officially agreed to continue to borrow back at long term what it lent at short term. Finally in 1971 came the New Economic Policy, a new program of subsidizing exports, curtailing imports, abdication of previous trade agreements, and sundry other methods to repair the crisis. Again Canada begged exemption, and it secured only partial satisfaction. Just how much sovereignty and wealth was bartered away in the corridors of power in Washington remains unknown.

For the private capital market the effects of American domination have been marked. The growth of wholly owned branch plants has caused a relative shrinkage in the volume of shares traded on the stock exchanges, especially in the already weak category of industrial shares. Canadian equity investment flows through its financial institutions to the US. In Wall Street too Canadian banks do over half the call loan business that keeps the American stock jobbers going. The result can only be to impede the marketing of new issues by independent companies in Canada. Precisely the same considerations hold with respect to corporate bond issues in Canada, impeded by a limited and illiquid market at the same time Canadian financial institutions carry large portfolios of American bonds. This twisting of the capital market which facilitates the trend to industrial dependence is in fact an outgrowth of a historical process of evolution as long as, if not longer than, the pattern of industrial domination itself.

Canadian Investment Abroad

At the same time that the Canadian economy provided the leading example of a capital 'borrowing' country in all the various possible forms—commercial credit, portfolio capital in government loans, utilities and the like, direct investment in manufacturing and resources—it also undertook the export of capital in its own right, making short- and long-term investments in the metropolitan economies as well as seeking its own hinterlands to dominate.

The flow of capital from Canada to other countries began in the French régime. Fur-trade fortunes accumulated in the colony often returned to France in the form of investments, especially in land. While some of this outflow was the 'natural' result of the return of the fur traders themselves to resume or begin residence in the metropolis, some of it constituted a flow of unaccompanied long-term capital, over and above simple remittances of profit to the French partners in the business. The Church in Quebec also made long-term investments in France from its earnings from land in the colony. And most substantial of all were the massive sums plundered from the public purse and the population at large by government officials who remitted these earnings to France for investment there.

The early years of British rule witnessed an export of capital in several directions. Accumulations by wholesale merchants in Montreal and Halifax sustained investments in the United Kingdom, including at least one case of investment in the British asset of the era that carried the highest rate of return—the purchase of a seat in the unreformed House of Commons. As in the French régime, a major objective of early merchants in British North America was to make as much money as quickly as possible in the colonies and to subsequently retire to the metropolis. Typically the very few Canadian wholesale houses that entered the timber trade to Britain had to establish a British branch house, but the British branch often evolved into the head office of the concern.

As their roots in the colonies became firmer, other external investments attracted the merchants' attention. While New York capital was being invested in the Welland Canal system, Montreal capital found its way into the equity of the Erie Canal. Canadian banks by the 1830s were solidly established in exchange speculation in New York; Maritime wholesale houses extended long credit to the West Indies followed in 1837 by the creation of a joint-venture of Halifax and London capital in the establishment of a bank in the West Indies, the first of a long series.

Towards mid-century, and especially after the negotiation of a reciprocal lowering of raw material tariffs between British North America and the US in 1854, Canadian banks grew in importance in financing international movements of produce in Chicago and expanded their role in New York. As well, Canadian railway investments in the US began on a large scale.

The decades between Confederation and 1896 witnessed a slow but steady growth in Canadian activity in the US and the Caribbean, but with no major innovation apart from a few industrial branch plants. After 1896 however major structural changes occurred. Canadian banks and insurance companies spread across the Caribbean into Latin America. Great utility promotions involving Canadian direct investment also dotted the area. In the US the Canadian banks and railroad investments multiplied; the banks by that time had become indispensable for the operation of Wall Street stock jobbers. They were joined by large insurance company portfolio investments in American utilities and by direct investments by Canadian firms in the secondary iron and steel industry.

There was a major distinction between Canadian investments in the Caribbean and South America and those in the US. Those in the Caribbean and South America were aggressive enterprises, involving substantial economic control and imposing a large net draining of funds on the areas concerned. Those in the US were rentier-type investments, or were geared to facilitating long-distance trade, or to call money operations in Wall Street. They thus represented a substantial drainage of funds from Canada to the US. The Latin American investments helped per-petuate the area's colonial status: the American investments helped perpetuate Canada's colonial status. The contrast is sharp between Canadian banks' drainage of deposit money out of the Caribbean to Canada and their drainage of deposit money out of Canada to the US. It is equally strong with utilities–Canadian direct investment and control of major operations in Latin America on the one hand and Canadian portfolio investments in American promotions in the US on the other. The Bank of Nova Scotia's portfolio investment in United Fruit Company bonds neatly summarizes the relations for all the areas concerned.

With the decline and fall of the British Empire, Canadian investment abroad in the underdeveloped world began to shrink in importance. The banks remained in place, as did the insurance companies, but the utility and railroad operations abroad dwindled. But as the Canadian hold on the underdeveloped areas declined, the volume of investments in the US in the form of railway extensions, portfolio investments by financial institutions, and bank activities, grew. The Canadian investments in secondary iron and steel in the US were eclipsed by the growing hold of the US secondary iron and steel industry in Canada. However, among industrial investments, partnerships with American racketeers during the prohibition era permitted a number of respectable old Canadian breweries and distilleries to lay the basis for further growth in the US. The post war period accelerated these trends as the Canadian capital market grew increasingly integrated into that of the US, both by virtue of the 'natural' growth of the banks and financial institutions and as a result of conscious government policies on both sides of the border.

The proliferation of multinational corporations in the period since the mid 1960s had its Canadian representatives as well. The Canadian Pacific Railway had evolved into a modern conglomerate, albeit still firmly rooted in transportation and communications. The banks' importance in Europe and beyond, either by themselves or as part of multinational bank consortia, was another development of the period. A few mining operations began, renewed, or strengthened themselves abroad. The creation of a badly misnamed Canada Development Corporation in 1972 was the federal government's response to the request of Canadian big business for public money to assist their international development. But despite a few spectacular successes, which because of their roots in the old established banking and transportation sector represent the exceptions that prove the rule, Canadian participation in the multinational scramble has remained necessarily feeble. And those cases where participation has occurred in sectors other than finance and transportation may well reflect the fact that expansion within Canada is blocked by the already existing American hold; hence the aspiring Canadian multinational is forced to move abroad, unlike the American which moves as a result of its internal growth.

Conclusions

Canadian dependence on foreign capital has deep historical roots. From the beginning of white exploitation of its natural resource base external capital in one form or another has been invariably an adjoint of its development process. The type of 'foreign' investments changed as the metropolitan economies developed and as their economic objectives vis-à-vis the hinterland economies altered. Commercial credit and loans or subsidies from metropolitan governments to the colonies dominate the early, preindustrial relationships based on looting of the surface resources. With the coming of the industrial age in Britain, larger scale, longer term commercial investments, plus long term loans to finance the construction of infrastructure to move industrial raw materials and foodstuffs from the colonies to British markets, became typical. As the nineteenth century drew to a close, Canada became an open field for British portfolio investment prompted directly or indirectly by the search for more raw materials and foodstuffs for the imperial market, and for American direct investment prompted by the growth of an internal Canadian market and the rise of American oligopolies. In time the second source of foreign investment displaced the first completely.

The relations between Canada and the two great metropolises of recent history bear in some ways a striking resemblance. During the golden age of British finance capital, the note issue of the dominion government was linked to its holdings of British government securities, and until the First World War virtually all of its coinage was struck in Britain. Its financial and banking institutions were in many ways linked to those of Britain through the flow of funds to the colony. British law reigned supreme in many fields. Not only was the dominion's political power directly circumscribed and ultimately subject to British judicial review, not only did legislators tremble at the prospect of inciting the ire of the lords of high finance, but statutes in the dominion explicitly acknowledged the ultimate rule of British finance. Canada eagerly participated in the imperial wars and zealously sought bilateral preferential arrangements with the metropole.

As the balance of world economic power shifted to the US, drawing Canada into its orbit, similar relations emerged. The Canadian capital market and its financial institutions became directly tributary to those of the US. Canadian governments pledged financial fidelity to the stars and stripes to maintain and reinforce the tributary relation, subjecting the Canadian financial system to direct US rule. American law entered Canada along with its capital just as in the heyday of the British empire. Canada directly profited from, as well as participated in, the imperial wars. And large parts of its industrial base survive only by virtue of bilateral preferential arrangements with the metropole.

It is tautological that a capitalist economy and the society built upon it takes its orders from a capitalist class. And it is certainly an unassailable proposition that economic power is unevenly distributed among the various capitalist economies of the world. It follows that every 'small' capitalist economy is susceptible to a degree of outside direction of its development process. However the degree to which the Canadian capitalist class not only has bowed to pressures from abroad but has deliberately and earnestly set out to induce those very pressures to which it has bowed results in a difference in kind in its external relations, rather than just in degree. It makes the Canadian experience approximate much more closely that of a Third World neo-colonial economy than that of a small Western European economy. The level of its national wealth and the extent of industrialisation, albeit dependent and derivative, are superimposed on a set of social relations and economic structures that are essentially neocolonial. The typical neocolonial economy, when measuring its poverty and the degradation of its people against the shameful abundance and waste of the Canadian social system might well retort that it would give a great deal to achieve Canada's hinterland status. So, it seems, would the Canadian ruling class, for as long as they have something left to give.

[1]The principal sources from which this paper is derived are two works by the author: *The History of Canadian Business, 1867-1914*, two volumes (Toronto: James Lorimer and Co. 1975), from which the Canadian material from the 1850s to the First World War is taken in summary form; and a preliminary draft, 'Economic History of Canada.' Full footnote references will be available in these books.

THE EMERGENCE OF THE CANADIAN WORKING CLASS MOVEMENT, 1845-75

Steven Langdon

"No important attempt has been made to base an analysis of our history on class," says S.R. Mealing, "nor is there any weight of research to suggest that such an analysis is possible."[1] That statement is accurate, particularly for the time when it was published (1965).[2] But the observation is less a reflection of Canada's actual development, than a serious criticism of Canadian historiography. Or so this article argues. At least for the 1845-75 period in central Canada, class was an emerging and powerful reality for many Canadians–a reality which shaped their thought and action, and influenced the future pattern of their country.

What do I mean by class? E.P. Thompson's definition is apt:[3]

Class happens when some men, as a result of common experiences (inherited or shared), feel and articulate the identity of their interests as between themselves and as against other men whose interests are different from (and usually opposed to) theirs. The class experience is largely determined by the productive relations into which men are born–or enter involuntarily.

Thus, Thompson adds, "class is a relationship, not a thing." And the emphasis in understanding the relationship must be on shared, subjective feelings of common objective situation and interest–on class consciousness, that is, developed historically.

Thompson applies this definition to England in the 1780-1832 period, and finds it fits: "Most English working people came to feel an identity of interests as between themselves, and as against their rulers and employers."[4] A somewhat similar process of class emergence is clear among central Canadian working people, in the 1845-75 period. It represents the making of the Canadian working class–using that phrase as Thompson does: "*Making*, because it is a study in an active process, which owes as much to agency as to conditioning."[5] Working people shaped *themselves* as a class, in interaction with a changing socio-economic environment; and they did so without the direction of that vanguard party or intellectual elite which it is now too often the patronizing fashion to believe must carry wisdom to the workingman.

This study traces that progress. It follows the gradual growth of organizational cohesion and of class consciousness among central Canadian working people from 1845 to 1875; it argues that this development had reached significant proportions, and a relatively radical political perspective, by the early seventies; and it demonstrates that this rise was intimately inter-related with the emergence of an industrial capitalist political economy in the area. The importance of the process is three-fold. First, at the time, it influenced Canadian development choices significantly. Second, historically, it established certain traditions and social roots which shaped today's working-class and radical movement in Canada. And third, historiographically, tracing this process of working-class emergence illustrates the basis and need for a class-oriented approach to interpreting Canadian development generally.[6]

I-The Industrial Capitalist Transformation

The sixties in central Canada, wrote *The People's Journal* in 1871, "set agoing an industrial revolution . . . ."[7] From points of commercial exchange in the 1840's, dominated by merchants and oriented around trade with Britain, central Canadian cities had by the 1870's become centres of industrial capitalist production—marked by dynamic factory complexes, shaped by powerful industrialists, and inhabited by a large industrial workforce. Given the leverage of these cities in patterning Canadian development,[8] this urban transformation meant central Canada had effectively become an industrial capitalist political economy.

The social process of capitalist industrialization of the first industrial revolution, in England, was thus mirrored at this later period in central Canada.[9] Large, increasingly mechanized factories rapidly expanded—especially in Montreal, Toronto and Hamilton. In Hamilton, for instance, a significant industrial sector had already emerged by 1864 (2,300 workers were employed in 46 factories—43% of these steam-mechanized—all in a city of 19,000). By 1870 this sector showed even further dramatic growth (the number of workers per factory was up 52%, the percentage of steam-powered plants up 32%, and so on).[10] This was the pattern across Canada. "Factories," wrote one 1872 observer, "are springing up in every part of the country . . . ."[11]

Similarly, a conscious class of industrial capitalists appeared, as these factories grew. Early industrial operators in Canada were usually merchants, for whom production was a sideline; and in their political action they followed the commercial capitalist lead—as in rejecting protective tariffs for industry.[12] By the 1860's and 1870's, though, independent industrialists were organizing their own collective institutions—some for co-operation in particular sectors (like the Canadian Iron Founders Association, formed by leading stove manufacturers)—others for cohesive action throughout the whole political economy (particularly the Association for the Promotion of Canadian Industry, run by Canada's most important industrialists by 1870). These class institutions increasingly influenced public attitudes and government activities to the benefit of industrial capitalism. Macdonald's National Policy, with its high protective tariffs, was the ultimate triumph of this industrialist action.[13]

Finally, there was that most characteristic feature of industrial capitalism—the emergence of a self-regulating, impersonal labour market.[14] As Pentland shows, this institution was also developing in central Canada after mid-century.[15] The breakdown of older, personal, paternalistic employment ties is obvious in the rising strike statistics for the time; the self-regulating nature of the new market is clear in the similar wage rates, by occupation, in different Canadian cities—and in the parallel ups and downs of such wage rates city by city. By the sixties and seventies, a mature impersonal labour market was operative in the area. In fact, central Canadian working people were part of a continental labour market, marked by large-scale movement back and forth across the Canadian-American border.[16]

In England, this process of capitalist industrialization (though it also produced "a vast movement of economic improvement") brought on an "avalanche of social dislocation for most ordinary Englishmen."[17] This was the case for many Canadian workers, too, in the 1860's and 1870's. The growing industrial cities were marked by grim housing conditions and serious health problems. Working conditions in the rising factory complexes were even worse. And the emergence of an impersonal labour market, especially, generated greater inequality, unemployment and poverty in central Canada.[18]

Two inter-related trends were responsible for this. First, the rise of an impersonal labour market undermined job security. Under the old system of personalized employment ties, in the isolation of Canada, a firm had to keep its workers on the payroll, even when business suffered a cyclic decline—or else it wouldn't have enough workers to take advantage of upturns in the future. Thus the social cost of cyclic depression was fully shared by employers and employees. In an impersonal labour market, though, the employer could readily hire the workers he needed, exactly when he needed them. So in a cyclic downturn, he could simply dismiss excess workers—and be sure of getting replacements when business boomed in the future. The result was rising unemployment during cyclic declines—and increased poverty for working people. What the change amounted to was this: the social cost of the capitalist trade cycle was no longer fully shared; it was predominantly borne by employees. That helped further industrialization—because it left capitalists with more resources, to respond to business up-turns when they came. But it also brought painful social dislocation to working men and women.

Second, this spreading labour market, and the driving mechanization of industry, combined to undercut the wages of employees, especially if they were unskilled. The introduction of new machines meant that old craft skills were no longer as necessary in the production process. So some of those with such skills (and appropriate good wages) could be dismissed; and the labour market could provide unskilled replacements (often children or apprentices), readily able to do the routine operations on a machine, at much lower wages. This effect was reflected in the significant increases in child labour use that ongoing mechanization brought to central Canada.[19] And, even where skilled workers kept their jobs, their wages ordinarily fell; machines meant there was less premium for their old skills. This process hit printers, tailors, shoemakers, cigarmakers and many others, as the material below illustrates.

So unemployment and poverty increased with industrialization. In Toronto, for instance, the number of people receiving poor relief increased by 478% from 1850 to 1865.[20] Cyclic unemployment became common; by 1869 a *Globe* reporter angrily wrote that "hundreds if not thousands of men are out of employment, families are starving, and the great cry of these men is for work. But that they cannot get."[21]

It was in response to such social dislocation in England (says Polanyi), that "a political and industrial working class movement sprang into being." The purpose was to slow down and regulate change, to enforce a collective community control over it—so that economic improvement should not also mean social distress.[22] This happened in central Canada, too. The rest of this study traces how. I look at three periods, in turn, in this process of developing class cohesion and consciousness: the forties and earlier fifties, when workers' collective action was tentative, isolated and trade-oriented; the later fifties and earlier sixties, when trade unionism expanded, mostly in a craft context; and the later sixties and seventies, when rapidly increasing organizational linkages marked the emergence of a working class *movement*, with a good base of support and distinctly radical views—insofar as radicalism implies a collective sense directed toward establishing social equality.

II—The Forties and Earlier Fifties

There were two significant sorts of collective action by workingmen in this period. The first involved *ad hoc* and non-institutional reaction, by workers, to particularly intolerable circumstances—without establishing a continuing organizational form after the immediate protest had either succeeded or failed. The strikes of Irish labourers, on Canada's public works, provide the best examples of this.

In 1843, for instance, workers on the Lachine and Beauharnois canal projects near Montreal struck against the further reduction of already extremely low wages, and against the way those wages were often paid—in "Store" pay, good only at the company store. Perhaps using secret Irish societies, and certainly relying on their tight sense of ethnic community, the Lachine workers struck unanimously: "we are all Irishmen . . ." their strike notice said. It appears that the strike was successful, too. But no continuing workingmen's organizations emerged from the event.[23]

Similarly, Irish labourers struck and rioted on the Welland canal works in 1842, protesting the fact that only 575 of 2,000 available workers had been hired for the season.[24] Irish labourers also struck, for higher wages, on the Great Western railroad near Hamilton in 1848.[25]

These strikes were all important as first signs of working people's efforts to control and regulate the impersonal labour market, which was growing around the infrastructure projects advanced by a commercial community. But they also illustrate how difficult sustained collective action was in circumstances of such shifting, seasonal and casual employment. And without more permanent institutions of class action a continuing growth of class consciousness was impossible; for it meant there was no way to assess collective actions and analyses, and improve on them in an ongoing process.

Secondly, though, there *were* some continuing workingmen's organizations that did develop in this period. Like the few trade unions that emerged in the 1820's and 1830's, however,[26] those of the forties and earlier fifties were small and confined to particular cities and particular trades. Still, there was a growing number of them: in Montreal, for example, a stonecutters' and a printers' union in the forties, and unions of shoemakers, bakers, and engineers in the early fifties;[27] in Toronto, unions of stonemasons, printers, and cordwainers (shoemakers) in the forties, and of tailors by the early fifties;[28] and in Hamilton, of printers in the forties and of tailors and shoemakers by the fifties.[29] These organizations were largely isolated from one another. There is, for instance, no mention in the Toronto Typographical Society (TTS) minutes from 1845 to 1851 of contact between the Society and any other Toronto union. And while there were some communications with Hamilton, Montreal and Quebec typographical societies, and even with the printers' union in Rochester, these contacts were far from extensive.

Because of this localization and isolation, such unions had a tenuous existence—as the absence of records from their short lives testifies. Even the TTS (whose records do survive) experienced some very weak periods after their 1844 formation; no meetings could be held, for lack of a quorum of nine members, for six months in 1845-46. TTS members felt a sense of public hostility, too; Thomas Hill, for instance, argued against an 1845 handbill

because the public to whom allusion is made in the statement . . . are adverse to any kind of combinations among workmen, how mild soever their form or righteous their intentions.[30]

Their isolation and sense of vulnerability were a part of the reason why workingmen in these early unions were trade-oriented rather than class-oriented in their attitudes; i.e., they seem, by and large, to have expressed an identity of interest with others in their particular trade (including their employers), rather than with other tradesmen or other workers generally. The TTS, for example, had for its "great" object "maintaining our own position in the Trade." Consequently, the Society stressed, the interests of employer and employee were one and the same—"one and indivisible," as the TTS President put it at an 1849 anniversary dinner for the union, at which employers were honoured guests. The union sought, it said,

a better understanding between two parties, who are sometimes carried away with the erroneous idea that their interests are antagonistical instead of being, as they in reality are, mutual and reciprocal.[31]

Similarly, after an 1852 dispute, the Journeymen Tailors' Operative Society of Toronto sat down to celebrate the settlement with their employers in the St. Lawrence Hall, over goose and cabbage.[32]

Much of this sentiment, though, was more wishful thinking than hard-held analysis. The process that was generating the early unions was placing those unions in conflict (if only occasional) with their employers; and that same process, the rise of industrial capitalism, was just as inevitably forcing workers to move beyond their trade consciousness. Consider two cases, printers and tailors.

Because newspapers were such important communication media in pre-1850 Canada, printing was one of the earliest sectors of potential large-scale production. So it was one of the earliest sectors of industrial mechanization; as early as 1844 George Brown's

Globe introduced extensive new machinery (the first cylinder press in Upper Canada).[33] As suggested above, this undermined job security and wages for skilled printers—through the much greater use printing firms were consequently able to make of unskilled "apprentices." This is clearly what the TTS was reacting to in its early formation; increasing use of apprentices was an angry preoccupation of the Society right from the beginning. Thus the mechanizing Brown was strongly attacked by the TTS in 1845 for "nearly filling his office with boys" (i.e. apprentices). The use of these men, stressed the TTS,

> would occupy the situation which regular hand otherwise be called upon to fill (sic)— and thus throw numbers of men out of employment and ultimately reduce the wages of the whole.

What the unionists opposed, of course, was not mechanization *per se,* but the use of unskilled labour on the new machinery; and their opposition grew increasingly fierce. By 1850, they were referring to "the Monster evil—the bane and curse of every printer . . . *the indiscriminate employment of apprentices.*'[34]

Similarly, the early tailors' unions were sparked into existence by the first stages of industrial mechanization—in this case by the introduction of the steam-run sewing machine. In Toronto the struggle began in 1851-2, when workmen there, "fearing for their craft," broke the first of these machines brought to the city and combined to prevent the introduction of others.[35] In Hamilton, the Journeymen Tailors' Protective Society reacted the same way in 1854, seing the new machine as "threatening extermination to the whole craft.''[36]

The significant point, though, and a further reason for the trade-consciousness of early unions, was that at first the strong solidarity of those skilled workers within the particular trade was sufficient to counter these dangers to jobs and wages. By organizing just about every skilled craftsman within a trade in any one city, and setting up a protective fund, a union's bargaining position could be strong indeed, simply because the undeveloped labour market for skilled workers meant that outside replacements for strikers

were hard to find. Thus the TTS was able to defeat attempts to lower printers' wages in both 1844 and 1847, without even undertaking a strike. Even if apprentices were being more widely used, the TTS was maintaining full employment for all its members at high wages. The tailors were even more successful, effectively preventing the introduction of the sewing machine in Toronto in 1852. In these circumstances, trade consciousness was natural, because it was sufficient to defend craftsmen's positions.

But the situation couldn't last, once the labour market spread more widely, and the drive toward mechanization gathered more momentum. Employers were forced to introduce technological innovations and to try to hire the lowest-cost workers possible—or else face undercutting from competitors at home or abroad. So they had to take aggressive action against the unions that limited their freedom of action. As a result, the trade-oriented unions were forced into clear, dramatic conflicts with those employers, in which unionists had first to abandon any idea of "one and indivisible" identity with their opponents, and then second to develop concepts of countervailing solidarity and assistance among all workingmen—across craft lines within one city, and across city lines within one craft.

This aggressive employer action was obvious by the early fifties. In 1853 and 1854, for instance, the TTS was forced into strikes to defend its pay position, and the printing firms began to find it possible to hire replacement workers. In 1854 the firms even organized themselves jointly to fight the "secret combinations and foul threats" of their employees, hiring female typesetters as replacements for strikers.[37] In such a context, any idea of identity of interests rang hollow. By 1854, the goose dinner had also given way to court action; the firm that sought to introduce sewing machines had the executive of the Journeymen Tailors' Protective Society arrested for conspiracy.[38] As the next section shows, a new consciousness among workers developed out of such conflict; they began to draw organizational links with each other and think in similar terms.

Throughout most of this period, though, interests *did* remain trade-oriented. This led to a singular concentration by unionists on the immediate and special concerns of employment in their particular trade. Thus, between 1845 and 1851, the TTS entirely ignored social or political concerns beyond the printing trade; and on the single occasion on which there was even a hint of politics intruding (the union considered inviting Lord Elgin, then the centre of controversy over the Rebellion Losses Bill, to its 1850 anniversary dinner), the result was a serious dispute within the TTS and the president's resignation "in consequence of the political and general ill-feeling which I have observed in several members of this Society."[39] One exception to this apolitical pattern was an unsuccessful 1852-3 effort, supported by workers' petitions from Brantford, Hamilton and London, to have the Legislative Assembly "prohibit the payment to mechanics . . . of wages in goods or way of truck."[40] But this *was* quite exceptional.

Still, the effort did preview later political action by working people. And likewise, within their city craft insititutions, workers were developing a collective sense that previewed wider collective action in the future. The TTS, for instance, established mutual benefit provisions in its constitution (which also helped keep the organization together); it committed itself to "rescue from privation our less fortunate fellow workmen, . . . administering to the wants of others of our Profession"; and it stressed, in 1847, that:[41]

esteeming one another as brothers of a glorious fraternity . . . we are knit together by ties that should be considered as indissoluble, being in the words of our motto, "United to Support–not combined to Injure."

The early stages of capitalist industrialization had generated that solidarity; and the continuing thrust of industrial capitalism would widen such feelings of common community much further.

III–The Later Fifties and Earlier Sixties:

This was the period when factory complexes first began to develop significantly in central Canadian cities. New sectors of mechanized industry emerged, producing machines, metal goods, shoes and tobacco particularly. In these new sectors new collective action by workers developed. At the same time, the spread of the self-regulating labour market was taking impersonal labour relations into all parts of the Canadian economy; so workers were organizing collective responses in a wide number of other sectors, too. In all these sectors the changing consciousness previewed last section was evident; workers were moving away from an identification with employers in their trade, to a greater sense of solidarity with their fellow employees, in other cities and in other trades.

The growing organization linkages of this period were one sign of the change. The first international unions, for instance, appeared in central Canada. In the machinery sector, various locals of the Amalgamated Society of Engineers, a British-based union, organized themselves; from one local with twenty-one members (in Montreal) in 1853, the ASE had grown to include four locals and 207 members (in Montreal, Hamilton, Toronto and Brantford) by 1867, forming a small union of highly skilled men.[42] In the metal-working sector, various local unions in Canada joined the newly-formed International Molders Union (IMU) in 1859; by 1867 there were eight locals with 270 members in central Canada (mostly in Toronto and Montreal). Moulders, too, were highly skilled craftsmen.[43]

In the boot and shoe sector, union organization also moved forward quickly. During the period local unions of shoemakers were reported at various times in Montreal, Toronto, Hamilton, Oshawa, St. Catharines and London.[44] Some of these were associated with the US-based Journeymen Shoemakers of the US and Canada–which was involved in a Toronto strike in 1857-58, and had a local in Hamilton in 1858.[45] But the most dramatic sign of increasing linkages came in 1867, when shoemakers gathered in Toronto to form a Boot and Shoemakers Union of the Province of Ontario; delegates were present from eight cities.[46] Cigarmakers showed the same pattern. Local unions formed in various Ontario centres, and organized a provincial Journeyman Cigarmakers Union in 1865.[47]

Similarly, the TTS widened its contacts considerably in the late fifties and early sixties. By 1865 it was in direct communication with two British unions and at least nineteen US city typographical unions.[48] This was a prelude to the Society's decision in 1866 to affiliate with the National Typographical

Union of the U.S. Thereafter, although the TTS was jealous of its local autonomy,[49] the Toronto printers were closely involved in affairs well beyond their own local milieu. By the end of 1867, the TTS president was a member of the International executive committee; the TTS standing committee was going office-to-office in Toronto discussing with members the proceedings of the International; and financial assistance was being granted to US strikers.[50] Contact among printers inside Canada increased as well—as shown by the encouragement the TTS sent striking Quebec printers in 1862.[51]

This pattern of organization linkages reflected the ongoing response of workers to industrial capitalism. First, industrialization remained the key to union emergence. It brought together workers into larger collective units of production, which permitted them to form continuing organizations with some strength. And it sparked workers toward such organization by the ongoing thrust of mechanization. The new unions were as much a response to the job security and wage threats of industrial capitalist change as the printers and tailors unions examined above. Thus the IMU, for instance, also focused on the apprenticeship issue in its struggles; that problem, the union said in 1861, "has given us more trouble than all others combined."[52] William Sylvis (the IMU President) explained why on his 1863 organizing trip through Canada; he noted that in Kingston where the IMU local had collapsed, there were now "boys without number," and moulders' wages had dropped severely.[53] That, of course, is exactly the sort of social dislocation that unregulated industrial capitalism usually generated. When employers in the US and Canada organized a grand lockout in 1866, they illustrated the importance of this unskilled labour issue too; one of their central objectives was to "proceed at once to introduce into our shops all the apprentices or helpers we deem advisable. . . ."[54]

Second, industrial capitalists continued to fight the restrictions which strong unions put on their freedom to benefit from the expanding labour market. The lockout against moulders was one example of this tough employer action; shoe manufacturers also used the courts against Toronto shoemakers in 1858; while the Butler and Jackson iron foundry in Brantford warned Sylvis in 1863 it would ultimately "break up" his union.[55] United action against the IMU was, in fact, the primary impetus toward formation of the employers' Canadian Iron Founders Association in 1865—reflecting Thompson's points about English industrialists developing class cohesion only in the face of workingmen's collective action against them.[56]

In these circumstances, tradesmen were forced to expand their organizational horizons. Three tactical imperatives, in particular, underlay this expansion.

The critical sanction that gave workers their power in the early period of mechanization was their ability to stop strikebreakers from finding jobs if a strike were won. That is, if a worker deserted his fellows during a strike, and the strike were ultimately successful, unionists would refuse to work with the deserter, and the firm that had hired him would have to fire him if it wanted union members to come back to it. So the strikebreaker would be without a job. This sanction in favour of solidarity, however, was less effective in the transience of North America if the strikebreaker could simply move to another city without penalty. So local unions began to trade "Ratting Registers," to enforce the ban on working with strikebreakers on a much wider basis. In 1860, for instance, TTS members in one office refused to work with a man who "had been guilty of 'Ratting' in Buffalo . . until he shall have made ample reparation to the Buffalo Union for his offence."[57] This tactical innovation was one factor in promoting wider union contact and cooperation.

A second imperative grew from the maturing spread of the impersonal labour market—because as a result of that spread, employers found it possible to import craftsmen from other cities during disputes. This too, was an impetus toward cross-city union co-operation; locals began to keep each other in touch with their affairs, to discourage cross-city movements into strike-breaking situations. In 1865, for instance, the Detroit Typographical Society wrote to the TTS of an upcoming strike in that city, "requesting that this society use its influence in preventing printers from going there at present."[58]

Finally, as conflicts with employers became more bitter, local resources and protective funds were no longer sufficient to buttress local unions during disputes. Access to outside funds became more and more important in winning fights. This was particularly true, for example, of the four year strike which Brantford moulders finally won against Butler and Jackson in 1864; financial aid had been give by the IMU central fund from early 1861.[59]

Wider organizational linkages developed naturally from these imperatives toward co-operation. And a correspondingly wider consciousness of common interests also developed among workers, at least insofar as the TTS provides evidence. By 1860, all the 1849 rhetoric was gone about "one and indivisible" identity with employers; instead the TTS stressed "the favourable opinion formed of us as a Typo body by our brethren of the craft in the US and Canada."[60] The point of reference had shifted from employers to fellow craftsmen throughout the continent.

There were even signs of this sense of common interest spreading outside the single craft context to encompass other craftsmen and other workers generally; unions' need to provide each other with mutual aid during disputes was a major impetus in this direction, too. Thus in 1862, local 26 of the IMU in Hamilton put its resources behind an effort by Journeymen Bakers to reduce their hours of work. The moulders resolved (and advertised to that effect in the press) that they would "not patronize those of the master Bakers of this city, who will not comply with the request of the Journeymen Bakers. . . ." They stressed their widening sense of common interests by appealing to "all the working class to join us in carrying out this resolution."[61] Similarly, the TTS loaned money to the Cigarmakers' Union of Toronto in 1867.[62] A more dramatic extension of linkages came in 1863, when a city Trades Assembly was formed in Hamilton. The body seems to have had the power to sanction or forbid strikes by affiliates, and to organize contributions from fellow members to sanctioned strikes.[63] There were also signs of such co-operation (at least to the extent of organizing joint union picnics) in Toronto by 1867.[64]

These new ties reflected the maturing labour market, which left most workers in similar relationships with their employers. And as that labour market spread, so union organization spread—beyond the large cities which had industrialized earliest, beyond those large-scale sectors which had mechanized earliest (printing, metal working, shoe manufacturing, etc.), and beyond the skilled craft segment of the urban industrial labour force.

The first trend was clear in the wide number of smaller central Canadian cities and towns in which there were locals of the cross-city unions–the ITU, IMU, ASE and provincial shoemakers and cigarmakers. Toronto, Hamilton and Montreal locals were joined by those in Quebec, Brantford, Guelph, Georgetown, Stratford, London, St. Catharines, Kingston, Oshawa and Ottawa at one time or another in these unions. The second trend was clear enough, too. Carpenters and stonecutters unions proliferated in the fifties and early sixties. And by 1867 there were also unions of bakers, brushmakers, tinsmiths and seamen in Hamilton; of cabinet makers, bakers, masons, bricklayers, brushmakers, plumbers, saddlers, carriage makers, blacksmiths, ship carpenters, caulkers and tinsmiths in Montreal; and of bakers, harnessmakers and locomotive engineers in Toronto.[65] The third trend was obvious in this range, as well. Though most unions still represented skilled workers,[66] (the printers, shoemakers, machinists, tailors, moulders, bricklayers, cabinet makers, engine drivers, harnessmakers, plumbers and tinsmiths), semi-skilled workers were also beginning to organize (the bakers, blacksmiths, carriage makers, masons and shipwrights). There were even signs of unskilled organization (the seamen). There was other evidence of the latter, too—particularly in the rise of the Quebec Ship Labourers' Benevolent Society, a union of several thousand Irish longshoremen which had been formed in 1857, and had reached a powerful strength by 1866.[67]

So workingmen's organizations were expanding widely. The large-scale, rapidly industrializing sectors were marked by cross-boundary and intra-provincial links among unions. These unions were recognizing and organizing their links with other working people. And these institutional developments were reflected in a consciousness that was closer to class perspectives than to trade feelings of mutual interest.

I must not exaggerate the state of central Canadian labour organization by the mid-sixties, though. Unions remained small and vulnerable, even when they had formal links with central bodies of workingmen. The IMU itself, for instance, briefly disintegrated at the International level in 1862; and various of its Canadian locals had to be reorganized several times before they stayed active.[68] Even the confidence and resources of the ASE in Britain couldn't stop Brantford and Kingston ASE branches from dying several times.[69] The TTS suffered too, seeing its membership fall from 76 in 1859 to 31 by 1866, because of the "great depression of business which prevailed throughout the larger part of the year."[70] Society meetings lacked quorums for five months in 1863 and five months in 1865. Conditions for non-affiliated unions were even more difficult; so organizations sometimes formed, disappeared and reformed in regular cycles of enthusiasm, difficulties, defeat—then resparked enthusiasm. Nor were any of the ongoing unions large at this stage; of locals for which the membership is known, none had 100 members by 1867.[71]

Nor had there been any significant movement in this period toward concern with wider social and political issues. Workingmen's organizations had not yet the strength, confidence and consciousness to move outside the immediate and direct concerns of employment. And even in *those* concerns, central Canadian workers at this period seemed still to be responding, often defensively, to the continuing drives of mechanization and market adjustment in the emerging industrial capitalist economy. They had not yet reached an institutional maturity sufficient to take collective *initiatives* in society. Signs were evident, then, of the rise of a central Canadian working class during these years; but the process still had far to go by the mid-sixties.

NOTES

[1]S.R. Mealing, "The Concept of Social Class and the Interpretation of Canadian History," *Canadian Historical Review*, Sept., 1965, 212.

[2]At that point, there had indeed been little weight of research presented on either the application of class analysis to Canada or, more specifically, the role of working people in Canadian history. There had, of course, been some work in the latter area—some of it cited in this study. But Forsey's judgement on much of it is justifiably brutal: "most of the work, even the academic work, which has been done on the general history of Canadian labour simply cannot be relied on." See E. Forsey, "Insights into Labour History in Canada," *Industrial Relations*, 20:3, July, 1965, 448. Since 1965, though, a marked increase of interest in Canadian labour history is apparent. Both an example of the trend, and a bibliography of recent and forthcoming material, see *Committee on Canadian Labour History*, Bulletin No. 1, York University, 1971.

[3]E.P. Thompson, *The Making of the English Working Class* (Harmondsworth, 1968), 9-11.

[4]Ibid., 12.

[5]Ibid., 9.

[6]Such an approach should not concentrate on class *per se* as a determining factor in historical interpretation. But an emphasis on class is a useful way to inter-relate so-called political, economic and social factors of development in a *politicial economy* approach to analysing social change. See S. Langdon, "The Political Economy of Capitalist Transformation: Central Canada from the 1840's to the 1870's," MA thesis, Institute of Canadian Studies, Carlton University, 1972, chap. 1.

[7]*The People's Journal*, Apr. 1, 1871–clipping in the Buchanan Papers, Public Archives of Canada (PAC), MG 24, D 16, vol. 112.

[8]See J.M.S. Careless, "Frontierism, Metropolitanism and Canadian History," *Canadian Historical Review*, 1954, 1-21; also such supporting evidence for his argument as D.G. Creighton, *The Empire of the St. Lawrence* (Toronto, 1956)–concentrating on Montreal's role in the earlier commercial capitalist period; D.C. Masters, *The Rise of Toronto* (Toronto, 1957); J. Spelt, *The Urban Development in South Central Ontario* (Assen, 1955)–both of which trace Toronto's dominance as it develops in southern Ontario and the rest of Canada.

[9]For description and analysis of the process in England, cf. K. Polanyi, *The Great Transformation* (Boston, 1967); E.J. Hobsbawm, *Industry and Empire* (Harmondsworth, 1969); Christopher Hill *Reformation to Industrial Revolution* (Harmondsworth, 1969); M. Dobb, *Studies in the Development of Capitalism* (London, 1963).

[10]The statistics for 1864 are from Sessional Paper 6, 1865, 142-7. The comparisons with 1870 draw on data for the same firms from the manuscript returns of the Census of 1871, PAC, RG 31, sections 695, 705, 712-16.

[11]*Report of the Ottawa Immigration Officer*, Sessional Paper 2A, 1872, 58.

[12]W.H. Merritt, the St. Catharines merchant who diversified into grain milling and ship-building, is a good example. See J.P. Merritt, *Biography of W.H. Merritt* (St. Catharines, 1875), 300 ff.

[13]See Langdon, chap. 5 and 6. The CIFA is discussed in C.B. Williams, "Canadian-American Trade Union Relations," Ph.D. thesis, Cornell, 1964, 92-4. The APCI is best documented in the Buchanan Papers.

[14]Polanyi explains why this market must inevitably emerge with industrial capitalism: "Since elaborate machines are expensive, they do not pay unless large amounts of goods are produced. They can be worked without a loss only if the vent of the goods is reasonably assured and if production need not be interrupted for want of the primary goods necessary to feed the machines. . . . (That means) that all the factors involved must be on sale. . . . Unless this condition is fulfilled, production with the help of specialized machines is too risky to be undertaken." Therefore, Polanyi continues, "the extension of the market mechanism to the elements of industry–labour, land and money–was the inevitable consequence of the introduction of the factory system in a commercial society. The elements of industry had to be on sale." *The Great Transformation*, 41, 75.

[15]See H.C. Pentland, "Labour and the Development of Industrial Capitalism in Canada," Ph.D. thesis, Toronto, 1960. A summary of part of the thesis is available in Pentland, "The Development of a Capitalistic Labour Market in Canada," *Canadian Journal of Economics and Political Science*, 1959, 450-61.

[16]Langdon, chap. 4.

[17]Polanyi, 40.

[18]*Report of the Select Committee on Hygiene and Public Health, House of Commons Journals*, App. 8, 1873; *Report of the Commission on Mills and Factories*, Sessional Paper 42, 1882–both offer some evidence on these matters. See also Langdon, chap. 7.

[19]In Hamilton, for instance, in 32 firms for which comparable statistics are available, child labour as a percentage of employees increased from 5.9% to 9.8% over 1864-70–at the same time mechanization increased. Langdon, chap. 7.

[20]*Globe*, Nov. 14, 1850; Sessional Paper 10, 1866, 26. From 674 to 3,895. The latter was some 9% of Toronto's 1861 population.

[21]*Globe*, Jan. 26, 1869. This increasing poverty was reflected in the emergence of new charitable institutions, too. Langdon, chap. 7.

[22]Polanyi, 83.

[23]See H.C. Pentland, "The Lachine Strike of 1843," *Canadian Historical Review*, 1948, 255-77.

[24]W.H. Merritt to the Governor-General, Aug. 17, 1842, Merritt Papers, PAC, MG 24, E 1.

[25]*Globe*, Jan. 19, 1848.

[26]On which see Forsey, 446; C. Lipton, *The Trade Union Movement of Canada* (Montreal, 1966), 3-8.

[27]Forsey, 446-7; *Globe*, May 1, 1854; Minutes of the Toronto Typographical Society (hereafter TTS), PAC, MG 28, I 72, Apr. 2, 1845; Canadian Labour Congress files on labour history (hereafter CLC), PAC, MG 28, I 103, vol. 247.

[28]Forsey, 446-7; TTS, Apr. 2, 1845; *Globe*, Nov. 17, 1847; Dec. 7, 1852.

[29]TTS, Aug. 5, 1846; CLC, vol. 249 (citing Hamilton *Gazette*, Feb. 16, 1854); *Globe*, June 15, 1854.

[30]TTS, July 2, 1845.

[31]TTS, Apr. 2, 1845; Mar. 7, 1849.

[32]J.M. Connor, "Trade Unions in Canada," in J.E. Middleton, *The Municipality of Toronto*, vol. 2 (Toronto, 1923), 558.

[33]J.M.S. Careless, *Brown of the Globe*, vol. 1 (Toronto, 1959), 46.

[34]TTS, July 2, 1845; Nov. 4, 1846; Jan. 5, 1850.

[35]*Globe*, Dec. 7, 1852.

[36]CLC, vol. 249 (citing Hamilton *Spectator*, Feb. 10, 1854).

[37]*Globe*, June 8, 1854; June 12, 1854.

[38]*Globe*, July 13, 1854; July 17, 1854. Note also the court action against the Toronto shoemakers' union in 1847–*Globe*, Nov. 17, 1847; and against Hamilton shoemakers in 1854–CLC, vol. 253.

[39]TTS, Jan. 19, 1850.

[40]*House of Commons Journal*, Index, 1852-66.

[41]TTS, Apr. 2, 1845; Feb. 10, 1847; Apr. 5, 1848; Feb., 1849.

[42]CLC, vol. 247–ASE file.

[43]Williams, 135ff; see also CLC, vol. 248–IMU file.

[44]CLC, various volumes.

[45]CLC, vol. 253.

[46]*Globe*, Sept. 20, 1867; see also CLC, vol. 249 (citing Hamilton *Evening Times*, Sept. 21, 1867).

[47]*Ibid.* (citing *Evening Times*, Nov. 18, 1865). Its officers were from Toronto, Hamilton and Brantford.

[48]TTS, Nov. 1, 1859. Between 1859-65, the TTS was in touch with printing unions in Buffalo, Louisville, San Francisco, Boston, New York, Mobile, Montgomery, Charleston, Milwaukee, Chicago, Leavenworth, Cincinnati, Indianapolis, Albany, Cleveland, Peoria, Sacramento, Memphis and Detroit.

[49]See the dispute over whether union locals in the ITU should have uniform constitutions–TTS, Oct. 9, 1867: Nov. 13, 1867.

[50]TTS, Dec. 12, 1866; Sept. 11, 1867; Nov. 13, 1867.

[51]TTS, Jan. 8, 1862.

[52]Williams, 97.

[53]*Ibid.*, 115.

[54]*Ibid.*, 120.

[55]*Ibid.*, 114; CLC, vol. 253.

[56]Thompson, 12.

[57]TTS, Sept. 7, 1860.

[58]TTS, June 14, 1865.

[59]Williams, 119.

[60]TTS, Jan. 17, 1860.

[61]CLC, vol. 249 (citing Hamilton *Evening Times*, Sept. 9, 1862).

[62]TTS, Jan. 9, 1867.

[63]CLC, vol. 249 (citing Hamilton *Spectator*, Dec. 12, 1863; Hamilton *Evening Times*, June 1, 1864; Nov. 10, 1864).

[64]TTS, Aug. 10, 1867.

[65]CLC, various volumes; *Globe*, May 11, 1854; July 25, 1867; Nov. 15, 1867; *The Locomotive Engineers' Monthly Journal* (hereafter LEJ), Department of Labour Library, Ottawa, Jan. 1867, 12.

[66]Using, with one change, the definitions and divisions used by P.G. Goheen, *Victorian Toronto, 1850-1900* (Chicago, 1970), 229. He puts printers in the "less-skilled" category; I place them in the "skilled" category.

[67]J.I. Cooper, "The Quebec Ship Labourers' Benevolent Society," *Canadian Historical Review*, 1949, 336-43.

[68]Williams, 111, 116-18.

[69]CLC, vol. 148–ASE file.

[70]TTS, Jan. 11, 1866.

[71]See Williams, 135; CLC, vol. 247–ASE file; TTS, Jan. 8, 1868, IMU local 28 (Toronto) had 96 members, Hamilton's ASE Branch 91, Montreal's ASE 77, the TTS 75 and IMU Local 26 in Hamilton 62.

THROUGH THE PRISM OF THE STRIKE: INDUSTRIAL CONFLICT IN SOUTHERN ONTARIO, 1901-14

Craig Heron and Bryan D. Palmer

The trouble with the heads of many industries is that they become money mad and drunk with the power that money brings. They think that they can do anything and everything in a high-handed and ruthless manner just because they have a fat bank account and gilt-edged securities lying in some safety deposit vault.

When an employer gets that notion into his head he is almost shaking hands with disaster. It is a purely selfish idea and is mainly responsible for strikes.

It is the unbusiness-like attitude that produces unrest among the toilers. It is the tidal wave that will some day engulf the greedy, grasping and gloating galoots who think they can do as they like because they happen to be rich and powerful.

The worm always turns on men like that.[1]

This outburst from the *Bobcaygeon Independent* in 1913 reflected a marked upswing in industrial conflict which accompanied the massive economic expansion in early twentieth-century Ontario.[2] Its dramatic description of the responsibility of the moneyed class for the conflict conveys both the characteristic tone and the analytical weaknesses of the 'people's press' of the period.[3] To go beyond such generalized condemnation and probe deeper into the contours and context of industrial strife, we have examined strike activity between 1901 and 1914 in ten southern Ontario cities that were emerging as major industrial centres.[4] In Berlin, Brantford, Guelph, Hamilton, London, Niagara Falls, Oshawa, Peterborough, St. Catharines, and Toronto, the 'toilers' and the 'greedy, grasping, and gloating galoots' clashed frequently after the turn of the century. Through an examination of this conflict, in which the strike looms large, we can learn much about class relationships in these early years of a maturing central Canadian capitalism.[5]

What emerges clearly from even the most superficial glance at strike activity in the years 1901-14 is the magnitude of the conflict between labour and capital. Stuart Marshall Jamieson's portrayal of the 'relative placidity of labour relations' in Ontario during these years seems strangely misplaced.[6] The ten cities under discussion experienced the trauma of 421 strikes and lockouts in this fourteen-year period and approximately 60,000 working men and women participated in these battles.

The pattern of this strike activity buttresses the classic contention that industrial unrest follows closely upon the heels of economic cycles of contraction and expansion. In the boom years prior to 1904 an unusually tight labour market brought about a sharp increase in the incidence of strikes. As years of economic retrenchment, 1904 and 1905 saw the pace of unrest slacken; a resurgence of strikes in 1906 and the early months of 1907 told of the return of more prosperous times. But with the economic downturn of 1908 strike activity came to a virtual standstill, and the severe depression year, 1908, witnessed the least number of conflicts in the entire period. Only in 1910 did the number of strikes begin to rise again significantly, reaching a peak in the early part of 1913. The prewar recession quickly stifled the growing conflict, however, and by 1914 strikes were once again quite uncommon. Strikes, then, were commonly resorted to in times of prosperity when concessions were more easily wrung from recalcitrant employers, and were more sparingly employed in years of recession, most

Table I
The Contours of strike activity, 1901-14

City	Number of strikes	Number of strikers
Berlin	13	552
Brantford	14	715
Guelph	24	1024
Hamilton	92	11249
London	38	1650
Niagara Falls	6	1356
Oshawa	1	263
Peterborough	11	302
St Catharines	24	2346
Toronto	198	38903
TOTALS	421	58356
Industry		
Building	110	23654
Metal	106	11216
Clothing	48	8675
Woodworking	33	3345
Food, Liquor, and Tobacco	31	2184
Miscellaneous	27	1779
Unskilled	24	3758
General Transport	14	2377
Printing and allied	11	591
Leather	9	259
Textile	8	518
TOTALS	421	58356

Source: *Labour Gazette*, 1901-14

prominently 1908 and 1913-14, when labour's chances of even the most marginal victories were slim indeed.[7]

Finally, the contours of industrial strife in these years reveal important patterns of geographical and industrial concentration. Predictably, the geographical locus of strike activity coincided with the concentration of population. Toronto and Hamilton, the largest urban centres under consideration, far outstripped the other cities in terms of the number of strikes and workers involved: Toronto sustained 198 strikes or lockouts in the years 1901-14, in which 38,903 workers participated, while Hamilton experienced 92 such conflicts, involving 11,249 working men and women. Oshawa, in contrast, saw only 263 workers strike on a single occasion in the entire period, in February 1903. Workers in the building and metal trades were clearly in the vanguard of this industrial upheaval, leading fully half of the total number of strikes in the ten cities. Trailing them, but playing a major role, were workers in the clothing, food, liquor and tobacco, and woodworking trades. More generally, it was the skilled that provided the cutting edge of opposition: unskilled labour participated in less than 6 per cent of the total number of strikes in the ten southern Ontario cities. In the following pages, therefore, it will be the craftsman who will be prominently in the foreground. From these broad contours we must turn to the context of industrial conflict if we are to capture an understanding of the forces precipitating the many strikes and lockouts of the period.

Perhaps the fundamental feature of the context of industrial strife in southern Ontario between 1901 and 1914 was the accelerating pace of industrial capitalist development. After more than thirty years of economic expansion, the first decade and a half of the twentieth century saw the pace of industrialization quickened and pushed to new heights. Penelope Hartland has argued that the years 1900 to 1914 represented the most rapid growth in the Canadian economy since the decade preceding Confederation, and the 1911 census noted 'the gratifying movement of the country's industrial prosperity during the last decade.'[8] Finally, the period witnessed the acceleration of the process of concentration and consolidation of business enterprises initiated in the late 1880s.

In his study of the Canadian 'merger movement,' H.G. Stapells documented fifty-six major consolidations in manufacturing industries in the years 1900-12.[9] As a result more and more southern Ontario workers found themselves working in large factories: in Hamilton, for example, 135 firms employed 18,695 of the city's 21,149 industrial workers in 1911.[10]

While this economic development was undoubtedly a national phenomenon, southern Ontario seemed destined to play a leading role: the area offered easy importation of raw materials, especially the coal and iron vital to the development of heavy industry; efficient and lucrative marketing facilities and transportation networks were close at hand; skilled and unskilled labour was long established in the area; cheap hydro, particularly after the turn of the century, was easily obtainable; and local politicians eagerly enticed firms, notably branches of large American corporations, with lucrative bonuses and tax exemptions. Under these conditions southern Ontario cities attracted industry and capital with relative ease, and new factories mushroomed while older concerns expanded. Table II conveys the dimensions of the growth in the cities under consideration.

Berlin developed thriving footware and furniture plants, while the smaller manufacturing businesses—producing rubber, motors, engines, pianos, organs, soup, sugar, and shirts—continued to thrive. Brantford quickly emerged as a major centre of the metal trades, while the tobacco, textile, and carriage construction industries remained active. Guelph, Niagara Falls, London, St. Catharines, Oshawa, and Peterborough all mixed heavy and light industry, as did Toronto, which embraced an impressive variety of establishments producing miscellaneous goods for a rapidly expanding home market. In Hamilton, long renowned for the vigour of its metal trades, heavy industry concentrated with amazing rapidity. With the introduction of steel production, undertaken by the Hamilton Steel and Iron Company in 1900, the city quickly established itself as the banner city of Ontario's heavy industry. By 1905 more men were employed in various realms of the city's metal trades than in any other industrial category; a host of ancillary trades— farm implements, electrical parts, machine and tool works, bearings, and elevator production–also located in the rising 'Birmingham of Canada,' grasping the opportunity to locate near ready supplies of raw material and skilled labour.

The impact of expansion of these years, of course, transcended the figures of aggregate growth and gross output compiled by statisticians and economists. As E.P. Thompson has stressed, 'the transition to mature industrial society entailed a severe restructuring of working habits–new disciplines, new incentives, and a new human nature upon which these incentives could bite effectively . . . '[11] Two such disciplines and incentives, mechanization and new conceptions of managerial authority or industrial efficiency, were of particular relevance in capital's quest for 'the restructuring of work habits' and the creation of a new, more pliable, human nature. Although set in motion a century earlier in the first throes of the Industrial Revolution, this process was accelerating rapidly by the early

Table II
Manufactures in ten southern Ontario cities for 1891, 1901, and 1911

City	Years	Establish-ments	Capital	Employees	Value of Products
Berlin	1891	94	1,499,486	1827	1,825,722
	1901	68	2,500,810	2758	3,307,513
	1911	76	8,501,844	3908	9,266,188
Brantford	1891	250	3,231,879	2841	4,280,999
	1901	44	6,830,871	3603	5,564,695
	1911	111	19,972,623	6492	15,866,229
Guelph	1891	159	2,199,931	1886	2,973,927
	1901	68	3,532,641	2206	3,689,183
	1911	78	7,152,635	3072	7,392,336
London	1891	805	6,192,342	6039	8,225,357
	1901	120	6,824,574	5675	8,122,185
	1911	180	15,469,635	9413	16,273,999
Hamilton	1891	1133	8,175,557	9609	14,044,521
	1901	232	13,494,953	10,196	17,122,346
	1911	364	58,013,768	21,149	55,125,946
Niagara Falls	1891	36	192,910	246	369,435
	1901	14	403,547	422	422,728
	1911	39	21,976,792	1085	3,266,651
Oshawa	1891	94	799,748	921	1,155,085
	1901	22	1,660,065	1206	1,343,100
	1911	24	6,179,062	3220	6,266,226
Peterborough	1891	216	1,993,615	1876	2,594,996
	1901	44	3,123,358	2166	3,789,164
	1911	65	6,415,466	4029	10,633,119
St. Catharines	1891	108	1,721,661	1310	2,444,680
	1901	40	1,841,423	1900	2,070,573
	1911	58	5,919,728	3139	6,024,017
Toronto	1891	2401	31,725,313	161,751	241,533,486
	1901	847	52,114,042	189,370	367,850,002
	1911	1100	145,799,281	238,817	579,810,225

SOURCE: From *Census of Canada*, 1911, III (Ottawa 1913), 351—3. The drastic decline in the number of establishments between 1891 and 1901 results, partially, from the changing criterion employed by the census. While in 1891 any productive unit was considered a manufacturing establishment, by 1901 the growing concentration of capital resulted in an alteration in the census' definition of an establishment: only those concerns employing over five individuals were to be considered.

twentieth century.

The disruptive impact of technology and mechanized production on the skilled crafts of the late nineteenth century in advanced capitalist countries is an often told tale, although the Canadian experience has only just begun to receive attention.[12] What has recently been stressed, however, is the other side of the historical coin: the degree to which skilled workers retained much of their craft status, pride, and economic security through a thorough organization and control of the productive process. Gregory S. Kealey has recently demonstrated the lasting power of iron molders and printers in the face of the mechanization of Toronto's skilled trades,[13] while David Montgomery's study of craft workers in the late nineteenth century in the United States regards skilled workers' control of the productive process as the touchstone of their self-conception of manhood: 'Technical knowledge acquired on the job was embodied in a mutualistic ethical code, also acquired on the job, and together these attributes provided skilled workers with considerable autonomy at their work and powers of resistance to the wishes of their employers.'[14] In many trades, as George Barnett early demonstrated in the case of the printers, mechanization had little disruptive impact, for craft unions were able to 'keep tabs' on the new machines by forcing employers to hire only skilled journeymen to run them.[15] Craft workers, as Benson Soffer has argued, cultivated a rich and varied collection of shop floor control mechanisms throughout the course of the nineteenth century. Such devices, assuring skilled workers a degree of autonomy at the work place, exercised a tenuous hold over work relationships in many nineteenth-century trades.[16] Underpinning these mechanisms was a resilient consciousness of pride and self-confidence in their social worth that would carry these workers through many struggles.

Yet, even granting the significant degrees of control over the work processes exercised by many craftsmen to the end of the nineteenth century, by the early twentieth century technology had made real strides in diluting skill and transforming the workers' status on the shop floor. Complementing this propensity of modern machinery, moreover, was another development. Aware of the impediments that the autonomy of the skilled worker had raised against productivity and authority, employers turned to an array of managerial innovations and efficiency schemes after the turn of the century. Ranging from the employment of autocratic foreman, pledged to drive men and women harder and faster, to the utilization of complex systems of task simplification, job standardization, time and motion study, cost accountancy, and piece and bonus systems of wage payment, this amalgam of tactics became known as 'scientific management.' This pervasive thrust for efficiency, coupled with the impact of mechanization, constituted a concerted assault upon the control mechanisms and customs of the trade embedded within the consciousness and shop practices of the skilled worker.[17]

While the drive to rationalize and intensify the productive process through the agency of scientific management and industrial efficiency has its greatest impact in the United States, the movement's presence was felt to some degree in all industrial capitalist countries.[18] Canada, and particularly southern Ontario, did not escape this generalized experience despite the recent skepticism of Michael Bliss.[19] Much of the efficiency zeal undoubtedly became transferred to Canadian settings via the introduction of branch plants, while the increasing size of corporate holdings, accentuated after 1907 by the accelerating merger movement, lent a logic to the introduction of managers and shop-floor planners. In Hamilton, for instance, where by 1913 forty-five companies attested to US parentage—including such major employers as Canadian Westinghouse, International Harvester, and the Imperial Cotton Company—it is unlikely that managerial personnel were unaware of recent conceptions of techniques gaining such widespread currency south of the border.[20] Frank Jones, of the Steel Company of Canada, described as the best manager of men the young country had yet produced, must have been in direct contact with many of the managerial innovators.[21] But the case of Canadian manufacturers' adoption of the new 'science of management' does not rest on inference alone.

Frederick Winslow Taylor, the proclaimed 'father of scientific management,' received an enthusiastic endorsement from the *Hamilton Spectator* as early as 1906.[22] By 1908 Taylor's hand-picked disciple, Henry L. Gantt, was introducing a sophisticated piece-work system on a number of North American railroad lines, including the Canadian Pacific.[23] Moreover, in the spring of 1913 the journal of the Canadian Manufacturer's Association, *Industrial Canada*, printed three articles by Taylor, outlining the essence of his system of job standardization, task simplification, and wage payment; on 18 January of the same year Taylor himself had addressed the Canadian Club of Ottawa on 'the principles of scientific management.'[24]

With the potential of innovative managerial techniques laid clearly before them, it is not surprising southern Ontario employers made tangible efforts to jump aboard the efficiency band-wagon. In a letter to the Royal Commission on Industrial Training and Technical Education, the CMA (largely a southern Ontario concern) made it very clear that developments in the United States were not passing them by. They had come to realize that

> The greatest difficulty manufacturers have to face is the securing of competent, well trained mechanical experts to act as foremen, superintendents, managers, etc. Such men must not only be well up in the actual trade practices but must also know the theory of their work. The old apprentice system would meet the first requirement, but it would have to undergo important modifications to fulfil the second condition. It is probable that it could be developed so as to provide theoretical training if it were free from restrictions. This has been amply demonstrated by the splendid systems developed by several firms in the United States, notably the Brown & Sharpe Machine Company of Providence, The General Electric Company of Schenectady, The Baldwin Locomotive Works, Philadelphia, The Hoe Press Company, New York, and several others. We would request that the Commission devote special attention to these systems when visiting the United States. They show in a very practical manner how theoretical training can be co-related with shop practice.[25]

Employers and their managers did more than simply study such systems, however; in the years preceding World War I the implementation of efficiency measures became common practice.

As early as 1906 H.L.C. Hall, a member of the International Accountants' Society, introduced a system of cost accountancy at the B. Greening Wire Company of Hamilton. Involving the transfer of authority from skilled workmen to foremen, job standardization, efforts to eliminate all lost time and motion, a record of the minutes required to complete each job, strict tabulation of all materials and tools employed, and the adoption of piece rates and premium plans, Hall's system exemplified the exactitude introduced on the shop floor by the new managers. Also characteristic was Hall's purpose: 'First to induce economy by the elimination of waste and second to induce economy by intensifying production.'[26] Similar cost accountancy schemes, born of similar motivations, were introduced at Copeland-Chatterson-Crain Ltd, Toronto, the London Machine Tool Company, and the Steel Company of Canada, where W.R. Cuthbert, an American accountant, with specialized experience in steel production, was imported as the new company's comptroller.[27]

The showplace of Canadian 'efficiency in production methods,' however, came to be the Lumen Bearing Company of Toronto. In 1911 *Industrial Canada* approvingly described the role of experts and the resulting jump in productivity:

> Practical assistance to the workmen must be given by an expert. In the Lumen Bearing Co.'s shop a man is placed on the floor in an advisory capacity to the foreman. His is not the work of administration or management. He is there to assist the workmen, to suggest short cuts, to evolve economical methods, to save time for the workman, and for the manager, to the material advantage of both . . .
>
> It is the place of the 'staff boss,' the 'expert advisor,' to show workmen where these minutes may be saved. He is on the floor all the time; he is corrective to slovenly practices. The stop watch is his gauge. By careful and accurate observations a basis is arrived at for piece work prices . . .
>
> In the Lumen Bearing Co.'s foundry a certain class of castings was formerly made at the rate of twenty-eight a day. That was in the day work era. To-day the average production per man of the same casting is

sixty-five. The history of the change in output from twenty-eight to sixty-five daily is the story in concentrated form of efficiency management. It was accomplished by showing the moulders how this, that and the other operation could be accomplished with greater speed and with less labor. It is the story of economy of time and energy; of making the head serve the hand; the story of developing more efficient workmen.[28]

Industrial Canada then went on to depict the general transformation efficiency-conscious employers and their managers were bringing about in many Canadian industries:

Formerly as in most shops, the mechanics did a large part of the planning how work was to be done. They studied their blue prints and decided what operations were necessary, which should come first, and how they should be accomplished. They hunted up the machine tools they needed, borrowing them with or without permission. They drove their planes and lathes at whatever feed or speed they thought right. Finishing a job, they left their tools where they dropped. The next man who needed them conducted his own search for them, lost time putting them into condition again or used them as they were at half efficiency. They 'soldiered' by the hour at times on 'fill-in' jobs while waiting for castings or drawings for their principal tasks. To list all the wastes would take pages; few manufacturers need to be told of them, however. They know.

Today, the workmen do no planning. Every detail of work on every job is thought out for them and put down in unmistakable black and white. Not merely general directions, but the specific instructions indicating operations necessary on each part and the factors bearing on these operations—the character and number of cuts, the depth of each, the tool to be used, the speed, the feed, the time allowed if a bonus or premium is to be earned, the hourly rate if the bonus time is not attained. Analyzing the drawings and specifications, the planning department reduces each machine or group of machines ordered to its primary elements and prepares an instructions card for each part or lot of similar parts required. Each operation has been standardized; the standards are either carried in the planners brain or in a convenient file: the instructions card carries these to the workman and his gang foreman.[29]

Southern Ontario craftsmen lost no time in pointing to the destructive impact of the twin processes of mechanization and modern management upon their callings: specialization, simplification, payment by the piece or on the bonus, the utter disregard of apprenticeship training, and the flooding of the labour market with unskilled, uninformed, 'green hands' all contributed to the demise of their skill and the erosion of their craft pride. James Simpson, a prominent trade unionist long associated with Toronto Typographical Union No 91, wrote in 1907 of the 'extension of the principle of the division of labour,' in which Canadian workingmen were required to specialize ever more narrowly in one small aspect of production. The Royal Commission on Industrial Training and Technical Education, on which Simpson served, received numerous letters from disgruntled workers and stressed in its report the degradation of skilled workers occasioned by modern methods of production.[30] Testifying before an Ontario Commission on Unemployment in 1915 Thomas Findley, vice-president of Massey-Harris, captured the plight of the modern mechanic when he characterized him as 'not a man who understands every process, but a specialist in a single process.' Findley's ironic conclusion was that the cure for this social problem lay in an ever large dose of what must have been part of the cause: 'The need is for more supervision than before.'[31] Given these developments and sentiments, the strike became an early weapon employed by skilled workers to curb impingements upon their manhood inflicted by the machine or the autocratic manager, superintendent, or arbitrary foreman.

Most trades, of course, by this late date accepted mechanized production as inevitable and attempted to control its ill effects through staunch enforcement of union rules, the introduction of training programmes, petitions for the establishment of technical schools, and, above all else, the thorough organization of their craft. Some workers, however, reacted bitterly when employers sought to utilize machinery to displace skilled labour. Such was obviously the case at the International Harvester plant in Hamilton in 1904, when 125 machinists led a three-month struggle against efforts to mechanize their craft.[32] Similarly, thirty-two stone masons left their Toronto work-place for five days in October of 1905, protesting the introduction of a planing machine. Upon their return they found their places filled by other workers prompting a sympathetic strike of seventy-two of their brothers employed at six other stone-cutting firms.[33] And in February 1912 sixty-five cloakmakers struck the T. Eaton Company of Toronto, refusing to work on new machines installed by their employer. The dispute soon encompassed over 800 employees, but my mid-summer the company appeared victorious.[34] Strikes such as these tended to be the exception and not the rule. Often they ended in defeat and demoralization. More to the point, as the *Industrial Banner* pointed out, was the extent to which the threat of mechanization was utilized to intimidate the skilled worker. In a cigarmakers' strike in London in June 1910, involving 278 members of the trade, 'the threat of . . . bringing in machines to replace hand work was brought forth once more to, if possible, intimidate the employees and prejudice the public.' The *Banner* concluded that 'This old chestnut has grown so stale that it is not even funny anymore.'[35]

Most often skilled workers rallied to the defence of their unions as a bulwark against a loss of their shop-floor power. Throughout the period thirty-two strikes were fought for union recognition;[36] a further seventy-three involved victimization of trade unionists, employment of non-union labour, and various violations of trade standards; and on at least fourteen occasions workers struck in sympathy with fellow trade unionists already on strike. It was this defiant trade unionism, attempting to consolidate and expand its range of influence in Ontario's industry in the opening years of this century, that raised the hackles of employers.

Moreover, the question of apprenticeship, which had raged during the late nineteenth century, continued to exert its presence in the years 1901-14.[37] Indeed, in at least a dozen instances, as employers sought to introduce unlimited numbers of apprentices into the mechanized shops and factories of southern Ontario, this issue became the apex of a violent labour-capital clash.

Toronto early became the focal point of this battle over apprenticeship. In September and October 1903, 150 bookbinders struck because an apprentice was doing a journeyman's work. On 20 July 1904 twenty woodworkers at the Adamson Moulding Company engaged in a similar job action and, like the bookbinders, reached a satisfactory settlement with their employer. Brookmakers [sic], wall-paper printers, and bakers waged summer-long fights to limit the number of apprentices in their respective trades in 1905, although their efforts were apparently unsuccessful. The following year saw sheet-metal workers victorious in a strike aimed at preventing helpers from doing skilled work. And, finally, in the autumn months of 1906, 600 employees of eight Toronto piano manufacturers staged a significant last-ditch attempt to prevent the flooding of their ships with 'green hands.' Their demands included the limitation of the number of apprentices to one for every five mechanics, and the extension of the term of apprenticeship to five years of service.[38]

The piano workers' battle was an unsuccessful one, however, and after 1906 the incidence of apprenticeship struggles lessened considerably. The worsening economic situation, in conjunction, perhaps, with the stepped-up rate of mechanization induced by the availability of cheap hydro-electrical power from Niagara Falls,[39] allowed employers new freedoms in their attempts to break down barriers raised by craft unions against lax apprenticeship practices. Yet, even where employers were able to flood their concerns with poorly trained men or young apprentices, their tactic often rebounded against them. For, as this description of conflict in a London foundry suggests, apprentices usually considered themselves as potential craftsmen, and often acted accordingly:

Some time since the Leonard's imported a real live, slick Yankee labor crusher from Buffalo to act as superintendent of their engine works, and it was fondly hoped that he would hustle the deluded Canadians employed, cut down expenses and squeeze out profits. His first endeavours were to hire a number of apprentices and bind them for four years on the munificent salary to start with of $2.50 per week. Then he began to fill the shop with cheap Johns who had done a little fiddling in other places, and who desired to steal the machinist trade. A few farmers were also brought in. As the apprentices were not getting a fair show, they sent a deputation to the office, but got no satisfaction. A new hand who had never run anything but a drill in his life was brought in and put on a lathe, and he knew about as much about it as a hen does of singing. The apprentices guyed him to their hearts' content and at last run him out of the shop. The firm offered a reward of $5 to any boy who would turn informer and show who had thrown snowballs in the shop. Then all at once the police force were withdrawn from Victoria Park where they were on duty guarding the snow, and put on duty in the machine shops to protect the slick Yankee and his dubs from respectable Canadian workmen, many of whom had made the money for the Leonard's father. On the second day the patrol force was increased. The apprentices then made another attempt to get justice from the office. They said if the firm wanted cheap dubs, they wanted them to start where they had to begin, and as they had bound themselves to learn the trade for a term of years they demanded to have a fair show. The conditions in the establishment at length became unbearable. It was war between the crushers and the apprentices. What with the police on the scene and the determination of the kids to have justice it was hardly a picnic. One of the most objectionable of the dubs was bodily run out of the shops, and the last developments have resulted in the labor crusher getting the shunt. Whether peace, quietness and the old time policy under which the Leonards prospered, or at least under which their papa made their money for them, will be returned to is something for time to decide. As it is the slick imported Yankee has come out second best with the Canadian kids. It is hoped the Leonards' will realize that it pays to treat even apprentices fairly, and though they did succeed in shunting all the old men who built up their business, they can't make mechanics out of dubs. It is now hoped the boys will get a show, and the police allowed to resume their duty of protecting the snow on Victoria Park.[40]

As an appropriate comment on the informal workings of the shop floor, the fraternal solidarity which bound workmates to one another, and the extreme methods often resorted to by employers to secure undisputed control over the work process, this passage deserves particular attention.

Not all workers, to be sure, were as successful in dealing with instances of managerial autocracy as London's foundry apprentices. Nevertheless, there is ample evidence that many southern Ontario workers, like their counterparts south of the border, firmly rejected attempts to rationalize trade practices and work procedures.[41] Strikes were frequently resorted to in order to curb the 'autocratic' and 'tyrannical' practices and attitudes of managers, foremen, and superintendents, many of whom had been imported from the United States. Garment workers and iron molders in London in 1901 and 1905, for instance, refused to work under supervisors they considered intolerable.[42] At Toronto's Dunlop Tire and Rubber Company thirty-one rubber workers turned out in 1906, objecting to the supervision of their work by an expert who they claimed was an alien.[43] In February 1908, 'when an officious foreman in the Morlock Brothers establishment, Guelph,' informed a committee of upholsterers that they could either accept a cut in wages' or get to h . . . out of the shop,' the furniture coverers, objecting to the 'ungentlemanly conduct of foreman Webber,' obliged their supervisor and abruptly left work.[44] James O'Connell, president of the International Association of Machinists, addressed an assembly of the IAM and the Amalgamated Society of Engineers–traditionally hostile craft bodies–drawn together in the Grand Trunk railworkers' strike of 1905: 'The battle is fiercer than ever before. "Produce, produce, produce," is the cry of the masters on every side. Machinists are speeded to a limit almost beyond belief and the strain upon the physical endurance of the operators is tremendous . . .'[45] In this context skilled workers frequently struck against the immediate source of irritation, an obnoxious company official: in all we have found eighteen strikes where the issue was clearly the workers' disapproval of a particular company employee, usually supervisory staff.

Beyond this hostile reception afforded 'crushers' and 'drivers' lay even more blatant rejections of the 'new management.' Hamilton's *Labour News* struck hard at the introduction of efficiency measures in many Canadian machine shops: 'The "one man two machines," the "Taylor," "Scientific," "Premium," "piece work" and other systems introduced in the metal shops are making of men what men are supposed to make of metals: machines.'[46] A worker in Alan Sullivan's 1917 novel, *The Inner Door*, condemned efficiency engineers as men 'who put your immortal soul in a box and say, "Don't get outside that because it's a waste of energy and a dead loss to the company." '[47] In many southern Ontario cities this distaste for efficiency systems resulted in the cessation of work.

Hamilton, for instance, witnessed a number of conflicts that appeared to have had their roots in working-class dissatisfaction with various modes of 'shop management.' Late in 1902 several hundred female employees of the Eagle Knitting Mill objected to a new system of cutting and work classification. Leaving their benches, they claimed the innovations would result in a wage reduction of upwards of $2 a week. The dispute was ultimately 'amicably adjusted,' management claiming the cutters would soon be doing more work and collecting larger wages. Forty hands at the Chapman-Holton Knitting Mills struck in 1910 against a system of deductions levelled against spoiled work. And in May 1911 one hundred coatmakers at the Coppley, Noyes, and Randall Company successfully blocked the introduction of a piecework system. Finally, in 1913, workers at the Canadian Westinghouse Company left the plant in an unsuccessful display of opposition to the introduction of time clocks. Like the machinists at the Watertown Arsenal in the United States, these electricians refused to be 'put under the clock.'[48]

Toronto, too, experienced similar struggles. In the summer of 1902 three hundred carpet weavers waged a protracted work stoppage over the introduction of a 'clock system.' Nine picture framers left work in 1904, protesting attempts to impose time sheets upon them; the next day they returned to work, the loathsome sheets withdrawn by their boss. From 17 May to 29 June 1905, in an apparently unsuccessful fight with the Canada Foundry Company, sixty-nine machinists opposed the introduction of both individual contracts and the premium system. And in December of the same year, at the Lowndes Company, two hundred garment workers refused to work under a 'checking system,' designed to keep closer accounts of work output, spoilage, and poor workmanship. The workers regarded such innovations as 'a modified form of introducing the sweating system.'[49]

Other centres also saw growing discontent with new, more rigorous, forms of management. A strike on the Grand Trunk line, affecting numerous southern Ontario cities, captures the character of much of this emerging unrest. For many months conductors, brakemen, baggagemen, and switchmen had grown wary of the practices of Manager Hays. His secret, like that of Taylor, lay in promising the men wage increases, '*or their equivalent.*' While the company was thus quick to grant wage hikes, manager Hays made quite sure that each increase followed larger and intensified work-loads, longer stints, diminishing numbers of days off, and an accelerated work tempo. As men paid by the month, Grand Trunk workers often found themselves wondering where the wage gains of earlier periods had been lost. Whatever their confusion, it was clear to the workers that they always fell 'in for the big end of the work and the small end of the increase . . . It was, indeed, the slickest trick any manager ever had up his sleeve.' Attacking Hays and 'his scientific system of exploitation on the Grand Trunk,' the trainmen, 'faced with the alternative of an abject surrender to an arrogant and overbearing corporation or a firm stand in defence of what they believed to be their rights,' chose the latter course, leaving work on 18 July 1910. A settlement was quickly negotiated in which *actual* wage increases were to be put into effect immediately and the subterfuges of the past discontinued.[50]

But perhaps the most vivid example of the impact of efficiency-conscious managers upon work processes, and the working-class distaste for such developments, was the 1907 Bell Telephone strike, involving women operators. In 1903, in an attempt to undercut unnecessary and inefficient work techniques, the company installed new equipment, demanded the completion of routine tasks in drastically reduced time periods, and cut the hours of work from eight to five per day. Two shifts of women catered to the needs of an 'overexacting public.' For many the severe nervous tension, heightened by the company's absolute refusal to consider work breaks and the constant flashing of lights and clicking of receivers attendant upon the work, proved unbearable. Maud Orton, Minnie Hanun, Aria Strong, and Laura Roch-all later testified that their employment at Toronto's Bell offices had brought about nervous breakdowns and frequent mental discomfort. Shocks from the switchboards were everyday occurrences and the women's seating apparatus, lacking back supports, produced constant irritation. Medical authorities were quick to condemn the unhealthy working conditions prevailing in the offices. Nor was this all that rendered the operatives' work oppressive. Lady supervisors paraded the aisles, making sure the working women violated no rules; talking was strictly forbidden; and a monitoring system, which management deemed essential, intensified the strain and tension seemingly inherent in the job.[51]

Yet from 1903 through 1906 the women at Bell Telephone endured their lot, albeit begrudgingly. Lacking the traditions and practices of control so embedded within the craft consciousness, existing outside the pale of trade unionism and only recently injected into modern work settings, these women had few benchmarks to guide them in their orientation towards an increasingly burdensome and exploitative job situation. If their dissatisfaction grew too great, they left, a frequent occurrence if we are to believe management's complaints of high turnovers in personnel; this process simply exacerbated the problem of inefficiency since trained staff did not always stay on the job long enough.[52] But the women's relatively passive acquiescence was not to last forever.

In March 1906 the company decided to assess the relative merits of the innovative five-hour day. Two studies were commissioned, one by James T. Baldwin and another by Hammond V. Hayes, both employees of the American Telephone and Telegraph Company. Completed late in 1906, the reports concurred in their findings. Through elaborate analyses of the speed and quality of service and minute calculations of the number of seconds allotted per call, as well as the number of calls handled in one hour, both

agreed that the eight-hour system, then in effect in Montreal, surpassed Toronto's five-hour plan in the efficient and effective utilization of labour.[53]

From these conclusions the company proceeded quickly. Overly confident of the pliability of its work force, Bell acted as it had in the past, reintroducing the eight-hour day as it had all previous changes in technical and organizational operations: without warning the women at Bell were told that they should once again work eight-hour shifts. Aware of the intensity of work under the old system, and with no assurance that they would receive increased relief or lessened pressures, the employees rightly feared that their new work load would become even heavier. Like their employer, the Bell women acted promptly, striking in January 1907 and soon after joining the International Electrical Workers Union. Within the city the strike was widely reported and discussed, and a Royal Commission consisting of deputy minister of labour William Lyon Mackenzie King and Judge John Winchester conducted a thorough investigation of the issues involved. Although the delay created by the investigation diffused the momentum of the women's protest and ultimately led to defeat for them, the strike serves to remind us that it was not only the skilled who suffered the consequences of managerial drives to perfect human efficiency.[54]

Struggles such as these—built around fundamental changes in the way work was to be organized and carried out—must be seen as efforts by the working class, especially the more skilled sectors, to secure or retain control over their job settings. Although tabulating precise statistics on the issues in dispute in prewar strikes is extremely difficult owing to the sketchiness of much of the Department of Labour's reporting, and although the analysis is further clouded by those strikes involving two or more clearly discernible issues, we have concluded that probably more than two hundred strikes involved conflict over some aspect of control of the workplace. It should be made clear, however, that the control we are referring to in this period bore little resemblance to the demands posed in later years by the more consciously revolutionary British shop stewards' movement, or the Western Canadian miners of the One Big Union.[55] These groups went far beyond the limited conception of control embedded within many prewar strikes, demanding workers' control of entire industries on a national basis.

Carter Goodrich long ago distinguished three types of control: restrictive control, shop control, and the more politically conceived control of an entire industry.[56] Restrictive control was widespread among skilled trades in the late nineteenth and early twentieth century, the most common examples of its presence being the limitation of output[57] and the demand for a ceiling on the number of apprentices allowed to enter a trade. It was seen as the bulwark of the wage differential that stood as the badge of craft status and price, separating the skilled from the unskilled. Shop control, also prevalent during the same period, was a somewhat more complex phenomenon, institutionalized in union rules, regulations, and standards: shop committees, controlling

Table III
Strike Issues

Category I

For higher earnings	212
Against wage reductions	28

Category II

For recognition of union	32
For shorter hours	58
Defence of trade unionism	73
Sympathy	14
Apprenticeship control	12
Objection to new system of work	20
Change in conditions of work	22
Objection to employment of particular persons, usually supervisors	18
Adjustment of procedures of wage payment	8

Figures represent our compilations from the *Labour Gazette*, 1901-14. Category II includes those strike issues we have considered struggles for control. Since some strikes involved two or more clearly discernible issues, we have found it necessary to 'double count' some strikes in order to avoid the mistaken impression that all conflicts revolved around a single issue. Therefore the total from this table does not correspond to the total number of strikes examined, but exceeds it.

hiring and firing, pricing of products, and the hours worked by members of the union were the backbone of this form of control. Some trades, most notably glass-workers, carried this form of control to the point of dictating when production would commence and when it would cease: from July until September every glass factory in North America closed its doors and the workers took their customary summer holiday.[58] The demands for industrial control of entire realms of the economy, raised in the war and postwar years, were an entirely different phenomenon, belonging to the epoch of the twentieth century, where concerns were often moulded by events like the Russian Revolution.[59] Both restrictive and shop control, then, were rooted in the nineteenth-century experience of skilled workers; they thrived as trade customs and were most potent on a localized level. Both were shaken by mechanization but, as we have argued, adapted and revitalized themselves in many crafts. With the introduction of twentieth-century innovative managerial systems geared to rationalize and intensify work processes, however, these forms of control came under severe attack. That is what concerns us in the years 1901-14.

Just how critical and contentious control struggles could become was illustrated in London.[60] In July and August of 1901 cigarmakers were locked out of one shop for refusing to make expensive, high-quality cigars at the same rates paid for cheaper variants. Twelve days later they returned to work under their own conditions. In 1913, with the prewar recession already well underway, fifty members of the same trade struck a local establishment for the right to control practices of hiring and firing. While their walkout was waged in vain, the stogie-makers' proposal that a committee of workmen regulate employment during the coming recession spoke of their deeply embedded conception of their rights as craftsmen.[61] Moulders, too, saw control of their trade as a vital issue. In a strike at McClary's in the summer of 1905, the firm's 'sand artists' presented a list of demands to the superintendent which included the establishment of a shop committee, selected by the workers, to be the sole determinant of pricing work done in the foundry.[62] Two years earlier 263 carriage workers had raised a similar demand in Oshawa's McLaughlin Carriage Company.[63] The Toronto garment industry saw even bolder efforts. During the summer of 1911 thirty-five workers waged a lengthy, unsuccessful strike against the Puritan Skirt Factory for the right to appoint committees to adjust all prices, to control hiring and firing, and to distribute all available work evenly in order to avoid layoffs. Another sixty cloakmakers, twenty-five of them women, walked out of M. Pullan & Sons the following January demanding a similar price control committee and the right to appoint a shop chairman with wide powers.[64]

But it was from another quarter that perhaps the most articulate statement of workers' repugnance for their employers' quest for control arose. In the depressed years of 1908-10 the London Trades and Labour Council established a co-operative toy factory to alleviate the distress of unemployment. Known as the 'London Experiment,' the concern was run collectively and employed over sixty craftsmen, providing work and relief for many London families. Expressing a long-established distaste for the rigidity of factory discipline, the co-operative venture issued the following circular: 'The committee of management believe that the promulgation of a set of cast-iron rules, with restrictive provisions is unnecessary, feeling assured the employees will heartily co-operate and recognize that the largest possible measure of liberty is not incompatible with the operation of an efficient system from which the best results shall accrue.' Pointing to the viability and potentiality of working-class self-management, the 'London Experiment' drew cheers from Canadian workers.[65]

Finally, our discussion of control struggles must make brief mention of working-class attempts to shorten the working day, a demand with a long and rich history. Fifty-eight of the 421 strikes and lockouts in the years 1901-14 involved this issue. At the beginning of our period a Toronto labour publication noted that in certain kinds of work, becoming increasingly common, 'workers cannot stand as many hours of toil as they used to stand. The man who tends a never slackening machine in a well-equipped factory works at a higher tension than did the man who hammered out the article to be produced on the anvil, or shaped at the bench . . . This growing tension ought to be accompanied with shorter hours, or the heavy strain will be too much for the men who have to stand it.' In the face

of technological and managerial innovation many workers undoubtedly invested energy previously devoted to 'soldiering' and other forms of restrictive control in the struggle for the eight- or nine-hour day.[66]

Not all conflicts centred directly on the issues of control of the workplace. Of the 421 strikes and lockouts examined, 212 involved the question of higher wages, and twenty-eight more were the consequence of resistance to wage reductions. Behind this activity undoubtedly lay, in large part, the widely discussed issue of the soaring cost of living in the two prewar decades. In an 1100-page statistical survey of this problem in the period under study, Robert Coats of the federal Department of Labour revealed increases in prices of food, fuel, and lighting in southern Ontario cities of 43 to 58 per cent and in rents of 35 to 90 per cent. Wages, he concluded, seldom kept pace.[67] Small wonder, then, that so many workers were prepared to strike over conditions that were eroding their real wages.

Yet it is these struggles which are the most difficult to classify, for as Knowles has argued, wage strikes 'tend to be symbolic of wider grievances'; to view them as simply conflicts over the size of a pay packet would be overly reductionist. Certainly disputes which pitted a working-class notion of 'a fair wage' against the employer's criteria of efficiency and productivity epitomized fundamentally opposed views of labour in the productive process. Moreover, many of these strikes for higher wages also involved issues that fell more clearly within the sphere of control struggles. And in the case of those conflicts arising out of efforts to impose wage cuts it is clear that many unionists saw such struggles as a defence of their unions, for employers were not above using wage reductions to destroy entrenched craft organizations. Then, too, we have no way of knowing how many workers, conscious of the loss of autonomy occasioned by the drift of modern industry, sought recompense in a higher wage. Nevertheless, it can not be denied that in the context of rampant inflation and declining real wages which, to many workers, became the encompassing reality of everyday life in the modern world, strikes over wage issues were an important feature of industrial unrest in the years 1901-14.[68]

However, if many of these strikes fought to

win increased rates of remuneration, resist the rising tide of inflation, or forestall attempts to reduce wages were not concerted attacks upon managerial prerogatives, neither were they passively accepted by capital as mere 'bread and butter' skirmishes. Rather, as Louis S. Reed long ago argued, strikes for higher wages often bit deeply into narrowing profit margins. To the employer, also feeling the pinch of inflation, such conflicts were viewed as the straw aimed at breaking the camel's back, and it is not surprising that capital soon organized a retaliatory assault.[69]

Labour's upsurge prompted an increasingly hostile reception on the part of employers. Most businessmen viewed with distinct displeasure, for example, the phenomenal growth of the American Federation of Labor in Canada–the association with which most of the skilled workers involved in our 421 strikes and lockouts were affiliated– in the years 1896-1904.[70] Capital's consternation, like that of labour, was to be an organized force, utilizing a plethora of sophisticated techniques that ranged from the open shop drive to the development of subtle forms of paternalistic manipulation of working-class needs and aspirations.[71]

Southern Ontario employers early learned the value of organization and collective, as opposed to individual, action.[72] In October 1903 the National Association of Manufacturers in the United States, an organization which was to provide the cutting edge of a nation-wide open-shop drive, held a special convention in Chicago where a national federation of employers' associations was born, the Citizens' Industrial Association of America; representatives from Toronto were present at the proceedings.[73] Many Canadian firms were connected to the American open-shop campaign through affiliations with American associations: the National Founders' Association, the National Metal Trades Association, and the United Typothetae of America, for instance, all had a Canadian membership.[74] Skilled workers, it seems, were not the only beneficiaries of international connections.

Canadian employers quickly learned important lessons in anti-union practices from their American confrères; strikebreaking in the years 1901-14 became something of an art, involving intricate infiltrations of plants and factories by spies, detectives, and 'spot-

ters,' as well as massive influxes of often notorious 'blacklegs.'[75] In a strike at the Canada Foundry Company in Toronto in 1903, a local officer of the moulders' union reported that the company was employing twenty-four to twenty-eight roving professional strikebreakers supplied by the National Founders' Association at $1.50 a day over and above regular moulder's wages; these men had been sent from Duluth and were encamped on company property.[76] The National Metal Trades Association also advised members in the handling of industrial disputes, furnished men and money to break strikes and troublesome unions, and operated an immense labour bureau where the records of hundreds of thousands of men were kept, allowing employers to determine the potential loyalty of prospective employees.[77] Moreover, the resources and expertise of American businessmen often proved quite useful, as in February 1903 when a prominent figure in the American open-shop drive, John Kirby of Dayton, Ohio, visited Toronto to help employers launch their anti-union offensive.[78]

While the American presence and example was thus critical in the origins of the southern Ontario employers' offensive, it was soon outstripped by indigenous developments. Canadian employers' associations mushroomed in the post-1901 years: the *Labour Gazette* found over sixty such organizations in 1905 in the ten cities under consideration. It was from these locally based bodies, as well as the newly reorganized CMA, predominantly an Ontario concern in its early years, that capital's counter-attack was initiated.[79]

In October 1902 two hundred Toronto manufacturers were invited to attend a meeting on 14 October to discuss the 'placing of business on a more stable and permanent basis by preventing strikes and providing means of arbitration upon an equitable footing in all matters of dispute between capital and labour . . .'[80] From this gathering emerged the Employers' Association of Toronto, led by men who had recently experienced some of the city's most bitter strikes and lockouts: James P. Murray of the Toronto Carpet Company, a prominent figure in the CMA; W.H. Carrick of the Gurney Foundry Works; and Frank Polson, a well-known local foundryman. In a clear rejection of the principle of collective bargaining,

Murray's presidential address revealed the impetus behind the group's formation: 'The growth of industry and of transportation facilities had so increased competition that stable prices, unreliable deliveries, and imperfect goods were now fatal to trade. The strike was the most productive agent of these conditions . . .' The artisan, according to the president, had no right to interfere with the prices another artisan might demand for his labour. Labour organizations he urged, by fixing a uniform price under which unionists must work, brought it about that the quality and quantity of work plays no part in relation to what is paid for it.' In their stated aim of assuring 'their rights to manage their respective businesses in such lawful manner as they deem proper,' the Toronto employers left no doubt as to where they thought control of the workplace should reside.[81] To the CMA the group was attempting 'to meet union with union'; after four years' experience with the Toronto body the *Tribune*, organ of the Toronto Trades and Labour Council, saw it as one more effort aimed at 'dragging down and crushing the working people.'[82]

Simultaneously, pressure was being exerted within the CMA for a more militant opposition to organized labour. 'Why should one body of men,' complained a committee set up in 1902 to consider the employers' relationship to organized labour, 'be permitted to unionize the shop or factory of their employer? In every trade or community there are many who are opposed to unionism and who stand for freedom of contract. This is their right. Yet the demand for unionism is to compel a man to join their organization or leave the shop.'[83] In their conclusions the committee struck sharply at working-class initiatives to control production, especially criticizing the growing numbers of struggles around the issue of apprentice limitation. Like the monumental US Special Report of the Commissioner of Labour, the employers were scathing in their indictment of 'soldiering,' 'ca'canny,' and other modes of restricting 'the output of our factories': 'Labour unions in general refuse to work "by the piece" and the daily output in many lines notwithstanding the introduction of labour-saving machinery is not more than two-thirds of what it was a few years ago. No man, nor any body of men, have the right to retard so unreasonably the growth of our national trade and commerce.'[84] Out of the committee's dissatisfaction flowed a 'Declaration of Principles' regarding 'the labour question,' subsequently adopted by the association. In language similar to that used by proponents of the open shop in the United States, all the major arguments against the aggressive craft unionism of the early twentieth century were transferred to Canadian settings.[85]

These developments added fuel to the anti-union fires burning in the breasts of many local employers. The most typical response of industrial capital, it seems, was to precipitate strikes, often in periods of economic crisis when labour could ill afford costly work stoppages, in the hope of ridding itself of the irksome presence of the trade unions. No case epitomizes this strategy more vividly than the running battle between the foundrymen of southern Ontario and the International Iron Molders' Union. Conspiracy seemed to shout at the unionists from the depths of one struggle after another:

> The iron moulders have been singled out by the Canadian manufacturers as the point of attack in the vain attempt to put International unionism out of business. The McClary trouble, followed by that of the Buck Company of Brantford, and the Moffat Company of Weston, and still later by the new struggle in Hamilton, are all details in a clearly laid plan. In each of these cases the manufacturers were so clearly in the wrong that no defence of their stand was possible. It was a manifest attempt to use the business depression as a lever to smash the labor organizations and put them out of business. In each instance the union was ready to reach an understanding. In each instance the fight was forced by the manufacturers and in each instance there was a lack of real cause for conflict.

These conflicts were seldom total victories, however, craft bodies proving more resilient than their employers bargained for. At the Buck Stove and Range Works in Brantford, the contours of the struggle, ultimately unsuccessful for the strikers, embraced mass importations of strikebreakers, gunplay, vicious assaults upon picketing workmen, drunken brawls inside the shop by 'scab' stove mounters, and ringing denunciations of the whole affair by large segments of the community; yet the conflict remained unresolved some sixteen months after its inception. On 1 April 1908 120 union mounters had walked out of the concern, and in August 1909, 'despite special inducements alluringly and temptingly dangled before their eyes, only two men were prevailed upon to betray their manhood.' For the iron moulders it was a 'most remarkable record.'[86]

The employers' assault had begun to check the growth of trade unionism by 1905, but they never managed to drive the unions completely from the field. In March 1908 the *Industrial Banner* reported on what is considered to be the dismal record of one open-shop campaigner:

> The Toronto Employers' Association, which has deliberately forced two-thirds of all the strikes occurring in Toronto during the last three years, is apparently disappointed with the results of that struggle. Despite the loss of thousands of dollars in these unnecessary battles, and the further loss of additional thousands in profits as a result of demoralization in business, they have not succeeded in destroying a single union; in fact, the contest has had a directly opposite effect. The machinists and plumbers, who have both borne the especial brunt of the attack, are as confident and determined as they were months ago.[87]

It was in this context of stalemate on the economic front, then, that capital was forced to adopt other, more indirect, means of repression.

For decades legislation had been a bone of contention between workingman and employer. *Industrial Canada* insisted that is was essential that 'no legislation should be adopted which will place our Canadian manufacturers at a disadvantage.'[88] From this premise the CMA consistently lobbied to roll back all pieces of legislation that appeared to grant concessions to organized labour. In 1901 the Alien Labour bill was amended so 'that nothing in this Act should be taken to prevent the importation of skilled labour requisite to the development of . . . industry in Canada';[89] as we shall see, the logic behind such a revision was to prove critical in capital's struggle for the open shop. Labour representatives, in their attempts to introduce legislation aimed at bettering the lot of their constituencies, also met the stern resistance of the CMA. The legalization of the union label was successfully blocked, while attempts to introduce eight-hour bills in the House of Commons were persistently deflected.[90] Employers also sought to promote legislation useful to their cause, bills prohibiting American labour officials from operating in Canada, restraining the activities of striking workmen, and attacking 'foreign agitators,' all gaining unqualified support from the CMA and local employers.[91]

The courts, too, became transformed into arenas of the growing conflict. George Denison, a Toronto magistrate, epitomized the bench's sympathy with anti-union employers. In 1903 he fined two garment workers, formerly employed by the W.R. Johnston Company, $75 and costs for intimidating strikebreakers; he administered the same penalty to a Gurney worker who persisted in yelling 'scab and other names' at an individual crossing the picket line established at the foundry. Denison imposed a similar fine on a striking cabman in 1907, and exacted a like penalty upon two employees who, in 1911, referred to strike-breakers at the Continental Costume Company as 'scabs.' 'I want it distinctly understood that I object to that word,' Denison told the men before imposing the fine.[92] Similar court proceedings occurred in other cities, most notably Brantford, where in the above mentioned Buck Stove and Range dispute, several charges were laid against strikers.[93]

But it was the injunction, the tried and true method of legalized opposition to labour's demands and actions, combined with the suit for damages, which were perhaps the most useful tools in capital's legal struggle to stifle opposition. Probably taking its cue from the famous Taff Vale case in Britain, the Metallic Roofing Company of Toronto, owned and operated by J.O. Thorn, chairman of the Toronto branch of the CMA, launched the systematic use of the weapon in 1902.[94] After prolonged attempts to secure the union shop in the Thorn concern, Local No. 30 of the Amalgamated Sheet Metal Workers International Association abandoned negotiations, informing workers in the trade that 'on or after August 20, your men refuse to handle any products of the Metallic Roofing Company of Toronto, as they are unfair to organized labour.'[95] The company immediately secured an injunction restraining the boycott and brought a suit of damages against the union. In 1905 Thorn was awarded $7500, but the union stalled payment by appeals to higher courts. Both capital and labour recognized the importance of the case, *Industrial Canada* stressing that it was of 'the greatest importance to every manufacturer in Canada,' and the *Toiler* contending that is was 'the battle of all trade union organizations.' Not until 1909 was the dispute resolved, plaintiff and defendant calling off the feud with a quiet, undisclosed agreement.[96] In the meantime, however, other employers were quick to follow Thorn's pioneering example. Two of the better known cases, the H. Krug Furniture Company's action of 1903 and the Gurney campaigns of 1903 and 1905 against prominent members of various metal trades unions, the Toronto Trades and Labour Council, and the *Toiler*, siphoned the strength of picketing and boycotting as union tactics and severely hampered the effectiveness of many strikes. Just how heavy-handed the courts could be was revealed in orders given to that labour council during the Gurney boycott of 1903, restraining it 'from interfering with or intimidating the company's workmen; from wrongfully interfering with the company's customers; from boycotting its goods and from publishing wrongful statements that they are made by incompetent workmen; and from wrongfully and maliciously conspiring against the company;' the council also had to pay for 'damages for having already committed these acts.'[97]

Employers supplemented these organizational, legislative, and judicial efforts with a drive to flood southern Ontario cities with foreign workmen. Such a tactic served the purposes of employers well, for immigrant workers could often be used to break strikes and, in generally increasing the supply of labour, they undermined the strength of craft bodies, whose power traditionally resided in their ability to restrict labour's availability.[98] But, because the unions were most often entrenched in the more highly skilled trades, recruitment necessarily had to attract a like class of workmen; unskilled labour posed a relatively minor threat to the trade unions.

In their attempts to import such labour,

Canadian industrialists and manufacturers were somewhat restricted by the Alien Labour Act, originally passed in 1897 in retaliation against American alien labour legislation. Although amended in 1901 in the employers' favour, the act retained some force in this period. James E. Merrick, secretary of the Toronto Employers' Association, was twice taken to court for his pains to secure contract labour from New York to work in two lithographing plants experiencing strikes for union recognition. In one instance the charges were dismissed, while his conviction in the second case brought a minimal $50 fine. A year later the same individual was acquitted on similar charges.[99] In 1906 four Toronto-based companies—the Toronto Carpet Company, run by the president of the CMA, the Freysburgh Cork Company, the Menzie Wall Paper Company, and the Gerhard Heintzman Company—were charged with similar offenses; each company was in the midst of a strike at the time of the transgression.[100] Thus, while the law was never rigorously enforced, the machinery for instituting criminal proceedings was clearly open to unions and their members, and for this reason employers tended to concentrate their efforts on the more distant, but less awkward, British labour market.

The CMA, *Industrial Canada*, and W.T.R. Preston, Canada's commissioner of emigration in Britain, openly encouraged the immigration of skilled English mechanics to Canada.[101] As early as June 1903 the Toronto District Labour Council felt compelled to publish an 'Open Letter to the Workmen of the United Kingdom,' in which the CMA's portrayal and promise of employment opportunities in Ontario was curtly dismissed as a sham. The letter summarized the context in which assisted immigration was being undertaken:

The struggle between capitalistic influences and the influences of the organized workers has become very acute here, and there is an aggressiveness characterizing the different employers' associations that has never been known before in Canada. Both illegitimate as well as legitimate means are being adopted by these associations to compel the workers to submit to conditions that are neither congenial nor appositive for the industrial classes, a determined effort is being made to disrupt the labour organizations that stand between the avarice of the employing class and the highest interests of the toilers.[102]

The letter apparently did little to stop the rising tide of foreign workmen, and the CMA's initiatives met with success after success, culminating that same year in the formation of a privately-run 'Canadian Labour Bureau' in England which promised employment in Ontario's rolling mills, machine shops, foundries, building trades, stove works, and agricultural implements plants. Three years later the operation of this bureau, functioning with Preston's complete co-operation, created a minor scandal for the Canadian government.[103]

Moreover, innumerable emigration societies and companies operated openly in Britain. One recently arrived English immigrant, unable to find the work he thought so plentiful, told Hamilton labour leader Samuel Landers how he had come to leave a good job in England to settle in southern Ontario: 'Why, agents are going all over England holding lectures with limelight views of Canadian industries, urging English mechanics and workmen to emigrate to Canada at once. At one lecture, I saw the International Harvester works of Hamilton thrown on canvas with its numerous buildings, and the Westinghouse industries of the same city, we were told that a thousand men were wanted in Hamilton at once, so I came.'[104] In a pamphlet issued by the Grand Trunk Company, 'which until late 1908 could be picked up in most towns in Britain,' Canada was glowingly pictured as labour's promised land; the Canadian Pacific Railway Company provided similar literature to all shipping agents in Britain.[105]

These practices continued to prevail in 1912. E.H. Glenn and Harry Gearry of Local 132 of the Journeyman Tailor's Union reported to the Trades and Labour Congress that manufacturers frequently advertised in English papers to secure operatives. Similarly, the International Molders' Union complained bitterly about the attempts of the Malleable Iron Foundry's St. Catharines and Brantford branches to secure foreign workers.[106] In the spring of 1914 the Dominion Emigration Department's Ontario branch undertook to prosecute seventeen employment agents who were fraudulently enticing immigrants to Canada.[107] Perhaps no single issue in this fourteen-year period so enraged the *Industrial Banner* as this deliberate importation of workingmen for the express purpose of breaking strikes and crushing unions.[108]

The stick, however, was not the only means employed by capital to stifle opposition and siphon working-class discontent. A more subtle tactic slowly developed and involved pre-empting the humanitarian appeal of the labour movement by offering employees numerous social amenities associated with the health, safety, recreational, and security requirements of working people. In an article entitled 'How about your Factory,' *Industrial Canada* argued that 'pleasant surroundings are conducive to the economic production of good work, while at the same time they attract a better class of working people.'[109] At the Berlin firm of Williams, Greene and Rome, manufacturers of shirts, collars, and cuffs, the 'Right Idea,' featuring employee dining-rooms, women's restrooms, a relief fund, athletic and benefit associations, a complaint department, and dramatic and literary societies, gained province-wide acclaim. The Frost Wire Fence Company, about to locate in Hamilton's East End in 1904, claimed that in its construction plans, 'Space has been set apart for a recreation room, which will be fitted up with pool tables and will be nicely furnished. Current literature will be kept on file for those of a more serious turn of mind. Some vacant property adjoining has been acquired, which will be turned into grounds for out-of-door sports, and the company will encourage their employees to enter a team in local hockey, football and baseball leagues.'[110]

Behind provisions like these the *Labour Gazette* perceived a conscious purpose: 'The officials of the company anticipate that they will get a return for their expenditure in better service from the man.'[111] *Industrial Canada* was even more blunt, arguing in a 1912 article, 'Homes for Workmen,' that, 'Workmen who have comfortable homes are more efficient, contented and reliable than those who have not . . . Out of the slums stalk the Socialist with his red flag, the Union agitator with the auctioneer's voice, and the Anarchist with his torch.'[112] To men like the efficiency-conscious H.L.C. Hall, efforts to alleviate the drudgery of modern work settings made good

64

business sense, and he chastized Canadian manufacturers: 'You will spend money everytime to increase the efficiency of your machinery. Then why not spend a little time and effort to increase the efficiency of your human machines? It will pay and pay handsomely. It is in some localities quite the fashion to beautify factory buildings and grounds. Civic pride you say. Not a bit of it. Certain wise ones have discovered that it pays to spend a little something on the comfort of the worker. It is a cold business proposition. You get more out of them.'[113]

Employer-sponsored welfare schemes for industrial workers were as old as the Industrial Revolution itself, but in the prewar years a new, more sophisticated form of welfare capitalsm was emerging throughout southern Ontario.[114] It is crucial to see the development of paternal modes of management as part of a continuum embracing force as well as manipulative coercion. In January 1904 the *Toiler* commented on welfare programmes in an article appropriately entitled 'The Wrong Idea': 'It can safely be said that the majority of them are designed to protect the firm in a systematic way by keeping the deluded employees under their special care so that they can be more easily robbed of what is their just dues as a return for their labour. These schemes are designed to keep out the trade union or if it is already in to bring about its destruction.'[115] For the workingman, welfare capitalism was simply one more chapter in a lengthy book written by capital in which other, preceding sections had been formulated around the themes of mechanization, 'scientific management,' strikebreaking, and the open shop.

The years 1901-14, then, are an important chapter in the history of Canadian industrial relations. Much of what transpired in this period was, of course, rooted in the nineteenth century. Conflicts which arose in response to mechanization or the abuse of apprenticeship regulations had been common since the 1860s, and often seem strangely archaic in the world of the twentieth century. Yet we should not be surprised that skilled workers continued to resist the encroachments of industrial capitalism, for their adaptation to the new disciplines of the factory had always been uneven and far from complete.[116] And when startlingly new developments were thrust upon them—such as the

innovative techniques of an efficiency-conscious management, or the militantly collectivist response of Canadian manufacturers to craft unionism—skilled workers naturally took refuge in the control mechanisms of the past. It is in this context that we have come to regard control as a vital issue in these years, linking the nineteenth and early twentieth century experience of skilled workingmen.

While the episodic quality of strikes poses problems for wide-ranging generalization, our examination of the contours and context of industrial conflict in the years 1901-14 suggests some conclusions. Skilled workers continued to use the strike to maintain shop-floor control rooted in nineteenth-century work practices, as well as to combat twentieth-century developments in work-shop organization and managerial innovation. At the same time their employers launched a concerted offensive against the institution that harboured and perpetuated much of the craftsman's autonomy, the trade union. By 1914 there was no definite resolution of the conflict between these forces. The cyclical depressions that began in 1908 and 1913 weakened organized labour as an adversary, but each time strikes resumed with the first signs of the return of prosperity. A tight labour market during the war restored strength lost in the prewar slump, and many scenes of the pre-1914 conflict were repeated in the next five or six years, with perhaps even greater intensity.[117]

From this perspective it would seem that the strike was *not* simply a battle over the division of the economic pie. Like Edward Shorter and Charles Tilly, whose massive compilation of data on strikes in France also stresses the role of craftsmen in pre-World War I industrial conflict, we have come to regard the strike as an implicitly political event, a clash over the distribution of power on the shop or factory floor flowing directly from the desire and ability of working people to act collectively.[118] In the same vein, the evidence presented here indicates that the analysis of American historians James Weinstein and Ronald Radosh, stressing 'corporate liberalism' as the foundation of a labour-capital alliance, has little relevance for Canada in this period.[119] Like David Bercuson, in his study of the roots of the Winnipeg General Strike, we find the prewar years an age of industrial violence.[120] To end, appropriately, where we began, we must note that if the *Bobcaygeon Independent*'s assessment of the causes of strikes lacked sophistication and subtlety, it nevertheless captured one prophetic truth: the worm, in these years 1901-14, had indeed turned.

Vol. VIII No 4 December 1977

Author's note: We are grateful for the critical comments on earlier drafts of this paper made by R.C. Brown, Michael Cross, Russell Hann, Gregory S. Kealey, Ian McKay, and Edward Shorter. While we have made efforts to incorporate suggested revisions, some of our critics are likely to remain unappeased. They bear no responsibility for the shortcomings of the paper. Bryan Palmer would also like to acknowledge the assistance of the Canada Council and the 1973 London Labour History Project.

NOTES

---

[1] *Bobcaygeon Independent,* 16 May 1913,2, from an article 'One of the Causes of Strikes,' reprinted from *The Windsor Record.*

[2] Statistical data on nineteenth-century strikes does not exist. Comparisons between the nineteenth- and early twentieth-century experiences are therefore difficult, and generalization demands caution. Yet it would seem, on the basis of local research currently in progress, that the years 1901-14 saw workers resort to the strike and employers turn to the lockout more often than in preceding years. Bryan Palmer's dissertation research on skilled workers in Hamilton in the years 1860-1914, as well as his previous study of the emergence of a labour movement in London, Ontario, in the years 1867-1914 [' "Give us the road and we will run it": The Social and Cultural Matrix of an Emerging Labour Movement,' in Gregory S. Kealey and Peter Warrian, eds., *Essays in Canadian Working Class History* (Toronto 1976), 106-24], suggests this. Kealey's forthcoming dissertation on the Victorian working class in Toronto makes it very clear that the strike was frequently resorted to in the years 1860-92, but it was not as common as it was in this later period, when Toronto experienced 198 industrial conflicts.

[3] On the 'people's press' see the viewpoints in Russell Hann, 'Brainworkers and the Knights of Labor: E.E. Sheppard, Phillips Thompson, and the Toronto *News,*' in *Essays in Canadian Working Class History,* 35-57; P.F.W. Rutherford, 'The People's Press: The Emergence of the New Journalism in Canada, 1869-1899,' *Canadian Historical Review,* LVI, 1975, 169-91.

[4] The basic source for much of what follows was the *Labour Gazette.* Because this publication provides only an introduction to the many strikes and lockouts of the period, and an often inadequate one at that, we have also turned to numerous local labour newspapers, the regional *Industrial Banner,* and the standard sources on Canadian trade union history and strike activity: Charles Lipton, *The Trade Union Movement of Canada, 1827-1959* (Montreal 1968), 98-161; H.A. Logan, *Trade Unions in Canada* (Toronto 1948); Stuart Marshall Jamieson, *Times of Trouble: Labour Unrest and Industrial Conflict in Canada, 1900-1966* (Ottawa 1968), 62-157. Finally, because strikes involving national or provincial transportation networks often involved cities outside of the regional concerns of this study, we did not include them in our quantitative analysis of the contours of strike activity. Where such strikes illuminated issues of particular relevance, however, we have included them in our impressionistic discussion of the context of industrial conflict.

[5] On the importance of the historical study of strike activity see Michelle Perrot, *Les Ouvriers en Grève: France 1871-1890,* I & II (Paris 1974); Peter N. Stearns, 'Measuring the Evolution of Strike Movements,' *International Review of Social History,* XIX, 1974, 1-27; Edward Shorter and Charles Tilly, *Strikes in France, 1830-1968* (London 1974); K.G.J.C. Knowles, *Strikes—A Study in Industrial Conflict* (Oxford 1952). Peter Stearns has outlined the main features of mature industrial society: the regularization and intensification of work; new forms of supervision; reduction of working time; reduction of personal initiative on the job; and a new infusion of technological change. As we shall see, such features were to play a prominent role in the evolution of industrial unrest in this period. See Peter Stearns, *Lives of Labour; Work in a Maturing Industrial Society* (London 1975), 343.

[6] Jamieson, *Times of Trouble,* 85

[7] Thirty-one strikes occurred in 1901, 48 in 1902, 53 in 1903, 35 in 1904, 24 in 1905, 47 in 1906, 43 in 1907, 7 in 1908, 10 in 1909, 20 in 1910, 24 in 1911, 30 in 1912, 36 in 1913, and 12 in 1914.

[8] Penelope Hartland, 'Factors in the Economic Growth of Canada,' *Journal of Economic History,* XV, 1955, 13; *Census of Canada,* 1911, III (Ottawa 1913), v. Cf, Gordon D. Bertram, 'Historical Statistics on Growth and Structure in Manufacturing in Canada, 1867-1957,' in J. Henripin and A. Asimakopulas, eds., Canadian Political Science Association Conference on Statistics, 1962-3, *Papers* (Toronto 1964), 93-146; O.J. Firestone, *Canada's Economic Development, 1863-1957* (London 1958), 209-10; Jacob Spelt, *Urban Development in South-Central Ontario* (Toronto 1972), 150-86

[9]H.G. Stapells, 'The Recent Consolidation Movement in Canadian Industry' (unpublished MA Thesis, University of Toronto, 1922)

[10]*Census*, 1911, III, 331

[11]E.P. Thompson, "Time, Work-Discipline and Industrial Capitalism," *Past & Present*, XXXVIII, 1967, 57. Cf Herbert Gutman, 'Work, Culture and Society in Industrializing America, 1815-1919.' *American Historical Review*, LXXVIII, 1973, 531-88; Sidney Pollard, "Factory Discipline in the Industrial Revolution," *Economic History Review*, XVI, 1963, 254-71

[12]See Gregory S. Kealey, 'Artisans Respond to Industrialism: Shoemakers, Shoes Factories, and the Knights of St. Crispin in Toronto,' *Canadian Historial Association, Papers*, 1973, 137-58; David Brody, *Steelworkers in America: The Non-Union Era* (Cambridge 1960), 27-79; Robert Ozanne, *A Century of Labor Management Relations at McCormick and International Harvester* (Madison 1967); George E. Barnett, *Chapters on Machinery and Labor* (Carbondale 1969); Robert A. Christie, *Empire in Wood: A History of the Carpenters' Union* (Ithaca 1956), 80-2; Gregory S. Kealey, ed., *Canada Investigates Industrialism: The Royal Commission on the Relations of Labor and Capital, 1889* (Toronto 1973).

[13]Gregory S. Kealey, ' "The Honest Workingman" and Workers' Control: the Experience of Toronto Skilled Workers, 1860-1892,' *Labour/Le Travailleur*, I, 1976, 32-68. For a discussion of the experience of skilled workers in Halifax see Ian McKay, 'The Working Class of Metropolitan Halifax, 1850-1889' (honours thesis, Dalhousie University, 1975), 53-67.

[14]David Montgomery, 'Workers' Control of Machine Production in the Nineteenth Century,' *Labor History*, XVII, 1976, 485-509

[15]Barnett, *Chapters on Machinery and Labor*, 3-29; Barnett, 'The Printers: A Study in American Trade Unionism,' *American Economic Association Quarterly*, X (Cambridge 1909), 182-208. Cf Wayne Roberts, The Last Artisans: Toronto Printers, 1896-1914,' in Kealey and Warrian, eds., *Essays in Canadian Working Class History* (Toronto 1976), 125-42

[16]Benson Soffer, 'A Theory of Trade Union Development: The Role of the "Autonomous Workman," ' *Labor History*, I, 1960, 141-63

[17]This paragraph draws on material in Bryan Palmer, 'Class, Conception and Conflict: The Thrust for Efficiency, Managerial Views of Labor and Working Class Rebellion, 1903-1922 *Review of Radical Political Economy*, VII, 1975, 31-49; David Montgomery, 'The "New Unionism" and the Transformation in Workers' Consciousness, 1909-1922,' *Journal of Social History*, VII, 1974, 509-29.

[18]See, for instance, Stearns, *Lives of Labour*, 193-228, for developments in France, Belgium, Germany, and England. On 'Taylorist' practices in the French auto industry see Alain Touraine, *L'Evolution du travail ouvrier aux usines Renault* (Paris 1955), 25, 48-53, 107, 115. 156-7; James Laux, 'Travail et Travailleurs dans l'industrie-automobile jusqu'en 1914,' *Mouvement Social*, 1972, 9-26. An interesting discussion of the rise of supervisory personnel in the Ruhr is Elaine Glovca Spencer, 'Between Capital and Labor: Supervisory Personnel in Ruhr Heavy Industry Before 1914,' *Journal of Social History*, IX, 1975, 178-92.

[19]Michael Bliss, in an important treatment of the Canadian businessman, has argued that there were few Canadian organization men or managerial specialists prior to 1920. Bliss *A Living Profit: Studies in the Social History of Canadian Business, 1883-1911* (Toronto 1974), II. While our findings, regionally based and preliminary in nature, do not demolish Bliss's argument, they do point to the need for more research in this area.

[20]On the rise of the branch-plant in southern Ontario in these years see *Labour Gazette* (Ottawa), III, 1902-3, 138; IV, 1903-4, 1207; *Hamilton, Canada, Its History, Commerce, Industries and Resources* (Hamilton 1913); Herbert Marshall, Frank A. Southard, Jr, and Kenneth W. Taylor, *Canadian-American Industry* (New Haven 1936). For the most recent discussion of the changes in the American management techniques, see Daniel Nelson, *Managers and Workers: Origins of the New Factory System in the United States, 1880-1920* (Madison 1975), 55-78.

[21]William Kilbourn, *The Elements Combined: A History of the Steel Company of Canada* (Toronto 1960), 72, 75

[22]*Hamilton Spectator*, 5 Dec. 1906, 1

[23]US Congress, *Final Report and Testimony Submitted to Congress By the Commission on Industrial Relations*, 64th Congress, Senate Document 415 (Washington 1916), X, 9761. Gantt would later outline 'the straight line to profit' for Canadian manufacturers in an article subtitled 'Scientific Management is the New Gospel in Industrial Progress.' See *Industrial Canada*, March 1911, 837-40.

[24]*Industrial Canada*, March 1913, 1105-6; April 1913, 1219-23; May 1913, 1349-50; Frederick Winslow Taylor, 'The Principles of Scientific Management,' in Canadian Club of Ottawa, *Yearbook, 1912-1913* (Ottawa 1913), 115-43. Our thanks to Russell Hann for making this latter source available to us.

[25]Canada, Royal Commission on Industrial Training and Technical Education, *Report of the Commissioners*, IV (Ottawa 1913), 2087

[26]*Industrial Canada*, June 1906, 732-5

[27]*Industrial Canada*, May 1908, 774-5; May 1909, 836-8; Kilbourn, *The Elements Combined*, 84-5

[28]*Industrial Canada*, May 1911, 1073-4

[29]Ibid., 1074

[30]Toronto District Labour Council, *Labour Day Souvenir, 1907* (Toronto 1907); Commission on Industrial Training and Technical Education, *Report*, I.63: II, 173; IV, 2125

[31]Ontario, Commission on Unemployment, *Report of the Commissioners* (Toronto 1916), 227

[32]Canada, Department of Labour, *Report on Strikes and Lockouts, 1901-1912* (Ottawa 1913), 189

[33]*Labour Gazette*, VI, 1905-6, 673

[34]*Labour Gazette*, XII, 1911-12, 857; *Labour News* (Hamilton), 15 March 1912, 1; 22 March 1912, 1; 5 April 1912, 1; 3 May 1912, 2

[35]*Industrial Banner*, June 1910, 2, 4

[36]Unfortunately the *Labour Gazette* did not always make a clear distinction between a demand for union recognition and opposition to the hiring of non-unionists in a closed shop; the *Gazette* probably also neglected to note this issue in strikes fought for higher wages.

[37]On the roots of the struggle against the indiscriminate use of apprentices and helpers see John H. Ashworth, *The Helper and American Trade Unions* (Baltimore 1915), 44, 75-95; Barnett, 'The Printers,' 160-81; Frank T. Stockton, *The International Molders Union of North America* (Baltimore 1921), 57-69, 170-85; *Iron Molders International Journal*, Oct. 1873, 131-2; 10 Nov. 1875, 484-5; *Palladium of Labor*, 14 Feb. 1885, 7; 21 Feb. 1885, 8

[38]*Report on Strikes and Lockouts*, 1901-12, 173, 184, 195; *Labour Gazette*, VI, 1905-6, 207; VII, 1906-7, 440, 612. Cf *Labour Gazette*, V, 1904-5, 85; *Report on Strikes and Lockouts, 1901-1912*, 184, 188; *Industrial Banner*, Dec. 1901, 1; Feb. 1903, 1; March 1905, 3; Sept. 1905, 3, on further apprenticeship struggles in Guelph, St Catharines, and London, where molders, smithers, painters, and carpet weavers were active.

[39]In 1901 census-takers found that 1426 of the 3468 Ontario firms reporting the use of power machinery used electricity. By 1911 7151 out of 8001, or 89 per cent had introduced electrical power. *Census*, 1911, III, 153-9

[40]'He got the Shunt,' *Industrial Banner*, Dec. 1901, 1

[41]On the working-class response to managerial innovation in the United States see James Duncan, 'Efficiency–Real, Unreal and Brutal,' *American Federationist*, XVIII, 1911, 380-4; John Golden, 'Scientific Management in the Textile Industry,' ibid., 603-4; Samuel Gompers, 'The "Miracles" of Efficiency,' ibid., 278-9; Gompers, 'Machinery to Perfect the Human Machine,' ibid., 116-17; Paul Hanna, 'The Flaw in Efficiency,' *Machinists Monthly Journal*, XXIII, 1911, 854-5; John R. Commons, 'Organized Labor's Attitude Towards Industrial Efficiency,' *American Economic Review*, I, 1911, 463-72; Sue Ainslie Clark, 'Efficiency, Scientific Management,' *Life and Labor*, I, 1911, 131; *The Typographical Journal*, Jan. 1914, 6; *International Molders' Journal*, Aug. 1911, 601-2; April 1911, 284-6; *The Shoeworkers' Journal*, Oct. 1911, 13-14; Jean Trepp McKelvey, *AFL Attitudes Toward Production, 1900-1932* (Ithaca 1952), 12-26; Milton J. Nadworny, *Scientific Management and the Unions* (Cambridge 1955).

[42]*Labour Gazette*, I, 1900-1, 250, 308; VI 1905-6, 207, 398; *Industrial Banner*, Sept. 1905, 1; Nov. 1905, 3; Jan. 1906, 1; April 1906, 1

[43]*Labour Gazette*, VII, 1906-7, 561-2

[44]*Industrial Banner*, Feb. 1908, 1

[45]Ibid., July 1905, 1

[46]*Labor News*, 1 March 1912, 1; 26 July 1912, 1; 2 Jan 1914, 1

[47]Alan Sullivan, *The Inner Door* (New York 1917), 133-4. Sullivan was a Canadian novelist trained as a civil engineer. Closely in touch with developments in the Canadian business community, he can be regarded as an astute social commentator. In this novel he chronicles the attempts of an impersonal management to utilize efficiency experts and speed-up to elicit greater production. The outcome is a violent strike, in which the workers seize the factory. Our thanks to Russell Hann for making us aware of this source. On Sullivan see Michael Bliss's Introduction to Sullivan's better-known novel, *The Rapids* (Toronto 1972). vi-xx.

[48]*Labour Gazette*, III, 1902-3, 479, 566; x, 1909-10, 1441; XIII, 1912-13, 1000; *Report on Strikes and Lockouts*, 1901-12, 224; Hugh G.J. Aitken, *Taylorism at Watertown Arsenal* (Cambridge 1960), 15

[49]*Report on Strikes and Lockouts, 1901-1912*, 180, 189, 193; *Labour Gazette*, VI, 1905-6, 802

[50]*Industrial Banner*, Aug. 1910, 1. Our account of the Grand Trunk strike has simplified an exceedingly complex conflict. The settlement of 1910 proved only temporary, and the strike dragged on for two more years. Other issues, besides Hays' dubious practices, were involved and heightened the trainmen's discontent. For fuller accounts see J.H. Tuck, 'Union Authority, Corporate Obstinacy, and the Grand Trunk Strike of 1910' (unpublished paper presented to the CHA meetings, 1976); H.S. Ferns and B. Ostry, *The Age of Mackenzie King: The Rise of the Leader* (London 1955), 99-145

[51]See *Industrial Banner*, May 1903, 2; Royal Commission on a Dispute Respecting Hours of Employment between the Bell Telephone Company of Canada and operators at Toronto, Ontario, *Report* (Ottawa 1907) 7, 13, 55-60, 98. It is deserving of comparison with Elinor Langer, 'Inside the New York Telephone Company,' *New York Review of Books*, XIV, 12 March 1970

[52]Royal Commission on Bell Dispute, *Report*, 13

[53]Ibid., 5-7

[54]Cf accounts on the strike in *Labour Gazette*, VII, 1906-7, 922; Alice Klein and Wayne Roberts, 'Be-

seiged Innocence: The "Problem" and the Problems of Working Women–Toronto, 1896-1914,' in *Women at Work: Ontario, 1850-1930* (Toronto 1974), 244-51; R. MacGregor Dawson, *Willim Lyon Mackenzie King: A Political Biography*, I: *1874-1923* (Toronto 1958), 144-6

[55] On the British shop stewards' movements see James Hinton, *The First Shop Stewards' Movement* (London 1973); Branko Privicevic, *The Shop Stewards' Movement and Workers' Control* (Oxford 1959); Arthur Gleason, 'The Shop Stewards and their Significance,' *Survey*, XLI 4 Jan. 1919, 417-22. On the revolutionary ideology of western Canadian miners in 1919 see Peter Warrian, 'The Challenge of the One Big Union Movement in Canada, 1919-1921' (unpublished MA thesis, University of Waterloo, 1971), 52-60

[56] Carter L. Goodrich, 'Problems of Workers' Control,' *Locomotive Engineers' Journal*, LVII, 1923, 365-6, 415. Cf Goodrich, *The Frontier of Control: A Study of British Workshop Practices* (New York 1920)

[57] The most exhaustive treatment of this phenomenon remains Carrol D. Wright, et al. Eleventh Special Report of the Commissioner of Labor, *Regulation and Restriction of Output* (Washington 1904). Restriction of output was extensive in southern Ontario in the late nineteenth century and retained much of its force in the years 1901-14. See Public Archives of Canada [PAC], M.A. Pigott (a Hamilton contractor) to Adam Brown, Esq., MP, 8 May 1888, Macdonald Papers, volume 155, 63160-4; PAC, Department of Labour, Strikes and Lockouts Records, RG 27, volume 296, Strike no 3124, on Hamilton molders and restriction of output.

[58] Montgomery, 'Workers' Control of Machine Production'; 'What One Trade has Done,' *John Swinton's Paper*, 23 March 1884, 1; *Report of the Royal Commission on the Relations of Labor and Capital in Canada* (Ottawa 1889), VI, 371-3

[59] While distinguishing between nineteenth-century variants of control and those of the twentieth century, we should not lose sight of the fact that the experience of restrictive and shop control may well have facilitated the rise of the demand for the more revolutionary workers' control of the later period. A shop steward told Carter Goodrich: 'People talk as if the demand for control was something that had to be created among the workers by a slow process, but it's there already!' Goodrich, *The Frontier of Control*, 31. Cf Montgomery, 'The "New Unionism," ' 509-29

[60] For background on these developments see Bryan D. Palmer, ' "Give us the Road and we will run it"– the Social and Cultural Matrix of an Emerging Labour Movement: The Case of London, 1867-1914,' in Kealey and Warrian, eds., *Essays in Canadian Working Class History*, 106-24

[61] *Labour Gazette*, II, 1901-2, 127, 144; XIII, 1912-13, 895

[62] *Industrial Banner*, Sept. 1905, 1. Cf *Labour Gazette*, I, 1900-1, 517, 590; IV, 1903-4, 86, 119-20, 308-9, 350; V, 1904-5, 150; VII, 1906-7, 139, 621; VIII, 1907-8, 234-7; XIII, 1912-13, 557-9, for similar control struggles waged by other London skilled workers

[63] *The Toiler*, 27 Feb. 1903, 1

[64] *Labour Gazette*, XII, 1911-12, 196, 784

[65] See *Labour Gazette*, IX, 1908-9, 993; *Industrial Banner*, Feb 1909, 4; March 1909. 1; April 1909, 1; May 1909, 1; *The Typographical Journal*, March 1909, 334. Cf *Industrial Banner*, Aug. 1905, 3, for two similar co-operative ventures in Berlin, emerging out of the 1892 Krug furniture factory strike and a later conflict involving broommakers, and *Labour Gazette*, IV, 1903-4, 24, for a Berlin woodworkers' co-operative factory at nearby Elmira.

[66] F.S. Spence, 'The Shorter Hours Movement'; Toronto Trades and Labour Council, *Labour Day Souvenir, 1900* (Toronto 1900), 13. On the relationship between the shorter hours movement and the thrust for control see Montgomery, 'Workers Control of Machine Production,' 16-17.

[67] On the inflationary surge of these years in southern Ontario see Canada, Department of Labour, Board of Inquiry into the Cost of Living, *Report* (Ottawa 1915), II, 3, 76, 80, 381; *Labour Gazette*, III, 1902-3, 308; V. 1904-5, 308, 437, 556, 689; VI, 1905-6, 388; VII, 1906-7, 689, 1082; XVIII, 1907-8, 271; X, 1909-10, 864; XI, 1910-11, 49, 53; XIV, 1913-14, 770; *Industrial Banner*, Feb. 1912, 4.

[68] Knowles, *Strikes*, 219. For further discussion of the wider significance of wage strikes see Montgomery, 'Workers' Control of Machine Production,' 496-7; and Jon Amsden and Stephen Briar, 'Coal Miners on Strike: The Transformation of Strike Demands and the Formation of the National Union in the U.S. Coal Industry, 1881-1884,' forthcoming in *The Journal of Interdisciplinary History*.

[69] Louis C. Reed, *The Labour Philosophy of Samuel Gompers* (New York 1930), 30

[70] On the rise of the AFL in Canada see Robert Babcock, *Gompers in Canada: A Study in American Continentalism Before the First World War* (Toronto 1974).

[71] This chapter in Canadian management relations has received only the most cursory treatment. See, for instance, Bliss, *A Living Profit*, 74-94; Michael J. Piva, 'The Decline of the Trade Union Movement in Toronto, 1900-1915' (paper delivered before the Canadian Historical Association Meetings, 1975), 8-17.

[72] On the nineteenth-century forerunners of employers' associations see *Hamilton Evening Times*, 23 Feb. 1866, 3; 23 March 1866, 2; *Iron Molders International Journal*, April 1866, 7.

[73] J. Castell Hopkins, *The Canadian Annual Review of Public Affairs, 1903* (Toronto 1904), 559; *Industrial Canada*, Jan. 1905, 379

[74] Clarence E. Bonnett, *Employers' Associations in the United States* (New York 1922), esp. 63; *The Toiler*, 2 Dec. 1904, 3, which noted the case of the National Metal Trades Council, on whose executive sat G.W. Watts of Toronto and J.M. Taylor of Guelph. For a contemporary discussion of this new employer

offensive in the United States, see Ray S. Baker, 'Organized Capital Challenges Organized Labour: the New Employers' Association Movement in the United States,' *McClure's*, XXI, 1904, 279-92.

[75] On the proliferation of these practices see *The Toiler*, 9 April 1903, 3; *Industrial Banner*, Dec. 1903,3; Jan. 1904, 1; Oct. 1905, 1; May 1906, 2; Sept. 1906, 1; May 1908, 1; Aug. 1908, 1; July 1911, 1.

[76] *The Toiler*, 10 July 1903, 1

[77] Bonnett, *Employers' Associations*, 109, 117-18

[78] On Kirby's visit and the working-class response to it see *The Toiler*, 6 Feb. 1903, 3; 15 May 1903, 1; *Industrial Banner*, Feb. 1903, 1; May 1903, 1.

[79] *Labour Gazette*, VI, 1905-6, 279-88

[80] Ibid., III, 1902-3, 374

[81] Ibid., 375-6

[82] Quoted in Piva, 'The Decline of the Toronto Trade Union Movement,' 8

[83] *Industrial Canada*, Oct. 1903, 133; Nov. 1905, 280

[84] Ibid., Oct. 1903, 133-4

[85] Ibid., 134

[86] *Industrial Banner*, April 1909, 4. On the resistance of the moulders, and consequent prewar strength, see *Industrial Banner*, 17 Oct. 1913, 1. For the moulders' strike at the Buck Stove and Range Works see *Industrial Banner*, Aug. 1909, 4; May 1908, 1; Aug. 1908, 1; June 1908, 1.

[87] *Industrial Banner*, March 1908, 1

[88] *Industrial Canada*, 20 Nov. 1900, 107

[89] Ibid., 22 April 1901, 233

[90] Ibid., 22 April 1901, 233; Sept. 1902, 90; Oct. 1903, 131; July 1904, 586

[91] Trades and Labour Congress of Canada, *Proceedings of the Annual Convention, 1909* (Toronto 1909), 58; Trades and Labour Congress of Canada, *Proceedings, 1910* (Toronto 1910), 54; *Industrial Canada*, Oct. 1903, 131; Aug. 1903, 13

[92] Ontario, Bureau of Labour, *Annual Report*, 1903 (Toronto 1904), 178; *Annual Report*, 1907, 178; *Annual Report*, 1911, 265

[93] See Ontario, Bureau of Labour, *Annual Report*, 1908, 252-3; *Industrial Banner*, June 1908, 1; Dec. 1903, 1, 3; Jan. 1904, 1, for similar cases in other cities.

[94] See John Saville, 'Trade Unions and Free Labour: The Background to the Taff Vale Decision,' in Asa Briggs and John Saville, ed., *Essays in Labour History* (London 1960), 317-50. The case of Metallic Roofing is also discussed in Wayne Roberts, 'Artisans, Aristocrats, and Handymen: Politics and Trade Unionism among Toronto Skilled Building Trades Workers, 1896-1914.' *Labour Le Travailleur*, I, 1976, 92-121

[95] Ontario, Bureau of Labour, *Annual Report*, 1905, 180

[96] *Industrial Canada*, Oct. 1903, 205; *The Toiler*, 3 April 1903, 4; Trades and Labour Congress of Canada, *Proceedings, 1906*, 76

[97] Ontario, Bureau of Labour, *Annual Report*, 1903, 179, 195; *The Toiler*, 19 June 1903, 2; Ontario, Bureau of Labour, *Annual Report*, 1905, 169, 180; *Industrial Canada*, Dec. 1903, 288; Trades and Labour Congress of Canada, *Proceedings*, 1906, 9-10; *Proceedings*, 1905, 16, on the use of the injunction and the union response.

[98] Forthcoming studies on this theme by Donald H. Avery should contribute greatly to our knowledge in this area. See his 'Canadian Immigration Policy and the Alien Question, 1896-1919: The Anglo Canadian Perspective' (unpublished PHD thesis, University of Western Ontario, 1973).

[99] Ontario, Bureau of Labour, *Annual Report, 1905*, 178-83; *Annual Report, 1906*, 138

[100] Canada, Department of Labour, *Annual Report, 1906-1907* (Ottawa 1908), 111-12; *Labour Gazette*, VII, 1906-7, 612

[101] *Industrial Canada*, May 1903, 436; June 1903, 480; May 1912, 1158-61; Hopkins, *Canadian Annual Review, 1903*, 556

[102] *The Toiler*, 5 June 1903, 1. Cf Hopkins, *Canadian Annual Review, 1903*, 556

[103] On the successful importation of foreign workmen see *Industrial Canada*, Oct. 1903, 129; Oct. 1907, 208-9; Oct. 1908, 235; S.D. Clark, *The Canadian Manufacturers' Association* (Toronto 1939), 47; *Labour Gazette*, IV, 1903-4, 150; *The Toiler*, 19 June 1903, 1; *The Tribune*, 26 May 1906, 1, 4; 7 April 1906, 1; May 1906, 1. The scandal, which revealed the government's involvement in the importation of strikebreakers, Preston's corrupt acceptance of large sums of money, and bonuses and subsidies to firms engaged in the increasingly lucrative promotion of immigration, is chronicled in *The Tribune*, 26 May 1906, 4.

[104] *The Toiler*, 25 March 1904, 1

[105] Cited in Trades and Labour Congress of Canada, *Proceedings of the Annual Convention, 1909*, 33-4

[106] Trades and Labour Congress of Canada, *Proceedings, 1912*, 77, 96

[107] *Labour Gazette*, XII, 1911-12, 1890

[108] *Industrial Banner*, July 1911, 1; Oct. 1910, 1; Feb. 1910, 1; Jan. 1910, 4. Cf. *Report on Strikes and Lockouts, 1901-1912*, 215

[109] *Industrial Canada*, 2 June 1902, 354. Cf *Industrial Canada*, April 1901, 205; March 1909, 664

[110] Canada, Department of Labour, *Annual Report, 1907-1908* (Ottawa 1908), 26; *Industrial Canada*, Dec. 1904, 327

[111]*Labour Gazette*, V, 1904-5, 466

[112]*Industrial Canada*, May 1912, 1064

[113]Ibid., Sept. 1906, 105

[114]See the accounts of various welfare schemes in *Labour Gazette*, V, 1904-5, 136; IX, 1908-9, 744; XI, 1910-11, 1056, 1352; III, 1902-3, 83; XIV, 1913-14, 757. For the best recent summary of the growth of these schemes in the United States, see Nelson, *Managers and Workers*, 101-21.

[115]*The Toiler*, 22 Jan. 1904, 1. For an analysis of the management thinking behind welfare capitalism at International Harvester (whose Hamilton plant was one of the city's largest) see Robert Ozanne, *A Century of Labour-Management Relations at McCormick and International Harvester* (Madison 1967), 71-95. See also Daniel Nelson, 'The New Factory System and the Unions,' *Labour History*, XV, 1974, 163-78. This evaluation of the implementation of welfare schemes at the National Cash Register Company, Dayton, Ohio, buttresses contemporary assessment of corporate motivations.

[116]See Gutman, 'Work, Culture, and Society,' 531-88; Thompson, 'Time, Work-Discipline, and Industrial Capitalism,' 56-97; Frank Thistlethwaite, Atlantic Migration of the Pottery Industry,' *Economic History Review*, X, 1957-8, 264-73; Sidney Pollard, *The Genesis of Modern Management* (Cambridge 1965), 160-200; Stearns, *Lives of Labour*, 342-3; Stearns, 'Adaptation to Industrialization: German Workers as a Test Case,' *Central European History*, IV, 1970, 303-31.

[117]For example, a massive strike of 1500-2000 machinists in Hamilton's munitions plants in 1916. PAC, RG 27, vol. 304, Strike no 27A

[118]Shorter and Tilly, *Strikes in France*, Cf Charles Tilly, Louise Tilly, Richard Tilly, *The Rebellious Century, 1830-1930* (Cambridge 1975); and a brilliant local study, Peter Friedlander, *The Emergence of U.A.W. Local 229, Hamtrack, Michigan: A Study in Class and Culture* (Pittsburgh 1975). Our conclusions, then, stand counterposed to those of Peter Stearns, who regards the main impetus behind strikes as the struggle for economic gain, realized in higher wages. See Stearns, *Revolutionary Syndicalism and French Labor: A Cause without Rebels* (New Brunswick 1971).

[119]James Weinstein, *The Corporate Ideal in the Liberal State, 1900-1918* (Boston 1968); Ronald Radosh, 'The Corporate Ideology of American Labor Leaders from Gompers to Hillman,' *Studies on the Left*, VI, 1966, 66-88. A recent attempt to apply portions of the above argument to the Canadian case is Michael J. Piva, 'The Workmen's Compensation Movement in Ontario,' *Ontario History*, LXVII, 1975, 39-56.

[120]David Bercuson, *Confrontation at Winnipeg: Labour, Industrial Relations, and the General Strike* (Montreal 1974), 1-31.

THE PENETRATION OF CAPITALISM IN QUEBEC AGRICULTURE

Bernard Bernier

In every region of the world, the development of capitalism has entailed the transformation of agricultural production. The expansion of capitalism, first in its mercantile form and later in its productive form, has brought with it the sale of land as a commodity, the sale of agricultural products, the purchase of agricultural means of production with the consequent necessity for the peasants to borrow money, and finally the expropriation of a good portion of the peasantry. Theoretically, the question of the transformation of agricultural production under the impact of the market can be formulated in this way: how do relations of production that are characteristic of capitalism penetrate and modify an economic sector whose internal relations of production are not specifically capitalist?

It is this process of capitalist expansion in Quebec agriculture from the establishment of the French colony to the present day that we examine here. Some historical periods will perforce be treated rather briefly. The analysis of Quebec agriculture will be divided into two parts, the second one being more detailed: (1) a presentation of the seigneurial system and its uses up to 1853: (2) an examination of the transformation up to the present of the system of independent commodity production which became dominant in 1853. In order to make sense of the analysis, it is necessary at first to examine how Marx and Marxist authors have treated the problem of the penetration of capitalism in agriculture.

I. Theoretical aspects

Violence

Marx (1969a and 1973) insisted that the establishment of capitalism requires the application of some kind of violence. The reason for this violence lies in the fact that pre- (or rather non-) capitalist relations of production and class interests resist the expansion of capitalism. For example, in France, the landed nobility resisted the advance of capitalism to such an extent that a bourgeois revolution was necessary in order to sever the rights of the nobility to the land and the peasants. In England, violence was used to expropriate peasants from communal land and even from family plots (see Marx, 1969a: section 8; and Moore, 1966: chaps. 1 and 2).

Violence was also used in Quebec in order to impose capitalist forms of production. However, violence against peasants was minimal because the colony was founded primarily for commercial purposes; thus, despite some quasi-feudal overtones, agriculture had from the start been geared at least partly to trade. Violence was used chiefly against the Indians, but this point is outside the topic of the present paper.

Marx and English agriculture

For Marx (1969a: section 8; 1969b: section 6), the model of the penetration of agriculture by capitalism was the English case. In England, not only was agriculture the source of workers for industries through the expropriation of peasants' land, but agriculture itself grew to be divided along the lines of the capitalist class antagonism.[1] From the fourteenth century on, there took place the expropriation of peasants from communal land and individual plots, the appropriation of large tracts of land by the nobility in order to gain from the sale of wool and wheat, and, finally, in most cases the renting of this land to capitalist farmers in return for a land rent. Capitalist farmers were hiring salaried workers, most of whom were drawn from the population of dispossessed peasants. Very few independent farmers were spared in this process of concentration of land (Moore, 1966: chap.1).

Thus we find in nineteenth-century English agriculture, three classes that Marx (1969b: section 6, and chap. 52) presented as characteristic of a capitalist agriculture: (1) a class of landowners, most of them nobles, that is, descendants of the dominant feudal class, who effected the concentration of land, and the majority of whom now lived off rented land;[2] (2) capitalist farmers who invested capital in agriculture in order to secure a profit; most of these farmers came from the peasantry itself – prosperous farmers who slowly became entrepreneurs–but some were merchants who decided to invest money in agriculture; (3) agricultural workers, who were dispossessed peasants or descendants of peasants who had earlier been expropriated. Since up to the late nineteenth century there was a surplus of labour, their wages were very low.

Marx presented this tripartite class division within agriculture as typical of capitalist development and as the model which would eventually (and rapidly) prevail in other capitalist countries. In fact, Marx recognized and analysed other forms of the penetration of agriculture by capitalism: in France, for example, where an agriculture of independent commodity producers[3] was retained, but was increasingly controlled by the bourgeoisie through mortgage, loans, and the sale of agricultural products (Marx, 1963). In this system, instead of the massive expropriation of peasants' land and the concentration of land in the hands of the aristocracy, who would rent it to agricultural entrepreneurs, one finds the maintenance of the small producers, who kept the ownership of the land, who were the nominal owners of means of production and who organized their labour process.[4] However, through the market, the bourgeoisie recuperated part of the value produced in agriculture. In the USA (Marx, 1970), the availability of land retarded the creation of capitalist agriculture; in order to offset a lack of manpower, the slavery system was used in the South. In fact it was only when the West had been opened up that a capitalist agriculture was created. But in other areas, independent commodity production was still prevalent, and in the South, after the Civil War, sharecropping was established. Thus in France and in the USA., small-holding family agriculture was retained. However, for Marx, this situation was only the prelude to the class differentiation between entrepreneurs and workers which was found in England.

Lenin (1899, 1917) and Kautsky (1900) by and large accepted Marx's view of capitalism and agriculture. Their insistence was primarily on the internal differentiation within the peasantry itself: the richer peasants become agricultural entrepreneurs and the poorer are expropriated and become workers. Both authors underlined other processes involved in the penetration of agriculture by capitalism. For example, Kautsky analysed the ways in which part of the returns of agricultural production are transferred as rent to the bourgeoisie, a process in which smallholding agriculture is kept because it profits the capitalists.

This remark by Kautsky is very important, for it underlines *one* important reason why the capitalization of agriculture predicted by Marx has not happened (yet?) in most capitalist countries. In fact, if one examines agriculture in other capitalist countries, one finds that none have followed the English model. Although all have seen the development of a small capitalist sector in agriculture, the bulk of their agriculture is still of the independent commodity production type, that is most farms are owner-operated, using family labour, although in some countries there still remains a residual sector of sharecropping or tenancy.[5] The reasons for the maintenance of the smallholding[6] farm are complex and numerous. First, monopolization of industrial capital, with its consequent increase in profit rate, has made investment in agriculture less interesting to investors. Second, there has been a transfer of value from the smallholders to capitalists (industrialists who sell agricultural means of production, industrialists who transform agricultural products, merchants who deal in agricultural products, bankers and financiers who loan money to farmers). These transfers, made through the money and commodity markets, according to the mechanisms of the equalization of profit rates (Marx, 1969b: section 3) and reinforced by the monopolies' control of the market, have revealed themselves to be very lucrative for the capitalists. Third, in many countries, the maintenance of an agricultural sector of smallholders, with slow and gradual expropriation, has been a political tool of the bourgeoisie against the working class. In preserving property, the dominant classes have enlisted farmers in support of policies of 'law and order' and of protection of social peace (for example in France, Quebec, and Japan). Finally, up to the 1960s, small-

holders, through the intensive use of family labour and low standards of living, have produced agricultural products at a low cost, thus insuring a flow of low-priced products in order to reproduce the industrial labour force, with the consequent possibility of keeping a check on wage increases.

Because of these various factors, the penetration of agriculture by capitalism and its consequent modification of this sector are complex processes. In fact only a small part of the transformation of agriculture reproduces the type of development which took place in England. This does not mean that a capitalist agricultural sector is not going to prevail in these countries if capitalism is maintained. However, one must be aware that the penetration by capitalism of agriculture in most countries has not followed the 'classic' case and that, until now, other forms of relations of production have been prevalent. These forms are in flux; they evolve through time. They depend on a complex interplay of factors. It is this complex interplay that we now examine for Quebec.

II. The seigneurial system: 1600-1853

The development of agriculture in Quebec in the seventeenth, eighteenth and the first half of the nineteenth centuries was marked by the seigneurial system and the dominant class position of the 'seigneurs'.[7] The seigneurial system was created by the French Crown in order to insure a type of appropriation of North American territory according to the agrarian structures and social class positions of the metropolis. It was a tenure system based on the establishment of quasi-feudal rights.

The seigneurs, in exchange for vast tracts of land given to them by the Crown, were supposed to pay for expenses of immigrant peasants who, according to the plans, would constitute the majority of the population. The right of ownership rested with the seigneurs, and this right gave them the privilege to exact various kinds of dues, the most important being a land rent, from the peasants. The peasants were given a hereditary right of use on a delimited area of land, but no right of ownership. In fact, the seigneurial system was from the start akin to a tenancy system.

From 1623 to 1763, 375 seigneuries were granted, a third of these to various religious orders and Catholic parishes. However, the seigneurial system was a failure from the standpoint of both population and agricultural production. The majority of seigneurs were involved in fur-trading and administration and were more interested in making profit from trade or speculation than in financing immigration. In 1760, the entire population of the French colony was only about 60,000, compared to 1.5 million for New England (see Ouellet, 1966:26). As for agricultural production, three points must be noted: (1) 'Peasants' who were brought to the colony were selected mainly from the urban poor or the military. Few were of peasant origin, thus few had the skills to engage profitably in agriculture. (2) The sparse population discouraged the establishment of commercial agriculture; most peasants were engaged in subsistence agriculture. As a consequence, rents were rarely paid. (3) The fur trade had a need for manpower and peasants were attracted to profits that could be made as 'coureurs de bois': thus the agricultural population was further depleted. The failure of the seigneurial system to populate the land was in fact one factor in the defeat by the British in 1760.

Paradoxically, the conquest prompted the revival of the seigneurial system (Bourque, 1970). The reason for the maintenance of the seigneurial system *de jure* and its revival *de facto* was the complex class situation which followed the conquest. The first element of this situation was the fact that the English military administration had to rule a population which was overwhelmingly French. Second, the administration, selected from the English lower nobility, had to counter the demands made by the counterparts of their metropolitan foes: the newly arrived English merchants. In this situation, the administrators were prone to lean on a French landed class, both sharing the same class background. Third, the dignitaries of the French administration, losing their administrative posts and their trading partners, had to live off the land; thus their interest in reviving old rights that had been marginally applied before. Fourth, this landed class convinced the English administration that its collaboration was needed in order to keep the French-speaking population quiet.

All these factors led to the maintenance of the French legal and land tenure system. Thus

the seigneurial system, which had existed legally but had not been applied in reality, was revived; and old rights and dues which had never been followed before, were now in force. One point to be noted on this subject is that language (French) and religion (Roman Catholicism), which the seigneurs had claimed to be elements that had to be preserved in order to counter potential unrest in the colony, were really the guarantee of the seigneurs' class dominance over the peasants. This explains the unfailing insistence of seigneurs on language and religion in the period that the followed the conquest.

It was the increase in urban population due to immigration and the arrival of English farmers which prompted the development of a merchant agriculture.[8] As the internal market was developing, wheat became a major export item to England (after 1780). English farmers, established first in Upper Canada, and later, after 1790, in the Eastern Townships, were the first to profit from this commercialization of agriculture. Even Quebec peasants living under the seigneurial system started specializing their production in order to gain from trade. However, unlike English-speaking farmers, Quebec peasants were not using new tools and techniques of soil regeneration and so productivity increases were very low. For example, up to 1850, manure from cattle, instead of being used as fertilizer, was thrown away in rivers as garbage. The ignorance of new tools and techniques, the urban origin of most peasants, as well as the inheritance system prevalent among the French-speaking farmers would become important forces in the agricultural crisis which started around 1810.

From that date until the dissolution of the seigneurial system in 1853 (and even after), Quebec agriculture was in severe difficulty. The first, but least important cause of the crisis was the difficulty in selling wheat to England from 1802 on. The second cause was the over-population of seigneurial land, due primarily to the very high birth rate, encouraged by the Church, and estimated at 60 per 1000. As long as there was enough land to cultivate, there were few problems. But when seigneurial land became scarce, population pressure was felt. This was aggravated by the stipulation of the inheritance system that all heirs inherit a piece of their father's land. Even this land partitioning would have been less important if proper tools and techniques had been used. But without fertilizing, crop rotation, or fallow, and with ploughs that were too shallow, productivity of the land was gradually decreasing (Ouellet, 1966: 152, 239).

The net effects of these trends were a decrease in productivity per acre and per worker; a return to subsistence agriculture centred on potatoes and peas; pauperization of peasants and seigneurs with near-starvation for many; a shrinking of the internal market, which is a basis of capitalist development; emigration to the USA.

Rural poverty was one factor in the revolt of 1837-8, but it was not its basic cause. The main element was the interest of a class of rural professionals and petty industrialists (Bourque, 1970). This class was trying to establish industries based on the transformation of agricultural products, such as breweries, distilleries, etc. In order to attain this goal, it needed a larger market for agricultural products, a market which had to be freed of seigneurial rights. Thus the opposition of this class to the seigneurs. Moreover, this class, bent on local production, by 1800 controlled the Legislative Assembly of Lower Canada and clashed with English-speaking merchants who were dependent on trade with England. Enlisting the support of peasants by promising them the abolition of the seigneurial system and ownership of the land, this class of bourgeois-to-be mounted a political campaign against the dominant interests of the seigneurs and English merchants and for the independence of Quebec. This campaign led to the uprisings of 1837-8 and ended in defeat, a defeat which meant the elimination of the class which had prompted that action. Henceforth, the commercial interests of the English-speaking bourgeoisie, with the cooperation of the seigneurs, the Church, and reactionary professionals, were to dominate.

However, the insurrection of 1837-8 had shown the failure of the seigneurial system, which was finally abolished in 1853. Abolition took the form of purchases by peasants of seigneurial land they were cultivating. Since the peasants were poor, they had to pay on a long-term basis. Thus the dependence on the seigneurs was maintained: the peasants were still giving sums of money to seigneurs. In fact some peasants were still indebted to the descendants of seigneurs in 1940, when the provincial government finally settled the debts.

The abolition of the seigneurial system was really a land reform, and its effect was the creation of smallholding independent commodity producers. Theoretically, the owners had become independent. But we will see below what this independence meant.

III. The evolution of independent commodity production: 1853-1974

From 1860 on, agricultural production was shifted to dairy products in order to satisfy the English demand for cheese and butter. There was thus a reorganization of production and a re-entry into the market. This specialization in dairy farming is still dominant in Quebec.

At first, production was carried out in a traditional way, without sophisticated tools and machines, and the products were sold to small local dairies and butter factories. However, this was to change with the post-1880 concentration of industries and trade linked to dairy products, a concentration which was but a small part of the monopolization of capital which occurred at that time in North America.

The concentration of capital had important effects on farmers: (1) The development of dairy farming meant that agricultural machinery, and later feeds, fertilizers, and insecticides whose production was increasingly concentrated in the hands of monopolies, became important elements in the production process. This trend entailed higher expenses, which in turn made necessary the recourse to credit. Thus the net effects were an increase in 'capital' expenses and indebtedness. While from the start purchases of machinery were made through monopolies, up to the 1940s loans were chiefly from local merchants, 'rentiers,' and usurers. (2) As the dependence on monopolies was being established through the purchase of means of production, monopolization was also increasing in the transformation of dairy products. Thus the farmers' dependence on monopoly capital was increasing both in the purchase of means of production and in the sale of agricultural products. This trend was to become stronger as the years passed. (3) The increased dependence of farmers on a monopoly-con-

Table I
Number and Acreage of Farms, Quebec, 1881-1971

Year	Number of farms	Average acreage
1881	137,863	91
1891	174,996	90.6
1901	140,110	96
1911	149,701	104
1921	137,613	125.5
1931	135,957	127
1941	154,669	114
1951	134,336	131
1961	95,777	148
1971	61,257	176

Source: Federal Bureau of Statistics: Agricultural Statistics

Table II
Total Value of Farm Capital Quebec, 1901-38

Year	Value of capital (in millions of dollars)
1901	436
1911	788
1921	1085
1931	877
1938	872

Source: Haythorne and Marsh, 1941: 547

trolled capitalist market had as a consequence a decrease in the number of farm families and in the farm population, with a considerable increase in the average acreage of farms (see Table 1). The stricter relation to the market was forcing marginal farmers out of agriculture, setting them 'free' to sell their labour as workers. Throughout the twentieth century, dispossessed farmers have been joining the ranks of the industrial workers, thus putting pressures on wage increases.

The First World War consolidated the commercial orientation of agriculture. Exports of dairy products to England increased and farmers were encouraged to shift a larger share of their production to commercial products. Industrial development and the increase in urban population in the 1920s furthered the trends to commercial farming. This is clear in the upward movement of total farm expenses (see Table II).

However the depression of the 1930s saw a return to subsistence agriculture, at least in regions without a nearby urban market, so the number of farms increased. The depression was a period of hardships for farmers: as Table III shows, their income decreased much more than urban wages, even though the cost of living was about the same for farmers and urban workers.

The Second World War marked a return to previous trends. The major element which appears in the examination of the transformation of the agricultural sector in the last three decades is the sharp decrease in the number of farms and in the farming population (see Table IV). From 1941 to 1971, the number of farms has decreased by 60 per cent, from over 150,000 to just above 60,000. On average, *nine farms have disappeared per day* in Quebec in these thirty years. At the same time, the farm population has decreased by more than 50 per cent, and in 1971, it accounted for only 5.6 per cent of the total population (3.5 per cent of the active population in 1973) compared to 27 per cent in 1931. Such a decrease represents the acceleration of trends which had appeared before the depression: concentration of agricultural production, increase of productivity, expropriation of marginal farmers.

At the same time, the acreage per farm increased by 85 per cent from 1901 to 1971 and by 38.5 per cent between 1931 and 1971 (see Table I). The acreage of utilized land per farm increased 50 per cent between 1931 and 1971. Average acreage, however, is not sufficient to evaluate the sweeping changes in farm operation, farm productivity, and farm expenses which have happened in Quebec since the beginning of the Second World War. Average production per farm has gone up tremendously: from $1217 in 1941 to $13,059 in 1971. In constant dollars, it represents an increase of more than 300 per cent (see Table V). The major cause of this increase has been the increased productivity which has followed the use of better machinery, feeds, fertilizers, and seeds.

In fact, total investment in agriculture almost tripled between 1941 and 1971, increasing in that period from $740 million to $22 billion. In the five-year period of 1961-6, the average investment per farm rose from $16,925 to $23,548, an increase of 33 per cent. For machinery alone, total investment has in-

Table III
Economic Comparative Trends, Measured by Income and Price Indexes, Canada 1913-40

| Year | Income | | Wage rates | | Wholesale prices | | Cost of living | |
	Farm revenue	Other entrepreneurs	Farm labour	Common factory labour	Farm products	Manufac- tures	Urban	Farm
1913	—	—	—	53	64	65	65	66
1914	—	—	40	54	70	66	66	68
1915	—	—	42	54	78	71	67	72
1916	—	—	50	59	90	85	73	78
1918	—	—	112	81	133	128	97	111
1920	—	—	141	115	161	156	124	144
1926	100	100	100	100	100	100	100	100
1928	113	115	100	100	101	95	99	98
1930	55	107	85	101	82	87	99	94
1932	20	77	46	93	48	70	81	81
1934	36	74	44	91	59	73	79	81
1936	54	86	54	96	69	74	81	81
1938	58	94	60	106	74	78	84	84
1939	69	97	64	107	64	75	83	82
1940	70	103	72	111	67	82	88	88

Source: Haythorne and Marsh, 1941: 492

Table IV
Number of Farms, Agricultural Population and its Percentage of Total Population, Quebec 1931-71

Year	Number of farms	Farming population	Percentage of total population
1931	135,957	777,000	27
1941	154,669	839,000	25.2
1951	134,336	792,000	19.5
1961	95,777	585,000	11.1
1971	61,257	334,519	5.6

Source: BFS Agricultural Statistics

Table V
Average Production per Farm, in Current and Constant Dollars, 1931-71

Year	Production (current dollars)	Index (1941 = 100) (constant dollars)
1931	1,359	124
1941	1,217	100
1951	3,356	168.9
1961	5,104	222.1
1971	13,509	445.2

Source: BFS, Agricultural Statistics:
Annuaire du Québec, 1973

creased from $97 million in 1931 to $427 million in 1971 (see Table VI). This increase in capital investment has been accelerated in recent years, as is shown clearly in Table VII, which presents number of farms according to the amount of invested capital in 1961 and 1971.

Such an increase in capital has entailed heavy indebtedness for Quebec farmers. In 1968, the average debt per farm was $33,000, for an average total value (including land, buildings, and machinery) of $42,000 per farm (UCC, 1969: 108-9). Thus debts, on av-

Table VI
Agricultural Capital Expenses, and Expense for
Machinery, Quebec, 1931-71

Year	Total expenses (in million dollars)	Machinery (in million dollars)
1931	—	97
1941	740	85
1951	1,339	211
1961	1,624	301
1971	2,200	427

Source: Lessard, 1974: 38

Table VII
Number of Farms, by Invested Capital,
Quebec 1961-71

Invested capital	1961	1971
0- 4949	7,786	1,383
4950- 9949	20,226	4,583
9950-14949	41,609	20,853
14950-49949	15,900	23,527
49950 +	256	11,911

Source: Lessard, 1974: 37

erage, are equivalent to 80 per cent of the average farm value.

Most of the loans now come from government sources: either the Farm Credit Corporation (federal government) which accounts for about one quarter of the total agricultural credit given in Quebec between 1929 and 1973; or the Quebec Farm Credit Bureau (provincial government) which accounts for about half of the credit between 1936 and 1973 (SCA, 1973:22). In 1971, banks and caisses populaires accounted for the last quarter, consisting mainly of the most lucrative short-term loans.

What is important to note is that large farms are in proportion more indebted than small ones (Table VIII). This means that large farms, despite their use of complex technology, do not become successful ventures. In fact, according to *La Terre de chez nous*, the newspaper published by the Union of Agricultural Producers, most auctions in the last few years have involved large farms (see Corriveau, 1974:10 sq.). In other words, in Quebec agriculture now, scale, at least up to a certain point, is not a guarantee of financial success. The main reason for this is that prices of farm products are rising much more slowly than prices of items necessary for agricultural production. This is amply illustrated in Figure I where the increase in prices of agricultural products at the farm is compared with price increases of manufactured goods, semi-manufactured goods, construction material, and consumption items. Moreover, it

Table VIII
Number of Mortgaged Farms, by Invested Capital, Quebec, 1971

Capital	Total no. of farms	No. of farms with mortgage	Percentage of mortgaged farms
2950- 7449	3,463	652	18.2
7450-14949	8,807	2,858	32.4
14950-24949	13,549	6,056	44.7
24950-49949	23,527	14,654	62.2
49950-74949	7,802	5,650	72.4
74950-19950	4,109	2,900	70.5

Sources: BFS Agricultural Statistics, 1971: 55

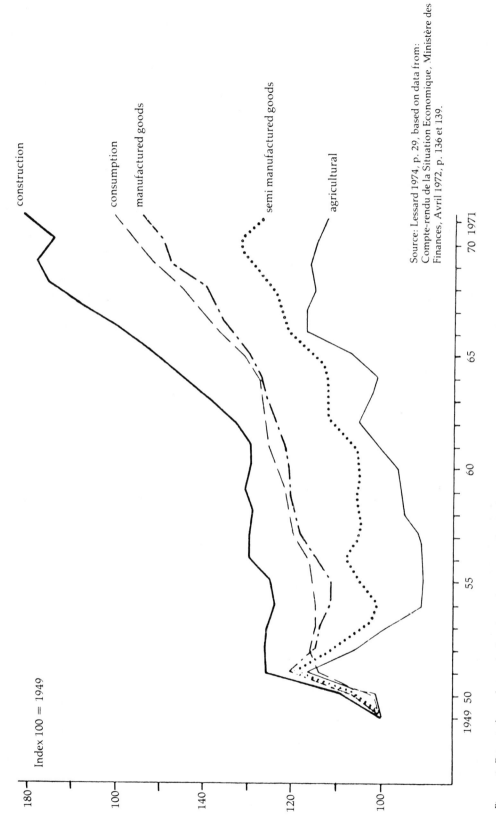

Figure 1 Price indexes for agricultural products, manufactured goods, semimanufactured goods, construction material, and consumption. Canada, 1949-71. Source: Lessard, 1974:29, based on data from Compte-rendu de la Situation Economique, Ministère des Finances, avril 1971 : 136, 139.

must be noted that prices of agricultural machinery have increased faster than prices of other finished products. For example, from 1956 to 1968, the price of machinery increased 50 per cent, compared to 10 per cent for cars and a decrease of 14 per cent for household electrical goods. Finally, the price of cereals, which are necessary as feed for animals, has increased by 120 per cent from 1970 to 1973. Grain accounted for 10 per cent of all feed in 1964, 24 per cent in 1966, and 45 per cent in 1974. In fact, feed accounted for 27 per cent of all farm expenses in 1970, and 36 per cent in 1973 (Corriveau, 1974:54.)

When one takes into account all means of production, the price increase from 1966 to 1972 has been 42 per cent, whereas prices of agricultural products in the same period have gone up 27 per cent (*Le Devoir,* 13 dec 73). This explains why the percentage of total retail food prices which is accounted for by expenses for means of production has gone up from 28 per cent in 1958 to 66 per cent in 1974.

What all this means is that an increase in scale is not a guarantee of rising income; for the increase in productivity is more than offset by larger increases in expenses. For example, an increase of 21 per cent in gross income from 1972 to 1973 has been eliminated by an increase of 23 per cent in expenses. In fact, since 1972, more productive machinery, which is necessary to pay back earlier loans, has not meant a rising income; rather it entails yearly deficits which are increasing. Thus scale has become one path to spiralling indebtedness.

Nor is scale a sign that capitalist relations of production are developing within the agricultural sector. In fact, with the exception of a small number of very large farms where one can find the use of fulltime agricultural workers, the great majority of Quebec farms are still of the family type, although some hire wage labour occasionally or at harvest time. Thus family farming is still the dominant form in agriculture. But as the rates of dispossession and indebtedness show, this type of agricultural venture meets with increasing difficulty.

Capitalists have found a way to profit from agriculture while maintaining some forms of agricultural production. Thus a new form of financing is now used in pig and chicken raising and in the production of eggs. Feed producers (Purina, Master, etc.), through their local agent, provide the buildings, equipment, animals, and feed. The farmer provides the land (a miminum amount is all that is needed) and labour. Thus farmers raise pigs or chickens or produce eggs with capital provided by monopolies. In return for this capital, farmers must sell the product, at a set price, to the agent of the feed companies.

This system has been profitable to both farmers and feed companies up to now: farmers have not had to pay directly for price rises in means of production and they have kept their land; companies have benefitted from a steady supply of products paid at a low price.

In this system, the farmer retains ownership of the land, but he loses the ownership of means of production. He controls his work process, but he is paid a certain amount per unit product. In fact, the farmer has become almost a wage-labourer. He is in a transition stage between the smallholder and the agricultural worker. Up to now, this organization has been successful, mainly because of government support prices. But with consumer prices increasing, there will have to be an increase in the price paid to the farmer for his products. However, with the overproduction of eggs and chickens which is now the case in Quebec, it is not probable that farmers will get such an increase.

It must be noted that this type of organization is limited to certain sectors of agricultural production. It has not penetrated the most important sector of Quebec agriculture: dairy farming. This sector has been hard hit by the current recession and its difficulties constitute the major trend in agricultural production.

The complex picture of the agricultural sector in Quebec which is suggested by the quoted figures can be summarized in a few major elements. (I) An increasing number of farmers are being dispossesed of their land and farms. Dispossession does not depend on violent or legal means: when farmers are indebted and when they judge that farm income is not even sufficient to insure a 'decent' living, they sell or auction off their farm. No need for lawsuits or foreclosures. Up to the late 1960s, it was mainly marginal farmers, i.e., farmers who marketed only a small part of their produce, who were the victims of dispossession. But in the last five or six years, owners of large farms, squeezed between the high prices of their means of production, interest on loans, and low prices of farm produce, have had to sell. The expropriation has become a danger for all farmers, and the ones who stick to agriculture have had to use more and more credit, thus hiking the proportion of debts to farm-value at a time when incomes are decreasing. (2) The reason agriculture has met with increasing hardships in Quebec must be sought in the workings of the capitalist system. On one hand, monopolies control the market both for products needed in agricultural production and for farm produce. Prices are thus controlled by capitalist entrepreneurs. Moreover, the government has devised programs to fix prices, but at a level which is not always sufficient for farm production to be maintained. On the other hand, farm producers, even when organized in cooperatives, have little control over the market.

In fact, the market is organized to insure maximum profits for agribusinesses. But in order to maintain that effect, the market has to pressure farmers. This pressure would not be too dramatic if, at the same time, the diversification of industrial products and the necessity to sell them had not managed to raise the level of needs, even of the farmers. Thus the market pressure on farmers has had the effect of forcing farmers out of the agricultural sector.

This trend, however, is contradictory. For the pressure needed in order to maintain profit rates has the ultimate effect of erasing the base on which the profit is made: profits come from farm products which farmers produce; if farmers leave agriculture, the products disappear. Thus the search for maximum profit, as analysed brilliantly by Marx, (1969b: section 3) entails conditions which hinder the base on which this profit is made. (3) The dispossession of farmers would not pose enormous problems if it were not for the impossibility, given current economic conditions of agricultural production in North America, to create a strong capitalist agriculture in Quebec. This is due partly to climate and soil fertility, but also to the fact that agricultural production is already organized in a capitalist and/or a more productive way in Ontario and the US. In fact, it is because the profits expected from capital investment in agriculture are low that it is impossible to establish more than a few thousand capitalist farms (20,000 at most). (4) Farmers find themselves collectively in a difficult situation at a time when their usefulness as a conservative political force has markedly decreased due to their low percentage of the total population. There is thus little that they can expect from the state unless they organize to get it. (5) Finally, farmers are being expropriated massively at a time when unemployment is increasing. This process of expropriation is one more element which contributes to the rise of the unemployment rate.

Conclusion

All these elements point to the contradictory development of capitalism in agriculture. Contradictions, stemming from the quest for profit, are apparent at various levels. (a) While profits of agribusinesses come in part from agricultural production and are based on the presence of agricultural products, the functioning of the market which is controlled by these businesses has as a consequence the disappearance of family agriculture. (b) This disappearance of family agriculture is not adequately replaced by the development of a local capitalist agricultural sector: total agricultural production has decreased since 1973 and the trend is likely to accelerate. (c) Farmers are being expropriated at a time when keeping them on the farm might be a necessity for the dominant class for economic and political reasons (i.e., to keep the unemployment rate down and for the maintenance of capitalist 'law and order'). (d) Agricultural production is endangered in Quebec at a time when food production on a worldwide basis must be increased.

The contradictions underlined here are not specific to Quebec agriculture: French and Japanese farmers, at least, are confronted with similar problems (see Servolin, 1972 for France; Bernier 1974 for Japan). But the examination of Quebec agriculture in detail has brought forth an understanding both of the peculiar situation which prevails in one particular area and of general problems which confront family farming of the independent commodity producer's type when pressed by capitalist interests. The general conclusion that can be reached is that capitalism, as Marx and others have predicted, is destroying pre-capitalist forms of agriculture. The corollary to that conclusion is that a capitalist agricultural sector is developing. However, the development of capitalist agriculture is characterized by the tendency inherent in capitalism, of unequal regional development, that Marx (1969b), Lenin

(1916), and Luxembourg (1969) have underlined. In the case of Quebec, the penetration of the market by agricultural goods produced in areas with better climatic conditions (in the US or Ontario) by capitalist farmers using a cheap labour force is a major obstacle to the creation of such an agricultural sector locally. In this situation, most farmers are confronted with increasing financial problems and finally expropriation. Moreover, agricultural production is decreasing.

The solution to these problems, inherent in capitalist development, cannot come from farmers alone. Already, as in Mirabel, where expropriation of farmers in order to build the new Montreal International Airport has taken place, farmers are becoming aware that their problems can be solved only if they co-operate with other classes which are exploited in capitalism, chiefly the working class (see Bouvette, 1975). They realize that they alone cannot keep agricultural production alive. They also realize that independent commodity production is impossible under the present economic conditions, that they will have to find new ways of organizing agricultural production.

Class alliances are only in an incipient stage; consciousness is still low. But a tradition of struggle has been developing in the last ten years mainly among workers, but also among farmers. All that is lacking is political leadership that would channel various kinds of protest into a movement for the transformation of the existing social order.

Rev. canad. Soc. & Anth./Canad. Rev. Soc. & Anth. 13(4) 1976.

REFERENCES

Bernier, Barnard, « *L'Economie et la société japonaises face à la crise monétaire de 1971* », Pp. 27-57 in Robert Garry, éd., Le Japon:Mythes et Réalités, Québec, CQRI, 1974.
Bourque, Gilles, *Classes sociales et Question nationale au Québec 1760-1840,* Montréal, Parti Pris, 1970.
Bouvette, André, « *Intervention étatique et luttes de classe* », MA thesis, Université de Montréal, anthropologie, 1975.
Chatillon, Colette, « *Le développement de l'agriculture au Québec* ». MA thesis, Université de Montréal, anthropologie, 1974.
Corriveau, Céline, « *Pour mieux comprendre les problèmes de la relève agricole* ». Miméo, 1974.
Dore, Ronald P., *Land Reform in Japan*, Berkeley, University of California Press, 1959.
Duby, Georges, *Guerriers et Paysans*, VII-XIIème siècle, Paris, Gallimard, 1973.
Hamelin, Jean, et Yves Roby, *Histoire Economique du Québec 1851-1896*, Montréal, Fidès, 1971.
Harris, Richard Colebrook, *The Seigneurial System in Early Canada*, Quebec, Presses de l'université Laval, 1966.
Haythorne, George V., et Leonard C. Marsh, Land and Labour, Toronto, McGill University Press, 1941.
Haythorne, George V., *Labor in Canadian Agriculture*, Cambridge, Mass, Harvard University Press, 1960.
Kautsky, Karl, *La Question Agraire*, Paris, Giard et Brière, 1900.
Hedley, Max, « *ndependent Commodity Production and the Dynamics of Tradition* *, Paper presented at the CSAA meeting, Toronto, 1974, 1974.
Henripin, Jacques, « *Notes de Cours, Démographie* », Universitê de Montréal, 1968.
Lénine, V.I., *Le développement du Capitalisme en Russie*, Moscou, Editions du Progrès, Euvres complètes, Tome 3, 1899.
Nouvelles Données sur les lois du développement du capitalisme dans l'agriculture, Moscou, Editions du Progrès, Euvres complètes, Tome 22, 1917.
L'impérialisme stade supréme du capitalisme, Moscou, Editions du Progrès, 1969, publié en 1916, 1969.
Leroi-Ladurie, Emmanual, *Les paysans du Languedoc*, Paris, SEVPEN, 1966.
Lessard, Diane, « *Les rapports de production dans l'agriculture Québécoise, 1941-1971, MA thesis, Université de Montréal, anthropologie, 1974.*
Luxembourg, Rosa, *L'Accumulation du Capital*, Paris, Maspéro, publié en 1918, 1969.
Marx, Karl, *Le 18 Brumaire de Louis Bonaparte*, Paris, Editions sociales publié en 1852, 1963.
Le Capital, livre 1, Paris, Gonthier-Flammarion, publié en 1867, 1969a.
Le Capital, livre 3, Paris, Editions Sociales, publié en 1893-4, 1969b.
La Guerre Civile aux, Etts-Unis, Paris 10/18, articles de journaux 1861-5, 1970.
Moore, Barrington, *The Social Origins of Dictatorship and Democracy*, Boston, Beacon Press, 1966.
Ouellet, Fernand, *Histoire économique et sociale du Québec 1760-1815*, Montréal, Fides, 1966.
Elements d'histoire sociale du Bas-Canada1, Montréal, HMH, /é°.

Postel-Vinay, Gilles, *La rente foncière dans le capitalisme agricole*, Paris, Maspéro 1974.
Rey, Pierre-Philippe, *Colonalisme, néo-colonalisme et transition au capitalisme*, Paris, Maspéro 1971.
Rey, Pierre-Philippe, *Les Alliances de classes*, Paris, Maspéro, Servolin, Claude, 1973.
« *L'absorption de l'agriculture dans le mode de production capitaliste* », In L'Univers politique des paysans, Paris, A. Colin, 1972.
Société de crédit agricole du Canada 1973 Rapport annuel, 1973. Ottawa, Imprimeur de la Reine, 1973.
Union catholique des cultivateurs Rapport dur l'exercice, 1968-69, Montréal, UCC, 1969.

NOTES

[1]This antagonism is based on the fact that one class, the bourgeoisie, owns the means of production and through this ownership controls the work process, and that the other, the working class, dispossessed of means of production, has only its labour to sell.

[2]Some landowners kept the management of their land and became capitalist agricultural entrepreneurs. Others did not rent their land: rather, they hired managers to run their farms for them. But the majority found it easier to simply let a farmer cultivate the land in exchange for a land rent. Part of this class was not of noble origin; it included merchants who succeeded in purchasing domains which they either managed themselves or rented out to farmers.

[3]For more detail on this type of agriculture, see Hedley, 1974.

[4]Of course, there were regional differences as documented in the works of Duby (1973), Leroi-Ladurie (1966), and Postel-Vinay (1974).

[5]Japan is an exception on this score. Up to 1946, the percentage of peasant who were tenants was around 30, and at one point (1940), it reached as high as 45. However, the land reform of 1946-7 created an agricultural sector of small independent family farms (cf. Dore, 1958).

[6]Here and thereafter, 'smallholding' refers chiefly to independent commodity production which is the dominant type of family agriculture in all capitalist countries.

[7]The information on the seigneurial system comes from Ouellet 1966 and 1972: Harris, 1966; Bourque, 1970; and Chatillon, 1974.

[8]This section on the period from 1760 to 1900 is based on Ouellet 1966; Hamelin et Roby, 1971; and Bourque, 1970.

CLASS CONTRADICTIONS IN CANADA'S INTERNATIONAL SETTING

Carl J. Cuneo / McMaster University

Materialist dialectical theorists locate transformations in economic, social, and political structures in the notion of "contradiction." A primary contradiction is usually posited between capital and labour, or between the capitalist class and working class (Mao, 1954: II, 13-53). Structural transformations are thus seen as ultimately rooted in class conflict. In countries that "dominate" important sectors of other countries, or in countries largely "dependent" on other countries, a nonprimary contradiction along the national international dimension cuts across the primary class contradiction. Two serious problems arise in the analyses of such countries.[1] First, the analysis of the national/international dimension often distorts a clear analysis of the class structure. The result is often a muddled picture of the country's class structure. Secondly, the relation between class conflict and social change often becomes lost in the complexities of the national/international dimension. Quite often no clear theory of the origin of change in the primary contradiction emerges.

Analyses of Canada suffer from both of these problems. Focusing on the first problem, the national/international dimension has often been analysed in lieu of the relationship between capital and labour and the way this is integrated into Canada's international context. At times this takes the form of posing Canada as almost totally dependent on the United States (e.g., Levitt, 1971; Laxer, 1973) while at other times it is suggested that Canada is an imperialist country in her own right exercising dominion over other countries (e.g., Moore and Wells, 1975). In both of these analyses, the relationship between the capitalist class and the working class is not treated in a central way. However, there is another tradition of studies that examines the activities or characteristics of various sections of the capitalist class in an international context, although once again the relationship between capital and labour is not of central concern (Naylor, 1975; Clement, 1977). These latter studies do contain information useful as guides for shedding light on the relationship between the capital/labour and national/international contradictions. The purpose of the present paper will be to theoretically examine this relationship in the Canadian context and to draw on some empirical illustrations.

For Karl Marx (1967; I, 177-230; Gough, 1972; O'Conner, 1975), the heart of the relation between the capitalist and working classes lay in the extraction of surplus value from productive labour by industrial capitalists. This contradiction between capital and labour intensifies with the advance of the capitalist mode of production. In this advance, capitalists invest relatively more capital in technology than in living labour. This allows for the greater production of surplus value on the basis of a comparatively smaller productive labour base. The term most often used for this advance is "monopoly capitalism." Since the focus of this paper will be on the most intense forms of class contradiction in Canada's international context, it is first necessary to examine some characteristics of monopoly capitalism before setting out four types of class contradiction.

Monopoly Capitalism

The most striking external indicator of monopoly capitalism is the domination of an economy by a few large corporations which account for a relatively high proportion of assets, profits, and sales. In the words of Paul Baran and Paul Sweezy (1966: 52): "Monopoly capitalism is a system made up of giant corporations." More precisely, they argue: ". . . we use the term 'monopoly' to include not only the case of a single seller of a commodity for which there are no substitutes, but also the much more common case of 'oligopoly,' i.e., a few sellers dominating the markets for products which are more or less satisfactory substitutes for one another" (p.6, n.3). However, this market structure is only the end result of the process of monopolization. We have to ask how a few corporations achieve such a dominant position in the market. The answer to this question leads us back into the sphere of production and its integration with financial capital at the national and international levels. This aspect of monopoly capitalism has been succinctly stated by V.I. Lenin. He argued that imperialism and "monopoly stage of capitalism" are synonymous, and focused on five central characteristics: the concentration of production and capital "playing a decisive role in economic life"; "the merging of bank capital with industrial capital" to create "finance capital"; the export of capital; "the formation of international monopolist combines which share the world among themselves"; and "the territorial division of the whole world among the biggest capitalist powers" (1973: 105-6).

Four general observations may be made about this characterization of monopoly capitalism. First, Lenin's definition explains Baran and Sweezy's definition. Corporations assume a commanding position in the commodity market because they have concentrated their production with financial help. Thus circulation must be traced back to production. Second, monopoly capitalism is not an absolute but a *tendency*. The concentration of production in a corporation is a tendency in the emergence of monopoly capitalism even though the particular corporation in question may not occupy a leading position in world cartels. Third, with increasing concentration of production, the primary industrial class contradiction between labour and capital intensifies. As noted earlier, this occurs mainly through the relative shift in capital investment from living labour to technology.[2] This has ramifications for other types of class contradiction in the sphere of circulation to be specified later. Fourth, monopoly capitalism always has a tendency to take on an international character. This point will become important later on when we locate different types of class contradiction in Canada in an international context. Before this is done, we will first present some rough empirical indicators of the growth of monopoly capitalism in Canada since the Second World War.

An indication of the growth of monopoly capitalism in Canada in the postwar era is provided by increases in the proportion of total assets, revenue, and profits in the entire economy controlled by a small number of corporations.

A year-by-year analysis of corporation taxation data from 1944 to 1964 reveals that during this period profitable corporations of $5 million net profit or more increased their hold over the Canadian economy while remaining a constant proportion of all corporations. During this period these few monopolistic corporations, representing 0.1%-0.2% of all profitable corporations, increased their share of total corporate assets from 26% to 33%, their share of fixed assets from 33% to 42%, and their share of all corporate investment in affiliates from 31% to 44%. Over the same period their share of total corporate revenue increased from 20% to 24%, and their share of all corporate profits from 25% to 38%. Although the proportion of all profitable corporations that these corporations represent never exceeds 0.2%,

their absolute numbers increased from 26 in 1944 to 111 in 1964 (calculated from Dept. of National Revenue, 1946-66).

Using assets rather than net profits to define monopoly corporations does not change the pattern of increasing monopolization. Between 1951-53 and 1963-64, corporations with assets of $100 million or more increased their share of all corporate assets from 25% to 40%, their share of all fixed corporate assets from 32% to 43%, and their share of all corporate investments in affiliates from 30% to 56% (see Table I). The latter increase, being the largest, at the same time gives one of the best indications of the control exercised by these corporations over the rest of the economy. During this same period, these top corporations also increased their share of all corporate revenues from 14% to 23% and their share of all corporate profits from 23% to 37%. During this entire period, the proportion that these monopoly corporations represented of all corporations did not change at all. This proportion remained constant at 0.1%.

Because of administrative and procedural changes in the sources of the data, corporation taxation statistics could not be profitably analysed beyond 1964. However, corporations reporting under the Corporations and Labour Unions Returns Act could be analysed from 1963 to 1972. Using a more liberal and less satisfactory definition of

Table I
Share of Corporate Economy Controlled by Top
Corporations,* 1951-64

	1951-53	1954-56	1957-59	1960-62	1963-64
Average number of top corporations	35	57	86	113	156
Top corporations as percentage of all corporations	0.1	0.1	0.1	0.1	0.1
Assets of top corporations as percentage of all corporate assets	25.4	29.3	32.9	34.9	39.7
Fixed assets of top corporations as percentage of all fixed corporate assets	32.4	35.3	39.2	41.0	43.1
Investments in affiliates by top corporations as percentage of all corporate investments in affiliates	30.0	44.7	47.4	49.0	55.6
Revenue of top corporations as percentage of all corporate revenue	13.7	16.6	17.4	19.1	22.6
Profits of top corporations as percentage of all corporate profits	22.9	27.0	26.4	34.7	37.4

*With assets of $100 million or more; figures are averages for several years.

85

Table II
Top Corporations (by sales), 1966-74*

	1966-68	1969-71	1972-74
Sales of top 100 corporations as percentage of all corporate sales†	42‡	46	54
Assets of top 5 banks as percentage of assets of top 25 financial institutions	60	63	66
Sales of top 10 merchandisers as percentage of sales of all merchandisers	—	21	21
Net income of top 10 merchandisers as percentage of net income of all merchandisers	—	16§	14

*According to *Financial Post* (see footnote 3).
†Includes manufacturing, resources, and utilities; excludes merchandising and finance.
‡Percentages are the average over a three-year period.
§Excludes 1970.

monopoly corporations, during this latest period, corporations with assets of $25 million or more increased their share of all corporate assets from 53% to 66%, their share of all corporate revenue from 37% to 44%, and their share of all corporate profits from 57% to 59%. During this period the proportion that these top corporations represented of all reporting corporations remained steady at 1.5%. Their absolute numbers increased from 414 in 1963 to 669 in 1972 (calculated from Dominion Bureau of Statistics, 1963-69; Statistics Canada, 1970-72; 1973; 1975a).

In all of the preceding data, the absolute number of top corporations increases with time, although not their proportion of all corporations. It is useful to show data extended over time where the absolute number of top corporations is held constant. In this case, their proportion of all corporations would decline, and any increase in their share of total assets, revenue, and net income would attain even greater significance. Such a trend can be constructed from the *Financial Post* which publishes annually a list of the top 100 corporations in manufacturing, resources, and utilities (ranked by sales between 1966 and 1974), the top twenty-five financial corporations, and the top ten merchandisers (see Table II). Between 1966-68 and 1972-74, the top 100 corporations increased their share of total sales from 42% to 54%. The top five chartered banks increased their share of the assets of the top twenty-five financial institutions from 60% to 66%. However, there does not appear to have been any increase in monopolization in merchandising during the

years for which data are available.[3]

The international dimension of monopoly capitalism can be indicated by the nationality of the ownership and control of the largest corporations operating in Canada. In 1975-76, seven of the top ten corporations in the *Financial Post* list of the top 200 industrials were foreign controlled (*Financial Post 300*, 1976: 15-19). These were Ford, General Motors, Imperial Oil, Chrysler, Alcan Aluminum, Shell and Gulf Oil. All except Shell (Royal Dutch) and Alcan were US controlled. Alcan is a special case because it appears to be controlled from several countries and so is a "true" multinational (Clement, 1977: 160-62). Only three of the top ten (Canadian Pacific, Bell Canada, and Massey-Ferguson) were Canadian controlled. Between 56% and 65% of the 200 top industrials were foreign controlled, mostly in the US. These 200 corporations accounted for 63% of all industrial sales in Canada in 1975-76 (*Financial Post 300*, 1976: 15-19). In contrast, banking is much more in Canadian hands. The top five banks (all Canadian) have consistently been the Royal Bank, Canadian Imperial Bank of Commerce, Bank of Montreal, Bank of Nova Scotia, and Toronto Dominion Bank in that order. In 1975-76, "the five biggest banks account for 90% of the assets of the 10 operating chartered banks and a remarkable 64% of the assets of the largest 35 financial organizations for which such data are available" (*Financial Post 300*, 1976: 29). Merchandising also tends to be in Canadian hands. Six of the top ten merchandising corporations in 1975-76 were Canadian controlled. These were George Weston, Dominion Stores, Steinberg's, Loeb, Oshawa Group, and Woodward Stores. In addition, Eaton's would be included in this group were it to reveal its financial figures. Two companies (Canada Safeway and Woolworth's) are completely controlled in the US, Simpsons-Sears is split between US and Canadian control, and Hudson's Bay is controlled in Britain. The top ten corporations accounted for 77% of the sales of the top twenty-five merchandising companies in 1975-76 (*Financial Post 300*, 1976: 40). Thus, while industrial corporations are heavily foreign controlled, financial and mercantile companies are much more in the hands of Canadian capitalists.

Behind these data lie national and international divisions in monopoly capitalism which are important in laying the groundwork for discussing types of class contradiction. The following patterns are the most important to emphasize. First, foreign (especially US) investment in Canada tends to be in the productive industrial sphere. This is centred in resources and manufacturing. In this regard, Clement (1977: 80) states:

in 1946, 35 per cent of Canada's manufacturing was foreign controlled; by 1953, foreign control had risen to 50 per cent, and by 1957 to 56 per cent; in mining and smelting the corresponding increases were from 38 per cent to 57 per cent to 70 per cent. In the course of a decade after the Second World War, both the manufacturing the the mining and smelting sectors of the Canadian economy, the productive cornerstones, ceased to be predominantly Canadian owned and became predominantly foreign owned.

Most of this foreign control tends to be centred in the United States. In 1970, the United States controlled 47% of Canada's manufacturing, 61% of its petroleum and gas, and 59% of its mining and smelting (Clement, 1977: 92). Secondly, large Canadian-controlled corporations have dominated the sphere of circulation of money and commodities. This is true of finance, wholesale trade, and retail trade. With the exception of the Mercantile Bank (which is controlled by Citicorp in the US), all federally chartered banks in Canada are indigenously controlled. Eighty-two per cent of the assets of all life in-

surance companies in Canada are also indigenously controlled (Clement, 1975: 400-1). In 1972, 58% of wholesale trade was indigenously controlled while 17% was controlled from the United States. Sixty-four per cent of retail trade was controlled from Canada and 14% from the United States (Clement, 1977: 306-7). Transportation and utilities are the two major exceptions to this split between the spheres of production and circulation by nationality of control. In 1970, 98% of railways and 93% of "other utilities" were Canadian controlled (Clement, 1977: 92). Transportation and utilities combine production and circulation in ways that manufacturing, resources, finance, and wholesale and retail trade do not. In the case of transportation, Marx (1967: II, 152) argued that ". . . its distinguishing feature is that it appears as a continuation of a process of production *within* the process of circulation and *for* the process of circulation." Transportation is in the sphere of production because value is *added* to commodities by their physical movement from one location to another and is in the sphere of circulation because value is *realized* through the buying and selling of goods permitted by transportation systems. Thirdly, the division between the spheres of production and circulation by nationality in Canada influences the origins of foreign investment in other countries by companies based in Canada. Clement (1977: 115) argues for a recognition of two types of foreign investment by Canadian corporations; a go-between investment in which Canadian companies that are subsidiaries or affiliates of foreign companies mediate the investment of parent companies in other countries, and indigenous-based investment in which Canadian-controlled corporations independently invest in other countries. Go-between investment tends to emerge from the sphere of production while indigenous-based foreign investment tends to originate from the sphere of circulation or combined production-circulation. The implications of this difference for types of class contradiction will be pointed out shortly. Finally, the average size of foreign corporations in Canada is larger than that of Canadian-controlled corporations. One measure of size is profits per corporation. The ratio of profits per Canadian-controlled corporations to profits per foreign-controlled corporations were calculated (Statistics Canada, 1970-72).

If these ratios exceed 1.00, Canadian-controlled corporations are larger than foreign-controlled corporations; if these ratios are less than 1.00, foreign-controlled corporations exceed the size of Canadian-controlled corporations. For the five years from 1968 through 1972, these ratios are respectively: 0.905, 0.845, 0.863, 0.891 and 0.927. This means that foreign-controlled corporations in Canada are, on the average, larger than Canadian-controlled corporations. The leading edge of monopoly capitalism in Canada tends to be foreign corporations rather than indigenously based corporations, although there are many exceptions to this pattern. It is within the context of these four points that the national and international dimensions of class contradictions in Canada will now be set out.

Types of Class Contradiction

There are two fundamental ideas expressed by the term "social class" in the capitalist mode of production. The one is the ownership and control of property and the other is the extraction of surplus. In the capitalist mode of production, the dominant capitalist class consists of those persons who own and control the *major* means of production and circulation and who thereby appropriate surplus primarily but not exclusively from the working class. The working class consists of all those persons who neither own nor control such means of production and circulation, are forced to sell their labour power to earn their means of subsistence, and produce the surplus which the capitalist class appropriates. Four different types of surplus may be distinguished: industrial surplus, circulation surplus, consumer surplus, and financial surplus. Their mode of extraction in class relations gives rise to four different types of contradiction: industrial class exploitation, circulation class oppression, consumer class oppression, and financial class oppression. The fundamental type of class contradiction is industrial class exploitation. Circulation, consumer, and financial class oppression directly or indirectly depend on it. The remaining parts of this paper will be devoted to an outline of the central characteristics of these four types of class contradiction and their relation to the question of nationality in Canada set within an international context.

Industrial class exploitation

Karl Marx attempted to answer the question of why the value of commodities at the end of production was greater than value at the beginning of production. He divided the value of commodities into three portions: constant capital (or the cost of the means of production, instruments of labour, and raw or semi-processed materials); variable capital (or the wages paid by capitalists to workers); and surplus value. Marx argued that the value of depreciated constant capital is simply transferred to the final commodities. It does not increase the value of the final commodities. The increase in the value of the final commodities must therefore be based on variable capital and surplus value, both of which arise from labour. Labour is thus the secret of the increase in the value of commodities in production. Marx divided the labourer's working day into necessary labour time and surplus labour time. Necessary labour time is that part of the working day for which the capitalist pays wages or variable capital to the workers. These are sufficient to pay for the cost of the workers' means of subsistence as determined by historical and cultural standards of the particular society. But since this covers only part of the working day, the labourers work the other part of the working day *gratis* for the capitalist. This is the origin of surplus value which is the amount by which the final value of commodities exceeds depreciated constant capital and variable capital. Surplus value itself is the origin of the profits and capital accumulation of the capitalist class.[4] *Industrial class exploitation* is the extraction of surplus value by the industrial fraction of the capitalist class from productive labourers in the working class primarily in manufacturing, resources, services, and transportation.[5] Its distinguishing characteristic is the *generation* of surplus value through the consumption of labour in the production and transformation of goods and services. It is important to note that only a part or fraction of both the capitalist and working classes is involved in this type of class contradiction.

Marx measured industrial class exploitation by what he called the "rate of surplus value" or the ratio of surplus value to the wages of productive workers (I, 216). An increase in the rate of surplus value suggests a corresponding increase in the extraction of surplus value by industrial captalists from industrial productive workers, and hence a more intense industrial class exploitation.

The rate of surplus value in the manufacturing industries of Canada has been calculated for the years between 1917 and 1971 (Cuneo, 1978a). Although the theoretical disputes and technical difficulties surrounding the calculations suggest that not much reliance can be placed on the absolute size of each annual rate of surplus value, more confidence can be placed on their broad trends over time.[6] Three distinctive patterns emerge. First, there was a great increase in the rate of surplus value from 1917 to 1971. For the most valid rates of surplus value, the increase was from 33% in 1917 to 262% in 1971. Second, the period of sharpest increase was in the postwar era (1948-69) when both American capitalism and monopoly capitalism witnessed their greatest growth in Canada. Third, a minor decrease in the rate of surplus value occurred between 1929 and 1935, the period of the Great Depression. Smaller decreases occurred immediately after the First and Second World Wars, both periods of considerable labour strife during which the working class asserted its rights against capitalism.

Three types of industrial class exploitation are set out in Figure 1. The first–(A) to (C)–is between Canadian comprador industrial capitalists (under the control of foreign industrial capitalists) and Canadian productive workers. For example, General Motors of Canada Ltd. is controlled from the United States and has five production plants in Ontario and one in Quebec. The second type (D) is between indigenous Canadian industrial capitalists and Canadian productive workers. One of the most prominent examples is the Steel Company of Canada which in Canada has plants in Hamilton, Saskatchewan, and Montreal. Thirdly, there are two subtypes of industrial class exploitation involving the thrust of corporations from Canada into third countries (which can include the United States). The one involves a route from (A) to (C) to (H) to (L) and is between comprador industrial capitalists in third countries (under the control of Canadian comprador and US indigenous industrial capitalists) and productive industrial workers in third countries. One example is the Ford Motor Company of Canada which is controlled from the United States but which, in turn, controls plants in Australia, South

Africa, New Zealand, and Malaysia. The other route runs from (D) to (I) to (L). This class contradiction is between comprador industrial capitalists in third countries (under the direction of indigenous Canadian industrial capitalists) and productive workers in these countries. As an illustration, Massey-Ferguson, a Toronto-based multinational, has plants in Brazil, Argentina, Australia, South Africa, Rhodesia, Malawi, United States, France, Italy, the Netherlands, and Germany.

The primary class contradiction in a Marxist theory of the generation of wealth is industrial class exploitation. In the case of Canada, this involves both national and international dimensions. Within the borders of Canada, industrial class exploitation takes place between productive workers in the Canadian working class and an alliance among foreign comprador and indigenous industrial capitalists (see arrows [B₁], [B₂], [A], [C], and [D] in Figure 1). However, since foreign multinationals operating in Canada are larger than indigenous corporations, and given that industrial class exploitation is more intense in more advanced forms of monopoly capitalism, the primary class contradiction in Canada is between comprador industrial capitalists and productive workers in the Canadian working class (C). The surplus value generated in this class exploitation serves as a basis for the expansion of US multinationals operating through Canada into other countries. In this way, the industrial class exploitation in other countries (L) is linked to the conditions of industrial class exploitation in Canada. Because indigenous Canadian corporations (with less developed technologies) have smaller scales of operation, a less intense form of industrial class exploitation occurs between indigenous Canadian industrial capitalists and productive workers in the Canadian working class. This is associated with an overall less intense form of industrial class exploitation by indigenous Canadian multinationals in other countries (route from [D] to [I] to [L]). All forms of industrial class exploitation are more fundamental than circulation, consumer, and financial class oppression (to be outlined shortly) because they generate the surplus value for the capitalists operating in the sphere of circulation. The national dependence of certain third world countries on

Figure 1 National and international dimensions of four class contradictions in the Canadian context

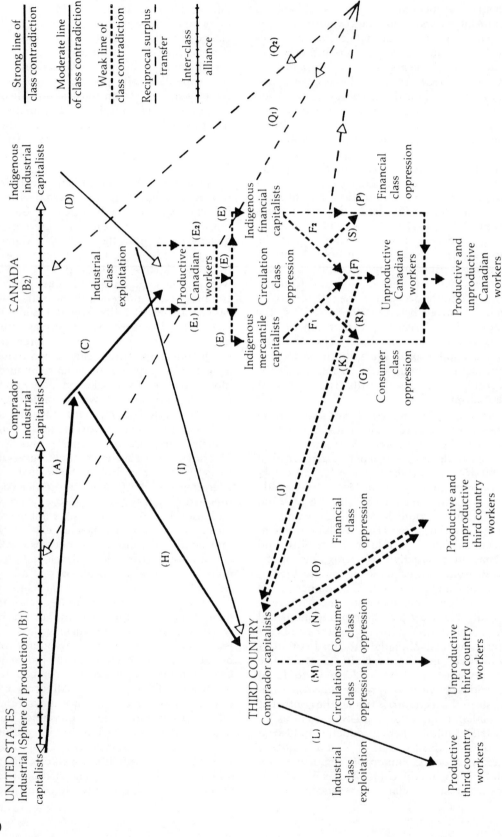

Canada, and of Canada on the United States, is therefore based primarily on the class dependencies in the international structure of industrial class exploitation. A class theory of structural transformations in Canada cannot be developed by ignoring the class linkages first of all with the United States, and secondly with other countries to which Canada directs industrial investments. A Marxist theory of social change would thus locate the objective base of class revolution among productive workers in Canada and other countries (experiencing industrial investment through Canada) ranged against an alliance among US indigenous industrial capitalists (with Canadian and multinational operations), comprador industrial capitalists in Canada, and indigenous Canadian industrial capitalists.

Three sets of related observations have often been made about the Canadian working class. First, radical working-class consciousness has been relatively weak. Secondly, a nationally organized working class based on an integrated trade union movement has failed to emerge. Thirdly, the working class in western Canada has traditionally been much more radical than its counterpart in central and eastern Canada (e.g., Porter, 1965: 36-37, 309-36). The uneven regional development of Canada in industrial class exploitation and Canada's distinctiveness in this regard in comparison with other western capitalist countries may lurk behind these observations. The interaction between social class and monopoly capitalism have produced unbalanced regional structures in Canada (Cuneo, 1978b). This is evident in the regional splits among productive workers in urban manufacturing and hinterland resources. The most intense form of foreign investment in Canada's productive sphere has occurred in the resource industries of its hinterland regions, especially in northern and western Canada, and the northern parts of Ontario and Quebec. This has produced intense industrial class exploitation in the country's hinterland. The result has been a more marked drain of surplus from Canada's hinterland regions than is true of other developed western capitalist societies. The combination of this intensity of exploitation and isolated conditions of work and existence have created some of the most radical working-class elements in hinterland areas. In other western capitalist countries, indigenous secondary manufacturing has developed more within their urban cores than is true in Canada where foreign investment in assembly-type production has stunted Canadian manufacturing in the central urban core. The different conditions of existence and work of productive workers in central urban Canada (Ontario and Quebec) have made it difficult for this part of the working class to identify with productive resource workers in the hinterland. As a result, the uneven regional development of industrial class exploitation in Canada has weakened the organization and consolidation of the working class at a national level. This is one of the limiting structural conditions that mitigates the kind of class revolution expected from Marxian theory discussed earlier.

Circulation class oppression

A second type of class contradiction given less prominence by Marx than industrial class exploitation is circulation class oppression. Marx argued that surplus value is not generated in the circulation of commodities and money (i.e., in mercantile and financial activities) but only distributed to these sectors from the industrial sector (III, chap XVII, 290-301). The wages of workers and profits of capitalists in trading and finance as well as such "circulation costs" as advertising and bookkeeping are all part of distributed industrial surplus. The working day of unproductive workers is divided into necessary and surplus labour time as is the day of the industrial productive worker. Necessary labour time, while expressed as wages or the cost of the workers' means of subsistence, now is part of distributed industrial surplus. Surplus labour time in these sectors does not generate surplus value but allows mercantile and financial capitalists to appropriate part of the industrial surplus without having to organize activities to generate surplus independently of industrial capitalists. *Circulation class oppression* for our purposes means the extraction of surplus labour time by mercantile and financial fractions of the capitalist class from unproductive workers in these sectors allowing such capitalists a share of industrial surplus value. This type of class contradiction does not directly involve the entire capitalist class but only its mercantile and financial fractions. Similarly, it does not involve the entire working class but only unproductive workers (see footnote 5).

Under entrepreneurial capitalism in the nineteenth century, the industrial, mercantile, and financial fractions of the capitalist class were relatively distinct. Similarly, productive and unproductive workers were relatively distinct. With the rise of monopoly capitalism, these fractions in each of the two main classes begin to merge somewhat, although this process is much further advanced in the capitalist class than in the working class. Thus, "finance capital" in Lenin's definition of imperialism introduced earlier represents a merger of industrial and financial capitalist class fractions although the working class employed by the corporations controlled by this alliance may still remain somewhat more separated into divisions specializing in productive labour and divisions specializing in unproductive labour.

As noted previously, indigenous Canadian capitalists exercise less control over the sphere of production than the sphere of circulation (cf. Naylor, 1975; Clement, 1977). Canada is distinctive in this regard in comparison with other developed western capitalist societies, but not necessarily in comparison with underdeveloped third world countries. In developed western capitalist countries, there is greater indigenous control over the sphere of production, but this is much less the case in underdeveloped third world countries. There are of course some exceptions to this pattern, e.g., India. The implications for Canada are that circulation class oppression relative to industrial class exploitation is more pervasive in comparison with other developed western capitalist societies. In a sense, circulation class oppression is overdeveloped and industrial class exploitation is underdeveloped or unevenly developed. However, the peculiar twist in this is that the surplus distributed as profits and wages in circulation class oppression comes from industrial class exploitation whose most intense forms are externally induced. This reduces the apparent national autonomy of circulation class oppression and of indigenous Canadian capitalists operating in the sphere of circulation. This is a class explanation of the dependence of even comparatively autonomous sections of Canadian society on the class links in the sphere of production between Canada and the United States. In terms of Figure 1, circulation class

oppression (F) occurs between unproductive Canadian workers and indigenous Canadian capitalists specializing in financial (F_2) and trading (F_1) activities. Tellers working for the Canadian Imperial Bank of Commerce and check-out clerks working for Dominion Stores (which is controlled by Argus Corporation) are examples of unproductive workers experiencing circulation class oppression; the former labour in the trading of money while the latter labour in the trading of physical commodities. However, the surplus distributed in the form of wages and profits in the sphere of circulation derives from industrial class exploitation. This comes *primarily* from comprador sources (route from [A] to [C] to [E_1] to [F]) and *secondarily* from indigenous sources (route from [D] to [E_2] to [F]).

It is difficult to estimate empirically circulation class oppression in Canada because so much of the surplus going to the mercantile-financial sector is hidden as circulation costs and is not expressed as profits or investment income. Thus, most estimates of this type of class contradiction will likely be understated. With this proviso, we can compare over time the proportion of investment income (part of the capitalist's surplus) and wages (the "workers' surplus") going to the mercantile and financial sectors in Canada. Between 1926 and 1972 the proportion of total investment income in the economy going to the wholesale sector almost doubled from 3.8% to 7.0% while the proportion of labour income going to this sector increased only slightly from 4.8% to 5.6%. In the retail sector, investment income decreased from 6.5% to 4.8% while labour income rose slightly from 7.6% to 7.7%. In the financial sector, investment income almost doubled from 13.4% to 22.6% while labour income increased only slightly from 4.3% to 5.4% (calculated from Dominion Bureau of Statistics, n.d.: Tables 29, 30). While these figures are only crude estimates, they suggest that in Canada circulation class oppression has increased the most in the financial sector and next in the wholesale sector, while a decrease in this type of class contradiction occurred in the retail sector. This is not unexpected since monopolisation has increased to a much greater extent in the financial and wholesale sectors than in the retail sector. This places the capitalist class in finance and wholesale in a much stronger position relative to the working class than in retail.

Previously it was noted that much of the indigenously-based foreign investment flowing from Canada to other countries tends to be in the sphere of circulation, such as banks and life insurance companies, or in spheres that combine production and circulation, such as railways and utility companies (cf. Naylor, 1975: I, 218-73; Clement, 1977: 115, 120). Although the origin of the surplus for expansion abroad often is circulation class oppression in Canada ([J] in Figure 1), the destination of the surplus in other countries may be industrial class exploitation (L), circulation class oppression (M), consumer class oppression (N), or financial class oppression (O). In the first case ([J] to [L]), Canadian banks are involved in financing industrial operations in other countries. Twenty per cent of the voting stock of the International Nickel Company of Canada is controlled by Canadian financial institutions (Clement, 1977: 155). This helps finance Inco's operations in such countries as Indonesia and Guatemala (*Toronto Star*, 29 October 1977: A 3). In the second case of arrows ([J] to [M]), Canadian banks and life insurance companies operate directly in many other countries, especially in the Caribbean (Chodos, 1977: 109-29). Employees in these countries working for such financial institutions experience circulation class oppression. In response, at least in Trinidad, attempts have been made to form bank unions to fight the Canadian banks (Chodos, 1977: 122-23). Circulation class oppression in other countries also emerges directly from industrial class exploitation in Canada (routes [H] to [M] and [I] to [M]). However, this form of international class linkage through Canada is not as pervasive as the ones just outlined. The conclusion to be drawn from this theoretical analysis is that circulation surplus and circulation class oppression in many countries arise out of class contradictions occurring outside of their borders. The class and international links in the chain are complicated, but essentially circulation class oppression in several third countries arises out of circulation class oppression in Canada which, in turn, emerges out of the surplus generated in industrial class exploitation also in Canada. The latter, in turn, is partly dependent on the class alliance between comprador industrial capitalists in Canada and their head office capitalists in the United States or in other foreign countries (B1). In this way, the conditions of class contradictions in many third countries in which Canadian indigenous capitalists have investments are tied into the nature of Canada's class dependence on the United States. Therefore, according to a Marxist class theory, a successful class revolution in several third world countries must objectively be based on the subtle class linkages at the international level, such as those just outlined.

Consumer class oppression

Consumer class oppression, the third class contradiction, goes a long way towards providing a class explanation of inflation. The growth of large wholesale and retail monopolies gives mercantile capitalists considerable leeway in raising the prices of consumer commodities over and above competitive levels. One might argue that the portion of wages extracted because of mercantile monopoly control in setting the cost of consumer commodities is part of necessary labour time. However, since this portion does not support the *real* cost of the means of subsistence of the working class, it clearly no longer represents necessary labour time but surplus labour time. *Consumer class oppression* is thus the extraction of part of the wages of the working class, now representing surplus labour, on the part of mercantile capitalists by the extent to which their exercise of monopoly raises the cost of consumer commodities over and above what is necessary to reproduce the labour power of the working class. Although the working class may be partly organized through trade and industrial unions which afford some protection against industrial class exploitation and circulation class oppression, this is not the case in consumer class oppression. Consumer pressure groups are largely ineffective.

Consumer class oppression appears similar to circulation class oppression because both occur in the sphere of circulation. However, there are two essential differences between these types of class contradiction. First, consumer class oppression occurs between the capitalist class as seller and working class as buyer while circulation class oppression takes place between the capitalist class as employer and working class as employee. Second,

Table III
Consumer Class Oppression in Postwar Canada*

Year	Gross weekly wages and salaries (1)	Real weekly wages and salaries (1949 = 100) (2)	Consumer class oppression	
			Absolute loss in weekly income (3) = (2)−(1)	% loss in weekly income (4) = (3)/(1)
1949	$ 42.96	$ 42.96	$− 0.00	0 %
1950-54	53.22	47.23	− 5.99	11 %
1955-59	67.46	55.52	−11.94	18 %
1960-64	80.88	61.65	−19.23	24 %
1965-69	103.52	69.69	−33.83	33 %
1970-74	152.25	86.20	−66.05	43 %

*Calculated from Urquhart and Buckley (1965: 103, 293, 304) and *Canada Year Book* (various years)

while both types of class contradiction involve the mercantile fraction of the capitalist class, consumer class oppression covers the entire working class while circulation class oppression includes only unproductive workers.

In contrast to industrial class exploitation, consumer class oppression within the borders of Canada occurs largely between indigenous mercantile *Canadian* capitalists and the *entire* Canadian working class (arrow [G] in Figure 1). Although consumer surplus can also be extracted from the new middle class, by and large its main source is the Canadian working class. Since this type of class contradiction has not been widely discussed in the Canadian or international class literature, we now turn to a detailed examination of empirical illustrations drawn from Canadian sources.

The wages and salaries that the working class has lost through inflation is one crude measure of consumer class oppression. The data which show this from 1949 to 1974 in Canada are displayed in Table III. Gross weekly wages and salaries are shown in column (1). This is the approximate real purchasing power the working class would have if consumer class oppression has *not* occurred. The degree to which the real income in column (2)–gross income controlled by the 1949 Consumer's Price Index–falls below the level of gross income in column (1) gives us a rough idea of the extent of consumer class oppression. This is shown in column (3) as the absolute average income per week lost by the working class through inflation. Column (4) shows the percentage of weekly income lost.

Both the absolute income loss in column (3) and the percentage loss in column (4) increased consistently from 1950 to 1974. Between 1950 and 1954 the working class lost an average of $5.99 or 11 % of its weekly income through inflation. By the 1970-74 period, this loss had increased dramatically to $66.05 or 43 % of weekly gross income. This suggests not only that consumer class oppression exists but also that it has increased in intensity throughout the entire period from 1950 to 1974. Defenders of capitalism often argue that both gross and real income have risen in the prosperity following the Second World War. They are essentially correct in a general sense, but they fail to grasp the significant import of these data which lies in the widening gap between gross and real income. Between the 1950-54 and 1970-74 periods, gross income rose by 186%, real income by only 82%, and income loss through inflation by a dramatic 1,003%. The use of the perspective of consumer class oppression allows us to explain this phenomenon in terms of social class and monopoly capitalism and so gives some pause to the statements of the optimists among us.

It would be wrong to assume that consumer class oppression has the same effects on the more well-to-do and less well-to-do within the working class. The more impoverished sections of the working class spend a greater proportion of their family budget on survival (essentially meaning food and, to a lesser extent, shelter and clothing). The more well-to-do sections of the working class as well as the capitalist class spend a far smaller proportion of their budget on survival items and a far greater proportion on self-indulgence (essentially meaning personal care, medical and health care, smoking and alcoholic beverages, travel, recreation, reading, and education). In 1972, families and unattached individuals earning a gross income under $4,000 spent 78% of their budget on survival items and 22% on self-indulgence; in contrast, families and unattached individuals earning $25,000 and over spent only 35% of their budget on survival but a full 64% on self-indulgence (see Table IV). It is therefore important to analyse separately price increases in different commodities to understand more fully the effects of consumer class oppression on different income levels of the working class. Since monopoly capitalism among mercantile corporations developed to its fullest extent in the 1960s and 1970s, our discussion will now be focused on this period.

Between 1961 and January 1975, the Consumer Price Index as a whole rose by 77%. However, during this time the cost of food increased by 102%. No other general category of commodities increased by so much. The smallest increase (55%) was for tobacco and alcohol (calculated from Statistics Canada, 1975d: 50). The effect of these differential price increases weighs particularly heavily on the lower sections of the working class which spends between one-quarter and one-third of its budget on food (Statistics Canada, 1975c: 10).

A detailed analysis of price increases in different types of food suggests that the eating habits of the poor may be deteriorating relative to the rich. Between 1961 and January 1975, the cost of fresh milk increased by 121% in contrast to a 96% increase in the cost of powdered skim milk. This gap seemed to increase in the latter part of that period. Between 1972 and January 1975, the cost of fresh milk increased by 46% compared to only 24% for powdered skim milk. These differential increases by quality of product are also true for other commodities. For instance, between 1961 and January 1975, the following increases were recorded: sirloin steak (115%); round steak (117%); prime rib roast (117%); veal (140%); fish (178%). In contrast, hamburger increased by only 81% and wieners by only 65% (calculated from Statistics Canada, 1975d: 51). The effect of these differential increases seems to be one of forc-

Table IV
Percentage of Annual Income (after taxes)
Spent on Survival and Self-indulgence by
Income Category, Canada, 1972*

Income category	Spent on survival (%)	Spent on self-indulgence (%)
$ 4,000-	78.1	21.9
4,000-4,999	63.3	36.7
5,000-5,999	6.14	38.6
6,000-6,999	57.8	42.2
7,000-7,999	53.1	46.9
8,000-8,999	53.2	46.8
9,000-9,999	52.1	47.9
10,000-11,999	48.4	51.6
12,000-14,999	45.8	54.2
15,000-19,999	42.3	57.7
20,000-24,999	40.2	59.8
25,000—	34.6	64.4

*Calculated from Statistics Canada, 1975c: 10-11

ing the poorer sections of the working class onto less nutritious diets.

Price increases by the capitalist class in other areas of consumer commodities also have had the effect of widening the gap in the living styles between the rich and the poor. In the area of housing, rent increased by 31% between 1961 and January 1975. In contrast, the cost of home ownership increased by 138%. In the latter category, the largest increases were mortgage interest (195%) and dwelling insurance (263%), both part of financial class oppression to be discussed shortly (calculated from Statistics Canada 1975d: 76-77). The apparent effect of these differential increases is to force the poorer sections of the working class into tenancy while allowing the more well-to-do to own their private homes. In view of the fact that finance is one of the most monopolized sectors in the economy while granting the lowest wage increases to its workers, it is significant that interest and insurance payments to the financial sector have contributed more than any other single item to the increase in the cost of home ownership. In lending out mortgages, the private financial institutions clearly favour the rich over the poor. For instance, in 1971, 53% of the mortgages held by household heads earning less than $1,000 were from banks, insurance companies, and trust and mortgage companies in contrast to 80% for household heads earning $25,000 and over (calculated from Statistics Canada, n.d.: Table 79). The state has had to subsidize the poor where private financial monopolies refuse to take "unwarranted risks."

What is the link between consumer class oppression and other types of class contradiction in Canada and other countries? The origin of consumer surplus lies in the circulation class oppression of unproductive Canadian workers by mercantile capitalists (route [R] from [F₁] to [G] in Figure 1). The large mercantile monopolies were built up on the basis of the unproductive workers employed by them. The extraction of consumer surplus in the market place is directly dependent on the unproductive labour of the employees of large wholesale and retail chains. Visible examples in Canada are Eaton's and Dominion Stores. Since circulation class oppression is ultimately based on industrial class exploitation, consumer class oppression is indirectly dependent on the industrial class exploitation exercised by the alliance of comprador and indigenous industrial capitalists in Canada (route from [E]a to [F₁] to [R] to [G]). The other part of the question has to do with the destination of consumer surplus. This has a potential thrust into other countries and can become active in any of the four types of class contradictions (routes from [K] to any of [L], [M], [N], and [O]). However, these destinations are not pervasive since most of the larger indigenous wholesale and retail trading corporations in

Canada do not extend very much into other countries.

Financial class oppression

The fourth type of class contradiction to be considered is financial class oppression. There are two aspects of this class oppression. The one is the ability of financial institutions to charge the working class high interest rates on consumer loans, whether these are in small amounts to cover the buying of household effects or in large amounts to cover the cost of buying automobiles and homes. Since these interest rates are not necessary to reproduce the labour power of the working class, the costs they represent are not part of necessary labour but become part of surplus labour. The second aspect of financial class oppression is the ability of financial institutions (banks and insurance companies) to gather up a significant proportion of the wages of the working class in various types of accounts and plans before they are spent on the means of subsistence of this class. Over the short term, such monies do not reproduce the working class's labour power. In bank accounts and insurance plans they become part of the surplus of financial capitalists. The portion of wages that these monies represent is therefore not necessary labour but also becomes part of surplus labour. *Financial class oppression* is the extraction of that part of the wages of the working class which is not immediately expended in the reproduction of labour power but is set aside in funds controlled by capitalists. Because Canada's financial institutions are mostly indigenously controlled, this type of class contradiction occurs mainly between indigenous financial capitalists and the entire Canadian working class (arrow [P] in Figure 1). Once again, because this type of class oppression is not commonly discussed in the class literature, considerable reference will be made to empirical materials to illustrate it. For this purpose, we shall focus on the banks.

During the first three-quarters of the twentieth century, the number of Canadian chartered banks declined through consolidation from thirty-four to eight banks, a 76% decrease (see colum [1], Table V). In the same period there was a vast expansion in the number of branches controlled by each bank. Between 1901 and 1910 there was an average

Table V
Growth of the Canadian Chartered Bank Monopoly, 1901-74%

Year	Average no. of banks (1)	Average no. of bank branches (2)	Average no. of branches per bank (3)= (2)/(1)	Average Canadian population (4)	Average no. of persons per bank (5)= (4)/(1)	Average personal savings in the banks (6)	Average personal savings per bank (7)= (6)/(1)	Average personal savings per person (8)= (6)/(4)
				'000	'000	$'000000	$'000000	$
1901-10	34	1,539	45	6,127	180	‡	‡	‡
1911-20	22	3,349	152	7,916	360	‡	‡	‡
1921-30	13	4,098	315	9,431	726	1,336	103	141.66
1931-40	10	3,503	350	10,890	1,089	1,460	146	134.07
1941-50	10	3,290	329	12,380	1,238	2,850	280	226.58
1951-60	10	4,344	434	15,942	1,594	5,758	576	361.18
1961-74	8	5,837†	730	20,432	2,554	14,432	1,804	706.34
% change (1901-10)-(1961-74)	−76.5%	279.3%	1,522.2%	233.5%	1,318.9%	‡	‡	‡
% change (1921-30)-(1961-74)	−38.5%	42.4%	131.8%	116.6%	251.8%	980.2%	1,651.5%	398.6%

*Calculated from Urquhart and Buckley (1965: 14,230, 246) and *Canadian Statistical Review* (1961-75)
†1961-72
‡Not available

of forty-five branches per chartered bank; by the 1961-74 period this figure had risen to 730, a 1,522.2% increase (column [3]). Because the Canadian population increased only by 233.5% during this three-quarters of a century, this meant that increasingly more people were being forced to deposit their money into fewer banks. In the 1901-10 period, there was an average of 180,000 persons per bank, but by the 1961-74 period this had risen to 2,554,000 persons per bank (column [5]). The fewer and larger banks were also becoming more efficient in gathering up the personal savings of the population in financial class oppression. In the earliest period for which data are available, 1921-30, each bank collected an average of $103 million in personal savings; by 1961-74 this figure had reached $1.8 billion (column [7]). Translated into personal terms, between 1921 and 1930 each bank took an average of $141.66 from each person in the form of savings deposits; by 1961-74, this had climbed to $706.34, nearly a 400% increase (column [8]). This is about four times the rate of inflation.

A closer examination of the social and fi-nancial history of bank monopolization in the twentieth century reveals two distinct patterns: first, bank expansion has not been steady; second, the amount of personal savings deposits gathered up by the banks is directly related to the speed of centralization in their organizational structure. In the twentieth century so far, there have been three periods of organizational changes in the banking structures: first, centralization, then retrenchment, and then renewed centralization. The first period of centralization was from 1901 to 1924. In this period, the number of banks declined through consolidation (mergers and failures) from 35 to 13, a 62% drop in only twenty-four years. But the number of bank branches increased from 750 to 4,040, a 439% increase. Thus, the centralization of banks (branches per bank) increased by 1,350%. Personal savings deposits in chartered banks increased from $625 million in 1913 (the earliest date for which comparable data are available) to $1,238 million in 1924, a 98% increase. This rapid increase in centralization and deposits was then followed by a period of retrenchment from 1925 to 1944, roughly corresponding to the end of the boom of the early 1920s, the depression of the 1930s and the Second World War. During this time, the number of banks only dropped from eleven to ten; the number of branches dropped from 3,840 to 3,087, a 20% decrease; there was now a 12% *decrease* in centralization; and the amount in personal savings accounts increased from $1,319 million to $2,173 million, only a 64% increase. After 1944, there was again a sharp acceleration in bank centralization, but it was of a different nature from the expansion in the early part of the twentieth century. While in the earlier period there was a large drop in the number of banks operating, between 1945 and 1972 the number of chartered banks fluctuated between eight and eleven. Yet during this later period, the number of branches went up from 3,106 to 6,508, a 109% increase. Expressed in branches per bank, this indicates a 132% increase in centralization. Therefore, the first period of bank centralization came about through the contraction in the number of banks and the expansion in the number of branches per bank. The second period of centralization occurred primarily through branch expansion. This means that in the last period, monopolization and centralization were qualitatively very different and were much more intense in the sense that each bank increased by more the extensiveness of its corporate structure. And it is also in this second expansionary period that we witness the greatest increase in personal savings deposits: they increase in amount from $2,635 million in 1945 to $19,949 million in 1972, a 657% increase. It appears, then, that even though the speed in centralization varied through time, its general direction was definitely towards a greater monopolization. As the pace of organizational centralization picked up, so did the financial class oppression of mainly working-class people.

These personal savings form the largest single source of bank funds. Between 1913 and 1968, personal savings deposits constituted from 51% to 71% of the value of all deposits in the Canadian chartered banks.[7] The majority of savings deposits are quite small. Between 1955 and 1972, about 52% of the personal savings deposits in Canadian chartered banks were of less than $100. Slightly more than 80% of all savings deposits were less than $1,000. In contrast, deposits of $100,000 or more constituted only 0.1% of all savings deposits.[8] These latter deposits are certainly those of the capitalist class while the majority of the former are those of the working class. These data would seem to suggest that not only do the chartered banks rely for a considerable portion of their capital on the working class, but also that it is the poorer sections of the working class which provide a sizable amount of banking funds.

To understand the relation between financial class oppression and other types of class contradiction, it is important to trace the destination of such funds. While some of the loans made by the banks certainly do go back to the working class, these pale by comparison with those that go to business. Between 1955 and 1972, the chartered banks gave more than half of the value of all general loans to business but consistently less than a third to individuals; for example, in 1972, 57% of all loans from the chartered banks went to businesses while only 30% went to individuals. The rest went to public institutions and various other agencies.[9] It is especially the larger national and multinational businesses that receive the lion's share of the business and corporate loans. Between 1951 and 1964, corporations with assets of $5 million or more, consisting of 2% of all corporations, received from 44% to 49% of the total value of bank loans going to corporations. In the same period, corporations with assets of $100,000 or less, making up 50% of all corporations, received consistently only about 4% of the total value of all corporate bank loans (calculated from Dept. of National Revenue, 1953-66). There is some indication that the Canadian chartered banks are increasingly favouring the large borrower to the detriment of the smaller borrower. In 1962, 14% of all business loans made by chartered banks had been worth $5 million or more; since 1962 this percentage had gradually climbed, and by 1972 it had reached 35%. In contrast, small business loans and loans made under the Small Business Loans Act have steadily declined. In 1962, 33% of the value of all business loans made by the chartered banks was less than $100,000; by 1972 this figure had dropped to 18% (Bank of Canada Review, July 1973: 10). These differences are not completely accounted for by inflation. Thus it seems that there is a net transfer of funds from the depths of the working class to the heights of the capitalist class. In terms of Figure 1 (arrows [Q1] and [Q2], the surplus labour of the working class becomes the capital accumulation of indigenous Canadian financial capitalists which then becomes the constant and variable capital of the alliance among US, Canadian comprador, and Canadian indigenous industrial capitalists at the top of multinational corporations investing in third countries. In this way, financial surplus becomes part of the sources of the expanded reproduction of monopoly capitalism on a world scale. However, it must be stressed that financial class oppression and financial surplus are rooted in industrial class exploitation through circulation class oppression (route from [E] to [F2] to [S] to [P]). Canadian banks have built up their monopoly structure on the basis of the unproductive labour of their employees. The surplus that forms their wages comes from the industrial surplus value extracted from productive workers in the sphere of production. Canadian banks receive the funds they loan to foreign multinationals to take over Canadian companies from the financial and circulation oppression and industrial exploitation of Canadian workers. These funds are then utilized to further intensify class contradictions in Canada and abroad. This is the class meaning of the Canadian debate over "capital shortage."

Transition in Types of Class Contradiction

The historical transition from entrepreneurial to monopoly capitalism has changed the way the working day is divided into necessary and surplus labour time. With the emergence of monopoly capitalism, necessary labour time contracts, surplus labour time expands, and the variety of class contradictions increases (see Figure 2). Under nineteenth century British capitalism studies by Marx, industrial class exploitation was the central class contradiction. Circulation class oppression, although existing, did not have the prominence it has today because of the "underdevelopment" of the vast bureaucracy of circulation in contrast to its "overdevelopment" once monopoly capitalism

emerges in full bloom. Consumer class oppression had not yet developed because of the greater competition among a large number of small firms operating in the market place. Financial class oppression had also not yet emerged because the early banks were formed by merchants who did not collect deposits from the working class. With the rise of monopoly capitalism, the capitalist class as a whole captures for itself a greater part of the working day through the growth of circulation class oppression and the emergence of consumer and financial class oppression. Industrial class exploitation is still the fundamental class contradiction but involves proportionately fewer productive workers because of the increase in labour productivity due to the revolution in productive technological forces and the introduction of scientific management (Braverman, 1974). A proportionately smaller productive industrial working-class base is thus able to produce a much larger surplus than was the case under entrepreneurial capitalism. We are therefore left with the proposition that the transition from entrepreneurial to monopoly capitalism has brought about an intensification and diversification in class contradictions.

ism in Canada has mainly been in the sphere of production rather than circulation, and since circulation, consumer, and financial class oppression depend on industrial class exploitation, the increasing foreign (US) ownership of the Canadian economy has both intensified and differentiated class contradictions in Canada. American industrial capitalists have specialized in industrial class exploitation, while indigenous Canadian mercantile and financial capitalists have specialized in circulation, consumer, and financial class oppression. This makes Canadian mercantile and financial capitalists dependent on American industrial capitalists. This theory explains Canada's dependence on the United States. But because investments flowing out of Canada into third countries reflect this internal differentiation in class contradictions, Canada's *relative dominance* in these countries is rooted in its class dependence on the United States. Any structural class theory of social change at the international level in which Canada is implicated must focus on Canada's industrial dependence on the United States.

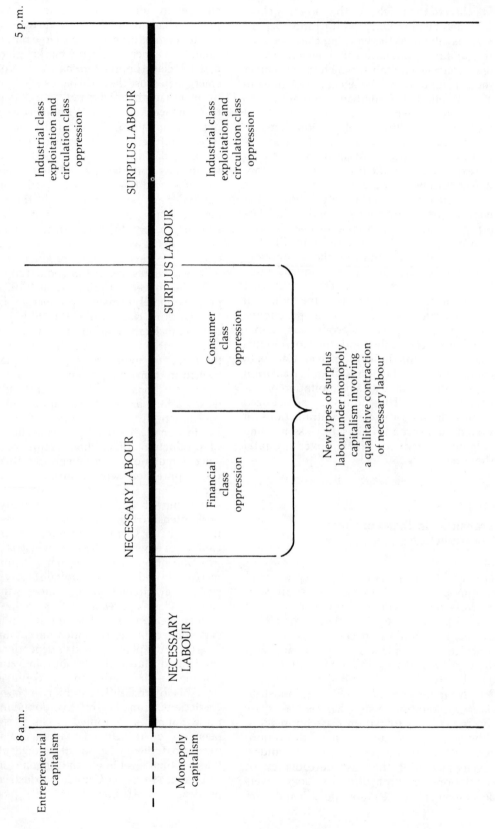

Figure 2 The working day: extraction of surplus from the working class under entrepreneurial and monopoly capitalism

100

REFERENCES

Bank of Canada. *Statistical Summary Supplements*. 1960, 1964, 1965, 1968, 1969.

Bank of Canada. *Bank of Canada Review*. 1973.

Baran, Paul, and Paul Sweezy. *Monopoly Capital*. New York: Monthly Review Press. 1966.

Braverman, Harry. *Labour and Monopoly Capital*. New York: Monthly Review Press. 1974.

Canada Year Book. Various years.

Canadian Statistical Review. 1961-75.

Chodos, Robert. *The Caribbean Connection*. Toronto: James Lorimer 1977.

Clement, Wallace. *The Canadian Corporate Elite*. Toronto: McClelland and Stewar. 1975.

    Continental Corporate Power. Toronto: McClelland and Stewar. 1977.

Corey, Lewis. *The Decline of American Capitalism*. New York: Covici-Friede. 1934.

Cuneo, Carl J. "Class exploitation in Canada." *Canadian Review of Sociology and Anthropology* 15(3). 1978a.

    "A class perspective on regionalism." Pp.132-56 in Daniel Glenday, Hubert Guindon, and Allan Turowetz (ed.), *Modernization and the Canadian State*. Toronto: Macmillan 1978b.

Dept. of National Revenue, Taxation Division. *Taxation Statistics: Corporation Statistics*. Ottawa: Queen's Printer 1946-66.

Dominion Bureau of Statistics n.d. *Annual National Income and Expenditure Account: Historical Revision,* Ottawa: Information Canada. 1926-72.

    Annual Report of the Minister of Trade and Commerce Under the Corporations and Labour Unions Returns Act (Part I: Corporations). Ottawa: Queen's Printer. 1963-69.

Financial Post. 1967-75.

Financial Post 300. 1976.

Gillman, Joseph. *The Falling Rate of Profit*. London: Dennis Dobson. 1957.

Gough, Ian. "Marx's theory of productive and unproductive labour." *New Left Review*, No. 76: 47-72. 1972.

Laxer, Jim. "Canadian manufacturing and US trade policy." Pp. 127-52 in Robert Laxer (ed.), (Canada Ltd.); *The Political Economy of Dependence*. Toronto: McClelland and Stewart. 1973.

Lenin, V.I. *Imperialism, the Highest Stage of Capitalism*. Peking: Foreign Language Press. 1973.

Levitt, Kari. *Silent Surrender: "The Multinational Corporation in Canada*. Toronto: Macmillan. 1971.

Mandel, Ernest. *Late Capitalism*. London: NLB. 1975.

Mao, Tse-tung. "On contradiction." Pp. 13-53 in his Selected Works, Vol. II. London: Lawrence and Wishart. 1954.

Marx, Karl. *Capital*. Vols. I-III. New York: International Publishers. 1967.

Moore, Steve, and Debi Wells. *Imperialism and the National Question in Canada*. Toronto: privately printed. 1975.

Naylor, R.T. *The History of Canadian Business. 2 Vols*. Toronto: James Lorimer. 1975.

O'Conner, James. "Productive and unproductive-labour." *Politics and Society* 53: 297-336. (1975).

Porter, John. *The Vertical Mosaic*. Toronto: University of Toronto Press. 1965.

Statistics Canada. *Census of Canada. Vol. II, Part I* (Bull. 2.1-11). Ottawa: Information Canada. n.d. 1971.

    Corporations and Labour Unions Returns Act (Part I: Corporations). Ottawa: Information Canada. 1970-72.

    Corporations and Labour Unions Returns Act (Part I: Corporations). Ottawa: Information Canada. 1973.

    Manufacturing Industries of Canada. Ottawa: Information Canada. 1974..

    Corporations and Labour Unions Returns Act (Part I: Corporations). Ottawa: Information Canada. 1975a.

    Manufacturing Industries of Canada. Ottawa: Information Canada 1975b.

    Urban Family Expenditure 1972. Ottawa: Information Canada. 1975c.

    Prices and Price Indexes, January 1975. Ottawa: Information Canada. 1975d.

Toronto Star 29 October. 1977.

Urquhart, M.C., and K.A. Buckley (eds.) *Historical Statistics of Canada*. Toronto: Macmillan. 1965.

Varga, E. *The Great Crisis and Its Political Consequences*. New York: International Publishers, n.d.

Varley, D. "On the computation of the rate of surplus value." *Science and Society* 2(3): 393-6. 1938.

Wright, Erik Olin. "Class boundaries in advanced capitalist societies." *New Left Review* No. 98: 3-41. 1976.

Rev. canad. Soc. & Anth. Canada. Rev. Soc. & Anth. 16(1) 1979 *Author's Note:* Thanks are due to Alan Banks, James Curtis, Robert Gardner, James Rinehart, Anupam Sen, and Gary Teeple for their comments on an earlier draft of this paper.

[1]Throughout the paper, "third world country" refers to underdeveloped or developing countries (such as India and Jamaica) while "third country" refers to *both* third world countries *and* developed capitalist countries (such as Britain and, at times, the United States). When "third country" is applied to the United States, it is the *recipient* of foreign investment *from* Canada rather than the *source* of foreign investment *in* Canada.

[2]On the nature and consequences of this shift, see Braverman (1974).

[3]Calculated from data in the *Financial Post* (15 July 1967; 20 July 1968; 2 August 1969; 11 July 1970; 24 July 1971; 5 August 1972; 23 June 1973; 3 August 1974; 26 July 1975).

[4]Marx, *Capital* (1967; I, chap. VII-IX, 177-230). The most important recent development of this theory is Braverman (1974).

[5]Productive labourers are directly involved in the production of surplus value while unproductive labourers are not. The latter work in the sphere of circulation and enable surplus value to be realized by merchants and financiers (Gough, 1972; O'Conner, 1975). While this broad distinction does exist within the working class, some workers combine both productive and unproductive labour. This makes a definitive separation of the working class into productive and unproductive fractions difficult (Wright, 1976: 15-16).

[6]Calculated from Urquhart and Buckley (1965: 463) and Statistics Canada (1974; 1975b). In these calculations, changes in the number of productive workers, depreciation, and inflation were taken into account. The estimates are likely to be low in that they do not include that part of industrial surplus distributed in circulation. Estimates of the discrepancy between the values and prices of commodities were not included in the calculations. However, assuming that a radical inversion over time in the organic composition of capital between manufacturing and other sectors of the economy has not taken place, considerable reliance can be placed in the broad trend. For comparable but somewhat less sophisticated calculations done in other countries, cf. Varga (n.d.: 174-75); Corey (1934: 83); Varley (1938); Gillman (1957: 33-65); Mandel (1975: 164, 175).

[7]Calculated from Urquhart and Buckley (1965: 230) and *Bank of Canada Statistical Summary–1968 Supplement* (20). The exception to this percentage range is the period from 1941 to 1945 when the figures dropped to less than 50%. Inconsistencies in the reporting of these banking data make a precise historical trend difficult to estimate.

[8]Calculated from *Bank of Canada Statistical Summary–1960 Supplement* (35); *1964 Supplement* (27); *Canada Year Book* (1967: 1131; 1969: 1154; 1970-71: 1235; 1973: 790).

[9]Calculated from *Bank of Canada Statistical Summary–supplements of 1960, 1965, and 1969* and *Bank of Canada Review* (July 1973: 10).

STATE

Introduction

In the General Introduction, reference was made to the instrumentalist and the structuralist views of the state. The former, it may be remembered, was based on the proposition that the informal and formal ties between business and state leaders went a long way toward explaining the tendency of state activities to promote the interests of the bourgeoisie. The latter started from the assumption that the state behaved in a fashion consistent with the preservation of the system of which it is a part. The articles in the current section, after providing an analysis of the general advanced capitalist context in which the state operates, accomplish two things: 1) examinations of the exact mechanisms whereby class interests are mediated by the state and find eventual embodiment in policy; 2) assessments of the relative merits of the instrumentalist and structuralist positions with regard to state activity.

Contemporary Canadian capitalism, Mellos argues in his article, has three underlying characteristics: 1) a large degree of economic concentration that finds embodiment in giant corporations, most of which are multinationals; 2) the application of science-based technology to the productive process; and 3) a great deal of state involvement in society. The last mentioned, which is of major concern here, finds expression in state-business co-operation in economic ventures such as Syncrude; in the attempts of the state, through various measures, to prevent eco-nomic and political crises. It should be noted, however, that state-business co-operation in Canada is nothing new.

In speaking of business-government relations prior to the nineteenth century, for example, Hugh Aitken (1967:209) remarks that, "The assertion that the state in the form of the federal government was merely acting as the agent or instrument of private economic interests . . . could probably be supported." In a similar manner, when speaking of the entire course of Canadian economic development, Naylor (1975 I:58) remarks that, "From an early date the process of economic development in Canada displayed a very close interfacing of politics and business, leading to inevitable hopeless compromises of the public finances as the government treasury was plundered with impunity by promoters of various projects." Similarly, Armstrong and Nelles argue that, "Because businessmen constituted the dominant class in Canadian society, they assumed that the state should be organized to meet their needs" (1973:22).

There are those who argue that without this type of relationship, Canadian economic development would have been an impossibility. S.D. Clark, for one, shares this view. Using Innis' terms, Clark points to the fact that Canada was "a 'hard' frontier. Canadian resources were hard to get at . . . What was called for in the opening up of this northern half of the continent," he continues, "were massive accumulations of capital, large-scale forms of economic organization, long lines of communication and transportation, and [importantly], extensive state support" (1975:27). The inhospitality of the environment—particularly that of the Canadian Shield—is also referred to by Nelles (1974) in accounting for large scale state involvement in the economy.

Most would agree with Clark in his recognition of the necessity of large scale state intervention in the face of the rigours of the Canadian landscape and environment. However, critics of the state's role focus on four aspects of its behaviour that warrant comment. First, state operations in the economy have been accompanied by massive corruption (John A. Macdonald was not immune to temptation). Second, it is doubtful, if the goal was to have been eventual industrialization, that the amount spent by the state in the provision of an infrastructure designed to promote the export of staples, was wise. The capital could have been more effectively channelled into manufacturing. Third, it is clear that state intervention, by and large, has promoted the interests of particular classes in Canadian society. Any benefits that may have trickled downward, were not in proportion to profits accrued at the top. Fourth, state policy, to the degree that it has promoted the interests of a mercantile-corporate fraction, actually worked to the long term disadvantage of the industrial fraction.

When the state intervened in the economy, particularly in early days, it was frequently a foreign state, that of Britain. After 1783, for example, Aitken observes that "The merchant capitalists of Nova Scotia and New Brunswick wished the ports of the British West Indies closed to all but British and colonial shipping, hoping that in this way they could monopolize the lucrative carrying trade, breadstuffs, livestock, staves, dried cod, molasses and rum" (1967:189). For a while, they got their wish. In a similar fashion, for a while, British preferences for colonial timber enabled the establishment of fortunes by those involved with this commodity.

The state—this time the colonial one of Upper Canada—also provided support to business interests in the form of financial assistance in the mammoth canal building projects of the last century. While the Welland Canal was at least initiated by private enterprise and only later taken over by the state, the Cornwall, Williamsburg, Beauharnois, and Lachine canals were later constructed by the government of the Canadas. These ventures, that resulted in an enormous burden of public debt, were typical of later state ventures in the provision of an infrastructure designed to meet the needs of the mercantile elements of the bourgeoisie. The most romanticized government undertakings, however, were the railways (Berton, 1970). The support received by these enterprises is legendary.

For example, the Guarantee Act, passed by the Canadian legislature in 1849, "provided a government guarantee for half the bond of any railroad over 75 miles in length, if half the line had already been built . . . Financial aid extended by the provincial government under this Act and later acts to assist the Grand Trunk Railway totalled approximately $33,000,000" (Aitken, 1967:198). Municipalities provided an additional $12,000,000 in support.

Canadian Confederation, described by Naylor as essentially a financial venture (1975:I:32), accelerated the trend of state support for certain ventures, serving primarily the interests of the mercantile fraction. Most importantly, the federal government's commitment to build a transcontinental railway exclusively through Canadian territory resulted in the granting of millions of acres, and other subsidies, to the Canadian Pacific Railway. This pattern of generosity was repeated when other railways were proposed.

The promotion particularly of a transcontinental railway, in addition to the initiation of a tariff designed ostensibly to protect Canadian manufacturers and raise revenue for a commercial infrastructure (Naylor, 1975 I:55), and the promotion of immigration, were the three major items of the Conservatives' National Policy of 1878. State activity in these areas was designed to fill up the West, provide a market for Canadian-manufactured products, and promote the trade in wheat between Canada and other nations. The historical record indicates that whatever the benefits derived from this exercise, they were not shared by all Canadians.

At "the same time that great fortunes were being consolidated," Naylor points out, "living standards for the working class were deteriorating: real wages fell during the great expansion of 1896. Even for a select group of highly skilled, well organized workers, money wages barely kept ahead of the cost of living. Rents," he continues, "rose more quickly than money wages, and the share of rent in total expenditures tended to rise. Food costs rose very quickly, and between 1900 and 1910 while per capita GNP rose 60 per cent in nominal terms, money wages for the selected group rose only 30 per cent" (1975 I:221). Observations such as these are confirmed by analysing contemporary inquiries into the plight of particularly the urban working classes (Ames, 1897/1972; Woodsworth, 1911/1972).

In the twentieth century, the state continued in the direction established earlier. Although it did not get as financially entangled as it had in earlier ventures, state support for the Trans-Canada Pipeline was essential. Without it, it is doubtful that the company involved would have succeeded in obtaining financial backing. One of the results of its role, however, as history shows, was the defeat of the Liberal government over the issue of closure while the pipeline was under the scrutiny of the House (Kilbourn, 1970). Also in the twentieth century, the state has played roles in the development of the St. Lawrence Seaway, the James Bay hydro electric development, and Syncrude.

In the last case, state support is massive. "The government," Pratt observes, "must shoulder the . . . burden of building the . . . infrastructure . . . providing equity and debt financing, royalty holidays, guaranteed returns and prices, ensure labour stability, train a work force, [and] underwrite environmental studies and costs . . ." (1976:95). The magnitude of support is such that while it costs "between $50,000 and $70,000 in manufacturing" to create one permanent job, in the tar sands project it will cost well over a million dollars (Pratt, 1976:111).

While the point has not been stressed in this description, it is important to note that the bourgeoisie, at different times, has used all three levels of government to attain its objectives. Also, there frequently has been conflict between the interests of different fractions comprising the bourgeoisie. On more than one occasion, the fractions have utilized the assistance of different levels of government to attain their objectives. Sometimes such assistance was offered;

sometimes it was demanded.

In the last century, as an example of the former, while the federal government was busy providing the mercantile interests with a commercial infrastructure, and financial institutions were spending their time promoting the shipment of staples to markets, municipalities were attempting to lure industry to their locations. The importance of this activity cannot be overemphasized. "In large measure," Naylor points out (1975 II:104), "bonusing was a stop-gap policy to plug the hole in the capital market left by the banks, the financial system in general and the federal government, which channelled funds off into commerce and the construction of a commercial infrastructure. Bonusing of industry," he suggests, "in effect converted the municipality into an investment banker, facilitating industrial capital accumulation by redistributing income and providing a further attraction to foreign capital."

While the municipalities offered government assistance, it was often demanded. At the turn of the century in Ontario, two different levels of government were used by different fractions of the bourgeoisie in an attempt to achieve their goals (Nelles, 1974). The issue this time was the provision of cheap and efficient hydro-electric power to municipalities and industry. When it appeared as though control of this valuable resource would fall into the hands of the mercantile fragment, a popular front of industrialists and 'the people', spearheaded by Adam Beck, demanded state intervention at the provincial level. Beck's success at the provincial level forced the mercantile fraction to appeal for disallowance at the federal level of legislation, putting hydro electricity under provincial control. While "Laurier and leading members of his cabinet took few pains to conceal their sympathies with injured entrepreneurs" (Armstrong and Nelles, 1973), they did not intervene. As a consequence, Beck and his allies were victorious.

A not completely unrelated example involves the governments of Alberta and Canada in a squabble over oil taxes. (The mercantile-corporate industrial difference is, however, less applicable in this case.) In this confrontation, Pratt observes that "Lougheed was . . . acting as Syncrude's political strategist, advising the groups on tactics, setting up meetings and trying to smooth the way to

Ottawa" (1976:141). At the same time, because the general position of the oil companies would result in greater costs to them, "The other larger industrial corporations do not seem . . . to have been very vocal in their support for the oil industry's position" (Berry, 1976:309).

Since 1867, there appear to have been some changes in the use that Canadian business has made of different levels of government. The changes, in turn, derive from long-term developments in Canadian economic activity mediated through the class structure. In an important article on this matter, Stevenson (1977) points to the fact that "Montreal and Winnipeg, the strongholds of the mercantile bourgeoisie whose interests required a strong central government, began to decline . . . after the First World War, and continued to do so . . . after the Second World War. The rise of Toronto, Vancouver, and later Calgary as the new strongholds of economic power," he feels, "reflected the shift to an economy . . . based on natural resources under provincial jurisdiction and relying heavily on American direct investment" (1977:78). This trend notwithstanding, it is Stevenson's feeling that a new fraction of the upper class, such as those associated with operations connected with the Canada Development Corporation, that rely on the protection of a strong central government, will resist further increases in provincial power. While Stevenson's analysis of the past has great credence, it is too early to comment on his predictions for the future.

Apart from conflicts based on the mercantile-corporate industrial dimension, there are examples of disagreement between fragments identified in the introduction to the section on class as indigenous and comprador. These are important. They are cases in which foreign capitalists operating in Canada have attempted to influence the Canadian state to take positions at variance with the long-term interests of indigenous fragments. Unfortunately, until recently, researchers, by and large, have ignored the nationality of capitalists when conducting political analyses. As a consequence, few detailed examples of the political operations of foreign capitalists are available. One important exception is Resnick (1977). He points out, in a discussion of post-Second World War Canada, that while indigenous fragments of

the bourgeoisie sometimes opposed what they regarded as increased dependence on the United States, their voices were unheeded.

Despite a scarcity of data, it is possible to give an example of conflict in which indigenous Canadian interests were victorious and one in which they were temporarily defeated. In both instances, the role of the state was crucial. In both cases the power of a foreign state was used to assist the compradors in the attainment of their objectives. The lesson should be obvious: where the interests of foreign capital operating in Canada are thwarted, they will use both the Canadian and foreign states in attempting to achieve their objectives.

The first example, which involves the introduction of the 'manufacturing condition' in Ontario in 1898, involves four major actors. First, and most directly involved, were two fragments of the indigenous bourgeoisie: the old established timber barons of the Ottawa Valley; a new group of timber interests operating in the Georgian Bay and Lake Superior regions. Of the latter, Nelles comments that, "They had to scrounge for timber limits, financial backing and markets. They were," he says, "an erratic, strident bunch who depended entirely upon the American export market . . . they lacked the stability—financial and social—afforded by British business connections of long standing. Although they were more numerous, they operated on a much smaller scale with less capital tied up in limits and mills [than the Ottawa lumbermen]" (Nelles, 1974:66). The other actors, in turn, were American timber exporters operating in Canada, the provincial and federal states, and the American state. The issue precipitating conflict was the Dingley Tariff of 1897 which restricted the free entry of lumber into the United States. At the same time, the tariff allowed the entry of logs with no restrictions. In essence, Canada was being allowed to ship unprocessed raw, but not semi-processed materials, to the United States. The consequence would have been the ruination of the new lumbermen.

While the Ottawa Valley interests still had certain British markets available to them, and, in any case, were more financially equipped to weather the storm, the new lumbermen had no such fallback position: their lumber markets were in the United States. Despite their better position, the Ottawa interests nonetheless dispatched a lobbyist to Washington to plead for concessions. He was unsuccessful.

At the same time, the new lumber interests approached the federal government to intercede on their behalf. But Ottawa, concerned with more grandiose matters, was unreceptive. Consequently, assisted by mounting public support for their cause, the new lumber interests approached the provincial government. Faced with an impending election, a somewhat reluctant provincial government introduced an amendment to the Crown Timber Act "requiring that pine timber cut on crown lands be sawn into lumber in Canada" (Nelles, 1974:73). The effective consequence of such legislation would be a cessation of the export of logs to the United States.

American reaction to the legislation was swift. "For their part," Nelles points out (1974:74), "the American exporters holding Canadian limits challenged the manufacturing clause in the courts, protested to their own Secretary of State, and joined some of their Canadian colleagues in petitioning the federal government to disallow the provincial legislation. It soon became apparent to the Laurier government, however, that any attempt to delay the implementation of the legislation, as had been urged by the American Secretary of State, would gain little public sympathy in Ontario. As a consequence, Laurier was finally placed in a position where he could do nothing but support the legitimacy of the provincial action. This was a wise move in light of the courts' subsequent upholding of the legality of the legislation.

Despite conflicts, virtually all concerned, with the exception of the Americans, were in the end pleased with the effects of the new law. It not only led to the establishment of both American and Canadian saw milling operations on the Canadian side of the border, but also it stimulated a rise in prices for Canadian lumber. In addition, it created the sentiment that was to be embodied in future action, that similar provisions should apply to the manufacture of pulp.

A second case in which there was disagreement between foreign and indigenous interests is one concerning foreign periodicals in Canada. In 1931, Bennett's Conservatives imposed a short lived tax on foreign period-icals entering Canada. With the return to office of William Lyon Mackenzie King in 1935, the tax was removed. It was not until 1956 that there was an attempt by the Liberals to reimpose a tax on foreign periodicals. But it was removed the following year, this time by the Conservatives. They opted instead for a Royal Commission on Publishing to make recommendations on the magazine industry in Canada.

In a real sense, *Time* and *Reader's Digest* emerged as the central concern of the Commission. By 1955, their Canadian editions, established in 1943, had accounted for one third of magazine subscriptions in Canada. It is not surprising, therefore, that the two magazines bore the brunt of the attacks of the Periodical Press Association (PPA) and Maclean-Hunter Limited. *Time* and *Reader's Digest*, they argued, were "seriously undermining the economic viability of domestic magazines" (Litvak and Maule, 1974:618). As a solution they advocated tariff protection from foreign competition.

There was, however, no unanimity among Canadian publishers on this matter. While central Canadian interests advocated a tariff on foreign imports, "publishers in the Maritimes and the West, operating within a regional context, did not experience the full impact of foreign competition" (Litvak and Maule, 1974:618). But this divergence of interests notwithstanding, the PPA and Maclean-Hunter view seems to have held some sway. The Commission recommended "1) that the deduction from income by a taxpayer of expenditures incurred for advertising directed at the Canadian market in a foreign periodical . . . be disallowed; and 2) that the entry into Canada from abroad of a periodical containing Canadian domestic advertising be excluded under Schedule 'C' of the Customs Act" (1974:619). It was not until the Liberals were returned to office in 1964, however, that the report was acted upon. They proposed legislation that prohibited "the entry into Canada of split runs or regional editions containing advertising specifically directed at the Canadian market, and of magazines including trade papers, if over 5 per cent of their advertising content was directed at Canadians. The second proposal was that the Income Tax Act be amended to prohibit a taxpayer from deducting from his income, for tax purposes, expenditures for advertising specifically directed at the Canadian market in a non-Canadian periodical" (1974:619). The proposed legislation, however, was ineffectual. Because of the peculiar definition given 'Canadian', *Time* and *Reader's Digest*, largely because of their 'Canadian' editions, were outside of the scope of the legislation.

The reason for this development, and previous attempts to impose import restrictions, can be traced to two processes. First, *Time* and *Reader's Digest* both conducted public relations campaigns designed to mobilize the Canadian public behind their position and made representations to appropriate committees, Cabinet Ministers, etc., outlining the benefits of their operation to the Canadian economy. As Litvak and Maule express it (1974:624), "A number of Liberal members appeared to have a direct political interest in the welfare of *Time* and *Reader's Digest*." Such individuals included C.M. Drury, Alan McNaughton, and John Turner. Second, and more importantly, as major U.S. corporations, *Time* and *Reader's Digest* were able to obtain the support of the U.S. State. It was made clear to Canada that "Canada's exemption from U.S. balance of payment policies might be discontinued, and that the Automotive Agreement was under heavy attack in Congress and was unlikely to receive Senate ratification if *Time* and *Reader's Digest* were threatened in Canada" (Litvak and Maule, 1974:623). Faced with odds like these, it would take a Special Senate Committee on Mass Media, a concerted effort by the Canadian business press and small magazines, and a further decade of wrangling before *Time* and *Reader's Digest* would be denied their privileged position in the Canadian periodical market.

The conclusions that can be drawn from the historical record are clear. The state has always been an important presence in Canadian economic development. Moreover, it is safe to say that its activities have been of most immediate benefit to the mercantile-corporate fraction of the bourgeoisie. Benefits that trickled down to the other classes were incidental. It is also clear that on occasion, different class fractions have used both the federal and provincial levels of government in attempts to realize their goals. In some circumstances, as with industry in the last century, the municipal government has

entered the equation in an important way. It is equally clear that the state has played a key role in disputes that may have emerged between domestic and foreign capitalists in Canada. The latter have had access to both the Canadian and U.S. states in attempting to pursue their interests.

The orientation underlaying the analysis to this point has been primarily instrumentalist—not because the editor favours this position but because the approach is implicit in most of the works referred to. (It must not be assumed, though, that most of the writers cited are Marxists.) State policies have been related to either personal links between the leaders of state and the bourgeoisie, or to the advantaged position enjoyed by certain fractions of the bourgeoisie in dealing with the state because of their superior resources and organizing ability. In two of the following articles included in this section the structuralist position is taken. Both Cuneo and Mahon, in their articles on the introduction of unemployment insurance and on the Textile and Clothing Board respectively, argue that the instrumentalist position is of little validity in dealing with matters they are concerned with. As argued in the General Introduction, it is likely that there are occasions on which the instrumentalist position is valid. On other occasions the structuralist viewpoint may have more to offer. The final article examines the consequence of the state's activity for strikes in Canada.

DEVELOPMENTS IN ADVANCED CAPITALIST IDEOLOGY
Koula Mellos

1. Developments of Advanced Capitalism

An increased incidence of state intervention in the economy and science-technology as a force of production are new developments specific to the advanced phase of capitalism. These developments are both the outcome of, and contributory to, the process of capital formation in this post-classical stage of capital accumulation, and have deep implications for class structure and the class struggle. Reflecting, and at the same time reinforcing these developments, are changes in the dominant ideology of advanced capitalism. In exploring this dialectic, we will briefly describe these material features of advanced capital formation and examine the corresponding changes in ideology, focussing for the most part on the Canadian example. The discussion will draw on published statements and interviews of senior executives and directors of major private enterprises in Canada as expression of the dominant ideology in this context.

Contemporary capitalism bears a number of distinguishing characteristics which set it apart from its previous classical stage of development. Currently, the process of capital accumulation proceeds in a setting in which economic concentration takes the form of gigantic national and multinational corporations and the far-reaching organization of goods, capital and labour. A competitive labour market dependent on unorganized labour, and numerous individual capitalists with competing interests (conditions of classical capitalism) have been replaced by the organization of labour in the form of trade unions and the concentration of capital in monolithic enterprises dominating or controlling whole economic sectors. The market operable under conditions of classical capitalism is now superseded. The state acts as an instrument for regulating the business cycle and attenuating its increasingly critical effects at each new stage of capital accumulation. In this role as regulator of the process of capital accumulation, the state performs new functions, both of the accumulation and the legitimation types.[1]

In an effort to create and maintain conditions in which profit accumulation proceeds smoothly, the state devises and executes a comprehensive economic policy involving fiscal and monetary measures in addition to loans, subsidies, credits and numerous other means. It enters bilateral or bloc economic and political agreements in order to strengthen its position in the international market. Further, by maintaining a permanent policy of war-preparedness the state creates unproductive consumption through armaments production, facilitating the realization of capital. It initiates, maintains and expands permanent construction programmes in the transportation, health, housing and education fields and thus contributes to the development of the material infrastructure. The imperative need of capitalist production for an increase in the productivity of labour seeks satisfaction through the state's manifold educational programmes including advanced technological research and development as well as manpower training and retraining. Related to this are a number of medical and social insurance arrangements which also contribute to the expansion of the productive capacity of the labour force. The state also maintains welfare programmes and programmes of unemployment compensation which, although unproductive in themselves, aim at winning mass loyalty by relieving the material cost of private appropriation of socially produced surplus.

Science-technology in the form of a highly skilled labour force and systematic technical innovation increases the productivity of labour power. It has been claimed that by so doing, it alters the organic composition of capital and counteracts the tendential fall in the rate of profit[2] thereby permitting the process of capital expansion to proceed with relatively little interruption in this advanced phase of capital accumulation.

These developments–a highly interventionary state, science-technology as a principal force of production, and economic concentration in the form of national and multinational corporations–mark the end of classical liberal capitalism. In these respects, Canada qualifies as an advanced capitalist system.[3]

Capital accumulation has now acquired global proportions as exemplified by the flow of capital from one nation state to another. Thus, capital concentration in one nation state must be situated within the network of world capitalism. This is a particularly salient question in the case of Canadian industry and resources as their ownership and control are shared by foreign, largely American, interests.[4] Alongside these, however, there are large Canadian-owned corporations operating in a large number of nation states and in many cases dominating whole economic sectors.[5] This pattern of foreign-owned corporations in Canada and Canadian-owned multinational corporations has given rise to a left-nationalist debate regarding the status of the Canadian bourgeoisie.[6] Although these debates have important implications for the critique of capitalism, for the identification of class contradiction and for the place of nationalism in the articulation of left political action programmes (which would vary depending on the relative strength of national bourgeoisies), we wish to focus here on the common features of monopoly capitalism and in particular its ideology rather than on the nationality of the controlling bourgeois class.

2. The Universality of Ideology

Just as the early liberal phase of capitalism required and nurtured an ideology as a mechanism of unification of all classes, so does the present phase of monopoly capitalism. Indeed, a class society marked by the fundamental contradiction of irreconcilable interests derived from the relations the classes bear to the means of production achieves integration to the degree to which a common ideology is shared by opposing classes. The ideology operates such that it explicitly promotes not class interests, that is, interests of the bourgeois class, but universal interests. In this way, it aims at concealing the fundamental contradiction in the private appropriation of socially-produced surplus value and

at preventing working class consciousness from emerging and generating opposing claims.

Ideology is constitutive of practice. It is dialectically generated in practice and at the same time serves to orient and justify practice. Appeals to universality thus involve the interpretations of the privatization of surplus–a bourgeois class interest–in terms of universal interest. The modifications at the level of practice which have emerged in the present phase of advanced capital concentration, are accompanied by corresponding modifications on the level of ideology including the specific appeals to universality. Furthermore, the particular nature of these modifications both at the material level and at the level of ideology is such as to facilitate, as we argue below, the appeal to universality.

Universality refers to a state of communal being in which man achieves emancipation in the unity of the individual and the society. Man's history is a long struggle for the realization of community and thus each class which makes a revolution appeals to universality and claims to be promoting not class interests but communal interests. As Marx argues in *The German Ideology*

[t]he class making a revolution appears from the very start, merely because it is opposed to a class, not as a class but as the representative of the whole of society; it appears as the whole mass of society confronting the one ruling class. It can do this because, to start with, its interest is really more connected with the common interest of all other nonruling classes. . . .[7]

Indeed, in the theory of historical materialism, history is a progression of class struggles, each advancing man's development one step closer to the achievement of conditions permitting the expression of his communal character. In this sense a revolutionary class, as was the French bourgeoisie in its overthrow of the French aristocracy, sets itself up as the emancipator of society and its claims to universality are justified in terms of the total historical project of man's liberation.

Liberalism, the ideology of the bourgeois class, claimed to be a vehicle of universality and not a means of promoting class interests. The material conditions, however, from which it emanates and which it justifies cannot permit the development of communal man. Marx argued that man in classical capitalist society is divided in two[8]–the citizen operating within the political society on the basis of universal criteria which promote communal interests, and the bourgeois operating within civil society in accordance with egotistical needs and privatistic interests. Thus, the possibility of a human community of universal rationality is denied under capitalist conditions which generate and are dependent on a divided rationality, that is, a public rationality and a private rationality.

In its claims to universality, this rationality must conceal the contradiction generated by its privatistic basis. It must depict itself as being something it is not. For it is not truly a universal rationality. The world view and norms of behaviour it promotes as universal advance the interests of a class of owners of the means of production who appropriate the socially-produced surplus in conformity with rules of capital accumulation. Many students of classical liberal ideology[9] have explored in detail the ways in which the principal themes of liberalism as the ideology of capitalism operate such that they favour the bourgeois class while appearing to promote universalistic interests. Individualism, equality and freedom emerge in capitalistic practice and ideology in a particularistic form but appear as universalistic.

The equality theme, for example, is generated and reinforced by the liberal market which appears to be based on exchange of equivalents. Marx, developing his labour theory of value, showed that the equal exchange between labour and capital is, in fact, an exchange of nonequivalents. While the labourer selling his labour-power receives its market price, its exchange value, the capitalist appropriates the value-creating capacity of living labour. The worker thus is selling his power to work, not his work. The exchange between capital and labour is the means by which the capitalist appropriates surplus value. The liberal market thus generates inequality not equality. While it frees labour from the fixed serf-master pattern of feudalism, it creates an assymetrical capital-labour exchange. But the freeing of labour and the subjection of it to universal exchange value is sufficient to generate an appearance of reciprocal exchange, to conceal the source

of surplus value in labour and thereby to hide the contradictory class interests. The particularistic bourgeois interests appear as universal.

3. Neo-Liberal Ideology and Its Material Roots

The transition to advanced capitalism facilitates the portrayal of bourgeois class interests as universalistic. The class contradiction of irreconcilable opposing interests is even further concealed within this phase of the capitalistic mode of production. Marcuse describes how "here in the economic structure of monopoly capitalist society are located the factual bases of universalism. But in the theory they are totally reinterpreted. The whole that it presents is not the unification achieved by the dominion of *one* class within the framework of classless society, but rather a unity that combines *all* classes, that is supposed to overcome the reality of struggle and thus classes themselves. . . . A classless society, in other words, is the goal but a classless society on the basis of and within the framework of the existing class society."[10]

Continued capital accumulation at this advanced state of capital concentration requires an alteration in the organic composition of capital in order to assure a profitable private appropriation of surplus value. Although the factors involved–capital concentration, state intervention in the economy, science-technology–are indivisible and interdependent as part of the same process, it is possible to distinguish the particular ways in which each contributes to facilitate appeals to universality.

(A) Capital Concentration

Capital concentration has involved a replacement of the market economy by a corporate economy which no longer allows the individual to "seek his fortune" according to the rules of exchange of the liberal market. The economic space is already occupied. It is divided, allocated and controlled. Individual entrepreneurship, to the extent that it is present, acquires a place allotted by corporate control. The free competitive basis of the liberal market has been replaced by corporate monopoly.

Monopolistic control of the already divided economic space tends toward concealment of the distinction between private

111

and public interests. This is so because corporate planning and control assumes a societal or global character encompassing both private and public interests and promoting them as universal interests. As sectoral planning expands to societal planning, the distinction between the private and public sphere–the economic interest of the private appropriating individual and the public interest of community well-being–appears to be brought to an end. The public interest seems to have absorbed the private interest and thereby to have resolved the contradiction. This distinction, of course, is not and cannot be eliminated in a system of privately-appropriated surplus value. It is merely concealed in the emerging neo-liberal ideology.

(B) The Interventionary State

The state in capitalistic society has traditionally been regarded as the uniquely appropriate instrument to oversee and promote the common good. Although specific interests have the legitimized right to pursue their particularistic claims, the state is recognized as the organism with the obligation to pursue the societal good. This has been regarded as its main responsibility from Locke to contemporary liberals. The ways in which the state is expected to achieve this have varied. The state in classical capitalism was seen as best doing least. The norms of state behaviour in the promotion of the common good were largely negative. The state was to abstain from intervention other than to secure peace and order, to regulate contracts, and to provide some material infrastructure such as means of transportation. It was rather the individual who was vested with the rationality to pursue his interests unobstructed by external agencies. This rationality, the property of the individual, equipped him to tend to his needs and fulfillment. This condition for the good of the total society was assured by the state in maintaining its distance, in refraining from visible interference in the individual's pursuit of his interests, and in providing a framework within which the full freedom of these interest-pursuing individuals could be achieved and maintained.

Although this is roughly the image of the state in liberal capitalist rhetoric, it is questionable whether the various capitalist states were ever in practice restricted to this passive role. Certainly, the Canadian experience deviates from this norm.[11] The Canadian state was involved in the process of capital formation in the latter part of the nineteenth century as exemplified by the National Policy. Conditions of advanced capitalism, however, have required the state to assume a new range of functions to such an extent that a relatively clear distinction can be made between the role of the state in liberal capitalism and in advanced capitalism. Indeed, the intervention of the state in the economy is indispensible in contemporary capitalism as a mechanism of containing its internal contradictions, heightened and intensified at this advanced stage of capital accumulation. This breaks the link between passive state and common good in the contemporary liberal rhetoric. The passive is now replaced by active as the means of achieving the common good. Health, welfare and unemployment compensation, monetary and fiscal management of the economy, intensified support for education, research and development are prominent examples of some of the new activities of the state, in its role of regulating the crisis-generating economy and hence in maintaining the private appropriation of socially-produced surplus value. They are promoted in the ideology as projects with egalitarian intent and consequence.[12]

The nature of a great deal of the accelerated economic activity of the state facilitates its characterization in the ideology as serving the total community good. State programmes required for profitable private accumulation[13] including the development of the material infrastructure (for example, road construction, housing construction, and health centres and hospitals) appear as instruments in the promotion of the common, societal good. These programmes of a universal public character project a unifying focus and appear as vehicles of common benefit. Programmes of the nonmaterial infrastructure, such as education programmes of various types and scientific research, contribute in like manner to apparent collectivism.

That which appears most directly collectivist are the various social welfare programmes and unemployment compensation, which, indeed, in the logic of capital expansion, are not even indirectly productive. They contribute perhaps to the stabilization of the economy by minimally assisting the realization of capital in expanding the purchasing power of the unemployed and unemployables. The principal if not sole function of these programmes, however, is the "selling" of the whole advanced capitalist order to the temporarily or permanently unproductive members of society—a society whose unjustice would with greater facility be challenged in the absence of such programmes. More recently the state has been initiating a variety of ecological programmes, requiring private enterprise to subscribe to standards of pollution control and in some cases purification of the environment.

While these state measures are dictated by considerations of averting crises generated by capital expansion, they are also means of redistributing social wealth. Being based on universal criteria, they generate an appearance of collective action for the common good. This serves to conceal the privatistic features of the material conditions and at the same time to diminish the explicitly individualist dimension of the ideology so prominent in the classical liberal period. Class interests of the bourgeoisie are disguised as universal interests, one and the same as those of the non-capitalist class. Insofar as they are disguised they remain closed to political consciousness and prevent the fundamental contradiction from constituting the basis for the articulation of class interests.

(C) Science-Technology

Another feature of advanced capitalism which contributes in large measure to the apparent collectivism is science-technology. It is social capital in the form of education, and research and development. It enters the productive process as a new force of production, making for an increase in productivity of labour, and hence counteracting the law of the tendential fall of the rate of profit. It increases the rate of surplus value and makes possible a compromise between labour and capital in the division of the surplus in that it allows both capital and labour an increased share of the surplus. Relative shares remain approximately the same while varying absolutely. The interests of labour and the interests of capital appear to coincide in that the enlargement of the "economic pie" appears to benefit the whole society. Continual economic expansion of capital accumulation which science-technology makes possible is promoted as a fruit of communal, societal character.[14]

The invocation of science-technology in the claim to universality is reaffirmed on another important level—the level of the rationality of science. Science-technology, of which the technically skilled labour is the medium of application, is depicted as an objectified knowledge which contains infallible truths. This claim appeals to the positive feed-back reactions resulting from an effective control of reality.[15] Rooted in a rationality in which fact is divided from value and in which the latter is seen as having spurious effects on the understanding and explanation of fact, science-technology assumes a position of neutrality vis-à-vis particularistic interests. The "neutral" character which this rationality claims for science, favours no group in particular, but society in general. Scientific solutions to problems appear to be not only correct but to reside on the level of universal interests. By virtue of its objectivity and neutrality, science-technology seems to serve all interests equally. It becomes an important unifying tool which conceals the relations of domination of one class by another by being placed not on the level of particularism but on the level of universalism. Science-technology thus becomes ideology.[16]

4. The Emergence of New Norms

These material developments are accompanied by a shift of action from the level of the individual to the level of the group. Whereas liberal capitalist practice and ideology required and emphasized the importance of individual action as the vehicle for the achievement of the total collective good, under conditions of advanced capitalism it is increasingly the group which is the unit of action instrumental in the attainment of collective good. The emerging norms of group action emphasize a cooperative, collaborative focus, and hence inherently contain universality claims, portraying collective action as necessary for the common good.

Pluralism, as a pattern of group action in liberal democratic capitalist societies, emerged early in this century but flourished especially after the Second World War, and is now increasingly giving way to corporatism. Both pluralism and corporatism are patterns of voluntary association organized around particular interests expressed in articulated goals or sets of goals which are actively promoted by lobbying techniques before authoritative decision-making centres. Pluralist associations, however, differ in origin, organization and behaviour from corporate associations. The former, as a student of these two phenomena describes, are marked by "controlled emergence, quantitative limitation, vertical stratification and complementary interdependence."[17] The corporate characteristics of group formation and behaviour are consistent with and indeed echo the centralization tendencies generated by the concentration of capital in the advanced stages of accumulation and its replacement of the market. This replacement involves the supersession of the mechanism of mechanically interconnected forces by a concerted functional adjustment of the whole—the supersession of competitive interaction by planning. Centralization accordingly involves the coordination of interest associations and requires the incorporation of groups by which ties with the state are formalized. Insofar as pluralism as a multiplicity of autonomous groups engaged in a competitive interaction was a modern extension of classical individual-based competitive action and as such was an anachronism in the conditions of advanced capitalism, it inevitably gave way to corporatism with its controlled links to decision-making centres in a planned advanced capitalist network. National and global planning requires the rationalization of decision-making which is rendered possible by the incorporation of groups. This incorporation of groups is portrayed in the ideology as collaborative interaction within an organic interdependent whole, each group action contributing to the general well-being.[18]

In this reality new norms compatible with and necessary for corporate capitalism are emerging. These new structures of practice are based on cooperation. They represent a common pursuit of the social good. Because they have cooperative, collaborative roots, they more easily carry out their ideological role to conceal the privatistic nature of the process of capitalist production than did the individualist norms of liberal capitalism. This is so because they are disguised and projected as public more naturally than the competitive, individualist norms of behaviour of liberal capitalism. In the ideology, these cooperative norms are portrayed as involving

collective action in a communal project. In this way the universality function of the ideology is facilitated.

As we suggested above, all ideologies of class societies must possess an apparent quality of universality if the privatized basis of surplus appropriation is to be legitimized. Classical liberal ideology justifies classical capitalist practice in the name of community, just as corporate ideology justifies advanced capitalist practice on the basis of universality. Appeals to universality, however, relate to different material realities. Although capitalist practice is justified in the name of the total public societal good so as to conceal the privatized appropriation of the socially produced surplus, the conditions under which this very surplus is produced and distributed differ between the liberal and corporate phases of capitalist development. In the analysis below of fragments of corporate ideology of the dominant fraction of the capitalist class, we examine the way in which ideology emerges in practice and at the same time directs and justifies practice in the name of community, noting that while this general feature of ideology characterizes the different phases of capitalism, it relates to different material realities. Indeed, now that which seeks justification is less the liberal market and individual competition and more the concentration of capital; less the state as regulator of contracts and more the state as regulator of wealth. We point out as well that the cooperative norms which accompany these major developments in advanced capitalism facilitate the appeal to universality.

The justification of material developments in capitalism in the name of community, although shared by all classes, would, we argue, prevail among the dominant fraction of the contemporary bourgeois class, that is, those in control of capital concentration in the form of national and multinational corporations. For the senior executive levels of large corporations constitute the centres of decision-making regarding the direction and scope of economic expansion. Such decisions touch the totality of social life. They determine type and degree of production including the means of production, both capital and labour. The type of goods and services produced set the parameters of consumption; they also lay down the specifications regarding the production technology which define the type and extent of work. These factors, in turn, provide the educational centres with directions for planning curricula with a view to preparing a smoother insertion of students into the job market. Decisions of how, when and where to expand are also decisions affecting total life styles.

These economic decisions of great political, cultural and social import are now made in collaboration with the state and organized labour. For advanced capitalism, requiring an active interventionary state, generates a highly integrated rapport between the various institutions. This, of course, cannot imply an equal partnership between corporate capital, the state, and labour in making decisions, for the setting is still one of private appropriation of socially-produced surplus. This involves labour remaining in the service of private capital even though it has achieved the politically sanctioned power to negotiate wages. (Indeed, it is this latter factor which gives the modern capital-labour relationship the semblance of equal partnership.) This tripartite association, which advanced capitalism requires, promotes the appearance of collective social action which in turn facilitates the appeal to universality by the dominant class. Thus, although we will not investigate it here, we would expect that cooperative categories of thought would pervade top governmental executive thinking and other levels of the state and, to a large extent, labour, whose pursuit of a more favourable division of the surplus between itself and private capital attests to the prevalence of a false consciousness.

5. Illustrations of Dominant Ideology

In our closer look at dominant ideology in advanced capitalism, we limit our observations to written texts from senior executives of large capitalist corporations as expressions of ideology. The texts are largely in the form of speeches delivered before professional associations, such as the various Chambers of Commerce, Manufacturers' Associations, Insurance Associations, Boards of Trade, Societies of Financial Analysts, etc.; service organizations, for example the various Lions and Rotary Clubs; and the annual meetings of shareholders. These statements are often printed as an introduction to the annual reports of corporations. Some texts are in the form of briefs to the Royal Commission on

Corporate Concentration or as communiqués to the mass media. This material is backed up by individual interviews the author conducted with a half-dozen senior executives. While the written data are public statements, the interviews were conducted in confidence. Consequently, the former will be quoted explicitly, and authorship attributed, but not the latter.[19]

Our analysis of these statements will link the three developments of advanced capitalism, that is, capital concentration, state intervention in the economy, and science-technology as an important force of production, to the cooperative relationship between corporations, corporation and the state, and corporation and technically-skilled labour respectively. At the same time we will focus on key themes of liberal and neo-liberal ideology to demonstrate the way in which individualist competitive basis of interaction is increasingly giving way to cooperation in reflecting the developments of advanced capitalism. An integral part of the perceptions and understandings of these themes is the justifications of these developments, grounded on the principle of common social good.

The question arises as to what extent the evidence to be presented here, drawn from contemporary Canadian sources, bears on the development of neo-liberal ideology as we have sketched it. Indeed, to what extent does the development of capitalism in Canada exemplify a passage from primitive to liberal and to corporate capitalism? Although present Canadian reality bears the principal features of advanced capitalism, namely capital concentration, intensified state intervention in the economy, science-technology as an important force of production, all of which emerged as a system rather clearly after the Second World War, Canada's history of economic and political dependence dictated against a development that showed each of the three successive phases of capital accumulation. The absence of a pure phase of competitive-liberal capital accumulation is linked to Canada's colonial and neo-colonial history whose implications and consequences for the pattern of capital formation is the subject of an ongoing debate.[20] Clearly, the state, wherever its locus may have been at any particular time or on any particular issue, had an integral involvement in the economy – the regulation of

115

commerce, the integration of a trans-continental economy, capital formation. Thus, at no time did capitalist development in Canada correspond to a pure competitive model of political economy in which a free market is the regulator of capital expansion. The period from the mid-nineteenth to the early twentieth century was marked by considerable capital concentration in some sectors and by state assistance including tariff protection. In this period, the pattern of competitive economic interaction typifying more clearly classical-liberal economic formations was in part absent, though, of course, not entirely. Nevertheless, competitive norms underlay much of the ideology of the period, even if this seems somewhat incongruent with practice. Bliss's analysis of businessmen's thought in the period 1883-1911 concludes that "the rhetoric of individualism in business was supplemented in practice by very considerable collectivism to minimize the impact of competition"[21] and that "[w]hen they talked about success in business, or anything else in life, businessmen were deeply individualist. They held each man personally responsible for any success or failure in life . . ."[22] The gap between individualist theory and collectivist practice was bridged by the expedient of justifying noncompetitive economic interaction in terms of competitive principles. The Retail Merchants Association argued in 1888: "Far better to permit and even encourage the regulation of competition than to foster an end to competition by making sane regulations illegal."[23] As documented by Goodwin, even the Canadian protectionists of the latter part of the nineteenth century acknowledged the theoretical primacy of free trade in the international market, and justified their position in terms of the special circumstances of an embryonic Canadian economy: "All respectable politicians before Confederation (many of whom were at the same time big businessmen) professed at least grudging approval of free trade . . . ."[24] A parliamentary committee in Nova Scotia sharing the views of the protectionist businessmen held in 1883 that "we are not in any manner reduced to the necessity of maintaining the position that perfect freedom of trade is not, in a politico-economical sense, sound in principle. Without in any manner offending the most fastidious advocates of free trade, we can, nevertheless . . . demand for our manufacturers . . . the same encour-

agement and protection of the home market as is awarded to their competitors."[25] It was argued just after Confederation that "[a]s respects free trade in the abstract, few of us will differ. We all like free trade, as we do sunshine and good roads; but sunshine and good roads are not always to be had, and if I should venture to use an umbrella to protect me in a storm, I trust that the man of one idea will not suppose that I am prejudiced against a bright sky, or that I consider that the acme of human happiness consists in going through life with an umbrella over my head. It is a temporary expedient only to escape the effect of a temporary inconvenience."[26]

One can make a case that the dominant ideology of mid-late nineteenth and early twentieth century Canadian capitalism, inherited from predominantly individualist classical European economic thought, served to justify a combined competitive and cooperative practice marked by combines, producers' guilds, state support in various forms. Even in today's advanced capitalist ideology in which cooperative norms prevail there remains distinctly classical liberal themes. This may, on the surface, suggest little change in the ideology from a century ago. The present cooperative norms, however, derive from the particular features of advanced capitalism while the competitive norms relate to the persisting but much weakened competitive sector of modern economy and serve to uphold a continuity in capitalist rationality. To the extent that the monopoly sector predominates and controls, it may be argued that not only a shift of emphasis has occurred in ideology in the balance between individualism and cooperatism, but that today's cooperatism is a product of advanced capitalism as distinct from the cooperatism of a century ago.

In any case our principal aim here is not to trace the development of capitalism in Canada but to compare principal trends in the ideology of two phases of capital accumulation, focussing on the present phase of capital concentration for which Canadian sources are appropriate and convenient, and using the generally well-known model of the theory of competitive capitalism as the implicit and explicit point of comparison. In spite of the fact that any given capital formation corresponds to the theory of classical capitalism more or less (and certainly the Canadian experience deviates considerably in practice),

116

this use of an ideal type as a benchmark serves to highlight contemporary trends in practice and ideology.

(A) Relationship Between Corporations and the Changing Classical Liberal Principles of Interaction

The competitive interaction between independent commodity producers has receded with the decline of the autonomous entrepreneur. What emerges is a combined cooperative and competitive interaction between corporations. Today the process of continued capital accumulation requires a rationality uniting individuals in collaborative concerns in addition to the independent competitive ventures. Increasing cooperation is exemplified by tendencies towards the centralization of capital, in the form of mergers, consortiums, cartels, takeovers, inter-corporation stock holdings and so forth. The rationality of continued capital expansion dictates a pooling of resources even though resistance to some takeovers may suggest an element of competition.

The cooperation which underlies these forms of capital concentration recurs in price-fixing. Prices of products arrived at by market forces in liberal capitalism are now set by agreements between apparently competitive corporations. The price of the labour-power commodity escapes competitive market forces as well, and is replaced, as we discuss below (sec. 5[c]), by the institution of collective bargaining as cooperative interaction between capital and labour.

The cooperative norms as a basis of interaction between corporation and corporation is highlighted in the following: "My competitors and I are not at each other's throats, so to speak . . . I am in constant communication with my counterparts in other corporations. We must keep an open line and cooperate to do the best we can for everybody."[27]

(i) Profit

In this context, the significance of profit, as the return on an investment whereby the individual is rewarded for his activity, is changing. Profit in classical capitalism was conceived as the tangible reward of the individual's unobstructed drive in the appropriation of nature. It was the visible means of the process of appropriation by which the indi-

vidual achieved pleasure and happiness and indirectly contributed to the common good. Profit in contemporary monopoly capitalism is losing its manifestly individualistic character. An insurance executive describes the basis of his enterprise as being a particularly cooperative collective venture: "Life insurance is not fundamentally a profit-making business itself. At its heart, life insurance is a cooperative, voluntary pooling arrangement through which 12 million Canadians share some of the financial risks of life."[28] Profit is conceived less as an instrument of individual private appropriation and more as having a public social function of serving wants. It is equated with salary or wages but whereas the salary as remuneration for work serves the individual, profit now is portrayed as serving the collectivity as reinvestments in the expansionary programmes of economic growth and development: "Profits are involved in satisfying a want. The want can be for a refrigerator, a toaster, a trip on an aircraft. . . . For these wants to be satisfied, it's always necessary that somebody puts up some money. The wages of that money is profit, and it's just as important and just as essential as the wages you pay to the people who work in the factory, fly the airplanes, serve in hotels.[29] "Profit is a measure of work well done, work that is in the interest of other people."[30]

The periodic phases of capital devaluation are transformed into permanent inflationary spirals as a means of attenuating the critical recessions of the business cycle and generally moderating business fluctuations. The beneficiary of this "solution" is monopoly capital which is also the generator of the inflation problem. It conceals this, however, by invoking norms of cooperation and appealing to the whole community to join in a common front to restrain demands and thus keep prices down. In this context, a low profile is kept on profits and when these are mentioned, they are justified as a means permitting reinvestment in maintenance and expansion programmes of communal benefit.

(ii) The Emergence of Planning and the Decline of the Market

Planning is increasingly replacing the market as regulator of the economic system. Indeed, planning is the modus operandi of monopoly capitalism and lends itself particularly well to the justification of corporate concentration in terms of universalistic values of communal well-being. Planning has indivisible but distinguishable means and ends aspects, the former relating to norms of interaction employed in the achievement of the goal, the ends. Planning involves by its very nature coordination, collaboration, cooperation, and consultation as norms of interaction. The singular objective in capitalist planning is the private appropriation of surplus value in capital expansion, where the principle of calculation is exchange value. The rationality of this objective contains the built-in contradiction between exchange value and use value. Planning with such an objective is based on what Habermas refers to as the capitalist organizational principle of "unplanned nature-like growth"[31] which generates crises of near-exhaustion of natural resources and environmental pollution.

In the ideology, both the means and objective planning are disguised. The constraining, repressive character of the coordination dictated by a capital expansion calculus is concealed by translating the collaboration in planning as universal cooperation towards a common goal of economic growth, the beneficiary of which is the whole community. Accordingly, the crises consequences of the objective of capital planning are interpreted as the consequences of community action and therefore of community responsibility. Somewhat paradoxically then, crises serve as a means of unification of opposing sectors of society in working for their solution, as exemplified by the intensified search by all for new energy resources. Increasingly the emerging world view is one in which the natural and social world are seen as a bundle of crises whose solution must be the preoccupation of each and all. Planning thus accomplishes two ideological functions: it unites disparate and objectively opposing classes behind the capitalist objective of private appropriation of surplus, by promoting it as a common objective contributing to the common good; it displaces the responsibility for any crisis from monopoly capital and diffuses it throughout the whole society by linking communal responsibility to communal action and emphasizing concerted efforts in the resolution of crises.

Inflation, for example, is depicted as a major problem resulting from community action and requiring community-wide cooperation to solve it:

All of us, in varying ways and to varying degrees, have played a part in the creation and nurturing of inflation. No one is blameless. . . . Business today is not just growth and profitability. It also demands ethical conduct, fair value for a fair price, enlightened employee relations, candour with the public and a host of other things which can be summed up by the word "accountability". . . . Government must use the appropriate tools of policy to create the conditions for economic health. There are those who have suggested that I believe government should not "interfere" in economic matters. Far from it. Every reasonable person recognizes the responsibility of governments to create conditions favourable to economic growth and to set the framework of law and regulation for individual and business activity.[32]

Capital charges the state with the function of creating and maintaining conditions for "economic health" at every stage of capital accumulation. As we argued above, however, the activities of the state in assuring conditions for capital expansion in the phase of classical capitalism involve what one scholar refers to as "minimal support,"[33] in contrast to the intensification of activity in some areas, or the penetration of others, in order to reduce the increasingly destructive effects of the economic cycle. The state's new activities as collective capitalist facilitates the diffusion of responsibility for economic and social problems such as inflation and unemployment to the whole society as a collective and singular unit.

(iii) Competition

Competition is another central category of classical capitalist practice and ideology. The superseding of basic elements in the material base involves, just as in the case of the market, a modification of its ideological meaning more in line with the changing context of capital formation. The significance attributed to competition now reflects and justifies the concentration of capital. The independent entreprenuer with his material resource base which constituted the foundation of classical capitalist competition is now replaced by the gigantic national and multinational corporation shifting the centre of gravity of competition from the level of individual interaction within the nation state to the level of multinational interaction of conglomerates on the global level. It is asserted, for example: "Without question, multinational corporations have accelerated the spread of technology around the world and there is more competition in many industries."[34] This shift of reference serves to justify the centralization of capital. For effective competition on the international level, it is argued that concentration and absence of competition is required on the national level, a factor which contributes to the societal well-being both national and international.

This emphasis on the international aspects of competition, however, is itself beginning to lose credibility with the emergence of international cartels. The nature and size of today's projects are seen as necessitating partnership and collaboration of many corporations in a common enterprise:

> In today's environment, it is rare that the sophisticated management, technology, raw materials, finance and markets required for a large project are available from the same corporate or even national source. As a result, international partnerships are becoming increasingly necessary to meet demands of these very large undertakings, involving as they do enormous capital outlays and complex technical and managerial skills and requiring advance commitments for both finance and the purchase of the output. . . . Nothing less than an absolute and unwavering commitment to the spirit of the partnership is likely to withstand the test to which such a relationship will be put over a period of time.[35]

The argument using size and complexity of modern projects is ideological in that the process of self-expanding capital, which is necessarily based on an exchange value calculus, is conveyed as being motivated by the value concerns. Accordingly, the above author refers to social demands for use value as being the basis of international partnerships concealing the fact that the exchange value rationality generates the very international consortiums themselves as a form of capital accumulation. Such a justification recurs, as we see below, in the collaboration of private-state capital ventures.

(iv) Concentration

Capital concentration as manifested in bigness is interpreted in the rhetoric as being essential for "winning and holding confidence" on the international level, once again concealing its basis in exchange value:

> We have been able to operate successfully in the international market because we are big and people have confidence in us. And that's important because external trade is a vital element of our economy. . . . If we are going to provide the kind of financial services that our exporters need, we have to stand shoulder to shoulder with other big banks who operate in international markets. And that means size and stability.[36]

In the classical capitalism of independent entrepreneurs, new ventures could weather an initial nonprofit period of moderate duration. The threat of bankruptcy was a factor in rejection and abandonment of such projects. With capital concentration, however, the corporation's capacity to withstand periods of non profit in comparable ventures is considerably extended. Furthermore, the threat of bankruptcy is largely eliminated in the modern context where the large corporation employs a network of mechanisms in controlling directions of development (and often receiving state subsidies in so doing). The corporation's capacity to expand in an isolated region or depressed area is considered to improve the well-being of all groups of society:

> The bank's size also brings benefits to Canadians. . . . Because of the wide-spread branch-banking system, the chartered banks are able to reach out to the public in every part of Canada . . . to meet a demand for banking services in new or remote areas where a branch may not be profitable for a few years . . . to provide mortgage financing on uniform terms in all areas of the country . . . and thus more money is made available to remote regions of the country than otherwise might be possible . . . most important of all, size gives us the ability to put large amounts of money into mortgage markets in response to government and public demands. . . . I don't think you'd get that kind of money from the combined efforts of a hundred

smaller banks each one-hundredth of the size.[37]

Using similar comparisons, capital concentration is further justified in terms of its response to economic crises. The smaller enterprise, in the face of a crisis, is incapable of coping and is likely to fold up. The large corporation, on the other hand, is able to "weather the blows" and remain in operation continuing to satisfy social wants while retaining employees. The ideology thus justifies continuing accumulation in terms of a capacity to overcome the very crises which monopoly capital generates. By emphasizing the qualities necessary to cope with crises, it discredits small enterprises, legitimizes large corporations and obscures the source of crises in the very process of continuing capital accumulation: "One of the reasons why even marginal copper mines are seldom closed by low prices is that they are increasingly operated by large companies or groups with financial ability to weather periods of low prices."[38]

The preservation of freedom is tied to the concentration of capital, the former justifying the latter. This is done by the intermediary of competition which has shifted focus from the level of individual interaction within the nation state to the level of multinational corporate interaction within the global framework. Just as a freedom principle was invoked to justify individual competition in classical liberalism, it is now invoked to justify multinational corporate competition and at the same time to justify the continuing concentration of capital which this involves. Thus the on-going process of capital expansion, involving increasing accumulation of capital and bringing the entire world within its sphere in an imperialist network, is interpreted in the ideology as the means which protects freedom. The contradiction between the material process and the ideological justification is evident: the more capital expands the more it stifles individual and cultural freedom by penetrating and controlling more of the geopolitical and social space, the very process which ideology portrays as one which preserves freedom: "The wealthy and socially responsible country enjoys a degree of freedom proportionate to its wealth . . . . If its wealth is diminished, so is its freedom of choice. Profits are the primary source, the basic source of freedom if you like, of future wealth."[39]

(v) The Social Role of the Corporation

The portrayal of the large corporation as a public service organism is a further justification of capital. The public image accorded to the executive and the corporation contrasts with that of the individual entrepreneur and his small-scale enterprise. Whereas in classical liberal ideology, the small entrepreneur and his business were regarded as necessary components of the competitive process of capital formation and hence as the means of achieving the common good, they are now depicted as engaging in an egotistical, privatistic and even shady pursuit of profit with a total disregard for the public good. The corporation executive and the enormous corporation he directs, on the other hand, are suited by virtue of the qualities they possess to promote the public interest. Their goal of long-term survival and growth are dependent on public support which in the ideology is a function of the corporation's capacity to promote the public good. This ideological relationship between the successful pursuit of corporation goals and the public good is less a coincidence of private and public interest and more a unity of interest, the corporation appearing as an organism of the communal good:

Corporations always eventually reject shysters, because business dealings can't work without co-operation and trust. When I sell you something, you trust me that the shipment I send you will match the sample, and that, when we shake hands on a deal, I'm going to stick by my word. In corporate business, that trustworthiness is essential. . . . Big business is under constant scrutiny. Nobody takes much notice of the fly-by-night operator who's here today and gone tomorrow and does a lot of damage. He's not as visible as big business is. Basically, big business is straightforward for another reason; it's under professional management. When the Royal Bank makes a gain, that's a little pat on the back for management, but it doesn't affect me personally, financially. But the fly-by-night entrepreneur puts every gain he makes into his pocket. Short term and long term factors come into it, too. The shady entrepreneur can afford to be interested only in immediate profit, because he can run to the next town. A big corporation can't run; it wants to stay in business for ten years,

120

twenty-five years, maybe forever. . . . Thus, while the basic goal of private enterprise is to survive and to earn optimum returns for the shareholders, this is really a consequence of the more fundamental corporate goal to serve society's needs.[40]

The continuing process of capital accumulation increasingly depends on generating social needs. The artificiality of an individual's needs today are well recognized by critical liberal economists[41] who correctly relate them to the pursuit of exchange value. In the dominant ideology, however, this process is distorted. The society is seen as determining production and the productive apparatus merely as responding to the already expressed, naturally emerging social needs, thereby attributing a servant role to the corporation as an instrument of communal well-being:

> Our long term interest whether it's in narrow terms, such as profitability, or broader terms such as survival, will not be served by knowingly financing things which are detrimental to the community. We depend on the health of our communities. If the community prospers, we prosper. . . . While the basic goal of private enterprise is to survive and to earn optimum returns for its shareholders, this is really a consequence of the more fundamental corporate goal to serve society's needs. Profit is a valid objective in this context, because it serves as an incentive to investment, as a measurement of performance and also because it is essential to long-term survival.[42]

(B) Relationship Between the Corporation and the State

(i) Norms of Cooperation

The relationship between the corporation and the state is based on norms of cooperation. This underlies the state concessions to monopoly capital for the exploitation of minerals and other natural resources. The joint private-public ventures into which the state enters with monopoly capital are generally motivated by the latter's need for additional capital assistance, which the state contributes directly and/or indirectly in its role of guarantor of additional loans on the international capital market. These joint ventures, depending on cooperative norms, pervade Western Europe, the Italian IRI and the French ELF-ERAP and Avions M. Dassault-Bréguet Aviation being prominent examples: and they are beginning to emerge in Canada as evidenced by the Canada Development Corporation and Syncrude. Joint state-monopoly capital advisory boards such as the National Energy Board of Canada constituted to advise the state on economic development exemplify, as well, the increasing pervasiveness of norms of cooperation.

Cooperation between the corporation and state is formulated in the ideology as being rooted in a harmony of societal interests. The opposing class interests of a capitalist society, based on the contradiction between capital and labour, are concealed in the ideology where the society is depicted as a unitary harmonious organism of interdependent parts engaged in the solution of common problems. The economic institution and the state are assigned the role of satisfying in collaborative, coordinate fashion, the common societal interest. Whereas the harmony of societal interests in liberal capitalism was a function of the competitively pursued individual interests, the harmony of interest now is portrayed as the unity of interests collectively pursued in universal cooperation:

> We need to spend more time and effort trying to understand what is going on and trying to reach a consensus on the direction we want our society to follow. And by definition, the reaching of consensus requires that the major segments of the society communicate effectively with one another . . . [;] business and government are key ones. . . . For both politician and businessman, the only acceptable basic purpose for today and tomorrow is to meet the needs of society. . . . Both government and business are institutions set up and maintained by society to fill needs and if a society's institutions don't seem to be doing this then sooner or later society will change them.[43]

> The key to that future requires the harmonization of the power of government and the capability of corporations. Each can reinforce the capacity of the other to serve the best interests of Canadians.[44]

This proposition of a harmony of total societal interest as a justification of the state-capital ventures and thereby of capital concentration, serves to conceal the privatistic basis of the continuing process of a capital accumulation by portraying it as a universal, public project of communal well-being: "The interests of Canada will be served if the power of government combines with the productive capability of industry . . . [;] government and business must work together in the interests of Canada and the consuming public."[45]

The joint ventures and the continuing concentration of capital are further justified in the ideology by the argument of complexity, cost and size of modern technological programmes. These features of modern projects such as the enormity of size of the Canadian Oil Sands Project are seen as requiring the collaboration of private industry and the state.[46] Often many banks are required to finance such a project and the state must enter its support as guarantor. It is argued that "we cannot afford futile bickering between various levels of government, nor mutual suspicion between business and government."[47] In the Bell Canada submission to the Royal Commission on Corporate Concentration it is reaffirmed that "Bell must share power with the regulator [state], customers, unions, investors and suppliers." A petroleum company spokesman said:

> The time is long overdue in this country to begin a non-partisan approach to our long-term needs for energy development, to rise above petty politics or regional parochialism. If Canadianism means anything to me, it means the ability to sit down and reason together in the determination that the overall national interest must prevail. . . . Confidence and trust must be established between both levels of government and between governments and the industry. We perhaps need a new forum to accomplish this—a fully participative energy council—wherein senior representatives from industry and the federal and provincial governments can exchange ideas and develop ideas for the best long-term interests of Canadians.[48]

This depiction of the state-corporation relationship is a collaborative, balanced partnership in pursuit of the communal interest conceals the corporation's employing the state in the promotion of the private interest of accelerated accumulation of capital. For example, an appeal to the state to encourage mergers between corporations where the corporations deem it desirable as a rational measure in the process of continuing capital accumulation, is justified on the grounds of promoting efficiency, eliminating social waste and thus contributing to the communal good. Holding the Japanese model as an example to follow, state-encouraged mergers are justified in these terms:

> The Japanese were not content to accept what was happening to their economy. When they acted, they acted powerfully and in unison. The national concern for survival resulted in consensus not confrontation. The Japanese planner not only proposed economic remedies. . . . Accelerated by the oil crisis, the Japanese are deliberately letting oil prices force closure of the weaker, less efficient [companies]. The Japanese government is encouraging merger of the weaker companies with the stronger and providing incentives to the acquiring companies. They are adapting to change while the Canadians opt for a temporary status quo.[49]

(ii) The State and the Market

The interventionary role of the state in the economy involves an enormous flexibility in that in attempting to avert crises of business cycles, it shifts the focus and, to a lesser extent, intensity of state economic activity from periods of recession to periods of economic expansion. What appears below as an apparent contradiction in the ideology between the justification of an active state at certain times and a less active state at others, can be understood in terms of the imperatives of the process of capital accumulation. In calling for the state's retreat from some of its economic activity, business leaders invoke principles of classical liberal ideology that persist in modified form in the neo-liberal ideology, such as competition and market. This is done by appealing to the re-establishment and maintenance of a balance between the state and the market. The "balance" device serves as a confirmation that the market is still in operation as a regulator of wealth and as a justification as well as a check on an interventionist state. Thus, the market mechanism is involved in instances of delimiting and separating and balancing the areas of activity of the state with those of the private sector of the economy. The appeal to the market is made to moderate the growth of the state and to maintain a balanced partnership rather than a partnership of subordination-superordination between state and economy:

> Social priorities are appropriately defined through the votes of our democratic government. But economic priorities are appropriately defined through the anonymous votes of the market-place. Mingling the two processes tends to distort the functioning of our markets, and eventually even the functioning of government itself.[50]

The balance mechanism delineates the healthy relationship between the economy and state. An imbalance is a prelude to danger or an expression of mature crises: "If government plays too large a role, the system itself cannot function properly, and we cannot beat inflation. A halt must be called to the growth of government."[51] Too much state regulation in the economy is criticized: "The overregulation or the regulation behind closed doors of the railways and the communications common carriers are recent examples of this phenomenon which prevents these industries from discharging their normal service obligations."[52] The proper interventionary role of the state is described in the following way:

> . . . there are good and valid reasons which explain, at least in part, the rapid growth of government. These include the increasing complexity of our society and the resulting needs for government services (e.g. urbanization). Increasing levels of affluence as well as changing social mores lead to the decision that we can afford expanded government services (e.g. education, income maintenance). . . . Government should obviously do the things required in the common interest. The provision of common services—roads, schools, hospitals, water—are all within the orbit of government, as is obviously the field of income redistribution, and the standard tools of fiscal and monetary policy.[53]

In addition, "We recognize the advantages of regulation where the intent is consistent with

the maintenance of growth, regulations which set the rules without restraining play."[54] It is suggested:

> We could reduce pressures on government and allow the market mechanism greater freedom and a larger role in achieving the goals of our society. This would not mean a return to a completely free market environment, but a conscious re-enforcement of beneficial market forces together with an insistence upon the affordability of any proposed social programme before it is implemented.[55]

The principle of balance between the market and the state, which parallels the private-public balance, contains as mentioned a built-in flexibility able to represent the swing of state activity between periods of expansion and periods of recession. The call for retreat or withdrawal of the state from some of its activity in the regulation of the economy is made in terms of a freedom principle which echoes the classical liberal rational for a passive state. The interventionary wage and price control policy of the Canadian government, for example, is justified as a means of re-establishing economic stability, but should be withdrawn upon resolution of the economic problems of inflation, in order to protect freedom:

> What, then, should government do in addressing the combined problem of inflation and unemployment? First, it should ensure that the present anti-inflation programme works well, so that its effect is positive, and its duration short. The longer such detailed controls remain in effect, the more we run serious risks of damming up pressures which will burst forth later. Moreover, the longer such detailed intervention continues, the more serious are the dangers to our freedoms and institutions.[56]

(C) Relationship Between Corporation and Labour

Science-technology as an important force of production and its consequences on the level of ideology in the promotion of universalistic values can be examined in terms of (i) the context of the cooperative relationship between the corporation and labour and particularly technically skilled, reflexive labour, and (ii) the objectivist rationality of science.

(i) The Labour Market, Labour Interests and Technology

The competitive dynamics of the labour market of liberal capitalism have been largely replaced by the institution of politically mediated collective agreement in the monopoly sector and the state sector. Competition within the labour force has shifted from the market to the school, which provides the skills and necessary technical qualifications for entry into the labour market. Thus the kind of job the worker will find and the wages he will receive depend less on the kind of work he is willing to do and the amount he is willing to sell his labour-power for and more on the availability of an opening and on his skill credentials to fill it. The availability of a job is determined not by competitive market forces but by planning within the monopoly and state sectors. The wages tied to a job are set by capital-labour agreements. Thus the state, which provides near-universal training and education, a need generated by the imperative of continually increasing productivity for accelerated capital accumulation, mediates the process of selling and buying of labour-power.[57] Wage scales are set by the politically-mediated institution of collective bargaining, exemplifying the pervasiveness of cooperative norms in the relations of production. As pointed out above, with the increasing productivity the relatively constant division of surplus wields a bigger share for both labour and capital. Thus, what appears as a harmony of interests between labour and capital is translated as universal interest.

Ideological themes of cooperation and of participation in a collective venture are bolstered by the institution of stock holding and its diffusion throughout society. Common stock, representing relatively small units of capital, universalizes ownership across the labour force and bourgeois class. In the rationality of capital accumulation, it is an indispensible mechanism for assembling and concentrating capital but it is interpreted in the rhetoric as evidence of the disappearance of both the class of owners of the means of production and the class of propertyless workers and of their replacement by one universal community in which the human individual can find fulfillment.

Cooperation forms the basis of the tripartite organisms of capital-labour-state for defining an economic policy of expansion. In Canada this is manifested in recurring economic summits which aim at achieving cooperation for self-imposed restraints.

Cooperation as a basis of interaction is interpenetrating structures of advanced capitalism of which the above are notable examples in uniting capital and labour. According to the ideology this cooperation is founded on identity of interests of labour and capital:

> In the area of industrial relations, there must be a recognition that the age of confrontation must be replaced by the age of cooperation based on a better understanding of the economic facts that are basic to the common interest of management and employees. . . . There must be a reappraisal of the collective bargaining process which seriously looks for modifications and new approaches to achieving the goals of all members of society. I am not suggesting we discard the process but it must be updated to meet the new and additional requirements. . . [;] business leaders and others meet to consider addressing themselves to the question of broader work values as concomitant of a climate of cooperation.[58]

This unity of interest is echoed by the proposition that "without profit, capital is destroyed and jobs are lost."[59] The ideological proposition of identity of interests between capital and labour recurs on the more general level of capital and society. This is done by attributing to capital the unique capacity to "produce wealth," hence generating economic expansion of benefit to the whole society: "What the private sector can do is marshall economic resources into productive investment to increase the size of the economic pie available to everyone."[60]

Much of capitalist activity is portrayed as a universal participatory method of uniting people to help themselves collectively:

> Life insurance industry has 12 million policy-owners in Canada. The earnings on the life companies' investments keep the cost of insurance down for these policy-owners, and to the extent that a good proportion of those investments are in profit-making corporations, every policy-owner has a very personal stake in the continued profitability of those corporations. What about participants in pension plans, owners of mutual funds, owners of savings

in banks and companies? All of those people have a very real financial interest in the profitability of corporations in which they are investing directly through intermediaries.[61]

Cooperation between labour and capital is reinforced while capital concentration in the form of large corporations is justified by the depiction of the corporation in the ideology as the means of providing avenues for work expression and creativity. The instrumental basis of the relationship between capital and worker, capital utilizing the labour-power of the worker as means of extracting surplus value is reversed in the ideology so that the corporation becomes the instrument, the servant of the worker, providing the condition for human development and fulfillment:

Large size creates opportunities for people. Not only are employees' needs met in the areas of working conditions, safety and benefits, but, more importantly, in the variety of career opportunities within the business. . . . Bell is responsive to needs for the communities it serves and supports programmes that help to improve the quality of community life.[62]

In this context, norms promoting productivity such as efficiency are emerging and interpreted in the ideology as the means of communal well-being. Assuring productivity involves capital centralization and not duplication, the former being based on norms of cooperation, the latter on competition. The well-being of consumers composing virtually the entire society is linked to the concentration of capital in the sole form of the large corporation able, in cooperation with skilled labour, to assure high productivity. It is the efficiency of the large corporation unit, through technically skilled labour, which is able to maintain low prices, rather than market competition involving the elimination of inefficient producers:

The presence in Canada of petroleum corporations that are large, well managed and staffed, highly-specialized and skilled, technologically-oriented and vertically and horizontally integrated is to benefit to consumers. . . . It results in improved service and improved quality of product and, as a consequence of efficiency and a high level of productivity, low product unit-cost.[63]

Also,

Domtar believes it makes a significant contribution to social as well as economic progress in its pursuit of the general objectives of constantly improving efficiency in every aspect of its operations, of maximum utilization over the long term of the capital, human and technological resources available to it.[64]

The generally recognized indispensibility of science-technology as a means of increasing the universal material standard of living is further distorted in the ideology in being portrayed as dependent on capital concentration. Indeed, as we have illustrated in section 5.(A)(iii) above, it is argued that the demands of the changed and evolving technology of many modern projects on a national and increasingly on an international level require great concentration of capital, thereby justifying the process of capital concentration:

Larger projects may be sponsored by several corporations which establish a separate project entity of such magnitude that it could not be initiated by one company or financed by one institution. Some developments being considered today are so large and so complex, with world-wide ramifications, that the traditional methods of financing are no longer adequate. The development of the Canadian oil sands is a recent example.[65]

By claiming an interdependence of science-technology and capital concentration, the ideology defends and justifies mergers, interpreting them as efficiency-promoting ventures. For example, an increase in merger ventures is called for in the following statement and the state is asked to promote rather than oppose them:

One of our Canadian problems is that excessive fragmentation of some of our manufacturing industries does not permit research and development to be justified at an effective level, and sometimes not at all. Current anti-combines legislation is based on the principle that the public is best served by a large number of competitors in each of the various industries. Government policy rather should encourage rationalization of industry so that producers can

125

achieve economies of scale needed for effective research and development and for costs competitive with global conditions.[66]

The mutual reinforcement of technology and capital concentration is illustrated in the claim that technological research and development is dependent on the rationality of capital expansion:

> Research has no validity per se unless it is part of some broader corporate or national purpose. No company is going to conduct research and development unless there is some commercial justification for the results. You cannot push research from behind if there is no justification for it at the front end. Research and development does not create a purpose, it responds to it. The best way to stimulate research is to create a need for it by stimulating a healthy environment for capital investment.[67]

(ii) The Ideological Rationality of Science-Technology

Scientific rationality, based on a fact-value separation, is attributed a neutral quality in the rhetoric, both in its logic and in its application to the productive process. Science-technology can thus be promoted as having a collectivist character. It is portrayed as being, by its very nature, in the service of all, its fruits being reaped by the total society. It is argued: "The benefit of corporation expansion of knowledge, of efficiency, of knowing how, flow to the people, directly or indirectly."[68] Scientific rationality is regarded as capable of solving any problem relating to the control of nature. It provides the key to overcoming all obstacles in man's way of appropriating nature for his use: "Our biggest struggles today are not technical: they are not with the elements, impossible terrain and geological formations. We have proved we can overcome these problems."[69]

The control-of-nature scientific rationality, however, is invoked as well for its identical applicability in the social domain. Its claimed capacity to provide correct solutions to social problems such as inflation, coupled with its objectivist posture, apparently maintaining a value-free, neutral position vis-à-vis any particular social group, serve an important ideological function. This rationality conceals the source of social problems such as inflation in the process of private appropriation of surplus, by implicitly depicting the social relations of production as nature-like, following the same logic as physical nature: "One day soon, we'll have developed our scientific knowledge to such an extent that we will be able to solve such nasty problems as inflation. And, of course, we'll all profit from that.[70]

6. Conclusion

The emerging cooperative norms which appear increasingly to pervade the structure of social interaction of advanced capitalism, accompany and strengthen the new material conditions, namely concentration of capital, state intervention in the economy and science-technology as a new force of production. The cooperative basis of social interaction underlies, as noted, such structures as consortiums, cartels, mergers, private-public ventures, joint advisory boards, collective bargaining and tripartite negotiations. This is replacing the competitive basis of interaction compatible with an earlier phase of capital formation but which in the reality of advanced capitalism is increasingly irrelevant.

The development of cooperative interaction on the level of material practice has important consequences on the level of ideology. The perpetration of claims to universality by the neo-liberal ideology is facilitated precisely because cooperation, universal participation and collaboration are categories which can be more easily promoted as related to the common good than the classical liberal structures of competitive individualism. This is so in that the link between these structures of action and the communal good is direct whereas in the conditions of classical capitalism the action/communal good link was mediated by the individual. The ideological portrayal of cooperation as a collective pursuit of the communal good more effectively conceals the particularistic nature of this mode of production in which the privatism of a divided man lies in the private appropriation of socially produced surplus, and drives the universality claims deeper into false consciousness. The universality claim thus appears to be satisfied in the material conditions which bring together the whole society in a programme of economic expansion which in turn yields fruits for the total society.

This ideology-practice dialectic of advanced capitalism has an important consequence for political practice. The class struggle is being fought almost solely within the institution of collective bargaining which, however, is based on a mutual recognition and reciprocal acceptance of a conflict of interest resolvable to the mutual satisfaction of both parties. Bound to this institution of collective bargaining, the working class defines its interests as the pursuit and acquisition of a greater share of the surplus and also better working conditions–a factor which, at least in the short run, makes for the institutionalization of the working class as working class and for the deflation of its revolutionary potential. That these interests so defined are reconcilable with the interests of the bourgeois class accounts in part for "the surprising vigor of an aged capitalism."[71] The interests of the working class and of the human community ultimately lie in the negation of the social relations in which one class serves as the instrument for the production of surplus value appropriated by another class. Action in this direction must involve the rejection of the cooperation in contemporary capitalist practice and ideology.

Canadian Journal of Political Science, XI:4 (December, 1978). *Author's note:* I am grateful to Léonard Beaulne for his assistance in the research phase of this study and to Professor Jayant Lele for his critical reading of previous drafts of this paper. Funds for the research of this study were provided by the Faculty of Social Sciences, University of Ottawa.

NOTES

[1]Following roughly James O'Connor's classification of modern capitalist state functions in the *Fiscal Crisis of the State* (New York: St. Martin's Press, 1973). Although this distinction is useful to emphasize the predominantly economic nature of the accumulation functions, we emphasize that all state activities aim ultimately at legitimizing the capitalist institutional order, that is, the private appropriation of socially-produced surplus. In this sense, then, all state functions are legitimation functions.

[2]Jürgen Habermas, *Legitimation Crisis* (Boston: Beacon Press, 1975). This position is opposed by a number of Marxists. See, for example, W. Müller and Neusüss, "The Illusion of State Socialism," *Telos* 25 (1975), 13-90; E. Altvater, "Notes on Some Problems of State Intervention," *Kapitalstate* 1 (1973), 96-108 and 2 (1973), 76-83.

[3]In particular its economic structure reflects heavy corporate concentration of production such that oligopoly dominance prevails in some major industries and monopoly in others. The 3,924 mining corporations operating in Canada range in asset size from under $150,000 to over $100,000,000. One per cent of these have 60.2 per cent of the total assets ($20,502,700,000) and 68.9 per cent of the profits after tax ($1,484,200,000). This pattern of concentration also appears in the manufacturing industry where in the same asset size range, the total of 24,218 corporations assume a distribution such that 14,187 or 58 per cent of corporations have total assets of a mere $1,203,000 but 98 or 0.4 per cent of the total number of corporations command 47.4 per cent of the total assets ($20,502,700,000) and 68.9 per cent of the profits after tax ($1,484,200,000). This pattern of concentration also appears in the manufacturing corporations, 9 or 2 per cent have 81.9 per cent of the assets and 68.5 per cent of the profits after tax and 239 corporations constituting 53.6 per cent of the total have 0.5 per cent of the assets and 5.2 per cent of the profits after tax. In the total nonfinancial industries of the 137,074 corporations, 76.2 per cent have 5.5 per cent of the total profits after tax whereas 0.1 per cent of the corporations have 49.2 per cent of the assets and 42.5 per cent of the profits after tax. These are statistics for 1973 from Statistics Canada, Business Finance Division.

[4]Recent statistics reveal that the total assets held by foreign- controlled corporations in nonfinancial industries is 34 per cent and their share of total taxable income is 46 per cent. (*Annual Report of the Minister of Trade and Commerce under the Corporations and Labour Unions Act*, Part 1, 1973, 16-21.)

[5]Farm implements, aluminum industries and finance capital may be cited as the most notable examples. Massey-Ferguson and Alcan figure among the top segment of the 300 largest non-American multinational corporations. ("The 300 Largest Industrials Outside the U.S." *Fortune Magazine* (1972), 155-59.)

[6]Some argue that the Canadian bourgeois class is dependent and subordinated to foreign capitalists not only economically but politically and culturally as well. Prominent among these are Gary Teeple in *Capitalism and the National Question in Canada* (Toronto: University of Toronto Press, 1972); James and Robert Laxer in *Canada Ltd.* (Toronto: McClelland and Stewart Limited, 1973); Kari Levitt in *Silent Surrender, The Multinational Corporation in Canada* (Toronto: Macmillan Company of Canada Ltd., 1970), and others. There are those who emphasize as well the fact of Canadian- owned multinationals and argue that Canada's bourgeois class is an imperialist one in successful pursuit of capital expansion wherever it can be achieved. Its command of a significant economic base situates it in an independent position, indeed, a controlling one in such industries as farm implements and aluminum in a number of countries. This group recognizes Canadian dependence but projects an increasingly imperialist future. See, for example,

Steve Moore and Debi Wells, *Imperialism and the National Question in Canada* (Toronto: S. Moore, 1975).

[7]Karl Marx and Frederick Engels, *The German Ideology* (New York: International Publishers, 1947), 41.

[8]Ibid., *The Holy Family* (Moscow: Progress Publishers, 1975), 131-40. This is also discussed in S. Avineri, *The Social and Political Thought of Karl Marx* (Cambridge: Cambridge University Press, 1968), 41-64.

[9]Harold Laski, *The Rise of European Liberalism* (London: Ruskin House, 1936); André Vachet, *L'idéologie libérale* (Paris: Editions Anthropos, 1970).

[10]Herbert Marcuse, "The Struggle Against Liberalism in the Totalitarian View of the State" in *Negations: Essays in Critical Theory*, trans. by Jeremy Shapiro (Boston: Beacon Press, 1968), 21.

[11]See, for example, Tom Naylor, *The History of Canadian Business 1867-1914*, Vols. I and II (Toronto: James Lorimer & Company, 1975).

[12]This interpretation of the modern capitalist state does not, of course, discount the dialectics of the class struggle in winning these benefits for the working class including the chronically unemployable. It emphasizes rather, that while the welfare programmes constitute economic relief, they assist in the regulation of the crisis-generating capitalist economy and thus, paradoxically, partly serve to reinforce capitalism.

[13]The activity of the Canadian state exemplifies this pattern. The federal budgetary estimates for the fiscal year ending March 31, 1976 shows $2,080,200,000 or 7.4 per cent of the allocated budget allotted to transportation and communications. The total estimate for health and welfare including infrastructural programmes is $7,835,900,000 or 27.8 per cent of the budget. Education assistance plus culture and recreation total 4.8 per cent or $1,362,900,000. (*Estimates, 1975-76,* Government of Canada.) In the Canadian federal system where education is an area of provincial jurisdiction, however, this figure is only partial. Ontario allotted 26.7 per cent of the total budget to education and 39 per cent to health and welfare. The corresponding figures for Quebec are 25 and 31 per cent respectively. (*Provincial Government Finance,* Statistics Canada, cat. no. L68-007, T.2, 1973.)

[14]Indeed, a major argument of ideologues of advanced capitalism is that economic expansion and growth are of benefit to the total society including the traditional working class or proletariat. It is this which deflates the revolutionary consciousness and precludes the class struggle foreseen by Marx, according to such prominent ideologues as Daniel Bell, Robert Dahl, Ralf Dahrendorf and others. (Daniel Bell, *The Coming of Post-Industrial Society* [New York: Basic Books, 1973]; Robert Dahl, *After the Revolution?* [New Haven: Yale University Press, 1970]; Ralf Dahrendorf, *Class and Class Struggle in Industrial Society* [Stanford: Stanford University Press, 1959].)

[15]The pervasiveness of this conception of knowledge both in the natural and social sciences is analyzed by Habermas, who points to consequent repression in the social realm where the unity of science principle and the assumptions of control of reality, both physical and social, permeates the whole scientific endeavour. (Jürgen Habermas, *Knowledge and Human Interests* [Boston: Beacon Press, 1971].)

[16]Habermas, "Technology and Science as 'Ideology,' " in his *Toward a Rational Society* (Boston: Beacon Press, 1970), 81-122.

[17]Philippe C. Schmitter, "Still the Century of Corporatism," *The Review of Politics* 36 (1974), 97.

[18]This development is but a tendency in Canada. In other more advanced capitalist societies a higher degree of corporatism can be determined.

[19]These texts are public statements of directors of some 200 largest corporations operating in Canada and representing the major corporate sectors of the Canadian economy namely the manufacturing industry, finance, insurance and real estate, transportation, communication, mining. The list of these corporations appears in the *Canadian Business Magazine* 48 (July 1975), 11-17. The classification of these economic sectors follows the *Standard Industrial Classification Manual* (Ottawa: Dominion Bureau of Statistics, 1970), and conforms with that used in *Concentration in the Manufacturing Industries of Canada* (Ottawa: Department of Consumer and Corporate Affairs, 1970), in which the extent of concentration is indicated. Although all texts received (80 per cent response which includes all corporations with assets over $100 million) and all interviews were carefully reviewed, the actual citations included in this paper were selected to assure the following: (1) that the executive of the biggest corporations in each of the above sectors of the corporate economy be represented, (b) that in cases of repetition of substance, directors of the larger or largest corporations be chosen so as to restrain the length of this paper. Every effort was made to ensure that selected quotations were characteristic of the larger texts from which they were drawn. All citations were quoted in context to prevent misinterpretation and ambiguity.

[20]Some of these issues surrounding the historical process of capital formation in Canada are raised by Tom Naylor in *The History of Canadian Business 1867-1914,* and critically discussed by Stanley Ryerson in "Who's Looking After Business," *This Magazine* 10 (December 1976) to which Naylor replies ("The Last Word," *This Magazine* 11 (May-June 1977). See also the Rosenblum-Naylor exchange in *Our Generation* 11 (1975-1976), 5-24.

[21]Michael Bliss, *A Living Profit, Studies in the Social History of Canadian Business, 1883-1911* (Toronto: McClelland and Stewart Limited, 1974), 134.

[22]Ibid., 183.

[23]Documented in ibid., 50.

[24]Craufurd D.W. Goodwin, *Canadian Economic Thought* (Durham: Duke University Press, 1961), 50.

[25]Documented in ibid., 55.

[26]Argued by R.G. Haliburton, lawyer and businessman, documented in ibid., 46.

[27]Confidential interview, April 1976.

[28]W.J.D. Lewis, Chairman, Canadian Life Insurance Association, President, Prudential Insurance Company of America, addressing the Rotary Club of Vancouver, April 1976.

[29]Ian Sinclair, Chairman, Canadian Pacific, in *A Case for the Enterprise System* (n.p.: n.p., September 1975).

[30]W.J.D. Lewis, addressing the Vancouver Rotary Club.

[31]Habermas, *Legitimation Crisis*, 42.

[32]Earle McLaughlin, Chairman and President, Royal Bank of Canada, addressing the Canadian Club of Montreal, March 1976.

[33]C.B. Macpherson, "Do We Need a Theory of State?" *Archives européennes de Sociologie* 18 (1977), 233-44.

[34]Albert A. Thornbrough, President, Massey-Ferguson, addressing the Seventeenth Annual Business Conference, University of Western Ontario, June 1973.

[35]William Mulholland, President, Bank of Montreal, addressing the Institute of Chartered Accountants of Ontario, October 1975.

[36]Earle McLaughlin, addressing the Vancouver Board of Trade, October 1975.

[37]Ibid.

[38]H. Ronald Fraser, Chairman, Hudson Bay Mining and Smelting Co. Ltd., addressing the Copper Forum, October 1975.

[39]D.K. McIvor, Vice-President, Imperial Oil, addressing the Empire Club of Canada, February 1976.

[40]Earle McLaughlin in *A Case for the Enterprise System*.

[41]Notably, John Kenneth Galbraith, *The Affluent Society* (New York: Mentor Books, 1970); *The New Industrial State* (Cambridge: Houghton Mifflin, 1967); *Economics and the Public Purpose* (Boston: Houghton Mifflin, 1972).

[42]Earle McLaughlin, in *A Case for the Enterprise System*.

[43]R.C. Frazee, Vice-President, Royal Bank of Canada, addressing the Canadian Association of Sickness Insurers, June 1973.

[44]William Daniel, President, Shell Canada Ltd., addressing the Canadian Club of Vancouver, December 1975.

[45]William Daniel, addressing the Faculty of Management Studies, University of Toronto, November 1975.

[46]Article in *La Presse*, October 23, 1976, referring to a recent statement by W.D.H. Gardiner, Vice-President of the Royal Bank of Canada.

[47]A.J. de Grandpré, President, Bell Canada, addressing the Canadian Institute of Chartered Accountants, September 1975.

[48]George Bevan, Vice-President, Shell Canada Ltd., addressing the Academy of Dentistry, Winter Clinic, Toronto, November 1975.

[49]Nathan Stan, Vice-President, Acklands Ltd., addressing the Toronto Club, June 1975.

[50]Earle McLaughlin, addressing the Canadian Chamber of Commerce, September 1973.

[51]Fred McNeil, Chairman and Chief Officer, Bank of Montreal, addressing the Employers' Council of British Columbia, February 1976.

[52]A.J. de Granpré, addressing the Canadian Institute of Chartered Accountants, September 1975.

[53]F. Burbridge, President, Canadian Pacific, addressing the Faculty of Management Studies, University of Toronto, November 1975.

[54]A.D. Hamilton, President and Chief Executive Officer, Domtar, addressing the Royal Commission on Corporate Concentration.

[55]R.C. Dawsett, President, Canadian Life Insurance Association, addressing the Edmonton Chamber of Commerce, April 1975.

[56]Earle McLaughlin, addressing the Canadian Club of Montreal, March 1976.

[57]It must be pointed out here that until the phase of advanced capital concentration in Canada covering roughly the post-Second World War period, the reproduction of labour power was not mainly the responsibility of the state. This can be accounted for by two factors. First, the required manual labour power in agriculture, railway construction, manufacturing and other sectors was supplied by waves of immigration. Secondly, the close link between education and science-technology as an important force of production had not yet fully emerged.

[58]Walter G. Ward, Chairman, Canadian General Electric Company Ltd., addressing the Conference Board of Canada, November 1974.

[59]W.J.D. Lewis, Chairman, Canadian Life Insurance Association, President, Prudential Insurance Company of America, addressing the Rotary Club of Vancouver, April 1976.

[60]F. Burbridge, President, Canadian Pacific, addressing the Faculty of Management Studies, University of Toronto, November 1975.

[61]W.J.D. Lewis, addressing the Vancouver Rotary Club.

[62]A.J. de Grandpré, addressing the Royal Commission on Corporate Concentration, October 1975.

[63]Shell Canada Ltd. submission to the Royal Commission on Corporate Concentration, October 1975.

[64]A.D. Hamilton, addressing the Royal Commission on Corporate Concentration.

[65]William Mulholland, President, Bank of Montreal, addressing the Institute of Chartered Accountants of Ontario, October 1975.

[66]Robert G. Richardson, President, Dupont of Canada, addressing the School of International Affairs, Carleton University, May 1975.

[67]Ibid.

[68]C. William Daniel, President, Shell Canada, addressing the Canadian Club of Vancouver, December 1975.

[69]John McCreedy, Vice-President, INCO, addressing the Convention of Prospectors and Developers Association, March 1976.

[70]Confidential interview, April 1976.

[71]Habermas, *Legitimation Crisis*, 17.

STATE, CLASS AND RESERVE LABOUR: THE CASE OF THE 1941 CANADIAN UNEMPLOYMENT INSURANCE ACT

Carl J. Cuneo

Canadian Review of Sociology and Anthropology, 16 (2), May, 1979. *Author's note*: Presented at the Second Conference on Blue Collar Workers and their Communities, University of Western Ontario, London Ontario, May 6, 1977.

Capital accumulation, the social control of labour, and labour's wage subsistence are three interests that coincide and conflict in the relations of the capitalist and working classes with one another through the state.

Capitalists are primarily interested in the accumulation of capital. They are interested in the control of labour mainly insofar as it aids capital accumulation. But at times these two interests conflict, such as when the costs of social control interfere with the capital accumulation process. Capitalists are interested in labour's wage subsistence only to the extent that it aids capital accumulation and labour control.

The state is primarily interested in the social control of labour. It is not as directly concerned as capitalists with the accumulation of capital, although the state does offer important 'support services' in accumulation and owns organizations directly concerned with the accumulation of capital. The state's interest in labour's wage subsistence is less important than its interests in labour and capital accumulation. The state's wage policy is likely to be tailored to its more primary concerns with the social control of labour and the accumulation of capital. But sometimes this is difficult. While granting labour a large wage subsistence may help to soothe industrial unrest, the state is forced to raise taxes to pay the costs of such control. These taxes reduce the purchasing power of the consumer which hinders the capital accumulation process.

Labour is primarily interested in raising its wage subsistence and displays much less interest in capital accumulation and the general control of the labour movement. However, the leadership of much of organized labour does co-operate with the state in keeping wages at levels generally acceptable to capitalists. The same leaders also become particularly interested in the accumulation of capital during crises (such as depressions and recessions) and in the control of labour when the security of their own positions is threatened from their rank and file.

In major pieces of legislation affecting the relations of the capitalist and working classes with one another and with the state, it is not always clear which of these interests prevail, nor the way they are implemented in state policy. Marxist *instrumentalist* theories of the state view the interests of the capitalist class as being implemented in state policy on the basis of *formal and informal ties between business and the state*. This tradition has been most amenable to 'ruling class theory' in which the state is seen as manipulated, either directly or indirectly, by the capitalist class as a whole or by its most powerful fraction. Marxist *structuralist* theories of the state tend to locate the basis of the implementation of capitalist class interests in *structural contradictions in the capitalist economy*. This tradition is most amenable to the theory of 'relative autonomy' in which the state is seen as exercising some independence from direct capitalist class manipulation. The structural basis of the relative autonomy of the state is rooted in two class contradictions: the splitting of the capitalist class into two or more fractions, and the antagonism between the capitalist and working classes. This theory opens the door for explaining how the state responds to working class demands while at the same time ensuring the implementation of the long-term interests of the capitalist class. Ruling class theory does not have this capability.[1]

It is likely that different interests do not act in the same way on each piece of state legislation. This reflects both the relative power of the state and the capitalist and working classes, and their degree of involvement in each piece of legislation. A general theory of the capitalist state must be based *ultimately* on a detailed examination of a series of case studies. These case studies should show what major interests are involved, which ones prevail, the reasons for this, and the conclusions that can be drawn.

One major piece of legislation is un-employment insurance, first successfully introduced in Canada at the Federal level in 1941.[2] The Federal state introduced this legislation to help keep the peace between labour and capital. However, keeping the peace in this instance appeared to interfere with the accumulation of capital. Capitalists were generally opposed to state unemployment insurance. However, during business de-pressions the capitalist class as a whole became economically and politically weak and this was reflected in splits and indecisiveness in

their ranks over unemployment insurance. Capitalists clearly were not concerned with how well unemployment insurance would control labour unrest. At least this concern was not uppermost in their minds. Labour was much more enthusiastic in supporting the legislation because of the wage subsistence it promised unemployed workers. Yet the Federal 1941 Unemployment Insurance Act provided the unemployed with a wage subsistence level less than half the general standard of living of employed workers.[3] The passage of the Act in 1941 reflected the greater weight of the state's interest in social control than the efficacy of labour's interest in wage subsistence or of capitalists' interest in accumulation.

This paper examines some of the interests of the federal state, capitalists and labour in the 1941 Unemployment Insurance Act, and the historical continuity and discontinuity of these interests. Provincial activity in this field goes beyond the scope of the paper, and the question of federal-provincial relations is considered only as they impinge on federal legislation. This case study suggests that in the area of unemployment insurance in 1941, the most appropriate Marxist theory of the Canadian federal state is the structural relative autonomy of the state rather than its direct instrumental control by the capitalist class.

I. State

The Political Control of Labour Through the 1941 Act

In the House of Commons during the 1940 debates on the introduction of the Unemployment Insurance Act, the Liberal Government of William Lyon Mackenzie King argued that this measure would be ". . . a contribution to industrial stability . . ."[4] Norman A. McLarty, the Minister of Labour in charge of introducing the Act, stated that it ". . . will be of some assistance in maintaining industrial peace."[5] He argued: "The surest foundation on which to base democratic government is a happy and contented people. Nothing militates more against happiness and contentment than fear. By this measure fear will be removed to some extent from 4,660,000 of the Canadian people."[6] This publicly expressed theme was communicated privately in a series of letters between King and the provincial premiers.[7] In an appeal to Premier Aberhart of Alberta, King argued that ". . . a national system of unemployment insurance would contribute materially to . . . industrial stability . . ."[8]

The state wanted to introduce unemployment insurance in 1940 to control industrial unrest because of the way it perceived the changing structure of the capitalist order. It saw two kinds of underlying changes requiring a political response. The first was the gradual displacement of labour by the introduction of technology and the second were the sudden crises the capitalist order was passing through. The two crises uppermost in the minds of the state were wars and depressions. Both crises disrupted the employed labour force and increased the size of the reserve army of labour.

In a much neglected classical critique of Bennett's ill-fated Employment and Social Insurance Act of 1935, Jacob Cohen argued that unemployment in the modern capitalist era was peculiarly "organic."[9] By this he meant that unemployment was part of the inner logic of capitalism rather than a temporary aberration. One aspect of this inner logic recognized by Cohen was the displacement of labour through the introduction of machinery. Automation increases production much more quickly than employment. This expands the reserve army of labour or the relative surplus population which, for the purposes of this paper, contains workers either temporarily or permanently unemployed in the private capitalist sector.

Various politicians seemed to understand the relations among the development of capitalism, technology and unemployment. Mr. E.G. Hansell, a Social Credit M.P., argued in the House of Commons during the 1940 debate on unemployment insurance that ". . . this resolution is indicative of the fact that the government evidently expects unemployment to be a permanent problem. We realize . . . that the old order has passed away, that we have reached a higher state of progress where the machine is continually putting men out of work."[10] Mackenzie King was not a stranger to this theoretical proposition. In 1930 he had in his possession a memorandum that summarized twenty points about unemployment insurance brought up in the House of Commons, one of which read

as follows: "A consideration of the boot and shoe industry, the steel industry, farming and the railroads indicated clearly the difficult situation which resulted from the displacement of man power by machinery."[11] Yet other notes by King indicate that, at least for the purposes of public debate, he did not accept this argument and developed a logic that employment, capital investment, and the expansion of home and world markets intimately reinforced one another.[12] King at least recognized that capitalism both expanded and contracted employment.

The state also recognized that the various crises of capitalism increased unemployment and for this reason considered the introduction of unemployment insurance during the Second World War. This was evident at different levels of the state. The Honourable Adelard Godbout, Premier of Quebec, favoured unemployment insurance partly on the grounds that ". . . serious problems . . . must be expected to arise at the end of the present conflict."[13] This argument was accepted by politicians in the House of Commons. McLarty, the Minister of Labour, argued that unemployment insurance ". . . is necessary at this time to anticipate and in some degree counteract the probable dislocation which will follow demobilization and the cessation of war work."[14] This line of reasoning was expressed more strongly by Mr. Neill, M.P., who was outraged at the opposition to unemployment insurance by the Canadian Manufacturer's Association and the Chamber of Commerce: "Cheap, short-sighted, ostrich-headed! Do they want a bloody revolution after the war? Think of all those idle men who will come back. They will not stand for the situation that prevailed last time."[15] The "last time" refers to the aftermath of the First World War during which unemployment rose considerably and labour unrest was particularly evident. MacKenzie King also accepted the argument that unemployment insurance was being introduced as a wartime measure. In a letter to Aberhart, he argued: "We consider that a system of national unemployment insurance, if established, will go far to prevent much of the . . . industrial dislocation which might otherwise be the aftermath of war."[16]

The other crisis of capitalism that lay at the basis of the state's introduction of unemployment insurance was the expectation of a depression after the war similar to the one that occurred during the 1930's. During the 1940 debate in the House of Commons, the Honourable R.B. Hanson, leader of the Conservative opposition, argued for unemployment insurance on the grounds that Canada could expect ". . . a tremendous dislocation at the end of the war, a dislocation much greater than was anticipated in the semi-depression period of 1935."[17] The Honourable A.A. Dysart, Premier of New Brunswick, argued for unemployment insurance because workmen must ". . . build for future security against the depression which must come."[18] King argued that ". . . we may expect a period of retrenchment and depression . . ." and therefore must build up an insurance fund during the peak of wartime prosperity when employment is high.[19]

These statements concerning the crises of wars and depressions indicate that the Canadian state seemed to view unemployment insurance as a partial means of coping with such contradictions of capitalism. An examination of the historical continuity of the state's interest and actions in the problems of employment, unemployment and unemployment insurance since the end of the First World War suggests that during periods of crises the state introduced measures designed to control industrial unrest in one form or another, but that during periods of relative calm the state was comparatively inactive in this field. There were two major crises of note: the industrial unrest in the immediate aftermath of the First World War between 1918 and 1921; and the crisis of the Depression during the 1930's. During these periods the state introduced many measures designed to cope with the problems of employment and unemployment. However, during the relative calm of the 1920's, especially from 1922 to 1929, the state was much less active in this area. Each period will now be briefly examined.

Historical Continuity of the State's Interest in Labour Control

The First World War caused a major disruption in the capitalist labour market. Unemployment was serious on the eve of war, especially during August, 1913, the winter months from 1913 to 1914, and June, 1914.[20] This resulted from the excess capacity that Canadian manufacturers experienced during 1913.[21] Canadian manufacturers welcomed the coming of the war as the stimulus the economy needed to expand production and markets. Capital investment increased, munition production expanded rapidly, and exports to Great Britain grew enormously.[22] With the expansion of munition production, employment increased.[23] But this was an atypical expansion in employment since, with the end of the war and the transition to peacetime production, munition workers were thrown out of work and the size of the reserve army of labour once again increased.[24] A similar disruption in the labour market occurred in the large recruitment of men for the armed services. Between 1914 and 1918 the total number of persons ever registered with the Canadian Expeditionary Force was 619,636.[25] Up to April, 1918, 62 per cent of the 364,750 men who had gone overseas were either skilled or unskilled labourers.[26] Demobilization at the end of the war occurred rapidly over an eighteen-month period. In July, 1918, the strength of the Canadian Expeditionary Force stood at 388,038; by November, 1919, this had plummeted to 11,565.[27] This rapid demobilization led to a large increase in the size of the reserve army of labour. Both the disruptions in capitalist industry caused by the transition to peacetime production and the rapid demobilization led to labour unrest.[28] While union membership in all of Canada decreased from 176,000 in 1913 to 160,000 in 1916, it jumped dramatically to 374,000 by 1920 but by 1922 dropped off to 278,000.[29] Similarly, the number of strikes and lockouts in Canada decreased from 152 in 1913 to 120 in 1916, but jumped dramatically to 322 by 1920 after which they decreased to 86 by 1923.[30] Three other official indicators of instability in industrial relations at the end of the war are the rapid increases in prices, wages and unemployment.[31]

The state responded by engaging in a series of actions designed to introduce some stability into the system of industrial relations. It did this partly by attempting to develop an employment policy for those out of work. It was out of these state moves in the aftermath of the First World War that the beginnings of unemployment insurance can be found.

Near the end of the war there were two notable types of reserve labour not employed by private industry: the soldiers being de-

133

mobilized from overseas and from units in Canada, and workers being released from munition factories. The state moved during and after the war to instil some stability into these two sectors to prevent an outbreak of unrest among them.

When war hostilities ceased, Canadian soldiers had to wait for a period up to twelve to eighteen months to be brought home. There was considerable dissatisfaction over this waiting period and rioting resulted.[32] "Between November, 1918, and June, 1919, there were thirteen instances of riots or disturbances involving Canadian troops in England." At Kimmel Park, 800 soldiers rioted and 5 men were killed and 23 wounded. Rioting occurred also at Witley and Epsom. The state, in the person of Lieut.-General Sir R.E.W. Turner, treated such acts as mutiny. Numerous arrests were made in an effort to quell the disturbances.[33]

The Canadian state recognized that demobilization was disruptive of a segment of the reserve army of labour and moved to institute some "soft measures" to keep the soldiers under control. In June, 1918, a committee was appointed by the Ministry of the Overseas Forces of Canada to study the question of demobilization. The committee recognized ". . . the steps which should be taken to keep the men employed and amused during the time which would inevitably prove trying to all concerned [i.e., during demobilization]. . . . the psychological problems of the demobilization period are quite as pressing as material problems. It is quite as difficult a matter to sustain morale as it is to organize repatriation."[34] Two plans for demobilization were considered. First, priority for coming home could be given to individual men on the basis of length of service overseas and marital status. Second, demobilization could be carried out by unit disregarding priority of the first type. The second plan was adopted because of its greater social control potential. "It was believed that the men would arrive in Canada happier and feel more contented and with discipline better maintained if the unit organization were adhered to until the last possible moment."[35] In the meantime, while demobilization began and disruptions occurred in the "normal" routine of military life, various agencies were either set up or expanded to keep the men occupied, amused and contented. The Ministry

of Overseas Military Forces of Canada reported: "Every effort has been made to keep the men intelligently occupied, interested and amused during the period preceding demobilization, both in England and France." Particularly prominent among organizations set up for these purposes were the Canadian Military Y.M.C.A., The Chaplin Service and the Khaki University of Canada.[36]

A more serious problem was the integration of the soldiers into civilian life, especially finding employment for them in the private capitalist sector. The state conducted a number of studies and set up a number of agencies to deal with such problems. In October of 1915, the secretary of the Military Hospitals Commission was asked to prepare a report of the possible employment and re-education of disabled soldiers. It produced "one of the first documents issued by any Government in connection with employment after the great war . . . ."[37] Since employers would not always take back partially disabled men, Sir Robert Borden reported that the Military Hospital Commission had by 1918

. . . established an artificial limb factory at which already 1,051 cases have been considered; a school for message, a school for instructors in remedial gymnastics, and various courses in re-education. They have established on a commercial basis industries such as a planning mill, a furniture factory, machine shops, motor mechanics, farm tractor operations, a woollen mill, and a power station. They give commercial instruction, instruction in dairying and in truck and glass gardening.[38]

For soldiers who could return to employment in the private sector, the Department of Soldiers' Civil Re-establishment was set up to ease this transition. "Through the dissemination of correct information, the Information and Service Branch of this Department proved a tranquillizing feature in the industrial life of the Dominion and in calming unrest among the returned men themselves."[39] In addition, a series of National Reconstruction Groups were set up across Canada "for the purposes of studying the problems arising from the war and making suggestions for their solution." These groups included representatives of capital, labour and the returned soldiers.[40] Other committees set up for similar purposes were the Repatriation and Employment Committee of the Dominion Government and the Returned Soldiers' Land Settlement Board.[41]

The state also moved along a more strictly civilian front to ease the transition to peacetime conditions. In May, 1918, it passed the Employment Offices Co-ordination Act which encouraged the setting up of a series of public employment offices across Canada through Dominion grants to the Provinces.[42] Under this Act, $50,000 was alloted in 1918-1919, and $100,000 in 1919-1920.[43] In addition, the state, acting under authority of this Act, set up the Employment Service Council of Canada

> to advise the Minister of Labour in the administration of the Act and to recommend ways of preventing unemployment. This body is composed of representatives of the Dominion and Provincial Government, the Canadian Manufacturers' Association, The Association of Canadian Building and Construction Industries, the Trades and Labour Congress of Canada, the Railway Association of Canada, the Canadian Railway Brotherhoods, the Canadian Lumberman's Association, the Canadian Council of Agriculture and the Great War Veterans' Association.[44]

This was one of several state moves to integrate capital and labour in its plans for the management of the reserve army of labour.

The degree to which the setting up of the employment offices under this Act was linked to problems of demobilization is indicated by the relative expansion and contraction in the number of offices throughout the period of demobilization. When demobilization was taking place, the number of employment offices expanded from 12 in May, 1918, to 15 in December, 1918, and to 92 in December, 1919. However, once the period of demobilization passed, the number of offices contracted to 76 by December, 1921. *The Canada Year Book* of 1921, an official publication of the Dominion Government, states: "As the demobilization period came to a close, the number of offices decreased . . ."[45] Thus, the state itself recognized the link between the period of demobilization of militarized reserve labour and the expansion and contraction in state employment offices.

It was out of the post-war crisis of unemployment, and political attempts to find employment for unemployed soldiers and munition workers, that the state began to make some overtures in the direction of unemployment insurance. The Dominion Government set up the Royal Commission on Industrial Relations which recommended in 1919 ". . . a system of state social insurance for those who . . . are unable to work . . . Such insurance would remove the spectre of fear which now haunts the wage earner and make him a more contented and better citizen."[46] This recommendation was also supported by the National Industrial Conference which the Dominion Government held in Ottawa in 1919.[47] By the latter part of 1919 it was discovered that not all the returned soldiers had found employment and that some unemployment relief would have to be provided for them over the winter months between 1919-1920. A total of $5 million was provided for relief and was expended by the Dominion Government through the Department of Soldiers' Civil Re-establishment and the Canadian Patriotic Fund.[48] Between 1920 and 1921, Arthur Meighen provided $1,232,758 in unemployment relief.[49] These were the first direct moves by the Dominion Government into the field of unemployment insurance. They emerged out of the state's attempt to smooth the transition from wartime to peacetime conditions by introducing some stability into the system of industrial relations during a period of considerable flux and unrest.

The period from 1922 to 1929 was marked by relative industrial calm and few significant state moves in the direction of setting up a major unemployment insurance scheme. Especially after 1925, employment was at a high level, wages and prices were relatively stable, and labour unions did not grow significantly in membership. There were some state commissions and reports suggesting unemployment insurance, such as the 1928 Committee on Industrial and International Relations,[50] but no major pieces of legislation setting up comprehensive unemployment insurance or unemployment relief were introduced.

All of this was to change with the coming of the Depression of the 1930's. Between 1922 and 1929, unemployment varied from 1.8 per cent and 4.5 per cent. However, by 1933 unemployment had climbed to 19.3 per cent and remained between 9.1 per cent and 14.6 per cent between 1934 and 1939. By 1941, with the coming of wartime prosperity, unemployment had dropped to 4.4 per cent.[51]

The state began to feel the pressure to take action to control the reserve labour that was developing during the Depression. In 1930, the prime minister's office of Mackenzie King began to receive requests from prominent people to move toward unemployment insurance. Secretary of the Prime Minister's Office, Harry Baldwin, wrote King a memo in 1930 in which he stated: "There is a growing sentiment among men whose opinion is valuable (such as Mr. Bradshaw of the Massey-Harris Company, Mr. G.F. Beer, who was on the Ontario Unemployment Commission in 1915, and the Officers of the Canadian Manufacturers Association), that sooner or later the question of unemployment insurance will have to be considered by the government."[52] However, the government was reluctant to move in this direction until popular opinion had built more strongly for unemployment insurance. Baldwin suggested the following delaying tactic: "In order to forestall precipitous action [on unemployment insurance] and the serious consequences devolving therefrom, the suggestion has been Mooted that a more or less permanent Royal Commission be set up which would study the whole question for a period of years, during which time political and public opinion would ripen and false steps would be avoided." King was anxious that such a strategy not be revealed to the public. He wrote over Baldwin's memo: "Do not want mentioned during campaign—leave alone."[53]

With rising unemployment and the coming to power of Bennett later in 1930, the state adopted some temporary measures between 1930 and 1935 to deal with the crisis. On September 22, 1930, the House of Commons passed the temporary Unemployment Relief Act, effective only until March 31, 1931. It provided $20 million to provinces and municipalities for public works to relieve unemployment.[54] By an Order-in-Council (P.C. 2246) instituted under the Act, the Dominion Government provided for one-third of direct relief expenditures of municipalities up to $4 million, one-quarter of the cost of municipal public works for the purposes of relieving un-

employment, and one-half of the cost of provincial public works and the Trans-Canada Highway.[55] However, not all of these monies went directly to assist unemployed workers. Under a further Order-in-Council (P.C. 2292), the Dominion Government agreed to pay out of the $20 million fund the interest at 5 per cent per annum for 18 months on $25 million to be spent by the C.P.R. and the C.N.R. "in the performance of certain works and the purchase of certain materials over and above the normal expenditure of the said Railways . . ."[56]

The Dominion Government also passed the Unemployment and Farm Relief Act of 1931. Besides the provisions of the Unemployment Relief Act, it included three additional features of note. It subsidized the costs of the production and distribution of farm products. It provided for loans to municipalities. And it contained broad social control powers. The Act conferred "certain powers upon the Governor-in-Council in respect to unemployment and farm relief, and the maintenance of peace, order and good government in Canada."[57]

In 1932 the Dominion Government passed the Unemployment and Farm Relief Continuance Act which extended the Unemployment and Farm Relief Act of 1931 from March 1, 1932 to May 1, 1933.[58] The other measure passed in 1932 was the Relief Act which provided assistance to municipalities in relief measures, gave assistance to drought-striken areas of Saskatchewan, provided monies for the National Park's program, and assisted the sale and distribution of natural resources.[59] In 1933, in the midst of growing unrest among the unemployed, the Act was amended by the addition of social control measures. When Parliament was not in session, the Relief Act of 1933 empowered the Governor-in-Council ". . . to take all such measures . . . to maintain, within the competence of Parliament, peace, order and good government throughout Canada."[60] The Relief Act of 1934 extended this Act to March 31, 1935, and provided for "special relief works and undertakings under the control and direction of the Department of National Defence and the Department of the Interior."[61] These were provisions for the labour camps for single unemployed workers under the control of the Department of National Defence that ended in the revolt of the unemployed on their on-to-Ottawa trek in 1935.[62] Bennett passed one further temporary measure, the Relief Act of 1935, which extended the 1934 Relief Act to March 31, 1936.[63]

Two significant points emerge out of these relief acts. First, they were temporary and as such did not give the state a permanent institutionalized mechanism at any level to control unemployed reserve labour. Secondly, despite their temporary nature, social control sections were built into the acts alongside those sections providing relief to the unemployed. This clearly indicates the degree to which the Dominion Government linked the provision of subsistence to the unemployed with their social control and, in fact, reveals one of the state's intents in setting up relief legislation during the crises of the Depression.

Prime Minister Bennett next moved to set up a more permanent mechanism of unemployment insurance in the form of the Employment and Social Insurance Act of 1935.[64] However, after his defeat and King's return to power, on June 17, 1936, the Supreme Court of Canada declared the Act ultra vires the Parliament of Canada because it invaded the area of civil rights which the B.N.A. act reserved to the provinces.[65] On January 28, 1937, the Dominion Government's appeal of this decision was turned down by the Privy Council on the same grounds.[66] Mackenzie King by this time was much more enthusiastic about unemployment insurance, given the crisis of the Depression. Between 1937 and 1940 he appealed several times in personal communications to the provincial premiers to agree to the necessary amendment to the B.N.A. Act that would allow the Federal Parliament to pass unemployment insurance. The last provincial premiers to agree were Aberhart of Alberta and Godbout of Quebec. This did not occur until May of 1940.[67] The stage was then set for the King Government to introduce the Unemployed Insurance Act in the House of Commons in July of 1940.

The State's Interest in Capital Accumulation

The Canadian state argued that the 1941 Unemployment Insurance Act would accumulate capital for war purposes. Contributions to the financing of the Act were to come from three sources: two-fifths from each of labour

and capital, and one-fifth from the federal state.[68] King argued that during the first year of the Act's operation, labour and capital would contribute $67,200,000 to the fund and the state $11,200,000.[69] He went on to argue that this insurance fund was a savings plan which could be invested to assist the war effort. "This $67,200,000 [labour and capital's portion] will be available for investment both in government securities and in industry. Against this, there will be an estimated administrative cost of $5,250,000. In short, the creation of the fund will represent the mobilization of more than $60,000,000 for investment purposes and for strengthening our war economy . . . ."[70]

The implementation of the Act largely supported King's contention. Between July 1, 1941 and March 31, 1943, labour and capital contributed $93,870,914 to the insurance fund and the Dominion Government contributed $18,774,183.[71] Since workers could not begin to collect benefits until January 27, 1942,[72] and given King's argument that wartime prosperity and high employment would mean that very few workers would be drawing from the fund,[73] it is not surprising that at the end of 1945 the par value of the reserves of the fund invested in Canada Savings Bonds stood at about $300 million and the accrued interest amounted to approximately $2 million.[74] Workers received only $19 million or 6 per cent of the amount invested in bonds and securities. This was entirely consistent with King's plans for the insurance fund. In a private memo he stated:

In the prosecution of the war, the whole emphasis of the national economy must be shifted from the production and distribution of consumer goods to a vastly increased production of the machines and implements of war. Satisfaction of the wants of individuals must be subordinated to the ends of national defence. This means that our people must spend less as individuals, and more as taxpayers of the government. While contributions under the scheme [i.e., unemployment insurance] will not be a tax, they will, nevertheless, achieve this same purpose of diverting a proportion of the national income from present private expenditures to place it at the disposal of the government.[75]

As several observers recognized, not only

would labour have to pay its own contribution of two-fifths, but it would also ultimately pay the majority of capital's contribution through increases in consumer prices and the state's contribution through increased taxation.[76] The 1941 Unemployment Insurance Act worked admirably well in transferring about $280 million throughout the war from the hands of labour to the coffers of the state.

The State's Interest in Wage Subsistence

The state's interest in protecting the economic standard of living of the worker through unemployment insurance seemed secondary to its interests in the control of industrial unrest and capital accumulation. The federal state never developed in detail a wage subsistence argument and preferred to tack it onto the end of its other two arguments for unemployment insurance.[77] The 1941 legislation was based on the contributory principle by which benefits paid to workers were based on their contributions which, in turn, were adjusted to their previous wages while employed. The Act set up seven categories of workers' wages that ranged from an average $6.44 per week to $32.24. Contributions were based on these categories. The lowest paid worker contributed 12 cents per week. Contributions increased gradually for higher paid workers. The highest paid worker contributed 36 cents per week. Benefits, in turn, were based on this sliding scale. The lowest paid workers received $4.08 in benefits per week. Benefits increased for each category of higher paid workers. The highest paid workers received $12.24 in benefits. Compared to wages in the employed labour force, these benefits ranged from 16 per cent for the lowest paid unemployed worker to 49 per cent for the highest paid unemployed worker.[78]

The state's income policy for unemployed workers had four far-reaching effects on the working class in general and unemployed workers in particular. First, the state's contributory principle *enforced poverty* on the lower sections of the working class. The contributory principle meant that, not only did workers contribute directly in subsidizing unemployment caused structurally by the forces of capitalism, but indirectly as well through increased taxation and consumer prices. Since benefits were always tied to con-

tributions, and contributions to past wages, it was impossible for workers to raise themselves out of poverty through the Act. In fact, the legislation did the reverse. It placed workers in a more severe state of poverty than they were in before becoming unemployed.[79] The Act maintained the unemployed at less than half the standard of living of employed workers. Second, the 1941 Act *reproduced the internal income stratification within the working class.* Because benefits were tied to past contributions and wages, workers poor before being unemployed remained poor after becoming unemployed. Workers who were more affluent before being unemployed remained comparatively so after. Third, the structure of benefits *regulated the flow of labour.* Because workers received fewer benefits than either their own past wages or the income of the employed labour force, they were forced through the experience of deprivation back into the employed labour force. Other provisions of the Act had the same intent. To qualify for benefits, the unemployed must prove ". . . that he is capable of and available for work . . . ."[80] Fourth, the income structure of the Act *divided the working class politically against itself.* The income differentiation among the unemployed themselves and between them and the employed divided them along similar political lines. This made any sustained attack by the working class against the structure and effects of unemployment insurance legislation difficult to sustain. This political effect may have been intended given that the 1941 Act was so closely modelled after Bennett's 1935 Employment and Social Insurance Act. The latter Act was introduced in the midst of the major revolt by the unemployed in the On-to-Ottawa trek.

II. Capital

Capitalist's Interest in Capital Accumulation

During the second reading of the Unemployment Insurance Act, a special House of Commons committee considered the bill in detail and invited submissions from interested groups.[81]

Most of the submissions were from capitalists. There were also some from labour and other interested groups. Generally, capital opposed the bill and labour supported it.

These positions were succinctly summarized by the *Canadian Congress Journal*, the official publication of the Trades and Labour Congress of Canada (T.L.C.):

> Presenting arguments against the enactment of the Bill at this session were the Canadian Manufacturers Association, Canadian Chamber of Commerce, Canadian Bankers Association of Canada, Canadian Transit Association, and the Canadian Life Insurance Officers Association.

> Supporting the Bill and urging its immediate enactment were the Trades and Labor Congress of Canada, The Legislative Committee of the Transportation Brotherhoods, the All-Canadian Congress of Labour, the C.I.O., and the Federation of Catholic Workers.[82]

The T.L.C. went on to identify the leader of capitalist opposition: "Opponents of the measure led by the Canadian Manufacturer's Association have lost no opportunity, especially during the past few years, to defeat its enactment."[83] Representatives of the Canadian state seemed in agreement with this assessment of capitalist opposition. Mackenzie King himself wrote a private memo: "The Canadian Manufacturer's Association is the principal organization opposed to the immediate establishment of a system of unemployment insurance."[84] And Mr. Angus MacInnis of the C.C.F., responding to the Canadian Chamber of Commerce's submission to the Commons Committee, stated: ". . . you are opposed to the enactment of this bill under any circumstances no matter how much opportunity you would have had to discuss it."[85]

Capitalists opposed the Act because it interfered with their own efforts to accumulate capital under wartime conditions. Mr. R.P. Jellett, vice-president of the Royal Trust and representative of the Chamber of Commerce, argued that the Act ". . . must hurt our one chief concern, which is our war effort, if on this particular measure we launch out on a scheme that would require . . . the contributions of millions dollars on the part of corporations and the government."[86] W.C. Coulter, Chairman of the Industrial Relations Committee of the Canadian Manufacturer's Association and president of Coulter Copper

and Brass Co. of Toronto, took exactly the same position.[87] He argued that the Act ". . . will inevitably entail a substantial amount of novel and troublesome work on the part of employers at a time when many of them are focusing their attention on war production."[88] Large employers would have to hire extra staff to keep records of employers' and employees' contributions for *each* employee. This represented a small but nonetheless real cost at a time when capitalists had their sights set during the war on cost efficiency.[89]

Capitalists viewed unemployment insurance impeding the process of capital accumulation in four ways.

First, they viewed unemployment insurance as a *tax* that would be an added burden on industry. Mr. Tolchard of the Toronto Board of Trade argued against unemployment insurance as an additional burden on business which is ". . . bearing the heaviest taxation in their history . . . ."[90] Mr. Norman J. Dawes, president of National Breweries and Representative of the Chamber of Commerce, outlined the taxes that business was bearing:

> Deductions from payrolls already include purchase of war loan B bonds and war savings certificates, national defence tax, group insurance, sickness insurance, medical fee deductions, war wage tax in Manitoba, check-off tax in Nova Scotia, collective labour agreement tax in Quebec, (and) hospital donations . . . ."[91]

Jellett argued that the addition of unemployment insurance to these taxes ". . . is the last straw that finally breaks the camel's back." He estimated that all of these taxes accounted for 40 per cent of the price of commodities.[92]

Capitalists did not object to these taxes because they themselves would ultimately have to pay for them. They saw their workers paying for such taxes. But *labour would then demand higher wages*. This was the second way capitalists viewed unemployment insurance impairing the capital accumulation process. Mr. Jellett submitted a letter to the Commons committee in which he stated: "Another addition to the present deductions from the workers' wages may lead to further demands from labour and add generally to its unsettlement in war times."[93]

The third way in which capitalists viewed unemployment insurance impeding the capital accumulation process was through a *reduction in consumer purchasing power.* Capitalists quite openly admitted that they would pass on the increased taxes and wages caused by unemployment insurance to the consumer in the form of higher commodity prices.[94] They were fearful that this would weaken the purchasing power of the consumer and thus reduce their own markets. Therefore, they opposed unemployment insurance, at least for the duration of the war when consumer prices were rising for other reasons.

Fourth, capitalists were worried about the effect of the cost of unemployment insurance on their *export markets.* Mr. Tolchard of the Toronto Board of Trade argued: "To the extent that unemployment insurance and other additional charges, such as higher taxation, cannot be absorbed by employers, high prices will be inevitable. The result will be to limit Canadian export possibilities because of the disadvantage under which Canadian exporters may be placed as compared with foreign competitors for export trade."[95] However, Tolchard neglected to mention the fact that many of Canada's foreign competitors had introduced unemployment insurance by 1940. Unemployment insurance was introduced around 1906 in St. Gall, Basle and Zurich in Switzerland, and in Bologna and Venice in Italy.[96] In 1911 Britain began state unemployment insurance.[97] In fact, Canadian unemployment insurance legislation was closely modelled after Britain's.[98] By 1922 unemployment insurance had also been introduced in Denmark the Netherlands, Austria, Luxembourg, Australia and several states in the United States.[99] Some arguments by Canadian capitalists were certainly vacuous.

Given the capitalist's position that the 1941 Act interfered with their drive for accumulation, what were their responses to the state? They formed five basic lines of defence, each one being somewhat weaker than the preceding one. First, they suggested that Canada could rely solely on the totally *private plans* already adopted in many industries. They next suggested a combined *public-private plan* involving state and capital in ways quite different from that envisaged by the 1941 Act. If the state rejected this, capitalists had a

third plan in which corporations with stable employment records could *opt out* of the 1941 Act. Fourthly, a much weaker plan called simply for *reduced contributions* for industries with good employment records. Finally, if all else failed, capitalists appealed to the state to *delay* introducing unemployment insurance hopefully until the end of the war. Each of these responses will now be examined.

(1) Private Plans

Canadian capitalists argued that they had introduced private company insurance and welfare plans which gave workers protection against unemployment.[100] G.V.V. Nicholls of the Canadian Manufacturer's Association's Industrial Relations Department stated: ". . . it would be a pity if federal legislation were to discourage still further the growing movement in these respects toward the self-regulation of industry."[101] Rather than state unemployment insurance, the Chamber of Commerce favoured "compulsory war savings or individual company assistance programs."[102] Mr. McLarty, Minister of Labour, estimated that at least 2,800 Canadian firms had "profit sharing co-operative savings funds."[103] Although businessmen argued that these plans protected the worker against unemployment (which was doubtful), they had at least one other hidden function: the accumulation of capital.

Capitalists said they had four different schemes for the protection of the unemployed.

Their *control of production* schemes ostensibly were an ". . . attempt to reduce layoffs by the careful planning of production." Employers ". . . plan their manufacturing activities in advance so as to insure as uniform a volume of employment as possible throughout the year."[104] The Canadian Banker's Association made a similar argument: ". . . the banks have followed the plan of maintaining at all times staff sufficiently large to take care of peak demands, including vacation season. Due to this policy the number released from employment is remarkably small . . . ."[105]

Companies made available *loan facilities* "to allow their employees advances to tide them over emergencies."[106] Unfortunately, no information on interest rates is provided, but it seems that such facilities increased the capital accumulation of employers by forcing the unemployed into debt.

A number of companies introduced *unemployment benefit plans*. Canadian Kodak Co. Ltd. set up its own ". . . reserve fund as a protection against unemployment, the primary responsibility of the fund resting on the company."[107] Both the company and employees contributed to the fund. This made available to the company one per cent of the wages of employees which represented a considerable accumulation of capital. General Foods Ltd. set up a termination plan which provided certain payments ". . . in the event of the worker's services being terminated prior to retirement."[108] However, this plan protected mainly the employed! The size of the benefits depended on how long the employee had been with the company. Employees who had been with the company for thirty-five or more years of continuous service received the maximum benefits of fifty-two weeks earnings. By definition, these were employees least in need of unemployment benefits. But employees who had put in five years or less of continuous service received only two weeks earnings.[109] Thus, workers most susceptible to unemployment received the least protection! Plans by Proctor and Gamble, L.S. Shaw, Somerville, and Taylor Instruments were similar to these.

A fourth kind of scheme came under the rubric of *savings plans*. Mr. Jellett of the Canadian Chamber of Commerce argued that he was "against unemployment insurance. We still feel that unemployment insurance does not cover as large a field [as private plans], and I personally feel that a company savings plan might fill the bill better and with less expense."[110] Although there were several different types, the general procedure was to have employees make contributions from their wages to a fund, sometimes matched by the company. Either the company or a bank or insurance company would have control over the fund. Employees could not withdraw from the fund unless they left the company. Only then could they receive some financial insurance against unemployment. The difficulty with several of these plans was that only workers who had been in the employ of the company for some time could make use of such funds. Thus, workers most susceptible to unemployment were again least likely to receive protection.[111] The funds were available to the company to invest in ways it saw fit. Companies using such plans increased the amount of capital available for their use.

Two such plans were instituted by Dominion Foundries and Steel Limited (Dofasco) of Hamilton. One was its Employees' Savings and Profit Sharing Fund adopted in 1938 and modelled after the well know plan of the Joslyn Manufacturing Company of Chicago. After three years of continuous service, employees could contribute three or five per cent of their wages to a fund up to a maximum of $150 per year. The company contributed at least ten per cent of its net operating earnings which was not to exceed four times the employees' contributions. The 'protection of the unemployed' came when workers voluntarily resigned or were fired from the company. At this point, the employee was to receive "his pro rata share of the employees' contributions to the fund, with interest and accumulated profits, and one-half of his pro rata share of the company's contributions, also with interest and accumulated profits.[112] Once again, protection, to the extent it existed, covered only the more permanently employed! Since employees could not withdraw from the fund when they were in the employ of the company, a relatively permanent capital fund was set up from which the company could make investments.

There is a long precedent in Canada to such plans. In 1894 Canadian manufacturers attempted to spread the model of profit sharing in Canada adopted by the United States by members of The Association for the Promotion of Profit Sharing.[113] While employees would share minimally in the profits of the company, no managerial rights would be shared with them. The control of labour unrest and the cementing of the loyalty of workers to the company were central aims of such schemes. Regarding the decision by capitalists to adopt such plans, the *Canadian Manufacturer* in 1894 had this to say: "The question then resolves itself into the proposition whether the employer, desiring to pocket all the profits he may make in his business, will take the chance of labor troubles and other annoyances that may arise, which would inevitably be the cause of loss to him, or whether, by agreeing to divide profits with employees, he secures a better and more economical class of labour whose interests are most thoroughly identified with his own, and where strikes and labour troubles would be practically impossible.[114]

The second plan suggested by Dofasco was called its "over-time savings" or "continuous pay day" plan. The hardly hidden object of the plan was to help the company accumulate extra capital while its ostensible purpose was to use the overtime pay of employees to tide them over periods of unemployment. Dofasco made the suggestion to its employees ". . . that they should allow their pay for everything over an eight-hour day to be held on their behalf in a special fund, the object being to build up a reserve to tide them over the slack time anticipated after the war. The scheme is simplicity itself. The employee authorizes the company to deduct from his wages each payday all money earned by overtime work in excess of the standard ninety-six hours per two week period. Amounts so deducted are deposited in a special account which may be withdrawn at any time the employee wishes."[115]

(2) Public-Private Plan

If the state rejected capitalists totally private plans as an alternative to unemployment insurance, a second weaker suggestion was a combined public-private plan participated in by capitalists, labour and the state in ways quite different from the 1941 Act. This plan was put forward by the Canadian Life Insurance Officers Association with the support of the Canadian Manufacturer's Association. It recommended:

> (1) the creation of an 'insurance fund' contributed equally by employers and employees to take care of short periods of unemployment, (2) the creation of a second 'savings fund' contributed to equally by the employees and the state to cover further periods of unemployment, (3) the creation of a relief fund sustained entirely by the state to pay relief for periods of unemployment longer than those covered by the two previously described funds.[116]

Under this plan capitalists would only have to contribute to the first 'insurance fund'. As Mackenzie King privately remarked: "The intention of this plan is obvious: to minimize the contribution of the employer as much as possible."[117] It would shift the cost of unemployment from the shoulders of businessmen to the state and labour much more than would the 1941 Act.

(3) Opt Out

Capitalists argued, as a third line of defence, that if the state was determined to go ahead with its unemployment insurance scheme, individual industries should be allowed to opt out of the 1941 Act on the basis of the three principles of good employment record, an imbalance between contributions and benefits, and a vote by employees to do so.

Both the Canadian Banker's Association and the Retail Merchant's Association of Canada made strong submissions that they be allowed to opt out of the 1941 Act on the basis of their good employment records. Canadian banks calculated that during the three pre-war years they had an "unemployment rato" of 1¼ per cent while the average unemployment ratio in 1942 for those covered under the Act would be 12 per cent.[118] Mr. H.T. Jaffray, President of the Canadian Banker's Association, stated: "The banks respectfully submit that instead of being included in a general plan of unemployment insurance, they and their employees should be exempted because, having regard to the normal practice of the employment, it is permanent in character."[119] The banks made two arguments in particular. They had instituted an apprenticeship system that reduced unemployment among their employees:

> Each young man, when he enters a bank's services, receives a careful training over a period of three or four years, a virtual apprenticeship. . . . Abrupt dismissals are avoided, the bank bearing the expense of continuing the employment for a time in cases where discharge would be immediate in many other businesses or industries."[120]

The banks also argued that they did not draw from the ordinary labour pool and therefore were no part of its problems. "There is . . . no group of temporarily unemployed bankers upon which the banks could or would draw, new employees being recruited almost entirely from young men emerging from the high schools and in some cases from the universities."[121] Curiously, most of the banks' arguments about stable employment were addressed using bank managers as illustrations rather than female clerical and sales personnel who had higher unemployment rates. The Retail Merchant's Association also wanted exemption from the Act on the basis of constant' employment among retail clerks, but did not develop the elaborate arguments put forward by the banks.[122] Other businessmen supported the ideas of the bankers and merchants. The Chamber of Commerce stated: "Employers whose staffs are subject to very little unemployment and who take care of the unemployment problems should be given the opportunity of being exempt from the general scheme of unemployment insurance . . ."[123]

Capitalists also tried to opt out of the 1941 Act by suggesting that some of their employees would make contributions to the insurance fund far in excess of the benefits they would draw out. The Canadian banks said ". . . bank employees as well as the banks, if forced to become contributors on the same basis as others in a general unemployment insurance plan, would have to pay amounts far higher than the insurance benefits which would be derived by such employees. . . . the proposed statutory plan, insofar as the bank employees and the banks are concerned, is nothing more than taxation."[124] On the basis of a bank "unemployment ratio" of 1¼ per cent, the banks estimated that they and their employees would have paid $560,000 into the insurance fund in 1942 while their employees would get back only $19,500 in benefits. "Bank employees and the banks would have paid into the fund some twenty-nine times as much as would normally have been received out of it.[125] Similarly, the Retail Merchant's Association of Canada wanted to opt out of the Act on the basis of a survey of 50 retail establishments in southern Ontario which showed that retail clerks would receive no more that 5 per cent of the contributions made by themselves and their employers.[126]

A third argument for opting out was based on a simple vote by employees that they preferred a private plan to the state insurance programme. The Canadian Manufacturer's Association suggested the following plan:

Even if the Government is determined to proceed with the present pool scheme, we propose to suggest that clauses should be added providing that if an overwhelming majority, say 75 per cent, of the employees in a particular industry vote in favour of a compulsory savings scheme, the details of which would of course be set out in the bill, such industry should be allowed to contract out."[127]

Of course, a considerable saving in capital would be had by those industries opting out.

(4) Reduced Contributions

A still weaker line of defence by capitalists against the 1941 Act was the suggestion that contributions in certain industries be reduced. The rationale was the same in the opt out schemes, but the solution deviated less radically from state policy. The Canadian banks suggested that if they were not allowed to opt out of the Act then their contributions should be reduced from twenty-nine times their employees' benefits to three times their benefits.[128] The Canadian Chamber of Commerce similarly argued that some industries ". . . should at least be entitled to a reduction in contributions in view of their favourable employment record. These employees should not be penalized for the benefit of the unemployed in another industry or even other establishments within the same class of business."[129] This, of course, would represent a saving to capitalists in industries with reduced contributions since there would be a weaker labour demand for wage increases to compensate for higher contributions.

(5) Delay

The weakest and final tactic by businessmen was to try to coax the state into delaying passing the 1941 Act anywhere from a few months to the end of the war. Both the Canadian Manufacturer's Association and the Canadian Chamber of Commerce argued that they had not been given sufficient time to study the bill and that the war was the wrong time to introduce such a measure given the demand for capital expenditures in other areas. Once they had studied the bill and had time to exert greater influence on its contents, it could be passed by Parliament at some future date.[130]

The State Rejects Capital's Position

The Canadian state ignored the schemes and complaints of capitalists. As H.T. Jaffray, president of the Canadian Banker's Association, remarked after the dust had settled: ". . . the [Commons] Committee [on Unemployment Insurance] unanimously reported to the House against any exemption or special treatment of any group of employees and employers covered by the Bill as introduced. With minor amendments the Bill was passed by the Commons and Senate and received the Royal Assent on 7th August [1940]".[131] The state rejected capitalists' arguments that the Act impeded the accumulation of capital. The accumulation objectives of state and capitalists apparently conflicted. While Mackenzie King argued that the Act would build up a reserve of capital to be invested for wartime purposes, capitalists themselves opposed this argument. The contradictory effects of the Act on capital accumulation explain the conflict between businessmen and the state. The state viewed the Act as accumulating capital in two ways: as a reserve to pay for *its own* wartime expenditures; and, as a reserve fund from which the unemployed could draw once the expected economic collapse occurred after the war. Clearly capitalists were not at all interested in the second of these objectives and only mildly interested in the first. Capitalists had slightly different interests in capital accumulation. They were worried about tax burdens on industries, labour costs, inflation in consumer prices, and their export markets. The 1941 Act, while accumulating capital for the state, apparently did impede the kinds of accumulation significant for capitalists.

The state opposed the various lines of defence against the Act devised by Canadian businessmen. Mackenzie King saw through some of the private and semi-private plans as reducing the contribution to unemployment insurance by employers.[132] The state also turned down capitalist's plans to opt out of the 1941 Act on the basis of stable employment. Politicians offered two arguments. They questioned the existence of stable employment in those industries wanting to opt out. Under repeated and close questioning by the Commons Committee, the Retail Merchant's Association admitted that ". . . an evolution has been taking place in merchandising in the last decade. . . . You are seeing established in Canada today a merchandising monopoly . . . distribution is getting into fewer and fewer hands." This has resulted in the ". . . closing of a lot of small local stores . . . with consequent unemployment."[133] Secondly, the state wanted to build up the insurance fund by including some industries where employment was fairly steady and where contributions were expected to exceed benefits. This would aid workers more susceptible to unemployment.[134] Politicians rejected capitalists' arguments for a delay in imple-

menting the bill because they were caught unaware by its sudden introduction in the House of Commons. Mr. Mackenzie from Vancouver Centre argued that Canadian industry had known since 1935 of the planned introduction of unemployment insurance and that a year's notice had been given by the present government.[135] Mr. Pottier of the Commons Committee thought that ". . . the manufacturers, the retailers and members of chambers of commerce . . ." stated they were caught unprepared because "they wanted delay." He further noted that labour did not argue this way.[136] Either the objections by businessmen were not strong enough or they decided not to exert stronger pressure to defeat the Bill.

Historical Continuity of Capitalist's Interest

During periods of economic growth or prosperity, capitalist class fractions appeared to agree in their opposition to state unemployment insurance. Between 1923 and 1929 business and industry formed a counterargument to numerous commissions proposing state unemployment insurance.[137] Before the 1928 Commons Committee on Industrial and International Relations, the Canadian Manufacturer's Association argued that ". . . unemployment insurance would put Canadian industry in an unfair position pertaining to the location of foreign industrial investment."[138] During the 1920's and the Second World War, markets were expanding and business did not want added taxation in the form of unemployment insurance that might weaken consumers' willingness to buy goods and services.

However, during the Depression of the 1930's, cracks began to appear in business opposition to state unemployment insurance. On the one hand, there was still considerable opposition to unemployment insurance. This was summarized in a letter sent in 1933 to Prime Minister R.B. Bennett from J.E. Walsh, General Manager of the Canadian Manufacturer's Association:

This subject [unemployment insurance] has engaged the serious attention and study of this Association for the past five years, and we have been on record as to our attitude since 1928. Copies are appended of resolutions and reports approved at largely-attended annual meetings in 1928, 1930, and 1932. That attitude is, in a word, that it would not be wise to introduce a system of unemployment insurance in this country."[139]

An analysis of the 16 letters sent to Bennett from businessmen between January 12, 1931 and January 10, 1933 reveals that 75 per cent of them opposed unemployment insurance and only 25 per cent were in favour of contributory unemployment insurance. None were in favour of non-contributory unemployment insurance.[140] As the Depression grew more serious, further splits began to appear among the ranks of businessmen. Alvin Finkel has listed some of the businessmen and business organizations which at one time or another during the Depression came out in *support* of state unemployment insurance. This list includes the Retail Merchant's Association, the Ontario Association of Real Estate Boards, the Canadian Manufacturer's Association (which apparently switched sides temporarily), the Canadian Chamber of Commerce, Pulp and Paper of Canada, the Bank of Nova Scotia, A.O. Dawson, president of the Canadian Chamber of Commerce and Canadian Cottons, and Sir Charles Gordon, president of the Bank of Montreal and Dominion Textiles.[141]

It is important to understand the basis of splits within business over unemployment insurance. While it is difficult to detect hard and fast lines between business fractions, much of the evidence seems to indicate that mercantile and financial capitalists were much more likely than industrial capitalists to temporarily support unemployment insurance during the Depression. This seems reasonable in view of the analysis of the Depression as rooted in contradictions in the sphere of circulation rather than in the sphere of production. Three arguments of businessmen seem cogent here. First, merchants were concerned about the purchasing power of the consumer in the marketplace. The unemployed without any monetary means of subsistence would not be able to purchase commodities. Transferring money to them through relief and unemployment insurance would stimulate their purchase of commodities, and so increase the circulation of goods.[142] Secondly, it was argued that municipal relief strained municipal budgets so much

that municipal credit was becoming worthless. This obviously was of some concern to the banks which loaned money to municipalities. Financial capitalists argued that Federal unemployment insurance would help to relieve the strain on municipal relief budgets and so help to restore the credit rating of municipal governments.[143] Third, real estate men were concerned that a heavy municipal relief budget, based in property taxes, was depressing the housing industry. Once again, federal unemployment insurance was seen as easing the tax load of municipalities.[144]

Once the Depression was over, businessmen lined up more solidly against state unemployment insurance. Both the opposition to state unemployment insurance during times of prosperity and the weakening of this opposition during times of depression are explained by the same general conditions—capital accumulation. What had changed during these different times were the specific conditions of capital accumulation. When the market in the trading of money and commodities was in a slump, state unemployment insurance was seen by some businessmen as restimulating the market. Since this market was 'healthy' during times of prosperity, there was no need at such times to call for state intervention in the marketplace.

III. Labour

Labour's Interests in the 1941 Act

Three noteworthy themes emerge out of labour's submissions to the 1940 *Commons Committee on Unemployment Insurance*. First, labour gave strong support to the 1941 Act even to the extent of co-operating with the state in its control of industrial relations. Labour took this position because the Act subtly tied the interest of labour in a minimal wage subsistence to the control objectives of the state. Secondly, labour did offer some criticisms of the Act. Most of these were in the direction of improving the structure of contributions and extending the Act's coverage to include more workers and industries. However, these objections were not strong enough to set labour against the Act's implementation. They hoped that some of their objections would be accommodated in future revisions. Thirdly, some divisions emerged

145

between craft and industrial unions. The Trades and Labour Congress (TLC) seemed more supportive and less critical of the Act than the All-Canadian Congress of Labour (ACCL) and the Congress of Industrial Organization (CIO). But even in the case of industrial unions, objections to the structure of contributions were not strong enough to turn them against state unemployment insurance. Not unexpectedly, the unorganized worker and the unemployed had no direct input in the formulation of the Act. Had this been the case, provided their submission was effective (which is doubtful), the Act would have offered greater protection and benefits to the unemployed.

Tom Moore, president of the Trades and Labour Congress, indicated the broad union support for unemployment insurance: "As the evidence given to the select committee of the House of Commons shows, all labour organizations, irrespective of their differences on other matters were a unit in urging immediate adoption of the bill and prompt establishment of the administrative machinery."[145] This general endorsement was supported by Mr. Dowd, secretary-treasurer of the All-Canadian Congress of Labour, and Mr. Millard, secretary of the Congress of Industrial Organization.[146]

Labour unions seemed generally satisfied with the financial security the Act provided unemployed workers. The Trades and Labour Congress argued that the Act ". . . does . . . provide a first line of defence for unemployed workers and will enable thousands who have been driven to seek public relief to get by without the necessity to do so."[147] Similarly, the Congress of Industrial Organization argued: ". . . we regard unemployment insurance as a form of collective security. Even those who are most regularly employed will welcome this scheme. Not only because it will provide added security to them as workers, but also because of the general improvement in social conditions and the labour market which results from the operation of such a scheme."[148] Labour did not argue for higher insurance benefits, even though the planned benefits under the Act were less than half of employed labour's income. R.J. Tallon, labour's representative on the Unemployment Insurance Commission, advised the rank and file of the Trades and Labour Congress that ". . . the un-employed worker's insurance income is necessarily smaller than his normal wages . . . ."[149] There are three reasons for this rather conservative position. First, Canadian labour had been pushing for state unemployment insurance since 1919 and seemed relieved to be finally attaining it after 21 years. Some insurance benefits were better than none and preferable to the humiliation of the relief dole. Secondly, the T.L.C., A.C.C.L., and C.I.O. represented workers with more stable employment than the unorganized. Unemployment for them was temporary and insurance benefits were supplementary to their main incomes earned while employed. Unemployed workers associations were not represented by these unions. There was therefore no push for greater benefits. Third, benefits were based on contributions. If benefits were to be raised, contributions under the contributory actuarial principle would also have to be raised.[150] This would present financial hardships for low-wage workers.

Labour accepted the schedule of contributions set up under the Act. Norman Dowd of the All-Canadian Congress of Labour stated: ". . . we believe that the workers are willing to make the contributions set forth in the bill, inspite of the fact that it will create a hardship for low-paid workers, and that many workers will contribute who will not, in the normal course of events, ever require the assistance which the insurance will afford."[151] At the same time labour offered four mildly critical comments of the contributions.

First, the more industrial unions argued in favour of exempting low paid workers from the necessity of having to contribute to the insurance fund at all. Dowd of the ACCL stated: "We have always taken the position that the low-paid workers, those receiving practically a subsistence wage, should be exempted from the necessity of contributing toward the insurance premiums . . . ; but we are not raising that as any objection to this measure. We are quite prepared to have any difficulties of that sort straightened out in the course of experience."[152] On the other hand, the craft-oriented Trades and Labour Congress argued only that contributions for low-paid workers "be kept to a minimum," not that they should be eliminated.[153]

Secondly, labour was critical of the suggestion by capitalists that their industries be allowed to opt out of unemployment insurance or have reduced contributions either on the basis of having their own private plans or because of stable employment records. Tom Moore of the TLC argued: "The fact that there has been over so many years hundreds of thousands of unemployed forced to seek public aid for their maintenance is sufficient answer that whatever has been done by individual savings schemes, etc., has been totally inadequate to meet even the temporary requirements of vast numbers of the unemployed."[154] Moore also opposed industries' attempt to opt out or give reduced contributions on the basis of stable employment: "The employer might show a very good employment record because of state assistance being rendered either through tariffs or subsidies which enables him to maintain his markets. In such cases, is it fair that he should be given the benefit of lower contributions because of the advantages so accorded?"[155] Labour thought industries should not be able to opt out on the basis of stable employment when stably employed workers themselves were willing to stay in the plan and contribute despite receiving few if any benefits. Dowd of the ACCL stated: ". . . in the railway industry there are some 90 per cent approximately permanent employees; I mean senior men who will never be laid off in the normal course of events. There is no objection [to unemployment insurance] on their part; in fact, they have consistently supported it and not only that they have advocated unemployment insurance right throughout."[156]

Labour also suggested a much broader occupational and industrial coverage of the Act. The 1941 Act defined insurable work as "employment in Canada under any contract of service or apprenticeship, written or oral . . ." with the *exception* of the following: agriculture, horticulture and forestry; fishing; lumbering and logging; hunting and trapping; transportation by water or air and stevedoring; domestic service; hospital or charitable institutions; professional nurses; teacher; armed forces; public service of Dominion and provincial governments; agents paid by commissions, fees, profits or other employment; moonlighting; unpaid family employment; jobs paid in kind; and sports.[157] The 1941 Act thus adhered to Winston Churchill's 1911 principle that unemployment insurance should protect workers in the advanced sectors of capitalist industry rather than in declining trades and industries.[158] The Act largely excluded occupations that were (a) declining, (b) in early rather than advanced capitalist modes of production, (c) white-collar, (d) having a high risk of unemployment, and, (e) belonging to the state sector. In 1942, the first full year of the Act's operation, only 50 per cent of the labour force was covered. Between 1942 and 1950 coverage varied from 44 per cent to 52 per cent.[159] Labour was concerned with this rather restrictive coverage. Mr. Millard of the Congress of Industrial Organization stated:

. . . we are in entire agreement that the present maximum of $2,000 should be raised to at least $2,500 and if possible higher. We are also concerned about many of the employments which are now excluded from the operation of the Act. Such as lumbering, logging, and the like. We hope that once the Act is put into operation, both the Commission and the Advisory Committee will consider the question of extending its operation to most of the workers now excluded, at the earliest possible moment."[160]

Millard was not to get his wish until after 1951 when coverage increased to 58 per cent of the labour force; by 1974 coverage had steadily increased to 89 per cent.[161]

Fourthly, industrial unions took a more radical stand than craft unions in suggesting a change in the balance of contributions to the insurance fund by labour and capital. Norman Dowd of the All-Canadian Congress of Labour suggested that ". . . ideally unemployment insurance should be a direct charge upon industry since the individual workers are not responsible for unemployment" but did not press this to the point of opposing the 1941 Act.[162]

The interests of organized labour were not radically different from the state's. The state wanted to build up a reserve insurance fund during the war to prepare for the economic collapse that was expected after the war. R.J. Tallon of the Trades and Labour Congress argued: "If a depression comes after the war, the reserve built up at the present time will be available to cushion the severity of unemployment. Unemployment insurance and its complement, the Employment Service,

147

offer an important means for readjustment during the post-war transitional period."[163] The state's interest in the stabilization of labour supply was also shared by organized labour. Dowd of the ACCL thought that the National Employment Service set up under the Act "will assist greatly to stabilize employment."[164] Moore of the TLC argued that ". . . the present situation calls for more active development of this [employment] service to meet war needs for labour supply. It will also be even more necessary to have a competent employment service during the demobilization and readjustment period."[165] Labour further co-operated with the state and employers in setting the Act up and in ensuring its smooth functioning. A three-person Unemployment Insurance Commission was set up with representatives from the state (Arthur McNamara), labour (Robert Tallon), and capital (Alan M. Mitchell, "a prominent Canadian employer").[166] In an editorial in the *Canadian Congress Journal*, Tom Moore, president of the TLC, recommended to the rank and file that it was in their self-interest to co-operate with state and capital. Since the editorial is so revealing, it is useful to quote it at length.

> . . . workers both individually and through their trade unions can be of material assistance to ensuring that the provisions of the Act are fully complied with.
>
> The first step in this direction is for every insurable worker to make certain that his employer registers with the Unemployment Insurance Commission, obtains the necessary insurance book, and regularly affixes the requisite stamps therein. While during employment the insurance book is held by the employer, workers are entitled to inspect their own books at any time to insure not only that stamps are affixed for each day or week of employment, but that they are of the proper value. It is from these stamps that the amount of benefit payable to the workers when unemployed will be computed, and as these benefits vary in amount according to stamps, it is of the utmost importance to the worker that the proper classification of stamps should be used.
>
> . . .
>
> It cannot be too strongly stressed that workers will be performing a useful duty

and protecting their own interests by lending every assistance to the administration officers charged with the carrying out of the provisions of this important measure of social security."[167]

Such labour co-operation helped the state to stabilize industrial relations between labour and capital. The type of outburst from the unemployed that so many feared would occur in the aftermath of the war was thus averted.

Historical Continuity of Labour's Interests

Labour supported state unemployment insurance since the First World War. Tom Moore of the TLC in 1940 stated; "For a quarter of a century workers in Canada have been looking forward to the protection which unemployment insurance affords and in 1935 thought they had secured this, but, to their intense disappointment, constitutional difficulties caused another five years delay which powerful opposing interests now seek to further extend."[168] The Trades and Labour Congress during the 1920's passed resolutions at several of its annual conventions urging the federal government to take action in this field.[169] In 1928, the Catholic Worker's Union of Canada appeared before the *Commons Committee on Industrial and International Relations* supporting unemployment insurance financed by contributions from state, labour and capital.[170] The All-Canadian Congress of Labour argued in 1940: "At almost every convention of the Congress since 1927, approval has been given by resolution to the principle of unemployment insurance and it has also been endorsed annually when delegations from the affiliated and chartered unions of the Congress submitted representations to the federal government with respect to legislative and other matters (of concern) to the workers."[171] This long support has been based on one main rationale: to increase the wage subsistence and purchasing power of the working class in general and the unemployed in particular.

Only during the Depression was there any serious split among different working class fractions over state unemployment insurance. However, this split was not over *whether or not* to institute state unemployment insurance. Rather, it was over the *type* of state unemployment insurance.

An analysis of 89 communications sent by labour organizations to Prime Minister Bennett between October 10, 1930 and May 10, 1932 reveals that 84 per cent of organizations of employed workers favoured contributory unemployment insurance compared to only 13 per cent of organizations of exclusively unemployed workers or mixed employed and unemployed workers. In contrast, 87 per cent of unemployed worker organizations favoured non-contributory unemployment insurance compared to only 16 per cent of employed worker organizations.[172] Non-contributory unemployment insurance, in which unemployment insurance would essentially be paid for by business and high-income earners, was the core of the Worker Unity League's "Working Class Unemployment Insurance Bill."[173] It had gathered 94,169 signatures from across Canada in the spring of 1931 in support of non-contributory unemployment insurance. The backbone of this drive were the numerous unemployed councils set up at the municipal level across the country. Organizations of employed workers, especially craft workers, lent little support to this political thrust against Bennett. The major lines of division within the working class appeared to be between employed and craft workers who supported contributory unemployment insurance, and unemployed workers and industrial unions which tended to support non-contributory unemployment insurance. No major labour organization opposed unemployment insurance, and this appears to be the major difference between the working class and business which displayed much greater opposition to unemployment insurance. By the Second World War, even these minor splits within the working class appeared to have all but disappeared.

In view of the long history of labour support, why did the state not introduce unemployment insurance sooner, especially given the way it apparently aided its social control objectives? A number of reasons can be given. The influence of labour on the state was much weaker than capital's which, through much of its history, opposed unemployment insurance. It took the Depression to erode some of capital's resistance. At that point the federal state fumbled for five years between 1935 and 1940 trying to work out constitutional arrangements that would allow it to pass the legislation. By the time the state finally moved into action in 1940, socio-economic conditions had changed, and capital had also changed its mind in the direction of more solid opposition. However, the state was determined to go ahead with its insurance programme. Its concern with a repetition after the Second World War of the post-World War I labour unrest and the revolts by the unemployed during the Depression were too fresh in its mind to risk pleasing the whims of capital. Organized labour in the end achieved its objectives, not through its own influence, but through changes in the capitalist order and the state's belated response to such changes.

IV. Epilogue

The fact that the Canadian state passed the 1941 Unemployment Insurance Act despite objections from capitalists suggests that the Marxist instrumental theory of the State, according to which the bourgeoisie directly manipulates the state, is not valid for the case under examination. More valid here is the Marxist structural theory of the state which suggests that the state is relatively autonomous of the capitalist class and responds primarily to structural changes in the underlying economic order. The Canadian state has historically been much more anxious to pass unemployment legislation controlling reserve labour during periods of crisis. This was true in the midst of the post-World War I period of turmoil as it was true for the Depression and the Second World War. But during the 1920's the state was much less active during a period of relatively peaceful industrial relations. Whether these remarks are also valid for other types of social security legislation must await the examination of further case studies, such as old age pensions, mother's allowance, and workmen's compensation.

It cannot be argued that capitalists publicly took one position and in private communications with the state took a different stand. Released state papers indicate a consistency between the two positions. Further, capital had no need of opposing unemployment insurance in public when there had developed such an overwhelming public opinion for support for it by 1940. There would be no advantage to capital in taking such an unpopular stand—unless it was based on a 'correct' reflection of their class interests.

It is ironic that unemployment insurance legislation was passed presumably to assist the finances of the unemployed when this was the major group in Canada that did not have a direct input in the legislation. This reflects the powerlessness of the unemployed in relation to the state, to capital and to organized labour. More importantly this reveals the state's intent. Since the legislation was passed in order to introduce stability into industrial relations that were beginning to come apart at the seams, there was no need for the state to consult the unemployed. The legislation was addressed more to organized labour and those more secure in employment who wanted a cushion to fall back on during times of temporary distress. The chronically unemployed received little help from such legislation. They would soon be disqualified from receiving insurance benefits because of the necessity to work for a period in the labour force to become recipients. They were thus thrown more onto the laps of provincial and municipal governments in their haphazard direct relief and public work's programmes. The political powerlessness of the unemployed was reflected in the inability of the 1941 Unemployment Insurance Act to relieve their distress on both a temporary and a more permanent basis.

NOTES

[1]The best summary of the "instrumentalist" and "structuralist" theories is by David Gold, Clarence Lo and Eric Olin Wright, "Recent Developments in Marxist Theories of the Capitalist State," *Monthly Review*, 27(5), Oct. 1975, pp.29-43. Representative of the instrumentalists is Ralph Miliband, *The State in Capitalist Society*, London: Weidenfeld and Nicholson, 1969, although there are structuralist subcurrents in Miliband's work. On this see especially Ralph Miliband, "Reply to Nicos Poulantzas," pp.253-62 in Robin Blackburn (ed.), *Ideology in Social Science*, London: Fontana, 1972 and his *Marxism and Politics*, Oxford: Oxford University Press, 1977. The structuralist literature is much more diverse. Some quite different examples are Nicos Poulantzas, *Political Power and Social Classes*, London: NLB, 1973; James O'Conner, *The Fiscal Crisis of the State*, New York: St. Martin's Press, 1973; Frances Fox Piven and Richard A. Cloward, *Regulating the Poor*, New York: Random House, 1971; Gosta Epsing-Anderson, Roger Friedland, Eric Olin Wright, "Modes of Class Struggle and the Capitalist State," *Kapitalistate*, 4-5, 1976, pp.186-220; and, Göran Therborn, "The Rule of Capital and the Rise of the Democracy," *New Left Review*, No. 103, 1977, pp.3-41.

[2]*Statutes of Canada*, 4 Geo. VI, 1940, c.44.

[3]Unemployment benefits varied from 16 per cent to 49 per cent of the average income of employed workers. Calculated from *ibid*, and Canada, Dept. of Labour, *Labour Gazette*, August, 1941, p.978.

[4]*Labour Gazette*, June, 1940, p.527.

[5]*Debates of the House of Commons*, July 16, 1940, p.1630.

[6]*Labour Gazette*, July, 1940, p.683.

[7]These letters attempted to arrange provincial co-operation to an amendment of the British North America Act that would allow the Federal Parliament to pass unemployment insurance legislation. See P.A.C., W.L. Mackenzie King Papers, "Unemployment Insurance Act," n.d., C231894-231901; Letters, King to Aberhart, Jan. 16, 1940, C231926-231929; Dysart to King, Jan. 25, 1940, C231922-231923; Godbout to King, May 13, 1940, C231924-231925.

[8]King Papers, King to Aberhart, Jan. 16, 1940, C231926.

[9]Jacob L. Cohen, *The Canadian Unemployment Insurance Act*, Toronto: T. Nelson, 1935.

[10]*Debates of the House of Commons*, July 16, 1940, p.1659.

[11]King Papers, "Summary of Debates on Unemployment," 1930, C103221.

[12]King Papers, "Suggested Unemployment Relief Commission," September 12, 1930, C103271.

[13]King Papers, Godbout to King, May 13, 1940, C231924.

[14]*Labour Gazette*, July, 1940, p.683.

[15]*Debates of the House of Commons*, July 16, 1940, p.1657.

[16]King Papers, King to Aberhart, Jan. 16, 1940, C231928. See also King's memorandum, "Reasons for Introducing the Unemployment Insurance Bill During the War," July 15, 1940, C232019-232021.

[17]*Debates of the House of Commons*, July 19, 1940, p.1768.

[18]King Papers, Dysart to King, Jan. 25, 1940, C231922.

[19]King Papers, "Reasons for Introducing the Unemployment Insurance Bill During the War," 1940, C231886-231889. (This is a revised version of the memorandum with the same title referred to in f.16, and will henceforth be noted by #2).

[20]*Labour Gazette*, September, 1913, p.221; December 1913, p.639; February 1914, p.944; July, 1914, p.1.

[21]*Industrial Canada*, January, 1914, p.773.

[22]*Industrial Canada*, May, 1915, p.70; June, 1915, p.166; July, 1915, pp.300, 310-12; *Canada Year Book*, 1916-17, pp.285, 294; *1918*, pp 308-09.

[23]*Labour Gazette*, May, 1915, p.84; July, 1915, pp.27, 33, 40; September, 1915, p.273.

[24]*Labour Gazette*, November, 1918, pp.905, 907; December, 1918, pp.1047, 1049; January, 1919, pp.5, 8.

[25]Colonel C.W.L. Nicholson, *Canadian Expeditionary Force, 1914-1918*, Ottawa: Queen's Printer, 1962, p.546.

[26]*Debates of the House of Commons*, April 22, 1918, p.978.

[27]Nicholson, *op. cit.*, p.547; *Canada Year Book*, 1920, p.26.

[28]*Debates of the House of Commons*, April 23, 1918, pp.1034-35.

[29]M.C. Urquhart and K.A. Buckley (eds.), *Historical Statistics of Canada*, Toronto: Macmillan, 1965, p.105.

[30]*Ibid*, p.107.

[31]*Ibid*, p.84, 303; *Canada Year Book*, 1921, pp.626-31. James Struthers notes that there was even "heavy unemployment in 1924 and 1925." See his "Prelude to Depression: The Federal Government and Unemployment," *Canadian Historical Review*, LVIII(3), 1977, p.277.

[32]Sir Andrew McPhail, *The Medical Services*, Ottawa: F.A. Aucland, 1925, p.400.

[33]Nicholson, *op. cit.*, p.532. P.A.C., Robert Borden Papers, RLB, Vol. 247, pp.238844-238869, Vol. 249, pp.139868-75; O.C., Vol. 114, pp.62458-62653.

[34]Overseas Military Forces of Canada. *Report of the Ministry of Overseas Military Forces of Canada*, London, 1918, p.516.

[35]*Ibid*, p.517.

[36]*Ibid*, p.525.

[37]*Canada Year Book*, 1920, p.26.

[38]*Debates of the House of Commons*, March 19, 1918, p.31.

[39]*Canada Year Book*, 1920, p.27.

[40]*Labour Gazette*, December, 1918, p.1041.

[41]*Ibid*, p.1041.

[42]*Statutes of Canada*, 8-9 Geo. V, 1918, c.2; Struthers, "Prelude to Depression . . . ," 1977, pp.279-81.

[43]*Canada Year Book*, 1921, p.623.

[44]*Ibid*, p.624.

[45]*Ibid*, p.623.

[46]*Debates of the House of Commons*, July 16, 1940, p.1648.

[47]Dept. of Labour. *National Industrial Conference. Official Report of Proceedings and Discussions*, Ottawa: J. de Labroquerie Tache, 1919, p.180.

[48]*Canada Year Book*, 1920, p.27.

[49]Struthers, "Prelude to Depression . . . ", 1977, p.284. Struthers further notes that the first state unemployment insurance scheme in Canada was devised in 1920.

[50]Canada. Parliament. House of Commons. *Select Standing Committee on Industrial and International Relations. Report . . . upon the Questions of Insurance Against Unemployment . . .* Ottawa: F.A. Aucland, 1928.

[51]These are very conservative estimates of unemployment since they are based on the percentage of unemployed seeking work out of the total labour force. Calculated from Urquhart and Buckley (eds.), *op. cit.*, p.61. Struthers cites some fairly high estimates of unemployment during the 1920s, especially during the winter months. See his "Prelude to Depression," 1977, p.277.

[52]King Papers, Memo, Baldwin to King, "Re. Professor Gilbert Jackson and Unemployment Insurance," May 22, 1930, C103135.

[53]*Ibid*, C103135.

[54]*Statutes of Canada*, 21 Geo. V, 1931, pp.4-5.

[55]Dept. of Labour. *Unemployment Relief Act, 1930. Report of Dominion Director of Unemployment Relief*, March 16, 1931. Ottawa: King's Printer, 1931, pp.4, 14, 15.

[56]*Ibid*, p.4.

[57]*Statutes of Canada*, 21-22 Geo. V, 1931, c.58, p.429.

[58]*Statutes of Canada*, 22-23 Geo. V, 1932, c.13.

[59]*Statutes of Canada*, 22-23 Geo. V, 1932, c.36.

[60]*Statutes of Canada*, 23-24 Geo. V, 1932-1933, c.18, pp.89-90.

[61]*Statutes of Canada*, 24-25 Geo. V, 1934, c.15, p.108.

[62]Ronald Liversedge, *The On-to-Ottawa Trek*, Toronto: McClelland and Stewart 1973; Lorne A. Brown, "Unemployment Relief Camps in Saskatchewan, 1933-1936." *Saskatchewan History*, XXIII (3), 1970, pp.81-104. P.A.C., Department of National Defence, "Unemployment Relief Scheme, 1932-1937," especially Vols. 3029, 3032-34, 3038, 3047-8.

[63] *Statutes of Canada*, 25-26 Geo. V, 1935, c.13.

[64] *Statutes of Canada*, 25-26, Geo. V, 1935, c.38.

[65] King Papers, Memorandum, "The Unemployment Insurance Act," n.d., C231894-231895.

[66] *Ibid*, C231896-231897.

[67] Thomas Cane, "A Test Case for Canadian Federalism: The Unemployment Insurance Issue, 1919-1940," M.A. Thesis, Dept. of Political Science, University of Western Ontario, 1971, pp.112-13.

[68] *Statutes of Canada*, 4 Geo. VI, 1940, c.44, pp.193-94.

[69] King Papers, Memorandum, "The Opposition to Unemployment Insurance" n.d., C231933.

[70] King Papers, Memorandum, "Reasons for Introducing the Unemployment Insurance Bill During the War," July 15, 1940, C232020.

[71] *Canada Year Book*, 1943-44, p.712.

[72] *Ibid*, p.712.

[73] King Papers, "Reasons for introducing . . . ," *op. cit.*, C232020.

[74] *Canada Year Book*, 1946, p.752.

[75] King Papers, Memorandum, "Reasons for introducing . . . ," (#2), *op. cit.*, C231886.

[76] P.M. Richards, "Unemployment Insurance," *Saturday Night*, January 6, 1940, p.7; B.K. Sandwell, "An Appeal to the Senate," *Saturday Night*, July 27, 1940, p.3; F. Gould Means, "Unemployment Insurance Means Increased Taxation," *Saturday Night*, July 27, 1940, p.7.

[77] For example, see King Papers, "Reasons for introducing . . . ," C232020.

[78] Calculated from *Statutes of Canada*, 4 Geo. VI, 1940, c.44, pp.223-24; *Labour Gazette*, August, 1941, p.978.

[79] For an excellent critique of the contributory principle, see Cohen, *op. cit.*, 1935.

[80] *Statutes of Canada*, 4 Geo. VI, 1940, c.44, p.197.

[81] Canada. Parliament. *House of Commons Special Committee on Bill 98 Respecting Unemployment Insurance. Minutes of Proceedings*. July 22-25, Ottawa: J.O. Patenaude, 1940. (In the following footnotes, the issue entirely in arabic pagination will be referred to as *Commons Committee on Unemployment Insurance, 1940*, while the issue with both Roman and Arabic pagination will have the addition of the symbol "RA").

[82] *Canadian Congress Journal*, August, 1940, p.15.

[83] *Ibid*, p.12.

[84] King Papers, Memo, "The Opposition to Unemployment Insurance," n.d., C231930.

[85] *Commons Committee on Unemployment Insurance, 1940*, R.A., p.141.

[86] *Commons Committee on Unemployment Insurance, 1940*, p.135. See also pp.134, 141.

[87] *Ibid*, p.87.

[88] *Industrial Canada*, August, 1940, p.39.

[89] See also P.M. Richards, "Unemployment Insurance," *Saturday Night*, January 6, 1940, p.7; P.M. Richards, "Costly Delusion," *Saturday Night*, February 3, 1940, p.9; B.K. Sandwell, "An Appeal to the Senate," *Saturday Night*, July 27, 1940, p.3.

[90] *Commons Committee on Unemployment Insurance, 1940*, R.A., p.137.

[91] *Commons Committee on Unemployment Insurance, 1940*, p.135.

[92] *Ibid*, p.137.

[93] *Ibid*, p.138; *Debates of the House of Commons*, July 16, 1940, pp.1651, 1657.

[94] *Commons Committee on Unemployment Insurance, 1940*, pp.135, 137; *Debates of the House of Commons*, July 16, 1940, pp.1657, 1661; B.K. Sandwell, "An Appeal to the Senate," *Saturday Night*, July 27, 1940, p.3.

[95] *Commons Committee on Unemployment Insurance, 1940*, R.A., pp.137-38.

[96] *Industrial Canada*, December 1906, p.442.

[97] Cohen, *op. cit.*, 1935, p.56.

[98] R.B. Bennett, *Debates of the House of Commons*, January 29, 1935, p.278.

[99] Cane, *op. cit.*, 1971, p.14; Marie Jahoda, Paul Lazarsfeld, and Hans Zeisel, *Marienthal: The Sociography of an Unemployed Community* Chicago: Aldine-Atherton, 1971 (1933), p.x.

[100] *The Canadian Banker*, October, 1940, pp.87-88, 90.

[101] *Industrial Canada*, February, 1940, p.35.

[102] *Commons Committee on Unemployment Insurance, 1940*, p.139.

[103] *Industrial Canada*, August, 1940, p.38; *Commons Committee on Unemployment Insurance, 1940*, p.86; B.K. Sandwell, "Creating a 'Counsel of Perfection,' " *Saturday Night*, July 13, 1940, p.11.

[104] *Industrial Canada*, February, 1940, p.35.

[105] *The Canadian Banker*, October, 1940, p.89.

[106] *Industrial Canada*, February, 1940, p.35.

[107] *Ibid*, p.36.

[108] *Ibid*, p.36.

[109] *Ibid*, p.36.

[110] *Commons Committee on Unemployment Insurance, 1940*, p.136.

[111] *Industrial Canada*, February, 1940, p.37.

[112]*Industrial Canada*, August, 1940, p.37.

[113]*The Canadian Manufacturer*, May 4, 1894, p.356.

[114]*The Canadian Manufacturer*, Feb.16, 1894. pp.136-37.

[115]*Industrial Canada*, August, 1940, p.53.

[116]King Papers, Memo, "The Opposition to Unemployment Insurance," n.d., C231931-231932.

[117]*Ibid*, C231932.

[118]*The Canadian Banker*, "Unemployment Insurance," April, 1942, p.311.

[119]*The Canadian Banker*, "Unemployment Insurance," October, 1940, pp.89-90.

[120]*Ibid*, pp.86-87.

[121]*Ibid*, p.87.

[122]*Commons Committee on Unemployment Insurance*, 1940, pp.129-30, 132.

[123]*Commons Committee on Unemployment Insurance*, 1940, R.A., p.137.

[124]*The Canadian Banker*, "Unemployment Insurance," October, 1940, p.89.

[125]*The Canadian Banker*, "Unemployment Insurance," April, 1942, p.311.

[126]*Commons Committee on Unemployment Insurance*, 1940, p.130.

[127]*Ibid*, p.86.

[128]*The Canadian Banker*, October, 1940, p.90.

[129]*Commons Committee on Unemployment Insurance*, 1940, R.A. p.137.

[130]King Papers, Memo, "The Opposition to Unemployment Insurance," n.d., C231930; *Commons Committee on Unemployment Insurance*, 1940, pp.87, 134-35.

[131]*The Canadian Banker*, October, 1940, p.86.

[132]King Papers, Memo, "The Opposition to Unemployment Insurance," n.d., C231932.

[133]*Commons Committee on Unemployment Insurance*, 1940, pp.133-34.

[134]The Canadian Banker, "Unemployment Insurance," April, 1942, pp.309-10.

[135]*Commons Committee on Unemployment Insurance*, 1940, R.A., p.138.

[136]*Ibid*, p.138.

[137]Cane, *op. cit.*, 1971, p.2.

[138]*Ibid*, pp.24-25.

[139]P.A.C., Bennett Papers, Walsh to Bennett, Jan. 10, 1933, p.502746.

[140]*Ibid*, pp.501889-2462.

[141]Alvin Finkel, "Origins of the Welfare State in Canada," in Leo Panitch (ed.), *The Canadian State: Political Economy and Political Power*, Toronto: University of Toronto Press, 1977, pp.349, 350, 352, 355, 357.

[142]*Ibid*, p.355.

[143]*Ibid*, p.349.

[144]*Ibid*, pp.355-36.

[145]*Canadian Congress Journal*, August, 1940, p.18. See also *ibid*, pp.12, 15.

[146]*Commons Committee on Unemployment Insurance*, 1940, R.A., pp.144, 146, 148.

[147]*Canadian Congress Journal*, August, 1940, p.12.

[148]*Commons Committee on Unemployment Insurance*, 1940, R.A., p.147.

[149]*Canadian Congress Journal*, September, 1941, p.31.

[150]See Andrew Watson, *Actuarial Report on the Contributions Required to Provide the Unemployment Insurance Benefits within the Scheme of the Draft of an Act Entitled, The Employment and Social Insurance Act*, Ottawa: J.O. Patenaude, 1935; Cohen, *op. cit.*, 1935.

[151]*Commons Committee on Unemployment Insurance*, 1940, R.A., p.145.

[152]*Ibid*, p.149.

[153]*Canadian Congress Journal*, August, 1940, p.19.

[154]*Ibid*, p.19.

[155]*Ibid*, p.19.

[156]*Commons Committee on Unemployment Insurance*, 1940, R.A., p.149.

[157]*Statutes of Canada*, 4 Geo. VI, 1940, c.44, pp.221-22.

[158]Cohen, *op. cit.*, 1935, p.114.

[159]Calculated from Dominion Bureau of Statistics, Labour Division, Unemployment Insurance Section, *Statistical Report on the Operation of the Unemployment Insurance Act*, July, 1961, Vol. 19, No. 7, Ottawa: Queen's Printer, 1961, p.6.

[160]*Commons Committee on Unemployment Insurance*, 1940, R.A., p.147.

[161]*Statistical Report . . .*, *op. cit.*, 1961, p.6; July, 1966, Vol. 25, Nov. 7, p.6; December, 1975, Vol. 34, No. 12, p.8.

[162]*Labour Gazette*, August, 1940, p.799.

[163]*Canadian Congress Journal*, September, 1941, p.31.

[164]*Commons Committee on Unemployment Insurance*, 1940, R.A., p.145.

[165]*Canadian Congress Journal*, August, 1940, p.19.

[166]*Canadian Congress Journal*, September, 1941, p.31.

[167]*Canadian Congress Journal*, July, 1941, p.7.

[168] *Canadian Congress Journal*, August, 1940, p.18.
[169] Cane, *op. cit.*, pp.11-14, 24; *Debates of the House of Commons*, September 10, 1930, p.63.
[170] *Ibid*, p.23.
[171] *Commons Committee on Unemployment Insurance*, 1940, R.A., p.144.
[172] Bennett Papers, pp.501739-2457.
[173] *Ibid*, p.501937.

REGULATORY AGENCIES: CAPTIVE AGENTS OR HEGEMONIC APPARATUSES

Rianne Mahon

The extension of the state's authority into the economic sphere in advanced capitalist formations has entailed not only the growth of the regular departmental apparatus but also the multiplication of independent boards and commissions whose legitimacy is seen to reside in their insulation from political pressure and their technical expertise. Critics of such agencies, however, have pointed to the ironic fact that rather than increasing the state's capacity to ensure that corporate decisions accord with the 'public interest' the proliferation of such institutions has rendered the state more vulnerable to corporate influence.[1] In other words, such agencies tend to become mere captive agents of the very forces they are to regulate. Liberals are not the sole proponents of the captive agents thesis. Certain radicals, too, support this interpretation although, for the latter, the 'captive' character of such agencies is but another instance in the functioning of the state as "an instrument in the hands of the ruling class for enforcing and guaranteeing the stability of the class itself."[2]

Yet the 'captive agents' thesis obscures far more than it reveals about the production of 'bias' in the state. While the radicals are correct in stressing that the 'bias' of regulatory agencies is linked to the ultimate character of the state as a capitalist state, neither regulatory agencies nor the state itself can be reduced to instruments in the hands of members of the bourgeoisie. 'Bias' in the activity of the state is produced in a complex way–through the unequal structure of representation inside the state, a structure expressive of inter- and intra-class relations of power. Through this structuration of class relations 'inside' the state, the interests of various social forces are combined in a particular way–organised around the long-term political interests of the hegemonic fraction of the dominant class.

Regulatory agencies constitute a 'special case' of this unequal structure of representation through which class hegemony is produced. Like other parts of the state apparatus, these institutions represent the interests of a specific fraction–but in a particular way, as they are effectively combined with the long-term interests of the hegemonic fraction. That is, they simultaneously represent and regulate. Such agencies derive their 'special' character from their origins in an issue that contains a particular kind of threat to the fundamental relations of a capitalist formation. Regulatory agencies thus constitute a particular compromise which is 'insulated' from the normal structure of representation. This does not mean, however, that such agencies are effectively exempted from the general pattern of compromise. In practice, a variety of means exist to subordinate the agency's functioning to the overall bias of the state.

The first section of this paper provides a theoretical elaboration, building from Nicos Poulantzas's concept of the capitalist state as "a factor for the establishment of the 'unstable equilibrium of compromises' [which] . . . is constitutively connected with its relative autonomy," to the notion of the unequal structure of representation of which regulatory agencies are a special case.[3] In order to illustrate the fruitfulness of this approach, the second section will discuss the Canadian Textile and Clothing Board–a semi-independent board established by the federal government

154

in 1970 to assist in the implementation of Canada's textile policy.[4] This will permit a comparison of the kinds of questions generated by the captive agents perspective with those posed by the alternative proposed in this paper.

I Theoretical Elaboration

It is not by chance that liberals (both classical and contemporary) and certain Marxists tend to the 'captive agents' interpretation of regulatory agencies. Although there are major differences in their respective views of 'society' and 'state,' both tend to conceive the relation, state/society, as one of externality: the state is a 'thing' whose power may be captured and utilised by private forces. In the recent Marxist literature on the state, a very different conceptualisation has been formulated, in which the capitalist state is understood as a structure—a relation between conflicting classes.[5]

1. The State as Structure

To conceive the state as a structure involves the rejection of the notion of 'state power' as something separate from and external to 'class power.' The authority of the state is, in the last analysis, the authority or hegemony of the leading fraction of the dominant class. At the same time, within the capitalist mode of production, this structure—as the 'universalizing' instance, the resultant of the political class struggle—is characterised by a relative autonomy from the dominant class(es). This seeming paradox is resolved when the role of the state is examined.

That is, the articulation of the class struggle in the state is that which 'produces' the authority of the hegemonic class or fraction. To cite Gramsci,

> . . . (T)he dominant group is coordinated concretely with the general interest of subordinate groups and the life of the state is conceived as a continual process of forming and superseding of unstable equilibria . . . between the interests of the fundamental group and those of subordinate groups—equilibria in which the interests of the dominant group prevail but only up to a certain point, i.e. stopping short of narrowly corporate economic interest.[6]

Through the state the interests of various fractions and classes are combined and recombined: the formation of 'authority' is a continuous process of 'incorporating' the interests of various forces. In this process, the unity of the power bloc is effected; at the same time, formation of 'the people'—an alliance of subordinate forces which poses a fundamental challenge to the system of domination—is inhibited.

The form of state 'typical' of advanced capitalist societies—the 'nation state,' 'rule of law,' 'universal franchise,' 'welfare state'—is thus more than an ideological screen masking the direct rule of the bourgeoisie. As Poulantzas notes,

> The notion of the general interest of the people, an ideological notion covering an institutional operation of the capitalist state, expresses a *real fact*: namely that this state, by its very structure, gives to the economic interests of certain dominated classes guarantees which may even be contrary to the short-term interests of the dominant class but which are compatible with their political interest . . . their hegemonic domination.[7]

The modern capitalist state makes 'real' concessions to the subordinate classes, concessions which serve to combine (in a subordinate fashion) their immediate interests with the general, politico-economic interests of the dominant class(es). In the post-war context, it may even be argued that the state has increasingly played a role in organizing the subordinate classes—but in such a way as to inhibit their political constitution as an autonomous revolutionary class.[8]

The effect of the relative autonomy of the capitalist state is not limited to securing the hegemony of the dominant class vis-à-vis the subordinate classes. It also permits the state to function as political organiser of the various dominant fractions and to arrange the 'corporate' compromises that provide the conditions for the expanded reproduction of capital and of the bourgeoisie as the dominant class. This is particularly important in the phase of monopoly capitalism. The divisions within the bourgeoisie produced by uneven development (between industries, sectors, regions), the global interpenetration of capital, and the whole series of 'irrational' differences introduced by the correspondence of economic and socio-cultural divisions have drawn the state into direct intervention in the economy in order to give to 'national development' a certain direction. In this instance, the direction tends to correspond to the long-term interests of the hegemonic fraction of the dominant class. To cite Gramsci again, through the nation state, "the development and expansion of a particular group are conceived of and presented as being the motor force of universal expansion, of a development of all national energies."[9] Although the 'national interest' may, in the final analysis, tend to the integration of the national economy into the global capitalist system, where a domestic fraction provides the political leadership (i.e., constitutes the hegemonic fraction) then the terms of integration are likely to take into account the political interests of that fraction. In other words, the 'national interest' cannot simply be reduced to 'imperialism in national guise.'[10]

The monopoly capitalist state, then, can be conceived as a structure characterised by a relative autonomy vis-à-vis the dominant class. Its relative autonomy is linked to its role as 'producer' of the authority of the hegemonic class of fraction: the state as "a factor for the establishment of the 'unstable equilibrium of compromises' serves to weld together a given class-divided social formation under the hegemony of a particular fraction." Yet how is this produced if the state is a 'structure' and not an 'instrument' in the hands of the ruling class?

Of the 'structuralist' theorists of the state, Nicos Poulantzas provides the strongest formulation–the best clue to a reading of the state in terms of the 'unequal structure of representation.' However, it is also worth considering the problems encountered by another critic of the instrumentalist concept, James O'Connor, in order to pinpoint some of the problems which require resolution.

2. Critique of O'Connor

James O'Connor has utilised a structuralist approach to produce some significant insights into the role of the state in advanced capitalist formations. For O'Connor, the relative autonomy of the state is linked to its contradictory functions. The state 'intervenes' in order to legitimate class domination and to provide the conditions for the stable accumulation of capital. It is these con-

tradictory functions that explain the tendency of the interests of monopoly capital to "emerge within the state apparatus 'unintentionally'." O'Connor utilises this concept of the functions of the capitalist state to develop categories for analysing state expenditure patterns: "state expenditure patterns have a two-fold character corresponding to the capitalist state's two basic functions: social capital and social expenses."[11] This framework enables him to provide an impressive account of the current fiscal crises of the state. However, O'Connor's method does not provide an adequate basis for analysing regulatory outputs.

That is, in examining the activity of the state it is important to distinguish between 'allocative' and 'regulatory' outputs:

> There is a fundamental distinction to be made between decisions which allocate tangible benefits directly to persons and groups, as expenditures generally do, and decisions which establish the rules of authority to guide future allocation.[12]

While O'Connor's categories help in analysing the first, his treatment of the second tends to an 'instrumentalist' position, despite his claims to the contrary. For instance, he argues that

> Interest groups have appropriated many small pieces of state power through a 'multiplicity of intimate contacts with the government.' They dominate most of the so-called regulatory agencies at the federal, state, and local levels. . . . [13]

This makes it difficult for O'Connor to explain the way in which the interests of monopoly capital "emerge within the state apparatus 'unintentionally'." Clearly, to establish this hypothesis (countering both pluralists and instrumentalists) the problem of cohesion within the state must be addressed–a fact which O'Connor recognises. However, he relies primarily on the introduction of new budgetary principles as the main mechanism of central control and coordination. He is therefore led to exempt regulatory agencies, yielding to the 'captive agents' position:

> These functions require effective central executive control over the federal budget and

administrative machinery. The exception is the interest group economic needs, to which the legislative branch and many executive agencies are highly responsive.[14]

To criticise O'Connor's analysis is not to suggest that interest group behaviour, and the 'sensitivity' of various parts of the state apparatus in the face of this, is irrelevant. However, it is to indicate that the concept of the state (and its relation to the class struggle) needs a more precise formulation. Poulantzas's theorisation of the capitalist state, as a structure through which political class domination (comprised of the moments of force and hegemony) is produced, emphasising the structured 'presence' of class relations, of class struggle inside the state. This suggests the notion of the unequal structure of representation which is inscribed in the state apparatus. It is this notion which provides the basis for analysing both 'regulatory' and 'allocative' outputs in a manner consistent with the principle of the relative autonomy of the state.

3. The Unequal Structure of Representation

For Poulantzas, to argue that the state is a structure is not to argue that the state is the 'sum total' of the institutions that comprise the state system. Rather, it is to emphasise the importance of discovering the hidden organising principle of these institutions, the form of state which is ultimately determined by the relations of production and the stage of class struggle.[15] The 'hidden principle' is linked to the particular relations of hegemony which obtain within a given social formation at a particular point in time. In turn, to argue that the state is a factor for producing the 'unstable equilibrium of compromises' (hegemony) suggests the necessity of analysing the way in which these compromises are arranged. It is here that the full significance of Poulantzas's emphasis on the form of state—which implies a reading of the state in terms of the unequal structure of representation inscribed in the state apparatus—emerges.

If relations of power within the state apparatus are understood as relations of power within and between classes, then:

. . . (C)onceiving of the capitalist State as a relation, as being shot through and constituted with and by class contradictions, means firmly grasping the fact that an institution (the state) that is destined to reproduce class divisions cannot really be a monolithic, fissureless bloc but is itself, by virtue of its very structure, divided. The various organs and branches of the State . . . reveal major contradictions among themselves, each of them constituting the seat and the representative . . . of this or that fraction of the power bloc . . . . In this context, the process whereby the general political interest of the power bloc is established and whereby the state intervenes to insure the reproduction of the overall system, may well . . . appear chaotic and contradictory, as a 'resultant' of these inter-organ and inter-branch contradictions.[16]

Thus the state, as articulated in the various institutions and branches that comprise the state system, appears to be composed of representatives of the various classes and class fractions—a particular level (the political) of the class struggle. However,

None of this means that the capitalist state is an ensemble of separate parts, expressing a 'share out' of political power among the various classes and fractions. On the contrary, over and beyond the contradictions within the State apparatus, the capitalist State always possesses *a specific internal unity, the unity of the power of the hegemonic class or fraction.* But this happens in a complex fashion. The functioning of the state system is assured by the *dominance* of certain apparatuses or branches over others; and the branch or apparatus which is dominant is generally the one which constitutes the seat of power of the hegemonic class or fraction.[17]

The state, then, expresses and organises the political relations of class domination. It is not 'captured' by the dominant class. Rather, inscribed in the state is an *unequal structure of representation* historically produced by the political class struggle. It is this structure of representation—guaranteed by the dominance of certain branches over others and by the central place occupied by that branch (or branches) which constitutes the 'seat of power' of the hegemonic fraction—through which the 'unstable equilibrium of compromises' is arranged.

This structure of representation cannot be reduced to a continuation of interest group politics. The specific internal unity of the state *qua* structure implies the contradictory functions performed by these 'representatives.' While one branch may 'represent' the interests of a particular fraction, it also performs the role of 'disciplining' that fraction in the name of the 'national interest' (the 'unstable equilibrium of compromises'), backed by its monopoly on the legitimate use of force. In contrast, while private interest groups may also discipline those they represent (particularly in a corporatist form of state where the line between private and public appears dissolved), this is done in the name of that particular interest and is not reinforced by 'legitimate coercion.'

This distinction is an important one, and one that O'Connor fails to make on a theoretical plane. O'Connor distinguishes between 'interest groups' and the 'class-conscious political directorate.'[18] The latter—which includes policy-making bodies, private, quasi-public and public in character—too closely identifies the members of the bourgeois class or with the (upper level) state personnel, an identification which, taken with the centralisation of budgetary control, becomes necessary, in O'Connor's framework, to ensuring that the class interests of monopoly capital prevail. In contrast, for Poulantzas, it is the form of state, the political logic inscribed in its internal relations, that permits the interests of the hegemonic fraction 'to emerge unintentionally.'

A brief discussion of the administrative apparatus—which in the stage of monopoly capitalism, comes to play an increasingly important role[19]—can indicate the way in which the unequal structure of representation operates.

In analysing the administrative apparatus, the conceptualisation adopted determines the particular features of the apparatus selected for special emphasis. Some writers focus on the social origins or 'class situation' of civil servants to explain their 'bias' in policy formation and implementation. Others focus on the effect of 'on-the-job socialisation,' arguing that their job definitions predispose them to identify their interests with the interests of that particular class or fraction which they

are to serve.[20] Both positions would lend support to an instrumentalist position. For Poulantzas, however, the civil service can be understood as a 'social category' and,

> The feature which distinguishes social categories from fractions and strata is the following: while political and ideological criteria can intervene in a more or less important fashion in determining fractions and strata, in the determination of social categories they have the dominant role.[21]

In 'explaining' the actions of this group, one must look to the (contradictory) unity characteristic of a social category, a contradictory unit produced by their position within the state apparatus. More specifically,

> (I)n the case of the administrative apparatus, the internal hierarchy of delegated authority characteristic of state apparatuses, the particular status attributed to functionaries, the specific internal ideology circulating within the state apparatuses (the 'neutral state' as arbitrator above classes, 'service to nation,' 'general interest,' etc.) allow the bureaucracy to present a unity of its own in certain conjunctures . . .[22]

Poulantzas is here referring to the possibility of the state bureaucracy acting as a distinct political force—just as the army may do in a military regime. However, these unifying factors also condition the role of the civil service in normal times.

Consider, for example, the role of a branch within the Canadian Department of Industry, Trade and Commerce (IT&C), charged with responsibility for a particular industry. To perform the job, the branch must strive for the 'health' of the industry. This may involve 'representing' that industry in intra- and inter-departmental policy discussions. It may also involve 'persuasive coercion,' inducing the industry to improve its performance (and hence profitability) through grants and assistance programmes tied to productivity improvements. Such an improvement corresponds with the long-run interests of the hegemonic fraction, by subordinating the industry's development to the direction of development that accords with the general economic and political strategy of the hegemonic fraction. This effect is produced

158

through the various means suggested by Poulantzas: internal hierarchy (subordinating the branch to the department which, in turn, is subordinated to seat of power of the hegemonic fraction), the civil servants' special status, the definition of the 'national interest' particular to a particular form of state and the character of the hegemonic fraction (its alliances). These means are far more subtle, comprehensive, and complex than those emphasised by O'Connor and go a lot further toward explaining the peculiar structural bias of the state.

4. Regulatory Agencies: Special Case of the Unequal Structure of Representation.

This conceptualisation of the state–which suggests that power relations within the state apparatus express and reinforce class relations of power, permitting the state to perform an important role in arranging the 'unstable equilibrium of compromises' that unify a social formation–offers a useful perspective from which to analyse regulatory agencies. This type of institution can be seen as a kind of 'special case' of the normal representational character of the various branches of the administrative apparatus. Like the latter, a regulatory agency's role can be conceived as a dual one: simultaneously to represent the interests of the regulated and to subordinate their interests to the long term political interests of the hegemonic fraction. Yet regulatory agencies also constitute a special case–they are 'independent' of the regular departmental and political apparatuses; they are 'open' to competing private inputs (adversary hearings); and their authority is specifically linked to their capacity to make 'politically neutral' technical judgements. These special characteristics may be traced to their origin.

John R. Baldwin has argued that a regulatory agency is most likely to have its origins in an issue that cannot be 'resolved' without threatening an important aspect of the existing system of juridical rights:

> The essential nature of the conflict that gives rise to a regulatory agency is the refusal of one of the parties concerned to accept the optimum that might be established via bargaining, *given the existing structure of legal rights.*[23]

This argument can be taken a step further: a regulatory agency is created to provide a framework for facilitating an 'exceptional' compromise in the face of a political challenge that can only be met by altering the juridical rights of capital. In advanced capitalist countries, a corporation's rights include the following: "...the right to determine the timing and extent of economic expansion, to invest or take over other companies, to distribute profits and dividends, to send sums abroad . . ."[24] Such an 'exceptional' limitation may be general in scope (e.g., labour relations, 'anti-trust') or be industry-specific (rates of production, exports, the direction of new investment). It may even involve a limitation on the corporate power of part of the hegemonic fraction. It may result from a challenge issued by subordinate forces or it may involve a conflict among different fractions of capital. These are matters to be determined empirically in each instance. What is distinctive is that this type of issue involves the general rights of property which, in certain exceptional instances, conflict with the political interests of the hegemonic fraction. In such a case, the issue can be more easily dealt with by establishing an 'independent' agency–one apparently insulated from partisan politics and the regular administrative apparatus which reflects "the existing structure of legal rights."

The origin of such agencies strongly suggests that they cannot function as mere captive agents. Such agencies cannot be 'captives' if they are to play the role of arranging particular compromises which reflect specific combinations of the demands of the 'rebels,' the 'regulated,' and the hegemonic fraction. This also suggests that there will be some means for ensuring that an agency's actions correspond (albeit in an exceptional way) to the 'national interest' which permeates the entire state. This may be achieved in a variety of ways: appointment of commissioners with long experience in the administrative apparatus, procedural rules, terms of reference, and the functioning of screening devices within the regular administrative apparatus. Of these, one of the most interesting and often neglected is the inter-departmental screening mechanism which may stand between the agency and the executive, for it is precisely the administrative apparatus (its structure of representation) that embodies the fundamental bias of the state due to its 'permanent' (but historically produced) character and its own specific combination of expertise. In any case, the agency's subordination to the 'national interest' is likely to occur in a complex way—and may only become explicit in times of crisis.

This leads to the final point: because the kind of issue which gives rise to the establishment of a regulatory agency—giving it its status as 'special case'—is a potentially explosive one, the threat may resurface, possibly necessitating renegotiation of the agency's terms, powers, and relationships to other parts of the state apparatus. That the particular compromise is institutionally located at an apparently greater distance than the rest of the apparatus from the overtly political institutions (the assembly and the executive) indicates the importance of neutralising or insulating the compromise. Yet it is precisely the special political nature of the issue that may lead to a future ruptue.

In summary: The theoretical perspective provided by the concept of the capitalist state as a structure characterised by a relative autonomy vis-à-vis the dominant class suggests an alternative to the thesis that regulatory agencies tend to become 'captive agents.' Such agencies function as instruments of the hegemony of a particular class or fraction whose leading position within a given social formation is specifically guaranteed by the state through the unequal structure of representation inscribed in the state apparatus.

Thus, a regulatory agency can best be understood, in relation to this unequal structure of representation, as a kind of 'special case' created in order to neutralise a threat to hegemony than cannot easily be contained by the normal functioning of the political and administrative apparatuses of the state. It represents a 'politically insulated' framework for the ongoing negotiation of this special compromise. Yet this does not mean that the compromise will not be subordinated to the 'national interest,' the general pattern of compromise inscribed in the state.

II The textile and Clothing Board: Captive Agent or Instrument of Hegemony?

The notion of regulatory agencies as instruments of hegemony poses a different set of questions from those raised in a study premised on a 'captive agents' perspective. The activity of interest groups, the two-way flow of personnel between industry and the agency, the way the agency's decisions tend to favour the industry: all of these are reduced from the pre-eminence received in the 'captive agents' approach. Instead, it becomes important to analyse the issue which produced the need for the agency not solely in terms of those forces directly invovled but also (and more importantly) in relation to the political interests of the hegemonic fraction. It is the latter aspect which is so often ignored by those who argue the 'captive agents' position, preventing recognition of the real 'mobilisation of bias.' Once the initial question is posed so as to include the presence of the hegemonic fraction, it becomes possible to analyse the way in which the agency 'resolves' the issue and thence to determine the conditions for its successful institutionalisation. Finally, such an analysis would not stop short of examining the means by which the agency is subordinated to the state. Liberals mourn the legislative assembly's apparent inability to control regulatory agencies, finding in this the root of the problem. However, a variety of means is likely to exist for exercising control—although these may differ according to the specific nature of the issue (including its level of politicisation, its centrality to the interests of the hegemonic fraction). Yet to uncover these, the relationship of regulatory agencies to the state (and thence, the 'national interest') needs to be examined critically and not in an ideological manner, i.e., not counterposing an abstract notion of the 'national interest' to an imputed sectional bias in government policy.

In what follows, Canada's Textile and Clothing Board will be examined from this perspective. A detailed analysis of the Board will not be provided for the object is merely to show that the 'instruments of hegemony' hypothesis poses questions which lead to significant insights obscured by the 'captive agents' perspective.

1. The Textile and Clothing Board

The Textile and Clothing Board is not, strictly speaking, a regulatory agency like the Canadian Radio-Television and Telecommunications Commission (CRTC). The

Board is not directly empowered to regulate matters like conditions of entry and pricing. It is, however, 'independent' of the regular departmental structure. In addition its recommendations can have a significant impact on the degree of competition and the price at which textile goods are sold in Canada. More importantly, the Board's powers include the right to examine the investment plans of the textile and clothing companies to determine whether such plans constitute sufficient attempts to become internationally viable. In addition, any decision by the Board to recommend import restraints is contingent upon its assessment of the adequacy of company's modernisation plans. This gives the industry a clear stake in the Board's decisions–yet it also provides it with an opportunity to exercise an influence on the Board's findings through 'confidential' discussions with the Board. It is thus possible for the Board to become particularly sensitive to the industry's needs (long term protection from import competition), leading it to recommend measures which would go against the 'national interest' (conceived of as a textile industry which is adjusting to the demands of an internationally competitive economy).

2. The Issue

An analysis premised on the 'captive agents' thesis would most likely look to the interest groups which originated the demand for the policy, finding tentative confirmation for the hypothesis in the fact that it was the industry itself which demanded government intervention to stem the tide of low-wage imports. However, working from the alternative hypothesis, it would seem essential to probe the issue more deeply to identify the way in which it affects the long term political interests of the hegemonic fraction. To do so requires identification of the hegemonic fraction within Canada and an attempt to locate the textile industry's place within a changing Canadian social formation.

The hegemonic fraction in Canada remains the 'merchant-financiers' whose formation has been studied by a significant group of Canadian political economists and whose continued centrality has been established by Wallace Clement.[25] A variety of arguments can be mounted as 'proof' of this hypothesis. The most important points, however, are the following. The old national policy, which laid the foundation for a continent-wide Canadian economy, expressed the politico-economic project of the central Canadian merchant-financiers. Creighton's analysis of the empire of the St. Lawrence traced the rise of this class to power. Vernon Fowke built on this, arguing that the first national policy was informed by this project:

> The economic objective of the first national policy [for which the federal government was created as "agent"] was the creation of a new frontier of investment opportunities for the commercial and financial interests of the St. Lawrence area.[26]

Fowke may have laid too much emphasis on the *narrow* interests served by the national policy. Through the political framework of the post-Confederation Canadian state and its 'national policy,' the interests of western Ontario farmers and manufacturers in Quebec and Ontario were combined and subordinated to the objectives of the commercial-financial fraction. At this point, national economic integration, the establishment of capitalist relations of production,[27] and expanded opportunities for servicing the flow of staples and manufactured goods, constituted the project through which this fraction achieved and maintained political and economic hegemony. However, Fowke and certain contemporary analysts have questioned whether this fraction has remained hegemonic, pointing to the preponderance of American capital in key resource and manufacturing industries and the (related) balkanisation of the Canadian state system.[28] However, Clement has produced sound evidence to suggest that although 'monopoly capital' in Canada is divided into two groups, the indigenous fraction has not only prospered with the deepening of foreign capital's hold on certain sectors but has also maintained its central position through the core institutions of the economy.[29] The indigenous fraction, still largely based in the service sector, occupies a position which gives it a perspective on (and a 'concern' for) the 'national' economy. The branch plants and foreign-controlled resource companies–American capitals–do not possess the institutional means for developing a consensus on the Canadian economy. In addition, despite the decentralisation of the Canadian state system, the federal government continues to symbolise Canadian unity. It continues to exercise jurisdiction over important areas (including interprovincial relations, fiscal and monetary policy, and external relations) and to act as co-ordinator in areas of mutual interest such as resources, labour, and social services.[30] Thus persuasive evidence exists to suggest that the indigenous bourgeoisie continues to exercise hegemony; it is their long term political interests (the health of the Canadian economy, national unity, and, ultimately, the maintenance of capitalist relations of production) that continue to be specifically 'guaranteed' through the Canadian state.

What place does the textile industry hold within the Canadian social formation? In the period of Fowke's "first national policy," the primary textile industry had gained a place as a subordinate fraction of the power bloc. As T.W. Acheson has shown, by the 1870s the Montreal-based merchant-financiers had begun to invest in the developing textile industry. In the 1890s textiles became the first industry to experience the merger movement, under the aegis of the Montreal-based fraction. In addition, the textile industry was, and remained, one of the main beneficiaries of the National Policy Tariff which, after 1920, encouraged foreign investment in the new synthetic fibre division.[31] However, the kind of economy which characterised postwar Canadian development was one in which non-renewable resources and new manufacturing industries performed the leading role in the goods producing sector. The textile (and related clothing) industry seemed no longer to warrant special protection, particularly in the face of growing markets for Canadian resources in the low-wage countries of the Pacific Rim. In other words, the relatively stagnant textile industry was seen to hold a minor position in the specifically economic objectives of the hegemonic fraction. By the late sixties, the industry—faced with the price effects of low-wage import competition and the need to undertake major new investment—found itself in a particularly disadvantageous position in the competition for external (to firm) capital controlled by the indigenous bourgeoisie.

Yet, the industry still employed a significant percentage of the manufacturing labour force in Quebec (roughly 22% when textiles

and clothing are combined). And in the late sixties it had become clear that in Quebec a significant separatist movement was developing, posing a potentially serious threat to 'national unity.' At the same time, the Quebec labour movement was becoming an autonomous, radical, social force.[32] Thus, should the domestic textile industry collapse in the face of import competition (and competition for investment capital from the subsidiaries of foreign-based multinationals in more dynamic industries) this could intensify the combined political threats of separatism and socialism. Thousands of unemployed textile workers could be available for mobilisation by one or both of these political forces.

In facing this situation, however, the federal government was not responding to an 'unmediated' threat from the textile industry. The political force which mounted the challenge was under the leadership of the dominant primary textile companies—the Canadian-owned firms of Dominion Textiles and Wabasso and the two leading foreign-controlled firms, Dupont and Celanese. These companies, through the Canadian Textile Institute, established an alliance with the three largest textile unions. It was under their leadership that the Quebec government was successfully approached for support. It was their carefully prepared strategy that forced the state to attempt to meet the threat. This mediation conditioned the response. Clearly, the underlying threat to the political and economic interests of the hegemonic fraction was a serious one. However, corporate—as opposed to labour union—leadership of the disaffected suggested that some form of special assistance to capital in the textile industry might suffice instead of a more radical approach.[33]

3. Negotiation of the Special Compromise

From the 'captive agents' perspective, the role of interest groups might be considered in explaining the original intent behind the establishment of a regulatory agency. Here, it might be conceded that such groups represented subordinate social forces demanding restrictions on the power of (a section) of the dominant class. Yet, it would be argued that although the original intent may have been to accede to popular demands, this tends to be

162

subverted as the agency becomes established due to its close and continuous contact with the industry. In this kind of analysis, the 'black box' of policy-formation process can indicate the way in which the 'exceptional' case is linked to the general pattern of compromise. In other words, it is important to examine the means by which the compromise was produced in order to determine how the policy combines the interests of the hegemonic fraction with the other interests involved.

In the textile case, an analysis of the parts of the state apparatus involved shows that from the outset, the policy was designed to achieve a specific combination of the interests of the hegemonic fraction with those of the leading textile companies. The 'representatives' of the latter (the Apparel and Textiles Branch of the Department of IT&C) worked 'in consultation' with representatives of the export interests and an interdepartmental committee which included a representative from the 'seat of power' of the hegemonic fraction.[34] This arrangement enabled the industry's representatives to establish two central points: that the industry, given the necessary protection, would continue to modernise and thus play its part in an expanding, 'open' economy; that, should the industry be permitted to collapse, the political repercussions would indeed be great. At the same time, the Branch was forced to concede the importance of expanding trade relations with low-wage countries and the necessity of the industry's adjustment to international competition.

The substance of the compromise was as follows. The industry's property rights would be subject to qualification in that future investment decisions would be oriented to the demands of meeting international competition. In exchange, short-term protection— a form of 'profit' support—would be granted. In addition, token adjustment benefits for workers were stipulated, developed by the Department of Labour.[35] Power to oversee the implementation of the compromise was vested in an independent investigative body (the Textile and Clothing Board) which would assess the situation on a case-by-case basis to determine whether, in fact, imports were disrupting the process of modernisation. The Board's terms of reference (to consider Canada's international obligations,

domestic 'regional and manpower' needs, the industry's plans for adaptation), its operating procedures (public adversary hearings, confidential discussions with industry representatives), the measures it could recommend (short term protection, bilaterally negotiated or unilaterally imposed) partly reflected the nature of the compromise. In addition two mechanisms were established to screen the Board's analysis: the Office of Special Import Policy (OSIP) and the Inter-departmental Committee on Special Import Policy—composed of those departments who sat on the original committee. OSIP, in consultation with the Textiles Branch and the branches representing the export interests would provide an initial assessment and negotiate import restraints. The Interdepartmental Committee would assist OSIP to assess the Board's reports. The latter's recommendations had, therefore, to pass careful scrutiny by these two agencies, both of which contained powerful supporters of the hegemonic fraction's development strategy.[36]

4. The Board in Action

If one were to argue the 'captive agents' position, it would be necessary to establish that the regulated industry drew especial benefit from the agency's functioning. The analysis presented thus far would create a different set of expectations: while 'confidence' might be restored, this would be linked to the industry's acceptance of the necessity of becoming 'internationally competitive'—not to generous protection engineered by the Board. Until 1976 this hypothesis seemed valid. Since then, the Government has strengthened the industry's (and Board's) bargaining position and has taken unilateral action to stem the tide of imports. However, the renegotiation which led to this occurred in response to a significant alteration in the political and economic conditions on which the compromise depended.

That 'health' was restored to the industry is indicated by rates of investment, financed partly through borrowing on the open market. Overall investment in the industry increased by 11% —with the leading textile firms accounting for a significant portion of this. The banks were prepared to support the industry. Annual bank loans to the industry increased from $320 million to 1971 to $553 million in 1973. Firms like Dominion Textiles and DuPont also had little trouble in placing large issues of debentures. More importantly, the leading primary textile companies all seemed to be adjusting to the requirement of international competition. For instance, both Celanese and DuPont planned to invest in world-scale fibre-producing facilities and to build new plants producing intermediates from Canadian raw materials. Dominion Textiles initially seemed to focus on diversification out of more traditional lines and into new, more capital-intensive areas such as woven plastics or 'fashion' materials. By the spring of 1975, however, Dominion Textiles had announced its acquisition of a sizeable American textile company, D H J Inc. This placed Dominion Textiles in a good position in the American market and provided sales and distribution outlets in eighty countries and manufacturing facilities in several major low-wage textile-producing countries. In addition, some of the more dynamic medium-sized firms like Consolidated Textiles expanded into the American market—at the price of ceding control to foreign capital.

While it would seem an exaggeration to attribute the industry's adjustment solely to the operation of the board, it is reasonable to suggest that this was not unimportant. The Board conducted ten inquiries and thirteen reviews between 1971 and 1974. Most of these resulted in short-term product-specific protection. Reviews in the 1973-74 period led to a relaxation of restraints on a wide range of items. In other words, the Board was not 'protectionist.' The rule continued to be, protection only to the extent necessary to permit adjustment. In addition, the inquiries and reviews included discussions between Board and Industry concerning modernisation. While such discussions were confidential, it does not seem unreasonable to link the kinds of decisions taken by the leading companies and the Board's administration of the policy.

However, toward the end of 1975 the industry began to mobilise against the policy as implemented. In the spring of 1976 the Senate Committee on Banking Trade and Commerce held an inquiry into the problems of the industry which resulted in an apparently dramatic shift in policy. J. Baldwin has made the general point that "If appeal is to be avoided, one would rarely expect either party to

achieve all they desire."[37] What explains the industry's successful appeal? Did the industry feel that the bargain had not been kept? In this context, it is important to note the industry's support for the Board and its criticism of the Interdepartmental Committee:

> The interdepartmental committees become involved in the act and months pass. I can't say as certain, but I believe that interdepartmental committees on occasion review facts which the Board has found to be facts. The Board is a fact-finding body. I don't think that any government bureaucrat or bureaucrats in general should look over the Board's shoulder as a fact-finding body.[38]

In turn, the Board's chairman supported a policy review to be conducted by government and industry.[39] Since then, the federal government has imposed global quotas on clothing imports, including those from the United States. An advisory committee, composed of representatives of the textile and clothing companies, the unions and the provinces concerned, has been established on a permanent basis. More importantly, the Department sponsored a task force on the future of the industry (part of the series resulting from the 1977 Conference of First Ministers). The task force facilitated the formation of an interesting consensus among textile and clothing companies and unions and representatives of the leading retail companies—an important step toward the establishment of 'voluntary' limits on imports. Yet it would be a mistake to conclude that the Board was a 'would-be' captive agent, inhibited only by the Interdepartmental Committee from fulfilling its destiny without any prior consideration of the general upheaval (global and domestic) this would cause, or of its effects on the strategy of the hegemonic fraction. That is, if the original compromise emerged from particular conditions, is it not important to consider whether these conditions had altered in any significant way?

The initial compromise was negotiated in the late sixties at a time when the state apparatus was permeated by an awareness that for Canada's integration into the international economy to occur on favourable terms, a new industrial strategy was needed, which would encourage rationalisation of the over-protected, 'branch plant' manufacturing sector.[40] In addition, the radicalisation of the Quebec labour movement and the rise of a separatist party posed a threat to Canadian capitalism. The leading primary textile companies had successfully manipulated the latter threat and the representatives of the hegemonic fraction had utilised this opportunity to negotiate a compromise whereby the textile industry would gradually prepare for 'freer trade'– with the United States, other advanced capitalist countries and indeed all countries participating in the global capitalist system. Further, as an analysis of the investment decisions of the leading primary textile companies suggests, the industry had begun to carry out its part of the bargain. What, then, caused the reversal?

Simply put, the factors on which the success of the strategy depended had altered significantly. First, the general energy crisis brought to the surface certain fundamental problems in the transition to a more highly developed international division of labour. The reactions of all the leading capitalist nations placed a heavy strain on the multilateral institutional framework that had facilitated the development of the new international division of labour organised under the aegis of the multinational corporations. In other words, the objective of free trade had received a serious setback. In these circumstances, a convincing argument could be mounted that the Canadian textile industry should receive additional protection–at least until other countries were prepared to reduce trade barriers, giving efficient Canadian manufacturers the enlarged markets necessary to derive economies of scale.

Second, the domestic situation had also altered. While Canada had experienced some of the impact of the global recession prior to 1974, by 1975 the Canadian economy was experiencing high rates of inflation and rising unemployment. In the fall of 1975, the federal government imposed wage and price controls with the cooperation of the provinces. In 1976 unemployment continued to rise while the labour movement across Canada mounted opposition to wage controls. This situation posed a particular threat in Quebec where the rate of unemployment was above the national average and where the labour movement, already more radical than the Canadian movement, was not divided by a link with a political party associated with the

wage control programme.[41] In addition, should a provincial election be called, the labour movement could support the parti Québécois, the independentist party whose social democratic programme aimed at forging an alliance among the Québécois petite bourgeoisie and workers. In this context, the industry could argue its political importance with effect.

Thus the apparent shift to protectionism must be understood in terms of a change in the conditions of realising the long-term objectives of the hegemonic fraction. Certainly the political action taken by the industry-led coalition was the means by which the significance of this change was 'recognised.' However, the Board-Committee mechanism remains in place and, should conditions become more favourable, the industry will again be induced to adjust to the demands of 'international competition.'

This discussion of the Textile and Clothing Board suggests that an analysis which considers such agencies as a special case of the unequal structure of representation is forced to examine the basic factors conditioning their operation. The discussion revealed, first, the nature of the challenge posed by textiles, going beyond the empiricist trap of locating the agency's origin in interest group activity. Second, it served to expose an important mechanism for limiting the extent to which the Board could function as an effective captive agent: the Interdepartmental Committee which contained a balance of representation reflective of the general bias of the Canadian state. Finally, the analysis of the apparent failure of the compromise again showed that overt political activity provides an insufficient explanation of the significance of change. Renegotiation was not due to the Committee's ability to inhibit the Board's development as a 'captive agent'–or to the industry's action to remove the Committee. Rather, it was linked to a significant change in the conditions necessary for the realisation of the long term political and economic interests of the hegemonic fraction.

Conclusion

The central thesis of this paper is that regulatory agencies–an important component of the state system in most advanced capitalist formations–can best be understood as a special case' of the unequal structure of re-presentation through which the authority of the dominant class and, in particular, of the leading fraction of that class, is dynamically reproduced. Thus, like other parts of the state apparatus, regulatory agencies contribute to the production of authority by simultaneously 'representing' and 'regulating.' This dual role is circumscribed by the nature of the particular compromise necessary to the maintenance of a particular pattern of domination. Second, regulatory agencies derive their special or exceptional character from their origins in an issue whose resolution demands a modification of the 'rights of capital' in a specific instance. By 'insulating' this compromise from the regular state apparatus, the exceptional character of this infringement is underlined. Yet formal independence does not imply that this compromise does not form part of the general structure of compromise. A variety of means exists to ensure that the agency performs its contradictory role: that it functions as an 'instrument of hegemony.'

This formulation, it has been argued, is more adequate to the task of critical analysis than the captive agents approach which views such agencies as 'captives' of the forces they are to regulate. It avoids the empiricist trap of interest group analysis (the analysis of the practical interconnection of corporate and political elites) in favour of the more incisive concept of class relations which makes possible the identification of the way in which the issue raises more fundamental questions. It avoids the ideological understanding that counterposes the 'public interest' (of which the nation-state is the imputed guardian) to a sectional bias induced by the functioning of regulatory agencies. Rather, the activity of such agencies is comprehended as a part of the general 'structure of bias': the dynamic 'equilibrium of compromise' that organises the interests of various social forces around the core interests of the hegemonic fraction.

This criticism is particularly pertinent in the Canadian context. In Canada, the high incidence of foreign (mainly American) ownership of key resource and manufacturing industries has prompted radical nationalists—like Jim Laxer and Ed Dosman—to argue that Canada is dominated economically, and hence politically, by the United States. They find support for this through their interpretation of the National Energy Board as a 'captive agent' of the foreign companies which dominate the energy sector.[42] They then recommend measures such as relieving the NEB of its responsibilities as 'watchdog of the national interest,' and nationalisation of Imperial Oil. Such analyses combine 'economism' and 'idealism' in their contradictory assertion that economic domination = political domination and that popular mobilisation can 'recapture' the state, permitting it to conform to its idealistic representation as 'guardian of the national interest.' In failing to come to grips with the complex character of political class domination, such analyses support reformist programmes—programmes which are ultimately bound to fail.

An analysis of the role of regulatory agencies which locates them within the general structure of authority could yield more fruitful political insights. For example, a re-reading of Dosman's material on the role of the NEB in the formation of northern development policy would help clarify the way in which the corporate interests of the powerful cluster of foreign interests are combined concretely with the 'national interest'–the way in which their interests are linked with the development strategy of the indigenous bourgeoisie. Similarly, Larry Pratt's work could provide a good basis for the development of a clearer understanding of the function of provincial governments in combining the interests of foreign capital, regional fractions of the indigenous bourgeoisie and petite bourgeoisie, and the hegemonic fraction.[43] Most importantly, an analysis of the role of the CRTC and the CTC (Canadian Transport Commission) could expose the way in which the narrow corporate interests of a group within the indigenous bourgeoisie are combined and subordinated to the long-run interests of this fraction.

Studies which pose questions about the way in which the state functions to 'produce' the hegemony of a particular class or fraction can make a useful contribution to the ultimate transformation of Canadian society. Only through a marriage of such analyses and political practice will the realization of socialism become a concrete possibility.

166

[1]Louis M. Kohlmeier, *The Regulators: Watchdog Agencies and the Public Interest*, (New York: Harper & Row, 1969); S. Krislov and Lloyd D. Musolf, *The Politics of Regulation: A Reader*, (Boston: Houghton-Mifflin, 1964); George J. Stigler, *The Citizen and the State* (Chicago: University of Chicago Press, 1975). Caroline Andrew and Rejean Pelletier, "The Regulators" in G. Bruce Doern (ed.) *The Regulatory Process in Canada*, (Toronto: Macmillan of Canada, 1978) do not theorise this relation but establish empirically the circulation of personnel. These assumptions shape the analysis presented in the series commissioned by the Canadian Consumer Council which includes G.B. Reschenthaler's interesting study, "The Performance of Selected Independent Regulatory Commissions in Alberta, Saskatchewan, and Manitoba," (October, 1972).

[2]P. Sweezy, "The Primary Function of the Capitalist State," in *The Capitalist System: A Radical Analysis of American Society*, edited by R.C. Edwards, Michael Reich, and T.E. Weisskopf, (Cambridge, Mass.: Prentice-Hall, 1972); excerpted from P.M. Sweezy, *The Theory of Capitalist Development*, (New York, Monthly Review, 1942). While Sweezy argues that the state is necessarily the instrument of the dominant class, Kolko's historical analysis of the Progressive era in the United States, suggests that the new regulatory agencies formed an important component of 'political capitalism': the corporate elite's strategy designed to limit competition and to forestall popular challenge, always latent in a democratic state. Gabriel Kolko, *The Triumph of Conservatism*, (New York: Free Press of Glencoe, 1963).

[3]In this formulation, I am particularly indebted to the theoretical insights provided by Nicos Poulantzas. *Political Power and Social Classes*, (London: New Left Books and Sheed and Ward, 1973); *Fascism and Dictatorship*, (London: New Left Books, 1974); *Classes in Contemporary Capitalism*, (London: New Left Books, 1975). Any errors or over-simplifications, however, are mine.

[4]See R. Mahon, "Canadian Public Policy: The Unequal Structure of Representation," in Leo Panitch (ed.) *The Canadian State*, (Toronto: University of Toronto Press, 1977) and "Canada's Textile Policy: A Case Study in the Politics of Industrial Policy Formation" (doctoral dissertation, University of Toronto, 1976).

[5]For example, Claus Offe and Volker Ronge, "Theses on the Theory of the State," *New German Critique*, Fall, 1975; and James O'Connor, *The Fiscal Crisis of the State*, (New York: St. Martin's Press, 1973).

[6]Antonio Gramsci, *The Prison Notebooks of Antonio Gramsci*, edited and translated by Quintin Hoare and G. Nowell Smith, (New York: International Publishers, 1971), p.182.

[7]Poulantzas, *Political Power*, p.191.

[8]See Philippe Schmitter, "Still the Century of Corporatism?" (*Review of Politics*, 36:1). L. Panitch, "The Development of Corporatism in Liberal Democracies," *Comparative Political Studies*, Vol. 10, No. 1.

[9]Gramsci, *Prison Notebooks*, p.182.

[10]N. Poulantzas, *The Crisis of the Dictatorships*, (London: New Left Books, 1976).

[11]O'Connor, *The Fiscal Crisis*, p.6.

[12]R. Salisbury and J. Heinz, "A Theory of Policy Analysis and Some Preliminary Applications," in *Policy Analysis in Political Science*, edited by Ira Sharkansky, (Chicago: Markham, 1970), p.40. Salisbury and Heinz are building on the insights of Theodore Lowi ("American Business, Public Policy, Case Studies, and Political Science," *World Politics*, July, 1964). For Canadian material utilizing this approach, see G.B. Doern and Peter Aucoin (eds.), *The Structure of Policy Making in Canada*, (Toronto: Macmillan of Canada, 1971).

[13]O'Connor, *The Fiscal Crisis*, p.66.

[14]*Ibid.*, p.70. O'Connor's treatment of regulatory agencies forms an integral part of his explanation of the 'immediate' cause of the fiscal crisis: the clash between rational (from the standpoint of monopoly capital) budgeting and incrementalism. The latter results from the capture of parts of the administration by 'interest-conscious' capital. In this, O'Connor fails to recognise the 'rationality of the irrational': the political importance of seemingly contradictory outputs which, in the absence of a popular-revolutionary challenge, maintains effective unity within the bloc.

[15]N. Poulantzas, "The Problem of the Capitalist State," in *Ideology in Social Science*, R. Blackburn (ed.), (Suffolk: Fontana, 1972), p.248.

[16]N. Poulantzas, "The Capitalist State: A Reply to Miliband and Laclau," *New Left Review*, 95, p.75.

[17]N. Poulantzas, "On Social Classes," *New Left Review*, March-April, 1974.

[18]O'Connor, *The Fiscal Crisis*, p.68.

[19]Poulantzas, *Classes* and *L'etat, le pouvoir, le Socialisme*, (Paris: Presses Universitaires de France, 1978). In the Introduction, Poulantzas elaborates on his original formulation, suggesting that the state produces a 'fragmented discourse' addressed to specific classes and fractions (in some respect akin to R. Manzer's notion of 'policy paradigms'–"Public Policies in Canada: A Development Perspective," presented to the Canadian Political Science Association, 1975–although Manzer does not link his paradigms to classes and fractions). In the fourth section, he stresses the significance of the shift to the executive and senior officials for the emergence of 'authoritarian statism.'

[20]Donald Gow, "Canadian Federal Administrative and Political Institutions: A Role Analysis," unpublished doctoral dissertation, Queen's University (Kingston, Ontario), 1973.

[21]Poulantzas, "On Social Classes," p.40.

[22]*Ibid.*, pp.40-41.

[23]John R. Baldwin, *The Regulatory Agency and the Public Corporation: The Canadian Air Transport Industry*, (Cambridge, Mass.: Ballinger, 1975), p.7. Emphasis added.

[24]A. Rotstein, "Introduction to Reclaiming the Canadian Economy by Gunnar Addler-Karlsson" in *Independence: the Canadian Challenge*, A. Rotstein and G. Law (eds.), (Committee for an Independent Canada, 1972), pp.79-80.

[25]This has received treatment in the work of various Canadian historians and political economists including Donald Creighton, *The Empire of the St. Lawrence*, (Toronto: MacMillan of Canada, 1970); V. Fowke, *The National Policy and the Wheat Economy*, (University of Toronto Press); H.A. Innis, *Essays in Canadian Economic History*, edited by Mary Innis, (Toronto: University of Toronto Press, 1956); R.T. Naylor, *The History of Canadian Business, 1867-1914*, (Toronto: James Lorimer, 1975); and T.W. Acheson, "The Social Origins of Canadian Industrialism: A Study in the Structure of Entrepreneurship," unpublished doctoral dissertation, University of Toronto, 1971. For the most systematic treatment of the place this fraction holds in the contemporary Canadian economy, see Wallace Clement's, *The Canadian Corporate Elite*, (Toronto: McClelland and Stewart, 1975) and *Continental Corporate Power*, (Toronto: McClelland and Stewart, 1977).

[26]V. Fowke, "The National Policy, Old and New," in *Approaches to Canadian Economic History*, p.243.

[27]Too little published material deals with this critical aspect. For a good overview of the role of the state in legitimating capitalist relations of production, see H. Clair Pentland, "The Background of the Canadian System of Industrial Relations," unpublished study done for the Federal Task Force on Labour Relations, 1968. For an analysis of the more overtly political aspects, see B. Ferns and B. Ostry, *The Age of MacKenzie King*, (Toronto: James Lorimer, 1976–reprint).

[28]See, for example, James Laxer, *Canada's Energy Crisis*, (Toronto: James Lorimer, 1975) or *(Canada) Ltd.: The Political Economy of Dependency*, R. Laxer (ed.), (Toronto: McClelland and Stewart, 1973).

[29]Clement, *Canadian Corporate Elite*, Chapter 3. In his recent work, Clement points to the tendency toward integration of this fraction with its American counterpart–a link 'from strength to strength,' joining Canadian circulating capital with American 'industrial' capital. It should be noted that a 'continental corporate elite' exists only as a *tendency*: its consolidation will not automatically develop.

[30]This interpretation is not in accord with Garth Stevenson's as advanced in "Federalism and the Political Economy of the Canadian State," in Panitch, op. cit. The area of disagreement warrants a more extensive discussion which is, however, beyond the scope of this paper. The main lines of my counterargument would focus on what D. Smiley has termed 'executive federalism' *(Canada in Question*, Toronto: McGraw-Hill Ryerson, second edition, 1976). While most agree that the provinces have assumed a more prominent role since the late fifties, a whole range of coordinating mechanisms permit the negotiation of an effective–though contradictory–compromise.

[31]O.J. MacDiarmid, *Commercial Policy in the Canadian Economy*, (Cambridge, Mass.: Harvard University Press, 1946).

[32]See D. Drache, *Quebec: Only the Beginning*, (Montreal: Black Rose) for a good collection of the major manifestoes of the Quebec labour movement.

[33]See "L'Avenir du Textile et Vetement au Quebec," (CSN, 1969) and the CSN's presentation to the Standing Senate Committee on Banking Trade and Commerce, April 1976 for more radical options that might have been followed had the labour movement in Quebec led the political alliance.

[34]The Department of Finance. See "Canadian Public Policy," (Note 4, above) for the argument substantiating this hypothesis.

[35]*Ibid.*

[36]This kind of bureaucratic screening mechanism is not uncommon in the Canadian state. For instance, E. Dosman's data indicate that a similar committee stands between the Cabinet and the National Energy Board, *The National Interest: the Politics of Northern Development, 1968-75*, (Toronto: McClelland and Stewart 1975), p.18.

[37]Baldwin, p. 11, note 23 above.

[38]Canada. Senate, *Proceedings of the Standing Senate Committee on Banking Trade and Commerce*, February 28, 1976. Canadian Textile Institute.

[39]Proceedings, March 10, 1976. Testimony of C. Annis.

[40]Dosman has noted that the Department of Finance had become particularly concerned: "After 1968, certain key Ottawa officials, particularly in the Department of Finance, progressively lost confidence in the so-called 'special relationship'; that had characterised Canadian-American relations after World War Two," *The National Interest*, p.177.

[41]That is, the labour movement in the rest of Canada is affiliated with the NDP, a party which, through the provincial government of Saskatchewan and Manitoba, had supported wage controls. The NDP is of minimal significance in Quebec.

[42]Dosman, *The National Interest*; J. Laxer, *Canada's Energy Crisis.*
[43]L.R. Pratt, "The State and Province Building: Alberta Development Strategy, 1971-76," *The Canadian State.*

THE STATE, COLLECTIVE BARGAINING AND THE SHAPE OF STRIKES IN CANADA

Christopher Huxley

Can. Journal of Sociology Vol. 4, No. 3 Summer 1979 pp.223-39.

A widely noted feature of Canadian industrial conflict in recent years, especially when compared with other western industrialized countries, has been the high number of working days lost due to strikes and lockouts per 1,000 workers.[1] This paper will consider the different dimensions of the postwar pattern of strike activity in Canada, paying particular attention to the long duration of stoppages. Previous explanations for the prolonged nature of strikes, which emphasize the respective economic power positions of employers and workers, are criticized for neglecting to consider the role played by the state.

The main argument presented in this article is that it is necessary to examine the impact of state regulation on collective bargaining, in order to account for the distinctive shape of Canadian strike activity. Two aspects of state involvement in industrial relations will be examined: direct forms of state intervention in the collective bargaining process, with special reference to limitations imposed on use of the strike weapon; and legislation aimed at legitimating the involvement by the state. This is followed by a consideration of why state intervention has taken this particular form. Previous explanations are viewed in the context of a more general theory of the institutionalization of industrial conflict. Lastly, countertrends to the process of institutionalization, and the likely pattern of state response to these countertrends, will be considered.

The shape of strikes in Canada

How have previous writers analyzed the pattern of strike activity in Canada? The most common approach has been to view the Canadian case as part of the wider North American variant of industrial conflict. For example, Lipset (1963:179) observes how the labor movements in the "new societies" of the United States and Canada have shown a willingness to pursue more militant tactics, and to tolerate a higher level of industrial conflict (i.e. "relatively frequent, long, and bitter strikes"), than in northwestern Europe. Ross and Hartman (1960), in a comparative study of strike trends in fifteen countries up to the mid-1950s, identify a *general* long-term decline in the duration of strikes;[2] but they also acknowledge that North American provides scant support for their thesis, since a distinguishing feature of North America strike activity has been the long average duration of stoppages. Shorter and Tilly (1974) concur. They propose that three dimensions make up the structure or shape of strike activity: duration (i.e. median number of days lost per strike[3]); size (i.e. mean number of strikers per strike); and frequency (i.e. number of strikes per 100,000 workers). When these three dimensions are graphed to depict American and Canadian strike activity, a cubic shape results. "Nowhere else in the postwar world," Shorter and Tilly (1974:329) report, "were even remotely similar shapes to be encountered," owing to the relatively long duration

Author's note: For helpful comments on an earlier version of this paper I wish to thank Robert Brym, Charlene Gannage, Dennis Magill, Richard Roman and the anonymous special reader for the Journal. Any shortcomings in the present article remain my responsibility.

169

of North American strikes. Finally, it deserves to be emphasized that during the post-war period the trend in Canada has been towards strikes of even longer duration. This is in contrast to the experience of several other countries, including the United States and the United Kingdom (Jamieson, 1973:137; *Labour Gazette,* January 1976).

Above all else, this pattern of protracted stoppages appears to account for the relatively high number of working days lost due to strikes in Canada (Malles, 1977; Kinsley, 1977; Huxley, 1977). How is this pattern to be explained? In contrast to the trend elsewhere, Ross and Hartman (1960:40) view strikes in North America in the post-1945 period as representing "a real test of economic strength between workers and employers." They propose that the economic dimension provides the key to explaining the relatively long duration of strikes. A similar argument is made by Shorter and Tilly:

> We associate this cubist pattern with business unionism, where the strike has a fundamental role to play within the collective bargaining process–the *ultima ratio* which brings the parties to the table–yet has few political functions. (1974:329)

Such a perspective is congruous with the dominant view of North American trade unionism as exemplifying the quintessence of economism (Mann, 1973:21). It finds specific expression in the many American studies dealing with the relationship between strike movements and economic fluctuations (Hansen, 1921; Griffin, 1939; Rees, 1954; Ashenfelter and Johnson, 1969), which attempt to show how oscillations in strike activity, usually measured by the number of strikes, or the number of workers involved in strikes, can be attributed to changes in such measures of business activity as fluctuations in the wholesale price index, the unemployment rate, real wages, profit levels or other similar indicators. In recent years there have been attempts to apply such techniques to Canadian data (Vanderkamp, 1970; Smith, 1972 and 1976; Walsh, 1975; Cousineau and Lacroix, 1976).

There are, however, certain limitations to any exclusively economic interpretation of strike movements, as was acknowledged by Griffin (1939:57) in his classic study of strikes in the United States:

In the case of strikes there are certain imponderables of great influence that cannot be reduced to quantitative terms. Among those elements are the general political climate, the type and ideology of the labor leaders, and the intellectual reactions and emotional conditions of the entrepreneur.

Since Griffin's work, various attempts have served to correct an exclusively economic interpretation of industrial conflict in North America. Rather than arguing that economic factors have had no influence on the behavior of the respective parties in collective bargaining, the main thrust of these contributions has been to show how economic influences have operated in conjunction with, or been mediated by, other processes deserving historical and sociological examination. For example, one perspective argues that economism notwithstanding, socialist or social movement unionism *has* represented an important competing pole of attraction in North American labor history with consequences for industrial conflict, at least until the early 1920s (Laslett, 1970), or the 1930s (Snyder, 1977),[4] and perhaps even up to the Cold War period (Green, 1975; Jamieson, 1968).

I shall follow this line of thought by proposing that another limitation of studies of industrial conflict which emphasize solely economic considerations is the neglect of the role played by the state. While briefly discussed by some authors (Ross and Hartman, 1960:175; Ingham, 1974:89; Jackson and Sisson, 1976:319), the influence of the state on the character of strike activity has generally failed to receive systematic sociological consideration, especially in the Canadian experience. The next section will review the role played by the Canadian state in attempting to institutionalize industrial conflict.

The state and collective bargaining

The Canadian state has, by and large, successfully institutionalized industrial conflict. That is to say, it has enacted legislation enabling employers and unions to reach agreement on certain norms and formal institutional mechanisms for the regulation of industrial conflict. It is useful to specify three functions of the capitalist state in order to develop a framework for the analysis of labor legislation[5] as a means of regulating industrial conflict. The first function, that of *accumu-*

lation, refers to the involvement by the state in policies aimed at ensuring favorable conditions for the long-term operation of capitalist enterprise (O'Connor, 1973:6). Second, the *coercion* function refers to "the use by the state of its monopoly over the legitimate use of force to maintain or impose social order" (Panitch, 1977:8).[6] These two functions are, in turn, supplemented by a third–*legitimation*–which refers to policies aimed at securing the legitimacy of the state. The legitimation aspect of industrial relations legislation is designed to ensure the loyalty of key sectors of the working class to the state and to facilitate their integration into capitalist society. In the words of Jackson and Sisson (1976:319):

> . . . intervention by the state which produces legislation on welfare and which encourages trade union recognition is not to be regarded as conflicting with the interests of employers but as complementary or alternative to independent action.

The enactment of different items of industrial relations legislation by the Canadian state has involved different aspects of each of these three functions. Of special relevance to the discussion that follows is the extent to which such legislation has been characterized by reliance on coercion. Jamieson (1973:3) notes the predisposition of federal and provincial governments in Canada toward legislation aimed at preventing strikes and lockouts, and the point is elaborated by Panitch (1977:19):

> What has been particularly notable about Canadian labour legislation, in comparison with the British and even in comparison with the American, is the extent to which the rights of unionization and free collective bargaining have been hedged around by, even embedded in, a massive legal and penal structure. This places such tremendous statutory restriction on labour and gives such a large role for the law and the courts to play, that the legitimation aspect of labour legislation in Canada's case seems at least balanced, if not actually overshadowed, by the coercive aspect.

The precise mix of functions which Canadian industrial relations legislation has been designed to perform can best be appreciated if we discuss in detail two major developments in Canadian labour legislation–the Industrial Disputes Investigation Act of 1907 and the Industrial Relations and Disputes Investigation Act of 1948. Both pieces of legislation were designed to regulate collective bargaining with a long term view to the accumulation function, making due provision for reliance, whenever necessary, on the coercion function. However, the legitimation aspect is rarely, if ever, found to be entirely absent.

Prior to World War II much of Canadian labor legislation, both federal and provincial, followed the British model (Logan, 1944:481). But this did not prevent the enactment of certain specific provisions for state intervention in collective bargaining that were to become the hallmark of Canadian industrial relations. Of all such legislation, "none has received more international comment and study than the Disputes Act of 1907" (Williams, 1964:315). Previous federal legislation, usually framed in direct response to labor relations crises in mining and rail, had provided for conciliation and the compulsory arbitration of disputes in those industries. The Industrial Disputes Investigation Act (IDIA) introduced compulsory conciliation with special provision for the obligatory postponement of any strike or lockout under federal jurisdiction until after a board of inquiry had conducted its investigation. This principle of delaying strikes and lockouts during a period of investigation was the one original element in the legislation.

Characteristically, some of the most extravagant claims for the IDIA, such as that it "would eliminate ninety per cent of lockouts and strikes," were made by its chief architect, the then deputy minister of labor, Mackenzie King (1918:510). Some authors have detected in King's own testimony and writings important clues for understanding the degree of acquiescence and, in some cases, even outright support given by important sections of the Canadian labor leadership to the IDIA.[7] One argument states that the main objective of the legislation was to promote employer recognition of, and negotiation with, trade unions at a time when a large number of industrial disputes arose over the issue of recognition. Citing King's testimony before the United States Commission on Industrial Relations in 1914, Woods (1955:462) concludes that:

171

The provision for a delay before striking was essentially a means of getting Parliament and the public to accept a piece of legislation which strongly favoured unionism and collective bargaining.[8]

This view, however, was not shared within the ranks of the coal miners, a group of workers directly affected by the IDIA. Shortly before Parliament passed the IDIA, delegates at a district convention in western Canada voiced their criticism. They argued that the legislation sought to forestall workers from taking prompt industrial action, while giving employers time to prepare for a strike (Selekman, 1927:151).

A more circumspect assessment of the IDIA is also offered by Ferns and Ostry (1976:331) who argue that: "The Industrial Disputes Investigation Act was promised to striking miners as a guarantee of union recognition. Its actual effect was to reduce the pressure of labour on employers." Ferns and Ostry (1976:65) view King's contribution to labor legislation as an innovative example of a "soft" attempt to solve social antagonisms, in stark contrast to "the virile, 'no nonsense' school of politicians who advocated 'hard' policies for the resolution of the social tensions of the nascent industrial community."

Thus, while Woods views the compulsory delay provision as a relatively mild concession to employers in order to obtain support for legislation which encouraged union recognition, Ferns and Ostry (1976:330) argue that the IDIA served to "weaken and divide the labour movement." The latter viewpoint suggests that the labor legislation was designed to ensure conditions that were conducive for capital accumulation.[9] This involved a coercive aspect, but equally important was King's attention to the need for legitimation, as evidenced in the way he sought to secure support for the IDIA among influential figures in the labor movement.

The IDIA was initially restricted to collective bargaining under federal jurisdiction. During both World Wars it was extended to cover war-related industries and in the interwar period provincial governments passed similar laws in their own jurisdictions.[10] The result was that by World War II the IDIA provided the bare framework for a nation-wide labor code; although it was not long before

state intervention in industrial relations took on a new form.

The key to understanding developments leading up to the Industrial Relations and Disputes Investigation Act of 1948 is the growing importance during the 1930s and 1940s of the unskilled and semi-skilled workforce in the resource and mass production industries. Compared to other advanced capitalist economies (including the United States) the workers in these basic industries in Canada were late in organizing. But as the movement for industrial unionism in Canada eventually gained ground, it became evident that the form of state response would broadly follow the American experience, while making due allowance for certain provisions from the original IDIA.

The upsurge of labor militancy in the United States, most notably among previously unorganized workers at the beginning of 1933, had produced a series of responses from the Roosevelt administration, first in Section 7(a) of the National Industrial Recovery Act of 1933 and later in the 1935 National Labor Relations Act, known as the Wagner Act (Preis, 1972:12). One of the key principles of this legislation was that of exclusive jurisdiction, providing for some form of election through which a bargaining body could gain certification as the exclusive representative of a group of workers.[11] The American state thereby assumed a special role in attempting to influence and, whenever possible, control the subsequent course of collective bargaining. This was emphasized by Trotsky (1977:90) when he noted how the Congress of Industrial Organization (CIO) "was no sooner founded than it fell into the steel embrace of the imperialist state." He describes the process as follows:

The US Department of Labour with its leftist bureaucracy has as its task the subordination of the trade union movement to the democratic state, and it must be said that this task has up to now been solved with some success (1977:91).

Compared to the American experience, Canadian legislation by the early years of World War II was still much more limited in scope, containing few provisions of any real substance (Woods, 1955:459). However, as the war continued, it became increasingly evident that the central principles of the

Wagner Act were finally going to the adopted. Legislation on the right of recognition, provision for certifying a group of employees as an appropriate bargaining unit, and compulsion to bargain in good faith was introduced, first in 1944 with the enactment of Privy Council (order-in-council) 1003 and later in the Industrial Relations and Disputes Investigation Act (IRDIA) of 1948. This last statute was restricted to federal jurisdiction but most of the provinces soon passed similar legislation (Jamieson, 1973:124). The result was a new Canadian labor code consisting of some central features of the American model but, at the same time, retaining provisions from the original IDIA. Specifically, this involved: (1) the IDIA principle of compulsory government conciliation and the postponement of strikes during investigation; and (2) stipulations affecting the content of agreements, especially the requirements "that a collective agreement contain a clause prohibiting strikes or lockouts during the term of an agreement" (Peach and Kuechle, 1975:48-9).

The role that was henceforth performed by the state in regulating strike activity can be summed up by considering four types of industrial disputes (Woods, 1955:447-8): recognition disputes, interest disputes, rights disputes and jurisdictional disputes. In three of these four areas of potential industrial conflict, the state has substituted adjudicating machinery for the strike. In the case of recognition disputes, legislation specifies procedures for the certification of a bargaining agency in which strike action, as a means to achieve recognition, is explicitly outlawed. Similar provisions apply for handling jurisdictional disputes. Rights disputes, arising while a collective agreement is in force, are supposed to be processed through a grievance procedure usually providing for some form of third-party arbitration. Again, strikes to resolve such disputes, before, during or following arbitration, are ruled illegal. The actual right to strike is limited to the fourth type of dispute—the interest dispute:

> Only in the case of disputes over the terms of an agreement in the making have we retained for the parties the role of ultimate decision-making. Here only is the right to resort to a work stoppage preserved and even that is seriously restrained by the compulsory conciliation requirements of the law. (Woods, 1955:451-2).

Canadian legislation has then significantly circumscribed the mechanism of free collective bargaining, up to and including the right to strike. This serves to introduce two questions. How have the coercive aspects of labor legislation, in the form of direct controls on the right to strike, affected strike activity? How has legislation concerned with union recognition and other legitimation aspects affected strike activity? These questions are pursued in the next section.

State regulation and the shape of strikes

It is sometimes argued that no amount of legislation can succeed in eliminating all expressions of industrial conflict (e.g., Goldenberg, 1969:310). However, this should not be interpreted to imply that state intervention has had no effect on the timing or the shape of strikes. This can be demonstrated by reviewing the Canadian experience, particularly in the post World War II period. Two main effects of intervention include: the reduction in the number of short strikes over union recognition, and the increased duration of strikes over interest disputes.

There are certain areas where formal procedures have gained some measure of acceptance as an alternative to strike action. For example, Canadian labor legislation, providing for highly formalized procedures to be substituted for strike action as a means of securing union recognition, did significantly reduce the number of strikes in this category. Jamieson (1973:138) reports that strikes over union recognition, or in defence of union activity, historically tended to be of shorter duration than those arising in the course of negotiations for a new agreement. In this case, then, labor legislation had the effect of eliminating some strikes of short duration.

The emphasis placed on the distinction between interest and rights disputes in North American industrial relations has had significant implications for the character of industrial conflict. Roberts (1959:100) argues that the distinction

> . . . inevitably leads to a way of looking at disputes that almost certainly promotes strikes, where a question of interest is in-

volved. Members of unions and employers have now become accustomed to the notion that a new collective agreement cannot be negotiated without a demonstration on both sides of militancy and a show of proof that they can take a strike.

The policy of attempting to settle rights disputes by arbitration has further repercussions for industrial conflict. Dissatisfaction over the handling and/or the outcome of a particular grievance may find an outlet in such forms of individual action as absenteeism, low productivity, work spoilage or minor acts of sabotage; or, resentment may simmer until the expiry of the contract, when it eventually finds expression in legal strike action over wage demands. Of course, the distinction between rights disputes which are arbitrable and interest disputes which are not, has not prevented Canadian workers from striking over issues of rights. As will be shown later, Canadian experience offers support for the following observation:

> Workers who have achieved such strength in the power relations that are real life in the workplace are unlikely to relinquish their liberty of action because lawyers tell them the issue is really one about "rights" rather than "interests." Instinctively they will know what is the case, namely, that this language of "rights" is too often used as though it served as self-evident proof that workers must be prohibited from using some sanction which might otherwise be available to them during periods when there is apparent or supposed agreement concerning the principles of relevance to determine disputes. The language is no such proof. (Wedderburn, 1969:89).

According to Jamieson (1973:138), Canada's system of regulation and disputes settlement legislation may have "rendered strikes more difficult to settle once they did develop." One special feature of state intervention that may have given rise to long stoppages in Canada is the legislated ban on strikes while a collective agreement is in force. This point was made by Dennis McDermott in a news release issued during his tenure as Canadian United Automobile Workers (UAW) Director and International Vice-President:

One of the reasons for the lengthy strikes, he noted, was that in Canada strikes are forbidden until a collective agreement expires. In anticipation, companies stockpile inventories and carry on business-as-usual for the first few weeks of a strike. Lengthy strikes were the result. (Canadian Industrial Relations and Personnel Developments, 1977:880).

Another result of the proscription on strikes during the term of a contract has been the tendency for managers to defer all sorts of questions to negotiations for the next collective agreement. Malles (1977:8-9) observes how management may take a highly legalistic approach to the solution of grievance problems, by refusing to negotiate or even to discuss questions not covered in the agreement and by referring them to the next negotiations.

Despite the extensive attention that the Canadian system of compulsory conciliation has received, there have been surprisingly few attempts to evaluate its effect on the pattern of industrial conflict. Exceptions include an investigation into compulsory conciliation in New Brunswick, in which Cunningham (1958) recommended that compulsory intervention in the form of conciliation officers be maintained, but that the second stage of conciliation, involving the appointment of conciliation boards, be placed on an entirely voluntary basis. Such a change did subsequently occur in New Brunswick, Ontario and Nova Scotia. Cunningham's (1969) follow-up study of the implications of this move suggested that one possible effect was a decline in Ontario's proportion of the total time lost due to strikes in Canada (Jamieson, 1973:139).

A second, more recent, investigation into the effect of compulsory conciliation on strike activity considers the case of Saskatchewan, the only province where access to conciliation has remained voluntary. Misick (1978) compares the record of "strike-days per union member" for Saskatchewan with that of Nova Scotia, a province which has continued to operate with the conventional system of compulsory first-stage conciliation. While his findings do not permit any firm conclusion as to the effect of compulsory conciliation on strike activity, it is noteworthy that the data provide no support for those who advocate compulsory conciliation as a way of reducing the number of days lost due to strikes.

Other sources have either questioned the effectiveness of compulsory conciliation in reducing industrial conflict, or have suggested that it tends actually to undermine collective bargaining. An example of the first is the low regard sometimes expressed–but, for obvious reasons, rarely documented–by experienced negotiators:

> It is not unknown for labour and management to agree mutually to dispose of the "conciliation obstacle" early in the negotiation process before settling down to serious bargaining. To achieve this end, labour and management go through some preliminary skirmishing during which they agree not to agree. They call for conciliation services, and the conciliator, being unable to bring about a settlement, submits his report to the minister. The parties then enter into serious negotiations unfettered by any conciliation or strike restrictions. (Misick, 1978:200).

The argument that compulsory conciliation weakens the effectiveness of collective bargaining is made by Woods (1955:464):

> The conception that the parties are assisted out of a deadlock by the conciliation agencies overlooks the fact that in many cases the deadlock has been reached because of the compulsory steps ahead, and at the expense of genuine bargaining. Each additional step tends to increase the administrative costs of collective bargaining.
>
> More important is the fact that the stoppage of work as a constructive social instrument is being replaced by the legal requirement of conciliation.

The intervention of the state in industrial relations has also facilitated the bureaucratization of trade union organizations, and this too, may have influenced the character of strike activity. Of special concern here are some implications of the legitimation aspects of post-World War II industrial relations legislation.

The role played by the state in the certification of bargaining units, involving the granting of exclusive rights of _____ sentation to a union within a _____ tion, has meant that union lead_____ quired a measure of protection fro_____ transferring to another union. The _____ also made provisions for some form _____ protection, ranging from "union shop _____ ments to the automatic "check-off" of union dues. But while such arrangements have often been presented as tangible gains won by trade unions, some observers have pointed to the associated burden of responsibilities which union leaders have assumed. Aronowitz (1973:217) reviews the United States case, but similar observations can be made for Canada. The most important obligations incurred by union leaders in both countries have been: (1) the undertaking not to strike, except under specific conditions, or until the expiry of the contract (legally required in Canada);(2) the acceptance of grievance procedure "during which the control over the grievance is systematically removed from the shop floor and from workers' control"; and (3) the agreement to accept the principle of managerial prerogatives stating the employer's right to manage on all questions referred to in the collective agreement. Aronowitz points to specific features of the typical labor contract which limit the union's automony. The automatic check-off of union dues from the worker's paycheck is seen as "a major barrier to close relations between union leaders and the rank and file" (1973:217), representing a mechanism to strengthen the ties between union leaders and employers. A related aspect is the pressure on union leaders to control and, if necessary, discipline their membership. In the case of rights disputes the union leadership is called upon to convince workers of the efficacy of binding arbitration.

The bureaucratized relationship between the union leadership and the membership may be a factor in explaining the long average duration of strikes for a new contract in North America. This theme emerges in Serrin's (1973) study of the lengthy 1970 UAW strike against General Motors. He argues that the protracted strike served various functions for both the corporation and the union leadership; the most important for the latter being that it helped secure the eventual membership ratification of a contract that the employer had always been prepared concede but which the membership had earlier considered unacceptable. According to Serrin, political considerations within the union rather than an economic trial of strength offer the key to understanding the length of that particular strike.

The reasons for state intervention

Why has the Canadian industrial relations experience been marked by this predisposition towards state intervention? Any satisfactory answer would need to explain the early involvement by the Canadian state in industrial relations legislation; the unique features of such legislation; and the subsequent shift towards the United States model of legislation, while preserving some distinctive Canadian features. Only the first steps towards addressing these points can be attempted at this time.

One explanation suggested by Woods (1955:453) is that the interdependent nature of the Canadian economy has increased the pressure on the Canadian state to reduce the economic loss resulting from work stoppages. Woods does not elaborate on the specificities of the national economy but he does note how the "importance of crises in stimulating labour legislation is clearly demonstrated in Canadian federal experience" (1955:454). Crises have repeatedly involved key industries, like railways and mining, as well as a variety of war-related industries during each of the world wars.

Jamieson is more specific in drawing attention to not only the internal interdependence of the Canadian economy, but also its international ties. In particular he notes

the vulnerability of a national economy that has depended far more than most countries upon foreign trade, and specialized to an extreme degree in the large-scale production and export of raw materials and semi-finished goods. (1973:117).

This vulnerability, according to Jamieson, helps to explain the willingness of Canadian legislators to make provisions for state intervention aimed at preventing, or at least delaying, strikes.

According to Garbarino (1969:334), American employers and managers have been willing to accept occasional lengthy stoppages *provided* they have been relatively infrequent

and predictable. Similarly, employers in Canada may have made a sanguine assessment of the relative cost advantage of occasional lengthy strikes over more frequent and more disruptive stoppages.[12]

The adoption of this perspective could have been prompted by more general developments in the economic structure of advanced capitalism. Thus, Goldthorpe (1977: 204) describes a common theme in the writings of contemporary economists, of both liberal (e.g., Galbraith, 1967) and Marxist (e.g., Kidron, 1968) persuasions:

Increases in the scale of production, advancing technology and more integrated and competitive markets place mounting pressure on industrial enterprises to engage in the long-term planning of their activities. It is no longer sufficient for managements simply to seek to adapt to new business conditions as they arise; they must attempt to foresee and, as far as possible, to control these conditions.

Countertrends to the institutionalization of industrial conflict

The institutionalization of industrial conflict described above need not exclude the possibility of industrial unrest finding expression in alternative forms. Unofficial or wildcat strike activity is specifically mentioned by Dahrendorf (1959:279) as one such countertrend. Since Canadian government statistics do not distinguish between official and unofficial strikes, estimates have had to be made. For example, an Ontario government study on the use of the labor injunction (Carrothers and Palmer, 1966:234) reported that 26.6 percent of all strikes in that province during 1966 occurred during the life of a collective agreement. Estimates for the whole country made by Flood (1972) indicate that approximately one-third of all strikes taking place between 1956 and 1969 represented some form of unofficial or "non-institutional" response.[13]

Both the number of wildcat strikes and the number of workers involved in wildcats increased during the second half of the 1960s (Crispo and Arthurs, 1968; Flood, 1972). In addition, Jamieson (1973:96-7) detects a change in the character of these unofficial strikes which, by 1965,

. . . numbered 149 or about 21 per cent of the total 501 strikes, and in 1966, 210 or about one-third of the total 617. Most of such strikes in the 1940s and 1950s had been relatively small walkouts of brief duration. During the 1960s, however, they included some of the costliest disputes. Outstanding among these were strikes in railways, postal services, trucking, primary steel, and nickel mining and smelting.

According to Dahrendorf (1959:279), increased unofficial strike activity might reflect "a new type of conflict, intra-union conflict" resulting from "the stabilization of an uneven authority distribution within the unions." One of Flood's (1972:611) case studies of a wildcat strike occurring in Canada during the 1960s provides an instance of this sort of intra-union conflict:

> The Lake Steel wildcat was found to be explicable in terms of the political situation within the union. Thus, it was an industrial wildcat, against the union, with the major sources of strain in the situation located within the union itself.

However, as Flood's other case study suggests, unofficial strike action need not necessarily be directed against the union:

> In the Northern Mining case, the workers did not reject the union. They simply defined the situation as one in which the union was unable to act due to the possibility of legal sanction being applied to them if they engaged in an illegal strike. Recognizing this fact, they did not reject the union but acted outside of the formal organization in a way that would not have repercussions for the union or its officers. (1972:613).

Here it is worth noting that the workers foresaw state intervention in any illegal strike that was endorsed by union officers. Wildcat action was therefore taken on the assumption (which turned out to be correct) that punitive repercussions from the state were less likely if union officers were deliberately excluded.

The increase in labor unrest during the mid-sixties in Canada was reflected in both the rising level of strike activity and in the widespread attention directed towards incidents involving illegality and violence

(Crispo and Arthurs, 1968; Jamieson, 1968). During 1966 growing concern prompted the state to authorize a major investigation of labor relations–the Prime Minister's Task Force on Labour Relations, headed by H.D. Woods.[14] Many of the specific proposals of the Task Force are still being debated. More important for the present discussion, however, are the main principles that inform the Task Force *Report* and which underscore it various recommendations. In this respect the *Report* can be regarded as representative of the ways in which an influential group of industrial relations experts proposed that employers and the state could effectively respond to the new expressions of industrial conflict.

Liberal-pluralism, the dominant approach in postwar industrial relations research, provided the underlying theoretical perspective for the Task Force *Report*. Thus, the authors (The Report of the Task Force on Labour Relations, 1968:169) stated their endorsement of "the collective bargaining process, including the right to strike and lockout, as the system most compatible with a mixed enterprise economy operating in a pluralist society based on liberal democratic values." Such an orientation involved a sophisticated appreciation of the role union leaders could play in the institutionalization of industrial conflict. This was most evident in the observations on rank-and-life militancy, especially where such collective action assumed an illegal character. In policy terms, emphasis was placed on how to build support for the existing union bureaucracy. Especially interesting was the warning that the "failure of management to stand up to such pressure not only invites repetition; it tends to undermine management credibility and the position of incumbent union leadership" (The Report of the Task Force on Labour Relations, 1968:101). The existing union leadership was thus viewed as a crucial mediating force which needed to be supported by both employers and the state if industrial conflict was to be contained within institutionalized channels. The Task Force authors viewed union officials as "managers of discontent" (The Report of the Task Force on Labour Relations, 1968:101)[15] who were in need of assistance and encouragement if they were to exert a moderating influence, especially in a climate of rising restlessness from below.

Many specific proposals made by the Task Force can best be understood in the context of this general orientation. One example is the recommendation to encourage the extension of collective bargaining to groups of employees not previously covered; another, to make the compulsory, irrevocable check-off of union dues available as a form of union security. As intended, such proposals for stressing the legitimation aspects of labour legislation were favorably received by certain prominent trade union leaders (*Labour Gazette*, June 1969:320).

The authors of the Task Force *Report* demurred at the proposition that any major overhaul of Canadian industrial relations was necessary. The call from the most frequently heard advocates of overhaul had been (and continues to be) in favor of even more restrictions on the right to strike than those already existing. Consequently, the *Report* came under fire from such quarters for not going far enough in its recommendations to contain strike activity, especially where an alleged "public interest" was involved. But despite the claim by the authors of the *Report* that they generally opposed any further limitations on the freedom to strike, they were not above advocating the imposition of other restrictive measures on trade unions. One controversial proposal was directed against union-controlled hiring halls; another involved increased state involvement in the internal processes of union decision making. The way the chairman of the Task Force viewed such proposals is best reflected in his own subsequent assessment of government labor policy:

On this continent, legislation designed to free unions and encourage collective bargaining has been matched by much legislation directed toward controlling the internal affairs of unions, and the operating relationship between the parties (Woods, 1973:38).

Conclusions

The central argument in this paper is that the extensive involvement of the Canadian state in attempting to regulate industrial conflict has had important consequences for the shape of strike activity. State intervention has reduced the number of authorized strikes over such issues as union recognition and rights disputes. More important, state regulation was a significant factor in accounting for the relatively long average duration of strikes.

This pattern of relatively protracted strikes appears to have been accepted by employers in Canada in preference to what was perceived as the more disruptive alternative: frequent, less predictable stoppages. However, the attempt to predict and control the pattern of industrial conflict was not always as successful as employers and the different levels of the state apparatus might have preferred, as indicated by the growth in non-institutional conflict. During the 1960s various policy recommendations aimed at counteracting the less predictable expressions of industrial unrest were made. The most important of these was contained in the Federal Task Force *Report*, which advocated special reliance on the official trade union leadership in restraining rank-and-file pressures, and new legislation aimed at further controlling the internal affairs of unions.

A more comprehensive investigation of the role played by different groups of employers in the formulation of Canadian industrial relations policy lies beyond the scope of the present work. This paper has, however, introduced a number of considerations that have relevance for general theorizing about the role played by the state in the institutionalization of industrial conflict, and for understanding some specific features of the Canadian case as it has developed historically, and as it may well develop in the near future.

REFERENCES

Aronowitz, Stanly. *False Promises: The Shaping of American Working Class Consciousness*. New York: McGraw-Hill. 1973.
Ashenfelter, Orley and George E. Johnson. "Bargaining theory, trade unions and industrial strike activity." *American Economic Review* 59:35-49. 1969.
Canadian Industrial Relations and Personnel Developments. *Newsletter* (December 7). 1977.

Carrothers, A.W.R. and E.E. Palmer, eds. *Report of a Study on the Labour Injunction in Ontario* Vol. 1-2. Toronto: Queen's Printer. 1966.

Cousineau, Jean-Michel and Robert Lacroix. "Activité économique, inflation et activité de grève." *Relations Industrielles* 31:341-58. 1976.

Crispo, John and H. Arthurs "Industrial unrest in Canada: a diagnosis of recent experience." *Relations Industrielles* 23:237-64. 1968.

Cunningham, W.B. *Compulsory Consiliation and Collective Bargaining: The New Brunswick Experience.* Fredericton: New Brunswick Department of Labour and Montreal: McGill University, Industrial Relations Centre. 1958.

"Conciliation: the end of conciliation boards." Paper presented at the 6th Annual Meeting of the Canadian Industrial Relations Research Institute. 1969.

Dahrendorf, Ralf. *Class and Class Conflict in Industrial Society.* Stanford: Stanford University Press. 1959.

Ferns, Henry and Bernard Ostry. *The Age of Mackenzie King.* Toronto: James Lorimer. 1976.

Fisher, Douglas and Harry Crowe. *What Do You Know About The Rand Report?* Don Mills: Ontario Federation of Labour. 1968.

Flood, Maxwell. "The growth of the non-institutional response in the Canadian industrial sector." *Relations Industrielles* 27:603-15. 1972.

Galbraith, John Kenneth. *The New Industrial State.* Boston: Houghton Mifflin. 1967.

Garbarino, Joseph W. "Managing conflict in industrial relations: US experience and current issues in Britain." *British Journal of Industrial Relations* 7:317-35. 1969.

Glenday, Daniel and CHristopher Schrenk. "Trade unions and the state: an interpretative essay on the historical development of class and state relations in Canada, 1889-1947." *Alternate Routes* 2:114-34. 1978.

Goldenberg, H. Carl. "The law and labour relations: a reaction to the Rand Report." *Relations Industrielles* 24:308-17. 1969.

Goldthorpe, J.H. "Industrial relations in Great Britain: a critique of reformism." In *Trade Unions under Capitalism,* edited by T. Clarke and L. Clements, pp.184-224. Glasgow: Fontana-Collins. 1977.

Great Britain. *Department of Employment Gazette.* London. 1977.

Green, James. "Fighting on two fronts: working class militancy in the 1940s." *Radical America* 9:7-47. 1975.

Griffin, John I. *Strikes: A Study in Quantitative Economics.* New York: Columbia University Press. 1939.

Hansen, Alvin H. "Cycles of strikes." *American Economic Review* 11:617-21. 1921.

Huxley, Christopher. "Industrial conflict in Britain and Canada: a comparative analysis of strike activity since 1945." Paper presented at the 2nd Conference on Blue Collar Workers and their Communities, University of Western Ontario. 1977.

Ingham, Geoffrey, K. *Strikes and Industrial Conflict.* London: Macmillan. 1974.

Jackson, Peter and Keith Sisson. "Employers' confederations in Sweden and the UK and the significance of industrial infrastructure." *British Journal of Industrial Relations* 14:306-33. 1976.

Jamieson, Stuart. *Times of Trouble: Labour Unrest and Industrial Conflict in Canada, 1900-1966.* Task Force on Labour Relations Study No. 22. Ottawa: Privy Council Office. 1968.

Industrial Relations in Canada. Second edition. Toronto: Macmillan. 1973.

Kidron, Michael. *Western Capitalism Since the War.* London: Weidenfeld and Nicolson. 1968.

King, W.L. Mackenzie. *Industry and Humanity.* Toronto: Thomas Allen. 1918.

Kinsley, B.L. "Strike activity and the industrial relations system: an international comparison." Paper presented at the Annual Meeting of the Canadian Sociology and ANthropology Association, Quebec City. 1977.

Labour Canada. *Labour Gazette.* Canadian Industrial Relations and Personnel Developments. 1969.

Laslett, John. *Labour and the Left.* New York: Basic. 1970.

Lipset, S.M. *The FIrst New Nation.* New York: Basic. 1963.

Logan, H.A. "The state and collective bargaining." *Canadian Journal of Economics and Political Science* 10:476-88. 1944.

Mahon, Rianne. "Canadian public policy: the unequal structure of representation." In *The Canadian State,* edited by L. Panitch, pp.165-98. Toronto: University of Toronto Press. 1977.

Malles, Paul. *Canadian Industrial Conflict in International erspective,* Ottawa: Information. 1977.

Mann, Michael. *Consciousness and Action among the Western Working Class,* London: Macmillan. 1973.

Mills, C. Wright. *The New Men of Power.* New York: Harcourt, Brace and Co. 1948.

Misick, John D. "Compulsory conciliation in Canada: do we need it? *Relations Industrielles* 33:193-204. 1978.

O'Connor, James R. *The Fiscal Crisis of the State.* New York: St. Martin's Press. 1973.

Panitch, Leo. "The role and nature of the Canadian State." In *The Canadian State,* edited by L. Panitch, pp.3-27. Toronto: University of Toronto Press. 1977.

Peach, David A. and David Kuechle. *The Practice of Industrial Relations.* Toronto: McGraw-Hill Ryerson. 1975.

Poulantzas, N. *Political Power and Social Classes.* London: New Left Books and Sheed and Ward. 1973.

Preis, Art. *Labor's Giant Step.* New York: Pathfinder Press. 1972.

Rand, I.C. et al. *Report of the Royal Commission Inquiry into Labour Disputes.* Toronto: Queen's Printer. 1968.

Rees, Albert. "Industrial conflict and business fluctuations." In *Industrial Conflict,* edited by A. Kornhauser et al., pp.213-20. New York: McGraw-Hill. 1954.

Roberts, B.C. *Unions in America: A British View.* Princeton, N.J.: Industrial Relations Section. Princeton University. 1959.

Ross, Arthur M. and Paul T. Hartman. *Changing Patterns of Industrial Conflict.* New York: Wiley. 1960.

Selekman, Ben. M. *Postponing Strikes: A Study of the Industrial Disputes Investigation Act of Canada.* New York: Russell Sage Foundation. 1927.

Serrin, William. *The Company and the Union.* New York: Alfred A. Knopf. 1973.

Shorter, Edward and Charles Tilly. *Strikes in France, 1830-1968.* London: Cambridge University Press. 1974.

Silver, Michael. "Recent British strike trends: a factual analysis." *British Journal of Industrial Relations* 11:66-104. 1973.

Smith, Dougals A. "The determinants of strike activity in Canada." *Relations Industrielles* 27:663-78. 1972.

"The impact of inflation on strike activity in Canada." *Relations Industrielles* 31:139-45. 1976.

Snyder, David. "Early North American strikes: a reinterpretation." *Industrial and Labor Relations Review* 30:325-41. 1977.

Trotsky, Leon. "Marxism and trade unionism." In *Trade Unions under Capitalism,* edited by T. Clarke and L. Clements, pp.77-92. Glasgow: Fontana/Collins. 1977.

Vanderkamp, John. "Economic activity and strikes in Canada." *Industrial Relations* 14:45-54. 1970.

Weber, Max. "Politics as a vocation." In *From Max Weber: Essays in Sociology,* edited by H.H. Gerth and C.W. Mills, pp.77-128. New York: Galaxy. 1958.

Wedderburn, K.W. "Conflicts of 'rights' and conflicts of 'interests' in labor disputes." In *Dispute Settlement Procedures in Five Western European Countries,* edited by B. Aaron, pp.65-90. Los Angeles: University of California, Institute of Industrial Relations. 1969.

Whitaker, Reg. "Images of the state in Canada." In *The Canadian State,* edited by L. Panitch, pp.28-68. Toronto: University of Toronto Press. 1977.

Williams, C. Brian. "Notes on the evolution of compulsory consiliation." *Relations Industrielles* 19:298-32. 1964.

Woods, H.D. "Canadian collective bargaining and dispute settlement policy: an appraisal." *Canadian Journal of Economics and Political Science* 21:447-65. 1955.

Labour Policy in Canada. Second edition. Toronto: Macmillan. 1975.

Woods, H.D. et al. *Canadian Industrial Relations. The Report of the Task Force on Labour Relations.* Ottawa: Pricy Council Office, Queen's Printer. 1968.

NOTES

[1]While numerous difficulties confront any attempt to make meaningful international comparisons of strike activity, working time lost (or forgone) through strikes and lockouts per 1,000 employees probably provides the most useful measure. The main reasons are conveniently summarized by Silver (1973:70):

. . . firstly because it automatically adjusts for differences between countries in the sizes of their labour forces, secondly because it constitutes a rough index of the economic cost of strikes, and thirdly because it is unlikely to be severely affected by international differences in the scope of strike statistics, since these differences mainly bear on the smallest and the shortest strikes (which usually contribute relatively little to the total number of days lost).

Using this measure, International Labour Office figures showed Canada leading all other industrial nations in strikes during 1975 (Great Britain, *Department of Employment Gazette,* January 1977).

[2]Ross and Hartman (1960:12) construct their ratio of strike duration "by dividing the number of workers involved into the number of working days lost for the particular year. In other words it shows time lost per striker."

[3]Shorter and Tilly (1974:51) use the median to avoid the distorting effect which one interminable strike could have on the mean.

[4]Snyder (1977) finds that the influential economic model proposed by Ashenfelter and Johnson (1969) does not fit the case of the United States or Canada for early periods of labor history. Nevertheless, like Shorter and Tilly, he continues to assign exclusive importance to economic deterrminants of strike activity occurring *since* World War II.

[5]Total bans on the right to strike, court injunctions, "emergency" back-to-work legislation and wage controls represent further variants of state intervention that are beyond the scope of the present paper.

[6]Strictly speaking, as Whitaker (1977:29) points out, the operation of the coercion function is not necessarily unique to capitalist societies, but could be considered part of the classic definition of the state for all manner of social formations proposed by Weber (1958:78). The reason given by Panitch (1977:8) for distinguishing between the coercion and the accumulation function is that the latter "does not *normally* rely on the coercion function, but operates independently of it" (Emphasis in original).

[7]With the notable exception of the miners and railway workers, the Trades and Labour Congress (TLC) supported the IDIA at its 1907 convention. In subsequent years, opposition began to develop and in 1916 the TLC convention went on record as "opposing the Lemieux (Disputes) Act in its entirety" (Selekman, 1972:167). This proved to be the only occasion that the TLC attempted to challenge openly the principles underlying the IDIA, as the next convention marked a return to the earlier position of seeking amendments rather than repeal of the legislation.

[8]However, as Woods (1955:462) acknowledges, the IDIA did *not* succeed in resolving the contentious issues of recognition; "the evidence is conclusive that in the years since 1907 employers generally remained hostile to collective bargaining."

[9]This viewpoint is supported by Mahon (1977:185) who states that the IDIA "was designed to curtail, and possibly prevent, work stoppages in industries considered essential to the National Policy."

[10]Glenday and Schrenk (1978:131) contend that the federal level of the Canadian state generally showed the way in industrial relations legislation "while the provincial state apparatus had to be dragged."

[11]The actual principle of exclusive jurisdiction was not the original idea of the legislators who framed the Wagner Act; it had long been championed as the central organizational tenet of the craft-dominated labor movement in North America.

[12]Here it is important to stress that the eventual form of state intervention in labor relations did not necessarily have to receive the unanimous approval of all employers and all those responsible for exercising influence over public policy affecting industrial relations. In this regard, Poulantzas (1973) speaks of the capitalist state exercising a relative degree of autonomy.

[13]Two methods are used by Flood: the first treats all short strikes of between one and five days duration as wildcat; the second method makes the assumption that most strikes occurring during the term of a contract are wildcat. Using the first approach, Flood estimates that between 1956 and 1969 wildcats constituted between approximately a third and a half of all strikes in Canada. The second approach suggests a slightly lower proportion.

[14]Another investigation ordered in 1966 was the Ontario Royal Commission on Labour Disputes. The ensuing Report under Justice Rand (1968) recommended that mass picketing be banned and that a system of selected compulsory arbitration be introduced. Most critics (e.g., Fisher and Crowe, 1968; Goldenberg, 1969) strongly objected to the idea of placing so much emphasis on the coercive aspect of labor legislations and the proposals were not implemented.

[15]The description of union leaders as "managers of discontent" was popularized by Mills (1948:224).

IDEOLOGY

Introduction

Ideologies, it was pointed out earlier, can be viewed as systems of belief that attempt to legitimize the rule of particular classes. They also serve as backdrops against which individuals interpret their everyday experience. One ideology that in Canada has received a considerable amount of attention is the ideology of conservatism.

It is now almost a social scientific cliché when examining Canada in comparison to the United States to refer to its conservative nature (Lipset, 1970; Hartz, 1964; Horowitz, 1966). Basically, so the argument goes, because of our essentially counter-revolutionary tradition and respect for law and order, Canadians have not experienced the consequences of a surfeit of liberalism and individualism that characterizes our neighbour to the south. Historically, those advocating the 'conservative thesis' maintain, this condition has been manifested in lower crime, divorce, etc. rates and a greater receptivity to state intervention in the economy (Lipsit, 1970). The reason for the latter is that society is regarded as somewhat of an organism with mutual responsibility among the parts (Horowitz: 1966). One consequence, to make a long story short, has been the development of a Canadian state that has been more concerned with the interests of the general population that the American state has. While the policy effects of this belief were supposedly more evident in early years of settlement, its mark on the Canadian social structure has not been erased. The Canadian Broadcasting Corporation, Air Canada, and hospitalization insurance schemes, to name only a few items, are here to prove it.

While there is little doubt regarding state intervention in the economy, there is less certainty concerning other aspects of the 'conservative thesis.' For one thing, it has been shown that many of the comparative assumptions underlying it simply are not true (Truman, 1971). More importantly, it is extremely doubtful that classes shared general notions of mutual responsibility.

In one of the few good analyses that can shed light on this matter, Smith, in the following article, has demonstrated that, at least in English Canada, contrary to the implications of the 'conservative thesis,' individualism was a dominant cultural force operative in society in the 1850-1914 period–a force that was consistent with continued bourgeoisie dominance. It was not long, however, before it was plain, even to its advocates, that hard work and initiative alone, in contrast to the individualist assumption, did not guarantee success. By the 1850s, increasing numbers of the bourgeoisie, or its spokesmen, were also stressing education as an invaluable aid to those desirous of social and economic advancement. To use Smith's own words, "Education's virtue . . . lay in the fact that in a universe of flux and change it equipped one to make his own way." Later in the century, however, further complications arose.

"The realization that Canadian society was complex," Smith argues, "did more than underscore the argument that the individual's chances of success would be seriously diminished if he did not equip himself with special skills; it also compelled some observers to admit that even if he had received schooling, and no matter how hard he worked, he might not alter his position in any appreciable way. Nor," some of them continued, (and this is the important part) "was it necessarily desirable that he should." In order to meet the challenge posed by the realization that neither toil nor education necessarily resulted in social mobility, a new stress was placed on the value of hard work as an end in itself.

As Smith puts it, "each man must work hard, look after himself, not expect great material success, and take satisfaction from the knowledge that his society was composed of men whose position and aspirations were the same." At the same time that moralists and businessmen were exhorting the working class to work hard, be contented with their lot, and to stand on their own two feet, they were petitioning the government for subsidies, tariffs, tax advantages, what-have-you, to ensure their own prosperity (Aitken, 1967).

The contradiction in this position is real, not apparent. The importance of what spokesmen for the bourgeoisie were saying, however, cannot be examined solely in terms of its truth or falsity. Its consequences must also be examined.

As Smith points out, the creed of individualism, "operated in a number of ways to induce satisfaction with existing forms of social organization and economic activity. By celebrating the work of the farmer, it strove to make that being happy with his lot and so encouraged activity essential to the development of an important sector of the national economy: by stressing the value of education," he continues, "it played its part in producing a skilled and semi-skilled workforce; by talking of success and fulfillment in terms of intangibles it reconciled workers to the fact of class; and," Smith concludes, "by obscuring the nature of the new collectivism, it masked the fact that society's thrust toward bureaucracy and rationalization was making it steadily more difficult to sustain the proposition that each man controlled his destiny." The reference to bureaucracy and rationalization is important. For by the closing years of the last century the merger movement was well under way (Naylor, 1975 I & II). In response to this and earlier developments, both farmers and the working class were engaged in new types of collective behaviour in attempts to better their positions in a changing capitalistic society–a society in which the myth of individualism was becoming increasingly more inconsistent with material surroundings.

With the merger movements, the Canadian economy, despite its continued reliance on staple production, passed from a stage of liberal to advanced capitalism. The former, to oversimplify greatly, can be characterized as a phase in which a number of small economic enterprises compete for the market. In the latter, a few large enterprises control the market. (It is clear that the former, in its pure form, really never existed in Canada.) Concomitant with this transition was a gradual transformation of the dominant emphasis on individualism to a stressing of co-operation. As Mellos pointed out in a former article, "Whereas liberal capitalist practice and ideology required and emphasized the importance of individual action as the vehicle for the achievement of the total collective good, under conditions of advanced capitalism it is increasingly the group which is the unit of action instrumental in the attainment of collective good." As a consequence, large scale enterprises and vertical integration of industry, trade unions, state intervention in the economy and close relations between business and state are acceptable within this general 'co-operative' cultural framework– far more so in fact than was true in earlier periods. Despite changes, in both liberal and advanced capitalism, dominant ideologies have buttressed the interests of the bourgeoisie. These facts notwithstanding it is unlikely that there ever was an uncritical and complete acceptance of dominant bourgeois ideology. The number of political protest movements that have emerged over the years attest to the validity of this statement. As early as the 1837 rebellions certain elements of the population of Upper and Lower Canada were questioning the legitimacy of relationships between commercial and state interests (Clark, 1959; Creighton, 1956; Ryerson, 1968). So did the Grange movement and the Patrons of Industry who entered Canadian farming communities in the closing years of the last century (Wood, 1924/1975).

After 1900, agrarian populist movements (Morton, 1950; Macpherson, 1953; Sharp, 1948), farmers' provincial governments (Irving, 1959; Lipset, 1950), union movements (Horowitz, 1968) and social democratic parties (Young, 1969) likewise manifested dissatisfaction with the implications of contemporary ideologies. Central to most of their beliefs was the idea that particular business interests in society worked against the well-being of the majority and that rather than assist these interests, the state should be mobilized against them. If analyses of the state offered earlier are valid, there was little chance that this goal would have been realized.

Although it is not well-documented, opposition to the dominant ideology has taken forms other than the overtly political. In working class journalism, for example, Watt (1957) discovered that challenges to some aspects of the dominant bourgeois ideology were offered in the nineteenth century. Such activities may not have attacked the fundamental assumptions of capitalism, but they certainly called into question a variety of practices. According to Lord (1974), in some instances, visual art had a similar impact. By the 1930s, as the following article by Grayson and Grayson demonstrates, rejection of the underlying assumptions of the dominant ideology were also evident in a number of English Canadian novels. Despite opposition, it is nonetheless evident that with its emphasis first on individualism and then on co-operation, the dominant ideology was well established.

While the main features of a dominant English-Canadian ideology, that was consistent with the interests of the bourgeoisie are summed up in the internally contradictory notions of individualism and co-operation as analysed here, there are a number of other closely related dimensions of ideology that find expression in the following readings. In his article, Rioux outlines how, since the Conquest, ideologies have been used by different classes in Quebec to consolidate their positions in society. More importantly, he demonstrates that the ideology of individualism as is stressed in English-Canada really did not extend to Quebec. In the period covered by Smith, a form of conservatism hostile to individualism was dominant. In his analysis, Layton points to the class roots of Canadian nationalism. Those members of the Canadian bourgeoisie who are most concerned with a drift into dependency are those with the fewest connections to the activities of multinationals operative in Canada. In the field of literature, Grayson and Grayson point out that changes in the ideological framework underlying the English-Canadian novel can in some cases be related to periods of crisis in capitalist development. In the final article, Smith points to the very important fact that all ideologies, in Canada, and elsewhere, by and large are reflections of male experience.

What does not receive adequate attention in the following articles is the possibility of the relative autonomy of ideology. As stated in the General Introduction, ideologies, to a degree, can develop in accordance with their own impetus. Then, at a crucial juncture, they may articulate with other forces in society. Unfortunately, rather than recognizing this possibility, most of the articles in this section lean toward variations of class reductionism as identified by Laclau. In short, ideologies tend to be viewed as derivative from the class relations extant in society.

THE MYTH OF THE SELF-MADE MAN IN ENGLISH CANADA, 1850-1914

Allan Smith

Recent scholarship concerning society and values in English Canada has placed much emphasis on the extent to which their evolution demonstrates a continuing Canadian attachment to conservative principle. Strongly concerned to establish the ways in which the Canadian nation may be distinguished from the American, scholars have drawn particular attention to the role played in its growth by deference, a belief in the rights of the community over those of the individual, and a sense that the collective experience of those who compose it gives society its substance and texture. The Canadian mind, they argue, has been characterized not so much by faith in the potency of the individual as by a conviction that men in society must accept the authority of those who preside over their affairs. Living in a community which has been shaped by metropolitan institutions—the church, the fur trade, government, corporations—has, they suggest, made Canadians inclined to value behaviour that allows an harmonious existence within a framework of organization, discipline, and order. Canadians, they continue, have doubted the wisdom of experimenting with new modes of political organization, preferring to cast their lot with institutions whose capacity to allow men to live together in peace, order, and good government has been clearly proved. It was, indeed, the Canadians' lack of enthusiasm for doctrines espousing the primacy of the individual that led them to structure a transcontinental nation dedicated to the furtherance of essentially conservative aims. In time their adherence to a value system in which a strong reverence for individualist modes of behaviour was displaced by a belief in class and community prepared the way for a measured but explicit commitment to social democracy. Even the businessman, contends a recent study, seriously qualified his individualism. In the midst of this welter of collectivist and quasi-collectivist belief, little room was left, scholars have concluded, for a Canadian assertion of faith in the power of the individual. In S.M. Lipset's formulation, 'Horatio Alger has never been a Canadian hero.'[1]

While there can be no doubt that the makers of this argument have contributed fundamentally to our understanding of Canadian society and the values, attitudes, and ideas of those who formed it, perhaps it is now time to look at the other side of the coin. Is there evidence to suggest that Canadians thought in individualist terms? Did they adopt individualist heroes? Were they, in short, men and women of their age? There can be little doubt that the answer to these questions is Yes. From the middle of the nineteenth century, when they first began to offer their compatriots sustained and regular instruction in what modes of behaviour were worthy of emulation, until the Great War, after which the emergence of new social and economic realities pushed discussion of these matters into a wholly new phase, English Canadians made it very clear indeed that the myth of the self-made man informed no small part of their thinking about society and its nature.

Many Canadians, certainly, did not hesitate to portray their society as one which at once allowed unlimited scope for, and had been shaped by, individual activity. Anxious to encourage the hard work which seemed so essential to the country's development, and convinced that the pain and struggle involved in doing that work would be more palatable if their results were seen to have special significance, these observers emphasized the degree to which individual effort was historically important, productive of great personal satisfaction, and likely to bring dramatic rewards. A deep-seated impulse to self-reliance, some of them insisted, was, in fact, to be found at the very core of the national experience. It was, they suggested, a matter of record that such figures as James Wolfe,[2] Sir Frederick Haldimand,[3] Sir William Phipps,[4] Lord Selkirk,[5] John Strachan,[6] and Tecumseh[7] had made their mark thanks in large part to the qualities of character, determination, and ingenuity which they so conspicuously displayed.

The commonly expressed contention—at its

187

most grandiose and explicit in the multi-volume *Makers of Canada,* published early in the twentieth century[8]–that individualist modes of behaviour had been exemplified by the founders of the nation, legitimized by the historical process itself, was accompanied by the equally widespread claim that the life of the present no less than the experience of the past was given shape and body by the latitude it allowed the creative, self-determining individual. There could be no doubt, insisted the popular historian C.R. Tuttle, that life in contemporary Canada provided anyone willing to work with ample opportunity to better himself. Incontrovertible proof of this proposition, Tuttle continued, was available to anyone who scrutinized the careers of the most eminent Canadians. One had only to consider the achievements of such men as Tupper, Mackenzie, and Macdonald to see that, in Canada, talent and ability could overcome the humblest of origins.[9]

What was demonstrated by the lives of Canada's leaders, claimed another chronicler of the Canadian experience, had been quite as clearly evidenced by those of its people. As historian John McMullen put it in 1855, what they were able to accomplish demonstrated beyond doubt that Canada was a society in which 'enterprise, economy, and prudence . . . are the avenues to wealth . . . everyday experience presents to our notice mechanics who, as the architects of their own fortunes, have won their way to positions alike well merited and honorable.'[10] As the figure who had been most intimately associated with one of the central features of Canada's existence–the clearing of the land–the pioneer farmer received particularly close attention from Canadian acolytes of the self-made man. By his hard work he at once advanced himself and gave content to his country's development. He was, claimed his literary friends, in the fullest sense his own master, free of all constraint and interference, quite literally able to shape his world as he wished, the heir to an abundant and fulfilling future. And what allowed him to attain these heights–the moral was driven home with unmistakable clarity by poet Isabella Valancy Crawford–was no more nor less than his own capability: '. . . all men,' insisted Crawford, 'may have the same/That owns an axe! an' has a strong right arm!'[11]

By the early years of the twentieth century the conviction that in Canada past and present combined to authenticate the individualist principle had become deeply rooted. As the University of Toronto's Pelham Edgar put it in 1909, the belief that Canada was 'the land of limitless possibilities . . .where old age may [never] lament . . . as in countries less rich in rewards, the life-long absence of opportunity . . . was so firmly entrenched that, he continued, it was past time to remind Canadians of Matthew Arnold's contention that an overweening concern with material advancement signified not progress but barbarism.[12] But if some of his compatriots heeded this and similar arguments, others continued to revere the man of success and accomplishment. Even Sir William Van Horne's none too scrupulous tactics in building the first Cuban railway justified his identification in the pages of the *Canadian Magazine* as a pre-eminent man of achievement whose industry, determination, and ingenuity had overcome all obstacles.[13]

If, in sum, the Canada of these years contained no scarcity of figures who could be shown to have shaped their careers in the finest traditions of the self-made man, it also contained no shortage of writers who thought it important that this fact be brought to the public's attention. Canadians, like the Americans and British, must be taught the virtues of self-help. What better way to do it than by showing them that what was best in their own society was the product of, gave ample encouragement to, and found its perfect expression in, individual effort?

For all its appeal, the uncomplicated picture painted by these partisans of the self-made man had serious shortcomings. The society in which their heroes functioned did not long remain–it had never really been–a place where unadorned virtue and simple hard work automatically brought fulfilment beyond mesure. It was, some observers had noted early on, a labyrinthine structure the mastery of whose byways depended on more than strength, fortitude, and determination. As early as the 1840s the transformation of Upper Canadian society into a more complex and differentiated entity had produced changes in the way it was viewed. It was no longer, some observers argued, to be seen as raw and unfinished, waiting for the hand of man who, in transforming it, would make his own career. It was instead a complicated and ever-changing mechanism. Success in coping with it involved more than will and initiative. Special training was required. In these circumstances, as the *Kingston Chronicle* put it in 1842, education was the 'young's man capital.' A tool in the struggle for self-sufficiency, it was 'the best assurance of further competency and happiness.'[14] Six years later, educator Egerton Ryerson pointed to the existence of a dynamic quality in society with which individuals must be trained to cope. This, he noted, was a time of 'sharp and skilful competition' and 'sleepless activity.' It was all, moreover, just beginning. 'The rising generation should, therefore, be educated not for Canada as it has been, or even now is, but for Canada as it is likely to be half a generation hence.'[15] Education's virtue thus lay in the fact that in a universe of flux and change it equipped one to make his own way: with schooling Canadians might, in the words of one of Ryerson's contempories, 'be prepared, at least, to make some near approach to that place in the social scale, which their more intelligent, because better educated, [American] neighbours, now threaten to monopolize.'[16]

Within twenty years this line of argument had become a familiar one. As one Canadian, recalling his early experiences, put it: 'I had heard that knowledge was power—and I looked upon Algebra and Euclid and the whole academic course as the rudimentary steam-engine with which I should sometime run a train of first-class cars, freighted full of hope and worldly success into some great depot of happiness. I looked upon education as a toolchest—as something to work with . . .'[17] The 1869 death of the American banker-philanthropist George Peabody provided the occasion for another observer to underscore the connection between success and education. Where Peabody's lack of schooling might once have been linked with his life of achievement to establish the fact that it was only by overcoming obstacles and relying upon oneself that one made his way, the connection was now made for quite a different reason. Peabody, readers of the *New Dominion Monthly* were assured, had always seen his failure to get an education as a handicap. His mature interest in it, therefore, 'probably arose in part from the fact that he was taken from school at eleven years, and thus himself felt the need of the advantage he

so liberally supplied for others.'[18]

What possession of those advantages might lead to was made clear to Canadians in a five-volume work published in 1891. Setting out to show what hard work, perseverance, and preparation could accomplish in almost any field, the title alone of the Reverend William Cochrane's *The Canadian Album, Men of Canada: or Success by Example, in Religion, Patriotism, Business, Law, Medicine, Education, and Agriculture* . . . clearly indicated that success was to be associated with special training—often professional—in a defined field of activity. Some commentators chose to add emphasis to the point by introducing fictional heroes who displayed a marked appetite for study and eventually became successful doctors or lawyers.[19] The living of a happy and fulfilling domestic life was in its turn shown to depend on the acquisition of certain skills.[20] The power of education to equip individuals with what was necessary to a successful career was, it seemed, unlimited. Even deficiencies of character which the individual could do nothing to ameliorate on his own might, claimed one educator, be overcome by training and example. That was why, argued John M. Sangster in 1892, teachers must exhibit no tendency towards laziness. Their deportment no less than the substance of their lessons had a role to play in fitting their pupils for life's struggle.[21]

Emphasis on learning as an adjunct to success was occasionally accompanied by a vigorous anti-intellectualism. It was necessary, some commentators insisted, to distinguish between learning that was useful and learning that was not. The training which had most to do with one's struggle to advance oneself did not, they claimed, come from the schools at all. 'Great men,' noted an 1868 observer, 'learn very little of what the world admires them for knowing, during what is called their 'educational' course. They are men who are constantly observing little things and great things passing around them . . . it is this knowledge obtained among men and from men that is the most useful in any walk of life, literary or commercial.'[22] Whatever its source, agreed another commentator, knowledge must be practical in its application. Schooling must produce 'a well-educated, properly finished man, ready to grapple with the numerous many-sided questions sure to present themselves in his day and generation.'[23] He who would be successful must also strive to broaden his practical experience. 'The young businessman who spends his whole life in the study of business in his own town or city has,' insisted a 1901 observer, 'far less chance of success than the man who has seen business done in a dozen cities.'[24]

One way of mastering the tasks of the workaday world within the context of a system of formal training was provided by the commercial and business schools of post-Confederation Canada. Their activities, in turn, were complemented by manuals offering systematic instruction in the steps necessary to achieve success in the world of commerce and practical affairs. Those who aspired to rise in that world might read John Macdonald's *Business Success*,[25] or, perhaps, listen to a series of lectures Macdonald gave to the students of Toronto's British American Commercial College. Published under the title *Business Character* in 1886, their statement of the relevance 'the old principles of truth and honesty and industry and patience . . . ' bore to the new situation earned them an enthusiastic response from *The Week*: the little book, it said, 'cannot fail to benefit every young man who is wise enough to make its precepts his.'[26]

Learning, whether formal or not, continued to be associated with mobility. One commentator drew the required lesson from Franklin's career. That luminary, he reminded his readers, had 'educated himself while fulfilling his labours as printer, editor, and bookseller . . .' This considerable accomplishment, moreover, was directly responsible for his success in later life. It had been 'by dint of his persevering struggle after improvement [that he became] an author, a philosopher, and a statesman.'[27] Another observer, more inclined to emphasize the value of schooling, insisted on its continuing relevance to those who wished to move in step with a changing world. 'The world,' she noted, 'is progressing, and he who would be successful in any calling must keep pace with the rapid onward march.'[28]

By the turn of the century the relevance of a university education to the plans of those who wished to advance themselves was being adumbrated. 'People are beginning to realize,' argued a supporter of post-secondary institutions in 1904, 'that the old orthodox way of making a fortune–to come to London or Montreal with fifty cents in your pocket and all the rest of it, is not the only way.' University training, and the mental discipline acquired in getting it, were, he continued, becoming more and more necessary, and those who have them will be the ones who will achieve success.[29] As another writer put it, the businessman who went to college would, other things being equal, be more successful than the one who did not.[30] More importantly, insisted a third observer, providing businessmen with a university education was likely to make them less bumptious and more humane. The self-made man, unadorned by anything save his money-making powers, was '. . . the pest of modern life . . . ' Transformed by a liberal education, he would be an altogether different being. When its civilizing capability was set alongside its relevance to income and status, the case for higher education in fact established itself.[31]

Some commentators, even more concerned to emphasize the fact that education must stimulate and develop the higher side of man's nature if his powers as a free and responsible individual were to be fully engaged, claimed that the educational enterprise itself was being perverted by emphasis on the acquisition of marketable skills and practical knowledge. 'The true aim of education,' contended an 1894 critic, 'is being lost sight of . . . The instruction that will fit for making money is considered of primal importance; the education that develops character, manliness, patriotism is considered of secondary importance.[32] The moral education of the young, agreed journalist J.A. Cooper, must not be neglected. Here the family had a special responsibility. It must not, Cooper argued in 1899, abandon it. This was, indeed, vital, for only the sort of sensitivity to the moral dimension of man's existence that would come from a proper family upbringing could create a truly self-directed and creative human being. Nowhere but in the midst of the family could young people be taught that 'education may come from within as well as without, that every individual is the architect and builder of his own life-building.'[33]

Other commentators were similarly persuaded that the development of character and a sense of responsibility could not be ignored.

They insisted, however, that the relationship this sort of moral improvement bore to self-reliance made it, like self-reliance, dependent on the acquisition of values, attitudes, and even skills that—in some circumstances at least—only schooling could provide. The arrival of the great wave of European immigrants in the early years of the twentieth century allowed this proposition to be illustrated in a particularly striking way. In their case, it was argued, schooling would provide not only needed skills—language, for example—but also the orientation towards society the newcomers required if they were to advance themselves. By inculcating the principles of self-reliance and initiative, it would overcome the bovine stolidity that so many observers found characteristic of the immigrants. This would at once lay the groundwork for their assimilation into Canadian society and make it possible for them to realize the opportunities—moral and material—open to them in their new situation.

Saskatchewan educator J.T.M. Anderson, anxious to show what a failure to equip themselves with knowledge of the language and *mores* of their new country had meant for many immigrants, advanced countless examples of men whose continuing attachment to the old ways had held them back. A young Polish immigrant who had got an education therefore emerged as one of his principal heroes. After overcoming a variety of obstacles, the Pole had become fluent in English, completed high school, and won his way through to a university education. That accomplishment, in equal measure the reward for past efforts and the means of future advancement, won him high marks from Anderson: 'What a splendid record of obstacles encountered and overcome, of worthy ambition, of loyal self-sacrifice, and youthful devotion to duty in the pursuance of a grand ideal!'[34] His feat, were it to be duplicated in immigrant communities across the prairies, would assure the advancement of the immigrant population in general. Schooling allied to character and initiative would help the new Canadians as it had the old to find their way to success and fulfilment.

The realization that Canadian society was complex did more than underscore the argument that the individual's chances of success would be seriously diminished if he did not equip himself with special skills; it also com-

pelled some observers to admit that even if he had received schooling, and no matter how hard he worked, he might not alter his position in any appreciable way. Nor, some of them continued, was it necessarily desirable that he should. Canada, they argued, needed nothing so much as a disciplined and productive work force. Getting [a work force] meant, in part, breeding up a race of men who would be content in the knowledge that their fate was to be hewers of wood and drawers of water. These points could not, however, be made without reservation. To cast them in categorical and unambiguous terms would be to take a dangerous step in the direction of denying mobility and affirming the existence of class. That, in its turn, would be to grant a major part of the case being framed by the critics of the individualist idea. Partisans of individualism, thus faced with the task of conceding what it seemed impossible to deny without, at the same time, doing violence to the essentials of their doctrine, sought to resolve their problem in the only way open to them. They would seek to persuade the individual frustrated by his lack of success that there was no real conflict between his situation and the idea that the social universe offered absolute scope for each man to live a happy and fulfilled life thanks to his own efforts alone. If the resources available for his use and pleasure sometimes seemed limited, that, he was assured, in no sense called the individualist idea into question. On the contrary, his modest stock of goods was a function of the fact that there existed a generally egalitarian system of apportioning society's bounty which was a necessary condition of individual fulfilment. By ensuring a more or less equitable distribution of what society had to offer, that system, argued its apologists, guaranteed everyone what he required to sustain his freedom and independence: limited means, quite simply, signified equality of condition, and equality of condition was to be viewed as the *sine qua non* of individual happiness and achievement. And if, continued some observers, there were occasions when opportunities leading in the direction in which he wished to move seemed few in number, that meant only that he should learn to find satisfaction in work in some field of activity where they were more abundant—and where, it was sometimes added, he was likely to be of more use. In nei-

191

ther of these cases, commentators insisted, was there reason to conclude that the individualist idea had lost its relevance. Each man remained the master of his fate. What he had to do to shape its contours perhaps involved paying more attention to circumstance than had once been thought necessary, but there could be no question that it remained within his power to make a full and satisfying life for himself.

The Toronto *Globe*, particularly concerned with influencing the wage earner's assessment of his position, played its readers a variation on the first of these themes in the early part of 1872. Far from being an impoverished exception in a community of the fabulously wealthy, the salaried worker was, that journal suggested, on a level with all Canadians. Canadian society was not to be thought of as a place whose representative figures were men of spectacular achievement. It remained open, to be sure, a place in which each man created his own destiny. 'We all work,' the newspaper insisted. 'We all began with nothing. We have all got by hard work all we own . . . ' Set alongside these familiar propositions, however, were others whose burden was that while hard work and self-reliance remained important, what should be expected to result from them were achievements of a modest and restrained sort. Each man's activity on his own behalf was, the *Globe* explained, attended not by dramatic and unlimited success, but by 'an ample independence.' Extravagant examples of good fortune were, in fact, specifically eschewed. 'We have,' it continued, 'no such class as those styled capitalists in other countries. The whole people are the capitalists in Canada.' The principal fact about the country, readers were assured, was that its people were 'frugal' and 'industrious,' the creators of a society in which 'the richest among us work still and like to do it.'[35] The moral to be extracted from all this was, then, clear: each man must work hard, look after himself, not expect great material success, and take satisfaction from the knowledge that his society was composed of men whose position and aspirations were the same.

There was, suggested a contributor to *Rose-Belford's Canadian Monthly*, another way in which the individual's limited share of the world's goods was compatible with the claim that he was an autonomous and self-di-

rected being. By throwing him back on his own resources his limited means called into play—indeed made mandatory the exercise of—the very qualities that allowed him to be defined in these terms. Far from rendering him impotent, the most straitened of circumstances thus had a special role to play in emphasizing the fact that he shaped his own fate. What became of him remained nothing more than a measure of the extent to which, thanks to his attributes of initiative and self-reliance, he turned to account whatever he had been given to work with. He must of course learn, explained *Rose-Belford's* correspondent, not to scorn what lay at hand. Even the finite and trivial, the most unprepossessing of means, had its uses. 'The great lesson'—here was the article's central message—'is not to despise the day of small things.'[36] Once, however, he had taken that injunction to heart, he would know that no matter how unpropitious his situation seemed, his life, still and as always, would be what he made of it.

The suggestion that his modest circumstances merely put the individual on his mettle, like the contention that they were proof of nothing more sinister than the fact that he lived in a society of equals, allowed the character of those circumstances to be conceded without making necessary a parallel concession that their existence deprived the individual of control over his fate. If, however, this careful avoidance of any suggestion that men no longer mastered their destiny played an important part in arguments designed to make society's members content with a limited share of the world's goods, it occupied a less prominent position in the case of those anxious that men who laboured for a living learn to derive pleasure and satisfaction from what they actually did rather than continually searching for some other livelihood the finding of which, as they seemed to think, would bring them happiness and enjoyment beyond measure. One commentator, single-mindedly striving to make the ordinary worker content with his lot, came in fact perilously close to arguing that he should learn to be satisfied with his daily round because he was likely to be involved with it for the rest of his working life. It was, argued L.R. O'Brien of the Ontario Society of Artists, imperative that society—and especially those of its members destined to be workingmen—understand that there was simply no room for everyone to advance. Only if this fact were grasped, O'Brien asserted, could those whose prospects were limited reach an accommodation with themselves and their situation that would enable them to live contented lives. That this should happen was in the interest of all of society, for only a real measure of satisfaction on the part of the worker with what he did would overcome the indifferent workmanship and—equally important for those anxious to curb labour agitation—the discontent with one's job that seemed characteristic of the age.

O'Brien's residual individualism moved him back, in the end, from fully embracing the claim that the workingman had lost the ability to move himself upwards in the social scale. His refusal to go so far had, however, the effect of reinforcing rather than qualifying his argument's principal theme: opportunity for advancement might indeed exist, but before the worker could take advantage of it he had to demonstrate his suitability for a more lucrative and responsible position by the exemplary performance of the duties now occupying his attention. Advancement in the future was thus tied to a willing acceptance of one's position and the tasks associated with it in the present. It was, as O'Brien put it, imperative that the wagearner see that he would 'rise by the excellence of his work, rather than by shirking it to seek for some easier mode of living or advancement.'[37]

Other observers agreed that the worker must keep his eye fixed firmly on what lay before him. To be sure, they, like O'Brien, avoided unambiguously suggesting that he be told that the social universe was a place of closed options and no hope. Equally, however, their concern that he be disabused of the idea that unlimited success and advancement automatically attended hard work led them to make an even stronger statement condemning what had become in their view a wholly spurious notion. The situation, argued the 1889 report of the federal commission investigating industrialism in Canada, was, in fact, urgent. Far too many children, their parents caught up in the belief that education was the highroad to success, were being enrolled in programmes meaningful only as preparation for professional and business careers. There were, however, few openings in these areas. At the same time the need—much more pressing in an industrializing society like Canada—for people trained to work with their hands was going largely unfilled. In these circumstances, the report suggested, those who gave the average child his picture of the society in which he must function had a duty to represent its character accurately. They must not continue the encouragement of extravagant expectations. Their task was to see to it that the child's training and, indeed, the whole of the socialization process to which he was exposed, contrive to make him content with a limited future. 'An effort should be made,' the report concluded, 'to instill in the minds of the young a preference for industrial avocations rather than the overstocked professional and commercial callings . . .'[38]

As much of the foregoing implies, an important part of the complicated business involved in conceding the reality of circumstance without denying the proposition that the individual was responsible for what befell him depended on getting that individual to accept an altered idea of what constituted success. Explaining to him what in many cases he already knew—that he did not operate in a wholly free and open universe—could not, by itself, do what was necessary. So long as he continued to covet wealth and power, his encounter with the limitations imposed by circumstance was, as O'Brien had suggested, likely to disillusion and embitter him, and so interfere with his interest in doing society's work. Equally disturbing, in the view of one observer, were the consequences that encounter entailed for society's moral tone. Some individuals, having recognized that circumstance was not to be overcome by hard work alone, were being led by their unmodified ambition to seek other means of dealing with it. The result, claimed J.A. Cooper in 1900, was a craven and undignified opportunism. Principled adherence to honourable behaviour was becoming a rarity. The ambitious were stooping to any level in their efforts to confound circumstance. 'The surest way to success,' as Cooper put it, was now 'by bending. Notice,' he continued, 'the politicians; they bend almost double. Notice the acrobatic actions of the successful businessman; they are the result of a long course of physical culture. Start out by accepting things as they are and proceed from that point.'[39]

Moving men away from an understanding of success that led in these directions required a sure and delicate touch. What replaced such an understanding must leave intact the idea that what one made of his life was a product of his own efforts. The result of those efforts had, moreover, to be attractive or one would have no incentive for doing the work necessary to achieve it. In their search for a goal that would be at once attainable and worth pursuing, philosophers of success found it difficult to do other than restate the idea that the proper end of human activity was a morally sound existence, one characterized by hard work, charity, and discipline. He who was successful was he who had shaped a moral life. In thus defining the goal in terms of the behaviour necessary to achieve it, they at once powerfully reinforced that behaviour and allowed wealth to be dispensed with as the object with which it would be rewarded.

This move, certainly, was consistent with Cooper's view of what was required. Only the man in whom means and ends were fused in one moral whole could, he thought, earn recognition as 'one of the world's truly great.'[40] It was, as well, a tactic that stood to have vitally important consequences so far as the worker was concerned. Winning his assent to this definition of success would play a central part in the difficult process of persuading him to accept the continuing validity of individualist assumptions even as his circumstances were compelling the conclusion that a life guided by them did not, in its externals at least, undergo significant change. Emphasis was, accordingly, laid on the notion that self-reliance, character, and discipline were to be their own rewards. Habits of thrift and industry were to be adopted by workers, not primarily as a means of moving themselves upward in the social scale, but as a way of ensuring a full, satisfying life for themselves where they were. The worker must identify himself with these values and attitudes, not so much because a life lived in accordance with them would ensure his rise, but because it would lead to the kind of satisfaction that could only come from the responsible and conscientious performance of one's task viewed as an end in itself. 'Let the workingmen of Canada learn,' as nine-hour day opponent C. Henry Stephens expressed the matter in 1872, '. . . to live frugally, temperately, and with a high and proper sense of the power and responsibility with which they are entrusted, and they will do more to ameliorate their position than by any reduction of their hours of labour, or by any fictitious appearance of material gain.'[41]

Material gain—at this juncture the influence of the Protestant tradition plainly revealed itself—could now in fact be pronounced incompatible with a truly successful life, In leading, as in its detractor's view it inevitably did, to self-indulgence and a weakening of moral fibre, it imposed a burden too great for any man to carry. As one writer, extracting the lesson from his story of a hickory tree felled in a storm, had put it in 1864: '. . . he had carried too large a top. Too great a wealth and growth of greenness had proved his ruin. Prosperity had been his bane. And many a one who walks the earth today, and many who do not, have thus, too, fallen!'[42] The awful inexorability with which this process worked itself out was dramatically illustrated for readers of the *New Dominion Monthly* a few years later. Storyteller J.R. Ramsay, chronicling the history of a fictional Canadian family, made a special point of the fact that one of its branches had undergone moral collapse owing to the failure of its members to cope with their success. A distillery started by one of them had prospered, but '. . . with wealth came luxury; with luxury temptation, disgrace.'[43]

Stephen was, of course, not alone in amplifying this theme. To be sure, those who joined him in embellishing it did not always take precisely the same tack. If writer-historian W.D. Le Sueur's 1875 statement—'To live worthily we must set before us an ideal, and that ideal must be something more than mere worldly success'[44] was quite categorical in its refusal to equate wealth and achievement, some observers declared themselves willing to countenance at least a measure of material prosperity. The fundamental concern in each case remained, however, the same. The moral content of one's life, commentators insisted, provided the true means of measuring its worth. Wealth in itself had no value. Achievement did not bestow the right to behave irresponsibly. It certainly conferred no right to demean oneself. A successful man must, in the words of Canniff Haight, 'guard against the enervating influences which are too apt to follow increase in wealth . . . Wealth can give much, but cannot make a man, in the proper and higher sense . . . '[45] The Reverend W.R.G. Mellen thought it imperative that wealth, once acquired, be put to proper use. Wealthy men must emulate the Peabodys, Vassars, Hopkins, and Cornells, and make their money available for the public good. It was delivered into their hands as a trust, and it must be used as such.[46] Personal deportment was also of great importance. Far from indulging himself, the man of wealth must adopt a style of life in which restraint, even unworldliness, figured prominently. He should, indeed, practice a kind of secular asceticism. The comment of British railway contractor Thomas Brassey's wife, that her husband 'was a most unworldly man,' was, then, suggested a Canadian commentator, worthy of special attention: 'This may,' he noted, 'seem a strange thing to say of a great contractor and a millionaire. Yet, in the highest sense, it was true. Mr. Brassey was not a monk: his life was passed in the world, and in the world's most engrossing, and, as it proves in too many cases, most contaminating business. Yet, if the picture of him presented to us be true, he kept himself "unspotted from the world." '[47]

By the early years of the new century, those who worked in the environment created by cities, industry, and commerce had been equipped with a definition of success in which material achievement played a relatively unimportant part. Although Toronto's Casa Loma was hardly the project of a man 'unspotted from the world,' its builder Sir Henry Pellatt won favourable mention in the pages of the *Canadian Magazine* because of his charitable activities. It was they, the journal implied, which had put the capstone on a successful career.[48] That journal could also proclaim railway magnate Sir William Whyte a truly successful man not simply because of his talents as a businessman, but also thanks to his adherence to Christian principle: 'It was what Mr. Whyte possessed in addition to business qualities,' journalist R.G. MacBeth assured his readers, 'that made him too great a human to be swallowed up by commercial concerns.'[49] Businessmen themselves fostered this understanding of what conferred worth and reputation. In their view, argues Michael Bliss, 'real success was not necessarily the achievement of wealth . . . In its ultimate implications the [businessman's] success ethic had little or nothing to do with making money, everything to do with the cultivation of moral character.'[50]

The realities of life in urban, industrial Canada had, in sum, made necessary a restatement of what composed a successful life. The promise of an abundant future might still inspire activity in less developed parts of the country, but in the cities the holding out of such a hope could only give rise to disillusionment and cynicism. The result would be, at the least, a recalcitrant and unco-operative work force, and, at the most, one likely to be driven into the arms of agitators animated by quite a different set of assumptions about the nature of man in society. If the myth of the self-made man was to retain its credibility, a new understanding of the kind of self he made had to be developed. Wealth, in consequence, ceased to be the yardstick of success and became its enemy. By thus falling back upon a restatement of the principles of the Protestant ethic, these commentators neatly squared a difficult circle. They were able to give up the untenable idea that wealth and position attended hard work without having to concede that the individual had no control over the shaping of his life. With the definition of success deprived of its materialist content, the way was open – in principle – for the worker to be adjusted to the fact that mobility did not exist. At the same time, he as an individual was left the master of his fate. If something which had to be defined as failure did occur, there could be no reason to attach blame to anything other than his own shortcomings. The ideologists of individualism were thus able to redefine their creed in a way that encouraged formation of a stable workforce, contributed to the adjusting of that force to the fact that social mobility was not a prominent feature of life in industrial Canada, and, by retaining the credibility of the individualist idea, helped to deny the legitimacy of opposing views of society and the individual.

By the end of the century theorists of individualism found themselves confronting another fact about life in society which seemed to raise questions about the accuracy with which their ideas represented it. Practice consistent with the principles of individualism was, it seemed clear, steadily receding from view. Collective action was assuming more and more importance in the shaping of the social and economic order. Labour, business, and government alike were yielding to the thrust towards bureaucracy and organization. The principles of *laissez-faire* might, as one observer put it in 1907, still constitute 'a good sermon, but it is to be feared that most of the congregation are away worshipping in other tabernacles.'[51]

These circumstances plainly required some response from those who wished to maintain the claim that the individualist view of the world continued to describe its dynamic. Removing the lack of congruence between their principles and the practice that now seemed so central a part of life in society was not, however, an easy task. To concede in principle that collectively organized behaviour was an integral part of life in society would be to modify in significant ways the individualist idea of reality as it had been expressed through much of the nineteenth century. To deny, on the other hand, that the new collectivism had implications for the individualist world view would be tantamount to rejecting the evidence of one's senses.

Those who were prepared to accommodate the new collectivism sought to reconcile this step with their continuing attachment to the individualist idea by suggesting that certain forms of collective behaviour were quite compatible with, and in some cases had become an indispensable condition of, individual fulfilment. To be sure, the doctrinaire assertions of the socialists were unacceptable. As Nova Scotia's attorney-general J.W. Longley put it in 1896, implementing their proposals would 'destroy the great stimulating influence of competitive exertion' and so deprive society's engine of its fuel. But, as he was equally concerned to make clear, once socialist orthodoxy was set aside one was left with a set of propositions whose acceptance depended only on a pragmatic recognition of the fact that a more subtle understanding of the individual's relation to society and the forces at work in it had become necessary. And once one grasped that, one would also see that 'socialist principles—especially in relation to such matters as education, public health, and communications—had informed public policy for decades. All of this made it clear, Longley continued, that the individualism of liberals like himself was not threatened by the new approaches. Socialism, properly understood, was in fact the ally of self-reliance. The two were alike 'consistent with true liberalism.' Viewed in this light, the new collectivism was quite compatible with the terms of individualist theory.[52]

The distinction Longley made between the dogmatic collectivism of the socialists and the more flexible kind validated by common sense allowed other partisans of the individualist idea to concede the existence of a collective dimension in society without requiring them to jettison their attachment to the individualist creed. Queen's University political economist Adam Shortt was thus able to pair a statement recognizing the importance of society's role in the shaping of individuals—it was 'our character . . . as a community' which determined their nature—with one reminding his readers that '. . . the dominance of men of exceptional capacity, force, and power [is essential] . . . the world never has got on, and never will get on without the one man power, that is, without leadership in every department of life . . . It all depends on the one man . . . '[53] O.D. Skelton, Shortt's successor as Sir John A. Macdonald Professor of Political and Economic Science at Queen's, similarly dealt with society in collectivist terms without abandoning his essential individualism. State intervention, he argued, might be welcomed in some circumstances as that which would accomplish what experience indicated individuals were not capable of doing on their own: it would introduce a measure of principled behaviour into their relations with one another. The state, functioning as a 'referee,' would ensure that the interests of the 'weak and helpless' did not suffer. They might be unable to look after themselves, but that did not mean that they should fall by the wayside. Yet, Skelton insisted, competition remained the fundamental fact of social life. Its 'ethical level' might be raised by state intervention, but society was still to be conceived of as an agglomeration of contending, self-interested individuals whose relations were to be characterized, in the classical metaphor of the Social Darwinists, as 'the struggle.'[54]

Other commentators took up the theme that a selective and limited collectivism might be the means to the realization of traditional individualist ends. Mackenzie King, as deputy minister in the newly-formed Department of Labour, was careful to argue that mechanisms which restrained individual action in one place might foster it in another.

Unionism was therefore to be defended on the ground that in restricting the rights of irresponsible employers it made it possible for the workingman, as King put it, 'to preserve his independence of character.' Collective action of this sort had, in fact, allowed the worker to resist what, in the view of the individualists, was the most demeaning of fates: 'he is now able,' King observed, 'to drive a bargain and does not have to accept a dole.'[55]

The discussion of old-age pensions which was sustained in these years provided a particularly illuminating example of the manner in which a careful distinction between means and ends allowed individualist thinkers to reconcile collectivist procedures with individualist principles. Generally upholding the view that the state should play a role in helping the worker prepare for his old age, they nonetheless insisted that it act only in ways that involved encouraging him to put aside money on his own behalf. Otherwise the effect would be to make him a charitable case, with the predictable result that his self-respect and moral fibre would be eroded. European plans were, therefore, to be favourably contrasted with those of other parts of the British Empire precisely because they sought to maintain the individual's responsibility for his own well-being. France's programme, argued one commentator, offered a good example of what should be done: it 'encourages thrift and a spirit of independence among the people, which would be entirely lacking in any government [financed] scheme . . . '[56] Bismarck's pioneering measure, said another, was a triumph just because it had so perfectly reconciled individualism and the general good: 'no man saw more clearly how the basic principle of self-help could be made to contribute to national and social stability and at the same time further the profoundest policy of the statesman.'[57] The Canadian government's 1909 annuity scheme, insisted a third observer, was to be praised on the ground that it, too, used the mechanisms of the state to assist individuals to help themselves. By demanding contributions from those who would benefit by it . . . 'it supplies a strong motive to thrift, and by the call which it makes on the personal responsibility of the annuitant, it tends to develop the valuable qualities of independence and self-reliance . . . '[58]

If these manoeuvres tended to deflect the full force of the collectivist onslaught by suggesting that some kinds of collectivist procedures were reducible to a description of them framed in terms compatible with individualist theory, those attempted by other commentators were more audacious. Their strategem was to close the gap between the new realities and their idea of what worked best in society by denying that gap's existence. The new practice, they insisted, was perverse and wrongheaded. The social universe remained comprehensible exclusively in terms of individualist theory. Those who claimed otherwise were dogmatic and irresponsible theorists whose ideas, if embodied in policy, would ruin society. 'The best of all governments,' insisted Goldwin Smith in 1893, 'is that which has least occasion to govern.' One could, in fact, scarcely imagine a more doubtful proposition than 'that society can be metamorphosed by the action of the State . . . ' Instead of speaking of unionism and strikes, labour spokesmen should be reminding the artisan of 'the improvement which [he] might make in his own condition by thrift, temperance, and husbandry of his means.' Even schooling was properly a private matter. It was the individual's responsibility to clothe and feed his children: so he ought to educate them.[59]

Clergyman John Hay, writing in the *Queen's Quarterly* three years later, was quite as firm in his belief that an unyielding statement of first principles was the most effective way of dealing with claims that the new realities made necessary a revolution in one's view of the way society worked. What was worthwhile in the socialist case, Hay insisted, amounted to a statement of the obvious: there were abuses in society and the state was the agency best equipped to deal with some of them. Conceding that truth, however, hardly represented an abandonment of principle. The traditional individualist view of man in society remained as vital as ever. And not only socialism, Hay continued, was built on 'false premises.' Every doctrine which failed to take account of the truths upon which individualism rested was equally doomed to fail. 'Any scheme,' as Hay put it, 'that tries to place all men on an equality, or that would abolish private property, contends against the law of man's being. In order that man may make progress he must indeed be free, and have access to those natural opportunities without which he can do nothing.'[60]

Smith and Hay were reacting to phenomena of whose existence they were merely observers; other turn-of-the-century partisans of self-reliance bore, however, a more complicated relation to the new realities. As men deeply involved in the world of practical affairs, they made extensive use of the collectivist procedures now available in it. Their claim that the individualist idea continued to describe reality thus involved them in denying the implications of their own behaviour. It appears, on this account, an even bolder step than that taken by those who occupied the manse or the study.

Some of those who followed this route seemed, indeed, scarcely to hesitate in offering a description of the way society worked which even a casual observer might have been expected to find seriously at odds with what the nature of their own actions signified. British Columbia's Sir Richard McBride, committed in practice to business collectivism, believing in the closest relationship between government and business, and persuaded that the power of the state must be used to create favourable conditions for economic growth, thus maintained a public and quite unequivocal enthusiasm for the individualist creed. 'All of his speeches,' writes Martin Robin, 'revealed a fervent belief in the mythology of the free enterprise system and the philosophy of Social Darwinism . . . He denied the significance of class differences, asserted a common interest in economic development spearheaded by private enterprise, and believed that British Columbia was an open system where the coal miner of today became the coal baron of tomorrow.'[61]

Language inconsistent with the nature of the reality it claimed to be describing was, in fact, used frequently on the frontier. Developments there which were primarily the result of carefully co-ordinated corporate activity were regularly offered as proof of what strong men acting individually could accomplish. McBride himself, having brought the power of government to bear on the development of British Columbia, continued to profess a belief in 'the ideology of frontier conquest through private enterprise.'[62] The opening of the farming frontier in the Ontario north, part of a concerted plan to promote economic development in that region, was similarly depicted in terms which suggested that it was to be understood in much the same way as the opening of the old agricultural frontier had been: as a project undertaken by self-reliant individuals bent on self-improvement. 'There is no means,' trumpeted an Ontario government publication in 1903, 'whereby the men without other capital than the power and will to labour can so readily attain a competence and a substantial position in the community as by taking up a bush farm.'[63] The myth of the self-sufficient pioneer, clearly at variance with the reality of his situation, survived for decades. 'Pioneer agricultural self-sufficiency . . . ' wrote V.C. Fowke as late as 1962, 'has been and remains a persistently fostered Canadian myth.'[64]

Plainly in evidence in the developing parts of the country, this espousal of a faith only marginally consistent with the actions it was meant to describe can also be discerned in other sections of it. To be sure, businessmen and manufacturers chastened by their proximity to the bewildering array of forces associated with Polanyi's 'great transformation' might, as Michael Bliss suggests, not only qualify their individualist practice; they also muted their expression of the individualist creed. They were, however, far from abandoning that creed altogether. Remaining, as Bliss puts it, 'deeply individualistic,' their ideas about others 'moulded in the categories of individualism,' they inevitably joined their progress towards 'self-interested collectivism' to a profession of faith hardly less inconsistent with it than McBride's ideology was at variance with the action he undertook.[65]

Large and substantial in retrospect, this gap between what the quasi-collectivist partisans of individualism said and what they did was not, however, particularly evident to their contemporaries. What helped hide it from view was, paradoxically, the very element which now points so clearly to its existence: the quasi-collectivists' continuing attachment to the individualist idea. Whether they were consciously engaged in a game of bluff and deception, whether they simply failed to perceive the contradiction between what they were saying and what they were doing, or whether they thought their recourse to collectivism a temporary and regrettable expedient which in no way invalidated basic principle, their insistence on the individualist faith played its part in sustaining a structure of belief and idea whose character did much to ensure that thought framed within its confines would remain oriented along individualist lines. The nature of what Quentin Skinner calls the 'formally crucial' process involved here is, of course, familiar enough, even if it remains 'empirically very elusive . . . The models and preconceptions in terms of which we unavoidably organize and adjust our perceptions and thoughts . . . themselves tend to act as determinants of what we think or perceive.'[66] Merely by dealing in the currency of the individualist idea, the quasi-collectivists were helping to ensure that the individualist system of 'models and preconceptions' did not languish and decay and so lose its capacity to shape the thought of those exposed to it.

This was an important development. Having come, like Dorothy in the Land of Oz, to view what lay before them through spectacles tinted with a particular hue, commentators framing their thoughts in terms of individualist categories would continue to consider the partial and imperfect picture so gotten as an accurate representation of reality only so long as they had no reason to doubt the integrity of the medium through whose agency it was made available. Rhetoric, the effect of which was to insist on that medium's undiminished relevance and utility, would thus play a critical role in ensuring that these observers continued to view the behaviour of the quasi-collectivists under its auspices—an operation that would, *pace* Skinner, throw individualist elements in that behaviour into high relief while simultaneously casting collectivist ones into the shadows. They would, in consequence, see, not the thrusts of government-supported ventures that were actually in front of them, but the enterprising and self-reliant individuals the architects of this important element in their society's ideological system told them were there.

This triumph of appearance over reality had profound effects. It left the quasi-collectivists at liberty to insist that the actions of others—labour organizers, reformers, anyone who sought collectivist action of a sort they judged incompatible with their own interests—be assessed in terms of an individualist standard from which, when circumstances demanded, they were in practice prepared to exempt themselves. The onus would be on those others to demonstrate why they should be permitted to use methods not sanctioned by the conventional individualist wisdom. By an exasperating irony they would be denied easy access to the collectivist procedures which were the logical consequence of their theory, while their opponents—still professing the individualist creed—were able to employ those procedures as they saw fit. The anxiety of socialists and reformers to escape this conundrum explains why they were so concerned to show that business and government had, as Canadian Socialist League member George Wrigley pointed out in 1900, collaborated on such undertakings as the Intercolonial Railway.[67] Only if the individualist idea could be shown to offer a fundamentally inadequate description of what even its staunchest defenders were doing could the way be opened for its rejection. The very fact that the point had to be argued demonstrates, however, how successfully the nature of the activities undertaken by practitioners of self-interested collectivism had been obscured. So potent did this expression of faith in the free and responsible individual remain that it affected the terms in which some of the enemies of the business-government alliance cast their own argument. Even after the pure milk of the individualist idea had gone noticeably sour, veteran socialist J.S. Woodsworth himself could be drawn onto the ground of his opponents. A moderate socialism was not, he would suggest to the founding convention of the CCF in 1933, merely a matter of tactics; the Canadian left must in fact qualify its attachment to collectivism in order to reflect the realities of the environment in which it found itself—an environment which, he continued, was in important ways susceptible of explanation only in terms of the individualist idea. He himself, he insisted, embodied the kind of individualism of whose existence the new creed must take account. 'I am,' he informed the assembled delegates, 'a Canadian of several generations, and have inherited the individualism common to all born on the American continent.'[68]

If, then, as H.V. Nelles has suggested, one part of Canada's ideological system—its 'much discussed' tory component—served in these years to rationalize and legitimate power concentrations, stratification, and class by stressing the harmony and interdependence of an ordered arrangement of groups and the idea of a community interest served by an activist state,[69] another element of it–the individualist idea–continued to mask the existence of these phenomena by insisting on the reality of competition, self-reliance, mobility, and the atomic individual. It thus played an important role in the process by which those who held power were able to control and manipulate the new forces in social and economic life. Particularly effective in containing the pretensions of the left, it managed either to limit the application of doctrines from that end of the political spectrum or to discredit them altogether. What, in short, might have signalled the beginning of the end for the individualist idea gave it a new lease on life. The range of ideological weaponry available to those whose activities shaped and defined their society remained very nearly as broad and ample as it had ever been.

All of this suggests that it is easy to paint an imperfect picture of the way English Canadians viewed their society if the individualist idea is ignored. Emphasis on the conservative principle, for all its utility in explaining what is uniquely Canadian, cannot tell us everything that we need to know about the character and function of the ideas English Canadians used to guide and shape their behaviour. Whatever may have been the objective circumstances of their collective existence–and evidence suggesting that society was organized along class lines with a minimum of social mobility and a high degree of government intervention, much of it on behalf of special interests, continues to mount[70]–there seems good reason to believe that many of those English Canadians who were able to articulate and promote a view of society wished, like other men in other nineteenth-century societies, their world to be viewed within the framework of a belief in the free and responsible individual. With its insistence on the capacity of that individual to master his fate, such a world view could legitimate both success and failure without reference to forces beyond his direct control. It would thus operate to deny the legitimacy of social theories which drew attention to such forces and so undermine the credibility and influence of those who put them forth. In this way the position of those who wished to organize their affairs unconstrained by any-

thing other than their own sense of what was just, possible, and in their interest would be materially strengthened, for what they did would appear to be action undertaken in a manner consistent with the way the social universe actually worked.[71]

This creed in fact operated in a number of ways to induce satisfaction with existing forms of social organization and economic activity. By celebrating the work of the farmer, it strove to make that being happy with his lot and so encouraged activity essential to the development of an important sector of the national economy; by stressing the value of education, it played its part in producing a skilled and semi-skilled workforce; by talking of success and fulfilment in terms of intangibles it reconciled workers to the fact of class; and by obscuring the nature of the new collectivism, it masked the fact that society's thrust toward bureaucracy and rationalization was making it steadily more difficult to sustain the proposition that each man controlled his destiny.

The individualist idea in Canada did not, to be sure, evolve neatly through a series of stages. Its different manifestations largely co-existed in time as functions of the varying social and economic circumstances which, in the view of the several commentators considered here, predominated in different parts of the country through the same several decades. English Canadians were not, then, confronted in their daily lives with a set of rigid and schematic variations on a theme; what, with cause, frequently appeared to them to be a confusion of proposals about the indiviual's prospects and capabilities served, in fact, to make the task of individualist theorists, striving to close the gap between theory and practice, more difficult. Equally, however, these patterns of belief exist as something more than analytical abstractions, having their being only, as it were, in the mind's eye of the historian. Linked in an intelligible way to social and economic circumstance, they were working ideas. Their role in investing a certain type of behaviour with normative significance and so encouraging activity consistent with it made their presence in the lives of nineteenth-century English Canadians no less real and immediate than that of those more tangible instruments–schools, factories, asylums, prisons–similarly operating to shape thought and action.

And if their undeniably variegated character was sometimes a cause of difficulties, it also pointed to a uniquely important source of strength. In signalling the presence within them of a suppleness and elasticity quite lacking in the structures set in place by the social engineers, it testified to the existence of a remarkable capacity to adapt to changing circumstance. The presence of this attribute, in the language of T.S. Kuhn,[72] gave the individualist paradigm an extraordinary facility in the assimilating or ignoring of anomalies. As late as the Great War its strength and appeal had been, in consequence, only marginally diminished. The vast collective efforts necessary to the prosecution of that war would of course deal its claims on behalf of the individual's power a serious blow. A decade later, the bankruptcy of individualist nostrums would be delineated even more clearly by the advent of the Great Depression. Even in the face of these challenges the individualist idea was, however, able to maintain in the minds of many the belief that it described something fundamental in the life of society. For all that Keynesianism, Social democracy, corporate planning, business conformity, and other manifestations of the new collectivism succeeded in complicating its existence, they did not, in the end, extinguish its appeal.

The search for a fully articulated picture of the English-Canadian value system has not, in sum, ended. In emphasizing its collectivist attributes scholars may, indeed, have been looking in the wrong direction. Perhaps, as students of Canadian society have recently been suggesting, a balanced representation of this phenomenon will be available only when an image of it framed in terms of what distinguishes it in North America is set beside one derived from an examination of the attributes it shares with other systems, North American as well as European. Certainly such a construct will be more comprehensive in scope than its predecessors; it will also probably be more accurate in detail. By shedding additional light on the character and function of ideas in Canadian life, it may even make clear how those ideas have helped give texture and shape to concrete historical circumstances at the same time that they themselves were being moulded by those circumstances. And if it does this, it will have succeeded in focussing attention on the manner in which society and thought in Canada were joined to each other in accordance with the same general principles that governed their relationship elsewhere–an accomplishment which will in its turn move the history of ideas in Canada onto a new plane of discussion and analysis.

NOTES

[1] These themes have been explored by a number of historians and social scientists. See, in particular, Donald Creighton, *Canada's First Century* (Toronto 1970): W.L. Morton. *The Canadian Identity* (Toronto 1961); S.F. Wise, Conservatism and Political Development: The Canadian Case, *South Atlanta Quarterly*. LXIX 2, spring 1970, 226-43: Gad Horowitz, *Canadian Labour in Politics* (Toronto 1968), 3-57: S.D. Clark. 'The Canadian Community and the American Continental System.' in his *The Developing Canadian Community* (Toronto 1962), 185-98: the same author's Canada and the American value System, in *La Dualité Canadienne à l'heure des États-Unis* (Quebec 1965), 93-192: J.M. Bliss, *A Living Profit: Studies in the Social History of Canadian Business 1883-1911* (Toronto 1974): and Seymour Martin Lipset, *The First New Nation. The United States in Historical and Comparative Perspective* (Garden City, NY 1967), 284-312 The Alger qote is on pages 287-88.

[2] John Mercier McMullen, *The HIstory of Canada from its First Discovery to the Present Time* (Brockville 1855), 158, 132, 159.

[3] H.J. Morgan, *Sketches of Celebrated Canadians and Persons Connected with Canada, from the Earliest Period in the History of the Province down to the Present Time* (Quebec 1862), 102.

[4] Elsie Trevor, 'Clarice: An Old Story of the New World,' *Canadian Monthly and National Review*, VI. 1, July 1874, 26.

[5] W.H. Withrow, *A History of Canada for the Use of Schools and General Readers* (Toronto 1876), 273.

[6] W.H. Withrow, *A Popular History of the Dominion of Canada from the Discovery of America to the Present Time* (Boston 1878), 355.

[7] Lynn Hetherington, 'Tecumseh,' *University Magazine*, VIII, 1, Feb, 1909, 137.

[8] See, in particular, Duncan Campbell Scott, *John Graves Simcoe* (Toronto 1909), 232-3; John Lewis, *George Brown* (Toronto 1909), 265; Robert Hamilton Coates and R.F. Gosnell, *Sir James Douglas* (Tor-

onto 1910), 353; and N.F. Dionne, *Champlain* (Toronto 1909), xiii. Local and regional histories also celebrated the individuals whose talent had allowed them to shape a civilzation out of the void. See R.E. Gosnell, *A History of British Columbia* (Vancouver [1906]); G.M. Adam, *Toronto, Old and New . . . with some sketches of the men who have made or are making the provincial capital* (Toronto 1891); Alexander Fraser, *A History of Ontario, its Resources, and Development,* 2 vols. (Toronto and Montreal 1907); Archibald Oswald MacRae, *History of the Province of Alberta,* 2 vols. ([Calgary?] 1912); and *The Story of Manitoba: Biographical–Illustrated,* 3 vols. (Winnipeg, Vancouver, Montreal 1913). Three-quarters of the MacRae study consisted of biographical sketches, while two-thirds of the Fraser and Gosnell books were composed in the same way. As well as insisting on the role of individual effort in creating new societies, these volumes also made much of the scope those societies offered men who wished to advance themselves. The remarks made in the Manitoba history on the career of railway man J.R. Turnbull were typical: 'The history of J.R. Turnbull is that of a man who worked his way upward by reason of the persistency of his purpose, the force of his character and the utilization of his opportunities. While he entered the employ of the Canadian Pacific Railroad in a minor capacity, the recognition of his merit won him advancement . . . ' II, 6. Similarly compiled on the assumption that Canada had been built by enterprising individuals whose virtue and accomplishments must be exhibited to the public, the biographical dictionaries which appeared in this period also fed and sustained the individualist vision of Canadian society. See, for example, *The Canadian Biographical Dictionary and Portrait Gallery of Eminent and Self-Made Men. Ontario Volume* (Toronto, Chicago 1880); *Quebec and the Maritime Provinces Volume* (Chicago 1881); George Maclean Rose, ed., *A Cyclopedia of Canadian Biography; being chiefly men of the time,* 2 vols. (Toronto 1886-88); G.M. Adam, ed., *Prominent Men of Canada: a collection of persons distinguished in professional and political life, and in the commerce and industry of Canada* (Toronto 1892); John Alexander Cooper, ed., *Men of Canada: a portrait gallery of men whose energy, ability, enterprise, and public spirit are responsible for the advancement of Canada, the premier colony of Great Britain* (Montreal and Toronto 1901-2); and *An Encyclopedia of Canadian Biography; containing brief sketches and steel engravings of Canada's prominent men,* 2 vols. (Montreal 1904-5).

[9]C.R. Tuttle, *Tuttle's Popular History of the Dominion of Canada . . . together with . . . biographical sketches of the most distinguished men of the nation,* 2 vols. (Montreal 1877).

[10]McMullen, *History of Canada,* Preface.

[11]Isabella Valancy Crawford, 'A Hungry Day,' in her *Old Spookses Pass, Malcolm's Katie, and Other Poems* (Toronto 1884). That the farmer was the creator of the nation's wealth, the builder of his own world, and a natural aristocrat unrivalled by those whose position was owing solely to lineage and descent were frequently articulated themes. For some variations on them, see R. Cooper, 'The Farming Interest.' *Anglo American Magazine,* I, 5, Nov. 1852, 401; W.S. Darling. 'The Emigrants: A Tale of the Backwoods,' *British American Magazine,* I, 1, May 1863, 53; D.W.. 'Canada,' *Canadian Monthly and National Review,* IV, 6, Dec. 1873, 472; A. Kemp and G.M. Grant, 'From Toronto to Lake Huron,' in G.M. Grant, ed., *Picturesque Canada: The Country as it was and is* (Toronto 1882), II, 584; Abraham Gesner, *New Brunswick; with Notes for Emigrants* (London 1847), 244-47. Cited in Michael S. Cross, ed., *The Workingman in the Nineteenth Century* (Toronto 1974), 24: *Canada Farmer,* I, 1847, 1, cited in Laurence Sidney Fallis Jr. 'The Idea of Progress in the Province of Canada: 1841-1867' (unpublished PH D thesis, University of Michigan, 1966), 145; Pamela S. Vining. 'Canada,' in Edward Hartley Dewart, ed., *Selections from Canadian Poets* (Montreal 1864), 105; W.W.S., 'A Settler's Own Tale,' *British American Magazine,* 12, June 1863, 193; Charles Sangster, 'Song for Canada,' in Dewart, *Selections,* 107; J.G. Bourinot. 'Titles in Canada,' *Canadian Monthly and National Review,* XII, 4, Oct. 1877, 350; Canniff Haight, 'Ontario Fifty Years Ago and Now,' *Rose-Belford's Canadian Monthly,* VI, 5, Nov. 1884, 449; and 'Buffalo Bill Abroad,' *The Week,* IV. 52, 24 Nov. 1887, 841.

[12]Pelham Edgar, 'A Confession of Faith and a Protest,' *University Magazine,* VIII, 2, April 1909, 305.

[13]C. Lintern Sibley, 'Van Horne and His Cuban Railway,' *Canadian Magazine,* XLI, 5, Sept. 1913, 444-51.

[14]Kingston Chronicle, 5 March 1842. Cited in R.D. Gidney, 'Upper Canadian Public Opinion and Common School Improvements in the 1830s,' *Histoire Sociale Social History.* V, 9, April 1972, 56.

[15]Egerton Ryerson, 'The Importance of Education to a Manufacturing and a Free People.' *Journal of Education of Upper Canada.* Oct. 1848, 300. Cited in Susan E. Houston. 'Politics, Schools and Social Change in Upper Canada. 'Canadian Historical Review. *LIII, 3, Sept. 1972, 271.*

[16]'Report of the Colborne District Council on the Gore Memorial,' in J. George Hodgins, ed., *Documentary History of Education in Upper Canada,* 8 vols, (Toronto 1894-1940), VII. 116. Cited in Houston, 'Politics,' 271.

[17]Anonymous, 'How I Made a Fortune in Wall Street . . . ' *Saturday Reader,* II, 27, 10 March, 1866, 14.

[18]'The Late George Peabody,' *New Dominion Monthly,* Jan. 1870, 64.

[19]See, for examaple, Jeannie Bell. 'The Highway to Honor; or the Secret of Lindsay Atwood's Success, *New Dominion Monthly,* July 1871, 37-40; Aug. 1871, 101-105; Sept. 1871, 174-75. This was the story of an orphan who became an apprentice in a lawyer's office and by 'diligence in study' advanced himself. See also Virna Sheard, 'Fortune's Hill.' a six-part serial which appeared in the *Canadian Magazine* from November 1902 to April 1903. It recounted the efforts of two medical students—one from a well-to-do family,

the other the son of a blacksmith. Both graduate, but it was the blacksmith's son who by study and hard work became a double gold medallist.

[20]'How to Succeed,' *New Dominion Monthly*, June 1875, 356-7.

[21]John M. Sangster, MD, 'Ontario's Schools,' *Education Journal*, 15 March, 1892, V, 21, 679.

[22]'Self-Education,' *New Dominion Monthly*, Feb. 1868, 299.

[23]C. Clarkson. 'A Liberal Education,' ibid., Oct. 1875, 262.

[24]'People and Affairs,' *Canadian Magazine*, XVII, 5, Sept. 1901, 483.

[25]Twelve copies of which were given to the Toronto Mechanics' Institute by Belford Brothers Publishers in 1876. [Ontario Archives] Mechanics Institutes of Toronto, Papers, Case A, no 3, Annual Reports 1838-82; Annual Report 1876, Appendix C.

[26]*The Week*, III, 31, 1 July, 1886, 504.

[27]J.J.Y., 'The Necessity of Improvement,' *Educational Journal*, V, 15, 15 Dec. 1891, 582.

[28]Miss M. Robertson, 'Growth,' ibid., V, 16, 1 Jan. 1892, 598.

[29]John Macnaughton, 'University Lecture,' *McGill University Magazine*, III, 2, April 1904, 33.

[30]A.W. Flux, 'Commercial Education,' ibid., I, 2, April 1902, 201-2.

[31]Norman DeWitt, 'The Educated Layman,' *University Magazine*, IX, 1, Feb. 1910, 28.

[32]Alexander Steele, 'Relation of Education to Our National Development,' Ontario Teachers' Association, *Proceedings*, 1894, 49. Cited in J. Donald Wilson, Robert M. Stamp, and Louis-Philippe Audet, eds., *Canadian Education: A History* (Toronto 1970), 293-94.

[33]'Editorial Comment,' *Canadian Magazine*, XII, 4, Feb. 1899, 368.

[34]J.T.M. Anderson, *The Education of the New Canadian; A Treatise on Canada's Greatest Educational Problem* (London and Toronto 1918), 177.

[35]*Daily Globe* (Toronto), 23 March 1872. Cited in Cross, ed., *Workingman*, 262.

[36]Hon. Wm. C. Howells, 'Superficial Learning,' *Rose-Belford's Canadian Monthly*, I, 4, Oct. 1878, 430, 432.

[37]L.R. O'Brien, 'Art Education–A Plea for the Artizan,' ibid., II, 5, May 1879, 584-91. All quotes are from 585.

[38]Greg Kealey, ed., *Canada Investigates Industrialism* (Toronto 1973), 58.

[39]J.A. Cooper, 'People and Affairs,' *Canadian Magazine*, XVI, 1, Nov. 1900, 88.

[40]Ibid.

[41]C. Henry Stephens, 'The Nine Hours Movement,' *Canadian Monthly and National Review*, I, 5, May 1872, 430.

[42]William Wye Smith, 'The Woods,' *British American Magazine*, II, 6, April 1864, 622.

[43]J.R. Ramsay, 'Chronicles of a Canadian Family,' *New Dominion Monthly*, June 1868, 147.

[44]W.D. Le Sueur, 'Old and New in Canada,' *Canadian Monthly National Review*, VII, 1, January 1875, 2.

[45]Haight, 'Ontario,' 454.

[46]Rev. W.R.G. Mellen, 'Wealth and its Uses,' *Rose-Belford's Canadian Monthly*, II, 3, March 1879, 341-50.

[47]'A True Captain of Industry,' *Canadian Monthly and National Review*, II, 4, Oct. 1872, 223.

[48]Newton McTavish, 'Henry Mill Pellatt: A Study in Achievement,' *Canadian Magazine*, XXXIX, 2, June 1912, 109-19.

[49]R.G. MacBeth, 'Sir William Whyte: A Builder of the West,' ibid., XLIII, 3, July 1914, 264.

[50]Bliss, *Living Profit*, 32.

[51]O.D. S[kelton?], review of Goldwin Smith, *Labour and Capital* (1907), *Queen's Quarterly*, XIV, 4, April 1907, 332.

[52]J.W. Longley, 'Socialism: Its Truths and Errors,' *Canadian Magazine*, VI, 4, Feb. 1896, 304, 301.

[53]Adam Shortt, 'In Defence of Millionaires,' *Canadian Magazine*, XIII, 6, Oct. 1899, 498.

[54]O.D. Skelton, *Socialism: A Critical Analysis* (Boston and New York 1911), 47-48.

[55]Canada, Department of Labour, *Reort of the Royal Commission on Industrial Disputes in the Province of British Columbia* (1903), 63. Cited in R. MacGregor Dawson, *William Lyon Mackenzie King* (Toronto 1958), I, 141.

[56]Andrew T. Drummond, 'A Social Experiment' *Queen's Quarterly*, VIII, 1, July 1900, 49.

[57]M.D. Grant, 'Old Age Pensions,' *University Magazine*, VIII, 1, Feb. 1909, 152.

[58]Francis Asbury Carman, 'Canada's Substitute for Old Age Pensions,' *University Magazine*, LX, 3, Oct. 1910, 437.

[59]Goldwin Smith, 'Social and Industrial Revolution,' in his *Essays on Questions of the Day, Political and Social* (New York and London 1893), 38, 36, 25, 13. See also Smith's *Labour and Capital: A Letter to a Labour Friend* (New York 1907).

[60]John Hay, 'A General View of Socialistic Schemes,' *Queen's Quarterly*, III, 4, April 1896, 292, 291.

[61]Martin Robin, *The Rush for Spoils: The Company Province 1871-1933* (Toronto 1972), 130.

[62]Ibid.

[63]Ontario, Crown Lands, *Land Settlement in New Ontario: A Short Account of the Advantages offered*

Land Seekers in Ontario (Toronto 1903), 21. Cited in Morris Zaslow, *The Opening of the Canadian North 1870-1914* (Toronto 1971), 179.

[64]V.C. Fowke, 'The Myth of the Self-Sufficient Canadian Pioneer,' Royal Society of Canada, *Transactions*, LIV, Series III, June 1962, 24.

[65]Bliss, *Living Profit*, Conclusion, 134-44, esp. 138, 142.

[66]Quentin Skinner, 'Meaning and Understanding in the History of Ideas,' *History and Theory*, VIII, 1, 1969, 6. There is an extensive literature on the manner in which the concepts, models, values, and attitudes in terms of which intellectual operations are carried out shape the view of reality that these operations yield. For the view of a social psychologist, who describes the process as 'one of being *prepared* to perceive or react in a certain way,' see Gloyd H. Allport, *Theories of Perception and the Concept of Structure* (New York 1955), 239. T.S. Kuhn's notion of the paradigm, a framework of theory, assumption, and idea which, he argues, conditions the way a scientist in any field in any epoch views and organizes his data has relevance for the understanding of intellectual activity in other areas–as the work of E.H. Gombrich in the history of art makes clear. See T.S. Kuhn, *The Structure of Scientific Revolutions* (Chicago 1962) and E.H. Gombrich, *Art and Illusion* (London 19600. Many commentators, inspired by the Marxist concept of ideology, have explained the emergence of these mediating ideas in terms of class structure and class interest. For the development of this notion, see George Lichthiem, 'The Concept of Ideology,' *History and Theory*, IV, 2, 1965. 164-95. For an application of Antonio Gramsci's marxist-based concept of hegemony, involving the argument that the dominant ideas in any society are not merely derivative and superstructural but possess a measure of autonomy which allows them to shape values and behaviour, see Eugene D. Genovese's *Roll, Jordan, Roll: The World the Slaves Made* (New York 1974). Some observers, unwilling to advance a categorically classed-based analysis of this phenomenon, have nonetheless emphasized the manner in which ideas, values, and attitudes are related to social structure. See Peter L. Berger and Thomas Luckmann, *The Social Construction of Reality: A Treatise in the Sociology of Knowledge* (New York 1966) and John Plamenatz, *Ideology* (London 1970). One cannot, finally, omit mention of two classic works, one in the marxist, the other in the non-marxist tradition. Georg Lukacs' *History and Class Consciousness: Studies in Marxist Dialectics* (trans. Rodney Livingstone, London 1968), framed under the influence of Lukacs' recovery of the Hegelian dimension in Marx's thought, emphasizes the dialectical relationship between ideas and circumstance, and, in particular, insists that the former simultaneously arise from, and shape, the latter. Karl Mannheim's argument, in some respects (as Louis Wirth points out) similar to that of the American pragmatists, depends on the claim that ideas condition the outlook of those exposed to them in ways that tend either to stabilize or undermine existing social arrangements. See his *Ideology and Utopia: An Introduction to the Sociology of Knowledge* (trans, Louis Wirth and Edward Shils, New York 1936).

[67]G.W. Wrigley, 'Socialism in Canada,' *Toronto Labour Day Sovereign*, 1900, 33. Cited in Martin Robin, *Radical Politics and Canadian Labour 1880-1930* (Kingston 1968), 34.

[68]Report of the First National Convention (1933) CCFP. Cited in Walter D. Young, *The Anatomy of a Party: The National CCF* (Toronto 1969), 45.

[69]H.V. Nelles, *The Politics of Development: Forests, Mines, and Hydro-Electric Power in Ontario, 1849-1941* (Toronto 1974), 494.

[70]Historians of nineteenth-century English-Canadian society have been revealing it as a place in which social mobility was low, economic and political decision-making monopolized by a few, and the formation of a work force dependent for survival on the sale of its labour an ongoing process. Nor is it now very controversial to note that public institutions were used in the furtherance of 'class' purposes. 'It would be difficult,' argues Michael Katz, 'to deny that class was a fundamental fact of life in mid-nineteenth century urban Canada.' See his *The People of Hamilton, Canada West: Family and Class in a Mid-Nineteenth-Century City* (Cambridge, Mass. 1975, 43. See also J.T. Copp, 'The Condition of the Working Class in Montreal, 1897-1920,' Canadian Historical Association, *Historical Papers*, 1972, 157-80, and his volume entitled *The Anatomy of Poverty: The Condition of the Working Class in Montreal, 1897-1929* (Toronto 1974). For the contribution Marxist scholars have made to this discussion, see especially H.C. Pentland, 'The Development of a Capitalistic Labour Market in Canada,' *Canadian Journal of Economics and Political Science*, XXV, 4, Nov. 1959, 450-61 and Gary Teeple, ed., *Capitalism and the National Question in Canada* (Toronto 1972), 43-66. That private groups, principally groups of businessmen, sought to use the power of government to promote their interests was noticed long ago. 'Canadian businessmen,' observed Elisabeth Wallace in 1950, 'while protesting their devotion to the principles of lassez faire, have never objected to state intervention in economic matters to benefit industry, and have frequently been clamorous in demanding it.' See her 'The Origin of the Social Welfare State in Canada, 1867-1900,' *Canadian Journal of Economics and Political Science*, XVI, 3, Aug. 1950, 383. More recently, the work of Gabriel Kolko and others in United States history has inspired an interpretation of Canadian government action in economic affairs which suggests that even action ostensibly taken to regulate the operations of businessmen was directed by them to their own ends. See, for example, the work of H.V. Nelles cited above.

[71]Some commentators, noting the Bendix-Lipset argument that rates of mobility in industrial societies– including the United States–have been more or less the same, have explained the failure of an explicitly class-related politics to establish itself in the US by pointing to the success with which the *belief* that indi-

vidual effort would be rewarded with advances in status, income, and property was maintained there. Michael Katz, following Stephan Thernstrom and Peter Knights, observes: ' . . . this expectation of mobility, in one line of argument . . . has kept the American working class committed to a capitalist social system . . . Has it been, then, the existence of an *ideology* of mobility that has kept American workers capitalist in contrast to their counterparts in much of the rest of the world?' See Seymour M. Lipset and Reinhard Bendix, *Social Mobility in Industrial Society* (Berkely 1960); Stephan Thernstrom and Peter Knights, 'Men in Motion: Some Data and Speculations about Urban Population mobility in Nineteenth Century America,' in Tamara K. Hareven, ed., *Anonymous Americans: Exploration in Nineteenth Century Social History* (Englewood Cliffs, NJ. 1971), 17-47; and Katz, *People of Hamilton*, 135. While this argument emphasizes how important ideology can be, it does not take account of the fact that modifications in it become necessary in order that it retain its credibility. As this paper has tried to suggest, the manner in which the ideology of mobility and the self-made man was altere was, in the Canadian case, an important factor in its continuing success.

[72]T.S. Kuhn, *The Structure of Scientific Revolutions* (Chicago 1962).

THE DEVELOPMENT OF IDEOLOGIES IN QUEBEC[1] *Marcel Rioux*

Historic Outline

In order to understand the recent evolution of ideologies in Quebec, it is necessary to establish where this period fits in the historical context. What ideas did the Quebecois, that is, the Francophone majority, have of themselves and their society? What goals did they, as a group, have and what means did they advocate for attaining them? The interpretation of ideologies proposed here will take two centuries of history into account and will, therefore, necessarily be schematic.

When can we begin to speak of an ideology for the Quebecois? Usually, as soon as a group has proved itself to be a distinct group and a strong enough "we" has been formed to oppose other "we's," individuals appear who define the situation and who clearly explain this collective consciousness. Under the French regime, it seems that the other group, which Canadiens were beginning to oppose, was still too close to them for the birth of an ideology. Canadiens had a feeling of non-identity toward French metropolitans, but this feeling was not yet used as an explicit concept.

Conquered in 1760, ruined by the war, deprived of their elites, the Quebec peasants spent their first forty years under English domination just surviving and a new elite slowly emerged from their ranks which assumed the function of defining the Quebec community and representing it politically. This new Francophone bourgeoisie, made up of people from the liberal professions, was to oppose the mercantile class which, in turn, was to represent the Anglophone minority. This social class made up of the liberal professions took it upon itself to define the Quebec nation; this brings us to our first ideology. Fernand Ouellet wrote that, with the appearance of a national consciousness at the heart of the bourgeoisie, its political vocation was greatly strengthened. From that time on, it no longer defended its class interests or proposed abstract values as far as the people were concerned; it represented the nation and its essential attributes. In 1810, Craig wrote:

> In truth, it seems to be their desire to be considered as forming a separate nation. The *Canadien* nation is their constant expression. . . .[2]

What is the relationship between this bourgeoisie and the people? Fernand Dumont gives the following explanation:

> The fact that this bourgeoisie was, at first, accepted by the people as their natural spokesman is clear, and can be explained, we feel, quite easily. As sons of the people, its members kept the essential attitudes of the peasantry from which they came.[3]

From the turn of the century to the 1830s, this new bourgeoisie got on well wth the clergy; both groups had approximately the

205

same views about Canadiens. But soon a division occurred in the Legislative Assembly: "with Papineau, the dream of an autonomous French-Canadian Republic began to take form."[4] The period known as the romantic period in French Canada was to finish badly: the Insurrection in 1837-38 was soon checked. The Church was seen more and more frequently by many of the bourgeoisie elite as an ally of the colonizers. When the Church, with Monseigneur Lartigue as spokesman, condemned the Insurrection, it realized that its directives were not well received in the Montreal region. Monseigneur Lartigue's intervention aroused anger which was expressed through popular demonstrations and violently anticlerical articles in patriotic newspapers. In Montreal, where 1200 *patriotes* paraded in front of the Saint-Jacques Cathedral during Vespers, it was said that the pastoral letter would hasten the "revolution," and in Chambly, three men left the church while the letter was being read. They formed a group to welcome Monseigneur Bourget and the clergy after Mass with cries of "Down with the movement!" and "Vive Papineau!" Elsewhere, priests were treated to the singing of the *Marseillaise* and the *Libera*.[5] In 1834, Papineau had already chastised the Church:

> This act [Quebec Act, 1774] retained all the rights, privileges and power of the clergy (although these advantages are better preserved through the confidence, religious persuasion, and conviction of the people), because it was fast losing its temporal authority with them as far as determining their ideas and opinions was concerned. The clergy eagerly welcomed this Act, took up the government's cause, and, ignoring that of the people, found it good because it was advantageous.[6]

Thus it can be seen that the first ideology of Quebec was formulated by a secular elite who defined Quebec as a nation. Independence was the aim of this nation. In an epilogue to the results of the Insurrection, Etienne Parent, a journalist, wrote in 1839:

> There were people, and we were among them, who thought that with the backing and the favour of England, the French Canadians could flatter themselves for having

retained and spread their nationality in such a way as to form an independent nation afterwards. . . .[7]

As Fernand Dumont writes:

> The Insurrection marks the failure in a sort of spasm of agony of this first attempt to define the situation and the future of the French-Canadian nation.[8]

The Rise of the Ideology of Conservation

The secular bourgeoisie which dominated the Assembly from 1820-1840 acted like a national bourgeoisie and took upon itself the task of defining the Quebec community and its future. It did not cause a great stir among the people who were afraid of the liberalism, anticlericalism, and anti-British ideas of the *patriotes*. On the whole, the clergy remained faithful to the British Crown. Derbyshire, who was an envoy from Durham, "also reported the noteworthy observation of the Abbé Ducharme, *curé* of Sainte-Thérèse":

> It was the educated men, the doctors, notaries, and lawyers, who were at the head of the rebellion and were the great seducers of the people, and he seemed to derive from it an argument against educating the lower orders.[9]

That is why, once the Rebellion had been suppressed and its leaders had fled, the clergy could regain its control over the people, with the aid of the British powers. The British, with Governor Durham as their spokesman, became aware of the prevailing situation in Quebec.

Durham stated that he had come to Canada thinking he would find a conflict between the people and the executive, but instead, he had found

> . . . two nations warring in the bosom of a single state: I found a struggle, not of principles, but of races . . . . The national feud forces itself on the very senses, irresistibly and palpably, as the origin or essence of every dispute which divides the community; we discover that dissensions, which appear to have another origin, are but forms of this constant and all-pervading quarrel; and that every contest is one of French and English in the outset, or becomes so ere it has run its course.[10]

Durham's solution was simple: he proposed the assimilation of Lower Canada, which was largely Francophone, with Upper Canada, which was mainly Anglophone.

> I entertain no doubt of the national character which must be given to Lower Canada; it must be that of the British Empire; that of the majority of British America; that of the great race which must, in the lapse of no long period of time, be predominant over the whole North American Continent. Without effecting the change so rapidly or roughly as to shock the feelings and trample on the welfare of the existing generation, it must henceforth be the first and steady purpose of the British Government to establish an English population, with English laws and language, in this Province, and to trust its government to none but a decidedly English Legislature.[11]

Durham added:

> I should indeed be surprised if the more reflecting part of the French Canadians entertain at present any hope of continuing to preserve their nationality. Much as they struggle against it, it is obvious that the process of assimilation to English habits is already commencing. The English language is gaining ground, as the language of the rich and of the employers of labour naturally will.[12]

It is hard to be more explicit.

The Durham Report and the Act of Union which followed the Insurrection, mark a very important turning point in the history of Quebec. It was not until the late 1950s, more than a hundred years later, that there appeared an equally important period, from an ideological point of view. We cannot overemphasize this period. Quebec's professional bourgeoisie was descended from the peasantry and had defended the traditional form of culture which had developed in Quebec since the Conquest. Was this, however, through choice or necessity? Being the ruling class of a people who were dominated politically, economically, and socially, the liberal bourgeoisie was obliged to defend what existed, and what existed was a people that the Conquest had relegated to agriculture. There is nothing to indicate that the Quebecois

chose to defend the traditional form of economy they practised. It was the dialectic of the situation which gave it momentum. These people that the liberal bourgeoisie wanted to lead to independence, "with the support and favour of England," were, for the time being, poor illiterate farmers. By opposing the dominators and the Anglophone mercantile class which represents it, the national bourgeoisie defended a way of life imposed on it since the Conquest and the failure of the Insurrection. There is nothing to lead us to believe that it was this way of life that they had defended. Above all, the liberal bourgeoisie was defending the right of the Quebec people to live as a total society. Papineau and his followers were insisting on the liberty of a majority group, which had been conquered militarily, economically, and politically by a minority.

However, everything changed after the 1840s. Despair beset even the most committed Quebecois. It was no longer a question of leading the people to independence, but of fighting against assimilation and Anglicization. With backing from Durham, the clergy became the main spokesman for the Quebec people; they no longer proclaimed an ideology of independence, but one of conservation. From the point of view of the ideology held in the first few decades of the nineteenth century, the new ideology they were expounding marks a tragic contraction. Sensing quite well that they were to become a minority, the Quebecois no longer sought to become an independent society, but strove to preserve their culture. The Quebec group was no longer a nation that had one day to obtain its independence, but an ethnic group with a particular culture (religion, language, customs); this culture would have to be preserved as a sacred heritage. Durham accused the Quebecois of having no history or literature; they had to prove to him that they had a past and that it was great—to such an extent that the period to be glorified by those who defined the situation was to become the past. The English soon realized that it was necessary to divide the Quebecois, both along the St. Lawrence, and later in Acadia, in order to establish a viable state that the English could control at will. Lord Elgin knew this well when he wrote:

> I believe that the problem of how to govern Canada would be solved if the French

would split into a Liberal and a Conservative Party and join the Upper Canadian parties bearing the corresponding names. The great difficulty hitherto has been that a Conservative Government has meant Government of Upper Canadians which is intolerable to the French—and a Radical Government a Government of the French which is no less hateful to the British. . . . The national lement would be merged in the political if the split to which I refer was accomplished.[13]

Dumont writes:

Politics will become a ground on which politicians will periodically defend their nationality; but it will only be one area among others for formulating nationalist ideologies.[14]

The arrival of responsible government enabled the elite in the liberal professions to find employment and to acquire a certain vertical mobility in administration and business. Georges-Etienne Cartier, a businessman and politician, is one of the first examples of a type of Quebecois who was to profit from the new regime. He took part in the 1837 Insurrection, but as Wade writes:

. . . he took no part in the second rising, having perhaps been led by his lifelong Sulpician friends to see that the clergy was right in condemning opposition to the constituted authorites, a view which he later recognized as "the only one that offered some chance of salvation for the French Canadians."[15]

With the backing of this same clergy, he and his party were to win all the elections in Quebec until the end of the century. Conservatism was triumphant. Some young people from the cities went to settle in the country, in the heart of traditional society. Gérin-Lajoie's novel, *Jean Rivard*, well explains this glorification of the earth. In 1849, the author wrote in his diary:

I have returned to my project of going to live in the country as soon as possible . . . . Oh, if only I were a farmer! . . . He does not become rich by beggaring others, as lawyers, doctors, and merchants some-times do. He draws his wealth from the earth: his is the state most natural to man. Farmers form the least egotistical and most virtuous class of the population. But this class has need of educated men who can serve its interests. The educated farmer has all the leisure necessary to do good; he can serve as guide to his neighbors, counsel the ignorant, sustain the weak, and defend him against the rapacity of the speculator. The enlightened and virtuous farmer is to my mind the best type of man.[16]

Several novels from this period were constructed around the theme of fidelity to agriculture and ancestral values. These romantic works, as well as historical studies, were to propagate the ideology of conservation that the petite-bourgeoisie and the Church were systematically building up. The historian Michel Brunet wrote:

From then on, the Canadian Church enjoyed a freedom it had not possessed since 1760. Without being fully aware of it, it benefitted from the establishment of ministerial responsibility and a new climate of religious tolerance among the Protestant elite in Great Britain and English Canada. . . . From 1840 to 1865, the Canadian episcopacy directed a Catholic counter-reform. This was necessary. Free thought had made considerable progress among the lay ruling classes and the population in general had become accustomed to neglecting its religious duties. . . . The clergy led a vigilant fight against the last representatives of liberal thought. Some of the Institut canadien and all of the anti-clericals who remained faithful to the revolutionary romanticism of the decade of 1830 continued to voice their opposition but they no longer influenced the bulk of the population.[17]

The Church profited from the liberty that the English were according them as a reward for their loyalist attitude during the Insurrection, and strove to get the people under their influence again. This thoroughly succeeded. From that time on, the Church fulfilled for the nation the role that it had filled for many minority groups: that of compensation. The minority should not be saddened by its existing situation because the rewards would come much later. If the Quebecois were to realize themselves fully, to become what they really are, it was out of the question to imitate the material successes of the English. It mattered little that they were conquered and poor, because they had a providential mission to accomplish in North America: to evangelize and civilize the continent. National history, particularly in the person of Garneau, helped the Church greatly to build the new ideology of conservation. Nourished by Voltaire and de Raynal, Garneau advocated prudence and fidelity to traditions. He wrote:

For us, part of our strength comes from our traditions; let us not separate ourselves from these as we change them gradually. We find good examples to follow in the history of our own mother country. Without laying claim to a similar destiny, our wisdom and our strong unity will greatly ease the difficulties of our situation and will arouse the interest of nations and make our cause appear more sacred to them.[18]

The "Catholic reaction,"[19] in the words of Father Léon Pouliot, s.j., took several years to sweep away all that remained of anticlericalism in Quebec. The greatest battle that the clergy had to wage was against the Institut canadien,[20] several members of which were free thinkers. August Viatte describes this struggle as follows:

A final battle remained to be waged. Quebec is evolving. Montreal is becoming inflexible. The Institut canadien is firing red cannon balls and Mgr. Bourget wishes to stop them. Starting in 1857, a priest destroyed 1500 "indexed" volumes at the Rolland Library, among which were the complete works of Lamartine, including *Jocelyn* and *Chute d'un ange*. In 1858, the Bishop also required the Institut to commit its manuscripts to flames.

Arthur Buies fought a final battle with his *Lanterne*.

In vain, he peddled his own journal. The depots refused him and the last number appeared in 1869. At this time, Garneau died and Crémazie was in flight; an era was ending; the spring rains that follow so prolonged a drought will disturb the fertility of the soil and will bring about a change in the climate.[21]

Buies resisted until 1869; the "Catholic reaction" had by then had many years to do its work and for the bulk of the population to have been taken into the hands of the Church.

It seems best to follow Dumont's interpretation that the predominance the Church acquired was achieved with the consent of

. . . leaders, even nonbelievers, who could not help but recognize that religion was an essential factor in social solidarity and a fundamental element in the differentiation of the French-Canadian nation from that of the English.[22]

The federation of the territories of British North America and the British North America Act, which should have been the constitutional document that consecrated this federation, was bound to accentuate what was embryonic in the Durham Report and in the Act of Union. In 1840, the Act which united English Upper Canada and French Lower Canada was supposed to have the result, in the spirit of Durham and the English lawmakers, of rapidly Anglicizing Lower Canada. It had done nothing. But with Confederation, that is, with the union of all British territories in North America (Upper Canada, Lower Canada, New Brunswick, Nova Scotia, and Prince Edward Island), the assimilation process appeared to be unavoidable. As a minority in this new political formation, the Quebecois again strengthened their ideology of defence and conservatism. Although the Quebecois remained the majority in Lower Canada, they were no longer the majority in Canada as a whole. Even inside Quebec, where they represented nearly 75 per cent of the population of nearly a million inhabitants, their economic and social position no longer corresponded to their numerical importance. The large cities, such as Montreal and Quebec, had just acquired a Francophone majority. But the English dominated commerce, industry, and finance. Thus even within Quebec, English and Canadiens were opposed to each other on all points: the Canadiens, rural and poor, were Catholics and French in their linguistic tradition; the English, urban and better off economically, were Protestants.

209

Although the period of Confederation marked a great economic boom in Canada, there was also a profound economic malaise in Quebec which was shown by a massive emigration to the United States. The Canadian economy was being displaced toward southern Ontario and the Quebecois were seeking work in New England. To counter this emigration, the clerical elite and the petite-bourgeoisie began a vast movement of colonization and a return to the land. Quebec followed in detail its ideology of conservation which forced it to remain within its borders:

. . . relatively sheltered from Anglo-Saxon influences, it (Lower Canada) is entirely taken up with the preservation of its personality which it wishes to keep immutable by time and space, in a sealed vase. [23]

An increasingly accentuated rift developed with France. In 1871, the year of the Commune, Mgr. Raymond wrote:

The capital of France, centre of these uprisings and of this filth, does not seem to me as more than a soiled land, like that of Babylon or Sodom, and as such calling for the vengeance of heaven. [24]

Gradually the theory of the two Frances was built up. Thomas Chapais gave it most explicit formulation:

There are now two Frances, radical France and conservative France, the infidel France and Catholic France, the France that blasphemes and the France that prays. Our France is this second one. [25]

This distancing from France was not compensated for by any rapprochement with the English in Canada.

In the decade of 1880, the Riel affair again seemed to harden the relations between Quebec and Canada. When Laurier, a Quebecois, became Prime Minister of Canada from 1896 to 1911, it seemed to mark a truce in the struggle between the two groups: he was elected as much by Quebec as by Canada.

During Laurier's term of office, the Quebec economy experienced an accelerated growth. Although the movement toward industrialization was mostly directed from the outside and activated in Quebec by the Anglophone element, it is possible to date the first decades of this century as those of radical transformation which the traditional lifestyle of the Quebecois had to go through. And it was from the perspective of the problem of the worker that Quebec first faced the consequences of its massive industrialization. [26] There, as elsewhere, the ideology of conservation played a strong role. To prevent the Quebecois from joining international unions, the clergy strongly encouraged the founding of Catholic unions that would protect them from the religious neutrality of the Americans.

In 1911, when Laurier left the government after fifteen years in power, Quebec had changed extensively. In 1871 Quebec was 77 percent rural, but forty years later, it was half urban. Because of its industrial and commercial development, Montreal had attracted many rural people who increased the ranks of labourers and salaried workers. The Anglophone minority continued to hold the wealth and the industrial and financial power. Already, at that time, the Quebecois writer Errol Bouchette earnestly advised his compatriots to invest in industry rather than land; for him, the future of Quebec was in industry rather than agriculture. Bouchette stated with bitterness that a Francophone population of 1,293,000 inhabitants sent only 722 students to university, whereas the English in Quebec sent 1358 for a population of 196,000. Only twenty-seven Francophone students were preparing for scientific careers, whereas there were 250 such students among the Anglophones in Quebec.

Viatte wrote:

About 1890, one would believe that Canadien literature (Quebecois) was going to die. Conformism becomes conservatism and any type of new wave, is censured. The critics deplored in vain "this quasi-inability to produce which results from language difficulties, the absence of graduate schools, the scarcity of books, the general indifference to any question that is a bit enlightened, political chicanery to the death, and from the progressive invasion of the American spirit." [27]

A few years later, in the first decade of the twentieth century, the Literary School of

Montreal aroused great hopes. But it was necessary to wait forty more years before the movement really had any momentum.

The encounter between Francophones and Anglophones that was evident during the Boer War in 1899, when the Quebecois refused to participate in an imperialist struggle, continued during the Great War of 1914-18. The question of the Ontario separate schools again aggravated the conflict between Quebec and the rest of Canada. In the Legislative Assembly in Quebec, a deputy minister presented a bill aimed at the withdrawal of Quebec from Confederation; the debates lasted for many days. In the end, the deputy withdrew his bill, the Prime Minister of Quebec, Lomer Gouin, declared himself against withdrawal from Confederation, invoking the fate of the Francophone minorities in Canada and the impossibility for Quebec alone to ensure her economic survival. It was during this period that Henri Bourassa, the grandson of Louis-Joseph Papineau, the leader of the 1837 Insurrection, became the champion of a type of pan-Canadian nationalism. Bourassa pleaded for an international policy that was Canadian and no longer British. Toward 1917, facing the facts as he saw them from the turn of events—conscription for overseas service, persecutions of the Francophone minorities in Ontario—he turned to the study of religious problems and published a book, *Le Pape, arbitre de la paix*, and arranged a big conference on "Language, Guardian of the Faith." His influence on generations of Quebecois was profound and explains certain positions of traditional nationalists who today still gravitate around *le Devoir* and *Action Nationale*.

During the early post-War years, Quebec continued to industrialize at an accelerated pace. The United States increasingly expanded its economic and cultural hold on Quebec. In 1921, the Francophone population of Canada reached its lowest level ever—27.9 percent. For the first time in history the urban population of Quebec, 56.01 percent, was greater than the rural population. Montreal had 618,506 inhabitants of whom 63.9 percent were Francophones. Many important industrial centres were developing: Three Rivers, Hull, Shawinigan, Grand'Mère, Chicoutimi, La Tuque. The national resources of Quebec continued to be exploited by foreigners. The last of capital

and technicians further accentuated the domination of the country. In the 1930s, a separatist movement arose which was directly descended from the traditional nationalist movement. The War came to put an end to this movement. Not that the conflict between Francophones and Anglophones was mitigated; as in 1899 and in 1914-18, the majority of the Francophone population of Quebec opposed sending troops overseas. The movement of industrialization and urbanization that was produced by the Second World War was bound to lay the ground for lively days ahead.

A Characterization of Quebecois Ideologies 1945-1965

We shall use the definition of a global ideology that was developed in the first part of these remarks to describe and characterize the ideologies of Quebec during the last two decades. In summary, a global ideology is a plan for living which is proposed to a society by one of its subgroups and which aims at expressing the total consciousness of the society and sharing its definition of the situation with the whole of the society. In a complex society, the conflict of ideologies expresses above all the conflict of subgroups which are competing for the majority's acceptance of their theory of society and, ultimately, to govern that society.

The Ideology of Conservation

When the Second World War broke out in 1939, the dominant ideology in Quebec was the ideology of conservation that had begun to develop in the second half of the nineteenth century. The majority of those in Quebec who had taken it upon themselves to define the nation and who had directed collective action had rallied to this ideology. For about one-hundred years, the ideology of conservation had been dominant, and the clergy and many of the liberal professions had been its champions. This does not imply that this was the only definition of Quebec that had existed during this century, but other definitions did not gain the favour of the public and did not guide the behaviour of the majority of Quebecois. The clergy and the liberal professions were at leisure to disseminate their ideology since they controlled, for all practical purposes, most of the information media, houses of learning, books and text-books. It is also necessary to add that the Quebecois also live in another political entity, that of Canada as a whole, they could and can, if necessary, forget the fact that they are Quebecois and participate in the ideology of Canada. The Quebecois can physically or otherwise escape their nationality and live as though they were Canadians or North Americans. Ideological conflicts cannot be produced for this precise reason. In addition, during all this time national education remained in the hands of the clergy, which was thus able to propagate and impose its own definition of the Quebecois group. How does one characterize this ideology? It defined the Quebecois group as the bearer of a culture, that is, as a group with an edifying history which became a minority in the nineteenth century and whose task it is to preserve this heritage it had received from its ancestors and which it must transmit intact to its descendants. This heritage is essentially composed of the Catholic religion, the French language, and an indeterminate number of traditions and customs. The privileged time of this ideology has passed. At the time when it was worked out, the Quebecois were becoming a minority and risking assimilation. It was to be expected that this ideology therefore idealized the traits of Quebec society in the second half of the nineteenth century when it was effectively Catholic, French speaking, agricultural, and traditional. Threatened with assimilation, this type of society and its principal characteristics were not supposed to change. Thus, it had to be rationalized and justified. This culture was not only that of the Quebecois, but the best culture that had ever existed. This ideology took hold over the years; from the end of the nineteenth century, it was transmitted almost intact to the beginning of the Second World War.

The Laval University sociologist Gérald Fortin has analysed the contents of *l'Action française,* later called *l'Action Nationale,* one of the principal reviews that transmitted this ideology over the course of years. His analysis extends from its appearance in 1917 until 1953[28] and brings out the principal themes of this ideology of conservation. It phrases the merits of the French language, the Catholic religion, the spiritual culture, the national history, rural life, and the family; it warns of the dangers of English imperialism, industrialization, urbanization, and the means of mass communication; it preaches about buying Quebecois and respect for the two cultures and the Francophone minorities. In the last decade, 1945-53, an interest in economic and social questions is growing and the question of the worker appears in the review. Fortin writes:

> If the ends and the means of the ideology are considered, it may be seen that the goals have not changed; they have been more strongly confirmed as new interpretations of the situation have been worked out.[29]

The Ideology of Contestation and Recoupment

After the Second World War, the ideology of conservation was seriously disputed by another strata of the population: union leaders, intellectuals, journalists, artists, students, and some members of the liberal professions. It is obvious that this form of contestation had its historical antecedents; it can, in many respects, be linked to the liberal tradition. This certainly does not question the fact that Quebec possessed a culture that is different from that of the rest of Canada, the principal elements of which must be preserved but, according to this ideology, the culture must be brought up-to-date. The ideological movement which arose during the Second World War was above all a movement of reaction against the old ideology of conservation. That is, its negative aspect, which opposed the old, was the most nebulous and almost always remained implicit.

It can be said that the ideology and old power structure in Quebec were becoming anachronistic in face of the demographic, economic, and social changes that Quebec went through between 1939 and 1945. Its irrationality was obvious. If, for convenience, we consider the decade between 1939 and 1950, it is noticeable, according to the study by Faucher and Lamontagne, that the labour force in Quebec doubled:

> This increase, in absolute terms, is equal to the growth witnessed during the whole century ending in 1939. . . . During the period under review, the rate of industrialization in Quebec has been higher than that of Canada as a whole. Since 1939, in volume

terms, output of manufacturing industries rose by 92 percent in Quebec and by 88 percent in Canada, while new investment in manufacturing increased by 181 percent in this province and by only 154 percent in the whole country.[30]

Nathan Keyfitz, in his work, shows the movement of the population of Quebec from agriculture to industry:

During the war and post-war years, the population in agriculture in the province of Quebec dropped from 252,000 to 188,000, a decline of 64,000. This decline more than counterbalanced the steady rise that had been shown from 1901, and hence the surprising result that, although the province of Quebec is almost three times as great in population in 1951 as it was in 1901, it contains fewer men in agriculture. The increase in non-agricultural industry is shown in every one of the thirteen main occupational groups, except fishing and trapping which, like farming, declined sharply. The rise from 79,000 to 237,000 in manufacturing occupations is especially conspicuous.[31]

Thus it appears that Quebec has undergone more important changes on a larger scale during the decade of 1939-49 than in any other decade of its history, except those of the Conquest and the Insurrection. The ideology of conservation which had survived all the other waves of industrialization and urbanization could not successfully resist the last. It must be added that this ideology, which had been dominant for so many years, had largely become inoperative on the level of everyday life. It continued to guide the general policies of the nation, but it no longer directed the behaviour of the more dynamic Quebecois who kept to themselves or withdrew into small groups which worked within other frames of reference. The patriotic societies continued to defend French-Canadian culture (our religion, our language, and our traditions) while the majority of individuals shared a number of core images concerning their nation; others were ideologically integrated into other North American societies, particularly into Canada.

The dispute of this ideology began in the post-War years. Clearly the sociologists and economists in the Faculty of Social Science at Laval University formed the most coherent centre for dispute at the end of the 1940s and during the 1950s. This group adopted reviews, *Cité Libre* is the most obvious example, and movements such as the Canadian Institute for Public Affairs (L'Institut Canadien des Affaires Publiques), which brought together intellectuals, professors, union leaders, journalists, and liberal politicians. Drawing their inspiration from the analyses of economists and sociologists from the Quebecois milieu and from their knowledge of other Western democracies, these movements and individuals undertook the systematic criticism of the ideology of conservation as well as of Quebecois culture.

Some writers have said that the 1950s was a decade when social problems were dealt with, that is, when the problems of the workers were recognized. These so-called social themes were even introduced into the pages of *Action Nationale,* which, as we have seen, had long been one of the most representative spokesmen of the ideology of conservation. Already by 1949, the reverberations that were provoked by the asbestos strike had brought about a realization that Quebec was no longer a traditional society living principally from agriculture, but a society in which the majority of citizens were salaried workers; a few years later, it was said that Quebec society was experiencing a slow proletarianization.

It is quite evident that in criticizing the ideology of conservation and Quebec culture in general, opponents had to criticize not only ideas, values, behaviour, and institutions, but also those groups and individuals who, according to them, were responsible for the global orientations that were influencing the direction Quebec was taking. Quite clearly this was a way of getting at the clergy who had always been responsible for national education in Quebec. Open discussions on education, religion, and the traditional interpretation of our history date from these years. There was bound to be criticism of Quebec Catholicism and those who had narrowed, particularized, and "Quebecisized" its content. This fact is well expressed by Maurice Tremblay:

Through this attitude of fierce defence against Protestant influences and French modernism, the Church has no doubt succeeded in keeping French-Canadian culture entirely Catholic; unfortunately, it must be recognized that this has been, to a great extent, at the expense of a narrow sterile dogmatism and an authoritarianism rooted in conservatism. On the whole, this French-Canadian Catholicism thus appears to us to be a canned Catholicism, at the rear guard of the radical changes the world is demanding of Christianity . . . . We have here an example of this narrow and unproductive ultramontanism that the Church has made its right arm in a general policy of conservation and defence of French-Canadian Christianity.

This Church has always sided with the traditional society for which it has been largely responsible, and has wished to preserve itself in the North American world which is repudiating and overtaking it in every respect. Tremblay further says:

> In effect, in a general manner the Church in French Canada tends to run against the increasing industrialization and urbanization, to maintain the structures and lifestyles of a rural civilzation that it can dominate and guide in its own ideal of a religious and Christian life for which it has an obvious nostalgia.[32]

The other power that was strongly attacked by this group who were trying to define the situation throughout this period, is the political power that was embedded in Quebec from 1936 until 1960[33] through the Union Nationale and its leader Maurice Duplessis. Relying on the population, this party put into practice the ideology of conservation that had been perpetuated in Quebec for many decades.

Acting completely pragmatically and distrusting intellectuals and idealogues, Duplessis implemented the most conservative policies in the name of autonomy and of coarse peasant good sense. In the best vein of traditional conservatism, he carried out a form of personal politics in which everyone knew each other and the prince grated his largesse to the good (those who voted for him) and left the wicked to sink (counties and regions which had shown some opposition). This manner of administering Quebec was as anachronistic as the ideology which inspired it. It included many characteristics of pre-

industrial society which tallied exactly with those of the ideology of conservation that had been developed expressly to ensure the preservation of the traditional society which Quebec had been in the middle of the nineteenth century.

The liberal opposition which was made up of partisans of the Liberal Party–and other opponents–took fifteen years to defeat these two powers, political and ideological, which were grafted together and worked shoulder to shoulder to rally a majority of electors. The traditionalists leaned on the two fundamental characteristics of the Quebec situation: the fact that the Quebecois have their own identity that clearly distinguishes them from other North American groups, and a second conviction which is a corollary of the first, the fact that they have remained a people whose culture is still traditional while living in a society that is largely industrialized and urbanized. In conclusion, the ideological opposition prior to 1960 wished to fill the gap that had formed between Quebec culture (ideas, values, symbols, attitudes, motivations) and Quebec society (technology, economy, urbanization, industrialization). This gap between culture and society in Quebec produced a global gap between Quebec and other North American countries. It can be said that those who opposed the regime (ideology and power) in Quebec during the period 1945-60, not only supported an ideology of contestation but also an ideology of recoupment.

In criticizing the delay experienced by Quebec in almost every aspect of human activity, the opponents have above all criticized the elites whom they held responsible for such a state of affairs. What did the new ideologists want for Quebec? What type of society did they want Quebec to become? It is necessary here, from the perspective of the analysis of ideologies, to make certain distinctions. It seems that the critical and negative part of this phase has been the most encouraged, the most systematic, and by far the most varied; this is easily explained. The ideology of conservation and the political powers had idealized Quebec culture to such an extent that it became an urgent necessity for opponents to deflate the balloons that had been blown up over decades. According to those in power, Quebec had the best educational system, the purest religion, the language closest to that of the Louis-fourteenth era, and the most humanist traditions. On top of that was grafted, a messianism which wished to make the rest of the world participate in these cultural treasures. According to the opinion that has been attributed to Duplessis, the Quebecois had become improved Frenchmen. It is not surprising that the first task of the post-War opponents was to criticize what Quebec had become and to compare the miserable reality to the fantasmagorias of the elites.

The opponents agreed relatively well over what they opposed, but they were not united in a similar manner over the positive objectives that they laid down for the society which they wished to construct. Furthermore, it seems that when mobilized by combat, they submitted to the rule of force and most of them did not question themselves about the positive aspect of their ideology. Opposition to the regime had brought together many individuals and groups who came from very different backgrounds: Catholic and progressive syndicalists, Catholic action leaders, Catholic and progressive intellectuals, members of the Liberal parties of Quebec and of Canada, and students from various disciplines. It would not be exaggerated to say that because of the history of Quebec and its political and intellectual climate, the only other model of society which the protestors could recognize as comparable was that of other North American societies. The majority of them wanted Quebec to become a liberal democracy, like Washington or Ottawa. Some of them had been influenced by European currents of thought, particularly French, for example, the review *Esprit*, but, for the majority it was the Ottawa model that consciously or unconsciously prevailed. During this period, a number of professors and students from the Faculty of Social Science at Laval University openly sided with Ottawa. The most typical example is that of Maurice Lamontagne[34] who was to rally to Ottawa after 1954. Three of the principal leaders of the post-War opposition movement, Marchand, Pelletier, and Trudeau were to join Lamontagne several years later. Others such as Sauvé and Pepin[35] also entered the Canadian government. Although many opposed the Ottawa regime during the 1950s, it is clear, after the fact, that their preferences unconsciously lay here and that the

positive aspect of their ideology was largely drawn from the model of the liberal democracy. We have tried to find articles from this period which expressed the positive aspect of the ideology of contestation. They are very rare. One of the few that we have found is that of Lamontagne to which we will return later.

From the point of view of the global ideologism of Quebec, that which we have taken here, we have laid out three principal ideologies: the ideology of conservation which was dominant for a century and which largely remained intact at the end of the War; the ideology of recoupment toward which most of the opposition of the 1950s would turn; the third, the ideology of development and participation, does not appear to have crystallized until the end of the 1950s. In Hegelian terms, a period of affirmation can be seen in the first ideology, in the second, the negation of the first, and, in the third, the negation of the negation.

The Ideology of Development and Participation

If we examine carefully the issues of *Cité Libre*, an organ of opinion which led the most systematic and coherent fight against the ideology of conservation, it will be seen that this was really a review of contestation against Duplessis, the clergy, the educational system, and many other subjects, but it never developed the positive aspect of its ideology in a systematic manner. At the outset, in 1950 and until the beginning of 1960, it fought against the ideology of conservation; beginning with the 1960s, it began to run up against the third ideology; it was only in 1964 that Pierre Elliott Trudeau wrote what seemed to be the most positive statement hat the review ever published: "Pour une politique fonctionnelle." We would like now to characterize third ideology which *Cité Libre* set itself against in the 1960s.

The ideology of recoupment largely contributed to the discrediting of traditional power elites and the ideology of conservation; essentially, it has directed its criticisms against the Quebecois themselves as a group; that is, it has been concerned with internal criticism. If one could schematize the thoughts of the principal spokesmen of this ideology, they do not seem to cast doubt on the fundamental postulate of the ideology of conservation, that Quebec forms a culture, that is, an ethnic group which possesses certain characteristics of language, religion, and traditions that distinguish it from other ethnic groups in Canada or the North American continent. If Quebec is behind compared to other ethnic groups, it is because of its elites which have misled it into the paths of conservatism, nationalism, chauvinism, and messianism. They now want this ethnic group to acquire a more open culture and ideology and integrate itself into Canadian society: according to Lamontagne, it is a question of a clear integration into Confederation. We thus see that this ideology of recoupment retains, for the most part, the essence of the ideology of conservation in that Quebec possesses a distinct culture and that it must accommodate itself to being implicated with Canada. The essential difference between conservation and recovery lies in the type of culture that Quebec should have. The first ideology is directed toward the past; the second is resolutely turned toward the present; it demands that Quebec culture be brought up-to-date and that it be reflected in the rest of Canada.

The third ideology also retains certain elements of the ideology of conservation in that it recognizes that Quebec possesses a different culture from other North American groups. Together with the ideology of recoupment, it recognizes that the elites of the past have perverted this heritage, that this culture and the ideology of conservation have become anachronistic, and that Quebec must move smoothly into the twentieth century. It recognizes that the lag between the social structure of Quebec and its culture must be filled. But the resemblance with the other ideologies ends there. It reaches back across the years to rejoin the first ideology of Quebec, before Confederation and even before Union. Quebec is not only a culture, that is, an ethnic group which possesses certain differences of language, religion, and traditions, but is a society that must be self-determined and gain its own independence. Now, because this ideology is set in the second half of the twentieth century and because Quebec has become an industrial society, it must, as any other industrial society, control its economy and polity. For the holders of this ideology, there can, therefore, be no question that Quebec should integrate itself with other societies such as Canada.

How do we explain the birth and development of this ideology? It could be suggested with some justification that it is written into the line of our traditional ideologies. But that is not the complete answer. The adherents of the two ideologies do not come from the same strata of society. The traditional nationalists or the liberals of the ideology of recoupment do not seem to have become, for the most part, partisans of the third and most recent ideology. Other groups in the population who have become active since 1960, workers, members of co-operatives, white-collar workers, teachers, civil servants, and students are the most active contributors to the development and diffusion of this ideology. It is true that there are several strata of the population who were already beginning to make their presence felt in the ideology of recoupment, but other strata have become more important and others, such as the newly unionized, are tending to subscribe, often implicitly, to this new definition of Quebec society.

In a phenomenon as diffuse as the birth of a new ideology, it is difficult to follow all the stages precisely. The criticism to which Quebec society has been submitted since the end of the last War has not happened without heart-rendering anguish and profound disequilibrium in a population which traditionally "was in quiet possession of the truth." The most firmly established truths, the most diffused myths, were attacked by more and more individuals and subgroups. Finally, in 1960, what has rapidly become known as the Quiet Revolution began and the time came to change the ideological climate of Quebec in a global manner. From the point of view that we are taking here, that is, of an ideology concerned with the theory that groups advance of their own accord, it is certain that one of the first effects of 1960 and the reforms that followed was to reaffirm the image that many Quebecois held of themselves and their society. One did not willingly boast about being a Quebecois during the dark years. To dethrone Duplessis, it was necessary to attack and to denounce all those teachers, politicians, and professional elites who were responsible for the fact that Quebec was the only feudal state "north of the Rio Grande." The day that more and more Quebecois realized that they could collectively escape from their rut, was the day that they acquired a taste for change and began to redefine themselves, set new goals for themselves, and seek the means to reach them. The ideology of recoupment, which wished to bring Quebec onto an equal footing with the rest of North America, served as a generator of many new policies and reforms. Now, in the same way as in the sixties it was a problem for the people of Quebec to progress to another stage of thinking and development, so the means available to do this and the direction that this reform should take could not be the same as those which had been used many decades ago by the Anglo-Saxon democracies of North America–the societies to which Quebec was catching up.

There had previously been independentist movements during the Duplessis regime. Although the new generation of independentists admitted almost all the critics who had been opposed to the state of Quebec society, they went further than the *Cité Libre* criticism and asked whether many of the problems of Quebec did not come from the fact that it had always been a dominated society; this explained the narrowing of their culture, their economic inferiority, and their morbid fear of losing their identity. They were thus exposing themselves to external criticism. And because on a worldwide scale there was increasing talk of decolonization and of national liberation, these terms quickly came to be used and new goals were set for the collective action of the Quebecois. From the beginning, however, these new movements split into two major factions: those who, like the Alliance Laurentienne, on the whole accepted the definition of the Quebecois group that the ideology of conservation had established; and those who, like Raoul Roy's *Revue Socialiste,* began to give another definition of the Quebec nation. The first more traditional group placed itself in the line of ideological choices that Quebec had known for decades; the second group was to define the ideology of development and participation which will now be discussed in greater detail.

On account of the homogeneity of the Quebecois and their culture (setting aside the Anglophone minority), the political options of Quebec since Confederation and the frame of reference of all political parties has always oscillated between certain more or less rightist tendencies. However, a considerable concensus has always existed between liberals and conservatives on the principal political options. It is still striking today to note that the differences between the partisans of the Union nationale and of the Liberal Party are quite minimal. The *Journal des Débats* of the Quebec Legislative Assembly gives the impression of a group whose ideas are interchangeable, who share the same values, and whose members are as thick as thieves. Often the only difference that separates them is the width of the corridor between the party in power and the opposition. Their differences are in tendencies rather than in doctrine. It is only recently that a more important cleavage has appeared between the left and the right. This phenomenon is so new in Quebec that at first it was said that these terms had no place in the political vocabulary of the nation since they did not correspond to any reality. Referring only to the members of the Assembly, it is quite evident that these terms do not mean very much. But with the third ideology which has appeared in the past few years, the terms right and left are beginning to refer to an increasingly clearly marked reality. Certainly, on the one hand, the Quebecois have not reinvented socialism, Marxism, self-management, state planning, or participatory democracy, but, on the other hand, it is also evident that the logic of the present situation has motivated them to take inspiration from these ideas to resolve problems that are demanding their attention in a very real way. It seems certain that it is above all the ideas of decolonization and national liberation that have awakened echoes among those who were troubled over the destiny and future of their nation. The phenomena of decolonization and of national liberation, which could be found in many nations of the world during the fifties, brought with them ideas of the good life and the good society, of the role of the economy, and of social classes, which were the same as those in the nineteenth century when the bourgeois classes of most Western nations undertook their national revolutions. Thus all these ideas finally reached a small part of Quebec youth who became aware that they could be applied to their own situation. But in explaining the development of ideologies in Quebec the influence of an international convergence must not be exaggerated; it is rather a case of a primarily local aid to phenomena that are the outcome of several decades of history. It must not be forgotten that the three ideologies are superimposed on each other and that they possess characteristics creating a chain of which the links are closely interrelated. The radical falling out of the third ideology is to a large extent developing away from a common understanding about Quebec society.

What precisely is this third ideology? It could be said that the three Quebecois ideologies are not mutually distinguishable and that there is no question, as some could believe, of a seesaw game between political parties. Let us first say that the distinguishing characteristic of the ideology of conservation is to consider the Quebecois group as a cultural minority within Canada; this group is largely centred in Quebec but has offshoots in other provinces. All these groups constitute the bearers of the French-Canadian culture (religion, language, and traditions) that must be preserved and transmitted as intact as possible over the generations. The ideology of recoupment also considers the French Canadians as a minority group spread across the country who must modernize their culture throughout that nation; this is a modern version of the ideology of conservation. There is here a difference between conservatives and liberals: the first want more autonomy for Quebec to ensure the conservation of its culture; the second want Quebec to become more integrated into Canada in order to profit from the advantages of the modern state while still preserving and enriching its culture and allowing it to spread across Canada.

The third ideology seems to be the most radical and from the beginning it was more strongly differentiated from the first two than these are differentiated from each other. It breaks from the other two by defining the Quebecois Francophone group not only as a culture but as a modern industrial society which has been dominated economically and politically by the rest of Canada; it ceases to speak of French Candians and speaks of Quebecois. For most of the people holding this ideology the minorities outside Quebec participate in French-Canadian culture but not in Quebec society. Of primary importance is that the Quebec nation be saved and liberated. This ideology is in accord with the ideology of recoupment in its fight against the ideology of conservation and in thinking that Quebecois culture must be modernized but not necessarily taking North American societies as models. In effect, the greatest mutation that this ideology represents in comparison with the others is that it develops a different idea of man and society in general, and of Quebecois man in his society in particular. It is here that we return to the Quiet Revolution and the international context in which it came into being.

Not only did the ideology of recoupment borrow its model of a good society from Canadian society, but it can also be said that the ideology of conservation was largely inspired by the same source. These two ideologies, one of which was dominant for many years and the other, long in a minority position, established itself after the Second World War, have both developed a kind of symbiosis with the dominant culture. It can be said that they borrowed from it their dominant ideas on the subject of life in society; that is, according to these ideologies, of a more or less developed capitalism which, however, fitted well with the philosophy of American society. The ideology of conservation has preserved or acquired some concepts derived from certain social encyclicals and from certain rightist dictatorships (Spain, Portugal) but, at its base, the model remained that of the so-called liberal democracies. In the 1950s nothing could predict that the upsetting of the Duplessis regime would result in this third ideology. Observers predicted that the ideology of recoupment, shared by the members of the Liberal Party, would become predominant and would take over from the ideology of conservation. But it happened otherwise.

But the independentist movements which had begun to arise again at the end of the fifties did much to attract attention to the idea of domination of one society by another. Still for many it was the question of political independence that was to facilitate the cultural expansion of Quebec. But the logic of the Quiet Revolution as carried out by the liberals must not be underestimated. Not only did their slogan of *Maîtres chez nous* contribute to the reinvigoration of Quebec and the Quebecois in their own eyes, but it also contributed to the launching of reform in the two major problem areas of Quebec both on the national level and on the economic level. It has also helped to link these two objectives which have tended to exclude each other: the national objectives remaining the prerogative of the right and the socio-economic objectives being traditionally those of the left. The task of catching up was initiated through a modern civil service, extensive reforms in education, nationalization of electricity, the S.G.F., conseil d'orientation économique, régime de rentes, caisse de dépôt et de placement, and the B.A.E.Q. The Liberals, through their dynamism, succeeded in interesting large sections of the population in their reforms (educators, civil servants, students, and underdeveloped regions), and kindling among them the desire to participate in this Quiet Revolution.

From an ideological point of view, challenging society and its myth quickly made the Quebecois aware that far from having built their society in its final form in the nineteenth century, it still remained to be built. Part of the population quickly came to see Quebec as a developing nation which not only removed them from their past conservatism but also differentiated them from other North American societies. This is another characteristic that brought them closer to colonized countries on the road to liberation and development. However, as opposed to countries that had developed in the nineteenth century and in the first decades of the twentieth century, the nations of today which are in the first phases of industrialization, or, like Quebec, are behind in relation to highly industrialized countries, have many models of development at their disposal. Even the concept of development no longer has the exclusive economic meaning that it acquired at the time of the triumph of capitalism. Not able or not desiring to entrust the problem of developing society to industrial entrepreneurs or financiers, the nations which are today on the path to development or who consider themselves to have already achieved it, must count on the state and on their whole population in order to reach their objectives.

In Quebec there are many intellectuals, youth, members of unions and co-operatives, and social activists who have realized that for the Quebecois to attain their desire of becoming *maître chez eux,* there must be planned socio-economic development and the establishment of a participatory democracy. The underdevelopment of Quebec, the relative homogeneity of the population, the exacerbation of national opinion, and the shallow roots of liberal democracy in Quebec have all encouraged the diffusion throughout the population of ideas of development and of participation. The powerful Quebec labour movement and the entry of new strata of the population into the unions give this ideology of development and participation great potential.

Must it be added that these ideologies are presently being disputed? Nothing definite has been achieved and there does not seem to be any way of predicting which of the three ideologies will become dominant in the near future. This should soon develop into a struggle between the two most recent ideologies, that of recoupment and that of participation.

Revue de l'Institut de Sociologie, No. 1, 1968 and *Communities and Change in French Canada,* Toronto: Holt, Rinehart and Winston, 1973.

NOTES

[1] Excerpt from *Revue de l'Institut de Sociologie,* No. 1 (1968), 95-124.
[2] F. Ouellet, *Histoire économique et sociale du Québec, 1760-1850* (Paris: Fides, 1966), p.210.
[3] F. Dumont, "Idéologie et conscience historique dans la société canadienne-francaise du XIX siècle," manuscript, 1965, p.11.
[4] *Ibid.,* p.16.
[5] M. Wade, *The French Canadians, 1760-1945,* Vol. 1 (London: Macmillan, 1967), p.192.
[6] T. Chapais, "Cours d'histoire du Canada" in *The French Canadians,* Vol. 4, *op. cit.,* p.27.
[7] G. Filteau, *Histoire des Patriotes,* Vol. 13 (Montréal: 1942), pp.243-44.
[8] Dumont, *op. cit., p.18.*
[9] Wade, *op. cit.,* p.186.
[10] *Ibid.,* p.197.

[11] *Ibid.*, p.208.

[12] *Ibid.*, p.212.

[13] *Ibid.*, p.252.

[14] Dumont, *op. cit.*, p.31.

[15] Wade, *op. cit.*, p.311.

[16] Louvigny de Montigny, *Antoine Gérin-Lajoie* (Toronto: 1849), p.13.

[17] Michel Brunet, "Trois dominantes de la pensée canadienne-francaise," *Ecrits du Canada francais,* 3 (1957), 98-100.

[18] F. S. Garneau, *Histoire du Canada* (1852), pp.401-02.

[19] Léon Pouliot, *La réaction catholique de Montréal,* 1840-1841 (Montréal: 1942).

[20] The Institut canadien was founded in 1844 and brought together young Canadiens who were interested in arts and sciences. This association, with its liberal spirit, came into conflict with the clergy until its dissolution in about 1878.

[21] Viatte, *op. cit.*, pp.95 and 98.

[22] Dumont, *op. cit.*

[23] Viatte, *op. cit.*, p.99.

[24] Mgr. Raymond, *Revue canadienne* (January 1, 1871), 38.

[25] Thomas Chapais, *Discours et conférences* (Québec: 1908), p.39.

[26] Louis Maheu has just written his thesis on this problem (Département de Sociologie, Université de Montréal, 1966).

[27] Viatte, *op. cit.* p.133.

[28] Gérald Fortin, "An Analysis of the Ideology of French-Canadian Nationalist Magazines: 1917-1954," manuscript, Cornell University, 1956.

[29] *Ibid.*, p.205.

[30] A. Faucher and M. Lamontagne, in *French-Canadian Society,* Vol. 1, M. Rioux and Y. Martin, eds. (Toronto: McClelland and Stewart, 1964), p.267.

[31] Nathan Keyfitz, "Population Problems," in *French Canadian Society,* Vol. 1, *op. cit.*, p.227.

[32] Maurice Tremblay, "La pensée sociale au Canada francais," manuscript, 1950, pp.33 and 36.

[33] With an interruption for the War years, 1939-1944.

[34] He was to become a minister in the Pearson government.

[35] These five men were then ministers in the Pearson government.

NATIONALISM AND THE CANADIAN BOURGEOISIE: CONTRADICTIONS OF DEPENDENCE

Jack Layton

Mel Watkins, a prominent theorist of the nationalist left in Canada, recently claimed that "the business class of this country has always been emasculated and cannot provide a base for a viable nationalism. I am increasingly of the view that nationalism for Canada must mean, and can only mean, a nationalism of the left."[1] In 1969, when this statement was made, the nationalism of the bourgeoisie in Canada largely consisted of the sentimental Canadianism of centennial year. Since that time, Canadian nationalism has appeared in many forms, emanating from many sectors of Canadian society. Obviously not all of this contemporary Canadian nationalism is "nationalism of the left." In fact, a good deal of the nationalist debate seems to be going on within the business class. Prominent promoters of what may loosely be called nationalist politics or policies include Walter Gordon (businessman, civil servant, and Cabinet Minister), Eric Kierans (President of the Montreal Stock Exchange, Cabinet Minister), the authors of the Gray Report[2] and the Honey Report,[3] the members of the Committee for an Independent Canada, the Minister of Health and Welfare, Marc Lalonde, and even, surprisingly, the former Minister for External Affairs, Mitchell Sharp, whose "option 3" calls for reduced dependence on the United States.[4] While some of these individuals and groups are not in the mainstream of business thinking, they nonetheless represent liberal or conservative nationalist views rather than any kind of socialist nationalism. Bourgeois nationalism appears to be gathering momentum. Do these developments belie Watkins' prediction? Is there a viable Canadian nationalism of the middle?

I

Conflicts between classes or between elements of the business class of a nation reveal some of the structural characteristics of its political economy. For example, the struggle between the monarchists and the whigs in seventeenth-century Britain was manifested through the conflict between the landed aristocracy and an emergent mercantile bourgeoisie—a struggle between classes; while the political conflict of nineteenth-century Britain over such issues as the Factory Act and the Corn Laws was a struggle involving merchant and industrial capital—an intraclass struggle. This study is primarily concerned with the latter, factional confrontation within the bourgeoisie.

In a novel interpretation of the nineteenth and early twentieth-century political economy of Canada, Tom Naylor has made the important distinction between two confronting types of capital (and capitalists). He argues that "the greatest contradiction among strata of the bourgeoisie appears between the industrial-capitalist entrepreneur and the mercantile-financial entrepreneur. The first operates in the sphere of production, the second in distribution. Thus, maximization of the mercantile surplus will minimize the industrial surplus."[5] There seems to be little doubt that during early periods of industrialization this distinction is relatively clearcut. Naylor demonstrates that in Canada, for example, the triumph of the mercantile ruling class over the Reform Movement, a victory incarnated in the institutions of Canadian Confederation and the National Policy in the nineteenth century, reveals, on the one hand, the conflict of interest between these two forms of capital, and on the other hand, the hinterland status of Canada within the British Empire. For if Canada's had been an autonomous, developing capitalist system, the industrialists might well have been victorious in

the conflict, as they had been in Britain only a few decades earlier. The question which Naylor's analysis raises is important for this study. Could it have been possible at that time, or indeed would it be possible today, for Canadian capitalism to become independent, or did the structural consolidation of Canada's hinterland status under the dominance of merchant/finance capital preclude the possibility of autonomy?[6]

An extensive historical analysis of the development of the mercantile and industrial sectors of the Canadian economy cannot be undertaken here. But some general trends must be identified to determine whether the split of the Canadian bourgeoisie in the late nineteenth century has remained an important feature of Canadian politics; whether this conflict has been transformed or whether discord has disappeared through the integration of the previously disparate interests of Canadian capitalists as a result of the new economic and political structures of the twentieth century. The first and most pervasive trend from 1900 to the present has been the transition from colonial status within the British Empire to "colonial" status within the American Empire.[7] Innis' term "colony" in the latter instance should be replaced by "dependency" in order to express the qualitative differences between the two empires and Canada's relationship to each.[8]

A second and related trend has been the tendency for Canada to maintain high levels of both unprocessed resource exports and manufactured imports. Canada continues to rely on its staple trade. Pulp and paper, minerals, oil and gas—have replaced the traditional fur trade, cod fisheries, square timber and lumber, and wheat.[9]

These new staples, as Mel Watkins has pointed out, have some important features. First, the export market is overwhelmingly in the United States, which has meant increasing integration of the Canadian economy into a continental structure. Also, the instrument of resource exploration is the multinational corporation, a highly efficient tool for appropriating not only the resource, but also the economic surplus for the benefit of the metropolis, with Canadian benefits coincidental and haphazard. Finally, staple production increasingly uses large amounts of capital or machinery, and relatively little labour—and much of the machinery is imported. As a result the new staple production has generated relatively less employment than did previous forms of production. Oil and gas, for example, have a decidedly lower labour component than does wheat, and it is that component and little else that benefits Canadians.[10]

This illustrates what André Gunder-Frank has called the "metropolis–hinterland structure," a fundamental relationship of world capitalism.[11] Canada fits this model because the economy performs a satellite function for the American metropole; and because central Canada functions as the metropolitan centre for the Canadian hinterland regions and for certain developing countries, such as those of the Caribbean.

The primary characteristic of this relationship is the continuing process of extracting economic surplus from the hinterland by the metropolis. The method of extracting surpluses in modern imperialist economies differs from that of earlier eras due primarily to the transformation within capitalist metropoles from mercantilism to industrialism. This has resulted in the institution of qualitatively different controls. Certainly, trading functions still exist, and resources must be transported to the industrial hub; but greater congruence is required in the relationship between the resources-rich sector and the productive sector. This is secured not so much through direct political control, since modern imperialism assumes primarily an "economic appearance" through the multinational corporation. An examination of the role and function of this central apparatus of American domination of the Canadian economy is essential for an analysis of the nature and structure of the contemporary Canadian bourgeoisie and of its positions on the "national question."[12]

The multinational corporation (MNC) is only "multinational" in the sense that it operates in more than one nation. In other respects, the MNC is a **national** entity. The MNC, rather than producing an "internationalization" of capital, turns out to be one of many ways in which American and European capital gains control over foreign capital.[13] Two hundred of the largest three hundred MNCs are based in the United States.[14] In Canada an even higher proportion of MNCs is American. Other mechanisms for American MNC control of

Canadian capital include raising capital from Canadian sources such as stock or bond issues; bank loans; tax concessions; reinvestment of surplus generated in Canada; and outright purchase of indigenous enterprise. This, then, is the process of "denationalization" of the capital of satellite nations which shapes the environment of the Canadian bourgeoisie. The process affects the various elements of the Canadian bourgeoisie differently and will provide the conditions determining the relative strength of these elements and their position on nationalism.[15]

One element of Canadian capitalism seems likely to profit directly from the activities of foreign investors and the MNCs in Canada, namely the Canadian financiers. The banks and financial institutions of the country are the instruments for the transferral of ownership and control of Canadian capital into foreign hands, using the mechanisms described above. These institutions developed out of the concentrations of mercantile capital which established their predominance in Canada during the nineteenth century.[16] Because, as a satellite, Canada has never been able to develop a strong, diverse, expansionist, industrial sector, and has not therefore been able to achieve an indigenous integration of finance and industrial capital after the fashion of the American metropole, the financial bourgeoisie which emerged originally from mercantile accumulation has remained the most powerful sector for the economy.

Oddly, Canadian finance capital was a strong force behind the nationalism of the "National Policy" which attempted to build an east-west mercantile system within Canada to guarantee their strength.[17] This policy was to be their undoing, because American industrial capital expanded into Canada by establishing branch operations in the protected Canadian market. This expansion was encouraged by the merchant financiers because it generated increased demand for resources, provided manufactured goods for exchange and created capital demand; all of which strengthened their position as distributors and bankers, or so it appeared. These encroachments of American capital set the stage for the development of a Canadian economy which became more and more dependent upon the United States and upon its expanding imperialist economy. The finance sector of the Canadian bourgeoisie has continued to profit handsomely by the expansion of American capital in Canada and consequently has continued to advocate this development and to shun the assertion of economic nationalism as it no longer serves their interests; unless, that is, American financiers attempt to encroach upon this sacred territory. Such a special case will be examined below.

We may now examine a second element of the Canadian bourgeoisie: the industrialists and the nature of their activities in the Canadian economy. While Canada is generally considered to be a developed nation, some aspects of her industrial structure and capacity resemble more closely that of an underdeveloped nation. Pierre Bourgault has shown that in the areas of innovation and structure of exports, Canada seems to lag well behind other industrialized countries, exhibiting very little innovative capability and low ratios of manufactured goods to raw material exports.[18] There are a number of reasons for this state of affairs in the Canadian economy. Firstly, Canada has always relied on exports of staple goods. The economic infrastructure is geared to this arrangement. The tariff in particular has on the one hand protected an east-west trade axis for Canadian mercantilists, while on the other hand it has created a "truncated" structure in Canada's industrial sector. There are too many firms competing to serve a relatively small home market, and this has given rise to inefficient production runs and low productivity. Consequently, Canadian industry, with only a few exceptions, has not been able to compete on world markets. The original design of Canada's economy in the National Policy advanced exactly this type of structure as its objective from the very beginning, representing the relative strength of the merchant/financiers by comparison with the small, emerging industrialists of the 1860s. The indigenous industrial bourgeoisie has remained at a disadvantage from that time, although there have been periods in the development of the Canadian economy which have witnessed some growth in Canadian industry, such as the period of the mergers at the turn of the century and wartime booms.

Although the Canadian industrial bourgeoisie has been a relatively weak element in Canada's economic structure, it has not resisted the process which maintains the inferior status of indigenous industrial capital. This brings us to the second reason for Canada's dependent and truncated economic structure. The industrial bourgeoisie in Canada is divided in three. First is the "second class citizen" of the multinational corporation—the Canadian manager. Next are two types of indigenous Canadian capitalists: the one whose enterprise depends on foreign-owned resource extractive or manufacturing operations in Canada for the greater part of his market; and the one who is truly "on his own"—serving a market in competition with American branch plants or imports. The latter category is quite small in number and size of firms involved and is frequently found in the service, rather than manufacturing sector, of the Canadian economy. This fragmentation has spawned an industrial bourgeoisie with conflicting attitudes on foreign investment. The first two types of the Canadian industrial bourgeoisie, the strongest elements of this group, have a strong interest in the maintenance of close relations with, and high levels of capital inflow from, the United States, while the third type of our industrialists might find themselves opposing this process and adopting a nationalist position.

Obstacles exist to such a development even among this relatively weak element of the Canadian bourgeoisie. First, it is the weakest of them all: the multinationals, their management in Canada, the merchant-financiers, and the indigenous industrialists providing services and products to the MNCs are all more powerful economic forces and all will likely resist nationalist economic policies in all but the most unusual circumstances. Second the common elements of the ideological position shared by all segments of the bourgeoisie, such as the primacy of unmolested free market forces in "producing" the "good society," generally outweigh the differences between the nationalist and continentalist interests—impeding the development of a viable nationalism among the bourgeoisie in Canada.

II

Catch the vision! Catch the vision of the kind of Canada this can be! . . . I've seen this vision; I've seen this future of Canada.

223

I ask you to have faith in this land and faith in our people.

John Diefenbaker, 10 March 1958

While Canadians were being exhorted to pursue an empty and undefined national objective from the hustings of the 1958 general election, the **Royal Commission Report on Canada's Economic Prospects** (the Gordon report) was awaiting publication to present to Canadians the question of the 1970s: Was foreign ownership of Canadian industry an issue requiring government policy decisions and intervention? Should the question of foreign control of the economy be the focus of national objectives?

Both a symbolic nationalism and a concrete economic nationalism emerged in 1958. The symbolic nationalism generated immediate popular response and approval but burned out because of its emptiness and its irrelevance, (with the help of continentalist dousing from Bay Street). However, the concrete nationalism was to encounter much more difficulty. The materials to sustain nationalist combustion were absent in the relative prosperity of the early sixties. Nevertheless, Walter Gordon desposited an insightful and persistent ember into the rhetorical nationalism of the Diefenbaker years.[19]

Why did Walter Gordon raise the question of Canadian economic independence in the mid-1950s? The fact that his concern was either ignored or rejected outright by leading businessmen and politicians at the time seems to suggest that Gordon stood alone amongst his peers. Denis Smith hypothesizes the role of an "entrepreneurial sense" in Gordon's awareness:

> Under the paternal guidance of the Minister of Trade and Commerce (C.D. Howe), Canada was going all-out for economic expansion, especially in the resource industries, and this expansion was being financed and directed largely from abroad.[20]
> C.D. Howe's unquestioned policy was that of the open door. Gordon believed in economic growth, but his **entrepreneurial sense** was offended by the increasing foreign role in the Canadian economy.[21]

The vague (but uncanny, from our perspective in the 1970s) nature of the "premonition"

is evident in the Gordon Report, which argued that political and economic instability could occur as a result of foreign investment.[22]

The perspective of Canada's economic elite toward American investment casts some doubt upon the idea that Walter Gordon's perceptions simply flowed from his "entrepreneurial sense." If this were the only cause, others would have been more receptive. Perhaps Abraham Rotstein's characterization of Gordon as possessing "the soundest political instinct of any of our political figures"[23] is a better explanation, but to refer to "political **instinct**" tends to ignore the fact that Gordon was in a position to examine the developing structure of the Canadian economy in more detail than other political figures of his time through his participation on the Royal Commission. His access to a broad analytical perspective and to factual information, combined with an enlightened political standpoint, enabled Gordon to predict with astonishing accuracy what others were only to observe in process: the reaction to foreign domination which would occur when the going got rough in the economy ten or fifteen years after his Report. Gordon, throughout his active political career, attempted to generate and encourage such a reaction and to establish mechanisms for dealing with the problem before it became so serious that reparations would be impossible.

All of this is not to deny that Gordon's nationalism was the nationalism of an entrepreneur, for it most certainly was not the nationalism of a conservative visionary such as John Diefenbaker, or of a proletarian radical responding to foreign exploitation and imperialism. The recommendations of the Gordon Report were based upon Gordon's perception of a threat to the ability of the indigenous business class of Canada to expand and prosper. The report recommended that the Government act to increase Canadian control of foreign branch-plants and subsidiaries through legislation which would require higher proportions of Canadians on their boards of directors, increased Canadian equity participation in these companies, and the publication of financial reports. In other words, Canadian business should be given greater opportunity to participate in the expansion of the Canadian economy which was being engineered under the aegis of foreign capitalists.

Response to the Gordon Report by the Canadian Government was cool. Diefenbaker did not understand the implications of the process of foreign domination which Gordon had documented. For instance, in 1960, the **Canadian Participation Provisions** (CPP) were introduced by the Conservative Government and provided that oil and gas leases be granted only to Canadian citizens or to Canadian corporations with (a) at least 50% of shares owned by Canadians, or (b) shares listed on Canadian stock exchanges, in order that Canadian citizens might have an opportunity to participate in the ownership of the corporation. The latter provision legalized the ability of the multi-national oil and gas companies to raise Canadian capital for the purposes of expanding their operations and legitimized the expropriation of Canadian resources through lease-hold arrangements. The nationalistic symbolism of the title of the Act was entirely misleading, and the CPP did not correspond to Gordon's recommendations. A second Government response, more in line with Gordon's suggestions (albeit the weakest and least substantial one from a nationalist perspective) was the **Corporations and Labour Unions Returns Act** (CALURA) which gave the Government power to collect financial and statistical information from corporations and labour unions carrying on activities within Canada.

The demise of Diefenbaker's "northern vision" in the wake of the pressures of continental defence arrangements and its replacement by the Liberal administration with Walter Gordon as Minister of Finance, provided Gordon with an opportunity to attack the problem of foreign ownership head-on— although he was to run into a brick wall of opposition. Gordon's 1963 budget announced measures to control foreign investment which were stronger than any advanced previously. They included a 30% "takeover tax" on the value of shares of Canadian firms sold to non-residents, the reduction of the 15% withholding tax on dividends paid to non-residents to 10% for corporations whose shares were at least one-quarter owned by Canadians, and an increase of the tax to 20% for firms with less than this level of Canadian ownership. Faster rates of depreciation were proposed for companies with at least 25% Canadian ownership.

The reaction of the financial elite of the country was immediate and hard-hitting. Eric Kierans, President of the Montreal Stock Exchange, in a published letter to Gordon on 18 June 1963, following the Budget Speech of 13 June, made clear the attitudes of the strongest element of the bourgeoisie in Canada concerning nationalist policies:

The financial capitals of the world have just about had enough from Canada. Last Friday, the initial reaction to the budget was one of bewilderment and dismay. Yesterday, it was anger and scorn. Today, our friends in the western world fully realize that we don't want them or their money and that Canadians who deal with them in even modest amounts will suffer a 30% expropriation of the assets involved . . . A non-resident take-over confers great benefits on the Canadian economy. . . . We must remember that we have sought, relied on and lived with foreign capital for generations and cannot now suddenly take an axe to murder the record of trust and confidence that has grown up over the years.[24]

The coercive power of threats by leaders of the financial community such as Kierans, when brought to bear on those politicians who had apparently stepped momentarily out of line, was sufficient to produce a rapid retreat by the Cabinet, and the offensive measures were withdrawn, while Walter Gordon tried weakly and absurdly to argue that the government's position had not been moved from its nationalist stance.[25]

Ironically, the next major event in the life of Canadian independence was an example of the dangers which Walter Gordon had anticipated five years earlier, and against which his budget had been directed. The American balance of payments situation had been deteriorating for some time, and in July 1963, President Kennedy announced an interest equalization tax on foreign borrowing in the New York money market—raising the interest cost to foreign borrowers to redress the drain of American capital. Panic ensued on the Canadian money market and Walter Gordon was forced to send Canadian government officials to Washington to plead for exemption. They were only partially successful, and only at the cost of an agreement to limit their foreign exchange reserves to $2.7 billion. This restriction limited the ability of the Canadian government to pursue independent monetary policies, for, as Diefenbaker noted in the House, the settlement still left "a veto with the president of the United States with regard to the expansion of Canada's economy, which is something . . . not in keeping with the sovereignty of this nation."[26] Of course, as Denis Smith has put it, "Walter Gordon did not need to be told."[27] Nevertheless, opposition and reaction to this significant event in the programme of continentalization was minimal and short-lived. This further integration of the two economies must have seemed to most of Canada's political and economic leaders to have been a matter of (the continentalist) course.

However, the course was by no means complete. In February 1965, the United States government announced voluntary guidelines for American corporations operating outside of the country for the purpose of overcoming continuing balance of payments difficulties. The guidelines included a reduction of investment abroad by these companies, an increased return flow of earnings by foreign subsidiaries to the metropole, and a policy of "buy American." Canada was exempted, at first, from the operation of the guidelines. But in December of the same year, the exemption was lifted in order that the objectives of the American policy might be more fully realized. Canada was, after all, the largest single repository for American direct investment in foreign countries, holding 31.0% of all such investment in the period from 1964 to 1966.[28]

This policy reveals once again the emptiness of the concept of the "multi-nationality" of the large American-based corporations. Secretary of the Treasury Henry Fowler expressed the relationship between the American government and these firms when lifting the Canadian exemption from the guidelines:

We must all recognize that the reconciliation of national interests and those of multinational corporations is essential to a future with freedom [and] therefore, they have not only a commercial importance—but a highly significant role in a U.S. foreign policy.[29]

Eric Kierans launched the first response to the application of the guidelines to Canada in what seemed a reversal of his anti-nationalist views on the 1963 Gordon budget. Writing to the American Secretary of the Treasury, he pointed out that Canada was contributing to a positive American balance of payments because more capital was being repatriated through income transfers from subsidiary companies to home offices than was being exported to Canada:

[The American] balance of payments problems are not caused by direct investment flows. They are caused by the heavy obligations and responsibilities of world leadership, by Vietnam, etc. Putting pressure, through your international corporations, on the economies of other nations, themselves struggling with problems of growth, productivity and welfare, is likely to cause a wave of hostility towards these corporations, and to revive the protectionist and nationalistic sentiments that lie close to the surface of any community.[30]

Kierans was very much aware of the interests of the Canadian business class in his response—pointing out that the Parliament was solely responsible for assuring growth of the Canadian economy, that Canadians would not be satisfied with "secondary staff positions of international units." The solution, for Canada, according to Kierans, was for the Canadian Government to create the atmosphere for Canadian citizens to play "creative and decisive roles in the growth of their own nation." In particular, Kierans proposed that **Canadian** multi-national corporations be established in order to absorb the "public and private initiative" of Canadians.[31]

Kierans thus personified the prototype Canadian bourgeois "nationalist," which was to develop into a more widely held position amongst elements of the Canadian business class in the following few years. But, an important contradiction in this form of nationalism—ultimately perhaps leading to its unviability—must be pointed out here. The multinational corporation is an instrument of the large economic imperialist nations of the world. Increasing the numbers of MNCs in Canada from 8 out of the 266 largest industrial corporations, as Kierans suggests, to 28 (assuming for the moment that this would be possible) would not increase Canadian independence, but will merely inaugurate greater and more complex types of integration between Canada and its large imperialist neighbour. It is fundamentally a "continentalist" rather than a "nationalist" proposal. It was not the structure of economic imperialism which concerned Kierans; he merely objected to a **symptom** of the pervasiveness and power of that structure–the overt application of political direction to the multinational corporations by the American metropolis. Kierans apparently misunderstood the roots of this problem: "We hope that international companies, unlike armies of occupation, will always have a role to play. To accomplish this, they must conduct themselves as true citizens of the host country."[32]

The Federal government responded to the American measure slowly and only symbolically. Walter Gordon had been removed as Minister of Finance, and a strong continentalist and multinational friend, Robert Winters (head of Rio Algom Mines–the Canadian branch of the English-owned Rio Tinto Zinc Corporation) had been installed as Minister of Trade and Commerce, largely at the insistence of the Bay Street business establishment.[33] Winters published, and distributed to MNCs in Canada, a pamphlet entitled: "Some Guiding Principles of Good Corporate Behaviour for Subsidiaries in Canada of Foreign Companies" (the Winters Guidelines). The list was a collection of motherhood phrases, qualified by "where possibles," "having in minds" and "fair and reasonables." This rendered them ineffectual.[34] Having tipped their hats to the nationalists, the government and the business class returned to their offices apparently unblemished. It is noteworthy, though, that, when stripped of their blandness, the Winters Guidelines formed a basis for many of the recommendations which were to emerge again and again in the political debate over foreign ownership in the years to come. In these debates, however, some legislative teeth were to be prescribed.

Two revealing cases of specific policy decisions made by the government on questions relating to foreign investment occurred in the mid-1960s on independent Canadian publishers and financiers. These two cases show how and why nationalist positions have developed within two of the components of the Canadian bourgeoisie. The success of these

components has varied, depending upon their economic and political strength. In the first case, a provision designed to reduce foreign involvement in the periodicals business in Canada through certain taxation measures which discriminated in favour of Canadian-owned publications was modified in order to exempt **Reader's Digest** and **Time Magazine**, the two largest-selling periodicals in Canada and both foreign-owned. This created the conditions for a nationalist response on the part of Canadian publishers as these two publications were the largest consumers of Canadian advertising dollars. Since that time, members of the Canadian publishing industry have provided leadership to the bourgeois nationalist movement in Canada. Note that these individuals fit the description of that relatively weak part of the Canadian bourgeoisie most likely to develop a nationalist position–namely, independent Canadian capitalists competing directly with the multinationals for the Canadian market. The eventual success of the publishers in this case can be explained in part by their position as generators of public opinion, thus making them more powerful than most other members of this independent sector of the bourgeoisie. Also, the **Time-Reader's Digest** case had become a symbol of American penetration into Canada, known to every school-child. It was therefore an important target for government response to growing nationalist sentiment among the population as a whole. Consequently, this represents a special case, not an indication of the general strength of bourgeois nationalism in Canada.

The second case concerns the modification of the **Bank Act** to protect Canadian content in the financial sector against the intrusion of the American-owned Mercantile Bank. Besides Canadian content on Boards of Directors, and the prohibition of new foreign-owned banks being established, there was a provision which limited the growth of banks (Mercantile in particular) presently owned by foreigners. The Canadian Government was pressured directly by J.S. Rockefeller, Chairman of Citibank, the new owner of the Mercantile Bank. In 1963, he worked to allow his bank purchase to proceed which it did despite Gordon's opposition and in advance of the legislated prohibitive modifications to the **Bank Act**. In 1967, he attempted to reduce the legislative impact on Mercantile's ownership

227

structure. Gordon succeeded in this second round and the bank was forced to comply within five years. The Trudeau government renegotiated the terms of the agreement in 1971, allowing Citibank a further nine years within which to expand its Canadian equity participation to the required levels, thus qualifying Gordon's earlier achievement.

Significant in this second example is the relative success with which the government was able to protect Canadian financial interests from encroachment by multinational finance. Again, this seems to conform to the model of nationalist responses by threatened elements of the Canadian bourgeoisie. Due to the strength of the financiers of Canadian capitalism, however, and in contrast to the first example, this nationalist response was rapidly and decisively successful and very much in the tradition of the privileged position which finance capital has maintained for itself in the Canadian economy.[35] The interests of Canadian financiers lie, therefore, with the multinationals and against nationalism **except** when their own territory is threatened.

In 1968, Gordon's pet project, the Task Force on the Structure of Canadian Industry, came to fruition in its Report, **"Foreign Ownership and the Structure of Canadian Industry"** (the Watkins Report). The nationalist debate in Canada entered a new phase. The Watkins Report introduced, for the first time, an analysis of the multinational firm and its effect on Canadian industrial structures as well as new statistics concerning the levels of foreign ownership of the Canadian economy. It maintained, however, Kierans' earlier viewpoint that MNCs were compatible with national independence because of the "harmony" between the desire of nations to pursue economic growth and the objective of MNCs to expand their global operations.[36] "Furthermore, economic benefit might cause national political benefit. A rich and growing country could pursue independent policies at home and abroad better than one poor and stagnant."[37]

Notwithstanding this shortsightedness, the Report did suggest that if Canada were to maximize the benefits obtainable from foreign investment, certain measures would be required. Of course, these recommendations operated within the framework of liberal, private enterprise capitalism and avoided the prohibited realms of nationalization. The proposals were merely designed to improve the functioning of an independent Canadian capitalism, and included suggestions such as the establishment of incentives for Canadian participation in new investments, the pursuit of greater competitiveness and efficiency in Canadian industry, the greater coordination and control of export trade, the establishment of a special agency to coordinate policies concerning multinational enterprise, and the creation of a Canadian Development Corporation to act as a holding company and to play a leadership role in the Canadian business environment.[38]

The government released the Watkins Report, but it failed to endorse it. Its refusal convinced Walter Gordon of the Pearson administration's anti-nationalism and precipitated his resignation from the Cabinet. The Gordon irritant removed, Pierre Trudeau's new government ignored the Task Force Report. During the following four years this administration faced increasingly nationalist groups and sentiments, indicated in public opinion polls, and more numerous exhortations by ex-Cabinet Ministers. Few legislative actions were taken. In 1970 and 1971, minor amendments to the **Canada Corporations Act** required foreign companies to publish financial reports. The **Loan Companies Act** and the **Investment Companies Act** amendments restricted foreign equity participation. This was also done provincially in Ontario, again as a result of successful "nationalist" pressure by finance capital. The Commons Standing Committee on External Affairs and National Defence report (the Wahn Report)[39] advocated 51% Canadian ownership of major foreign subsidiaries, but no action was taken by the government. But the most publicized measure was, as Paul Craven has described a similar Ontario tactic, a "smoke-screen."[40] This diversion was a report on **Foreign Direct Investment in Canada** (the Gray Report).[41] Although tabled in the House, it was, as in the case of the Watkins Report, "not a statement of government policy."[42]

The Gray Report was the most substantial attempt thus far to analyse the impact of foreign investment in Canada. It documented the threat to Canadian independence, and to an independent Canadian bourgeoisie, a menace looming from the "dangers of excessive concentration on natural resource extraction" and the "few jobs" it generates, from the "truncation" of firms, i.e., that foreign firm subsidiaries had "less opportunity for innovation and entrepreneurship, fewer export sales, fewer supporting services, less training of Canadian personnel in various skills, and less specialized product development aimed at Canadian needs or tastes."[43] Further, the report described how foreign direct investment weakened domestic control of the Canadian economy, and charged that multinational corporations were unresponsive to macroeconomic tools, such as monetary and fiscal policy. In addition, it predicted that direct American investment would prove to have a deficit impact on the Canadian balance of payments within ten years, and that new capital inflows would tend to force up the exchange rate and make Canadian industry less competitive.[44]

The effects of foreign direct investment which the Gray Report observed had been developing for some time. The traditional surplus on capital account, which Canadian leaders had claimed was demonstrative of the benefits which Canada derived from foreign investment in the form of economic growth, was steadily reduced, and Canada largely ceased to be a capital importer. In 1966, Canada began to have a net capital export. As well, the rate of expansion in the manufacturing sector was slower than should have been expected in the late 1960s.[45] Jim Laxer has argued that this phenomenon is an indication that "Canada's economy is moving from one phase of development to another."[46] Evidence for this claim is presented in a study of the "deindustrialization" of the Ontario economy.[47] A qualitative shift from a truncated manufacturing sector to a deindustrialized, resource-based, over-serviced economy has been under way since the mid-1960s. This transformation is a direct result of American trade policy and the level and nature of American penetration of the Canadian economy.[48]

Contemporaneous American trade policy endeavoured unsuccessfully to reverse the difficult trade position in which the United States found itself as it faced renewed competition from growing manufacturing centres in Europe (particularly Germany) and in Japan, through the creation of the Domestic International Sales Corporation (DISC), and the 10% surcharge on imports imposed in 15 August 1971, caustically referred to as "Nixonomics" by Canadian nationalists. The Ca-

nadian government responded to these programmes with the budget of 1972, which proposed to reduce corporation taxes in order to offset the ill effects to the Canadian economy. The theory behind this apparently non-nationalist response was faith in the "invisible hand" of free market economics; namely, that a cut in Canadian taxes would encourage the multinational corporations to remain in Canada, rather than appropriating capital earned in Canada for expansion in Europe, or for consolidation in the United States as they had been doing. Such reasoning misconstrues the relationship between the imperialist metropolis and its institutional apparatus, the multinational corporation, where the strength of the imperial economy outweighs the importance of the short-term profitability for the multinationals.

How could such a misunderstanding occur when the Government had in its possession the Gray Report, which attempted to illuminate at least some of the aspects of this relationship? The answer lies in the interests of Canada's bourgeoisie. Canadian business suffers no immediate harm if the American-owned manufacturing sector becomes deindustrialized (except insofar as high unemployment rates are bothersome), because the Canadian-owned sector seemingly expands (albeit modestly). Furthermore, increased emphasis on the resource extraction sector enables Canadian financiers to participate in large-scale, capital intensive projects for long-range benefit. And finally, the Canadian business class has always maintained considerable strength in the tertiary economic sector, particularly in transportation, and consequently it finds the "new mercantilism" to be quite satisfactory from the point of view of expanded demand for their services. The government can therefore be expected to pursue actively the development of such projects as the MacKenzie Valley Gas Pipeline, the James Bay Hydro Project, and the development of the Athabasca Tar Sands.

Despite the government's unconcern for the findings of the Gray Report, there was considerable discussion by various groups of Canadians concerning a new industrial strategy. The Committee for an Independent Canada (CIC) typified Canadian bourgeois nationalist response. Founded in 1970, the CIC attracted Walter Gordon, Abraham Rotstein, Peter Newman, Jack McClelland, Mel

Hurtig, Eddie Goodman and later many others, such as Minister of Trade and Commerce, Alistair Gillespie.[49] Many of these individuals, particularly the charter members, are in the publishing industry, which has precipitated specific confrontations between foreign-owned entrepreneurs and Canadian capitalists. This struggle is characteristic of the CIC's general approach to foreign investment problems and Canadian nationalism. That is, the CIC advances an economic nationalism oriented primarily towards the expansion and/or protection of Canadian business—a typical bourgeois nationalism. It has over time become the vehicle for the elaboration of the nationalism of a threatened class, although the organization has denied that its "positive nationalism" could be associated with the interests of a particular class. It claims a universal applicability:[50] "The premise we share is that the regaining of our independent powers of decision will require a common effort from all groups in the community: businessmen, educators, students, trade unionists, housewives, professional persons, journalists and so on."[51]

Recently the CIC moved from pressuring governments on an issue-by-issue basis to formulating a comprehensive set of policies to combat American penetration of the Canadian economy. A collection of papers at the CIC Convention in September 1972, commented:

> The policies proposed here are deliberately geared to the mainstream of public opinion in this country. We have avoided appeals to sectarian philosophies or special interests. We lean to the pragmatic rather than the doctrinaire and expect that all three major political parties should have no difficulty in accepting any of these suggestions within the context of their own economic and political philosophy.[52]

This statement dismisses the existence of competing or antagonistic elements within Canadian society beyond fringe or doctrinaire elements. It also implies erroneously that there is a "public opinion" or a "public interest" which applies generally to all sectors of the society, and that this public interest is definable in pragmatic terms. The Canadian party system is presented as a somewhat arbitrary division of the polity along undefined lines which, when reduced to the level of concrete policy-making, are largely irrelevant. These views originate from a liberal, pluralist conception of politics (a normative formulation advanced primarily by **American** theorists of democracy) and are, as such, ideological—despite the wishes and protestations of the CIC. This is not to condemn the CIC, but to place its activities, policies, objectives, and potentials into proper perspective.

The ideological perspective (and objective class interest) of the CIC is clearly revealed in policies which they advance, policies which may be described as a more coherent, more adventurous, and a more formalized version of the recommendations of the Gray Report. Under the general title of **Policies for Canadian Survival**, the CIC proposes what amounts to a new "industrial strategy" for Canada. This strategy is designed to improve employment and productivity in Canada through the preservation of natural resources, the rationalization of Canadian industry to improve competitiveness, the screening and policing of foreign investment, the development of Canadian technology, the improvement of Canadian entrepreneurship, a principle of corporate accountability in order that the "Canadian interest" might be pursued, the control of land sales, the pursuit of increased Canadian content in education, the strengthening of the Canadian publishing industry (not a surprising suggestion in light of the membership of the CIC), the control of communications, and the encouragement of the Canadian arts.[53]

The clearest indicator of the orientation of these policies is found in the specific proposals concerning entrepreneurship. The distinction between finance capitalists and industrial capitalists is clearly revealed when the CIC argues that there is a need for the creation of new institutions and the expansion of existing ones to provide merchant banking services to new Canadian businesses. The government, it claims, should ask or even require the chartered banks to devote more of their vast resources to higher risk enterprises.[54] The CIC thus recognizes the conflict between the powerful financiers of the Canadian economy and the struggling Canadian industrial entrepreneurs. It directs its proposals towards saving this element of the Canadian bourgeoisie. Many of the influential CIC members belong to this element, which pursues their interest through nationalist activities.

Sophisticated CIC analysts such as Abraham Rotstein understand that the multinational corporation and its junior partner, Canadian finance, have a firm grip on the Canadian economy and polity. Therefore, they conclude that more than simple free enterprise will be required if independent capitalists are to be set on their feet in Canada. Consequently, various kinds of government intervention and direction are recommended. One form of this intervention would result in what Adler-Karlsson calls "functional socialism."[55] Theoretically, functional socialism separates property ownership from the functions of property, allowing society to appropriate some of the rights traditionally associated with property in order that it may pursue the "public interest." On the one hand, this technique will allow governments to allocate resources within the country in such a way as to promote rational industrial growth, presumably by Canadian entrepreneurs; and on the other hand, it will permit the government merely to legislate out of existence the constraints placed upon it by high levels of foreign ownership. The major fallacy of this argument is that the multinational corporation is concerned with the functions as well as the ownership of capital. In some ways, the MNC is more concerned with the function of capital because it is through the control of resources, the market, and capital flows that the MNC can minimize uncertainty, maximize profit, and allocate surplus. (Note, for example, that the conditions of sale of American-owned oil companies in Libya involve the maintenance of certainty of supply for many years.) The objectives of the CIC and the independent entrepreneurs of Canada face these and other insurmountable hurdles which are inherent in the structure of the Canadian economy, and they face the overwhelming opposition from the commanding heights of our economic and political structure.

An example of government response to the Gray Report and to CIC proposals will serve to demonstrate the difficult road ahead for this fledgling bourgeois nationalism. The Trudeau Government introduced the **Foreign Investment Review Bill** on 24 January 1973. (It had been introduced but not enacted in 1972.) The Bill provided for the now famous "review procedure," whereby all acquisitions by foreign investors of Canadian firms with assets of more than $250,000 or gross revenues of more than $3 million would be subject to review by a special agency which would make recommendations to the Cabinet; the latter would be responsible for the final review decisions. The review board would determine whether the takeover would significantly benefit Canada in terms of employment, productivity, research and development, and capital flows. At some unspecified future date the review procedure would be extended to foreign investors not already operating in Canada, and even to new businesses by existing foreign-controlled firms in Canada in unrelated lines. This review extension seems highly unlikely as it would encounter tremendous opposition from multinational businesses and from Canadian finance. Provincial opposition could also be expected, as review procedures would conflict with the recruitment of new investment. Far more likely is the adoption of a registration procedure for new investments, such as that suggested by Industry, Trade and Commerce Minister Gillespie.[56] This would require little change of behaviour by foreign investors. Another possibility is that the screening process will result in most foreign investments receiving approval, in which case the review could be extended with nominal, symbolic effect.

The screening and registration procedures suggested by the government are unlikely to have more than limited effects on the behaviour of foreign firms in Canada, a limitation recognized even by the Liberal government. One observer puts it this way: "One may reasonably assess their proposals, therefore, as a masterful combination of practical goals, satisfactions for public opinion, and diffusion of responsibility."[57] In other words, the review procedure is merely another defusing of effective nationalism, another "smokescreen."

III

The expression of nationalism by the bourgeoisie in Canada has taken symbolic forms from time to time; this includes John Diefenbaker's "vision," and the preoccupation with Canadian unity of the Pearson years, culminating in a new Canadian flag and the Canadian Centennial. This analysis has discovered only one palpable, concrete

Canadian bourgeois nationalism, namely a capitalist response to an external threat. Furthermore, this bourgeoisie is weakened by being fragmented through special interests into various segments. There are those directly connected with the foreign investors as employees or associates. This is the financial sector, which thrives on maintaining foreign investment and the "new" mercantile economy. The "independent" industrialists depend upon the presence of American capital to provide them with a market (e.g., auto parts) or a function (e.g., transportation, public or private services). Both elements rely on Canada's dependent status for their existence and profit. The symbolic nationalism which they espouse from time to time has been aptly characterized by Danny Drache as "the nationalism of subordination."[58] In other words, their nationalism is a contradiction, an illusion, a pseudo-nationalism.

There is also the independent Canadian bourgeoisie operating in direct competition with foreign enterprise—a breed decreasing in number and never a powerful force in the Canadian economy, certainly not as powerful as the dependent bourgeoisie. It is within this independent element that a Canadian nationalistic capitalism might be expected to develop. This study has attempted to show this expectation to be valid. But the nationalism which has developed thus far has been weak and impotent, thanks to the opposition of the more powerful segments of the economy, and owing to the tenuous position within the economic structure which it occupies; it simply lacks a strong base. Independent Canadian business, particularly the manufacturing sector, probably the best bourgeois nationalist hope, has generally been weak, inefficient, and oriented towards the domestic market.[59] It is not surprising therefore that we find little in the way of an assertive, dynamic, bourgeois movement in nationalist politics.

On the basis of this analysis, we can conclude that there is scant possibility for a viable Canadian "nationalism of the middle" that might generate a strong independent Canadian economy: that the appearances suggesting the growth of such a nationalism are based upon contradictions inherent in the political economy of Canada, and are either symbolic pacifiers, or weak and largely ineffectual pursuits of self-interest by components of the bourgeoisie. While it may be true that the inadequate, unrealistic nationalism of the bourgeoisie may spawn an assertion of nationalist demands by other classes in Canadian society, this contribution will probably be its only one.

NOTES

[1]Melville Watkins, "The Multinational Corporation and Canada," in Dimitrios I. Roussopoulos, editor, *Canada and Radical Social Change* (Montreal, 1973), p.165.

[2]Government of Canada, *Foreign Direct Investment in Canada* (Ottawa, 1972). (The Gray Report).

[3]Government of Ontario, *Report of the Interdepartmental Task Force on Foreign Investment* (Toronto, 1971). (The Honey Report).

[4]Mitchell Sharp, "Canada-U.S. Relations: Options for the Future" (Special Issue), *International Perspectives,* Autumn (Ottawa, 1972). (Note that even Sharp's moderate position on independence in this article has not been adopted as government policy).

[5]Tom Naylor, "The Rise and Fall of the Third Commercial Empire of the St. Lawrence," in Gary Teeple, editor, *Capitalism and the National Question in Canada* (Toronto, 1972), p.3.

[6]Recent criticism of the Naylor thesis suggests that its representation of Canadian economic development is "too flat," i.e., schematic, or that it could be strengthened with the inclusion of a theory of "import substitution" as an explanation of the extent and nature of industrial development during the "third commercial empire." See Kevin Park, "Industrialization in Canada 1896-1912" (Toronto, mimeo, 1974); and Glen Williams, "Independent Canadian Industrial Capitalists, Where are you?" (Toronto, mimeo, 1974). These criticisms nevertheless affirm the fundamental hypotheses and conclusions of Naylor's argument.

[7]"Canada moved from colony to nation to colony." H. A. Innis, *Essays in Canadian Economic History* (Toronto, 1956), p.405.

[8]The term "dependency" is used in this way by authors in a collection of essays entitled: *[Canada] Ltd., The Political Economy of Dependency,* edited by Robert Laxer (Toronto, 1973).

[9]See Melville Watkins, "Resources and Underdevelopment," in Laxer, *[Canada] Ltd., pp. 107-26.*

[10]Ibid., p.121.

[11]André Gunder-Frank, *Latin America: Underdevelopment or Revolution* (New York, 1969), p.6.

[12]Kari Levitt, *Silent Surrender: The Multinational Corporation in Canada,* student edition (Toronto, 1971). p.103.

[13]Harry Magdoff and Paul M. Sweezy, "Notes on the Multinational Corporation," in K. T. Fann and Donald C. Hodges, editors, *Readings in U.S. Imperialism* (Boston, 1971), p.96.

[14]The Gray Report, p.54.

[15]Complementing this development is the "denationalization" of segments of the satellite ruling class. Within the MNC, for instance, managers must share the interests of the parent corporation and metropolis. The high levels of integration which develop between the economies of the satellite and the metropolis combined with the immediate benefits accruing to the bourgeoisie of the hinterland, produce a pervasive "integrationist" (in Canada, "continentalist") attitude amongst most components of the hinterland capitalist class. Some, as we shall see, may resist this trend in specific instances. Continentalism occurs not because of political allegiance or coercion, but due to the complex and pervasive structures of economic imperialism. See James O'Connor, "The Meaning of Economic Imperialism," in Fann and Hodges, editors, Readings, pp. 40-41.

[16]See Naylor, "The Rise and Fall . . . ," p.13.

[17]Ibid., p.21.

[18]Pierre L. Bourgault, *Innovation and the Structure of Canadian Industry* (Ottawa, 1972), Part III.

[19]This study will concern itself primarily with the latter form of nationalism–economic nationalism. There will be no consideration given to the emergent nationalism of French-Canada here, because its distinctiveness deserves separrate study. The author has presented the outlines of such an analysis in "Nationalism and Social Change: The Case of Quebec" (Toronto, mimeo, 1973).

[20]W.L. Morton, *The Kingdom of Canada,* second edition (Toronto, 1969), pp.509-510; paraphrased in Denis Smith, Gentle Patriot: A Political Boigraphy of Walter Gordon (Edmonton, 1973), p.31.

[21]Ibid., pp.31-32.

[22]From the Royal Commission on Canada's Economic Prospects (the Gordon Report) (Ottawa, 1958). Cited in Dave Godfrey and Melville Watkins, editors, Gordon To Watkins To You (Toronto, 1970), pp.15-16.

[23]Ibid., p.16.

[24]Ibid., p.20.

[25]House of Commons, Debates, 19 June 1963, p.1321. Cited in Smith, Gentle Patriot, p.161).

[26]Debates, 22 July 1963, p.2428.

[27]Smith, Gentle Patriot, p.175.

[28]Levitt, Silent Surrender, pp.160-161.

[29]Quoted in a letter to Mr. Fowler from Eric Kierans, then Acting Minister of Revenue of the Province of Quebec, dated 4 January 1966, a partial text of which appears in Godfrey and Watkins, Gordon To Watkins, pp.47-51. (Fowler's quotation appears on p.47).

[30]Ibid., p.49.

[31]Ibid., p.50.

[32]Ibid., p.51.

[33]See Smith, Gentle Patriot, chapters 11 and 12. See also Godfrey and Watkins, Gordon To Watkins, pp.9-25.

[34]The "Winters Guidelines" are reprinted in ibid., pp.52-53.

[35]Lest it be construed by the reader that Canadian politics was moving towards a more nationalist position on all fronts, it should be emphasized that the reverse was in fact occurring in the most important sectors of the political economy of Canada. The Columbia River Treaty and the Autopact are outstanding examples of these trends, signifying the continentalization of resoures and of manufacturing in Canada.

[36]Canada, Privy Council, Foreign Ownership and the Structure of Canadian Industry: Report of the Task Force on the Structurre of Canadian Industrry, (the Watkins Report) (Ottawa, 1968), p.36ff.

[37]Ibid., p.37.

[38]Ibid., pp.393-416.

[39]Canada, Commons Standing Committee on External Affairs and National Defence, Report (11th) of the Committee Respecting Canada - U.S. Relations (Ottawa, 1970).

[40]Paul Craven, "Two Faces of Ontario Tories: Love of Foreign Investment; Fear of Public Pressure," North Country, Vol. 1, No. 2 (April-May 1974), p.30. This article analyses the recent policies of the Ontario government relating to economic nationalism along similar lines to those being pursued here.

[41]Canada, Foreign Direct Investment in Canada (Ottawa, 1972).

[42]Ibid., p.v.

[43]Quotations from the Grray Report as reported in A. Rotstein, The Precarious Homestead (Toronto, 1973). p.56.

[44]Ibid.

[45]Canada Year Book, 1970-1971 (Ottawa, 1971), p.1200, Table 18: Balance of International Indebtedness Between Canada and All Countries. When interest and dividend receipts and payments are treated

as capital account items rather than as currrent account items, the table reveals a capital outflow in 1966, 1967, 1968, and 1969.

[46]In Laxer, [Canada] Ltd., p.145.

[47]Ibid., pp.147-148. Aggregate data reveal that there was a small absolute decline in manufacturing employment in Ontario (and in Canada) for the period 1966-1974. In June 1966 there were 776,831 workers employed in manufacturing in Ontario; by June 1974, the number was 772,200. However, during this period the work force in Ontario grew by approximately 27%.

[48]The deindustrialization study documents the difference in behaviour between the American-owned manufacturing firms in Ontario and the Canadian-owned ones during the period 1966-1974. Employment in the American-owned firms studied grew by only 8.1%, while that in Canadian-owned firms grew by 21.2%. Ibid., p.151.

[49]Walter Gordon was Minister of Finance in various Liberal governments in the 1960s; Abrraham Rotstein is an economist who worked on the preparation of the Watkins Report; Peter Newman, author, was editor of MacLean's Magazine and of the Toronto Star; Jack McClelland and Mel Ilurtig are publishers; Eddie Goodman is a prominent lawyer and occasional writer.

[50]It is a common characteristic of ideologies that they attempt to universalize their conception of reality; and this is parrticularly the case with nationalism, which has been married to many different ideologies in order to assist in the achievement of their philosophies or programmes.

[51]Abrraham Rotstein and Gary Lax, editors, for the Committee for an Independent Canada, Getting it Back: A Program for Canadian Independence (Toronto, 1974), p.xiv.

[52]Ibid., p.xii.

[53]Ibid., pp.295-394.

[54]Ibid., pp.299-300.

[55]Gunnar Adler-Karlsson, Reclaiming the Canadian Economy: A Swedish Approach through Functional Socialism (Toronto, 1970).

[56]House of Commons, Debates, 10 January 1973, p.154.

[57]John Fayerweather, Foreign Investment in Canada (Toronto, 1974), p.164.

[58]D. Drache, "The Canadian Bourgeoisie and Its National Consciousness," in I. Lumsden, editor, Close the 19th Parellel, Etc.: The Americanization of Canada (Toronto, 1970). p.10.

[59]Of the strong Canadian industrial corporations, most are resource-based concerns (Brascan, International Nickel, Alcan), while a very few others constitute exceptions to this general rule (Massey-Ferguson, Stelco), whose strength derives from unusual historical circumstances. Some of these are discussed in Tom Naylor, The History of Canadian Business, Vols, I and II (Toronto, 1975).

CLASS AND IDEOLOGIES OF CLASS IN THE ENGLISH-CANADIAN NOVEL

J. PAUL GRAYSON

L.M. GRAYSON

In Canada, the social scientific study of literature has aroused little interest outside of Quebec.[1] The reasons for this are at best speculative. But a good argument can be made that in English Canada, where the influence of American social science has been overwhelmimg, a generation of "radical empiricists" may have left the indelible imprint that somehow the study of literature is "soft" and that social scientists had better spend their time in other pursuits.[2] Perhaps also, the events of the sixties and early seventies have left some social scientists more concerned with the material structure of society than with its culture. And finally, it may be that

Canadian literature is simply not considered a worthy topic for study.

Whatever the reason, the study of English-Canadian literature has received short shrift. This is not to say that some social scientists have not considered literature, albeit briefly, in more general analyses of social processes.[3] Usually, dominant themes in our literature are used to buttress general claims relating to the basically conservative nature of Canada as compared to the United States and to the "non-creative" quality of our politics (see Porter, 1965).

For example, Porter, in his analysis of "Canadian Character in the Twentieth Century," writes that: "It is tempting to trace in Canadian institutions [a] quality which critics have found in Canadian literature, that is, the lack of social relevance, the lack of commitment to and the ambiguity about social ends and purposes" (1971:5). A similar interpretation is echoed elsewhere. In *Ideological Perspectives on Canadian Society,* Marchak argues that: "Canadian novels reinforce [a] classless image of Canada. They are not, in the main, about classes, let alone class struggles" (1975:15). This conventional wisdom is reiterated by Zureik and Pike: "Social class," they point out, "does not play a significant role in Canadian fiction" (1975:22).

It is interesting that in all three cases the authors base their impressions on literary critic McDougall's, "The Dodo And The Cruising Auk: Class In Canadian Literature" (1971), first published over a decade ago in *Canadian Literature.* Since this work first appeared, no other scholars have subjected his propositions to empirical scrutiny. There is, therefore, a grave risk that individuals using this work may be making assumptions about English-Canadian literature that in fact require further verification.

Contrary to McDougall, literary historian F.W. Watt (1957; 1976) argues that there has been a working-class tradition in Canadian literature dating from the nineteenth century. Watt, however, takes a broader definition of literature than [does] McDougall—who deals primarily with novels—and includes journalism in his analysis. The firm establishment of class components in Canadian fiction, according to Watt, occurred in the years of the Great Depression.

Through an examination of some English-Canadian novels, we intend, first, to outline the ways in which class and ideologies of class have found expression in English-Canadian novels since the last century. Second, in modification of Watt, we will show that class and ideologies of class have found embodiment in English-Canadian novels more or less continuously since the early nineteenth century. We will also demonstrate the way in which class and ideologies of class have changed over time. More importantly, we will suggest that these changes can be related to a number of complex changes in the socioeconomic and cultural environments in which Canadians have found themselves. There is, however, no simple formula by which the effects of broad environmental factors and a literary tradition on class and ideologies of class in Canadian novels can be assessed.

We will not argue that class and ideologies of class form a dominant part of the conscious literary tradition in Canada. To this extent we are in agreement with McDougall. Evidence suggests, however, that commentators may have been over-zealous in their references to the extent of the class component in British and American novels, the usual bases of comparison.[4]

In the analysis, we will be forced to rely on publication date in allotting novels to particular periods. We are painfully aware of the fact that they may have been written long before publication, but in the majority of cases there is no way of our knowing the gestation period. We also can appreciate that in a capitalist society most often works of literature are published when there is a perceived market. In this sense, publishing houses serve as censors over what we read. But, given market constraints, perhaps we can consider the mere fact of publication important. It indicates that a publisher perceives some connection between what is expressed in a novel and what some individuals in society are prepared to accept.[5] To this extent, date of publication is extremely important. Our analysis will proceed on the basis of this assumption.

Logic of Inquiry

The sample

The first problem we face is obviously one of sampling. In a bibliography of Canadian literature to 1960, Reginald Watters (1972) records approximately 16,000 entries. Since that date, as the bibliographical entries of *Canadian Literature* and the *Journal of Canadian Fiction* show, the number has swelled by several thousand.

If we believe that few English-Canadian novels have class components, it stands to reason that a random sample of bibliographical entries would be likely to yield very few novels showing the characteristics we are concerned with.[6] While such a finding would be a sound comment on class in English-Canadian literature, we would be prevented from any substantive discussion of the ways in which class and ideologies of class are manifested. As a consequence, we de-

engage in sleuth work; that is, we relied on the opinions of literary historians, crtics, and our colleagues in tracking down novels in which the class component is clear. Having once identified these works, we were then able to analyse the ideologies of class embodied in them. Obviously, because of space limitations, it was not possible to present information on all novels selected for analysis. Those that are discussed, however, are typical of the remainder. A complete list of these works can be found in the appendix.

Definitions

A second problem was one of providing workable definitions for class and ideologies of class. There are, of course, a number of existing usages from which to draw.[7] Most important of these is the distinction made by Marx and Engels between class and class ideologies: the former refers to the relationship of groups of individuals to the means of production; the latter to the ideational content of consciousness that legitimizes the existence of certain classes in societies and forms a backdrop against which the individual interprets his/her everyday experience (Baxandall and Morawski, 1973). In later writings on literature per se, scholars working within the Marxist tradition modified this particular conceptualization of ideology.[8] It is not, however, our intention to list these individuals. Suffice it to say that in this school the works of Georg Lukacs (1964; 1965; 1971) and Lucien Goldmann (1964a, b) have most affected our thinking.

In much of his work, Lukacs treats ideology more or less as a synonym for world view or "Weltanschauung" (1963). Goldmann, by way of contrast, identifies ideology as one component of a larger collective consciousness: ideology refers to bodies of thought used to justify "improving particular positions within a given social structure" (1973: 114). The relation of this formulation to that of Marx and Engels is clear. A second form of consciousness is not necessarily used to cloak material self-interest. Instead, it outlines possible types of relations between man and society and between man and nature. In order to clearly distinguish this type of consciousness from ideology, Goldmann terms it "world view" (1973: 114). In great works of literature, the world view of the author provides an inner coherence that is responsible for lifting the work from the level of the mundane. Great work, in fact, is to a large degree identified as work in which the inner coherence is evident.

In our analysis of English-Canadian novels, we accepted, to a limited degree, Goldmann's analytical distinctions between ideology and world view. In concrete cases, however, it was difficult, if not impossible, to assess the degree to which a work was structured more by self-interest than by the author's concern with the inner coherence of his/her work. While we can therefore accept Goldmann's conceptualization at an analytical level, at an operational level it was unworkable. We therefore decided to treat ideology in much the same fashion as Lukacs. That is, world view will be used more or less synonymously with the world view embodied in the novel. World view, for our purposes, includes the author's views of man, society, and the relation between them, as well as notions regarding the way society should be. When we speak of ideologies of class, we are therefore concerned with the ways in which and the degree to which the ideology underlying the novel includes class as a component of the social environment.

With the concept of class there were equal problems. Although class can be defined in terms of relations to the means of production, this usage seldom appears in literature.[9] As a consequence, it was necessary to think of class in a slightly different way.

Class, as we will be using it, can be thought of as the degree to which the author acknowledges, either implicitly or explicitly, class as a component part of Canadian society. The implicit definition used by the author may be less systematic than that used by the social scientist, but the writer at least admits that membership in particular groups has consequences for the ways in which people talk, the type of food they eat, the work they do, and where they live. Passages that reveal what we mean by this usage can be found in Hugh Garner's *Cabbagetown* (1951) and *The Intruders* (1976). In the latter, for example, a middle-class woman talking to a working class youth compares the area in which she grew up to Toronto's Cabbagetown. "We were the well-to-do or well-bred," she comments, "and you who lived down here the working-class, some of whose mothers came in once a week as cleaning women. Some people up there," she adds, "dismissed you as a barely mentioned segment of society, some acted as if they were better in every way than you, some were outright snobs, and others, I'd say the majority, were just conscious of their class, money and position in society" (1976:22). It is difficult to be more explicit than this.

The typology

Given the ways in which class and ideologies of class have been defined, there are a number of perspectives that can be brought to bear on the study of Canadian literature.[10] Likewise, ideology and its relation to literature can be analysed on a number of levels. First, and most obvious, are analyses that are restricted to an examination of the ideologies underlying one work. At the second level, efforts are concentrated on the ways in which, over time, the work of one novelist is affected by different ideologies. On the third level attention focuses on the extent to which the works of various authors share similar ideologies. It is on this third plane that our analysis is carried out.

More specifically, we will focus on the way in which class finds expression in a number of novels written in various periods. At the ideological level, we are concerned with the degree to which the existing class structure is accepted, questioned, or rejected (ACCEPTABILITY). Having once determined this factor, we can examine the response to the class structure as embodied in the novels (RESPONSE). Lastly, it is possible to determine the level at which the response occurs (LEVEL). Here again there are two options: the response can either be at an individual or a collective level. Clearly, by focusing on these concerns, we are confining our analysis of ideology to the relationship between man and society and the way society should be, at least as these matters relate to the class structure.

The logically possible combinations of "acceptability," "response," and "level" are summarized in Figure 1. In total, there are twelve logical categories into which novels can be grouped depending upon the ways in which the class structure is treated.

The degree to which the class structure was accepted, questioned, or rejected in most cases was easy to specify. Problems arose, however, in attempting to convey what ac-

ceptance means. A certain class structure may be accepted in the sense that it is regarded as legitimate; it may be accepted because it is felt that little can be done to change it. Our problem was that of identifying which of these alternatives seemed most plausible. For the other two options in the "acceptability" category, question and reject, there is less ambiguity.

A related problem stems from the usage of "response." If the class structure is accepted, a passive response was defined as one in which the novel conveys the idea of working within the existing class structure. An active response in this case refers to action in which the intent is to buttress the existing class structure as might be the case in a counter-revolutionary situation. Given the complexity of this latter category, we were fortunate in having no cases to deal with.

The "response" category for questioning or rejecting the class structure provided few problems in conceptualization. Similarly, "level" posed no insurmountable hurdles: the novels conveyed the notion of dealing with the class structure at either an individual or a collective level.

To illustrate the way in which this scheme was applied in actual cases, we can take one fairly well-known novel and show how it was categorized using these dimensions. Hugh Garner's *Cabbagetown* will suffice. Basically, the novel embodies a rejection of the class structure of the 1930s. Moreover, the rejection is active–emphasis is on change. Change, in turn, is to be brought about through collective action. Using a similar logic we were able to classify a number of other works written at different periods over the past hundred or so years.

Assumptions underlying evidence

Perhaps the most difficult problem of all is that of determining the ways in which the contents of the novels can be used to both prove and illustrate the points we are concerned with. So far as class is concerned, we have little difficulty: the type of passage cited earlier can be given to prove that the idea of class is not absent from the novel. With the underlying *ideology* of class we have a little more difficulty insofar as it *must be inferred* from what characters say, do, and think in various passages of the novel.

In taking this position we are in agreement

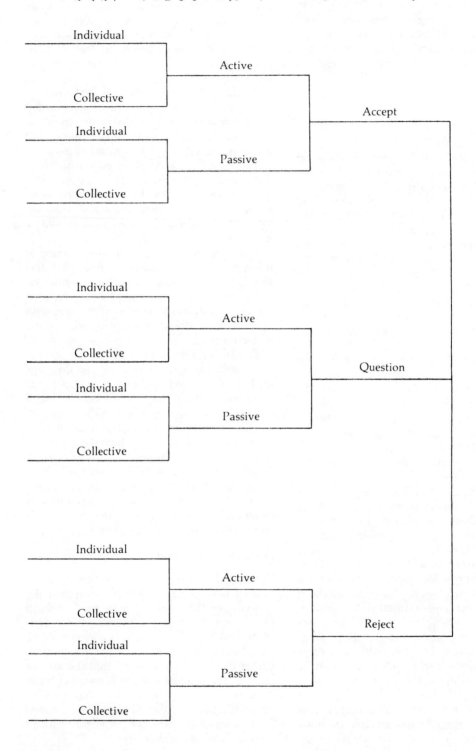

FIGURE 1: Approach to the class structure embodied in the novel

with Michel Zeraffa (1976) that "reality seems to be spread out before [the writer] with all its conflicting forces . . . which the writer is then able to synthesize in his work by setting them out in terms, and through the means, of some basic ideological principle." In this analysis, one of our major concerns is with the degree to which the ideological principle underlying the novel embodies an acceptance, questioning, or rejection of the class structure; whether the response to the class structure is active or passive; whether action to deal with the class structure is suggested at either the individual or collective levels.

Given this intent, it is necessary, in the presentation of evidence, to do four things. First, we must cite passages in these novels to verify the existence of ideas of class. Second, we must classify these novels in to those in which, at the ideological level, the class structure is accepted, questioned, or rejected. Third, quotations from the novels must be used to show how the underlying ideological principle becomes embodied in concrete thought, speech, or action. It must be stressed that passages will be presented in evidence *only if they embody the general notions underlying the novel with regard to class and ideologies of class.* Fourth, we must attempt to place the ideological principles into a broader sociohistorical framework: we are in agreement with Zeraffa that "the sociology of the novel should enable the history of a society to be read not in its literature, *but through* its literature, through the formally constituted literary artifacts it produces" (1976:64).

Novels in which the social structure is accepted

The idea of class

Novels in which the social structure is accepted, unlike those in which it is questioned or rejected, can be found among the early works of Canadian literature. Of significance in the early period is Susanna Moodie's *Roughing It In The Bush* ([1852] 1962).[11] This work is perhaps the first in Canada in which class is *clearly* seen as an objective part of the social structure. In addition, behind the description of trials encountered by a British gentlewoman in the backwoods of Upper Canada, lurks an obvious ideology of class.

For Mrs Moodie, society was legitimately comprised of classes, each of which was obliged to carry out certain tasks with a sense of duty. Her outrage at Canadian domestics who suggested that they should sit at the master's table is therefore understandable. Her condemnation of the rebels of 1837, who were bent upon changing the power of certain classes in society, also makes sense when seen against this ideological background. Likewise, her revulsion for "Yankee squatters," who were prone to unseemly behaviour, is just one part of a general concern with "respectability" as she understood it.

For all her concern with what was proper, Moodie was not insensitive to those who were less fortunate than she. Her defence of the Indian provides partial support for this statement. In addition, she almost understands the reasons underlying the "improper" behaviour of certain groups of English immigrants. "The most unnatural restraint which society imposes upon people at home," she writes, "forces them to treat their more fortunate brethren with a servile deference which is repugnant to their feelings, and is thrust upon them by the dependent circumstances in which they are placed. . . . But let them once emigrate," she adds, "the clog which fettered them is suddenly removed . . . and the dearest privilege of this freedom is to wreak upon their superiors the long locked-up hatred of their hearts" ([1852] 1962:139).

While she may not condone bad manners, Moodie is obviously aware of the fact that certain people have forms of behaviour imposed upon them, particularly in England, simply because the class structure provides no alternative. The blend of paternalism and moral indignation that seems to underlie Moodie's sentiments marks her as typical of the brand of Tory found among the upper classes of the last century.

Like *Roughing It In The Bush, The Imperialist,* by Sara Jeannette Duncan, published in 1905, treats class as an objective category in which people are placed. Also, particular behaviour can be thought of as natural for individuals in different classes. Woe betide those who contemplated transgressing accepted class boundaries, such as those middle-class individuals who would ride the workers' train from Elgin (Brantford) to Niagara Falls. Of individuals considering this course of action Duncan writes that "it was a question in Elgin whether one might sink one's dignity or go as a hand for the sake of the fifty cent opportunity, a question usually decided in the negative. . . . It will be clear at a glance," she continues, "that nobody whose occupation prescribed a clean face could be expected to travel cheek by jowl, as a privilege, with persons who were habitually seen with smutty ones, barefaced smut, streaming out at the polite afternoon hour of six, jangling an empty dinner pail" ([1905] 1961:14).

Although classes were well defined, there was at least the possibility of mobility. What improvement was allowed the individual, however–such as the hero of the novel–was to be won through personal achievement. There was no hint of any form of collective action designed to change the position of certain groups in society. To this extent, the ideology conveyed by *The Imperialist*, like that of *Roughing It In The Bush*, is supportive of the status quo.

With both *Roughing It In The Bush* and *The Imperialist*, it is tempting to link the ways in which class is depicted in the novels, and the ideologies underlying the novels, to more general systems of thought prevalent in society during the period. Indeed, concepts of class and ideologies of class portrayed in the novels come very close to a more embracing Victorian ideology analysed by W.L. Morton. Class, Morton points out, was simply taken for granted by Victorian Canadians: "What they did not include in their thinking was the concept of class conflict" (1968:326). This is not to say that the notion of class conflict was absent during this period for all classes. Quite the contrary, as will be shown in the discussion of novels in which the class structure was questioned, notions of class conflict were not entirely absent. What might be suggested–and understandably so– is that for the novels in which there is a clear expression of class as an objective category, and in which at the ideological level there is a clear acceptance of the class structure, there is a parallel between the general ideological principles underlying the novel and the ideology of particular classes in society–classes that felt more at home in the country drawing room than in the offices of newly founded urban factories (see Cross, 1974).

Unlike *Roughing It In The Bush* and *The Imperialist*, novels written in the twentieth century in which the class structure is clearly accepted tend to focus more directly upon the working classes in society. In many cases the portrayal of working-class life is inadequate but class is at least recognized as an objective dimension in which particular forms of behaviour occur or in which certain things are possible. In addition, although the recognition that divisions between classes are deep continues to be either implicit or explicit in the novels, class conflict is absent. Changes in circumstances, in turn, are to come only through the exercise of individual initiative.

That class is considered an objective category is brought out in a number of novels in which there is an underlying acceptance of the class structure. In Jessie Sime's *Our Little Life* (1921), centred on life in a Montreal slum immediately after the First World War, for example, the Irish-Canadian working-class heroine is uneasy in her relationship with a young, downwardly mobile middle-class Englishman, Robert Fulton: " 'What roight have I,' " she said to herself bitterly, "to be takin' part with such as him? He's as far above me as the starlight. He's not loike me. He's a gen'lemen bor'rn" (1921:183). Fulton, for his part, was equally uneasy about "rubbing shoulders" with the "lower orders." "It is one thing," he thinks, "to try to write sympathetically of the manual worker and quite another to sit beside him at supper" (1921:221).

Impressions similar to these are conveyed by *Delight* written in approximately the same period (1926) by Mazo de la Roche. The focus of this novel is on the experiences of a beautiful English immigrant domestic. Interestingly, some of the class barriers that may have confronted the heroine's real life counterpart in Britain also appear in a Canadian setting. When faced with the prospect of escorting the heroine to supper after dancing with her at a town ball, a shipper in a tannery comments that: "It was one thing to dance with a servant–a lord of the manor might do that–but to take her in to supper was quite another thing." His solution was therefore to take "in the daughter . . . of the jeweller, and [to sit] with a select few at one of the small tables in a corner" ([1926] 1961:60).

The existence of and the distance between classes is equally evident in *Under The Ribs Of Death* by John Marlyn (1957). That class is considered a major division in society is aptly portrayed by circumstances in which the main character feels, at least for the moment, that he has in some way shed the limitations imposed by his class affiliation. For Sandor Hunyadi, the mere establishment of a friendship with a rich English (Canadian) boy in the better part of town was a source of jubilation: it symbolized the crossing of erstwhile immutable class boundaries. "[A] vast gulf separated this world from his," he reflects, "but he had spanned it; in one stride had crossed over to taste, to see, and forever to invest his dreams with the vision of it. . . . [One] distant day," he promises himself, "he would return here to stay" ([1957] 1964:74). For Sandor, the Depression intervened between him and his dreams.

In a more recent novel, *Cabbagetown Diary* (1970) by Juan Butler, class is once again seen as an objective part of the social structure. To the main character this point is forcibly brought home by the non-intervention of police in a fight arising out of a middle-class political demonstration. "Goddam it," he rages, "just try to have a fight like this in Cabbagetown and you'll get your head busted in two by the Law. . . . And here these clowns pull off the same deal right on Yonge Street and the cops just pull them apart" (1970:205). The source of his outrage is obvious.

Ideology: passive acceptance at the individual level

As stated at the outset, in novels discussed so far, there is an acceptance of the class structure. In some cases mobility for individuals is possible but only through their own efforts. Usually, this acceptance is implicit in the ideology underlying the novel. In a few cases, the acceptance is more explicit.

In *Our Little Life*, for example, Miss McGee "didn't question things. She just took what came, and except in acute moments when she wished she were dead, she didn't complain–even to herself" (1921:133). In a discussion with a politically oriented friend, the main character of *Cabbagetown Diary* expresses his reluctant acceptance of the class structure, perhaps for the simple reason that no alternatives seem possible. "Look George," he argues, "What the hell am I going to get out of this? Is it politics that's going to keep me in spending money? What the hell do I care if there's poor people in Cabbagetown? There always has been and there always will

be" (1970:177). An even more negative attitude to collective action designed to better the lot of his fellow workers is expressed by the despicable hero of *Chipmunk* (1949). "Just when he was about to get a raise," he complains to himself, "the radicals had to start stirring up a lot of ill feeling" by organizing a union (1949:6).

A more positive orientation towards acceptance of the class structure is embodied in *Under The Ribs Of Death* and *The Apprenticeship Of Duddy Kravitz* (1959). In the former, at least the suggestion of mobility is present. Thus Sandor's father can promise that "you [Sandor] will go further than I. . . . Things will be easier for you" ([1957] 1964:25). In the latter, mobility is also presented as a possibility. For "Duddy wanted to be a somebody. Another Boy Wonder maybe. Not a loser certainly" ([1959] 1968:62). In these two novels there is an acceptance of the class structure, but an acceptance not necessarily based on the feeling that there are no alternatives; it derives more from a sense that perhaps self-improvement is not impossible.

With these novels it is difficult to clearly determine whether or not there is a parallel between the ideological principle(s) underlying the novels and the ideologies of particular groups in society. For one thing, the novels span a great number of years in which numerous changes were occurring in Canadian society.[12] The Canada of Jessie Sime is not the Canada of Mordecai Richler. Perhaps, however, some clue to the ideological structure of the novels can be found in the liberal-individualist ethos which to a certain extent accompanied industrialization in Canada. Given the nature of Canadian development, this ideology was perhaps less pronounced than elsewhere, but it certainly was present.[13] Failure to move upward in the class structure, according to this philosophy, is a consequence not of any structural impediments in society itself, but of some deficiency on the part of the individual. Such an ideology might lead individuals to passively accept their fate. As a consequence, they might never attempt to change their position in society. (Miss McGee in *Our Little Life* seems to display this type of resignation.) If individuals do attempt to change, and fail, they have no one to blame but themselves. Clearly, these notions are not inconsistent with the idea that the social structure none-theless is composed of classes or that certain types of behaviour only occur within certain class contexts. While the links between the liberal ideology and concrete manifestations in literature are difficult to draw, they must not be dismissed.

Novels in which the social structure is questioned

The idea of class

Not surprisingly, novels in which there is an underlying questioning of the class structure also contain some notions that class is an objective component of the social structure. In addition, certain behaviour is depicted that could only occur within a particular class context. For these novels, however, class, in both manifestations, is a prominent feature. In some cases we are even treated to the spectre of class conflict. By definition, they are also novels in which there is some discontent with aspects of the class structure. Most often, there is a belief that undesirable aspects of the class structure can be changed within the existing structure of society. In other cases, while the class structure is questioned, there is little hint as to the possibility of change.

Two of the most interesting facts that emerge from an overview of these works are, first, that a great number of them appeared in the last years of the nineteenth century and in the early years of the twentieth. Their appearance perhaps can be linked with general currents of reform present at that time. Second, in more recent novels, the underlying ideology of class is more muted. It is tempting to link this development with the "end of ideology" perspective that was perhaps as fashionable in Canadian as in American society in the 1940s, 50s, and early 60s.[14]

In *The Other Side* (1886), a nineteenth century novel by M.A. Foran, first serialized in a labour newspaper, class is clearly seen as a part of the social structure by an employer concerned with the prospect of nascent trade unionism. "Since the dawn of history," he comments, "there have been classes in society and while the world lasts there will be rich men and poor men. This is an inevitable law of human nature, and labour unions tend to make the poor dissatisfied" (1886:148). A

similar belief is affirmed by a businessman in Alan Sullivan's *The Inner Door* (1917). It is argued that "these working people have their place—like ourselves. It would take a rash man to alter it. The surest way . . . to achieve happiness is to confine one's interest to one's own sort. . . . " (1917:21). While J.P. Buschlen in *A Canadian Bankclerk* (1913) does not deal as extensively with class as the previous two authors, the imagery he uses to describe farmers at a bank is nonetheless telling. "Before the wicket farm-folk stampeded struggling to get their noses against the iron railing and to blow their breath on the weary-looking teller. A heap of germ laden money," he continues, "temptingly within reach of the rustics, only separated from those grimy, grasping fingernails by plate glass" ([1913] 1973:57). The sentiments underlying this description provide a clear example of a negative predisposition to a disadvantaged group of people in a novel that is otherwise sympathetic to another exploited group, bank tellers.

Often in the novels, women make comments similar to those of their husbands confirming the class nature of society. The situation is so bad for Mrs Masterson, wife of a factory owner in Albert R. Carman's *The Preparation Of Ryerson Embry* (1900), that she feels "one cannot venture to have a plan without consulting one's servants. The homes are ruled from the kitchen and the 'works' from the boiler room" (1900:73). In *The Course Of Impatience Carningham* (1911) by M. Burkholder, the friend of a factory owner's wife cautions her to "beware of trying to help the lower classes. They are a greedy and thankless lot. They will ride over you if you give them a ghost of a chance" (1911:58). To this sound advice the ungrateful woman has the gall to ask: "Are they not just ourselves stripped of the advantages money can give? Are they not just you and I working in a factory?" (1911:60). The very idea!

It should not be assumed that comments such as these are confined to businessmen or their wives. In more than one novel a recognition of the objective nature of class is offered by a preacher or his wife. Thus in Ralph Connor's *To Him That Hath* (1921), a preacher's wife comments that "there must be social distinctions and there are classes. I mean . . . we must inevitably draw to our own set by our natural or acquired tastes and by our traditions and breeding" (1921:71). In *The Magpie* (1923), by Douglas Durkin, statements made by a political leftist are equally categorical. To her "the Nansons and their kind may be kindly intentioned–they may be generous–they may be considerate–but they are rich and that makes them wrong" ([1923] 1974:167). It seems that not only is there a class structure but also that one's bank account determines the extent to which he/she can be trusted.

The objective nature of class is forcefully brought home once again in Phillip Grove's *The Master Of The Mill* (1944). In this, as in many of the novels, passage after passage could be cited in support of this contention. In one instance, for example, revellers returning home from a party behave in such a way as to warrant the comment: "It did look as if they were of a different race from the toilers who, in their white-dusted jeans, were trudging along to their toil while the sons and daughters of the gods were returning to sleep off the effects of their revels" ([1944] 1961:132). An equally telling passage is found in Hugh Garner's *The Intruders* (1976). In this case, a middle-class woman is describing to a working-class youth the difference between the area in which she grew up and Toronto's Cabbagetown. "We were the well-to-do or well-bred," she comments, "and you who lived down here the working-class, some of whose mothers came in once a week as cleaning women. Some people up there," she adds, "dismissed you as a barely mentioned segment of society, some acted as if they were better in every way than you, some were outright snobs, and others, I'd say the majority, were just conscious of their class, money and position in society" (1976:72). As stated earlier in this paper, it is difficult to be more explicit than this.

Ideology: active questioning at the collective level

The defining characteristic of novels analysed in this section, their questioning of the class structure, and in many cases, their attendant class conflict, provides a striking contrast to those discussed in the previous section. Often, the questioning is tied to ideas as to the ways in which society could be improved. Still, there are a number of novels in which the questioning is less obvious and no solutions are offered for social ills. As mentioned previously, early novels tend to fall in the former category. More recent ones are most often found in the latter.

A questioning of the existing state of society underlies the comments of a worker in *The Other Side*. "[To] admit that the time will come when all men will be equal in physical, social and mental power," he stresses, "is to admit that it is possible to eliminate from the earth, sin and disease and replace the race again in the Garden of Eden" (1886:441). Obviously, there is no passive acceptance of the status quo implicit in these words. Perhaps an even more obvious questioning is suggested by the words of a Knight of Labour in A.M. Machar's *Roland Graeme: Knight* (1892). To the Knight, "no entirely unprejudiced person can help feeling nowadays, that our working classes do not get fair play in the great battle going on around us; that here the 'battle' is emphatically 'to the strong,' and that the weaker are being, perforce, driven to the wall–crushed beneath the great iron wheels of Progress, Capital, Combination, and Protection" (1892:124).[15]

Questions as to the nature of progress were found in a number of other novels written around the turn of the century. A trade unionist in Alan Sullivan's *The Inner Door* makes a telling point in this regard. He argues that "We're using ourselves up to no purpose and we're bringing children into the world to do the same thing over again. You talk about progress, but progress is something that's got now so it feeds on men and sucks 'em dry and throws 'em away and reaches out for more" (1917:207). This point is lost on many members of the owning classes of the period.

In *The Preparation of Ryerson Embry* by Albert Carman, the sentiments expressed by a striking worker provide insight into the final position adopted by the hero, a theology student. "It is justice I'm after," the worker argues, "the masters shall not lie to us with impunity. . . . The time is coming when they will give us our fair share of the earnings of the 'works' or neither we nor they nor anyone else shall work" (1900:127). Comments made by a shoemaker in John Galbraith's *In The New Capital* (1897:24) reflect on the actual nature of wage labour. "Have you ever thought of it" he questions, "that, although slavery is abolished in English-speaking countries, that there is yet another kind of slavery coming up which is almost as bad as any kind that ever existed, and that is the slavery of labour under the mighty hand of capital?"

The position underlying J.P. Buschlen's *A Canadian Bankclerk* is even more easily discerned: the author actually states his purpose in writing the book. "My object in publishing 'Evan Nelson's history,' " he writes, "is to enlighten the public concerning life behind the wicket and thus pave the way for the legitimate organization of bankclerks into a fraternal association, for their financial and social betterment" ([1913] 1973:9). It is fair to say that, although the concept of social justice is not extended to all groups in society, the novel itself adequately embodies the author's purpose.

Although many of the novels written at the turn of the century appear to have been influenced by the teachings of the social gospel movement, clergymen themselves are frequently criticized for views that reinforce the status quo. One such attack is delivered by a labour leader in Ralph Connor's *To Him That Hath*. "I have heard you say something in the pulpit at times in regard to the value of men's immortal souls. What care can men take of their bodies and minds," he demands of the preacher, "if you work them ten hours a day?" (1921:213). Also questioned in this novel is the treatment accorded men returning from war.

More forceful in this latter regard, however, is Douglas Durkin's *The Magpie*. For soldiers returning from the First World War, the capitalist system had little to offer. "We've spent four years of the best part of our lives fighting for the big fellows," a returned sergeant bitterly complains, "and we'll spend the rest of our days working for them just the same as we did before the war. The only real difference is that we had a band or two and a chaplain or two to remind us that we were fighting for the glory of God and the brotherhood of mankind, and now we have the squalls of hungry kids and the insults of a few God damned slackers to cheer us on our way" ([1923]1974:12).

In some ways sounding remarkably Marxist, *The Master Of The Mill* by Phillip Grove, traces the evolution of a small mill to a technological giant. The dynamic of technosocial systems that leads to class conflict is clearly revealed in the words of the "master's" son

when he comments that the "system began to break down when the first inventor fashioned the first tool. Every system is born with the germs of its death in it" ([1944] 1961:312). While the novel is not directly concerned with the movement to a better state of society, class and class conflict resulting from increased mechanization are clearly portrayed as fundamental social realities.

It can be argued that there is a marked contrast between novels analysed in this section and those in which there is an acceptance of the social structure, whatever the reason. In many cases the novels carry a sense of anger—in some cases indignation. Unlike novels yet to be discussed in which there is a clear rejection of the class structure, however, there is a sense that things can be "fixed up" as it were. But there is also the realization that any change requires an active response on the part of certain groups to collectively bring about the change.

The belief that certain inequitable aspects of the class structure can be remedied through collective action is particularly evident in novels written at the turn of the century. The solutions to social ills embodied in these works tend, to a certain extent, to focus on the possibility of a "change of heart" on the part of the capitalist owning class. Such possibilities are frequently linked with the importance of religion in a moral society. If more recent novels are omitted from discussion, it is because their ideology is so diffuse little can be said regarding collective action to change things.

In Alan Sullivan's *The Inner Door*, the collective action designed to change society supports this generalization. The main character is aware that certain important social developments are afoot. "Beneath the polished surface of society," he surmises, "moved an inchoate mass, divided for the time by its very intensity, but drawing inevitably nearer to some stupendous climax" (1917:370). Despite this type of observation, it is difficult to avoid the impression that change should not occur through the conflict of classes; rather, it should result from the development of a higher morality on the part of those in power. Thus, a working-class leader comments that "It is elsewhere that the change should begin; I mean on top. Let them at home commence, and say not that the worker is dirty and perhaps underpaid but ask of themselves—I—am I overpaid for what I do? And if so, why is it?" (1917:313).

Despite an emphasis on the merits of collective action through trade unionism, the underlying thrust of *Roland Graeme: Knight* is also towards some type of moral improvement. For the abuses of contemporary society, the hero of the novel argued "there was only one radical remedy, and that was a fuller extension and wider use of the principle of brotherly trust or cooperation. It must govern all thought. It must be extended to the labourer as well as to the capitalist" (1892:167). In an earlier work, *The Other Side*, there is a similar assumption that a change of heart on the part of certain groups will have important consequences for the down-trodden. "[A] revolution in the sphere of matter, to be successful," it is argued, "must be preceded by a revolution in the realm of mind" (1886:437). In this case, though, religion as a rejuvenating force is absent from discussion. Instead, the major emphasis is on more secular measures: "The remedy [for wage slavery] is profit sharing, equitable participation in the product of labour and capital, and collective ownership in the great engines of production and agencies of distribution" (1886: viii).

In other novels in which the class situation is questioned, there is sometimes the notion that the capitalist class through their own volition can introduce certain improvements. In *The Course of Impatience Carningham* the owner of a factory reveals to his wife ideas he has regarding desirable changes in his factory. "In my dream," he fantasizes, "there is a model lunchroom and a rest and reading-room for the girl employees. Oh, if I had the means, I shouldn't mind buying that field on the opposite slope and turning it into an athletic ground, where they could indulge in football and tennis during the summer evenings, and tobogganing and skating in the winter" (1911:46).

In a number of novels it is clear that political action is viewed as the most effective means for introducing change. While trade union activity is not ruled out, the main character in *The Preparation of Ryerson Embry* says to a gathering of strikers: "I'd just like to ask you whether you or the 'bosses' have the most votes . . . you can govern the country that way . . . I believe in Trade Unions as a war measure; and labour is always at war

with its oppressors" (1900:174). The desirability of large-scale political action is emphasized once again in *The Gleaming Archway* (1929). In commenting on some labour activity, the main character states that "We have built the beginnings of a political party here that in time, will send its members to Parliament to fight the workers' battle" (1929:220). In this novel, however, the hero eventually becomes somewhat skeptical of the efficacy and even desirability of change.

This sentiment, in fact, is present in other novels. The main character in *The Magpie*, for example, comments that "The trouble is . . . if the Labor element took over the reins from the present governing bodies, it's a question of whether we'd be any better off for it" ([1923] 1974:14). Perhaps comparable reservations underlay the realization reached by a farmer turned radical in *Music At The Close* (1947). In a skuffle with a policeman during a strike " . . . it came to him in an inexplicable flash of intuition that between the miners and the policeman there was no difference; both were caught in the same trap" (1947:165).

Despite the emphasis on politial action as a means whereby workers can achieve some of their goals, it seems fair to say that trade unionism per se is just as often proposed as a mechanism whereby change can be affected. The reason for this latter course is suggested in *A Canadian Bankclerk*. "But men in my trade or calling can make themselves necessary to an employer collectively by cooperating;" the main character summarizes, "and," he continues, "co-operation is the only way. . . . If the bankclerks of Canada were united they could talk as a body, and the banks of Canada would be compelled to listen" ([1913] 1973:337).

Not surprisingly, whatever course of action is implicit in the novel, the owning classes do not passively sit by and allow events to take their course. In *To Him That Hath*, the action proposed to deal with a strike at a meeting of businessmen is "Fight them to a finish! Smash the unions!" (1921:206). When changes that might lead to a strike are proposed in *The Master Of The Mill*, the response of the master's son is that "Police and soldiering will have to protect that mill, with machine guns and tanks if need be, for the good of the masses themselves" ([1944] 1961:227). Similarly, in *The Magpie*, it is the opinion of a professional union

245

breaker that "There is only one cure for the condition in which we find the world today. Deal with these professional agitators as you would deal with enemy spies in camp" ([1923] 1974:138). In these cases, the vested interests are proposing collective action to counter that of the working classes.

In this, as in the previous section, it is tempting to link the ideological principles underlying the novels to general ideological principles present in society. For works published around the turn of the century, this is a relatively simple task. The abuses brought about by industrialization were being attacked by an emerging trade union movement, socialists in certain parts of the country, and adherents to the social gospel.[16] While there were a few exceptions, members of these groups questioned the existing relationships between classes and advocated reform, but did not propose wholesale rejection of Canadian capitalist society. It is therefore understandable that sentiments similar to these should find embodiment in some of the literature of the period.

Perhaps less understandable are novels written later in the century. Clearly, although the social gospel gasped its way into oblivion in the twenties, the union movement, while it had some difficult times, continued to grow. So did the number of socialists (Miller, 1971; Young, 1969). The more subtle embodiment of a questioning of the class structure in the later novels is, therefore, difficult to understand. At best, this section an be concluded with the comment that although class continues to find embodiment in various novels in which there is a questioning of the class structure of Canadian society, this questioning finds a more systematic form in novels published around the turn of the century than in later ones.

Novels in which the social structure is rejected

The idea of class

Relatively few novels can be placed in the category in which there is an underlying rejection of the class structure and a manifestation of class conflict. Most novels in this category were written since the Great Depression. More importantly, of those written recently, the background for most has been Quebec after 1960. As the major concern of this analysis is the English-Canadian novel, we will not dwell on the latter point.

It should come as no surprise that in novels analysed in this section, class is treated as an objective part of the social structure. It would be difficult to actively reject a class structure that was not perceived as real. It is equally understandable that class would be seen as a context within which certain types of behaviour can be understood.

Two novels in which the former can be seen are *Waste Heritage* (1939) and *Forgotten Men* (1933), although some might dispute the inclusion of the latter in this category. Both were written in the Depression and both are different from novels on the Depression written later. It is fair to say that neither of these two novels embodies the sense of naive—and perhaps wasted—effort that can be found in Earl Birney's *Down The Long Table* (1955) or Hugh MacLennan's *The Watch That Ends The Night* (1959), although the latter does not reject the social structure. The most obvious explanation for this omission is that these latter two works were written some time after the Depression in a climate of relative prosperity.

In *Waste Heritage*, the extent to which class is an objective part of the social structure is conveyed in a number of ways, ranging from the presentation of situations in which class is actually viewed as being responsible for events to those in which conflict becomes manifest in the behaviour of individuals. The situation in which, after a fruitless discussion with a police officer, the hero of the novel betrays the belief that "Uniforms were another bit of class oppression the same way that wars were cooked up by a bunch of pot-bellied financiers" ([1939] 1973:136), is an example of the latter phenomenon.

Although *Forgotten Men* also embodies the notion that classes are part of the social structure, there is an overall inconsistency with regard to class conflict. In one instance, for example, the hero, the reform-bent son of a wealthy industrialist, wants to tell his working-class companions "that they were wrong about Barlow Worth, and many other men like his father. He would tell them that he would fight with them, for their right to live, for their right to feed, and clothe, and house their wives and children comfortably" (1933:44). By the end of the novel, however, the hero is less sanguine about men of wealth taken as a class.

Although the ending note of *Down The Long Table* (1955) is disillusionment, class is clearly seen as an objective part of the social structure. The words of Comrade Kay, a communist, are therefore understandable. Anything "we can pin on the coppers is all for the good," she argues. "They're the repressive arm of the state, comrade, and we have to make thousands of un-class conscious workers who read the Herald aware of that fact" (1955:64). In Hugh Garner's *Cabbagetown*, also centred on the Depression, overall references to class are more subtle, but none the less obvious. For example, Ken Tilling, the main character, muses with regard to a wealthy area of town that "the district represented a way of life that he would never know, and which he really didn't care to ever achieve. He was satisfied to remain a member of his class and station in life" (1951:87). It is also true that in *Cabbagetown*, conflict between classes is not as immediate as in other novels.

The same cannot be said of *Fatherless Sons* (1955) where the ebb and flow of class strife are written into a novel that centres on life in a Canadian mining town. "[All] of this immeasurably valuable metal," it is commented, "and the fabulous profits derived from it, flow from the hands and the heads of the workers. Nickel is silvery clean when it turns up in columns of dividends. The stuff is black, sulfurous and stinking in the clothes of the men who mine it" (1955:117).

Ideology: active rejection at the collective level

In most of the novels under discussion, it is relatively easy to detect an underlying rejection of the social structure. For example, after suffering humiliation and abuse at the hands of his jailors, the hero of *Forgotten Men*, comes to the understanding as to why "those terrible things happened when there was a revolution in a country, as there had been, even in his own lifetime. Now he understood why the men who had been exploited and outraged, had no pity for the class that was responsible" (1933:382). While he likewise rejected the class structure, Ken Tilling in *Cabbagetown* was reluctant to formally associate himself with political groups. This stance was

a result of his political philosophy which "leaned toward the anarcho-syndicalism of the Wobblies" (1951:246). Thus, while he saw the need for collective action to bring about change, his own political views, to a certain degree, stood in the way of the achievement of his goal.

Less concerned with avoiding group affiliation, the main character of *Down The Long Table* clearly states that he rejects "the stupidities of our laissez-faire society . . . it is," he comments, "an outdated and destructive system and it must change, because change is the law of life (1955:78). With less distinction, but with a great degree of passion and conviction that things should change, the writer in Dyson Carter's *Fatherless Sons* sums up the sentiment of muted outrage embodied in the novel. Using the annual Christmas dinner as a backdrop, he rages that "it wasn't turkey we ate today, but human flesh! I tell you it's not mining you do, it's slaughter . . . every dollar you're paid," he concludes, "is soaking crimson wet with the blood of grandfathers and boys and soldiers and babies dead in the wombs of their bombed mothers" (1955:227).

In virtually all novels the way in which the rejected class structure can be changed is through collective action. Thus, in *Waste Heritage*, a man who gives some unemployed workers a ride comments on events that might lead even him to join others in their fight against certain injustices. "I never had no use for Reds . . . !" he insists, ' "nor for Red talk, but a man gets to look at things different when they hit him where he lives." His voice, the narrator continues, "rose suddenly in anger, 'Lookit!' he cried, 'look at the bunch of you boys here . . . no jobs, no place to go, no future, runnin' around the country like a pack of dogs. Give me another coupla years of this kind of thing,' " he promises, "an' goddamit, I'll be headin' a parade myself," ([1939] 1973:152). Despite his final disillusionment, the hero of *Down The Long Table*, an unemployed university teacher, is even more committed to collective efforts towards change. The role he sees for himself, and for others like him, however, may be somewhat grandiose. "[We] are the natural revolutionaries," he challenges, "We, not the work-drugged, half-educated machine-workers and the crestfallen workless of North America. It's we who are in the tradition of . . . Karl Marx and Nikolai Lenin . . . of

Friedrich Engels [and] Leon Trotsky" (1955:82).

In comparison to novels discussed earlier, the ideological principle embodied in novels in which there is an underlying rejection of the class structure is relatively easy to relate to more general ideological principles present in society. It is not by chance that the first of these novels as written in the Great Depression. In times of change, interpretations of the "way in which society works" that may have fallen on deaf ears in earlier, more prosperous decades, now had an audience.[17] (This no doubt explains the relatively large number of contemporary French-Canadian novels in which there is a rejection of the class structure.) Central to many of these interpretations was the notion that there must be a change in the class structure of society before any redress of the Depression's ills could be expected—notions that found expression in works discussed here.

After the Depression, a number of novels appeared in which the circumstances of the years 1929-39 were the main focus. In these, despite a general sense of disillusionment, there is still in some an underlying rejection of the class structure. That an end to the Depression and the coming of relative prosperity muted the embodied rejection is obvious.[18] Indeed, in English Canada, over the past few years there appear to be no published novels in which a rejection of the class structure is as obvious as in earlier periods.

Conclusion

We began this analysis with a number of purposes in mind. Our first intention was to show the ways in which the idea of class has found expression in English-Canadian novels and of revealing the ideological matrices in which the idea of class has been embodied.

Our second task involved the tracing, over time, of changes in these ideological matrices. The third concern was that of suggesting how the ideological configurations underlying the novel might be related to more general ideological principles present in society.

Perhaps one simple way to bring this endeavour to a conclusion is to outline, in table form, the presence or absence of particular ideological formations in novels written in various periods of our history. It is clear from Figure 2 that prior to 1870, where the idea of class did find expression in English-Canadian fiction, there was an underlying acceptance of the class structure (it must be borne in mind that very few works were produced in this period). This underlying ideology has persisted to the present. Between 1871 and 1900, by way of contrast, there emerged a clear questioning of the class structure. This tendency also has continued to the present. It was not until the 1930s, however, that there was an unmistakable rejection of the class structure embodied in the English-Canadian novel. This observation is congruent with Watt's belief that in the Great Depression a class tradition became firmly established in Canadian literature. Our contention is simply that it was in this period that the class structure was rejected in some novels. The idea of class per se had existed for some time. From the 1930s, the rejection of the class structure has continued in the English-Canadian novel; however, it has not been as pronounced as other ideologies.

If we assume that the developments suggested by Figure 2 are related to what was occurring elsewhere in society, it is obvious that a questioning of the class structure first occurred with Canadian industrialization. Indeed, a great part of the subject matter of such works concerns the abuses of machine technology in a capitalist society and reflects the concerns of certain groups in Canadian society at that time. In turn, a rejection of the class structure first occurred when the capitalist system ceased to function, even in accordance with its own assumptions. In circumstances such as these, it is not uncommon for individuals to question or reject previously held beliefs.

By suggesting this link, we do not mean to imply a mechanistic relationship between social change and the ideological principles underlying the novel. On the other hand, it

Figure II
Ideological structure of novel by period

	to 1870	1871 to 1900	1901 to 1930	1931 to 1960	1961 +
Class Structure					
Accepted	X	X	X	X	X
Questioned		X	X	X	X
Rejected				X	X

would be stretching the idea of coincidence too far to maintain that there was no link whatsoever. A clarification of this question, insofar as it relates to the English-Canadian novel, obviously awaits further inquiries.

Author's Note: We would like to thank Delores Broten, Leo Davids, Ray Ellenwood, and Judy Posner for useful comments made on an earlier draft of this paper.

Rev. canad. *Soc. & Anth./Canad. Rev. Soc. & Anth.* 15(3) 1978.

NOTES

[1]Works by French-Canadian sociologists on their literature include the following: the entire edition of *Recherches Sociographiques* 5 (1-2, 1964); Falardeau (1967); Vachon (1966). By way of contrast, there are no comparable sociological studies of English-Canadian literature.

[2]For an analysis of the influence of the United States on the sociology of English Canada see Symons (1975).

[3]For a dicussion of some themes in Canadian literature see the following: Atwood (1972); Frye (1971); Klinck et al. (1976); Moss (1974).

[4]For a dicussion of this point with respect to the United States see Ridout (1965). For information on Great Britain see Keating (1971).

[5]Throughout the study, no claims will be made as to the literary merit of the works in question. Essentially, two positions have been taken on this matter. Lucien Goldmann, for one, has argued that only great literature is worthy of study. See "Gentle structuralism in the sociology of literature" in Burns and Burns (1973). Richard Hoggart (1966), among others, in *America Scholar,* stresses the need also to study popular writing. We tend toward the latter position.

[6]A *very crude* quantitative expression of class themes in Canadian literature can be obtained from Fee and Cawker (1976). One of the undertakings of this bibliography is a rough thematic grouping of Canadian novels that appeared in *Canadian Books in Print* in 1973 and 1974. It is possible to express the novels appearing in various categories in percentage terms (see below). One of the important conclusions that can be drawn from the data is that there are few truly dominant themes in Canadian fiction, although death, marriage, Native peoples, and religion account for 24 per cent of all themes. If terrain is added to this list, 29 per cent of all novels are accounted for. Thus, despite wide diversity, it takes little iimagination to realize that there may be some quantitative support for critics who emphasize survival, etc. as dominant aspects of our literrature. A second conclusion is that social class is not a dominant theme. It nonetheless is as represented as other themes, such as immigrants. It is also important to point out that Sorokin (1962), in a mammoth study of art, sculpture, etc., over a 2,500 year span of Western civilization, found little representation of other than dominant classes in societies. In short, it seems to be the case in literature and in other forms of art that representation of other than dominant classes is the exception rather than the rule.
Themes in Canadian novels (in percentages); pioneers, 4; Depression, 2; World War I, 1; World War II, 2; animals, 3; terrain, 5; Canadian identity, 2; politics, 4; US influence, 2; Atlantic provinces, 3; BC, 2; North, 2; Quebec, 4; Prairies, 3; rural, 4; small town, 4; urban, 2; crime, 4; death, 6; human sexuality, 3; immigrants, 3; Jews, 3; magic, 1; marriage, 6; Native people, 6; poverty, 3; religion, 6; social class, 3; technology, 2; and women, 4 per cent; 99 per cent ($N = 1011$).

[7]For an overview see Harris (1968).

[8]Marx and Engels' thoughts as they relate to ideology in art and literature can be found in Baxandall and Morawski (1973) and Craig (1975). A good discussion of the early controversy in the Soviet Union over the position of literature in Marxist thought can be found in Strelka, ed. (1973).

[9]Although it has some problems, Johnson's (1972) article is a good example of a Canadian work that employs this definition.

[10]For collections of general approaches to sociology of literature see Albrecht, Barnett, and Griff, eds. (1970) and Burns and Burns (1973).

[11]Although technically not a novel, *Roughing It* is generally considered when early English-Canadian writing is analysed. Consequently, it was included here.

[12]For some discussion of these changes, see Brown and Cook (1974) and Clark (1965).

[13]See Naylor (1975) for a statement of this position.

[14]For a brief history of this concept see Lipset (1968:213 n).

[15]For a discussion of this and some other novels in this section see Vipond (1975).

[16]For the Social Gospel and Allan (1971) and Crysdale (1961). For trade unions and socialists see Horowitz (1968) and Kwavnick (1972).

[17]For discussions of the Depression see Grayson and Bliss, eds. (1971) and Gray (1966).

[18]For an assessment of the general consequences of prosperity see Clark (1970).

APPENDIX

Ted Allan, *This Time A Better Earth,* 1939.
Irene Baird, *Waste Heritage,* [1939] Toronto: Macmillan. 1973.
Earle Birney, *Down The Long Table,* Toronto: McClelland and Stewart. 1955.
Harry J. Boyle, *The Great Canadian Novel,* 1972.
Francis Brooke, *The History of Emily Montague,* 1769.
Mabel Burkholder, *The Course of Impatience Carningham,* Toronto: Musson. 1911.
J.P. Buschlen, *A Canadian Bankclerk,* [1913] Toronto: University of Toronto Press. 1973.
Juan Butler, *Cabbagetown Diary,* Toronto: Peter Martin. 1970.
Morley Callaghan, *They Shall Inherit the Earth,* 1936.
Albert R. Carman, *The Preparation of Ryerson Embry,* Toronto: The Publishers Syndicate. 1900.
Ralph Connor. *The Foreigner,* 1909.
To Him that Hath. New York: H.L. Burt, 1921.
Dyson Carter. *Fatherless Sons.* Toronto: Process Books. 1955.
Mazo de la Roche. *Delight.* Toronto: McClelland and Stewart. [1926] 1961.
S.J. Duncan. *The Imperialist.* Toronto: McClelland and Stewart. [1905] 1961.
Douglas Durkin. *The Magpie.* Toronto: University of Toronto Press. [1923] 1974.
M.A. Foran. *The Other Side.* Cleveland: Ingham, Clarke. 1886.
Sylvia Fraser. *Pandora,* 1972.
John Galbraith. *In the New Capital.* Toronto: Toronto News Co. 1897.
Hugh Garner. *Cabbagetown.* Toronto: Ryerson Press. 1951.
The Intruders. Toronto: McGraw Hill-Ryerson. 1976.
Gwethalyn Graham. *Earth and High Heaven,* 1944.
Claudius Gregory. *Forgotten Men.* Hamilton: Davis-Lisson. 1933.
F.P. Grove. *The Master of the Mill.* Toronto: McClelland and Stewart. [1944] 1961.
Hugh Hood. *The Swing in the Garden,* 1975.
Harold Horwood. *Tomorrow will be Sunday,* 1966.
Margaret Laurence. *The Diviners,* 1974.
Agnes Mayle Machar. *Roland Graeme: Knight.* Montreal: William Drysdale. 1892.
Hugh MacLennan. *Return of the Sphinx,* 1967.
The Watch that Ends the Night. Toronto: Macmillan. 1959.
John Marlyn. *Under the Ribs of Death.* Toronto: McClelland and Stewart. [1957] 1964.
Edward A. McCourt. *Music at the Close.* Toronto: Ryerson. 1947.
Ken Mitchell, *Wandering Rafferty,* 1972.
Susanna Moodie. *Roughing it in the Bush.* Toronto: McClelland and Stewart. [1852] 1962.
Len Peterson. *Chipmunk.* Toronto: McClelland and Stewart. 1949.
Mordecai Richler. *The Apprenticeship of Duddy Kravitz.* Harmondsworth: Penguin. (1959) 1968.
Jessie G. Sime. *Our Little Life,* 1921.
A.M. Stephen. *The Gleaming Archway.* Toronto: J.M. Dent and Sons. 1929.
Alan Sullivan. *The Inner Door.* Toronto: S.B. Gundy. 1917.
Scott Symons, *Civic Square,* 1969.
Catharine Parr Traill. *The Backwoods of Canada,* 1836.

REFERENCES

Albrecht, Milton C., James H. Barnett, and Mason Griff, eds. *The Sociology of Art and Literature.* New York: Praeger. 1970.
Allen, R. *The Social Passion.* Toronto: University of Toronto Press. 1971.
Atwood, Margaret. *Survival.* Toronto: Anansi. 1972.
Bohne, Harald, ed. *Canadian Books in Print.* Toronto: University of Toronto Press. 1973, 1974.
Baxandall, Lee, and Stefan Morawski. *Marx and Engels on Literature and Art.* St. Louis: Telos Press. 1973.
Brown, R.C., and Ramsay Cook. *Canada, 1896-1921: A Nation Transformed.* Toronto: McClelland and Stewart. 1974.
Burns. E. and T., eds. *Sociology of Literature and Drama.* Harmondsworth: Penguin. 1973.
Clark, S.D. *The Developing Canadian Community.* Toronto: University of Toronto Press. 1965.
"Movements of protest in postwar Canadian society." *Transactions of the Royal Society of Canada* (Series 4) 8. 1970.

Craig, David. *Marxists on Literature.* Harmondsworth: Penguin. 1975.

Cross, Michael, ed. *The Workingman in the Nineteenth Century.* Toronto: Oxford University Press. 1974.

Crysdale, S. *The Industrial Struggle and Protestant Ethics in Canada.* Toronto: Ryerson. 1961.

Falardeau, Jean-Charles. *Notre société et son roman.* Montreal: Editions HMH. 1967.

Fee, Margery, and Ruth Cawker. *Canadian Fiction: An Annotated Bibliography.* Toronto: Peter Martin Associates. 1976.

Frye, Northrop. *The Bush Garden.* Toronto: Anansi. 1971.

Goldmann, Lucien. *The Hidden God.* London: Routledge and Kegan Paul. 1964.

Pour une sociologie du roman. Paris: Gallimard. 1964.

"Genetic structuralism in the sociology of literature." In Burns and Burns, eds., *Sociology of Literature and Drama.* Harmondsworth: Penguin. 1973.

Gray, James. *The Winter Years.* Toronto: Macmillan. 1966.

Grayson, L.M., and Michael Bliss, eds. *The Wretched of Canada.* Toronto: University of Toronto Press. 1971.

Harris, Nigel. *Beliefs in Society.* London: C.A. Watts and Co. 1968.

Hoggart, Richard. "Literature and society." *American Scholar.* 35. 1966.

Horowitz, Gad. *Canadian Labour in Politics.* Toronto: University of Toronto Press. 1968.

Johnson, Leo. "The development of class in Canada in the twentieth century." In Gary Teeple, ed., *Capitalism and the National Question in Canada.* Toronto: University of Toronto Press. 1972.

Keating, P.J. *The Working Classes in Victorian Fiction.* London: Routledge and Kegan Paul. 1971.

Klinck, Carl, et al., eds. *Literary History of Canada* (Second ed.). Toronto: University of Toronto Press. 1976.

Kwavnick, David. *Organized Labour and Pressure Politics.* Montreal: McGill-Queen's University Press. 1972.

Lipset, S.M. *Revolution and Counterrevolution.* New York: Basic Books. 1963.

Lukacs, Georg. *The Meaning of Contemporary Realism.* London: Merlin Press. 1963.

Realism in our Time. New York: Harper and Row. 1964.

The Historical Novel. New York: Humanities Press. 1965.

The Theory of the Novel. Cambridge: MIT Press. 1971.

McDougall, Robert J. "The dodo and the cruising auk: class in Canadian literature." In Eli Mandel, ed., *Contexts of Canadian Criticism.* Chicago: University of Chicago Press. 1971.

Marchak, Patricia. *Ideological Perspectives on Canada.* Toronto: McGraw-Hill Ryerson. 1975.

Miller, R.U. et al., eds. *Canadian Labour in Transition.* Scarborough: Prentice-Hall. 1971.

Morton, W.L. "Victorian Canada." In W.L. Morton, ed., *The Shield of Achilles.* Toronto: McClelland and Stewart, 1968.

Moss, John. *Patterns of Isolation.* Toronto: McClelland and Stewart. 1974.

Naylor, Tom. *The History of Canadian Business. 1867-1914.* Toronto: James Lorimer. 1975.

Porter, John. *The Vertical Mosaic.* Toronto: University of Toronto Press. 1965.

"Canadian character in the twentieth century." In W.E. Mann, ed., *Canada: a Sociological Profile.* Toronto: Copp Clark. 1971.

Recherches Sociographiques 1964 5(1-2, janvier-août).

Rideout, Walter B. *The Radical Novel in the United States, 1900-1954: Some Interrelations of Literature and Society.* Cambridge: Harvard University Press. 1965.

Sorokin, Pitirim. *Social and Cultural Dynamics 1.* New York: The Bedminister Press. 1962.

Strelka, Joseph P., ed., *Literary Criticism and Sociology.* University Park: Pennsylvania State University Press. 1973.

Symons, T.H.B. *To Know Ourselves. Report of the Commission on Canadian Studies.* Ottawa: AUCC. 1975.

Vachon, Georges A. "L'espace politique et social dans le roman Québécois." *Recherches Sociographiques* 7(3). 1966.

Vipond, M. "Blessed are the peacemakers." *Journal of Canadian Studies* 10(3). 1975.

Watt, F.W. "Radicalism in English Canadian literature since Confederation." Ph.D. thesis, University of Toronto. 1957.

"Literature of protest." In Carl F. Klinck, *Literary History of Canada.* Toronto: University of Toronto Press. 1976.

Watters, Reginald E. *A Checklist of Canadian Literature* (Second ed.). Toronto: University of Toronto Press. 1972.

Young, W.D. *The Anatomy of a Party.* Toronto: University of Toronto Press. 1969.

Zeraffa, Michel. *Fictions: The Novel and Social Reality.* Harmondsworth: Penguin. 1976.

Zureik, Elia, and Robert M. Pike, eds. *Socialization and Values in Canadian Society*, Vol 1. Toronto: McClelland and Stewart. 1975.

251

AN ANALYSIS OF IDEOLOGICAL STRUCTURES AND HOW WOMEN ARE EXCLUDED: CONSIDERATIONS FOR ACADEMIC WOMEN

Dorothy E. Smith

In our society men, to a large extent, appropriate the positions that govern, administer, and manage the community. Men hold the positions from which the work of organizing the society is initiated and controlled. A distinctive feature of this social form is that the work or organizing is largely done symbolically. Things get done, or rather their doing originates and is coordinated, in words, in mathematical and other symbolic forms, on paper. It is an ideologically structured mode of action. Images, vocabularies, concepts, knowledge of and methods of knowing the world are integral to the practice of power. The work of creating the concepts and categories, and of developing the knowledge and skills which transform the actualities of the empirical into forms in which they may be governed, the work of producing the social forms of consciousness in art and literature, in news, in TV shows, plays, soap operas, etc.—this work is done by institutions which are themselves an integral part of the ruling structure. Universities, schools, broadcasting and publishing corporations, and the like are the ideological institutions of the society. They produce, distribute, and socialize in the ideological forms upon which this social organization depends.

The mode of organizing society ideologically had its origin some four or five hundred years ago in Western Europe. It is an integral aspect of the development of a capitalist mode of production. Women have been at work in its making as much as men, though their work has been of a different kind and location. But women have been largely excluded from the work of producing the forms of thought and the images and symbols in which thought is expressed and ordered. There is a circle effect. Men attend to and treat as significant only what men say. The circle of men whose writing and talk was significant to each other extends backwards in time as far as our records reach. What men were doing was relevant to men, was written by men about men for men. Men listened and listen to what one another said. A tradition is formed in this discourse of the past within the present. The themes, problematics, assumptions, metaphors, and images are formed as the circle of those present draws upon the work of the past. From this circle women have been to a large extent excluded. They have been admitted to it only by special licence and as individuals, not as representative of their sex. They can share in it only by receiving its terms and relevances and these are the terms and relevances of a discourse among men.

Throughout this period in which ideologies become of increasing importance first as a mode of thinking, legitimating, and sanctioning a social order, and then as integral in the organization of society, women have been deprived of the means to participate in creating forms of thought relevant or adequate to express their own experience or to define and raise social consciousness about their situation and concerns. They have never controlled the material or social means to the making of a tradition among themselves or to acting as equals in the ongoing discourse of intellectuals. They have had no economic status independent of men. They have not had until very recently access to the educational skills necessary to develop, sustain, and participate in it. The scope of their action has indeed over time been *progressively narrowed* to the domestic.

Women have of course had access to and used the limited and largely domestic zone of women's magazines, television programs, women's novels, poetry, soap operas, etc.

But this *is* a limited zone. It follows the contours of their restricted role in the society. The universe of ideas, images, and themes—the symbolic modes which are the general currency of thought—have been either produced by men or controlled by them. Insofar as women's work has been entered into it, it has been on terms decided by men and because it has been approved by men. This applies of course even to the writers of the women's movement.

In this paper I shall be concerned with some aspects of how the socially organized production and transmission of ideas and images deprives women of access to the means to reflect on, formulate, and express their experience and their situation. It is aimed at defining the distinctive role for women's studies which follows from the analysis. Much of what I shall say is not new as information. In fact what I want to do is to make observable some of the socially organized aspects of what we already know. It is a problem of tying things into a single framework which shows how they belong together. I want therefore to make use of the familiar in drawing up an account as a context within which the character and objectives of women's studies in sociology and in other academic fields might be conceived.

The Concept of Ideology

The conceptual framework used in the analysis makes the concept of ideology its key. In developing this analytic framework, I have returned to the formulation made by Marx and Engels in *The German Ideology* (1970), bypassing some of the very different traditions of use which are built into the contemporary practice. The meaning of the word ideology has been reduced to the notion of political beliefs.

There are two aspects of Marx's and Engels' formulation of the concept, only the second of which will be used here. First, they use ideology as a key term in a methodological critique of ways of thinking of social concepts and categories (the forms of thought) as if they were autonomous powers or agents in society, independent of those who think them and of the actual practical situations in which that thought arises and to which it is relevant. Second, they are concerned with ideology as a means through which the class that rules a society orders and sanctions the social relations which support its hegemony. The concept of ideology here focuses on social forms of consciousness (the ways in which people think and talk with one another) which originate outside the actual working relations of people going about their everyday business and are imposed upon them.

Marx and Engels held that how people think about their social relations and the social order and the ways in which they define themselves and their environment in relation to the social order arise out of their actual working relations and the discourse which accompanies and expresses them. 'The production of ideas, of conceptions, of consciousness, is at first directly interwoven with the material activity and the material intercourse of men, the language of real life. Conceiving, thinking, the mental intercourse of men appear at this stage as the direct efflux of their material behaviour. The same applies to mental production as expressed in the language of politics, laws, morality, religion, metaphysics, etc., of a people' (Marx and Engels, 1970:47). Originally then and perhaps in some sense 'naturally' (though this term must always be used with caution) the forms of thought arise directly out of and express people's working relations, their actual situation, their experience. With the emergence of a class society, however, 'mental production' becomes the privilege of a ruling class. Note here that Marx and Engels do not use the term ruling class as it has come to be used since then. It does not with them refer to a political elite. It refers rather to that class which dominates a society by virtue of its control of the means of production (1970:64). Among those means are the means of mental production.

In following their use of the concept of ideology we attend to the production of ideas by a specialized set of persons located in a ruling class. The ideas, images, etc., are produced for others to use, to analyse, to understand, and to interpret their social relations, what is happening, the world that they experience and act in. These systems of ideas are a pervasive and fundamental mode in which the organizing and control of this form of society is done. It is important to recognize that these social forms of thought originate in a practice of ruling—or management, or administration, or other forms of social control. They are located in and originate from definite positions of dominance in the society. They are not merely that neutral floating thing, the 'culture'.

The contrast implicit in their formulation is on the one hand between ideas, images—the social forms of thought—which are directly expressive of a world directly known and which arise where it needs to be thought and to be said and, on the other, the social forms of thought which come to us from outside, which do not arise out of experience and the needs to communicate with others in working contexts. Characteristic of the latter is a way of proceedings which *begins* from a knowledge of the ideas and images and how to use them and examines, interprets, assembles, and formulates the world of direct experience as instances of them. We come thus to know it in the terms in which it is ruled.

The forms of thought are learned. We receive them in what we read, whether books, magazines, comic-books, newspapers, or whatever; we receive them both conceptually and as images (a powerful and new ideological form in this type of society) on television and in movies; we hear them on the radio and second-hand in the ways in which the ordinary talk depends upon these media resources. The scope and intensiveness of the production of the social forms of thought is greater in this type of society than in any previously known.

The ideas and images are a pervasive and fundamental mode which serves to organize, order, and control the social relations, the working practices, the ideals and objectives, of individual members of the society. These are the forms given to people to understand what is happening to them, what other people are doing, particularly those not directly part of their lives. These are the means we are given to examine our experience, our needs and anxieties, and find out how they can be made objective and realized (made real) as a basis for action. Ideology in our form of society provides an authorization of social reality. Perhaps more than that which can become recognized as real in the socially constructed reality is what is already interpretable in the ideological forms of thought. The practice of the ideological analysis of experience is circular. Not proceeding by hypothesis, inference, and evidence, but by a process called 'typification' (Schutz, 1966) which analyses and assembles what is given

in experience to find in it the type which it intends.

The concept of ideology as I am developing its use here identifies a *practice* or *method* in the use of ideas and images which is ideological rather than a determinate object or type of object. I want to be able to recognize the ideological aspects of, or methods of using, the work of poets and artists and religious thinkers as well as the work of sociologists, political scientists, economists, etc. I do not, however, want to reduce the poem to its ideological use. I am not trying to suggest that everything that is produced by an intelligentsia can be reduced to this. I am holding rather that many types of literary as well as religious work have an ideological dimension and lend themselves to ideological uses. Works of many kinds may serve to order, legitimate, and organize social relations and the socially relevant aspects of experience. It is this function which is identified as ideology here. Insofar as these works are produced by that section of a ruling class known as the intelligentsia; insofar as they present as generally valid and authoritative the view and sense of the world from the specific position of its ruling class; insofar as they sanction and formulate determinate forms of social relations and serve to organize the local, particular, and directly known into the social forms of thought and discourse in which it is or can be ruled—they are ideological.

The model of manipulation from behind the scenes, the model of ideology as ideas designed to deceive and fool the innocent and ignorant put forward consciously and with malign intent by a ruling elite, is quite inadequate to analyse the phenomena we are concerned with. We are describing a class phenomenon. This means that we are locating a determinate set of positions in relation to a structure of power which constitute a common perspective, set of relevances, conditions of experience, interests, and objectives. People who occupy these positions arrogate certain powers. They have these powers because of their positions. Because of their positions they view the world in particular ways; they experience common conditions with others similarly placed. Things make sense to them in terms of projects and relevances which are not only similar but often directly related to one another. This class of positions controls the

254

means of 'mental production' as Marx and Engels describe it. Hence what is produced takes for granted the conditions of their experiences their interests and relevances. The forms of thought which are produced in this way assume the background conditions and knowledges which these positions are embedded in. They assume the moral and political values of the discourses of which they are part. They assume the dilemmas and contradictions and anxieties they give rise to. *And above all they take for granted the silences of those who do not hold these positions, who are outside.*

And as we know, those who occupy and appropriate those positions are men. Marx and Engels' account of ideology identifies it with the ruling class. It is now clear that the class basis of ideology is articulated yet further to a sex basis. For it is men who produce for women, as well as for other members of the society, the means to think and image. In the various social apparatuses concerned with the production and distribution of ideas and images, or with the training of people to participate in and respond to these forms of thought, it is men who occupy the positions of authority, men who predominate in the production of ideas and social knowledge, and men who control what enters the discourse by occupying the positions which do the work of gatekeeping and the positions from which people and their 'mental products' are evaluated.

Women's Exclusion Actively Enforced

The exclusion of women from these positions is not a function of their biology. Of course there have existed bases of exclusion in the social determinants of their role, but in this sphere there is a history of active repression. Women who have claimed the right to speak authoritatively as women have been repressed. I have made up from various sources a short list of instances.

Though we cannot assign a definite date to the emergence of ideological formations, the translation of the Bible into the vernacular languages of Europe is a good place to begin. At this point a written source which sanctified direct interpretations of moral and cosmological order became accessible to anyone who could read. The authority of the scriptures thus became anyone's authority and women were among those who could

grasp it. Our first example then is from this period.

1/Sylvia Thrupp in *The Merchant Class of Mediaeval London* tells us of Joan Boughton and her daughter Lady Yonge: 'The only evidence of heretical leanings in the city's merchant class concerns women. Sir John Yonge's mother-in-law, Joan Boughton, was burnt as a heretic in 1495, at the age of eighty, defying all the doctors in London to shake her faith in the tenets of Wycliffe, and a few years later Lady Yonge followed her to the stake. Pecock had complained of women "which maken hem self so wise bi the Bible," who would insist on disputing with the clergy and would admit no practice to be virtuous, "save what thei kunnen fynde expresseli in the Bible" ' (Thrupp, 1962:252).

2/Sheila Rowbotham gives an account of the trial and banishment of Anne Hutchison from Massachusetts in the seventeenth century: ' "You have stepped out of your place," the Calvinist church fathers in the Massachusetts Bay colony told Anne Hutchison in the mid-seventeenth century. "You have rather been a husband than a wife, and a preacher than a hearer, and a magistrate than a subject, and so you have thought to carry all things in Church and Commonwealth as you would and have not been humbled for it" ' (Rowbotham, 1973:17). Notice here a theme which we shall find again. It is not what she said that she is condemned for. It is rather that as a woman she claimed to speak as one who had authority. 'They worked hard at humbling her. She had gathered round her a group of followers, mostly women. They met together and Anne Hutchison preached on texts, criticized some of the ministers, and became respected for her knowledge of scripture and of healing herbs . . . She upset Calvinist dogma, political differentiation, and masculine superiority. She was accordingly tried by both civil and religious authority. Pregnant and ill, at one stage while she was being questioned she almost collapsed, but they wouldn't let her sit down . . . Finally she faltered and confessed to heresy. But they were still not satisfied. "Her repentence is not in her countenance." She was banished from the colony' (Rowbotham, 1973:17).

3/Many women were active in the French revolution. They were organized in active revolutionary clubs. In the fall of 1793 after

Marat's assassination, the Convention decided to prohibit women's clubs and societies. Two of the leading women, Olympe de Gouges (on 3 November 1793) and Manon Roland (on 8 November 1793) were guillotined. Here is the official interpretation of what women were to learn from their deaths: 'In a short time the Revolutionary Tribunal has given women a good lesson which will no doubt not be lost on them . . . Olympe de Gouges wished to be a statesman, and it seems that the law has punished that conspiratress for having forgotten the virtues appropriate to her sex. The woman Roland was a mother, but wished to rise above herself; the desire to be a savant led her to forget her sex, and that forgetfulness, always dangerous, finished by causing her to perish on the scaffold' (des Jacques, 1972:139).

4/ Mrs Packard was imprisoned in the State of Illinois Insane Asylum for three years from 1860 to 1863 under a law which permitted a man to commit his wife or child to an asylum on his word alone and without other evidence of insanity. Mrs Packard was married to a Calvinist minister. She came to hold religious and political views very different from those of her husband. Her attorney describes the difference as follows: 'Her views of religion are more in accordance with the liberal views of the age in which we live (than those of her husband). She scouts the Calvinistic doctrine of man's total depravity, and that God has foreordained some to be saved and others to be damned. She stands fully on the platform of man's free agency and accountability to God for his actions . . . She believes slavery to be a national sin, and the church and the pulpit a proper place to combat this sin. These, in brief, are the points in her religious creed which were combated by Mr Packard, and were denominated by him as "emanations from the devil," or "the vagaries of a crazed brain" ' (Szasz, 1973:57-58). It was not, however, the content of her beliefs alone which led to the decision that she was insane. Her husband had called in three physicians who as expert witnesses testified in the court procedures to her insanity. Her claim to speak as authority in religious and moral matters was judged insane: 'QUESTION: What else did she say or do there, that showed marks of insanity? ANSWER: She claimed to be better than her husband–that she was right– and that he was wrong–and that all she did

was good, and all he did was bad . . . (Szasz, 1973:66). Her case became a *cause célèbre*. After her release from the asylum in which she had been held, Mrs Packard was active in getting the law changed in Illinois.

5/ In Paris during the student uprising of 1968 a feminist group on the Left had prepared leaflets: 'As we walked around we handed out leaflets, particularly to women. A crowd of about a hundred people followed us around; most of them were hostile. We had been prepared for significant opposition from men, even afraid of it; but even so were not prepared for such depth and breadth of outrage. Here were "movement" men shouting insults at us: "Lesbians," "Strip;" "What you need is a good fuck . . . " ' (quoted by Mitchell, 1972:86).

6/ In 1969 a major demonstration in Washington was organized on the occasion of Nixon's inauguration. A women's group had arranged to burn their voter's registration cards to demonstrate how little getting the vote had done to change women's oppression. As the rally went on, the group began to sense that they were not going to be given a chance to speak. 'Dave Dellinger introduces the rally with a stirring denunciation of the war and racism. "What about women, you schmuck," I shout. "And, uh, a special message from Women's Liberation," he adds. Our moment comes. M., from the Washington group, stands up to speak. This isn't the protest against the movement men, which is the second on the agenda, just fairly innocuous radical rhetoric–except that it's a good looking woman talking about women. The men go crazy. "Take it off!" "Take her off the stage and fuck her!" ' (Ellen Willis, quoted by Mitchell, 1972:85).

This is the rough stuff. It points to a boundary which we are not aware of until we read such instances. They show us that more is involved than can be met simply by a work of reasoning and persuasion. There is a social structuring of authority which is prior to and a condition of the development among women of the means to express themselves and to make their condition actionable. Women are defined as persons who have no right to speak as authorities in religious or political settings. Deprived of this right, how can what they might have to say become a basis for knowledge, symbol, moral sanction, complaints, claims, or action? In most of the instances I have cited, it is the claim to authority which is the crucial impiety.

Male Control of the Educational System

The exclusion of women from participating actively in making and creating the forms under which social relations are thought and spoken of has seldom to be so violently repressed. The ordinary socially organized processes of socialization, education, work, and communication performs a more routine, generalized, and effective repression. The educational system is an important aspect of this practice. It trains people in the skills they need in order to participate, at various levels, in the ideological forms of social control (they must be able to read); it trains them in the images and the forms of what the ideology sanctions as real; it trains them in the appropriate relations and in the how to identify authoritative ideological sources (what kinds of books, newspapers, etc., to credit, what to discredit, *who* are the authoritative writers or speakers and who are not). It is part of the system which distributes ideas and ensures the dissemination of new ideological forms as these are produced by the intelligentsia. It is also active itself in producing ideology, both in forms of knowledge in the social sciences, psychology, and education, and in the forms of critical ideas and theories in philosophy and literature.

Prior to the late nineteenth century women were almost completely denied access to any form of higher education beyond the skills of reading and writing. One of the first major feminist works, Mary Wollstonecraft's *Vindication of the Rights of Women*, places their right to education at the centre of her argument. She is responding specifically to Rousseau's prescriptions for educating women which aim to train them for dependency, for permanent childishness, and for permanent incapacity for the autonomous exercise of mind (Wollstonecraft, 1967). During the latter part of the nineteenth century in both Europe and North America opportunities for women in higher education were a major focus of women's struggle. Though women's participation in the educational process at all levels has increased in this century, this participation remains within marked boundaries. Among the most important of these boundaries, I would argue, is that which reserves to men control of the policy-making

and decision-making apparatus in the educational system.

In this section I am going to present some of the by now familiar figures which describe how women are located in the educational system as teachers and administrators. I shall not be concerned with viewing these under the aspect of social justice. I am not concerned here with equality of opportunity. I want rather to draw attention to the significance of the inequalities we find for how women are located in the processes of setting standards, producing social knowledge, acting as 'gate-keepers' over what is admitted into the systems of distribution, innovating in thought or knowledge or values and in other ways participating as authorities in the ideological work done in the educational process.

In 1970-1, according to the Department of Labour statistics, women were 62.6 per cent of teachers in public schools at all levels.[1] In 1969-70 at the elementary school level where the major focus is the teaching of basic skills, they formed 75.0 per cent of teachers (this figure is for eight provinces only. Quebec and Ontario data were not available).[2] At the secondary school level young people receive not only a training in academic and vocational skills. They are also given substantive training in the ideological forms which regulate the social relations of the society (in sports as much as in history or English literature). At this level men predominated, and only 34.0 per cent of teachers were women (eight provinces only).

At each next point upward in the hierarchy of control over the educational process, the proportion of women declines. In 1969-70 only 23.6 per cent of principals were women (eight provinces only), though there is considerable varition by province.[3] The figures showing the proportion of women school superintendents or the location of women in Departments of Education are not readily available, but there is no reason to believe that we would see a different over-all picture.[4]

Figures on the educational staffs of community colleges show distributions in the same direction. In 1970-1 women were only 18.6 per cent.[5] At the university level the same pattern is apparent. Gladys Hitchman has brought together the data from studies of six Canadian universities (Alberta, Queen's, McGill, McMaster, UBC, Waterloo). An av-

257

Table I
Percentage of Women in Academic Status Categories for Six Canadian
Universities*

	Alberta (1971)	Queen's (1972)	McGill (1970-71)	McMaster (1969)	UBC (1972)	Waterloo (1972)
Lecturers/instructors	68.1	25.0	46.3	26.6	41.9	11.9
Assistant professors	20.0	13.0	19.2	11.9	18.7	9.5
Associate professors	9.1	3.5	12.3	7.2	9.3	3.6
Full professors	4.8	0.5	5.5	3.1	3.4	1.5
Chairpersons	n.d.	0.0	n.d.	n.d.	n.d.	0.0
Total faculty	16.1	7.7	16.8	11.0	18.1	5.3
(n.d. = no data)						

* Based on Hitchman, 1974.

Table II
Percentage Of Women In Non-Tenured And Tenured Positions For Six Canadian
Universities*

	Alberta (1971)	Queen's (1972)	McGill (1970-71)	McMaster (1969)	UBC (1972)	Waterloo (1972)
Non-tenured	44.5	19.0	32.75	19.25	30.3	10.7
Tenured	6.95	2.0	8.9	5.15	6.35	3.55
Difference	37.55	17.0	23.85	14.10	23.95	8.15

* Estimate based on Hitchman, 1974.

erage of the percentages of women at all ranks in these six is 12.54 per cent. Over-all the figures from schools, community colleges, and universities indicate an inverse relation between level in the education 'hierarchy' and the proportion of women.

Within the university the same pattern is repeated. The data brought together by Gladys Hitchman (1974) appear in Table I. The inverse relation between status level and proportion of women is obvious at every level and in all six universities. Women are most heavily concentrated in the positions of lecturer and instructor which are not part of the promotional system leading to professorial rank (the so-called 'ladder' positions), and are usually held on only a one-year contract. There is an appreciable drop even to the next level of junior positions, the assistant professors—the first step on the promotion ladder. Women form a very small proportion of full professors.

It is important to keep in mind that we are looking at rather powerful structures of professional control. It is through this structure of ranks and the procedures by which people are advanced from one to another that the professions maintain control over the nature and quality of work that is done and the kinds of people who are admitted to its ranks and to influential positions within it. Two points are of special importance: first the concentration of women in the relatively temporary non-ladder positions. This means that they are largely restricted to teaching, that their work is subject to continual review, and that reappointment is conditional upon conformity. The second point to note is the marked break in the proportion of women between tenured and non-tenured positions. I have made averages from Hitchman's tables in order to bring this out (see Table II). However, please note that this is a rather rough procedure and the results can be treated as estimates only.

There are considerable variations between universities, largely produced by the differences in proportions of women at the lecturer and instructor level. However, here we are concerned not with accounting for the variations or the over-all pattern but with looking at what it tells us about the structures of professional control in the university. The fig-

Table III
Percentage Of Women By Rank In Fields With Ideological Functions, UBC, 1972

	Arts	Education	Commerce	Law
Lecturer	44.8	44.4	0	0
Instructor	57.0	38.0	0	0
Assistant professor	21.2	33.3	0	0
Associate professor	10.8	17.0	0	0
Full professor	2.7	15.0	0	0

Source: Report on the Status of Women at the University of British Columbia, Table VIII.

ures show very clearly a marked jump between proportions of women in tenured and non-tenured positions, ranging from a difference of 8.15 percentage points at Waterloo to 37.55 at Alberta. (The lower break at Waterloo is a function of the lower proportions of women employed at any rank.)

These figures show us that at these six Canadian universities women are markedly underrepresented in positions of full membership of university and profession. These are positions in which their continued employment is no longer subject to the continual scrutiny of their senior colleagues. They are also those from which decisions are made about the continued employment of those as yet without tenure. If we look at these figures as if they represented votes, we find women woefully underrepresented. Only two votes in every hundred at Queen's, and at best only about nine in every hundred at McGill.

The tenured faculty to a large extent control who shall be admitted to its ranks and what shall be recognized as properly scholarly work.[6] This minimal 'voting power' of women helps us to understand why women in more senior positions in the university do not ordinarily represent women's perspectives. They are those who have been passed through this very rigorous filter. They are those whose work and style of work and conduct have met the approval of judges who are largely men. And, in any case, *they are very few.*

There is, I have suggested, more than one type of ideological function in contemporary society. There is that which is concerned with the general moral and expressive modes and with the political and philosophical interpretations which are generalized in the society. There is also that which is directly built into the modes of organizing the various corporate, bureaucratic and professional enterprises which govern the society. There are, we might say, two forms of ideology – the ideologies of expression, evaluation, and theory, and the ideologies of organized action. Women's relation to these two modes are different. Their access to the means of expression and the means of representation of their interests and perspectives in the ideological forms which govern the society are very differently structured. Some figures from a study done by the Women's Action Group (1972) at the University of British Columbia give us a clearer picture of the effect I am now trying to describe. The faculties of arts (which at the University of British Columbia includes the social sciences) and education represent the ideologies of expression and theory; the fields of commerce and law represent ideologies of organized action. These have of course very different relations to the power structures of the society – the latter being directly implicated in the formations and media in which power is exercised, while the former exercises primarily a control of regulatory function. Table III shows how women are located in these fields. It shows quite clearly that from those ideological fields which are directly involved in preparing people for positions in the managerial and governing structure, namely commerce and law, women are completely excluded. They are excluded thereby from occupying the positions in which innovative thinking in those professions is most likely to be done. Therefore they do not participate, at least from positions of authority from which their thinking may enter directly into the training and preparation of professionals, in forming the conceptual framework and relevances in which professionals in these fields are trained.

The differences between arts and education

are also suggestive. Faculties of education are concerned with training and distribution of knowledge, skills, and the forms of thought. Though innovative work is done in educational theory and practice, it is innovative as a means of transmitting a substance which originates elsewhere. At least in some of the arts fields, critical standards and procedures are being developed and concepts and knowledges originate. The direction of the difference between education and arts indicates the same effect. In the 'ladder' positions from assistant professors up, there are lower percentages of women at each rank in arts than in education. The loci of ideological production are largely controlled by men.

In this section I have suggested that we can see two major aspects with respect to how women are located in the educational system. One is that the closer positions come to policy-making or innovation in ideological forms, the smaller the proportion of women. The second is that the closer the ideological forms are to the conceptual and symbolic forms in which power is exercised, the less likely women are to be found in the relevant professional educational structures.

Authority

The control by men of the ideological forms which regulate social relations in this form of society is structured socially by an authority they hold as individuals by virtue of their membership in a class. Authority is a form of power which is a distinctive capacity to get things done in words. What is said or written merely means what the words mean until and unless it is given force by the authority attributed to its 'author.' When we speak of authority we are speaking of what makes what one person says count. Men are invested with authority as individuals not because they have as individuals special competencies or expertise but because as men they appear as representative of the power and authority of the institutionalized structures which govern the society. Their authority as *individuals* in actual situations of action is generated by a social organization. They do not appear as themselves alone. They are those whose words count, both for each other and for those who are not members of this class (note, I am not using the term 'class' here in a Marxist sense. It bears its ordinary dictionary meaning only.).

We have by now and in various forms a good deal of evidence of the ways in which this social effect works. It is one which Mary Ellman has described as a distinction between women and men in intellectual matters, 'which is simple, sensuous and insignificant: the male body lends credence to assertions, while the female takes it away' (Ellman, 1968:148). A study done by Philip Goldberg which was concerned with finding out whether women were prejudiced against women demonstrates this effect very clearly (Goldberg, (1969). Here is Jo Freeman's description: 'He gave college girls sets of booklets containing six identical professional articles in traditional male, female and neutral fields. The articles were identical, but the names of the authors were not. For example, an article in one set would bear the name John T. McKay and in another set the same article would be authored Joan T. McKay. Each booklet contained three articles by "women" and three by "men". Questions at the end of each article asked the students to rate the articles on value, persuasiveness and profundity and the authors on writing style and competence. The male authors fared better in every field, even such "feminine" areas as Art History and Dietetics' (Freeman, 1970). There seems to be something like a plus factor which adds force and persuasiveness to what men say and a minus factor which depreciates and weakens what is said by women.

A study reported by Jessie Bernard describes this effect in the context of teaching. A woman and a man were chosen by their department as being roughly equal in their ability to communicate. Each gave two identical lectures, which were in fact chapters from books by established sociologists. The study was concerned with finding out whether students learned more from one sex than the other. As determined by examination results, there was no difference. However, other differences did emerge and it is these that are relevant here. 'The young woman had less impact than the young man. Many more of her listeners gave neutral or impersonal résumés of the talk when tested. The young man evoked much more reaction' (Bernard, 1964:256). There was a difference in 'credibility': 'Fewer of the young man's listeners than of the young woman's hid behind the "he said" dodge. They accepted what he said as fact. The implication is that material presented by a man is more likely to be accepted at face value than material presented by a woman: it seems to have more authority; it is more important' (Bernard, 1964:257). This effect must generally diminish the authority of women teachers (at all levels) vis-à-vis students. I refer the reader to a moving retrospective account by one of Suzanne Langer's students which expresses this (Pochoda, 1972). Once brought into focus it is, I believe, an effect which academic women can recognize at once as an ordinary working condition.

It is not of course confined to academia. The way in which the sex of the speaker modifies the authority of the message has been observed in other ideological fields. Lucy Komisar reports that in advertising women 'receive instructions about how to do their housework from men: Arthur Godfrey, who probably never put his hands into soapsuds, tells women across the country why they ought to add still another step to their washing routine with Axion Pre-Soak. Joseph Daley, president of Grey Advertising, says that *men are used because the male voice is the voice of authority*' (Komisar, 1972, my emphasis). Chesler's study of preferences among psychotherapists and their patients shows that the majority of women patients prefer male therapists and that the majority of male psychotherapists prefer women patients. The reasons women give for preferring male psychotherapists are that they generally feel more comfortable with them and that they have more respect for and confidence in a man's competence and authority. Chesler reports that both men and women in her sample said that they trusted and respected men as people and as authorities more than they did women (Chesler, 1972).

A study done by Fidell on sex discrimination in university hiring practices in psychology shows the intersection of this effect with the educational system of controls described in the preceding section. She used an approach very similar to Goldberg's, constructing two sets of fictional descriptions of academic background and qualifications (including the PH D). Identical descriptions in one set had a woman's name attached and in the other a man's. The sets of descriptions were sent to chairpersons of all colleges and universities in the United States offering graduate degrees in psychology. They were asked to estimate the chance of the individuals described getting an offer of a position and at what level, etc. Her findings supported the hypothesis of discrimination on the basis of sex: 'The distributions of level of appointment were higher for men that for women. Further, men received more "on line" (academic positions leading to tenure) responses than women. Only men were offered full professorships' (Fidell, 1970). It seems as though the class attribution of authority which increases the value of men's work constitutes something rather like a special title to the positions of control and influence and hence to full active membership in the intelligentsia.

This effect is socially constructed. It is not a biological attribute. This becomes more observable when we attend to the social class dimensions of authority. It is not, as Ellman (1968) suggests, merely the male *body*, but rather the male body literally *clothed* in the trappings of his class which 'lends credence to assertions.' The working man, the native Indian, the black man are also depreciated. It is a social effect which preserves the status and control of male members of the ruling classes over the ideological forms and at the same time renders that control effective as authority.

These patterns are integral to the *social organization* of the ideological formations of this type of society. More than one study has shown that well-educated and middle-class people have what may be described as greater deference[7] to the opinions and perspectives of interviewers who represent the 'university' than do people with relatively little education (Schatzman and Strauss, 1966: Komarovsky, 1967). Pheterson's findings in a study using procedures similar to Goldberg's but limiting the topics of articles to matters within the women's domain, found that middle-aged 'uneducated' women did not respond as Goldberg's college student respondents had (Goldberg, 1969). Hochschild describes her findings thus: 'Pheterson (1969) explored prejudice against women among middle-aged, uneducated women. This time the professional articles were on child discipline, special education, and marriage. The women judged female work to be equal to and even a bit better than male work' (1973). Some women at least appear not to be fully integrated into the social organization of ideological formation. In some areas of discourse at least men are not constituted as authority. The class structure mediated by educational institutions is differentially articulated to this social organization. 'Educated' middle-class women are fully part of it. Their subordination is the second term which constitutes the grammar of authority. Their silence is integrated into and generated by its organization (Gornick, 1972: Smith, 1974).

Circles

The metaphor of a 'circle' of speakers and hearers relevant to one another is helpful in conceptualizing this as an aspect of the social organization of ideology. It seems likely that the process of developing ideological forms is controlled by restricting participation in such 'circles' to properly authorized participants. Only the perspectives and thinking of these get *entered* into the discourse as its themes and topics. Jessie Bernard describes this in the academic context as 'the stag effect' (Bernard, 1964:157) and refers to an informal experiment in which professional subjects were asked to name the top 10 in their field. Leading women members of the profession were unlikely to be mentioned. 'When this was pointed out to the subjects, they tended to look sheepish and say they never thought of her. She was not in the same image of their profession as were the men . . . It is not that the work of distinguished women scholars was not taken seriously; it was only that in most disciplines the image of the professional did not include them' (Bernard, 1964:176).

It seems that women as a social category lack proper title to membership in the circle of those who count for one another in the making of ideological forms. To identify a woman novelist as a woman novelist is to place her in a special class outside that of novelists in general. The minus factor attached to what they say, write, or image described in the previous section, is another way of seeing how what they say, write, or image is not 'automatically' part of the discourse. I suggest that if we observe how these things get done in our professions, in literary reviews, and in ordinary situations of meeting among professionals, we would see that what women say and do has a conditional status only. It awaits recognition by a fully qualified male participant. It awaits sanction. It must be picked up (and sometimes taken over) by a man if it is to become part of the discourse.

The previous discussion has been concerned largely with the authority of the written or printed word. But these are patterns which are clearly observable in face to face interaction also. We can and have observed them ourselves. There are by now a number of studies which serve to fill out our description of how male control over the topics and themes of discourse is maintained in actual situations of interaction. For example, Strodt-beck and Marm in their study of jury deliberations report that men talked considerably more than women. The differences however were more than quantitative. They also describe what seems to be a general pattern of interaction between women and men. Men's talk was more directed towards the group task while women reacted with agreement, passive acceptance, and understanding (Strodt-beck and Marm, 1956). The pattern I have observed also involves women becoming virtually an audience, facilitating with support or comments, but not becoming among those who carry the talk and whose remarks are directed towards one another.

Characteristically women talking with men use styles of talk which throw the control to others. As for example by interspersing their talk with interjections which reassign the responsibility for its meaning to others, as by saying 'you know' or failing to name objects or things or to complete sentences. Expectations for men's and women's speech differs and must have an effect on how people are seen with respect to how and how much to talk. Caudill describes a supervisor of nurses as 'an assertive person,' willing to express her opinion in unequivocal terms.' Yet his data show that in meetings she spoke less on the average than the hospital administrative and psychiatric personnel, including a resident described as 'passive and withdrawn' (Caudill, 1958:249).

Candy West has made a study of differences between single sex and mixed sex conversations which focuses upon the differential rights to speak of men and women (1974). She observed a variety of different 'devices' used by men apparently with women's consent which serve to maintain male control of the topics of conversation. For example, men tended to complete women's sentences, to give minimal responses to topics initiated and carried by women, and to interrupt without being sanctioned. She gives one example from a transcribed conversation which went as follows: 'After thirty lines of talk, during which the female lays out a problem she's having and the male responds minimally on every occasion of his turn arising, a twenty-five second pause ensues. Then he commences to discuss a paper *he's* working on—without semantically having *ever* acknowledged her subject' (West, 1974:37). Her study describes 'a pattern of male control of conversation, principally through the use of interruptions and the withdrawal of active participation in topic development' (West, 1974:19-20).

In professional conversations we can also identify a collection of devices which may be used to restrict women's control of what West calls 'topic development.' Among them are devices which are used to recognize or enter what women have said into the discourse under male sanction. For example a suggestion or point contributed by a woman may be ignored at its point of origin. When it is re-introduced at a later point by a man, it is then 'recognized' and becomes part of the topic. Or if it is recognized at the time, it is re-attributed by the responder to another male (in the minutes of the meeting, it will appear as having been said by someone else). Or the next speaker after the woman may use a device such as 'What Dorothy really means is . . . ' Or the woman's turn is followed by a pause following which the topic is picked up at the previous speaker's turn as if she had not spoken. We can I am sure add to the list of these devices and also cite many exceptions to these patterns. They arise, however, out of very general assumptions about the socially organized relations of men and women in relation to control of the ideological forms of the society. Their specifics may vary, but the over-all patterns of control over topics and themes recur. The social organization of men-women relations in such contexts can be understood as generating the appropriate practices, devices, and perceptions as these are situationally relevant and appropriate. The grammar of these relations is understood by both sexes. It is not simply imposed by men upon women. Women participate in the ways in which they are silenced.

Women as Subject

I have focused here on the various ways in which women have been and are excluded from full participation in creating the forms of thought which constitute the social consciousness of a society. By this point in the women's movement I believe we must be familiar with the effect of this. Modes of thinking and imaging our experience are produced for us by others who do not share our experience or position in the world. They are produced by those who hold the superordinate positions in the society and whose consciousness extends into the world as a reflection of the structures of power within which they act upon and know it. De Beauvoir in *The Second Sex* (1961) has made an important distinction between men as subjects and women as other. It is as if the world is thought from the position of a consciousness which has its centre in a ruling class of men—what Kate Millett has described as 'the patriarchy' (Millett, 1971). From this centre women appear as objects. In relation to men of these classes women's consciousness does not appear as autonomous origin of knowledge, an authoritative perspective on the world from a different position in and experience of it. Women do not appear to men as men do to one another, as persons who might share in the common construction of a social reality. It is the social organizational substructure of this relation which we have been assembling in the preceding sections. We have begun to look at this relation as it is actually practised and enforced. If women have failed to find a position from which we might reflect back upon men as subjects, it is these institutionalized structures and practices excluding us from functioning *as* subject which *enforce* our failure.

It is important to recognize that the deprivation of authority and the ways in which women have been trained to practise the complement of male control of 'topic development' (West, 1974:20) have the effect of making it difficult for women to treat one another as relevant figures. We have difficulty in asserting authority for ourselves. We have difficulty in grasping authority for women's voices and for what women have to say. We are thus deprived of the essential basis for developing among ourselves the discourse out of which symbolic structures, concepts, images, and knowledges might develop which would be adequate to our experience and to devising forms of organization and action relevant to our situations and interests. In participating in the world of ideas as objects rather than as subjects we have come to take for granted that our thinking is to be authorized by an external source of authority. Thus as Bostock says: 'One of the consequences of living in a world intellectually dominated by men . . . is that women try to have opinions which will satisfy the approved standards of the world; and in the last analysis these are standards imposed on them by men, which, in practice, means that our opinions are kept fairly rigorously separated from our own lived experience. If a woman today wants to have opinions which are truly her own, she has to check them against her experience; and often not against her personal experience alone, *but against a collective one'* (Bostock, 1972, my emphasis). Bostock is laying down an essential condition to the development by women for women of social forms of consciousness. But it has not been easy for women to take what women have to say as authoritative, nor is it easy for women to find their own voices convincing. It is hard for us to listen to ourselves. The voice of our own experience is equally defective.

Lack of authority then is lack of authority for ourselves and for other women. We have become familiar in the women's movement with the importance of women learning to *relate* to one another. We need also to learn how to treat what other women say as a source and basis for our own work and thinking.

The institutionalized practices of excluding women from the ideological work of society is the reason we have a history constructed largely from the perspective of men, and largely about men. This is why we have so few women poets and why the records of those who survived the hazards of attempting poetry are so imperfect (Bernikow, 1974). This is why we know so little of women visionaries, thinkers, and political organizers (Rowbotham, 1973). This is why we have an anthropology which tells us about other societies from the perspective of men and hence has so distorted the cross-cultural record that it may now be impossible to learn what we might have known about how women lived in other forms of society. This is why we have a sociology which is written from the perspective of positions in a male-dominated ruling class and is set up in terms of the relevances of the institutional power structures which con-

stitute those positions (Bernard, 1973). This is why in English literature there is a corner called women in literature or women novelists or the like, but an over-all critical approach to literature which assumes that it is written by men and perhaps even largely for men.

The ideological practices of our society provide us with forms of thought and knowledge which constrain us to treat ourselves as objects. We have learned to practise, as Rowbotham points out, a nihilistic relation to our own subjectivity and experience (Rowbotham, 1974:29-37). We have learned to live inside a discourse which is not ours and which expresses and describes a landscape in which we are alienated and which preserves that alienation as integral to its practice. In a short story Doris Lessing describes a girl growing up in Africa whose consciousness has been wholly formed within traditional British literary culture. Her landscape, her cosmology, her moral relations, her botany, are those of the English novels and fairytales. Her own landscape, its forms of life, her immediate everyday world do not fully penetrate and occupy her consciousness. They are not *named* (Lessing, 1966). This is the ideological rupture which Marx and Engels have given us the means to understand. Lessing's story is a paradigm of the situation of women in our society.

It is important I think to remember that we are not alone in this. Sheila Rowbotham has drawn a parallel between the experience of women in this relation and that of working class men (alas she does not refer to working class women, but we are all learning all the time). She writes:

There is a long inchoate period during which the struggle between the language of experience and the language of theory becomes a kind of agony. In the making of the working class in Britain the conflict of silence with 'their' language, the problem of paralysis and connection has been continuous. Every man who has worked up through the labour movement expressed this in some form. The embarrassment about dialect, the divorce between home talking and educated language, the otherness of 'culture'–their culture is intense and painful. The struggle is happening now every time a worker on strike has to justify his position in the alien structures of the television studio before the interrogatory camera of the dominant class, or every time a working-class child encounters a middle-class teacher (Rowbotham, 1974:32).

In insisting that women appear as subjects in the formation of a social consciousness we represent ourselves. We cannot break though we can be aware of the other enforced silences. And we can assert that there is not one way of seeing the world, not one way from which it may be known. There is not one universal subject from whose perspective knowledge can be simply transformed into an objective and universal account. We can recognize and explore the implications of this recognition. We can also confront the institutional practices which in an everyday and routine way constitute women as other in the ideological relation. These are the same or similar practices by which others are excluded and by which the appearance of a single subject is created out of the silences of many.

Conclusion

The implications of this analysis for women academics are far-reaching. Matters are not improved simply by including women in the professional and academic positions of influence. The professional discourse has by now a momentum of its own. The structures which have been developed have become the criteria and standards of proper professional performance. Being a professional involves knowing how to do it this way and doing it this way is how we recognize ourselves as professionals. The perspective of men is not apparent as such for it has become institutionalized as the 'field' or the 'discipline.' Similar considerations apply to the left-wing intelligentsia where the perspectives of men are institutionalized as the issues and topics of radical discourse in relation to which people locate themselves and are located politically.

We cannot be content with working as academics in the box created by the male monopoly of artistic, ideological, and other symbolic resources so that what we do in relation to women and arising out of our interests and experience as women is defined as 'women's business' and confined in the same way as women's magazines, women's novels, women's programs, etc. This essentially re-

stricts our topics to those of the relevance of women's roles. I now distrust that orientation in sociology (undoubtedly with its parallels in other disciplines) which makes the topic of 'sex roles' a central aspect of women's studies courses. Further, if I teach a sociology *of* women I am perpetuating the status of women as objects in relation to the ideological constructions written from the position of men. We must, it seems to me, begin an examination and critique of how women are constituted as other in the ideological formations which establish the hegemony of male consciousness.

In developing forms of thought and knowledge *for* women, academic women must offer a major critique of the existing disciplines and theoretical frames. We are confronted virtually with the problem of reinventing the world of knowledge, of thought, of symbols and images. Not of course by repudiating everything that has been done but by subjecting it to exacting scrutiny and criticism from the position of women as subject (or knower). This means, for example, claiming the right to examine literature from the perspective of women. That is to do much more than to establish the right of women to honour and examine the work of women poets and novelists or to study the role of women in fiction or drama. In sociology it means I think constructing a sociology *for* women rather than *of* women. By this I mean a sociology which will analyse and account for women's position in society and is capable of examining social structure from the perspective of women as subjects. Research is needed which begins with questions that could not have been posed before. I have learned from colleagues with whom I share an interdisciplinary course in women's studies what it means to examine anthropology and psychology from this point of view. I have begun to have a sense of the extraordinary depth and extent of what remains to be discovered by women working from the perspective and experience of women. I believe it goes much farther than I could have thought before participating in this course and approaching it from this (shared) perspective.

There are other implications. Some of them are difficult to come to terms with given the social organization of ideological formation and the productive organization of which it is part, but we should begin to find out how to think them anyway. Insisting on constituting women as subject (rather than that abstract mythical 'woman') raises questions about the relation of women members of the intelligentsia and their work to the existence and experience of other women. Exploration of what it means to be *responsible* to women in the society as *subjects*; what it means to develop forms of thought and knowledge capable of expressing their experience, examining and being capable of making intelligible to them how the world as they know and suffer it is determined, providing them with the knowledge, information, and means to think and act in relation to it; these are tasks proposed by the contradiction implicit in our situation as academic women (as it has been analysed here). We cannot just turn our backs on it by opting for membership in an elite whose ideological forms claim a spurious universality. A critique of the social organization of the academic enterprise is indicated which would examine how it is rendered academic, that is, how the forms of knowledge, relevances, conceptual frameworks, etc., are bounded by an institutionalized discourse which is an integral part of the institutions doing the work of ruling in this type of society.

NOTES

[1] *Women in the Labour Force: Facts and Figures* (1973 edition). Table 78, p.201

[2] *Women in the Labour Force: Facts and Figures* (1971 edition). Table 37, p.91. The percentages are my computation. The 1973 edition of *Women in the Labour Force* did not give this information, so I used the 1971 edition.

[3] *Women in the Labour Force: Facts and Figures* (1971), Table 35, p.87.

[4] Linda Shuto of the British Columbia Teachers' Federation in an address to the Department of Education Workshop on 'Sexism in Schools' (North Vancouver, 12-13 June 1975) reported that there were no women superintendents in British Columbia and no women senior officials in the Department of Education.

[5] *Women in the Labour Force: Facts and Figures (1973).* Table 71. p.187. This percentage is my computation. For both high school and community college we need to take into account the effect of a second factor on these percentages. In both, vocational and technical courses are a significant part of the curriculum. However even the 19 subjects *most* representative of women show only 39 per cent women (my computation from Table 76, p.197).

[6] This is generally true at least in a negative sense. The administrative structures of the universities provide for various forms of control over the collegial decision-making process, but it is only in exceptional cases that renewal, tenure, or promotions awards are made *against* collegial recommendation.

[7] Differences between middle and working class respondents are described in terms of greater ability on the part of middle-class respondents to 'take the role of the other' etc. My renaming is ironic but not I think unwarranted by the descriptions. See in particular Komarovsky's discussion of the differences between her interviews with wives of 'blue-collar' workers and earlier studies of college-educated women (Komarovsky, 1967: 14–22). She notices the respondents' relative 'unconcern with the interviewer's attitude' (p. 15).

Rev. canad. *Soc. & Anth./Canada. Rev. Soc. & Anth.* 12(4) Part I 1975. *Author's note:* The original version of this paper was presented at the Conference on *Women's Studies in Higher Education,* University of Calgary, 1–3 May 1975. Much of the thinking in this paper comes out of the Interdisciplinary Women's Studies Course at the University of British Columbia. I am indebted to the students, who are too many to name, and to Dawn Aspinall, Helga Jacobson, Meredith Kimball, and Annette Kolodny, who taught with me. My thanks also to Jane Douglas who typed the original, to Yvana Christie who put it on stencil, and to Steven Smith who helped to get it together.

REFERENCES

de Beauvoir, Simone. *The Second Sex.* New York: Bantam Books. 1961.
Bernard, Jessie. *Academic Women.* New York: New American Library. 1964.
'My four revolutions: an autobiographical history of the ASA' *American Journal of Sociology* 78(4) 1973.

Benikow, Louise. *The World Split Open: Four Centuries of Women Poets in England and America*. 1552–1950. New York: Vintage Books. 1974.

Bostock, Anya. Talk on BBC Third Programme published in *The Listener* (August). 1972.

Caudill, William. *The Psychiatric Hospital as a Small Society*. Cambridge, Mass.: Harvard University Press. 1958.

Chester, Phyllis. 'Patient and patriarch: women in the psychotherapeutic relationship,' pp.362–92 in Gornick, Vivian, and Barbara Moran (eds.) *Women in Sexist Society: Studies in Power and Powerlessness*. New York: Signet Books. 1972.

Ellman, Mary. *Thinking About Women*. New York: Harcourt Brace Jovanovich. 1968.

Fidell, L.S. 'Empirical verification of sex discrimination in hiring practices in psychology.' *American Psychologist* 25(12): 1094–7. 1970.

Freeman, Jo. 'The social construction of the second sex,' pp.123–41 in Garskof, Michele Hoffnung (ed.) *Roles Women Play: Readings Toward Women's Liberation*. Belmont, California: Brooks/Cole Publishing. 1971.

Goldberg, Philip. 'Are women prejudiced against women?' *Transaction* (April): 28–30. 1969.

Gornick, V. 'Woman as outsider,' pp.126–44 in Gornick, Vivian, and Barbara Moran (eds.) *Women in Sexist Society: Studies in Power and Powerlessness*. New York: Signet Books. 1972.

Hitchman, Gladys Symons. 'A report on the reports: the status of women in Canadian sociology.' *Bulletin of the Canadian Sociology Anthropology Association*. October 1974: 11–13. 1974.

Hochschild, Arlie Russell. 'A review of sex role research.' *American Journal of Sociology* 78(4). 1973.

des Jacques, Smache. 'Women in the French Revolution: the thirteenth prumaire of Olympe De Gouges, with notes on French Amazon Battalions.' Pp. 131–40 in Ann Forfreedom (ed.), *Women Out of History: A Herstory*. Culver City, Calif.: Peace Press. 1972.

Komarovsky, Mirra. *Blue-Collar Marriage*. New York: Vintage Books, 1967.

Komisar, Lucy. 'The image of woman in advertising.' Pp.304–17 in Gornick, Vivian, and Barbara Moran (eds.) *Women in Sexist Society: Studies in Power and Powerlessness*. New York: Signet Books. 1972.

Labour, Department of: Women's Bureau. *Women in the Labour Force: Facts and Figures*. 1971.
Women in the Labour Force: Facts and Figures. 1973.

Lessing, Doris. 'The old chief MshLanga.' Pp.83–106 in *The Black Madonna*. St Albans, Herts: Panther Books. 1966.

Marx, Karl, and Friedrich Engels *The German Ideology*. *Part One*. New York: International Publishers, 1970.

Millett, Kate. *Sexual Politics*. New York: Avon Books. 1971.

Mitchell, Juliet. *Women's Estate*. Harmondsworth, Middlesex: Penguin Books. 1972.

Pochoda, Elizabeth T. 'Heroines.' Pp.177–86 in Edwards, L.R., M. Heath, and L. Baskin (eds.) *Woman: an Issue*. Boston: Little, Brown. 1972.

Rowbotham, Sheila. *Women, Resistance and Revolution*. Harmondsworth, Middlesex: Penguin Books, 1973.

Women's Consciousness, Man's World. Harmondsworth, Middlesex: Penguin Books. 1974.

Schatzman, Leonard, and Anselm Strauss. 'Social class and modes of communication.' In A.G. Smith (ed.), *Communication and Culture*. New York: Holt, Rinehart and Winston. 1966.

Schutz, Alfred. *Collected Papers*, III: 116–32. The Hague: Martinus Nijhoff. 1966.

Smith, Dorothy E. 'Women's perspective as a radical critique of sociology.' *Sociological Inquiry* 44(1). 1974.

Strodtbeck, F.L., and R.D. Marm. 'Sex role differentiation in jury deliberations.' *Sociometry* 19(March): 9–10, 1956.

Szasz, Thomas S. (ed.). *The Age of Madness: The History of Involuntary Hospitalization Presented in Selected Texts*. Garden City, New York: Doubleday Anchor Books. 1973.

Thrupp, Sylvia L. *The Merchant Class of Mediaeval London 1300–1500*. Ann Arbor, Michigan: Ann Arbor Paperbacks, University of Michigan Press. 1962.

West, Candy. *Sexism and Conversation: Everything You Always Wanted to Know About Sachs (But Were Afraid to Ask)*. MA Thesis, Dept. of Sociology, University of California, Santa Barbara, California. 1973.

Wollstonecraft, Mary. *A Vindication of the Rights of Women*. New York: W.W. Norton. 1967.

Women's Action Group of the University of British Columbia. *A Report on the Status of Women at the University of British Columbia* (January). 1973.

CHANGE

Introduction

Over the past century or so, a number of changes have occurred in Canadian society. One of the most important was the transition from liberal to advanced capitalism. The former, it will be remembered, is characterized by, among other things, a situation in which a number of small enterprises compete for a market. The latter can be viewed as a situation in which a small number of enterprises control the market. Also important is that in English Canada, liberal capitalism was accompanied by an internally inconsistent ideology of individualism, dominance by the mercantile fraction of the bourgeoisie, and state activity designed to further the interests of this fraction. In advanced capitalism, co-operation has displaced the rhetoric of individualism, the mercantile fraction of the bourgeoisie has taken on corporate capitalist characteristics, and state activity, while it has continued to support the interests of the dominant sector of the bourgeoisie, has, of necessity, expanded its scope into activities that have the ostensible function of providing all classes with benefits such as old-age pensions, mother's allowance, and so on.

For the working class, the transition to advanced capitalism has been marked by an increase in the amount of surplus value that accrues to the bourgeoisie–i.e. an increase in the exploitation of labour, an increase in the trivialization of the work process, and, it can be argued, consequent increased alienation. The same period has also been marked by a relative decrease in the numbers of blue collar, as compared to white collar, workers. In addition, the expanded activities of the state have been largely responsible for the development of a new class, the new petty bourgeoisie. At the same time, 'rationalization' of agriculture has resulted in large decreases in the numbers of petty bourgeois farmers. Largely as a result of the emergence of monopolies, the number of petty bourgeois businessmen has also declined.

If we take a broad definition of mode of production, and include in it non-material factors like ideologies that have the consequence of misleading certain classes as to the real nature of social domination, it is clear that all of the above fall within the realm of changes in the productive forces of society. Despite the ebb and flow in the numbers of individuals belonging to this or that class, there has been no change in the relations of classes to the means of production. Private ownership and production for profit are still well entrenched maxims of Canadian capitalism.

Despite the continued operation of Canadian capitalism in accordance with certain principles, there have been a number of attempts on the part of members of different classes to change their position within society. The efforts of the majority of individuals engaged in the union movement attests to this fact. So do the number of farmer-based movements that have emerged over the years. Contemporary new petty bourgeois and working-class supporters of what is left of the nationalist movement can also be viewed as concerned with their position vis à vis other classes in society.

It is also clear from the preceding articles that since the first days of European settlement, the form of the relationship Canada has had with other societies has not varied to any great extent. Canada, that is, has been a dependency of France, Britain and the United States. In all cases, Canada has supplied these societies with its raw materials or staple products. In all cases the terms of exchange have tended to favour the metropolitan societies. This subordination in economic matters has tended to have its parallels in the political, cultural and military realms as well.

In the General Introduction it was mentioned that the metropolis-hinterland relationship—which is what those previously described events signify—is often duplicated within one society. Despite the odd reference here and there to this possibility, the preceding articles have not really dealt with this matter. In view of the amount of material that has already been supplied on the other aspects of change, it was decided, therefore, that the articles in this section would focus on metropolis-hinterland relationships within Canada. It will be readily apparent that a discussion of this dynamic involves considerations pertaining to changes in the forces of production and Canada's relationship to other societies as just outlined. In other words, despite their primary focus, the articles in this section will also include discussions of changes associated with the forces of production and Canada's relations to other societies.

In the article following this introduction, Veltmeyer elaborates on some of the general dynamics operative between metropolitan and hinterland regions. The most important point he makes is that regional differences in Canada and elsewhere can be viewed as a result of the normal operation of capitalism. In efforts to increase profits, capitalist enterprises become more and more centralized. The result is the deindustrialization of some areas and the creation in these of large numbers of unemployed or underemployed workers. Such individuals serve as a reserve army of labour that can be utilized when required.

One example of the general process outlined by Veltmeyer is traced by Frank in his article on the Cape Breton coal industry. He observes that for a while in the nineteenth and twentieth centuries, Cape Breton supplied an important raw material, coal, for consumption in the steel industry and elsewhere in Canada. As a consequence of changes in the nature of Canadian capitalism, that involved the consolidation of economic control in the hands of a Toronto-Ottawa-Montreal based bourgeoisie, Cape Breton changed from a relatively viable industrial area to an emergency supplier of raw materials and labour. A similar pattern was repeated throughout the Maritimes. One consequence of these and other changes was the Maritime Rights movement. Its goal was to promote the union of Nova Scotia, New Brunswick and Prince Edward Island in the hopes that such an alliance would "provide a more efficient use of available resources" (Forbes, 1975:65). Unfortunately for Maritimers, the movement failed.

Although it had never been an industrial area, the West also has experienced the consequences of metropolitan domination. For years farmers have been at the mercy of eastern financial and industrial interests who charge what have been regarded as exorbitant prices for their services and products. In an effort to change this and other conditions, farmers have engaged in a number of collective political protests, particularly in the first forty years of the century. Efforts to introduce change were undertaken by, among others, the United Farmers of Alberta, the Progressives, the Social Credit and the Co-operative Commonwealth Federation (CCF). Despite some successes, these movements failed to alter the position of those in the western provinces vis à vis eastern interests. A discussion of these movements, and the ways in which they have been analysed, is given in the article by Conway.

In their work, Bélanger and Saint-Pierre focus attention on Quebec. A number of the problems faced by various classes in this province are similar in origin to those of the Maritimes and the West. In Quebec, however, the situation is exacerbated by unique linguistic and cultural factors. The ways in which changing relations between classes have resulted in different perceptions concerning Quebec's position in Canada is also touched on by Bélanger and Saint-Pierre.

The final article in this section concentrates

on the unequal regional distribution of writers. Such individuals are important as, along with others, they are responsible for the creation of ideologies that have the functions referred to in an earlier section. Writers and poets, however, are not found in the various regions in reasonable proportions. Rather, over a long period, there has been a drain of creative writers from hinterland areas to the metropolis. In essence, their migration patterns have followed the general movement of economic surplus and labour across the land. It is suggested by Grayson and Grayson that such a pattern contributes to the impossibility of strong regional cultures and continued domination of the metropolis in cultural matters.

DEPENDENCY AND UNDERDEVELOPMENT: SOME QUESTIONS AND PROBLEMS

Henry Veltmeyer

A long outstanding but increasingly pressing problem of social and historical analysis is that of uneven regional development. Over the years, a surprising number of theories have been applied to this problem and have shared the fate of well-deserved disrepute.[1] More recently, however, a more promising line of questioning about this problem has been introduced by an emergent *dependency theory* based on the proposition that development and underdevelopment are reciprocal conditions of one and the same process of capital accumulation.[2] Deriving from a revised Marxist analysis of conditions that apply to countries on the periphery of an international system, and, by extension, to peripheral regions of countries at the centre, this theory boils down to two alternative theses: (1) capitalist development on the periphery is based on a hyper-exploitation of productive labour, and a massive capital drain that distorts the industrial structure of the economy, limits growth of the internal market, and generates misery, chronic unemployment, and marginality;[3] (2) industrial-finance capital on the periphery expands the production of relative surplus value, and, if it generates unemployment in the phase of economic contraction, it absorbs labour-power in the expansive cycles, creating an effect similar to capitalism at the Centre, where unemployment and absorption, wealth and misery, coexist within the same structure.[4]

Development of Underdevelopment or Dependent capitalist development: which thesis can be said to apply in Canada? To raise this question forces us to come to terms with a conceptual ambiguity deeply rooted in *dependency theory*. On the one hand, its ultimate centre of reference is a method of class analysis and a theory of capitalist development outlined by Marx. On the other hand, its conception of the capitalist system in terms of a *centre* (metropole) and a *periphery* (hinterland) has formed the framework of a regional not a class analysis of dependency and as such more often than not has proved to be its Achilles heel. To properly pose the problem of underdevelopment is to connect the class and regional conditions of dependency under capitalism, to show how the exploitative relation of wage-labour is reproduced in the regional structure of production and exchange.

The necessary groundwork for such an analysis is still being laid, and with respect to both Atlantic and Western Canada several points of principle remain unsettled.[5] It is the purpose of this paper to raise if not settle some of these questions of theory and method.

Point of Departure: Production or Exchange?

The major question over which dependency theorists are split can be traced back to the problematic relationship between production and exchange within the capitalist system. The major models of dependency are based on an analysis of exchange relationships, the conditions which are formed by an international market.[6] Departing from capitalism so defined, i.e. with reference to a market, the object in each case is to analyse the workings of this system in terms of a theory of unequal exchange. Because of the way the problem of capitalist development is posed, the resulting theories provide variations on the same theme: underdevelopment on the periphery is a product of development in the centre.[7]

This model has been criticised on the basis of a principle established by Marx, namely that the system of exchange (the structure of distribution) is, "entirely determined by the structure of production".[8] At issue is the point

273

of departure for a dependency analysis. By defining capitalism in terms of a market, and basing their analysis on relations of exchange rather than production, these studies are forced to conclude (they assume) that the world is captialist through and through; that all forms of productive activity in most regions of the world have been penetrated by capitalism and subjugated to its laws of development by virtue of a link to an international market. Commerce in commodities, and its medium of money, is seen here as the force behind an unbalanced international division of labour, and consequently, its structure of production. As such, capital is attributed with the power to break down, transform, or otherwise subjugate the various *traditional* (pre-capitalist) forms of more community-based productive activity.

Apart from its conceptual ambiguities (market relations are not specific to capitalism) the theoretical—and ultimately political—implications of this position are momentous. For one thing, it implies that a people can free itself from the rule of capital, and thus regain control over their lives, by a mere improvement in the conditions of exchange or terms of trade. To escape the consequences of this position, and to cut through this entire debate, I will argue for a closer reading of Marx's theory of capitalist development.

The Theory of Capitalist Development

The central problem in the analysis of regional underdevelopment under capitalism is to determine how the conditions of its class structure are reproduced in the colonial relationship of a central metropolis to its hinterland. Clearly, this problem can only be posed in terms of the conditions required for the emergence and expanded reproduction of capital. For this reason, analysis necessarily concentrates on the process of capital accumulation formed by these conditions. What is not so clear is how to approach such an analysis which involves both relations of production and relations of exchange built on them. On the one hand, most of the relevant studies focus their attention on relations of exchange, and consequently trace the source of capital accumulation to the monetary wealth accumulated primarily in commodity trade and concentrated in the hands of a merchant class.[9] On the other hand, although monetary wealth is clearly a source of capital accumu-

lation, commerce does not necessarily entail nor lead to industrial capitalism. The role of commerce in capitalist development is contingent on certain conditions and relations of production. What these necessary conditions are can be ascertained by reference to the distinction made by Marx between money as a medium of exchange and money as capital:

> It is inherent in the concept of capital . . . that it begins with *money* . . . as the *product* of circulation . . . . What enables money—wealth—to become capital is the encounter, on one side, with free workers; and on the other side, with the necessaries and materials, etc., which previously were in one way or another the property of the masses who have now become objectless and are also *free* and purchasable . . . . The *original formation* of capital does not happen, as is sometimes imagined, with capital *heaping up* necessaries of life and instruments of labour and raw materials . . . [but it is the] exchange [of] money for the *living labour* of the workers who have been set free . . . which enables money to transform itself into capital.[10]

In other words, the existence of *free workers*, an available supply of labourers formed by the expropriation of their means of subsistence and production, is an indispensable condition of capital accumulation, the basis not only of industrial capitalism but of commercial capitalism as well. Under this condition of dependence the capitalist relation of wage-labour is formed whereby surplus-value is extracted from the direct producer. This connection between free labour and the appropriation of surplus-value is based on the conversion of labour-power into a commodity which unlike any other commodity produces value greater than itself. This surplus-value, extracted under conditions formed by the accumulation of free labour and commercial wealth, is the source of profit and thus the basis of capitalist development.[11] However, in order for the capitalist class as a whole to generate an adequate rate of profit, it must realise the surplus-value embodied in the products of labour. The condition of this realization is: the formation of a market in which all commodities including labour-power, are exchanged at value (cost of production).[12]

To conclude, there are three essential (i.e.

structural) conditions of capital accumulation: (1) free labour; (2) monetary wealth; and (3) a market. Since each of these conditions can be treated as factors in the emergence and expanded reproduction of industrial capitalism it is necessary to specify the principles that govern their analysis.

First of all, the accumulation of capital under these conditions involve relations of production formed in the extraction of surplus-value and relations of exchange formed in its realisation. With respect to these relations, it is important to distinguish between the conditions under which surplus-value is appropriated (wage-labour) and the mechanisms through which it is transferred (unequal exchange). Strictly speaking Marx's concept of exploitation applies only to the class conditions of wage-labour. However, its extension to the inter-regional relation of unequal exchange is possible under the specified conditions of capital accumulation whereby the law of value, operating through the price mechanism, regulates social production.[13] Under these conditions, the process of capital accumulation is based not only on the exploitation of labour but on unequal exchange between regions which can be placed at the same level as a cause of underdevelopment.

How does the law of value operate through these conditions of capital accumulation to necessarily produce an inequality of regional development? To seek an answer to this question we must refer to Marx's theory of capitalist development based on the proposition of a "law of the falling tendency of the rate of profit". According to this theory, the development of the capitalist system, the expanded reproduction of capital, is based on its capacity to produce conditions that counteract this inherent (structural) tendency. These conditions can vary, but essentially involve either the intensification of the existing rate of exploitation (depression of wages, increased productivity, longer labour hours) or its increase by discovery of new sources of cheap labour (partially reflected in the cost of raw materials) or, in times of crisis, of new markets.[14]

The production of these conditions requires mobility in both labour and capital under the necessary framework of a market, which can operate under both competitive and monopoly conditions according to the dictates of an inevitable process. By breaking down the barriers to the free circulation of merchandise, labour and capital, the market mechanism allows for their redistribution according to the law of value based on the profit imperative.

It is this mobility in the distribution of labour and capital that explains the role of regional underdevelopment in the growth and consolidation of the capitalist system. First, with respect to the labour factor, the conditions of an uneven, polarised development can be connected to what Marx termed the "General Law of Capital Accumulation". Concomitant with the fundamental tendency for capital to centralise (concentrate in industrial centres) is the equally fundamental tendency for its expanded, reproduction to create a *relative surplus population,* an *industrial reserve army,* which takes the following forms: (a) a *floating surplus* formed by the alternate expansion and contraction of production, alternatively throwing some workers out and drawing them into production; (b) a *latent surplus* formed by the conditions that contract the economic basis of subsistence or independent commodity production (peasants, artisans, etc.); (c) a *stagnant surplus* formed by workers in marginal, very irregular employment; and (d) a yet lower stratum of individuals unable to sell their labour at any price, the, "hospital . . . and the dead weight of the industrial reserve army."[15]

As a pool of reserve labour, the existence of this surplus population functions as a mechanism that prevents wages from rising above value, and as such, a lever of capital accumulation, which works on the condition of an uneven development: the greater the social wealth, the mass of functioning capital *at one pole,* the greater the mass of exploited labour and with it the formation of a reserve army, the source of poverty and misery, at the other.[16]

Within the context of this polarised, uneven process of capital accumulation, the fundamental role of regional underdevelopment is clear: to furnish the industrial centres with reserves of cheap labour. The conditions of this role are very complex, but they can be analysed particularly in terms of a labour-force flow from non-industrial areas to industrial centres.[17] The general pattern of this movement has been empirically well established at both the international and the inter-regional levels. The vast movements of overseas migration of the labour-force to the United States, Canada, Brazil and Argentina in the nineteenth and the early twentieth century, has its close parallel to the migrationary movement within the Maritimes and from the Atlantic region to central Canada and can be explained in the same terms: as a response to conditions of capitalist development in the centre.

However, this is but one side of the picture. The unequal development of various regions and nations under capitalism is not entirely determined by conditions of labour mobility. There are limits to this process by which labour is freed and mobilised in peripheral areas for industrial capitalism at the centre. With these limiting conditions and given the fact that capital is more mobile than labour, the traditional pattern is reversed with a tendency for capital to move to non-industrial regions.[18] In these cases, industries go where they find concentrations of huge labour reserves, rather than drawing these reserves to the traditional industrial zones. This reversal of previous patterns can sometimes be explained by geographic factors, but its basic cause is the same: the pursuit of an adequate profit rate, determined in this case by a regional inequality of wages. This pattern is also applicable to both nations and regions within them. The falling rate of profit at the centre brings about a capital flow to the periphery where the cheaper source of labour allows for a higher rate of exploitation. Although de-emphasized by most *dependistas*, this export of capital to the periphery tends to reproduce in these regions some of the conditions of industrial capitalism, i.e. wage labour and investment in industry.[19]

However, the form, scale and direction of this investment is inevitably determined by the requirements of capital accumulation at the centre. As a result, capital on the periphery tends to concentrate in the extractive sector (mining, agriculture) which promotes an unbalanced division of labour and trade on an international scale. Typically, peripheral areas are led to specialise in the production and export of raw materials necessary for industrial expansion at the centre.[20] In this regard Canada has stood in the same relation first to England and then to the United States as the Atlantic region has stood in relation to the central provinces, and at a different level

again, the rural areas stand in relation to urban centres.

There is another dimension to this regional structure formed by an unbalanced division of commodity production, one that is more generally stressed by dependency theorists. This is that it supports peripheral areas in the role of securing a market for the growth of capitalist industry at the centre.[21] In this connection, the inequality of regional development is generally traced back to capitalist control not over the means of production but over the conditions of exchange.[22] This control forms the basis of a series of unequal exchange relationships between industry and agriculture, developed and underdeveloped regions or nations, involving a transfer of surplus-value, a process of capital drain from the periphery to the centre.[23] The mechanisms of this surplus transfer, for the most part hidden as in the conditions of trade, are brought to the surface by the various theories of unequal exchange produced in the dependency tradition. Within Canada, there is no comparably systematic analysis of unequal exchange at the regional level, although the same principles apply and there are numerous studies that move in this direction.[24]

Class and Region in Capitalism

The analysis advanced thus far is based on the thesis that an inequality of regional development is the necessary product of conditions created by capital accumulation. This thesis implies the systematic transformation, and in some sense the destruction of formerly dominant modes of production in the regions penetrated by capitalism. Presumably, production in these regions is reorganised to satisfy the requirements of capital accumulation, and with production thus placed on a capitalist basis (land, labour, and its products, transformed into commodities) the complex of pre-capitalist relations give way to the capitalist relation of wage labour, with conditions which overdevelop some regions and underdevelop others.

To the degree that it supports this assumption of a global system that swallows or destroys all prior modes of production in the process of its expansion, the thesis in question is misleading. It is unquestionably the case that the expansion of capitalism does not necessarily involve the destruction of pre-

276

capitalist relations. In fact, it can even be argued that the capitalist system reproduces certain pre-capitalist relations as a condition of its own expansion.[25] In any case, it is certainly a fact that capitalism either co-exists with or is integrated into systems based on subsistence, domestic and independent commodity or feudal modes of production; it combines with work relations formed by other modes. This is of the utmost importance for an analysis of regional underdevelopment.

Marx himself posed this problem of the relationship of capitalism to pre-capitalist formations only in historical terms, as a question of the conditions required for the emergence of capital. However, given the simultaneous co-existence of pre-capitalist and capitalist modes of production, with the integration of the former into a structure dominated by the latter and the continued reproduction of the former within this structure, the problem is clearly a structural one as well. As such, the question of a connection between pre-capitalist and capitalist formations can be applied not only to the analysis of primitive accumulation but also to the later stages of capitalist development.

To pose this problem of a structure formed by the combination of pre-capitalist and capitalist relations, raises questions not only about the Capitalist Mode of Production (CMP), the internal dynamic of which we have partially traced out, but also about the internal structure of the various pre-capitalist modes. With respect to the Asiatic modes of production, Marx emphasised that certain pre-capitalist modes are much more resilient than others to capitalist penetration for reasons that have little to do with the psychology of the producers, but a lot to do with the internal structure of the modes in question. However, since it is not merely a question of resistance but of the continued reproduction of pre-capitalist relations within a structure dominated by capitalism, the essential problem is still one of capital accumulation. In this connection, there are two possible positions on the articulation of the CMP with pre-capitalist formations: (1) it is necessary at a certain stage of capitalist development (Lenin, 1948); (2) it is necessary at all stages of capitalist development (Luxembourg, 1951). In either case, it is assumed that a purely internal accumulation of capital is impossible.

Given the assumed tendency for a falling rate of profit at the centre, the capitalist penetration of pre-capitalist formations is required for *access to the material elements necessary for expanding reproduction*, namely raw materials and labour, or at times of crisis, by the need for an *external market*.[26]

If not an answer, we have at least the framework of an analysis. To pose the problem in this form, however, still begs the question of why capitalist penetration of pre-capitalist formations would lead to their continued reproduction rather than their destruction as generally assumed. To raise this *unasked* question suggests that the reproduction of pre-capitalist relations is actually functional for capitalist development.

To properly pose this problem requires its placement in the context created by a capitalist penetration of production in periphral areas. On the one hand, the capitalisation of production in these areas creates conditions that contract the economic and social basis of self-subsistent, simple commodity, and other pre-capitalist modes of production. On the other hand, with the concentration of investment in the extractive sector, and the consequent specialisation in the production and export of staples, industry does not keep pace with the supply of labour thus created. This is one of the most characteristic features of dependent capitalist development, resulting in the formation of a large industrial reserve army. There are a number of problems created by this development, a major one of which is how to hold this labour in reserve for periods of capitalist expansion. Some of the surplus population is absorbed by a heterogeneous sector which forms to service capitalist production.[27] Another portion of the surplus population migrates towards the industrial centres to form the basis of a working class at the centre, and to a lesser degree on the periphery. However, with industrial capital largely concentrated at the centre of the system, this surplus population on the periphery forms the basis of a semiproletariat and a large underclass of dispossessed farmers, poor fishermen, and other *lumpen* elements on the fringe of the capitalist labour market that surface only as an unemployment statistic.[28] Clearly a more satisfactory solution for capitalism is for as much of this surplus population as possible to stay on the land or be otherwise involved in pre-capitalist work relations, while securing the instruments of its mobilization as required.

And this is precisely what happens in underdeveloped countries and regions in which a significant sector of production has a petty commodity form, is based on subsistence (agriculture, hunting, fishing, etc.), or (and this does not apply to Canada) is still governed by feudal relations. These pre-capitalist modes of production form the basis of complex social formations that ensure the vital needs of all members—productive and nonproductive—of the community. The significance of these social formations is that they do not exist in isolation but, as postulated by Luxembourg, are structurally linked to the CMP. Typically, the productive members of pre-capitalist formations exchange their labour-power for a wage either on a seasonal or a temporary basis, or even for an extended period involving a move of the immediate family.[29] The form and conditions of this structural tie to a wage-labour economy is quite variable, and requires careful empirical analysis, but its essential function in the expanded reproduction of capital is clear. Apart from the question of an industrial labour reserve, the reproduction of pre-capitalist relations, including those that derive from domestic production,[30] serve to increase the rate of exploitation, and thus offset the falling rate of profit at the centre. The mechanisms of this exploitation are specific to the structures that link these pre-capitalist relations to the conditions of a dependent capitalist development.[31]

First, both domestic labour and subsistence production, pockets of pre-capitalist relations, contribute towards the reproduction of labour-power, a pre-condition of capitalist development. Although the family and the self-subsistent community thus create conditions vital to the expansion of the CMP, their internal structure is pre-capitalist in form; the commodity labour-power is produced and reproduced within the framework of non-capitalist institutions. Under these conditions, capitalists dispose of a labour-force towards whose formation it has made no investment.

Second, given the conditions under which the productive members of pre-capitalist formations are forced to sell their labour-power, the capitalist extracts a labour-rent on top of surplus-value. It requires an exploitation of the complex mechanisms of migrations to and

from, and setting up a double labour market.[32] Added to the direct exploitation of productive workers is the indirect exploitation of the labour required of their wives and kin through the provision of services (domestic, social, security, etc.) which the capitalist would rather not assume, but which are necessary both for the reproduction of labour-power and for the preservation of an industrial reserve army.[33]

Although the conditions of this superexploitation require much empirical study, its central point is clear enough, and in conclusion can be established as a principle of analysis, a working hypothesis. The CMP creates conditions of class dependence reproduced at the social level through an inequality of regional development, and the preservation of certain pre-capitalist relations. A strategy of research on regional underdevelopment would do well to concentrate on an analysis of these conditions.

Methodological Notes on Surplus Value

(1)

As defined by Marx, the value of a commodity is determined by the "labour time socially necessary . . . for its production". (*Capital*, vol. 1, p. 16) The characteristic feature of the CMP is the need for workers to sell their labour for a wage, which, on Marx's assumption that "commodities are sold at their value", (519) represents the value of labour-power. On this assumption, surplus-value represents the difference between the value created by labour and the value of labour-power paid to workers in the form of wages. "The production of surplus-value", Marx argues, "is the absolute law of [the capitalist] mode of production". (618) Its necessary condition is: "Labour-power is saleable so far as it preserves the means of production in their capacity of capital, reproduced its own value as capital, and yields in unpaid labour a source of additional capital". (618) Under this condition, "the correlation between the accumulation of capital and the rate of wages is . . . at bottom, only the relation between . . . unpaid and paid labour." (621) As such, this relation of exploitation is expressed in the formula of surplus-value: surplus-value/value of labour-power. (531-4) Since the value of labour-power, received in the form of wages, represents the amount of labour-time necessary for labour to pay for itself, this formula can also be expressed in the form: surplus-labour/necessary labour. In this form (measured in time units), the value terms of the relation can be inferred and thus calculated in terms of price as the share of total profits to wages in the industrial output or national income. Needless to say, such a measure has its problems. Even if one sidesteps the theoretical problem of transforming values into prices there is the problem raised by the distinction between productive and unproductive labour. (Yaffe, 1973: 191ff) If one accepts Yaffe's position that *variable capital* represents only the wages of productive labour, not that of the total labour force, then the share of wages and profits in national income is a poor measure of the rate of exploitation.

<h2 align="center">(2)</h2>

The various theories of unequal exchange to which we have referred raise several questions about the calculations of the rate of exploitation. Of particular relevance to our conception of the problem is Emmanuel's theory based on the assumption not only of an unequal productivity of labour at the centre and on the periphery, but also on the hypothetical assumption of equal wages. In brief, if labour at both poles of the system were equally valued (rewarded as a factor of production), then the export price of goods produced on the underdeveloped periphery would be considerably higher. On this basis, trade constitutes a system of unequal exchange, a hidden mechanism of surplus transfer involving a drain of capital from the periphery to the centre. Put differently, labour is paid below value on the periphery, above value at the centre. In effect, Emmanuel treats wages as an independent variable: export prices are low because wages are low. This, of course, goes against Marx's insistence that in relation to the rate of capital accumulation, "the rate of wages [is] the dependent, not the independent, variable". (620) The source of Emmanuel's mistake is that he forgets at this crucial point that wages, as the value of labour-power, represents the cost of producing this labour-power, and that this cost varies not only historically but also across regional and national boundaries. (559ff) The cost of the expanded re-

production of labour-power within a structure of regional divisions is quite variable, and in itself a sufficient explanation of regional inequalities of wages, without resorting to the assumption that labour is paid well below value in some instances, and above value in others. This latter assumption never fully applies, given that the price of labour-power, strictly speaking, can occasionally rise above its value but can never sink below it. (519) It is true, nevertheless, that under monopoly conditions of external control, this law of exchange need not—and often does not—apply. However, even here there are strict limits to the process of unequal exchange (buying cheap and selling expensive). It can only apply when exchange involves the import of wage goods into the industrialised centre as a condition of lowering the cost of labour-power, and their import into the underdeveloped regions as a condition of raising this cost. Thus one can explain the frequent occurrence on the periphery of dramatic long-term decreases in the exchange-value of their staple-industry products without a corresponding fall in either or both wage goods or capital stock. Such a fall in industrial output relative to the cost of labour and the mass of fixed capital when it occurs in the centre is, of course, a classic example of the declining rate of profit as Marx conceived it. However, when it occurs in the underdeveloped regions of the periphery, the question of an unequal exchange applies only to the degree that the capitalist mode of production is generalised. As suggested above this is not typically the case. The costs of developing labour-power on the periphery are usually only partially capitalised, with a significant contribution of labour organised on a non-capitalist basis. Under these conditions the question of unequal exchange only complicates the real problem, which is to calculate the value of labour-power in each instance.

<h2 align="center">(3)</h2>

In calculating the relative value of labour-power, Marx assumes that commodities are generally sold at their value. (519) On this basis, Marx makes reference to the following factors:

(1) "The price and the extent of the prime necessaries of life as naturally and histor-

ically developed", which Marx points out, "varies with the mode of production"; (519)

(2) the cost of training the labourers;

(3) the part played by the labour of women and children;

(4) the productiveness of labour;

(5) its extensive . . . magnitude (number of work hours);

(6) its intensive magnitude (number of workers per machine).

A comparison on these factors requires, first of all, the following controls:

(1) an *average day wage* for the same trades and for different wage forms (time wage, piece wage).

(2) an *average intensity of labour* for the production of commodities, which, as Marx points out, changes from country to country—and we may add, from region to region.

(3) relative differences of the value of money (560-3).

With respect to the first two controls, it is a question of forming a scale of the appropriate units of measure. (560) The third control touches on a further problem. Here Marx points out that *relative values of money will . . . be less in the nation with a more developed CMP than in the nation . . . less developed.* (56) From this, "it follows that *nominal wages,* the equivalent of labour-power expressed in money, will also be higher in the first nation than in the second". (560) However, Marx adds, this, "does not at all prove [true] . . . for *real wages,* i.e., for the means of subsistence placed at the disposal of the labourer". (560) In this connection, Marx observes that even if we control for relative differences in the value of money,

frequently . . . the wage in the first nation is higher than in the second, whilst the relative price of labour, i.e. . . . as compared both with surplus-value and with the value of the product stands higher in the second than in the first. (560)

In other words, labour tends to be cheaper in rich countries than in poorer ones in relation to capital costs *within* (but not between) their respective boundaries. (560 n2)

This is in fact the problem requiring explanation: the difference in the relative price of labour expressed in real wages. Marx himself at this point does not essay a solution beyond various illustrations that point to the average intensity of labour and dismisses the theory that wages rise and fall in proportion to labour productivity. (561-3) Where he does move towards a solution is earlier in chapter XVII of *Capital* volume one. Here Marx makes passing reference to the first three of the above factors, each of which has an effect not easily measured, but excludes them in an analysis based on the last three. (520-30) In this analysis, Marx considers the many different possible combinations according to which many of the three factors are held constant or treated as variables. With reference to these considerations, it is clear that the regional structure of this variation can easily enough explain the relative costs of labour power, which, after Johnson, can be measured via an *average purchasing power index.*

(4)

One point of principle is clear: acts of exchange, do not add to value or produce profit. If wages are equal to the value of labour-power, then unequal exchange via trade cannot affect them. All it can do under conditions of regional inequality is transfer surplus value from one region to another, which is merely to re-distribute profit extracted under varying conditions of social production. Under these conditions of regional inequality the market mechanism can function to reduce the value of labour-power at the centre and thus offset the tendency of a falling rate of profit. This is clear enough in principle. The problem under these conditions of regional inequality is to calculate the ratio of the value of labour-power to the value produced by labour. Clearly capitalists at the centre appropriate an added surplus value by internal migration, a double labour market, the product market, etc., through which capitalists acquire labour without having to bear the cost of its development. The question is how to measure the value of this labour power under conditions such as domestic labour or subsistence agriculture involving other modes of production in which there is no direct exchange with capital, and in effect, no market. Without a market in labour, the magnitudes of value cannot be measured. No matter how clear it is in theory that capital is accumulated through an indirect exploitation of labour organised on a non-capitalist basis, it cannot be empirically determined. This is, for the most part, a problem without solution.

NOTES

[1] A selected range of these theories (staples, Development, NeoClassical, regional science), for what they are worth, are briefly outlined in Economic Council of Canada, *Living Together* (Ottawa: 1977). pp.23-30. The thinking behind this book shifts loosely among these theories, none of which admittedly serves as a general explanation of the well-known facts of regional disparity.

[2] Key points of reference for this theory are Samir Amin, "Accumulation on a World Scale" (New York: *Monthly Review*, 1974) and "Unequal Development" (New York: *Monthly Review*, 1970); Fernando Cardoso, "Dependencia y Desarrolo en America Latina" (Mexico, D.F.: *Siglo* XXI, 1969); Emanuel, "Unequal Exchange" (London: NLB, 1972); and Andre Gunder Frank, "Capitalism and Underdevelopment in Latin America" (New York: *Monthly Review*, 1967). The dominant Latin American tradition of this theory is reviewed in Ronald Chilcote. "A Critical Synthesis of the Dependency Literature", *Latin American Perspectives*, vol. 1, no. 1 (Spring 1974). Although Frank and Amin's work are the main points of reference, the underlying Latin American tradition of dependency theory has raised the questions of political economy increasingly taken up by a network of Canadian scholars. See *A User's Guide to Canadian Political Economy* (Sept. 1977) compiled by W. Clement and D. Drache, which suggest that Canadian studies are no longer sidetracked by the national question but like the articles in Gary Teeple (ed.), *Canada and the National Question* (University of Toronto, 1972), analyse it in terms of the social question.

[3] This form of dependency theory (*the development of underdevelopment*) is most clearly represented by Andre Gunder Frank. "Capitalism and Underdevelopment in Latin America" (New York: *MR*, 1967). At a certain level the assumptions on which this theory is based is shared by the theory of "Unequal Exchange" outlinted by Arghiri Emmanuel, "Unequal Exchange" (London: NLB) and Samir Amin. "Accumulation on a World Scale" (New York: *MR*, 1974).

[4] This second form of dependency theory (*dependent capitalist development*) is best represented in Fernando Henrique Cardoso "Dependency and development in Latin America", *NLR*, vol. 74 (July-August, 1972): *Dependencia y Desarrollo en America Latina* (Mexico: Siglo Veintiuno, 1969).

[5] As illustrated by *A User's Guide to Canadian Political Economy* a considerable range of studies have addressed and are raising questions of political economy from a shared perspective. However, the guiding principles of this perspective are still being worked out. A debate on problems of theory and method in relation to historical fact is but in its early stages.

[6] See Amin, *op cit.*; Emmanuel, *op. cit*; and Frank, *op. cit.*

[7] A good centre of reference for this concept of development and underdevelopment is the distinction made by Amin (1974) between an integrated *autocentric* economy wherein internal or domestic exchange is more important than external exchange (*i.e.*, imports and exports) and an economy *disarticulated* because of the domination of external over internal exchange. As brought out by Williams (1976) the theory based on this conceptual distinction lays emphasis on the size of the internal market as the crucial condition of independent capitalist development. However, Williams' analysis suggests that on the basis of Amin's theory it is also possible to explain the relatively high development of Canada's economic system within a framework of dependency.

[8] Karl Marx, *A Contribution to the Critique Political Economy* (Moscow, 1970). p.200.

[9] See for example Tom Naylor, "The Rise and Fall fo the Third Commercial Empire of the St. Lawrence", in Gary Teeple, *op. cit*. In actual fact, primitive accumulation both in Europe and Canada derives not so much from commerce as it does from a direct or indirect exploitation of labour, land grabs, monopoly control of the means of production, extortion of rent, piracy, currency manipulation. In the case of Canada not much is known, even today, of the specific origins of the first Capitalists, and Marx had nothing in the way of concrete historical material to offer on this matter. He does indicate, however, that there are two contrasting historical modes of progression into capitalist production. The first is where a segment of the merchant class moves over from purely trading operations into direct production. This occurred in the early development of capitalism in Italy, and in England in the late fifteenth/early sixteenth centuries. However, this form of capitalist formation soon becomes "an obstacle of the CMP and declines with the development of the latter". (*Capital*, vol. III, p.329). The second avenue of capitalist development is, according to Marx, "the really revolutionary way". Here individual producers themselves accumulate capital, and move from production to expand into trade. While Marx gives only a few hints of how this second mode of development occurs in manufacture, the analysis of Naylor (1972) and Teeple (1972) points to its necessary social conditions.

[10] Marx, *The Grundrisee* (London: Penguin Books, 1973), pp.505-7. Emphasis in original.

[11] It is this exploitation of wage-labour by capital, the appropriation by the latter of surplus produced by

281

the former, that constitutes the *innermost secret*, the hidden basis of the *entire social* structure and with it the . . . relation of . . . dependency. Accordingly, the mechanism of surplus appropriation based on the capitalist relation of wage-labour should be taken as the defining characteristic of the capitalist mode of production (*Capital*, vol. 1, p.217).

[12] The importance of this distinction between the extraction and realisation of profit can be traced back to the opening chapter of *Capital*, vol. one. Here Marx advances a complex argument based on the principle that an exchange of commodities cannot be understood on its own terms, but must be placed in the context of social production. On this basis, Marx argues that despite appearances the real source of profits is found not in acts of exchange but in relationships of production. The confusion of the realisation of profits with their real production arises from a tendency to view the process of capitalist production from the standpoint of the individual firm. This confusion is compounded by the existence of specialised firms that make profits through buying and selling without engaging in production at all—wholesalers, retailers and banks fall into this category: the cheaper they buy and the more expensively they sell the greater their profit. However, this obvious fact has no bearing on the general proposition that profits as a whole originate in production as the surplus of the social product over the consumption necessary for its production. The magnitude of social profit is not affected by acts of exchange, although its distribution between different firms is subject to market conditions. The forces that determine the distribution of profits should not be confused with those that determine its magnitude. They are of strictly secondary importance. (Marx, *The Grundisse* (London, Penguin Books, 1973, p.424). The proposition of such a long-term tendency is the theoretical basis of Marx's analysis of capitalist development. It is also the ultimate centre of reference for a dependency analysis of underdevelopment. Without the assumption of a structural tendency of a falling rate of profit, the phenomenon of exploitation loses its *objective* basis. No longer is it a question of *necessity*. Marx's theory of a falling rate of profit is based on the assumption of a tendency under capitalism for a rise in the organic composition of capital. Since labour is the source of value, and given Marx's formula for the rate of profit (s/c + v), a tendency for the organic composition of capital necessarily leads to a falling rate of profit. The problem is that the organic composition of capital is calculable in principle, but, as pointed out by Steedman (1975: 80), has never been established in fact. Moreover, the whole theory of a falling rate of profit is in serious dispute (Hodgson, 1974; Colletti, 1974; Rowthorn, 1974). What has to be squarely faced, however, is that without the assumption of a falling rate of profit, an analysis of dependent capitalist development has no theoretical basis.

[13] Some of the methodological problems involved in this extension are discussed in the Appendix.

[14] *Capital*, vol. 1, ch. XVII.

[15] *Ibid.*, p.664.

[16] *Ibid.*, p.632.

[17] This pattern forms the basis of a well-worn thesis in many studies of modernisation based on alleged but unexplained (assumed) *forces of spatial concentration and diffusion*. A very representative case of this tradition is Michael Ray, *Canadian Urban Trends* (Toronto: Copp Clark Publishing, 1976).

[18] This only happens in certain circumstances. The historical and structural conditions of these circumstances are not given in principle (beyond a general reference to the profit dynamic) and require a systematic analysis. Some halting steps toward such an analysis are essayed in my 'The Underdevelopment of Atlantic Canada', forthcoming publication in *Radical Review of Political Economy*.

[19] One of the basic tenets of dependency theory is that dependent status tends to block the development of industrial capitalism (Frank, 1969; Naylor, 1973). This widely accepted thesis in the case of Latin America has been challenged by a careful empirical analysis (Warren, 1973) and defended on the same basis (Emmanuel, 1974). In the case of Canada, Naylor's version of the thesis has been criticised by Ryerson (1976) and others.

[20] This pattern is so well established that it is taken as the key indicator of an unbalanced, dependent capitalist development. In the case of Latin American there are a great number of historical studies organised around a sequence of *export enclaves*, (coffee, sugar, cocoa, bananas, copper, tin, oil, etc.) developing in response to the needs of metropolitan interests (Abad, 1970; Furtado, 1970; Sunkel, 1969). These studies have their counterpart in the Canadian studies based on a staple theory (Creighton, 1959; H.A. Innis, 1956; M.Q. Innis, 1954; Watkins, 1963). Both the enclave and the staple theories take the national economy as their unit of analysis. Needless to say, the same principles can be applied to a regional analysis.

[21] The theory of this can be traced back to Rosa Luxembourg *The Accumulation of Capital*, London: Rutledge & Kegan Paul, 1951) who argued its necessity at all stages of capitalist development. On the concentration of production and manufactured goods in Canada's central provinces see Buckley (1974: 10-11).

[22] The mechanisms and institutional framework of this monopoly control have been analysed at length on the basis of a theory of imperialism (Dos Santos, 1970; Hayter, 1972; Magdoff, 1969; O'Connor). A study by Vaitsos (1974) does not fall into this tradition but provides a close analysis of the specific mechanisms of surplus transfer used by transnational corporations at the monopoly stage of capitalist development.

[23] This proposition of capital drain is shares by all dependency theories of underdevelopment, although it has been suggested that "the so-called [Capital] drain may merely be the foreign exchange price paid for the establishment of productive facilities" (Warren, 1973: 39).

[24]See, for example, the study by Bruce Archibald, "Atlantic Regional Underdevelopment and Socialism", in Laurier LaPierre *et al*, eds., *Essays on the Left* (Toronto, 1971), pp.103-20; Archibald, "The Development of Underdevelopment in the Atlantic Provinces" (M.A. thesis, Dalhousie University, 1971).

[25]See Barbara Bradby, "The Destruction of Natural Economy", *Economy and Society*, 4, 2(1975); and Claude Meillassoux, "From Reproduction to Production", *Economy and Society*, 1, 1(1972).

[26]Rosa Luxembourg, *The Accumulation of Capital* (London: Routledge & Kegan Paul, 1951).

[27]The characteristic feature of urban centres on the periphery of the capitalist system, whether in Lima, Guayaquil, or Halifax, is the predominance of a heterogeneous service sector, the social basis of its new *middle* class defined by an indirect relation to capitalist production. The socio-economic status of this broad class grouping is extremely variable as it involves a range of services from those that fulfill the function of capital, management, banking, etc. to a series of professional and white-collar functions, all the way to a number of petty services. These economic services, as the basis for government planning, are very well understood in occupational terms, but rarely analysed in terms of class studies in the Latin American context (e.g. Anibal Quijano, *Nationalism and Capitalism in Peru*, New York: 1971) but as far as I know there are no Canadian equivalents of such a systematic class analysis.

[28]See Leo Johnson, 'The Development of Class in Canada in the Twentieth Century', in Gary Teeple, *op. cit.*; and *Poverty in Wealth* (Toronto: New Hogtown Press, 1974).

[29]This is a problem well known to exist, and partially reflected in statistics on internal migration and employment, but little studied. For preliminary indications of such an analysis see Mike Beliveau, 'Canso, Cabinda and the "Weltury" Boys: The Gulf Oil Story', *Round One* 12 (Feb. 1974).

[30]Our analysis of the regional question could as easily be applied to the question of domestic production in its separation from social production under conditions of a sexual division of labour. This question recently has been subject to a serious theoretical debate (Benston, 1969; Coulson/Magas/Wainwright, 1974; Seacombe, 1974). An entire issue of *Latin American Perspectives* (vol. 4, Nos. 1-2, 1977) has been devoted to an analysis of this question in the Latin American context. The Canadian case is currently being explored with studies such as Connelly (1976).

[31]Again we have here a problem too little studied, although the following papers move in the right direction: B. Bernier 'Capitalism in Quebec Agriculture', *The Canadian Review of Sociology and Anthropology*, 13, 4 (1976); Max Hedley, 'Independent Commodity Production', *The Canadian Review of Sociology and Anthropology*, 13, 4 (1976); Meillassoux, *op. cit.*

[32]See Patricia Connelly, *Canadian Women as a Reserve Army of Labour*, Ph. D. dissertation, O.I.S.E., University of Toronto (1976), to be published by *The Women's Press*; and Meillassoux, *op. cit.*

[33]Marx himself suggests the concept of such an analysis in 'the appropriation of Supplementary Labour-Power by Capital: the employment of Women and Children' 1967: 394-402). However, since the principles of Marx's analysis apply only to the production of surplus-value, there is no basis in Marx for an analysis of super-exploitation under conditions that combine various modes of production. As noted in the Appendix, without a direct exchange with capital, the contribution of 'supplementary labour-power' no matter how clear in principle cannot be calculated in fact.

THE CAPE BRETON COAL INDUSTRY AND THE RISE AND FALL OF THE BRITISH EMPIRE STEEL CORPORATION

David Frank

Our understanding of regional underdevelopment in Atlantic Canada has been slow to develop. For more than 50 years we have had extensive documentation of the existence of serious regional inequality in Canada. Attempts to explain the reasons for this have been less common. In the 1920s politicians active in the Maritime Rights movement catalogued the "unfilled promises" and "betrayals" of Confederation and demanded increased federal subsidies as compensation.[1] A less subjective interpretation was proposed by S.A. Saunders, C.R. Fay and Harold Innis, who attributed the region's troubles to the new era of industrialism. For the Maritimes it was "prosperity so long as their face was towards the sea, and . . . struggle against adversity when the pull of the land increased". Like an "economic seismograph", the Maritimes registered the shockwaves of a

283

"rising tide of continental forces that were destined to dominate the economy of the Maritime Provinces".[2] Recent studies have questioned this approach: an economic historian has challenged the myth of the "Golden Age"; an historical geographer has traced the domination of the region by outside forces during the colonial era; an economist has pointed out that during a decisive period in the 1830s and 1840s local entrepreneurs neglected the region's industrial potential.[3]

The most important revisionist studies were those published in the early 1970s by Bruce Archibald and T.W. Acheson. In 1971 Bruce Archibald applied a sweeping metropolis/satellite interpretation to the economic history of the region. He argued that the region has "always existed in a dependent relationship with a larger controlling metropolis" and the region must be seen as "the back yard of a dominant economic centre rather than an autonomous but struggling unit". His survey stressed the role of outside exploitation in the underdevelopment of the region: the extraction of resources and capital in response to the needs of outside forces divided the loyalties of local entrepreneurs and produced growing regional underdevelopment.[4] In 1972 T.W. Acheson challenged the view that the Maritimes did not experience economic growth after Confederation; his study found that the Maritimes sustained a significant amount of industrial expansion in the late nineteenth century, as a group of "community-oriented" entrepreneurs transferred capital from traditional pursuits to new industrial investments. By the 1920s, however, this industrial structure had collapsed, mainly because no "viable regional metropolis"had emerged to take leadership and central Canadian business and finance had asserted control over the region's economic life.[5]

In the light of these studies, it seems clear that a new framework is necessary for understanding regional underdevelopment. A tentative approach may be drawn from the Marxist analysis of regional inequalities under industrial capitalism, which explains uneven development between regions as a natural feature of capitalistic economic growth. The continuing search for new economic surpluses, better rates of profit, new raw materials, markets and sources of labour supply, all caused an expansion in the scale of capital accumulation. As part of this process, the operation of the free market system generally led to the concentration and centralization of capital; economic wealth and power tended to become concentrated in fewer hands and centralized in fewer places. Once the structure of an inter-regional market in goods, labour and capital was established, relationships of domination and dependency emerged between regions. As the process continued, regional disparities deepened and the subordinate communities entered a cycle of capital deficiencies, population losses and economic powerlessness.[6]

By the 1880s industrial capitalism had become well-established in central Canada and began to extend its hegemony over regions and sectors where the growth of industrial capitalism was less advanced. The emergence of this trend towards the concentration and centralization of capital had devastating consequences for economic development in the weaker regions and communities of the country. The domination of central Canada over the Maritimes was completed by the 1920s. Much of the social and political turmoil of that decade expressed the community's response to the crisis of the regional economy.[7]

Nowhere can the results of these developments be seen more clearly than in industrial Cape Breton, where the process of national economic integration was of decisive importance in the exploitation of one of the region's richest natural resources, the coalfields. At the beginning of the twentieth century, industrial Cape Breton seemed a dynamic and prosperous industrial community. The population of the industrial area, which numbered 18,005 people in 1891, had increased to 57,263 people by 1911.[8] The largest and most valuable in eastern Canada, the Sydney coal-field stretches about 30 miles along the northeastern shore of Cape Breton Island and in the 1920s the field's proven reserves were known to exceed one billion tons. The accessibility and quality of the coal supply gave the Sydney field considerable economic importance. Cape Breton's bituminous coal compared favourably with other industrial coals, although it was no rival for anthracite as a domestic fuel.[9] The inexpensive water route to Quebec enabled Cape Breton coal to penetrate the central Canadian market, and the extensive iron ore reserves at Bell Island, Newfoundland, assisted the establishment of an iron and steel industry in Cape Breton; these two markets consumed the bulk of the coal industry's output. By the time of the First World War industrial Cape Breton occupied an important place in the national economy. The coal mines supplied more than 44 per cent of Canada's annual coal production, and the iron and steel industry produced more than one-third of the country's pig iron.[10]

Although the condition of the local economy at the peak of its fortunes inspired widespread optimism, at least one thoughtful observer was troubled by the emerging pattern of industrial development. In 1917 a Yorkshire mining engineer who had immigrated to Cape Breton, Francis W. Gray, lamented the underdevelopment of the coal resources:

Nova Scotia, as a province, has not reached the stage of industrial and manufacturing activity that should have accompanied a coal mining industry 100 years old. . . . It must be confessed that the potentialities of Nova Scotia have been but meagrely realized. Take away the steel industry from Nova Scotia, and what other manufacturing activity has the province to show as a reflex of the production of 7,000,000 tons of coal annually?. . . . The coal mined in Nova Scotia has, for generations, gone to provide the driving power for the industries of New England, Quebec and Ontario, and has, in large part, been followed by the youth and energy of the Province. For almost a century, Nova Scotia has been exporting the raw material that lies at the base of all modern industry. . . .

"Briefly", Gray concluded, "Nova Scotia has achieved the status of a mining camp, whereas its full stature should be that of a metropolis of industry".[11] Gray's worries proved well-founded. After the First World War, the local economy experienced a crisis from which it has never recovered. In 1921 the British Empire Steel Corporation assumed control of the coal and steel industries in Nova Scotia. The outcome of a well-established pattern of regional underdevelopment in Atlantic Canada, the rise and fall of the British Empire Steel Corporation marked a decisive turning point in the economic history of industrial Cape Breton.

Before the 1860s the growth of the coal industry in Nova Scotia was restricted by imperial policy. In 1826, under a royal charter, the General Mining Association (GMA) of London took exclusive control of the mineral resources of Nova Scotia, but advocates of colonial economic development, including Abraham Gesner and Joseph Howe, helped lead a popular campaign against the monopoly. In 1858 the Association's rights were restricted and control of mineral rights was vested in the colony. This successful revolt against colonial underdevelopment opened the way for expansion of the coal industry. Numerous mining companies were formed and a brief boom followed. Under the unusual conditions of the 1854 Reciprocity Treaty and the high demand for coal during the American Civil War, Cape Breton coal entered the long-coveted United States market on a large scale. The boom ended in 1867, however, when Congress restored prohibitive import duties.[12]

The collapse of the export trade led to growing protectionist sentiment in the coal industry. The example of British industrial growth, where the coal resources fueled the industrialization of the Black Country, provoked hopes for a large local market based on "home manufactures".[13] But the dominant protectionist impulse was support for a federal tariff to enable Nova Scotia coal to enter the central Canadian market. The idea was influential among pro-Confederates in the 1860s.[14] A short-lived duty in 1870 demonstrated the effectiveness of a coal tariff, and during the 1870s the Cape Breton coal operators campaigned for "the same just and reasonable protection as has been afforded to other Dominion industries".[15] This agitation was successful in 1879 when the National Policy established a .50 per ton duty on coal imports, which was raised to .60 the next year. Nova Scotia's coal sales in Quebec rose sharply, and the local market also became important, as the Maritimes experienced industrial expansion under the National Policy. Based on this twin foundation, the coal industry's long expansionist cycle continued until the First World War.

During this expansionist period the growth of the coal industry demonstrated several aspects of the uneven development between regions which characterized the emergence and consolidation of industrial capitalism in Canada. The growing concentration and centralization of capital in the Canadian economy created a national economic structure based on inter-regional linkages and dependencies. National economic policies encouraged the expansion of the coal industry, but did not promote stability or prosperity for the hinterland resource area. The creation of national markets led to a division of labour between regions, which established the Cape Breton coal industry as a source of industrial energy filling the needs of the central Canadian market. With the growth of strong Canadian financial centres, a corporate consolidation movement unified the coal industry into a few large companies and delivered control of the industry into the hands of powerful financial interests in central Canada.

The division of labour between regions established the coal industry in Nova Scotia as an important–but vulnerable–source of industrial energy in Canada. After the 1870s, imports of British coal into Canada declined sharply. Under the tariff, shipments of Nova Scotia coal to the Quebec market grew from 83,710 tons in 1878 to 795,060 tons in 1896 and 2,381,582 tons in 1914. Simultaneously, imports of American coal into Canada increased heavily, from 331,323 tons in 1878 to 1,451,508 tons in 1896 and 18,145,769 tons in 1913. By the eve of the First World War, Nova Scotia supplied 54 per cent of Canada's coal production–but 57 per cent of the coal consumed in Canada was imported from the United States.[16] Although the tariff promoted expansion of the domestic coal industry, it provided only partial protection. The Ontario market remained beyond the economic reach of the industry, and in Quebec Nova Scotia coal continually faced keen competition. Despite protests from Nova Scotia, the tariff on bituminous coal was reduced to .53 per ton in 1897 and remained at this figure until 1925. As coal prices approximately doubled during this period, the effect of the fixed duty, which had amounted to more than 20 per cent in the 1880s, was seriously diminished.[17] Under a national policy that was never truly national, the coal trade occupied a vulnerable position in the Canadian market.

The coal market in the Maritimes also grew during this period, reaching a peak of more than three million tons in 1913,[18] but the key factor in the coal market was a single customer. In 1913 the steel plant at Sydney consumed 1,362,000 tons of coal, more than half the total coal sales in Nova Scotia.[19] A vital customer for the coal industry, the Nova Scotia steel industry suffered from chronic instability throughout its history; dependence on this market was a source of further vulnerability for the coal industry.[20] In general, the industrial structure of the Maritimes was limited in scope and suffered seriously from its own pattern of underdevelopment and deindustrialization.[21]

The second main trend in the coal industry was the growth of a consolidation movement in the coal-fields. Completion of the railway to central Canada in the 1870s was followed by mergers dominated by Montreal interests in the mainland coal-fields in 1884 (Cumberland Railway and Coal Co.) and 1886 (Acadia Coal Co.). Plagued by the insecurities of seasonal operations, distant markets and inadequate capital, the Cape Breton coal operators also turned to mergers. The formation of the Provincial Workmen's Association prompted a short-lived defensive alliance among the coal operators in the early 1880s, the Cape Breton Colliery Association.[22] The battle for "survival of the fittest" continued, however, and of the 20 mines opened in Cape Breton after 1858, only eight remained in operation in 1892. The coal operators welcomed the formation of the Dominion Coal Company.[23]

The Dominion Coal Company played an important part in integrating the Cape Breton coal industry into the national structure of industrial capitalism in Canada, although ironically, this was not the original aim of the company's promoters. The formation of Dominion Coal in 1893 was sponsored by an alliance between Boston financier Henry M. Whitney, who promised to invest capital and revive the lost coal trade to New England, and a group of Nova Scotia coal operators and politicians anxious to expand the coal industry and restore dwindling provincial revenues. An experienced promoter, in 1886 Whitney has created Boston's West End Street Railway Company, the first extensive electrified rail system in the country. Whitney's interest in Cape Breton was designed to

286

secure an inexpensive coal supply and improve the financial position of his other companies. The financial arrangements indicate that the formation of Dominion Coal was a typical episode in an age of corporate carpet-bagging.[24] Dominion Coal also received considerable encouragement from the provincial government. The legislature approved a 99-year lease on all the unassigned coal resources of Cape Breton and the company was permitted to purchase any others; in return Dominion Coal guaranteed a minimum annual royalty at a fixed rate of 12 1/2c per ton for the duration of the lease. Premier W.S. Fielding predicted the coal industry would grow tenfold as Whitney accomplished "what nature intended . . . the shipment of large quantities of coal to the United States".[25]

The creation of Dominion Coal marked the integration of the coal industry in Cape Breton into a metropolitan network of financial control. The composition of Dominion's first board of directors revealed an alliance of New England, Nova Scotia and Montreal capitalists under Whitney's presidency.[26] The establishment of the merger also marked the triumph of the strategy of exporting the province's coal resources in large volume. Dominion Coal soon acquired control of all the existing operations in the Sydney coal-field, except the GMA's holdings at Sydney Mines. The unification of the south Cape Breton field under one management rationalized exploitation of the coal resource and the new coal company applied a much-needed infusion of capital and technology. Hopes of capturing the New England market were disappointed,[27] but the trade into the St. Lawrence ports continued to grow rapidly and Dominion Coal established an extensive network of railways, shipping piers, coal carriers and coal yards to serve this market.

Control of the coal industry again changed as the integration of the regional economy into the national economic structure accelerated after the 1890s. In 1901 Whitney sold control of Dominion Coal to James Ross, the prominent Montreal capitalist. Dominion Iron and Steel, another Whitney company launched with great fanfare in 1899, was abandoned to central Canadian interests at the same time. Ross and his backers briefly controlled both the coal and steel companies, but in 1903 separate control was established,

with J.H. Plummer of Toronto as president of the steel company.[28] Ross and Plummer were both important figures in Canadian business circles: in 1906 Ross held 15 directorships in addition to Dominion coal, including seats on the Bank of Montreal and Montreal Rolling Mills boards, and Plummer, formerly assistant general manager of the Bank of Commerce, held seven directorships in addition to Dominion Iron and Steel.[29] The two companies quarrelled continually; Ross attempted to take over the steel company in 1907, but in 1910 Plummer triumphed and merged the two companies into the new Dominion Steel Corporation. The merger also took over the Cumberland Railway and Coal Company, but failed to win control of the Nova Scotia Steel and Coal Company, the New Glasgow industrial complex.[30] With Plummer as president and Sir William C. Van Horne as vice-president, Dominion Steel represented a powerful alliance of Toronto and Montreal interests. Closely linked to the Bank of Montreal and the Bank of Commerce, the Dominion Steel directors as a group held more than 179 company directorships.[31] Thus, by the eve of the First World War the Cape Breton coal industry had become not only an important source of industrial energy for the Canadian economy, but also an attractive field of investment for Canadian businessmen. These two aspects of the Canadianization of the region's economic life would contribute heavily to the crisis of markets and corporate welfare which gripped the coal industry in the 1920s.

The emergence of the British Empire Steel Corporation (Besco), which was incorporated in the spring of 1920, was the result of extended manoeuvres for further consolidation of the coal and steel industries in Nova Scotia. By 1917 American financial interests had gained control of the Nova Scotia Steel and Coal Company (Scotia) and were actively pursuing a merger with the much larger Dominion Steel Corporation. The same idea attracted interest in Britain at the end of the war, and in 1919 a syndicate of British industrialists began to buy control of Dominion Steel. At the same time, a third group also appeared on the scene; based in Canada Steamship Lines and led by two Montreal entrepreneurs, J.W. Norcross and Roy M. Wolvin.

The Nova Scotia Steel and Coal Company

boasted a strong reputation for cautious management, technical excellence and financial success. From humble beginnings in the 1870s in New Glasgow, the Scotia companies had pioneered the growth of the Canadian steel industry, smelting the first steel ingots in Canada in 1883. In 1899 Whitney had attempted to include Scotia in his new Dominion Iron and Steel Company. In 1900 Scotia entered Cape Breton by taking over the GMA's holdings at Sydney Mines and building a steel plant there. Despite growing links with Toronto interests, especially through customers like Massey-Harris and financial backers like the Bank of Nova Scotia, the company remained dominated by Nova Scotia financiers and industrialists.[32]

In 1915 a number of steps signaled the closer integration of Scotia into the metropolitan financial structure. President since 1905, Robert Harris, the prominent Halifax financier, resigned to take a seat on the province's Supreme Court. He was replaced as president by Thomas Cantley, Scotia's longtime general manager. W.D. Ross, a native Cape Bretoner active in Toronto financial circles (and ultimately Lieuteant-Governor of Ontario), became financial vice-president, and N.B. McKelvie of New York joined the Scotia board as a representative of the New York investment house of Hayden, Stone and Company. In 1917 McKelvie's group supplied a large investment of working capital for Scotia and secured control of the company. Cantley was replaced as president by Frank H. Crockard, formerly vice-president of a Tennessee coal and steel company, "one of the bright stars of the United States Steel Corporation's galaxy of subsidiary corporations".[33] The New York investment banker, Galen L. Stone, became chairman of Scotia's finance committee. Speculation in the press suggested the giant U.S. Steel Corporation was behind the influx of American investment, but Scotia denied this rumour.[34] President Crockard explored plans for amalgamation with Dominion Steel, which he regarded as "absolutely essential" to develop local resources "along broad lines as followed in the States in the Iron and Steel industry".[35] Efforts to purchase shares in Dominion Steel met resistance and direct negotiations for a merger also failed in the spring of 1918. Dominion Steel President Mark Workman commented favourably on the idea, but insisted

that control must remain in Canadian hands.[36] Soon Scotia recruited the general manager of Dominion Steel to its side. A native Cape Bretoner, D.H. McDougall had worked for the Dominion companies for almost 20 years, rising from mechanic's apprentice to general manager, but in 1919 he accepted an appointment as president of Scotia.[37] A mining engineer, McDougall strongly favoured a merger of the coal operations in the Sydney coal-field, as the haphazard distribution of submarine coal leases threatened to cause mine closures and costly duplication of effort by the two rival companies.[38]

The next steps towards merger took place within Dominion Steel. In 1916 a Montreal clothing manufacturer, Mark Workman, had succeeded Plummer as president, but otherwise the controlling group remained stable. In October 1919 new merger rumours circulated; the "inside story", denied by Workman, was that Lord Beaverbrook had accomplished a merger of the Scotia and Dominion companies.[39] Soon it was revealed that a British syndicate had purchased a large quantity of Dominion Steel shares and that a London Advisory Committee had been formed to represent the British interests.[40] The London syndicate included a blue-ribbon committee of industrialists from the British steel and shipbuilding industries: Viscount Marmaduke Furness, chairman of the Furness iron, steel and shipbuilding companies; Benjamin Talbot, managing director of the Furness group; Sir Trevor Dawson, managing director of Vickers Ltd.; Henry Steel, chairman of the United Steel Companies of Great Britain; and Sir William Beardmore (soon Lord Invernairn), chairman of the large Glasgow shipbuilding company.[41] The most active members of the London group were Sir Newton Moore and Lt. Col. W. Grant Morden. Prominent in the Australian mining and steel industries, Moore had been active in Australian politics before removing to London during the war. There he sat in the House of Commons and pursued his business interests, especially in General Electric and various empire mining and steel companies. Chairman of the London group was Lt. Col. Morden, a Toronto-born entrepreneur who first came to prominence as promoter of the Canada Steamship Lines (CSL) merger in 1912, which had been backed by Vickers and

Furness. Morden himself had moved to London, engaged in industrial espionage in Germany and Switzerland during the war, chaired a British chemical firm and sat in the House of Commons. And according to a sketch in the *Sydney Record*, Morden was also "above all an accountant to the nth degree, lightning-like in his grasp of detail".[42]

During 1919 a third group also displayed interest in Dominion Steel. Led by J.W. Norcross and Roy Wolvin of Montreal, this group appeared to be working independently of the London syndicate. Norcross had started steam-boating on Lake Ontario as a youth and eventually became managing director of Canada Steamship Lines. In a bitter battle early in 1919, Norcross insisted on a distribution of common shares dividends and supplanted CSL president James Carruthers. Vice-President of the Collingwood Shipbuilding Company, Norcross was also a director of the Canadian branch of Vickers. Like Norcross, Wolvin was an aggressive young entrepreneur who came to prominence on the Great Lakes. Born in Michigan in 1880, Wolvin became a leading transportation expert in the shipping trade. As early as 1902, when he was working out of Duluth, Wolvin was known in Halifax as "one of the shrewdest shipping men on the lakes" and praised for his efforts to improve the capacity of the St. Lawrence canal system. Later Wolvin established the Montreal Transportation Company and joined Norcross in CSL and Collingwood Shipbuilding.[43] In the wake of the Halifax Explosion, Wolvin was invited by the Minister of Marine to consider the potential for establishing steel shipbuilding at Halifax, long a fond local hope. The result was the formation of Halifax Shipyards Ltd. in 1918 under the control of Wolvin, Norcross and their associates. Events then proceeded rapidly. Wolvin was impressed by the immense advantages of the Nova Scotia coal and steel industries and hoped to link them to his shipbuilding and shipping concerns. Following a chance shipboard conversation with Mark Workman, Wolvin began to purchase shares in Dominion Steel and entered the board as a director in July 1919. At some point during the year, Wolvin later recalled, he established a "friendly understanding, you might say", with the London interests. In January 1920 Norcross also entered the board and in March 1920 the London group proved their control

of Dominion Steel by installing Wolvin as the new president. A "silent revolution" had taken place in the affairs of Dominion Steel.[44]

Plans for creation of the British Empire Steel Corporation were unveiled in a speech by Morden at a meeting of the Empire Parliamentary Association in Ottawa on 14 April 1920. "If we can combine the capital and experience of the Old Mother Land with the resources of our Overseas Dominions", he explained, "we are going to put ourselves in an economic position that will forever maintain us as the greatest Empire in the world. I have long felt that the so-called 'silken thread of sentiment' should be reinforced by 'golden chains of commerce', but the difficulty was how to do it".[45] In its earliest form, the proposal was to create a $500 million merger which would join Canadian coal, iron and steel resources to the British steel and shipbuilding industries; the frankly predatory design was to use Canadian resources to revitalize British industry in the face of American competition. The proposal involved nine companies. In addition to the Dominion and Scotia companies, the merger would include three companies controlled by Wolvin's group (CSL, Halifax Shipyards and Collingwood Shipbuilding) and four smaller companies (Canada Foundries and Forgings, Port Arthur Shipbuilding, Davie Shipbuilding and Repairing, and the Maritime Nail Company). The book value of the corporation's assets was set at $486 million, including an estimated valuation of the coal and ore reserves at $200 million. The plan was to issue four types of shares, to a total value of $207 million: 8 per cent cumulative first preference ($25 million), 7 per cent cumulative second preference ($37 million), 7 per cent non-cumulative preference ($68 million) and common shares ($77 million). The first class of shares was reserved to raise new capital on the British financial market and the remainder were to be issued at advantageous rates of exchange for the securities of the merging companies.[46]

The proposal generated immediate controversy, including a three-hour debate in the House of Commons on the subject of "cosmopolitan grafters". "Members are afraid that it is some great stock jobbing scheme", reported the *Monetary Times*. "They will have to be convinced that there is no huge watered stock promotion job". Rather than face a threatened investigation, Besco quickly re-incorporated in Nova Scotia, where the province was pleased to receive a $75,000 fee and granted a charter specifying wide powers.[47] The proposed basis of share exchanges aroused criticism from directors of the Dominion and Scotia companies, who questioned the inclusion of the lesser companies, on which they lacked adequate financial information and on which the promoters of the merger stood to gain substantially through the merger. In response, the organizers made several revisions, dropping Halifax Shipyards and allowing better terms for the Scotia shareholders. But by the time of Dominion Steel's annual meeting in June 1920, a small group of veteran directors were in open revolt against the merger. In addition to Workman and Plummer, the dissident group included E.R. Wood and Sir Williams Mackenzie of Toronto and George Caverhill, William McMaster and Senator Raoul Dandurand of Montreal. A stormy session followed, as Wood, a Bank of Commerce director, pinpointed irregularities in the Besco balance sheet and protested the dilution of the steel company shares by the inclusion of the weaker companies.[48] Relying on the backing of the British group and his own holdings, Wolvin was able to control the outcome of the meeting.[49] The old board was defeated and only five members were retained on the new board: Wolvin, Norcross, Senator Frede-ric Nicholls and Sir Henry Pellatt (both vigorous defenders of the merger), and the aging Sir William Mackenzie. New members of the Dominion Steel board included Stanley Elkin, manager of the Saint John Maritime Nail Company, Senators Sir Clifford Sifton and C.P. Beaubien, and three of Wolvin's associates from the CSL, Halifax Shipyards, Collingwood and Davie Shipbuilding group. Three representatives of the London group also entered the board at this time: Moore, Talbot and Furness. In July D.H. McDougall of Scotia and Senator W.L. McDougald of Montreal, both directors of companies involved in the merger, were also added to the board.[50]

Ratified by the three principal companies, the merger was never completed.[51] First, an uproar took place over the arrangements with CSL. Cantley suddenly learned that instead of bringing the shipping firm in as one of the merging companies, Wolvin now planned to sign a 25-year lease guaranteeing a fixed return of 7 per cent to CSL shareholders. In effect, this would make dividends to Steamship shareholders a fixed charge on the earnings of Besco, to be paid ahead of returns to other Besco shareholders. Enraged, Cantley protested that Scotia was being "jockeyed out of its property and its resources and earnings" and denounced the lease as a violation of the merger terms; Galen Stone in New York agreed the news was "a tremendous shock" and suggested the merger might be voided as a result.[52] Furthermore, the new corporation encountered great difficulty in raising capital; completion of the merger remained conditional on the issue of the $25 million first preference shares, shown on the balance sheet as available working capital. The London financial market was not receptive. Besco had earned a poor reputation on the London "street". Initially enthusiastic, the *Financial Times* grew exasperated at the repeated revisions in the plans and in July 1920 denounced Besco's "Merger Mysteries". The lack of adequate information on the merging companies revealed that "so far as British investors are concerned, they have been very cavalierly treated" and the editors warned investors to be cautious:

> The efforts of the promoters of the deal seemed to have been concentrated to rush the matter through as quickly and with as little discussion as possible. . . . We do not like this way of doing business, and those interested in Canadian enterprise and anxious to secure the good opinion of the public on this side cannot learn the fact too quickly.[53]

Moreover, the collapse of the postwar speculative boom during the spring and summer of 1920 caused a contraction of British capital markets and, under an adverse exchange situation, Canadian borrowing in London became more difficult. Wolvin later estimated that the Besco merger "missed the boat" by about two weeks.[54]

A less frenzied pace characterized the reconstruction of Besco in 1921. Wolvin persisted in his plans for the merger by secretly buying Scotia shares on the open market and had gained about 10 per cent of the stock before his activity became known. The London shareholders, heavily committed to

290

Dominion Steel, also continued to favour the merger. The London Committee arranged a meeting in London in January 1921, where Wolvin reached an agreement with D.H. McDougall of Scotia.[55] A new merger plan was prepared, under which Scotia enjoyed improved terms and Wolvin was forced to exclude CSL, although Halifax Shipyards was admitted. The terms were approved by the shareholders of all three companies and the merger went into effect smoothly on 15 April 1921. Variously described as a "British" or "Montreal" company, it was difficult to identify Besco with any one geographic locale. The head office was in the Canada Cement Building in Montreal, but in 1922 the board's directors were distributed by residence among six locations: Toronto 4, Montreal 5, Britain 5, Nova Scotia 1, Boston 1, Quebec City 1. The directors fell into several interest groups. The first board was dominated by Wolvin and his partners Norcross and H.B. Smith. Three directors represented the Scotia company: President McDougall, W.D. Ross of Toronto and Galen Stone of New York and Boston. With expansion of the board the following year, there were several changes. Quarrelling with Wolvin over CSL and Halifax Shipyards, Norcross left Besco; Wolvin added J.F.M. Stewart, Frank Ross and Senator McDougald, all associates from shipping firms and coal agencies in Quebec and Ontario. Bank of Nova Scotia director Hector McInnes of Halifax joined fellow director W.D. Ross on the Besco board. And Sir Newton Moore led a group of five members of the London Committee onto the directorate. The changing structure of the Besco board in the 1920s is shown in Table 1.

Restricted to three companies, two of them well-known, the creation of the new holding company seemed less open to charges of stockwatering, although the inclusion of Halifax Shipyards reminded one critic of the "family compact element in the original merger that repelled the average investor".[56] The basis of share exchanges in the creation of Besco is shown in Table II. The share capitalization of the merging companies amounted to $82.75 million; in the merger this was transformed into $101.75 million, an increase of $19 million in stock value. The capital structure of the various merging companies included previous accumulations of "water" amounting to $38.5 million and the distribu-

tion of shares among the various classes of stock also allowed a considerable inflation of stock values. All the cumulative stock of the merging companies was exchanged, mainly on a share for share basis (except where 6 per cent stock became 7 per cent) for Series B first preference cumulative stock. On the other hand, the common stock of the merging companies, which amounted to $63.0 million, mainly at 6 per cent, was translated into a small number of common shares and a large block of second preference shares paying 7 per cent. The creation of this new class of stock was probably the most flagrant aspect of the merger and prompted Eugene Forsey to comment, in 1926: "Bless thee, Bottom, thou art translated".[57] The capital structure of the corporation also allowed the issue of two further categories of stock: 7 per cent non-cumulative preference shares, which would be paid ahead of common stock dividends, and Series A first preference 8 per cent cumulative shares, which would have first priority on the corporation's earnings. The plan was to issue $24.45 million of the Series A stock as soon as possible in order to raise new capital for the merger's operations.

While the Besco merger was before the House of Assembly in 1921, acting Nova Scotia Premier E.H. Armstrong requested an independent opinion of the merger arrangements from Ontario Liberal politician Newton W. Rowell, who visited Halifax to deliver the convocation address at Dalhousie University. Rowell alerted Armstrong to the dangers the capitalization of the company created. The high authorized capitalization of $500 million might lead to the acquisition of new companies, possibly above their fair value. The lack of working capital in the consolidation might require the issue of further stock, possibly below par value. As the terms of such arrangements could not be foreseen, there was a danger of new water entering the merger at a later date, and Rowell suggested that the province require Besco to seek approval of any stock issues or exchanges. As for the exchanges already outlined, a considerable danger existed: "without any addition to the tangible assets of any of these companies and without providing any additional capital for their operation or development", the share exchanges created a large volume of new stock:

This change in the character of the securities and this increase in the capital stock issued will undoubtedly involve sooner or later a serious Demand from Directors and Shareholders for a substantial increase in the earnings of the coal companies in order to pay dividends on these huge blocks of stock. These dividends can only come from increased efficiency in operation or an increase in price of coal over what would be necessary to pay a reasonable dividend on the old capitalization.[58]

Despite this warning, Armstrong loyally backed the merger, speaking out springly against "any action that would intimidate capital from embarking in Nova Scotia enterprises at such a critical time as the present".[59]

The British Empire Steel Corporation commenced operations in the unstable economic conditions of the early 1920s. Hopes for an enhanced level of profits were soon defeated, as were visions of new markets for the output of the Nova Scotia coal and steel industries. Throughout its short history, the British Empire Steel Corporation remained in financial crisis. The corporation's financial structure required minimum earnings of about $3 million a year to meet fixed charges. Dividends on the first preference stock required an additional $1.3 million. To make payments on the cumulative second preference stock would require about $4 million annually. Thus Besco required an annual operating profit of more than $8 million in order to meet financial commitments. Additional profits would be needed to build a reserve against less profitable years, to establish a surplus for capital expansion, or to pay dividends on the common stock. As Table III shows, Besco never met these expectations. No dividends were ever paid on the common or second preference shares. About $3.6 million was distributed in first preference dividends, until payments were suspended in early 1924. In 1924 and 1925 profits were too meagre to meet fixed charges and the corporation turned to bank loans and prior surpluses to meet these payments. By the end of 1925 Besco had accumulated a deficit of $5.7 million. Burdened with the unrealistic expectations embodied in Besco's corporate structure, Wolvin and his directors pursued an increasingly desperate strategy of corporate survival during the 1920s. As the industry's traditional markets were thrown into crises during this period, Wolvin and his directors pursued two central goals: to reduce the cost of labour power in the coal industry and to recruit state support for the coal and steel industries in the national market.

Firmly convinced his corporation possessed "the greatest known deposits of coal and iron ore, splendidly situated", Wolvin hoped to implement a programme of capital expansion and enlarge the scope and capacity of the steel industry at Sydney.[60] Under Besco in 1922 the Sydney steel plant for the first time in its history made a brief entry into foreign markets for finished steel.[61] Symbolic of the steel industry's aspirations for diversified production was the opening of Canada's first ship plate mill in February 1920; producing steel plate for shipbuilding, the mill represented a key addition to the industrial structure of the Maritimes. The federal government encouraged establishment of the mill during the war by contracting advance orders and in 1920 the new mill had some success in selling plate to British yards. But in 1920 the federal government cancelled its orders and a long dispute ultimately yielded Besco a $4 million settlement. The plate mill closed and was forgotten for 20 years.[62] Another desultory symbol of Besco's expansionist hopes was an unfulfilled agreement to construct a steel plant in Newfoundland by 1926.[63] Demand for the output of the Nova Scotia steel industry fell sharply after 1919. During the 1920s the steel industry at Sydney eked out a hand-to-mouth existence as it lobbied for orders to keep the plant open for months at a time. The smaller Scotia plant at Sydney Mines, though equipped with a new blast furnace at the end of the war, was closed in November 1920 and never reopened. Pig iron production at Sydney dropped from a near-capacity output of 421,560 tons in 1917 to 296,869 tons in 1920 and 120,769 tons in 1922; production then rose slowly but did not exceed 250,000 tons again until 1928. In 1922 the export to the Ruhr of more than 720,000 tons of iron ore, about three-quarters the annual production of the Bell Island mines, signified clearly the failure of Besco's hopes for expansion of the local steel industry.[64]

The coal industry also suffered seriously at the end of the war. The sharp drop in steel production curtailed the coal industry's largest single market; by the end of 1920 the

292

Sydney steel plant's consumption of coal had fallen from more than 100,000 tons per month to 40,000 tons.[65] The war itself had also disrupted the traditional pattern of markets for coal. The loss of the coal fleet to war service closed the St. Lawrence market, though this loss was compensated during the war by the vigorous local demand and the wartime shipping trade. When the war ended, readjustment was necessary. The return of coal vessels was slow and the Quebec market could not be entered aggressively until the 1921 season. Always costly, the alternative of rail shipments was uneconomic and the capacity of this route was limited by the Canso Strait. Also, high prices in the postwar bunker trade and potential export markets in France, Belgium and Britain tempted the coal operators more than the resumption of sharp competition in Quebec.[66] Recapturing Nova Scotia's share of the Quebec market took place slowly and with difficulty. The most formidable obstacle was the entrenched position of American coal suppliers, who shipped more than 3.5 million tons of coal to Quebec in 1920. Overexpansion of the U.S. coal industry during the war had led to the entry of large quantities of cheap coal into the Canadian market and the Nova Scotia coal industry did not regain its former share of this market until 1927.[67] In the Sydney coal-field, where production had reached a peak of 6.3 million tons in 1913, output fell to 4.5 million tons in 1920. The number of man-days worked in the coal industry plunged by one-third, from a peak of 4.5 million man-days in 1917 to 3.0 million in 1921; for the next two decades the level of activity never exceeded 3.3 million man-days per year and the industry was marked by irregular employment and a declining work force.[68]

Wage reductions in the coal industry promised substantial savings for Besco. The coal industry remained surprisingly labour-intensive and the potential for generating surpluses from the coal operations without new capital investment or a large amount of working capital, was attractive. Furthermore, since Whitney's time the coal operations had supplied hidden subsidies to allied companies, through below-cost contracts for coal (which the New England Gas and Coke Company and the Sydney steel plant enjoyed) or through the transfer of credits and surpluses

within mergers (which took place within Dominion Steel after 1910).[69] Wolvin made no secret of the fact that he regarded all assets within the merger as common ones and the transfer of earnings or materials from one to the other was the equivalent of changing money from one pocket to the other.[70] The Duncan Commission criticized this policy in 1926 and revealed that Dominion Coal had remained a profitable operation during most years in the early 1920s, in spite of Besco's claims that losses had required wage reductions.[71] David Schwartzman has reconstructed a series of estimates to show the financial position of Dominion Coal during the period when Besco did not issue separate reports for its constituents. When set beside the corporation's financial record, these figures reveal that in the merger's first years the coal operations contributed profits to the merger; by 1923, however, Besco could no longer lean on the coal operations to sustain the corporation.[72]

The coal miners' resistance to Besco's campaign of wage reductions made it impossible for Besco to implement this strategy of survival. In 1920 Wolvin reluctantly signed an agreement for substantial increases for the coal miners. When this contract ended, Besco began its campaign to reduce wages. In 1922 the corporation sought a reduction of about one-third, but after a dramatic struggle was able to win only half this amount. In 1924 and 1925 Besco sought 20 per cent reductions; in 1924 the coal miners won a small increase and in 1925, after a long and bitter strike, a royal commission allowed the corporation a 10 per cent reduction. The outstanding feature of industrial relations in the coal-fields in the 1920s was the tenacity of the coal miners' resistance to wage reductions. Besco's notorious labour policies did little to endear the corporation to public opinion and the coal miners' determined resistance placed an insuperable obstacle in the path of Besco's survival.[73]

To improve the competitive position of the coal and steel industries in the national market had long been a goal of the coal industry in Cape Breton. The coal duty never provided effective protection for a national market in coal. Wartime shortages alerted central Canadian consumers to the vulnerability of their fuel supply, as did postwar disruptions in the coal trade. Sentiment for an

293

all-Canadian coal market rose high during the early 1920s, but had little impact on public policy.[74] After a thorough review of proposals for more protection for coal, the *Monetary Times* concluded that higher duties would "restrict the operation of Ontario and Quebec industries and increase general living and production costs throughout these provinces".[75] In Nova Scotia improved protection for coal was a major theme of the Maritime Rights movement, a coalition which harnessed various regional grievances to the political ambitions of the Nova Scotia Conservative Party. The main demand was for an increase of the 14c per ton duty on slack coal to the general level of 53c and for a programme of subsidies to help Nova Scotia coal penetrate deeper into the central Canadian market.[76]

The relationship of Besco to this agitation was a complex one. In 1924 and 1925 the corporation did not participate in the large Maritime Rights delegations which visited Ottawa. In February 1925, however, Besco commenced publication of the *Besco Bulletin*, which campaigned for a "Bluenose tariff" to protect local industry. Besco's campaign grew most active in 1926, when the federal government appointed a tariff board to consider changes in protection for iron and steel. Wolvin in 1926 appealed for a 75c duty on coal and blamed the deteriorating protection for primary iron and steel over the previous two decades as the chief difficulty facing his corporation.[77] Yet Besco's enlistment in the ranks of Maritime Rights did not present a credible appearance. "At once the giant and the ogre of the Maritimes", Besco earned frequent attacks from local politicians and small businessmen who regarded the corporation as an embodiment of the outside exploitation which had destroyed the region's economy.[78] When Arthur Meighen came out "flatfooted for protection" for the coal industry in February 1925, he provoked dismay among party leaders in Nova Scotia. Gordon Harrington, the Glace Bay lawyer and future premier, warned Meighen that it would be unwise to become associated with protection for Besco, "until some very severe restrictions are placed upon it in the handling of the monopoly it has obtained of the industries based on the natural resources of our country. The absurdity of this corporation asking for tariff concessions on the one hand, and the reduction in already

too meagre wage scales on the other hand, must be apparent. Further, the corporation appears to be financially hopelessly unsound and its direction is beyond comment".[79]

The campaign for state intervention in the coal industry did meet some success by the end of the 1920s. In 1924-25 a limited system of rail subventions was tested, but abandoned. The intense lobbying in the winter of that year, the bleakest and most desperate months in the coalfields in the 1920s, caused the Liberal government that spring to standardize the duty on all bituminous coal at 50c per ton. While the Duncan Report failed to endorse tariff changes or subsidies, it called for wider use of Canadian coke in central Canada. The report concluded with an eloquent personal appeal by commissioner Hume Cronyn, a native Maritimer and Ontario businessman, who called on residents of Ontario and Quebec to make sacrifices to help this important Maritime industry. In the comfort of a steamship en route to Nassau that winter, Cronyn also penned a second addendum to the report in a private letter to Sir Robert L. Borden:

There are two main difficulties in Nova Scotia which could not be set forth openly in a public document. In the first place the industry is economically unsound and must remain so until the cheaper Virginian and Kentucky coals cease being dumped on our market. Next (quite confidentially) the company (Besco) is in the wrong hands. If it could be re-organized under a new President and staff and could obtain some relief by way of duties or bounties there would be hope for the future. Otherwise I can see nothing ahead but liquidation with all its attendant distress and loss.[80]

As a result of the tariff board hearings, protection for iron and steel was raised substantially in 1930 and 1931, and the coal duty was increased to 75c in 1931. Railway subventions were renewed in 1928 and soon became a large factor in the transportation of coal to central Canada.[81] But these important changes came too late to help Besco, and too late to rescue industrial Cape Breton from a condition of economic dependency and decline.

At stake in Besco's strategy of corporate

survival was the corporation's inability to raise new capital or to return a satisfactory profit. As Besco's fortunes deteriorates, internal tensions grew. To one observer, Besco in the 1920s was "a vicious circle of ancient ri valries and new antagonisms".[82] The battle on the board of Dominion Steel in the summer of 1920 was followed by new manoeuvres two years later, at Besco's first annual meeting. The most powerful financial figure in Canada, Royal Bank President Sir Herbert Holt, was reported ready to assume the presidency of Besco and provide the financial backing the corporation needed. Besco stock values rose with this speculation, but the London group continued to support Wolvin and retained control of the corporation for him.[83] In November 1922 Wolvin raised new capital by issuing Dominion Iron and Steel mortage bonds worth $4.6 million, which were financed by director Galen Stone's investment house.[84] At the next annual meeting, in an effort to make the corporation more attractive to investors, Wolvin reduced the corporation's authorized capital by half to $250 million.[85] The intense labour conflict of the summer of 1923 created more anxieties for the corporation. The popular vice-president and general manager, D.H. McDougall, resigned and was replaced by J.E. McLurg, general manager of Halifax Shipyards.[86] The most influential of the directors, Moore and Stone, remained active behind the scenes attempting to raise capital. In September 1923 Moore pleaded with Prime Minister Mackenzie King not to obstruct their efforts by appointing a royal commission to investigate the summer's labour strife. Moore sounded a plaintive note:

> A good many of us have put the savings of years into this Canadian enterprise and have been bitterly disappointed that the Company has not been able to return some interest on the capital invested . . . the present market value of our shares represents only 1/4 of the amounts of the purchase money.[87]

The turning point in the rise and fall of Besco was evident in the record of financial success. Operating profits fell sharply from $4.4 million in 1923 to $.9 million in 1924, when the corporation lost $2.3 million. In March 1924 the directors suspended dividend payments on all stock. Though additional capital was secured through the issue of Dominion Coal bonds, the year ended with a net loss of $1.3 million.[88] Besco's dividend policy awakened shareholder dissatisfaction. Wolvin received a "great many" letters criticizing the non-payment of dividends on the second preference stock and with the suspension of all payments, complaints multiplied.[89] The condition of Besco grew worse in the winter of 1924-1925, and the hardship and suffering of the local community starkly dramatized the plight of the coal industry. After the annual meeting in March 1925, a dejected Besco shareholder and director, *Montreal Herald* publisher Senator J.P.B. Casgrain, poured his heart out to Mackenzie King:

> I am a director of the British Empire Steel Corporation, and an unfortunate shareholder for a very large amount. I have never had one cent of dividend on that merger-stock. However, that is my own affair. . . . I do not plead for myself—although since the merger I have very foolishly invested, in money, in that enterprise $123,000. My wife, 25 years ago, after a visit to Sydney with Sir Laurier, Lady Laurier and myself, invested of her money $40,000. I know all this has nothing to do with the question of bounties and duties and it is not for that that I write. Forget about us but think of the 22,500 men who will be out of work when we close up. With their families, there will be over 100,000 who will probably have to leave Nova Scotia.[90]

Wolvin's intransigence in the 1925 strike, when he and McLurg refused to meet union leaders and closed company stores, further damaged the corporation's reputation. In June 1925 the Liberal government was overwhelmingly defeated in a provincial election, partly as a result of their association with the corporation.[91] Tory premier E.N. Rhodes, who had promised to settle the five-month strike, now found it impossible to deal with Wolvin: "Wolvin is, I think, the most stubborn man with whom I have ever come in contact", he complained to Borden, "and his stubborness [sic] is increased by the fact that his Companies are almost bankrupt".[92] E.R. Forbes has found evidence that Wolvin finally came to terms as a result of financial pressure from Bank of Commerce chairman Sir Joseph Flavelle, whose bank threatened to deny short-term money to Dominion Coal.[93] The strike ended with a temporary agreement and the appointment of a provincial royal commission, which, under the chairmanship of British coal expert Sir Andrew Rae Duncan, vice-president of the British Shipbuilding Employers' Federation, criticized Besco's unrealistic capital structure and financial policies.[94]

In the spring of 1926 the Bank of Commerce and Bank of Montreal refused Besco additional short-term financing, and Wolvin resolved to allow Dominion Iron and Steel, the weakest part of the merger, to go into receivership. In July 1926 Dominion Iron and Steel defaulted on bond payments and National Trust, closely linked to the Bank of Commerce, was appointed receiver for the company. No surprise, the collapse nevertheless caused a sharp fall in Canadian bond prices that summer and marked the beginning of Besco's disintegration.[95] Bondholders' committees were appointed to guard the interests of various investors, and early in 1927 National Trust began court proceedings for the winding up of Besco and Dominion Steel.[96] The Supreme Court of Nova Scotia refused to wind up Besco, but agreed to the liquidation of Dominion Steel, appointing Royal Trust, which was allied to the Bank of Montreal and the Royal Bank, as the receiver. In July 1927 Wolvin submitted a reorganization scheme to his shareholders, but could not win their support.[97] Soon Wolvin agreed to sell his holdings to Herbert Holt and a group of his Royal Bank associates. At the annual meeting in January 1928 Wolvin resigned as president of Besco.[98]

Wolvin's successor as Besco president was C.B. McNaught, a Toronto director of the Royal Bank. With the entry of seven new directors onto the Besco board in 1928, the coal and steel industries passed into the hands of a financial grouping dominated by the Royal Bank. The group began plans to reorganize the corporation. McNaught and J.H. Gundy visited London to reach agreement with the British investors. In March 1928 the group incorporated a new holding and operating company, the Dominion Steel and Coal Corporation, which was capitalized at $65 million and took over the Besco properties.[99] With the completion of this transfer in May

1930, the British Empire Steel Corporation ceased to exist. The new company represented an alliance of old and new interests. The Royal Bank group held half the seats on the Dosco board, but Sir Newton Moore and Lord Invernairn remained as directors to represent the continued British interest; Moore served as vice-president and from 1932 to 1936 was president of the corporation. The new company ended a decade of financial turmoil and disappointment and placed the corporation in a strong position to weather the troubles of the 1930s.

As an episode in Canadian economic history, the development of industrial Cape Breton between the 1880s and 1920s revealed a pattern of rapid growth culminating in severe crisis. Far from a backwater of economic inactivity, industrial Cape Breton performed important and useful functions for the national economy. Through the coal industry, the region supplied a basic industrial raw material, supported the local iron and steel industry and provided a lucrative arena for the financial wizardry of various investors. But industrial capitalism could not provide balanced and harmonious economic growth between regions; on the contrary, the national economic structure which emerged in Canada during this period promoted uneven development and regional dependency. This pattern of uneven development led to the crisis of markets and corporate welfare in the coal industry during the 1920s. Vulnerable in its distant markets and unable to rely on a stable local market, the importance of the Cape Breton coal industry declined. At the same time, the metropolitan search for economic surpluses continued, and in the case of Besco, reached unrealistic proportions. After the 1920s, the main functions of industrial Cape Breton in the national economy changed: the community was now called upon to provide a large pool of labour for the national labour market, and, in time of need, to supply reserve capacity for the national energy and steel markets. The rise and fall of the British Empire Steel Corporation provided the occasion, though not the root cause, for a structural turning point in the economic history of industrial Cape Breton.

The growth of the coal industry in Cape Breton expressed above all the financial opportunism of its successive owners, rather than any commitment to principles of regional economic welfare. Spokesmen for the coal industry from Richard Brown to Roy Wolvin endorsed local industrial development as a strategy for utilization of the local coal and iron resources, but in practice they sought trading links with distant markets and pursued policies of rapid resource depletion. The local business class offered no effective resistance to the integration of the coal industry into the national economy: native Cape Bretoners like D.H. McDougall and W.D. Ross were capitalists foremost and proved no more loyal to the region's welfare than Whitney, Ross, Plummer or Wolvin. The experience of industrial Cape Breton also suggests that in the period between 1890 and 1930 Canadian capitalism features a powerful and aggressive business class, associated in common purposes although often divided by rivalries. The resources of industrial Cape Breton attracted the interest of American and British investors, but except for the frustrated intentions of Whitney in the 1890s and the London syndicate in 1920, they preferred to leave direct control in Canadian hands. The passage of control over the coal industry from Bank of Montreal circles to a Bank of Montreal-Bank of Commerce alliance before the war, and ultimately to the Royal Bank in the 1920s, paralleled the successive domination of Canadian capitalism by these financial groupings. The route from Van Horne and James Ross to Sir Herbert Holt was interrupted in the 1920s by the intervention of Roy Wolvin and his allies on the Great Lakes and St. Lawrence and in London. But the extreme brevity and catastrophic failure of their regime during the 1920s indicated the distance that separated this group from the real seats of power in Canadian capitalism.

The most important conclusions to this episode in Canadian economic history were those reached by the local community in industrial Cape Breton. At a time when the labour movement was on the defensive across the country, the resistance of the coal miners to the British Empire Steel Corporation caused the eventual collapse of that enfeebled enterprise. the emergence of a militant labour movement in Canada helped begin a new stage in the history of Canadian capitalism. After the 1920s and 1930s, an ever closer collaboration between state and capital was needed to maintain the essential structure of the national economy. In industrial Cape Breton the deteriorating local economy would be propped up by government subsidies, enabling private capital to continue profitably to exploit the region's economic assets, while the deepening underdevelopment of the region would drive Cape Bretoners to leave their homes and enter the national labour market. The local working class continued to resist the progressive destruction of their community by campaigning for improved social standards and equitable national policies, and for public ownership of the coal and steel industries, which was achieved in 1967 and 1968. In 1928 hopeful members of the Cape Breton Board of Trade celebrated the arrival of the new Besco president, C.B. McNaught, with a ceremonial banquet. But the rise and fall of the British Empire Steel Corporation left most Cape Bretoners with a permanent distrust of outside capitalists.

Table I
Directors, British Empire Steel Corporation, 1921-1929

	Residence	1921	22	23	24	25	26	27	28	29	30 (Dominion Steel and Coal Corporation)
R.M. Wolvin	M	P	P	P	P	P	P	P	-	-	
D.H. McDougall	M	V	V	V	-	-	-	-	-	-	-
W. Mackenzie	T	X	-	-	-	-	-	-	-	-	-
J.W. Norcross	M	X	-	-	-	-	-	-	-	-	-
W.D. Ross	T	X	X	X	X	X	X	X	-	-	
H.B. Smith	T	X	X	X	-	-	-	-	-	-	
G.L. Stone	B	X	X	X	X	-	-	-	-	-	
H.M. Pellatt	T	X	-	-	-	-	-	-	-	-	
C.S. Cameron	M							V,S	V,S	V,S	V,S
C.P. Beaubien	M		X	X	X	X	X	X	X	X	X
Vt. Furness	L		X	X	X	-	-	-	-	-	
T. Dawson	L		X	X	X	X	X	-	-	-	
N. Moore	L		X	X	X	X	X	X	X	X	V
H. McInnis	H		X	X	X	X	X	-	-	-	
J.F.M. Stewart	T		X	X	X	-	-	-	-	-	
B. Talbot	L		X	X	X	-	-	-	-	-	
Invernairn	G		X	X	X	X	X	X	X	X	X
W.L. McDougald	M		X	X	-	-	-	-	-	-	
F. Ross	Q		X	X	X	X	X	X	X	X	
G.S. Campbell	H		X	-	-	-	-	-	-	-	
J.P.B. Casgrain	M		X	X	X	X	X	X	X	X	X
J.E. McLurg	S			V	V	V	V	V	V		
G.F. Downs	NY			X	X	X	X	X	X	V	
R.F. Hoyt	NY			X	X	X	X	X	X		
L.C. Webster	M					X	X	X	X	X	X
C.B. McNaught	T							P	P		P
C.J. Burchell	M							X	X		X
G.H. Duggan	M							X	X		X
J.H. Gundy	T							X	X		X
H.S. Holt	M							X	X		X
G. Montgomery	M							X	X		X
W.E. Wilder	T							X	X		-
H.J. Kelley	X										V,G
C.B. Gordon	M										X
J. Kilpatrick	T										X

Key: B   Boston   P   President
       G   Glasgow   V   Vice-President
       H   Halifax   X   Director
       L   London   S   Secretary and Treasurer
       M Montreal   G   General Manager
       NY New York
       Q   Quebec City
       S   Sydney
       T   Toronto

Source: *Houston's Canadian Annual Financial Review*, XX-XXXI (1920-1931)

Table II
Formation of the British Empire Steel Corporation, 1921
($ - millions)

| | Stock issued by Merging Companies | | Stock issued by British Empire Steel Corporation | | | | |
| | | | 1st pf A 8% cum | 1st pf B 7% cum | 2nd pf 7% cum | noncum | |
	cum pf	cmmn	cum	cum	cum	noncum	cmmn
Dominion Steel	6% $ 7.0	6% $43.0		$ 7.0	$40.85		$17.2
Dominion Coal	7% $ 3.0			$ 3.0			
Dominion Iron and Steel	7% $ 5.0			$ 5.0			
Nova Scotia Steel and Coal	8% $ 1.0	5% $15.0		$ 1.2	$13.5		$ 6.0
Eastern Car	6% $ .75			$ .75			
Halifax Shipyards	7% $ 3.0	$ 5.0	$ 3.0	$ 3.0			$ 1.25
	$19.75	$63.0	-	$19.95	$57.35	-	$24.45
Total Stock Issued	$82.75		$101.75				

Key: cum — cumulative
pf — preference
noncum — non-cumulative
cmmn — comm

Sources: *Houston's Review*, XXI, XXII (1921, 1922); *Duncan Report*, pp.25-8.

Table III
Financial Settlements, British Empire Steel Corporation, 1921-1926
($ - millions)

	1921	1922	1923	1924	1925	1926
Operating profit	4.416	6.917*	4.444	.924	−1.133	4.424
Sinking funds and depreciation	1.501	3.628	1.113	1.113	1.342	1.462
Bond and debenture interest	1.182	1.677	1.978	2.024	1.936	1.824
Net profit	1.734	1.613	1.354	−2.213	−4.411	1.138
Dividends	.978	1.344	1.347	.145	—	—
Net surplus	.756	.268	.007	−2.358	−4.411	1.138
Balance	.756	1.024	1.031	−1.327	−5.738	−4.600

*including $4 million settlement from the federal government.

Sources: *Houston's Review* XX-XXX (1920-1930); *Monetary Times*, 1920-1928.

Acadiensis, 7:1, Autumn 1977.

NOTES

[1]Nova Scotia, *A Submission of its Claims with Respect to Maritime Disabilities within Confederation* (Halifax, 1926; Nova Scotia, *A Submission on Dominion-Provincial Relations and the Fiscal Disabilities of Nova Scotia within the Canadian Federation* (Halifax, 1934).
[2]C.R. Fay and H.A. Innis, "The Economic Development of Canada, 1867-1921: The Maritime Prov-

inces", *Cambridge History of the British Empire* (Cambridge, 1930), vol. VI, pp.657-71; S.A. Saunders, "Trends in the Economic History of the Maritime Provinces", *Studies in the Economy of the Maritime Provinces* (Toronto, 1939), pp.245-65.

[3]P.D. McClelland, "The New Brunswick Economy in the 19th Century", *Journal of Economic History*, XXV (1965), pp.686-90; A.H. Clark, "Contributions of its Southern Neighbours to the Underdevelopment of the Maritime Provinces Area, 1710-1867", in R.A. Preston, ed., *The Influence of the United States on Canadian Development* (Durham, N.C., 1972), pp.164-84; R.F. Neill, "National Policy and Regional Underdevelopment", *Journal of Canadian Studies*, IX (May, 1974), pp.12-20.

[4]Bruce Archibald, "Atlantic Regional Underdevelopment and Socialism", in Laurier LaPierre et. al., eds., *Essays on the Left* (Toronto, 1971), pp.103-20; Archibald, "The Development of Underdevelopment in the Atlantic Provinces" (M.A. thesis, Dalhousie University, 1971); Archibald's work was based on an application of André Gunder Frank, "The Development of Underdevelopment", *Monthly Review*, XVIII (September, 1966), pp.17-31.

[5]"The National Policy and the Industrialization of the Maritimes, 1880-1910", *Acadiensis*, I (Spring, 1972), pp.3-28. Similar in approach was J.M.S. Careless, "Aspects of Metropolitanism in Atlantic Canada", in Mason Wade, ed., *Regionalism in the Canadian Community 1867-1967* (Toronto, 1969), pp.117-29.

[6]Karl Marx, *Capital* (New York, 1967), vol. I, especially ch. XXV; Paul Baran, *The Political Economy of Growth* (New York, 1968); Ernest Mandel, *Capitalism and Regional Disparities* (Toronto, 1970); Henry Veltmeyer, "The Methodology of Dependency Analysis; An Outline for a Strategy of Research on Regional Underdevelopment" (unpublished paper, Saint Mary's University, 1977).

[7]Recent work on regional underdevelopment includes E.R. Forbes, "The Maritime Rights Movement, 1919-1927: A Study in Canadian Regionalism" (Ph.D. thesis, Queen's University, 1975); David Alexander, "Newfoundland's Traditional Economy and Development to 1934", *Acadiensis*, V (Spring, 1976), pp.56-78; see also the contributions by C.D. Howell, Carman Miller, E.R. Forbes and T.W. Acheson to D.J. Bercuson, ed., *Canada and the Burden of Unity* (Toronto, 1977). The concentration and centralization of the Canadian economy affected the Maritimes in everal ways. First, national economic policies under Confederation promoted regional underdevelopment. The political hegemony of central Canada helped shape state policy to aid central Canadian goals and to injure or neglect regional interests, especially in tariff, railway, trade, marine and fisheries matters. The completion of the railway network added a key instrument of national economic integration; the railways brought western goods in and took eastern people out. The creation of a national market in goods undermined local industry as outside competitors conquered the regional market, and the creation of an inter-regional labour market tended to make the region a reserve pool of labour for neighbouring regions. A fourth aspect was the growing division of labour between regions, which often took the form of the export of raw materials and specialized products to the metropolitan market, but also resulted in the location of resource-based and labour-intensive industries to take advantage of raw materials and low wages in the underdeveloped region. A corollary was the emergence of economic sectors, which, because they were not important to the national economy, suffered capital deficiencies (the fisheries) or were absorbed into other economic empires (the forest industries). A fifth aspect of the "Canadianization" of the region was the steady import of central Canadian social and cultural norms; by the time they reached Ottawa, political figures like W.S. Fielding and R.L. Borden readily accepted the assumptions of central Canadian hegemony. Finally, the most effective form of regional subordination was the extension of direct metropolitan financial control over the region through mergers and takeovers in all the region's important industries and financial institutions.

[8]D.A. Muise, "The Making of an Industrial Community: Cape Breton Coal Towns, 1867-1900" (paper presented to the Atlantic Canada Studies Conference, Fredericton, 1976), Appendix I.

[9]M.J. Patton, "The Coal Resources of Canada", *Economic Geography*, I (1925), pp.84-5; A.L. Hay, "Coal-mining Operations in the Sydney Coal Field, American Institute of Mining and Metallurgical Engineers, *Technical Publication No. 198* (New York, 1929), pp.3-6.

[10]F.W. Gray, "The Coal Fields and Coal Industry of Eastern Canada", Canada, Mines Branch, *Bulletin No. 14* (Ottawa, 1917), p.14; W.J. Donald, *The Canadian Iron and Steel Industry* (Boston, 1915), Appendix B. In 1913 Nova Scotia produced 8,135,104 short tons of coal; of this total the Sydney field supplied 6,313,275 tons. For production data see Canada, *Report of the Royal Commission on Coal, 1946* (Ottawa, 1947), pp.64-5.

[11]Gray, "The Coal Fields of Eastern Canada", pp.13-14. The same question puzzled historians V.C. Fowke, S.A. Saunders and Harold Innis, who briefly examined the coal industry in the 1920s and 1930s. They observed that Canada's coal industry was located at the ends of the country, while most industry was clustered at the centre. They stressed the difficulties in shipping a cheap, bulky commodity like coal long distances to market and lamented the inadequacy of local markets within the region. By failing fo attract other production factors to generate industrial growth in its own geographic locale, the coal industry seemed to follow an anomalous growth strategy. To explain this, Innis and his associates began to point out the dominant role of central Canada in the construction of the national economy. This approach was supplemented by economist David Schwartzman and labour historian C.B. Wade, who drew attention to the manipulative and exploitative financial policies of the coal companies. They found that the ideas of

O.D. Skelton's "financial buccanneers" had blossomed handsomely in the coalfields and concluded that the industry's chornic instability and mismanagement stemmed largely from this source. See V.C. Fowke, "Economic Realities of the Canadian Coal Situation–1929" (M.A. thesis, University of Saskatchewan, 1929); S.A. Saunders, *The Economic Welfare of the Maritime Provinces* (Wolfville, 1932), pp.30-46; H.A. Innis, "Editor's Foreword", in E.S. Moore, *American Influence in Canadian Mining* (Toronto, 1941), pp. v-xvii; C.B. Wade, *Robbing the Mines* (Glace Bay, 194-);Wade, "History of District 26, United Mine Workers of America, 1919-1941" (unpublished manuscript, Beaton Institute of Cape Breton Studies, Sydney, 1950); David Schwartzman, "Mergers in the Nova Scotia Coal Fields: A History of the Dominion Coal Company, 1893-1940" (Ph.D. thesis, University of California, Berkeley, 1953).

[12]Abraham Gesner, *The Industrial Resources of Nova Scotia* (Halifax, 1849); Richard Brown, *The Coal-Fields and Coal Trade of the Island of Cape Breton* (London, 1871); C.B. Fergusson, ed., *Uniacke's Sketches of Cape Breton* (Halifax, 1958), pp.117-29; J.S. Martell, "Early Coal Mining in Nova Scotia", *Dalhousie Review*, XXV (1945-1946), pp.156-72; Saunders, "The Maritime Provinces and the Reciprocity Treaty", *Dalhousie Review*, XIV (1934), pp.355-71; Phyllis Blakeley, "Samuel Cunard", and David Frank, "Richard Smith", *Dictionary of Canadian Biography*, IX (Toronto, 1976), pp.172-84, 730-32.

[13]C.O. Macdonald, *The Coal and Iron Industries of Nova Scotia* (Halifax, 1909), p.42; G.A. White, *Halifax and its Business* (Halifax, 1876), pp.108-9.

[14]B.D. Tennyson, "Economic Nationalism and Confederation: A Case Study in Cape Breton", *Acadiensis*, II (Spring, 1973), pp.39-53; D.A. Muise, "The Federal Election of 1867 in Nova Scotia: An Economic Interpretation", Nova Scotia Historical Society *Collections*, XXXVI (1967), pp.327-51.

[15]J.R. Lithgow, *A Letter to the House of Comons of Canada on Behalf of the Coal Interests of Canada* (Halifax, 1877), p.9.

[16]Importance of the Canadian Coal Industry (n.p., n.d., probably 1897), pp.50-5; Canada, Dominion Bureau of Statistics, *Coal Statistics for Canada, 1927* (Ottawa, 1928), p.27.

[17]*Importance of the Canadian Coal Industry*, p.21. Tariff changes on coal are summarized in *Royal Commission on Coal, 1946*, pp.575-77.

[18]*Report of the Royal Commission on Coal Mining Industry in Nova Scotia* [Duncan Report], Supplement to the *Labour Gazette* (January, 1926), p.13.

[19]E.H. Armstrong, untitled manuscript on the coal industry in Nova Scotia, 1921, E.H. Armstrong Papers, Box 41, Public Archives of Nova Scotia (PANS).

[20]Basic accounts of the steel industry include Donald, *The Canadian Iron and Steel Industry*; E.J. McCracken, "The Steel Industry of Nova Scotia" (M.A. thesis, McGill University, 1932); W.D.R. Eldon, "American Influence on the Canadian Iron and Steel Industry" (Ph.D. thesis, Harvard University, 1952).

[21]Important studies of this process are Acheson, "Industrialization of the Maritimes", and Nolan Reilly, "The Origins of the Amherst General Strike, 1890-1919" (paper presented to the Canadian Historical Association Annual Meeting, Fredericton, 1977).

[22]*Canadian Mining Review* (August, 1894), p.131.

[23]Robert Drummond, "Appendix", in Richard Brown, *The Coal Fields and Coal Trade of the Island of Cape Breton* (reprint, Stellarton, 1899), pp.123-25.

[24]Robert Drummond, *Minerals and Mining, Nova Scotia* (Stellarton, 1918), pp.192-205; *The National Cyclopedia of American Biography*, X (1900; Ann Arbor, 1967), p.155; *Who Was Who in America*, I (Chicago, 1943), p.1340; Schwartzman, "Dominion Coal", pp.109-21. The most accurate study of Whitney and the origins of Dominion Coal is Don Macgillivray, "From Conway, Massachusetts to Cape Breton Island: The Whitney Saga" *Acadiensis*, IX, (Autumn, 1979).

[25]Nova Scotia, *Debates and Proceedings of the House of Assembly*, 1893, p.15. Conservative Party critics attacked the generous lease provisions and warned that the future of the coal industry would now depend "upon a thousand and one financial considerations . . . and not upon any consideration for the coal mines or for the people of Nova Scotia". One protectionist critic opposed the export of a single ton of coal: "This commodity is essential to our success as a manufacturing centre. If we jealously guard this commodity, the day may yet dawn when Nova Scotia will become to the Dominion of Canada what Manchester is today to England, Ireland and Scotland". *Debates*, 1893, pp.41-2, 71-3.

[26]*Canadian Mining Review*, (August, 1894), pp.131-33. In addition to Whitney, the board included his brother-in-law H.F. Dimock, a Mr. Winsor representing Kidder, Peabody and Company, the Boston investment house, and F.S. Pearson, a Boston engineer employed by Whitney. The Canadians included two local coal operators, J.S. McLennan, who became treasurer, and David McKeen, resident manager, two Halifax lawyers, W.B. Ross and B.F. Pearson, and three Montreal capitalists, Hugh McLennan, Donald Smith and Sir W.C. Van Horne.

[27]Reduced in 1894, the U.S. coal duty was restored near full strength in 1897; except for long-term contracts with Whitney's coke company, shipments to the U.S. remained small. Donald, *The Canadian Iron and Steel Industry*, p.200.

[28]*Canadian Mining Review* (March, 1902), pp.45-6; *ibid.* (December, 1903), pp.241-42. The rapid transfer from American to Canadian control is often overlooked, as in R.T. Naylor, *The History of Canadian Business* (Toronto, 1975), II, pp.176-77, 210.

[29]W.R. Houston, ed., *Directory of Directors in Canada* (Toronto, 1906).

[30]Acheson, "Industrialization of the Maritimes", pp.25-7, discusses the struggle for Scotia.

[31]W.R. Houston, ed., *Directory of Directors in Canada, 1912* (Toronto, 1912). In 1912 the Dominion Steel directors included from Toronto, J.H. Plummer, George Cox, Frederic Nicholls, William Mackenzie, James Mason, Henry Pellatt, and from Montreal, W.C. Van Horne, J.R. Wilson, William McMaster, H. Montagu Allan, George Caverhill, Robert MacKay, W.G. Ross, Raoul Dandurand, David McKeen of Halifax was the lone Maritimer. The board of Dominion Coal was very similar; Toronto: Plummer, Cox, Mason, Pellatt, Mackenzie, W.D. Matthews, E.R. Wood; Montreal: Wilson, Van Horne, Dandurand, MacKay, McMaster, Lord Strathcona (formerly Donald Smith), F.L. Wanklyn. W.R. Houston, comp., *The Annual Financial Review, Canadian (Houston's Review)*, XII (1912). An important study of the Canadian financial community in 1910 graphically situates Dominion Steel between financial groupings surrounding the Montreal and Commerce banks. The board of Dominion Coal had four or more directors in common with the following: Bank of Montreal, National Trust, Canadian Pacific Railway, Toronto Railway Company, Electrical Development Company, Canada Life Assurance Company, Gilles Piédalue, "Les groupes financiers au Canada, (1900-1930", *Revue d'Histoire de l'Amérique Francaise*, XXX (1976), pp.28-9.

[32]J.M. Cameron, *Industrial History of the New Glasgow District* (New Glasgow, 1960), ch. III; Donald, *The Canadian Iron and Steel Industry*, pp.194-99, 254-56. The Scotia board included J.W. Allison, Robert Harris, Thomas Cantley, G.S. Campbell, Frank Stanfield, G.F. McKay, J.D. McGregor, J.C. McGregor, all of Nova Scotia; W.D. Ross and Robert Jaffray, Toronto; Lorne Webster and K.W. Blackwell, Montreal; Frank Ross, Quebec City; J.S. Pitts and R.E. Chambers, St. John's, Newfoundland. *Houston's Review*, XII (1912). The Scotia board was closely linked to the Bank of Nova Scotia and the Eastern Trust Company, itself also close to the Royal Bank; Piédalue, "Les groupes financiers", p.28. From 1902-1909 Lyman Melvin-Jones, president of Massey-Harris, was a director of Scotia; according to Cantley, half of Scotia's sales were to agricultural implement manufacturers; Eldon, "The Canadian Iron and Steel Industry", p.489.

[33]*Financial Post* (Toronto), 30 June 1917; *Monetary Times* (Toronto), 22 February 1918, 22 June 1917. The new directors included D.C. Jackling, New York, and W. Hinckle Smith, Philadelphia, capitalists interested in mining investments and associated with Boston banker Charles Hayden, prominent in Kennecott Copper, Utah Copper and the International Nickel Company, *Who Was Who in America*, I, p.538; II (Chicago, 1950), p.498; III (Chicago, 1963), pp.195, 440-41.

[34]*Montreal Herald*, 10 July 1917.

[35]F.H. Crockard to N.B. McKelvie, 6 February 1918, Thomas Cantley Papers, Box 175, PANS.

[36]*Montreal Gazette*, 5 February 1918, *Canadian Annual Review 1918*; *Monetary Times*, 22 February 1918.

[37]*Canadian Mining Journal* (30 April 1919); ibid., (14 September 1923); *Who's Who and Why, 1921* (Toronto, 1921), p.885.

[38]Dominion Steel resisted accommodation with Scotia and both the provincial government and the Dominion Fuel Controller were forced to intervene in the dispute. Armstrong Papers, vol. II, Folders 3,4,5, PANS.

[39]*Sydney Post*, 3 October 1919. Evidence for Max Aitken's involvement is circumstantial. In February 1919 Aitken was meeting with both Cantley and Workman in London, and in June 1919 he was accompanied on his trip to Canada by W.D. Ross. "Daily Memorandum Covering European Visit, 1919", Cantley Papers, Box 167, PANS; *Montreal Star*, 25 June 1919. Grant Morden, the main Besco promoter, admitted in a New York interview that he was an associate of Aitken; *Sydney Post*, 13 February 1920. The rhetoric of the Besco promoters reflected Beaverbrook's vision of imperial economic cooperation.

[40]*Monetary Times*, 28 November 1919; *Sydney Post*, 15 December 1919, 10 January 1920.

[41]*Houston's Review*, XX (1920), p.166; *Who Was Who, 1929-40*; *Who Was Who, 1941-1950*; *Who's Who, 1920* (London, 1920).

[42]*Who Was Who, 1929-1940*, pp.963, 965; clipping, 1920, in Stuart McCawley Scrapbook, p.6, Miners' Memorial Museum, Glace Bay; *Sydney Record*, 1 May 1920; *Canadian Mining Journal* (March, 1934). Two ships in the CSL fleet reflected the links with Vickers: the *W.G. Morden* and the *Sir Trevor Dawson*, clipping, Cantley Papers, Box 175, PANS.

[43]*Monetary Times*, 14 February 1919; *Sydney Post*, 16 October 1919, 31 March 1920; *Monetary Times*, 26 March 1920; H.J. Crowe to G.B. Hunter, April 1902, H. Crowe Letterbook, PANS.

[44]Nova Scotia, Royal Commission on Coal Mines, 1925, "Minutes of Evidence", p.2061; *Sydney Post*, 22 March 1920; *Monetary Times*, 26 March 1920.

[45]*Saturday Night*, 8 May 1920; *Salient Facts of the Steel Merger* (n.p., 1 June 1920); *Press Opinions of 'Empire Steel'* (n.p., 1 July 1920). The crisis of the British economy in the post-war period led to efforts by prominent industrialists to revitalize the national economy, but they could not always rely on the support of the London financial community. For short summaries, see Sidney Pollard, *The Development of the British Economy, 1914-1950* (London, 1962), and John Foster "British Imperialism and the Labour Aristocracy", in Jeffrey Skelley, ed., *The General Strike, 1926* (London, 1976), pp.3-16. According to Wolvin, the two financiers in the original Besco promotion, Morden and an Austrian banker named Szarvassy, also tried to recruit American support; Duncan Commission, "Minutes of Evidence", p.2063.

[46]*Monetary Times*, 7 May 1920.

[47]Canada, House of Commons, *Debates*, 1920, pp.1945-67; *Monetary Times*, 7, 28 May 1920. Letters patent authorizing a capitalization of $100,000 were obtained from the federal government on 15 March 1920; the increase to $500 million was obtained in Nova Scotia on 22 May 1920; *Besco Bulletin*, 11 April 1925.

[48]*Monetary Times*, 18 June 1920; *Sydney Post*, 15, 16, 18 June 1920.

[49]By this time the London group held about 180,000 shares in Dominion Steel; Wolvin held 50,000 himself and as President controlled another 50,000. The dissident directors polled only 3,000 shares against the merger, which received 298,000 votes. Newton Moore to W.L. Mackenzie King, 1 September 1923, W.L. Mackenzie King Papers, Public Archives of Canada (PAC); *Sydney Post*, 23 June, 16 July 1920.

[50]*Monetary Times*, 25 June, 2 July 1920; *Sydney Post*, 23 June, 19 July 1920. The changing composition of the board may be followed in Table 1.

[51]W.D. Ross and D.H. McDougall encountered little resistance in gaining approval for the merger from Scotia shareholders. In New Glasgow their argument was that "the merger is going through with or without us", that the smaller company could not withstand the competition and that Scotia needed the capital which would be available through the merger; "Special Meeting, Scotia Shareholders, YMCA Building, New Glasgow, 25 June 1920", Cantley Papers, Box 175, PANS. The controlling interest in Scotia was held by the American investors, but the character of U.S. interest in Scotia had changed by 1920; during the inter-war period the American steel industry favoured a policy of retrenchment and did not engage in expansionist policies abroad; Mira Wilkins, *The Maturing of Multinational Enterprise: American Business Abroad from 1914 to 1970* (Cambridge, 1974), pp.151, 153.

[52]Cantley to Stone, 21, 26 July 1920; Stone to Cantley, 26 July 1920; Cantley Papers, Box 175, PANS. Also, before entering the merger, CSL shareholders purchased Wolvin's Montreal Transportation Company; *Monetary Times*, 2, 30 July 1920.

[53]*Sydney Post*, 28 July 1920; *Financial Times* (London), 23, 24, 29 July 1920, 4 May 1920.

[54]*Monetary Times*, 9 January, 2 July, 1 October 1920, 7 January 1921; Duncan Commission, "Minutes of Evidence", p.2070.

[55]Duncan Commission, "Minutes of Evidence", p.2062.

[56]Clipping, 25 February 1921, Armstrong Papers, Box 674, PANS.

[57]Eugene Forsey, *Economic and Social Aspects of the Nova Scotia Coal Industry* (Montreal, 1926), p.40.

[58]N.W. Rowell to E.H. Armstrong, 9, 12 May 1921, Armstrong Papers, Box 663, PANS.

[59]*Sydney Post*, 28 May 1921.

[60]*Monetary Times*, 2 July 1920.

[61]*Ibid.*, 14 July 1922.

[62]McCracken, "Steel Industry", pp.154-66; *Monetary Times*, 17 September, 26 November 1920.

[63]*Monetary Times*, 9 June 1922.

[64]*Monetary Times*, 13, 27 May 1921; McCracken, "Steel Industry", Appendix; *Houston's Review*, 1923, p.180. Overexpansion, competitive disadvantages and deteriorating tariff protection caused a general problem of excess capacity in the Canadian steel industry during the 1920s; the hinterland steel plants at Sydney and Sault Ste Marie, specializing in basic steel and rails and located at a distance from the industrial heartland, suffered the greatest contraction; Eldon, "The Canadian Iron and Steel Industry", p.132.

[65]Armstrong, untitled manuscript, 1921, PANS.

[66]*Sydney Post*, 28 November 1919, 26 February, 27 March 1920.

[67]The Quebec market normally obtained two-thirds of its coal supply from Nova Scotia, but in 1920 Canadian coal accounted for only 250,880 tons; by 1923 Canadian coal accounted for 1,540,284 tons and U.S. coal 2,922,991; by 1927 the more normal proportions were re-established: Canada 2,307,185, U.S. 1,572,692 tons. As late as the 1940s, central Canada continued to derive half its energy needs from coal. See Canada, DBS, *Coal Statistics for Canada*, 1922, pp.23-4; *ibid.*, 1927, pp.22-7; J.H. Dales, "Fuel, Power and Industrial Development in Central Canada", *American Economic Review*, XLIII (1953), pp.182-83.

[68]Nova Scotia, *Journals of the House of Assembly*, 1940, App. 9, p.148.

[69]Donald, *The Canadian Iron and Steel Industry*, p.257; Schwartzman, "Dominion Coal", pp.113, 125-37.

[70]Canada, Special Committee of the House of Commons on the Future Fuel Supply of Canada, *Official Report of Evidence* (Ottawa, 1921), p.137.

[71]*Duncan Report*, p.15. The financial data convinced the commissioners that no reduction of miners' wages was justified in 1922, that a reduction in 1923 would have been suitable, that the 1924 increase was not justified and that a ten per cent reduction was appropriate in 1925.

[72]Schwartzman, "Dominion Coal", p.182, estimates that for the year ending March 1921 Dominion Coal's profits were $4.2 million gross ($2.9 net), for December 1921 $3.4 million gross ($2.4 net), for December 1922 $2.6 million gross ($1.3 net), for December 1923 $1.4 million gross ($.1 net), for December 1924 $.7 million gross ($-.6 net).

[73]Don Macgillivray, "Industrial Unrest in Cape Breton, 1919-1925" (M.A. thesis, University of New Brunswick, 1971); David Frank, "Class Conflict in the Coal Industry: Cape Breton 1922" in G.S. Kealey

and P. Warrian, eds., *Essays in Canadian Working Class History* (Toronto, 1976), pp.161-84, 226-31.

[74]*Monetary Times*, 3 January 1919, 15 September 1922. "Canada can only be politically independent so far as she controls and supplies her own bituminous coal", warned F.W. Gray; by his estimate Nova Scotia was producing two million tons less than capacity during the 1920s and with adequate capital investment could supply 10 million tons of coal per year. F.W. Gray, "Canada's Coal Supply", Canadian Institute of Mining and Metallurgy and the Mining Society of Nova Scotia, *Transactions*, XXIII (1920), pp.300-1, 304; Gray, "Canada's Coal Problem", *ibid.*, XXV (1922), pp.293-300.

[75]*Monetary Times*, 6 March 1925. To economic historian J.H. Dales, the coal tariff "appears to be nothing but a mischievous hidden tax on Canadian manufacturing" whose effect was to "retard the industrial development" of central Canada; Dales, "Fuel, Power and Industrial Development in Central Canada", p.183.

[76]Forbes, "The Maritime Rights Movement", pp.147-49, 222-27, 280-82; Associated Boards of Trade of the Island of Cape Breton, *Memorandum with Regard to the Conditions Presently Existing in the Coal and Steel Industries of the Province of Nova Scotia* (n.p., 1925). Slack coal provided 1/5 of imported coal in 1920, but almost 2/5 in 1923. The lobby also sought abolition of the 99 per cent rebate on the coal duty allowed since 1907 to consumers using coal for steelmaking. Cantley favoured a duty of $1.50 per ton; *Monetary Times*, 10 February 1928.

[77]*Besco Bulletin*, 6 June 1925; *Houston's Review*, 1926, pp.165-66; Canada, House of Commons Special Committee Investigating the Coal Resources of Canada, *Minutes of Proceedings and Evidence* (Ottawa, 1926), pp.105-23.

[78]*Monetary Times*, 25 March 1927; *Halifax Herald*, 14 March 1924.

[79]G.S. Harrington to Arthur Meighen, 16 March 1925, Arthur Meighen Papers, PAC.

[80]Duncan Report, pp.30-1; Hume Cronyn to R.L. Borden, 14 February 1926, Robert L. Borden Papers, PAC.

[81]Eldon, "The Canadian Iron and Steel Industry", p.366; F.W. Gray, "The History of Transportation Subventions on Nova Scotia Coal" (unpublished manuscript, Miners' Memorial Museum, Glace Bay, 1944); O.J. McDiarmid, *Commercial Policy in the Canadian Economy* (Cambridge, 1946), p.276.

[82]*Canadian Mining Journal* (26 August 1927).

[83]*New York Times*, 21, 27 June 1922; *Financial Post*, 30 June 1922; *Financial Post Survey*, 1927, pp.233,235.

[84]*Monetary Times*, 8 December 1922.

[85]*Monetary Times*, 30 March 1923.

[86]*Houston's Review*, 1924, p.175.

[87]Newton Moore to W.L. Mackenzie King, 1 September 1923, King Papers, PAC.

[88]*Monetary Times*, 4 April, 29 August 1924. See Table III.

[89]Roy Wolvin to E.H. Armstrong, 4 March 1924, M.C. Smith to Br Emp S Co [sic], 1 March 1924, Armstrong Papers, PANS.

[90]J.P.B. Casgrain to W.L.M. King, 19 March 1925, King Papers, PAC.

[91]Paul MacEwan, *Miners and Steelworkers* (Toronto, 1976), p.145.

[92]E.N. Rhodes to R.L. Borden, 3 August 1925, Borden Papers, PAC.

[93]Forbes, "The Maritime Rights Movement", pp.263-68.

[94]*Who Was Who, 1951-1960*, p.326; Duncan Report, pp.26-8.

[95]Forbes, "The Maritime Rights Movement", pp. 392-97; *Monetary Times*, 11 June 1926; *Houston's Review*, 1926, pp.165-66; *Financial Post Survey*, 1927, p.233.

[96]*Monetary Times*, 10 September 1926, 25 March 1927.

[97]*Houston's Review*, 1928, pp.216-17; *ibid.*, 1927, pp.182-83; *Monetary Times*, 28 October 1927.

[98]*Monetary Times*, 3 February 1928. Wolvin re-established himself in the Canadian shipping and shipbuilding industry and on his death was chairman of the executive board of Canadian Vickers Ltd.; *New York Times*, 8 April 1945.

[99]*Monetary Times*, 30 March, 18 May 1928.

POPULISM IN THE UNITED STATES, RUSSIA, AND CANADA: EXPLAINING THE ROOTS OF CANADA'S THIRD PARTIES

J.F. Conway

The third parties which emerged in the prairie West of Canada–the Social Credit in Alberta and the CCF in Saskatchewan and their predecessors–are among the most studied political, social and economic phenomena in Canadian scholarship. Indeed, no single region, historical period, or political agitation in the country has been the subject of so many articles, books, theses, and dissertations. Yet despite this plethora of scholarly attention, no generally accepted theoretical organizing principle has emerged to make this work a coherent whole. At the risk of treading such well-beaten scholarly paths once again, this essay explores the possibility of seeking such a theoretical synthesis.

The argument presented in this paper suggests that the evidence culled over many years by Canadian historians and social scientists cries out for a more systematic explanation than has been heretofore provided. That explanation, it will be argued, lies in understanding a particular Canadian variant of the social movement we have come to know as Populism. I acknowledge that it has been long recognized that the Social Credit in Alberta and the Co-operative Commonwealth Federation (CCF)[1] in Saskatchewan were to some extent Populist formations. Yet that recognition is seldom a central aspect of the analyses–indeed most works seem more committed to a notion of Canadian exceptionalism than to locating such movements alongside cousin Populist movements in other times and places. Here it will be argued that the Populist aspect ought to be central to a complete analysis of these movements.

It would be useful to attempt a concise statement of the hypothesis at this point. The CCF and Social Credit can be best viewed as Populist resistance to the effects of the National Policy on the prairie West. (By "National Policy" we refer to those persisting policies of the federal government to settle the West, to build an all-Canada transcontinental railway, and to industrialize central Canada behind a wall of protective tariffs.) Detailed work around such a revisionist hypothesis would contribute greatly to the development of our insights into the political and social history of the prairie West. The starting point for such a systematic revisionist approach is a thorough discussion of the nature of Populism.

One finds it a remarkable deficiency, but in order theoretically to grasp the nature of Populism one must go to works on the subject by scholars in Europe and the United States, rather than in Canada. It is surprising since Populist movements in Europe and the United States were largely transitory and comparatively unsuccessful, whereas in Canada such movements not only won and held power in a number of provinces,[2] but laid the foundations for political parties that have survived on the Canadian political stage.[3] This deficiency in Canadian historiography is of course not total in that most works on Social Credit and the CCF at least implicitly recognize their Populist roots, yet few of the works grasp the theoretical essence of Populism. We will return to the question of the limitations of Canadian scholarship in this area later in this essay.

Populism in America

In the literature on American Populism one can discern two basic and contradictory perspectives. Each has useful insights to offer, but neither taken alone can be accepted completely since each relies on a highly selective analysis of the evidence.

One view, given perhaps its most consistent expression in the revisionist historical perspective on American Populism begun by

Richard Hofstadter in *The Age of Reform: From Bryan to F.D.R.*, holds that American Populism was narrow and provincial, deeply nostalgic for a permanently lost past, and racist and bigoted in its response to the ethnically diverse flow of immigration into the United States. In Hofstadter's words,

> [i]n the attempts of the Populists and Progressives to hold on to some of the values of agrarian life, to save personal entrepreneurship and individual opportunity and the character type they engendered, and to maintain a homogeneous Yankee civilization, I have found much that was retrograde and delusive, a little that was vicious, and a great deal that was comic.[4]

In a sense, Hofstadter began a process which legitimated (and quite properly so) a more critical perspective on American Populism. His work was followed by many others which developed Hofstadter's basic themes.[5]

The American revisionist perspective on Populism can be fairly characterized as follows:

> . . . the movement was unable to confront the facts of industrialism but sought instead to turn its back on social change in favor of the restoration of a golden age in the past. This retrogressive view of history insured the irrationality of Populist solutions. A movement cannot possibly ascertain the nature of its grievance and propose appropriate remedies when it refuses to recognize the changing circumstances of its environment.[6]

Until the emergence of this revisionist school, interpretations of Populism by American scholars had been largely sympathetic. "Historians once confidently believed that they understood Populism. Almost unanimous in their sympathetic portrayal of the movement, they saw it as a lineal descendant of Jeffersonian and Jacksonian Democracy, a precursor of progressive reform."[7] The classic study had remained John D. Hick's *The Populist Revolt* which had emphasized the positive features of Populism, asserting that, while most of the major reforms around which the Populists had agitated were never implemented, the overall historical impact of Populism on American society was overwhelmingly positive.

Thanks to this triumph of Populist principles, one may almost say that, insofar as political devices can insure it, the people now rule. Political dishonesty has not altogether disappeared and the people may yet be betrayed by the men they elect to office, but on the whole the acts of government have come to reflect fairly clearly the will of the people. Efforts to assert this newly won power in such a way as to crush the economic supremacy of the predatory few have also been numerous and not wholly unsuccessful. The gigantic corporations of today, dwarfing into insignificance the trusts of yesterday, are, in spite of their size, far more circumspect in their conduct than their predecessors.[8]

The other classic study of American Populism had been Roscoe C. Martin's sympathetic examination of the People's party of Texas.[9] He deeply shared Hicks's view that Populism was a movement of mass, popular resistance to the worst features of American capitalism and to the rampant corruption and dishonesty in American politics. Such was the friendly unanimity one found in the scholarship on American Populism which the onslaught of Hofstadter and the other revisionists shattered with finality.

With the shattering of this unanimity scholars in the Hicks and Martin tradition struck back vigorously. A school of counter-revisionists led by Norman Pollack set themselves the task of refurbishing the badly tarnished image of American Populism.

> Ignoring what came before, proponents of this framework [the revisionists] adopt the following line of reasoning: Populism did not adjust to industrialism; hence, the movement occupied an untenable historical position. And because it looked backward, its long-range solutions were, by definition, unrealistic. This meant that by not comprehending the basis for its discontent, Populism was forced to search for simplistic explanations and, ultimately, scapegoats. The result is a cumulatively deteriorating position; as protest becomes emotional, it bears less resemblance to reality. The final image is that of a movement of opportunists, crackpots, and anti-Semites, whose perception of the world conforms to the dictates of a conspiracy

theory of history. The overall consequence of this image is that Populism has been denied its traditional place as a democratic social force. Rather, its significance for American history is altered so greatly that it has come to stand as the source for later proto-fascist groups. McCarthyism, anti-Semitism, xenophobia, and anti-intellectualism. One senses the proportions of this denigration process when it is seen that the very term "populistic" has passed into the working vocabulary of many intellectuals as an epithet, signifying the traits just enumerated.[10]

Having thus characterized the revisionist argument, Pollack, studying only midwestern Populist thought, goes on to assert:

While primarily an agrarian movement, it [Populism] also contained significant support from industrial labor, social reformers, and intellectuals. The interaction between these groups was expressed not in terms of pre-industrial producer of values, but of a common ideology stemming from a shared critique of existing conditions. In a word, Populism regarded itself as a class movement, reasoning that farmers and workers were assuming the same material position in society. Thus, it accepted industrialism but opposed its capitalistic form, seeking instead a more equitable distribution of wealth. But Populism went further in its criticism: Industrial capitalism not only impoverished the individual, it alienated and degraded him. The threat was not only subsistence living, but the destruction of human faculties. According to Populism, there was an inverse relation between industrialism and freedom, because the machine was being made to exploit rather than serve man. Is Populism, then, a socialist movement? Here labels become unimportant; it was far more radical than is generally assumed. Had Populism succeeded, it could have fundamentally altered American society in a socialist direction. Clearly, Populism was a progressive social force.[11]

Pollack proceeds to buttress his contention by an appeal to primary sources illustrating that Populism was a progressive reform movement.[12] One leaves Pollack's defence

quite convinced that the revisionists have slandered a basically positive and humane popular movement. At the same time one notes that Pollack, by focussing on midwestern Populism, has been excessively selective in both his analysis and the primary documents he marshals to defend his case. As the debate rages, one cannot help agreeing with much in the revisionist school. The overall impression is one of ambiguity and contradiction—the evidence appears to support both cases strongly.[13]

Fortunately, the debate between the revisionists and counterrevisionists has led to a new spate of studies of American Populism. These efforts have served to develop a somewhat more balanced perspective on the issues. Studies of Kansas Populism clearly illustrate that there is no denying the many bread-and-butter reforms gained by the movement.[14] Abrams' collection of documents illustrating the issues of the Populist era emphasizes that, whatever the limitations inherent in the movement, Populism remained a popular movement making a serious attempt to grapple with the problems of capitalism and democracy in the heyday of America's modernization.[15] Further studies, such as Tindall's moving collection of selections from the writings of Populist leaders[16] and Durden's sympathetic, but clear-sighted, analysis of the defeat and absorption of American Populism by the Democratic party,[17] all tend to confirm the fact that Populism was clearly a response to serious problems inherent in American capitalism and in the American democracy of the late nineteenth and early twentieth century.

At the same time, it is foolish to ignore all that was pernicious and backward-looking in American Populism. Woodward's study of Georgia's Tom Watson shows that his career simultaneously epitomizes all that was best and all that was worst in the movement.[18] Tom Watson was one of the most prominent national figures in the People's party, finally running as one of William Jennings Bryan's vice-presidential running mates on the 1896 election fusionist ticket.[19] In his early career Tom Watson had fought corporations on behalf of the worker and farmer, had combatted racism in Georgia (a not inconsiderable feat), and had refused to "sell-out" Populist principles for the sake of political success. Yet after the decline of the People's party, Tom Watson became a rather typical southern US politician–personally opportunistic, a raging anti-Semite, and a panderer to the fear of blacks so endemic among the southern white population. The tragic and twisted story of Tom Watson makes it impossible to ignore the case made by the revisionists at the same time as his early career insists that we also listen seriously to the counterrevisionists' case. Populism, like the career of Tom Watson, had much that was both pernicious and progressive in it.

Combining the story of Tom Watson with the stories of T.G. Bilbo and James K. Vardaman, the famous (and infamous) Mississippi Populist,[20] who effectively combined racist demogoguery with agrarian social reform, and political opportunism with anti-corporation agitation, further illustrates the tensions within this movement. Albert Kirwan has written that Bilbo and Vardaman directed their campaigns against the interests of the corporations and against the Negro, and that "their appeal was directed to poor as against rich, to farmer as against townsman, to the 'common man' as against the aristocrat."[21] One cannot dismiss this tension by suggesting that it was merely a case of the peculiarities of Southern politics. The same tension existed in midwestern Populism, held up by Pollack as the most progressive section of the movement. Clinch's study of Populism in Montana clearly reveals this. In summing up its accomplishments, Clinch says, "Despite the flaws in its record, the Populist party had been a progressive force dedicated to reform. Its arguments for free silver, the eight-hour day, and mine safety legislation advocated the primacy of human over property rights. . . . [Populism] envisioned a widening of democracy in America and a greater responsiveness on the part of government to popular needs."[22] Yet in his next breath Clinch is compelled by the record to say, "The most glaring blot on the record of Montana's Populists was their unabashed espousal of Chinese exclusion. . . ."[23]

Perhaps this survey of the highlights of the debate among American scholars regarding the progessive and regressive nature of the American variant of Populism is sufficient to draw certain lessons. One may conclude that the debate has been an indecisive exercise since each school of thought can marshal evidence to support its various contradictory contentions. Although there have been a few signal efforts to develop a synthesis which adequately encompasses the contradictory features of American Populism,[24] American political historiography has generally been content to continue the polarization. There are those who embrace Populism and its heirs as the embodiment of effective reform in American history and those who reject Populism and its heirs as a misguided and irrational protest against the inevitable course of American development. For an outside observer, in all fairness, however, the debate has been useful in that the major feature of American Populism that stands out again and again is its two-sidedness–the one side, progressive and reformist; the other side, backward-looking and confused.

The richness of the literature on American Populism perhaps reflects its surprising effectiveness. The movement elected congressmen to both Houses, mayors in large cities, governors and state legislators in many states, and, during the fusion campaign of 1896, Populism made a major try for the White House. The result of the 1896 fusion election was, of course, to co-opt Populism and its heirs as a major element of the Democratic party.[25] It was no doubt here, as a wing of the Democratic party, expressed later in its New Deal guise, that Populism had its greatest effect.

It was in this great party that Populism finally reconciled itself to capitalism and at the same time sought to broaden the opportunity for all to "get ahead" by championing the slogan "Equal rights for all, special privileges for none." By advocating that many problems of American society could be solved, not by destroying and reconstructing the political and economic order, but by the positive and active intervention of government in defence of a common welfare and a common minimum security, Populism may have prepared the political ground for the New Deal's salvation of American capitalism. It is perhaps ironic, but the often confused efforts of the Populists of the 1890's who fought tooth and nail to save mankind from "crucifixion on a cross of gold,"[26] became the popular political underpinnings of an effective reconstruction of American capitalism in the 1930's and 1940's.

Perhaps American Populism's very effectiveness has also been the cause of the theoretical shallowness of the scholarship that has sought to understand it. By becoming a major thrust in the Democratic party, by becoming a source of many reforms in the American economic and constitutional order, Populism (or rather a particular refurbished interpretation of it) also became a major part of the mythology of America. Given the lack of any major challenge from the left to the course of America's development, it is not surprising that many have elevated Populism and its heirs (like George McGovern) to the role of major challengers to the course of American history. Equally, it is not surprising that many in America, witnessing the rather easy absorption of the Populist challenge by the American establishment, have dismissed Populism as an irrelevant and irrational by-product of the necessarily rough evolution of the American political economy. Either way, the theoretical significance of the Populist resistance becomes a mere footnote to the overall course of American history—either it was a significant stream that fed and enriched the great American tributary or it was a stagnant pool that was bypassed by the rushing current of American capitalism. Either way, the movement has been regarded as having little theoretical, indeed, practical, significance in its own right. It is perhaps here that one can seek and find an explanation of the inability of American scholarship in developing any theoretical sophistication in grappling with the Populist interlude.

Populism in Russia

Almost coincident with the Populist movement in America, a similar movement flourished briefly in Russia. As Minogue puts it, "[Populism had] two brief historical episodes in Russia and America. They were almost contemporaneous; they presented themselves as movements against established power by or on behalf of little men living on the land; and both placed great emphasis upon the 'people' as the oppressed agents of future changes."[27]

For our purposes, the most salient feature of the Russian case is that, due to the great nineteenth-century debate between Russian Marxism and Russian Populism, the scholarship on Russian Populism does not suffer from the theoretical underdevelopment that characterizes the work on the American case.

Probably the most reasonable explanation for the richness of theoretical development in the literature on Russian Populism would lie in the fact that, in the epoch leading up to the Russian revolution, all social, economic, and political questions were posed more urgently and sharply in an age when a number of revolutionary solutions were in contention. In such a context, it is easy to understand why Russian Marxist scholars and political leaders were forced to deal critically with Populism, their main political competitor for the leadership of the revolutionary current.[28] Yet for all the peculiarities of the Russian case, including the widespread revolutionary agitation, much of the content of Russian Populism bears a remarkable similarity to its American cousin.

Indeed, one can discern a recurring theme in the scholarship on both American and Russian Populism: Populism is the characteristic response of the independent commodity producer, or the agrarian petit-bourgeoisie,[29] to the threat of capitalist industrial modernization. Such modernization is a threat, firstly, because of the inevitable consequences of capitalist economic organization for small producers—either they become larger in order to survive or they are pushed out of business. This applies equally to handicraft production and to agriculture. In handicraft production it is clear: as capitalist industrial techniques are applied to the production of commodities (textiles, shoes, iron goods, etc.), the small producer using preindustrial and labour-intensive techniques simply cannot compete. Yet the same principle holds true in agriculture; inevitably industrial techniques come to be applied to the production of agriculture commodities, particularly in the area of the modernization of technology, especially machinery, to the point where the individual producer must apply the modern techniques and expand his land holding in order to produce more as the new competition lowers the prices paid for agricultural goods on the market.

The same threat applies at a more profound social structural level. Someone must bear the burden of the costs of industrial modernization of whatever variety.[30] Capital must be accumulated. Accumulated capital must be diverted into new investment areas—plant, machinery, raw materials, marketing, wages, etc. This capital must be extracted

309

somewhere, it must be diverted from its traditional uses. Under capitalist industrial modernization, capital is accumulated in the first (and obviously most important) instance through the extraction of surplus value from wage-labour.[31] Yet even before the exploitation of wage-labour can be accelerated, certain problems must be solved by capitalism. First on the agenda is the modernization of agriculture–the traditional rural social structure based on subsistence agriculture[32] must be transformed for a variety of reasons. As Hobsbawm puts it,

> [a]griculture [must be] prepared to carry out its three fundamental functions in an era of industrialization; to increase production and productivity, so as to feed a rapidly rising non-agricultural population; to provide a large and rising surplus of potential recruits for the towns and industries; and to provide a mechanism for the accumulation of capital to be used in the more modern sectors of the economy.[33]

Overall, the initial and often the heaviest costs of industrial modernization must be borne by the agricultural sector, which is overwhelmingly agrarian petit-bourgeois. This is obvious since in preindustrial societies the basic source of wealth is land and labour and the most significant commodities are agricultural. Capital must be accumulated in this sector initially and diverted to industrialization. Techniques must be improved, and holding size enlarged, both to increase production and to free labour from the land so that it may be diverted, under threat of starvation with capitalist modernization, to industrial wage labour. Consequently the two classes which must bear the costs of capitalist modernization are the agrarian petit-bourgeoisie (also, the landless and tenant agricultural worker) and the emerging industrial proletariat[34]–indeed in the process of capitalist modernization (and continuously) the agrarian petit-bourgeoisie (and those who depend upon it) are faced with the Draconian and remorseless prospect of successfully enlarging themselves at the expense of others or of losing everything and being forced onto the wage labour market. This threat is continuous, as the means of production are constantly revolutionized.[35]

Yet this fundamental social structural consequence of capitalist modernization is unevenly expressed by many scholars of Populism involved in the polarized debate of American scholarship. Unwilling to recognize the roots of Populism in the interests of a concrete social class, the agrarian petit-bourgeoisie, both the revisionists and the counterrevisionists fall into the trap of partisanship. One side, like Hofstadter et al., sees Populism cynically–as the reactionary and blind response of rural small holders to the threat of modernization. The other side, like Hicks and Pollack, ignores this very real threat and sees only the progressive aspects of the movement. In Russian scholarship there is a clearer and somewhat more balanced perspective on Populism–it is the response of a threatened class, but its totality cannot merely be understood in crass and vulgar class-interest terms. Populism was also a conscientious effort by a class not only to save itself materially, but to build a better society. Both sorts of insights were expressed in the writings of Lenin long before either perspective in American scholarship was enunciated. Indeed, Walicki's classic, *The Controversy over Capitalism: studies in the social philosophy of the Russian Populists*, takes very serious account of Lenin's work on Populism. Much of Walicki's work, through an analysis of primary sources in Russian Populism, essentially confirms Lenin's view. At one point Walicki concedes: "It was Lenin who gave it a more concrete historical and sociological connotation by pointing out that Populism was a protest against capitalism from the point of view of the small immediate producers, who, being ruined by capitalist development, saw in it only a retrogression but, at the same time demanded the abolition of the older, feudal forms of exploitation."[36]

Lenin's scholarship has long gone unrecognized by North American social science, including Marxist scholars. Lenin seems to be regarded solely as the architect of the Russian revolution who, as a Marxist intellectual, made his primary contribution in the realm of theories of organization and practical revolution. Again one has to go to Europe to find Lenin recognized as a Marxist scholar in his own right. Given the fact that it was Lenin, as Walicki admits, who initially argued that Populism was a protest against capitalism from the point of view of the small producer, and further given that this insight is central to scholarship on both the American and Russian cases, it is essential to appeal to Lenin's works in order to flesh out this perspective and to examine it in some detail to see if, indeed, it does commend itself as the most fruitful theoretical orientation in an analysis of Populism.

For Lenin, Populism was "a theoretical doctrine that gives a particular solution to highly important sociological and economic problems . . . ."[37] The essence of the particular solution had as its starting point "a protest against serfdom . . . and bourgeoisdom [capitalism] *from the peasant's, the small producer's point of view* . . . ."[38] The solution is one of rejection for Lenin, a rejection of elements of the past and of the future at the same time as certain selected features of the past are glorified. "[T]he Narodnik, in matters of theory, is just as much a Janus, looking with one face to the past and the other to the future, as in real life the small producer is, who looks with one face to the past, wishing to strengthen his small farm without knowing or wishing to know anything about the general economic system and about the need to reckon with the class that controls it—and with the other face to the future, adopting a hostile attitude to the capitalism that is ruining him."[39] The Populists extolled the "ethics of the thrifty peasant"[40] as the basis and bedrock of a permanent social morality. Rejecting, on the one hand, feudalism, it "regarded small-scale production as a natural system" and, on the other, "was up in arms against big capital" which it regarded as foreign, un-Russian, "an extraneous element."[41] Populism glorified the small peasant economy, extolling small production, arguing that such a form of social and economic organization ensured the independence of the producers and consequently eliminated the unnatural contradictions in the social structure being introduced by this "extraneous element," big capital.[42] As the foundation of a safeguard against the ravages of big capital, the Populists held true individualism up as the watchword and banner of the peasant movement.

Fundamentally, the struggle of the Populists in Russia was a struggle for their right to existence as small holders on the one hand, demanding democratic concessions from Tsarist absolutism so that they might engage in unfettered production for a free market,

and on the other, proposing measures to control the negative effects of big capital on their capacity to survive and flourish. Yet at the same time Lenin retained a balanced view: he saw the Populists as having "good intentions" and "fine wishes," however "impractical."[43] Indeed, he went so far as to argue that Populism "occupied a foremost place among the progressive trends of Russian social thought,"[44] and "made a big step forward . . . by *posing* the question of capitalism in Russia."[45] Lenin maintained that one cannot ignore the "historically real and progressive historical content of Narodism as a theory of the mass *petit-bourgeoisie* struggle of democratic capitalism against liberal-landlord capitalism. . . . "[46]

Clearly Lenin's arguments anticipated those which the American revisionists on Populism (Hofstadter, et al.) would marshal to diminish the significance of the Populist resistance in America. Yet his analysis also concedes many of the positive features of Populism recognized by Hicks, and later the counterrevisionists like Pollack, namely, the movement's commitment to democratic reforms and its frequent espousal of measures that bordered on the utopian socialist. Correctly, Lenin's view seems to account for both observations. Indeed, the movement did resist and lament capitalist modernization insofar as the small producer was threatened, but hardly in as cynical and irrational manner as Hofstadter et al., seem to suggest. What the movement was resisting was not Progress itself, as Hofstadter and others would seem to imply, but an historically specific form of progress led by a minority class, a form of unregulated capitalist modernization that threatened the very existence of the class of small producers.

In agriculture the Russian Populists decried the commercialization of agriculture (with its pressure toward larger and larger holdings utilizing modern techniques due to market forces) on the one hand, and landlordism (emcompassing a variety of remnants from feudalism) on the other. They advocated breaking up and dividing large land holdings and the distribution of land among small producers and communes.[47] That was one thrust of their agrarian program. Another was a broad program to reorganize land and labour around a ressurected form of the traditional Russian peasant commune—a holdover from

311

feudalism which still existed here and there and remained based on "the family labour principle," which the Narodniks glorified despite its cruel exploitation of women and children.[48] Such land tenure reforms and principles of labour reorganization were their maximum agriculture program. In the meantime, they fought for a variety of small reforms—peasant unions and associations to act as pressure groups, cooperatives in agricultural production and marketing,[49] stricter regulation of the capitalist market,[50] programs to reverse rural depopulation,[51] controls on the marketing of agricultural products, inexpensive loans to small producers, government intervention to aid in technical improvements in agriculture and handicraft industry,[52] free education programs to increase the people's knowledge,[53] and a retardation of "the money economy"[54]—all these and more were advocated as concrete measures to protect the small producer in agriculture.[55] As an aside, the similarity of such reforms to many of the reforms advocated by American Populism, and by the Social Credit and CCF, is interesting, particularly since it appears that such movements were addressing themselves to the obviously universal problems faced by small producers in the face of an aggressive and unremitting capitalist modernization.

Although most of their attention was focussed on the agricultural sector, the Narodniks also had a complete industrial program which they presented as an alternative to capitalist industrialization. They saw in capitalist industrialization the source of all the suffering of the great rural masses of Russia—the destruction of the small producer and the consequent decline of rural communities, the obliteration of the traditional skills of home handicraft industry, the irresistible magnet of urban, industrial jobs with a better standard of living that drew the landless peasants remorselessly to the new industrial centres, and so on. They also recognized the validity of many of the technical advances made in industrial production. Like Populist movements everywhere, they faced the problem of how to extract the best of both worlds; that is, to keep what was good from the past—the rural community, strong family and kinship ties, independence, traditional skills, etc.—and what was best from the present and future—inventions in machinery, new tech-

niques, the application of the natural sciences, etc. Their solution was easy: extend the principle of the peasant commune and home industry to industrial production—this was the basic strategy to resist the increasing migration of people from agriculture to industry.[56] "Bring industry to the traditional community," was their cry.[57] Lenin sums up their industrial program:

1) condemnation of money economy and sympathy for natural economy and primitive artisan production; 2) various measures for the encouragement of small peasant production, such as credits, technical developments, etc.; 3) the spreading of associations and societies of all kinds [co-operatives]among the masters, big and small—raw material, warehousing, loan-and-savings, credit, consumers' and producers' societies; 4) organization of labour [along communal lines]. . . .[58]

There was also a negative aspect to the program, that of resisting capitalist industrialization and suggesting that the state use its power to do so.

Side by side with the measures indicated above, which are usually described as a liberal economic policy, and which have always been inscribed on the banners of bourgeois leaders in the West, the Narodniks contrive to cling to their intention of *retarding* comtemporary economic development, of *preventing* the progress of capitalism, and of *supporting* small production, which is being bled white in the struggle against large-scale production.[59]

"[T]he Narodniks try to drag history back, to halt development, beg and plead that it be 'forbidden,' 'not allowed' . . . ."[60]

The basic orientation of both their agrarian and industrial programs was, of course, to use the state to defend[61] and extend small, independent production and production based on a reorganized peasant commune as over against the large-scale production of urban, big industry and of commercially-oriented, large-scale agriculture.

Besides this general economic program—encompassing the social reorganization of production in agriculture and industry—the Russian Populists, like their cousins in America, stood staunchly for democracy. For Lenin, this aspect of their program was enormously positive, since it reflected the deep democratic striving of the masses of rural Russia as well as being on the immediate and practical political agenda. Whereas he saw their general economic program as hopelessly impractical if well-intended, he took their struggle for democracy very seriously indeed. Their demands for universal, state-supported education, for universal suffrage, for responsive and responsible government, were among the Narodniks' most politically successful policies in terms of gathering mass support. Lenin saw the Populist democratic insurgence as the "struggle of democratic capitalism against liberal-landlord capitalism, of 'American' capitalism against 'Prussian' capitalism."[62] He called on all socialist revolutionaries to support "the republican-democratic trends"[63] and the "general democratic measures"[64] represented by and advocated by the Populists. "Narodnik *democracy*, while fallacious from the formal economic point of view, is correct from the *historical* point of view; *this* democracy, while fallacious as a socialist utopia, is *correct* in terms of the peculiar, historically conditioned democratic struggle of the peasant masses . . . ."[65] Further, the task of revolutionaries was to "extract the sound and valuable kernel of the sincere, resolute, militant democracy of the peasant masses from the husk of Narodnik utopias."[66] "The only real content and social significance of Narodism is peasant democracy."[67] The political support of the Populists must be sought by the revolutionary movement because the Populists were "honest, sincere, ardent, and strong democrats."[68] But there was little else Lenin found in the political posturing of the Populists to commend them. His critique was systematic and unsparing, and strongly reminiscent of the position taken by Hofstadter and the revisionists, although it was based in a much more concrete economic analysis than the American revisionists provide.

Lacking "sociological realism"[69] and unwilling to face the fact that the small producer too is locked into the capitalist economy, the Narodnik (according to Lenin) focussed his attack on "peculiarities *of policy*–land, taxation, industrial–and not on the peculiarities *of the social organization of production*,"[70]

and he extolled the "sugary Narodnik fairy tale"[71] of the independence and "naturalness" of small peasant production.

> The *petit-bourgeoisie* . . . is afraid to look things straight in the face, and to call a spade a spade. He turns his back on . . . undoubted facts, and begins to dream. He considers only small independent undertakings (*for the market*–he keeps a modest silence about that) to be "moral," while wage-labour is "immoral." He does not understand the tie–an indissoluble tie–between the one and the other, and considers bourgeois morality to be chance disease, and not a direct product of the bourgeois order that grows out of commodity economy (which, in fact, he has nothing against).[72]

This moral idealization of small production, disregarding its market goals, reveals the petit-bourgeois character of the Narodnik social and economic critique of capitalism, a critique which reveals "an extremely superficial understanding, that it is the artificial and incorrect singling out of one form of commodity economy (large-scale industrial capital) and condemnation of it, while utopianly idealizing *another form of the same* commodity economy (small production)."[73] Having ignored (or never understood) their real location in the larger economy, it is not surprising that the Narodniks failed to see themselves as representing a class from the past which stands between the working class and the capitalist class and whose interests lie with neither, yet whose fate it is necessarily to join one or the other as the logic of capitalist competition threatens it members' capacity to exist. Lenin sums up:

> [The Narodniks] invent for themselves a sort of abstract small production existing outside of the social relations of production, and *overlook* the trifling circumstance that this small production actually exists in an environment of *commodity production*. . . . *Actually*, the small producer, whom the romanticists and the Narodniks place on a pedestal, is therefore a *petty-bourgeois* who exists in the same antagonistic relations as every other member of capitalist society, and who also defends his interests by means of a struggle which,

313

on the one hand, is constantly creating a small minority of big bourgeois, and on the other, pushes the majority into the proletariat. Actually, as everybody sees and knows, there are no small producers who do not stand *between* these two opposite classes, and this middle position necessarily determines the specific character of the *petty-bourgeoisie*, its dual character, its two-facedness, its gravitation towards the minority which has emerged from the struggle successfully, its hostility towards the "failures," i.e., the majority. The more commodity economy develops, the more strongly and sharply do these qualities stand out, and the more evident does it become that the idealisation of small production merely expresses a reactionary, *petty-bourgeois* point of view.[74]

If our earlier survey of American scholarship of Populism revealed anything, it revealed the basic duality of the phenomenon—the one side, progressive and reformist, the other, regressive and reactionary. The point to be made is that each perspective is correct—evidence from the American Populist interlude can be adduced to support both features of the phenomenon. American scholarship has failed to reconcile the fact that the movement contained both progressive and regressive features simultaneously. Our examination of Lenin's approach to Russian Populism suggests that his theoretical schema can, in fact, cope with the facts of the case as presented by each side in the polarized debate in American scholarship.

We have spent some time on Lenin's analysis of Populism, but not simply because scholars like Walicki claim he provides the best theoretical framework nor, for that matter, because partial echoes of Lenin's perspective recur throughout the literature on Populism (although such reasons would be sufficient). The basic reason is that Lenin has provided, potentially, the most *complete* framework for an analysis of the Populist phenomenon in general. Unlike the Hickses and the Martins, and later the Pollacks, Lenin does not exaggerate the extent of the critique of capitalism made by the movement, nor does he ignore the less commendable features of the movement.

While not denying the progressive features of Populism, Lenin attempts to explain such features, as well as the seemingly contradictory reactionary excesses of the phenomenon, not by an analysis of the good or bad intentions of the leaders, not by a psychological explanation discussing the limitations of the leaders or the limitations imposed by the era; but rather by attempting to locate the movement and its supporters in the concrete class structure of a developing capitalism and by teasing out the consequences of an unfettered development of modern capitalism for the class of small producers. By doing so he has successfully explained the Russian case in all its contradiction.

On the one hand, we see the populists' general assault on capitalist modernization which was transforming the small property of the many into the big property of the few and imposing, as industrialization must, heavy costs on the agricultural sector to provide the capital, labour, and cheaper food required for modernization. On the other hand, we note that the Populists' unwillingness to reject the fundamental principles of capitalist economy—private property, commodity production, self-enrichment—forced them to adopt solutions which had the tendency to oppose development and modernization. Thus recognizing that Populism was the political expression of the agrarian petit-bourgeoisie in the class struggle, one can understand clearly both the reactionary and progressive faces of the movement.

At the same time Lenin does not fall into the errors of the Hofstadter and Bell revisionist perspective which emphasizes, with some discernible contempt, the crass class motives of the movement while at least implicitly supporting the effects of capitalist modernization on the small producer. This tradition ferrets out the negative and reactionary features of American Populism—the support of individual private property, the racism and anti-Semitism, its easy transition to more blatantly right-wing political tendencies—and downplays the progressive features of the movement. Unwilling to recognize the existence of a class struggle, unable or unwilling clear-sightedly to perceive the negative consequences of capitalist modernization for masses of people, the Hofstadters and Bells content themselves with dismissing the movement as an irrational rural protest against capital "P" Progress and capital "C" Civilization. On the other hand, Lenin, in the Russian case, attempts to locate the phenomenon in all its complexity and contradiction in a larger political and economic structure undergoing rapid transformation.

The extent to which Lenin's perspective is applicable to Canada is a question to be explored seriously by Canadian scholars. On the face of it, in terms of our examination of the American and Russian cases, there is a strong case for arguing that Lenin's view goes further in providing a systematic understanding of Populism than any of the main streams in the North American literature. Rather than further enmeshing us in the polarized debate on American Populism, his view explains the correctness of the main thrusts of both apparently contradictory cases. However, our task here is not to apply and test Lenin's orientation in terms of American Populism fully–that would be another and separate undertaking.

Populism in Canada

Our task here is to investigate *in an introductory and preliminary way* whether the CCF in Saskatchewan and Social Credit in Alberta can both best be viewed as Populist responses to the Canadian National Policy. By Populist, like Lenin, we mean the political expression of a critique of capitalism and a proposed developmental alternative from the point of view of the agrarian petit-bourgeoisie. We must ascertain whether such a perspective goes further in explaining both movements than the normal treatment provided in Canadian scholarship. In examining this argument, we ought not simply to marshal the usual evidence–their roots in pre-existing farm protest movements, the social and economic bases of the two movements, their political programmes, their rhetoric and whom it appealed to, the beliefs of their leaders and spokesmen–although such evidence must continue to be examined; but we must also begin to examine in detail their records as provincial governments to see if there, too, we can find evidence of the agrarian petit-bourgeois character of the two movements.[75]

The scholarship on Canadian Populism is strangely less rich and dynamic than that on the US or Russian variants. It is strange because in Canada the Populist reactions gained power in a number of provinces under the

banner of a number of organizations and, indeed, the heirs to that tradition remain permanent fixtures in Canadian politics. No one denies the essentially Populist nature of the early movements of agrarian protest in Canada, yet the various analyses of the CCF and Social Credit are at great variance with one another. As early as the late 1800's, American experiments in rural Populist protest were successfully transplanted in Canada–the Dominion Grange of the Patrons of Husbandry came to Ontario in 1874, organized by the American National Grange; the Grand Association of the Patrons of Industry came to Ontario in 1889, organized out of Michigan. Both had some degree of initial success (for example, the Patrons of Industry entered politics and won seventeen seats in the Ontario 1894 election).[76] Both organizations declined rapidly, but clearly laid out the foundations for the later successes of the United Farmers of Ontario which formed a government in 1919.[77]

In the West, similar agrarian protest organizations emerged almost as quickly as agricultural settlement established itself permanently. The Manitoba and North West Farmer's Protective Union was formed in 1883, but it was absorbed by the Manitoba Liberal party.[78] The Patrons of Industry, organized out of Ontario, also appeared briefly in Manitoba.[79] The more successful movements of agrarian protest in the West initially concerned themselves with the practical problems faced by grain producers. In 1901, the Territorial Grain Growers' Association of Assiniboia was organized, with its main membership in what is now Saskatchewan.[80] This move was followed quickly by provincial organizations, especially after Saskatchewan and Alberta were founded in 1905. In 1903, the Manitoba Grain Growers' Association was established. A similar organization was established in Alberta in 1905 which later joined with the Alberta Society of Equity to become the United Farmers of Alberta in 1909.[81]

The primary purpose of the new organizations was to educate their members in collective action, a knowledge of their legal and political rights, and an appreciation of the dignity of their calling. The organized farmers began with a deep conviction that the root of the farmer's plight was his individualism, his isolation, and his ignorance of matters outside his narrow practical experience. They sought to arouse class-consciousness in the farmer. . . . [82]

However, the organization also advocated and took practical action to alleviate the economic plight of the grain producer.

The grain grower was at a disadvantage as a producer and as a consumer; he sold on a buyer's, and bought on a seller's, market. To break this system of exploitation, action was taken in two ways. Producers' and consumers' co-operatives were organized, and pressure was put on government to take over the ownership of the elevators through which the grain passed and in which it was stored. The organized farmers were groping their way towards the elimination of the middleman and the control by the farmers of storage and sale of the annual harvest. [83]

This tendency toward practical action inevitably led the organized farmers into provincial politics in the West (and in central Canada), as the governments of the old-line parties proved unresponsive to their demands. This was to lead to the astonishing, but short-lived, success of the Progressive party on the federal scene in 1921 and the victory of the UFA in the Alberta election of the same year. A year later the United Farmers of Manitoba won power there too. [84] Suffice it to say that the political groundwork was laid for the successful emergence of the CCF and Social Credit after the initial ineffectiveness of the various organized farmers' rather unsuccessful early political adventures.

All works on these earlier movements of agrarian discontent accept them as Populist movements, basically representing the agrarian petit-bourgeoisie (although many make altogether too much of the American influences present). And indeed most seem to recognize the roots of the CCF and Social Credit in these earlier agitations and experiments, yet the application of the Populist theoretical schema seems most often to stop with the founding of the two new, and more successfully permanent, movements. W.L. Morton provides an example of this—he admits the roots of the CCF in the earlier Populist for-

mations but implies that the Federation transcended these roots. [85] He similarly locates the roots of the Social Credit movement. [86] The implication, though, clearly remains that these two movements were decisive political breaks with their Populist heritage.

S.M. Lipset, in his study of the CCF in Saskatchewan, also recognizes the roots of the Federation in the Populist agitations, [87] but coins a new theoretical phrase to characterize the CCF, "agrarian socialism." He essentially argues that the organized farmers' movement in Saskatchewan "went socialist," [88] giving birth to a completely new political phenomenon. Strangely enough, despite his title, Lipset gives the lie to his own analysis when he is forced by the facts to admit that increasingly the socialist rhetoric of the CCF was abandoned.

Some of the agrarian CCF candidates realized that greater strength could be achieved for an independent farmers' party that opposed the eastern capitalists than for a socialist party. *Even before the first election in 1934*, party leaders began to omit all reference to socialism in their propaganda. . . . The party leaders were trying to popularize the CCF by speaking in the traditional language of agrarian radicalism. . . . [89]

Clearly, even by his own admission, the CCF had long abandoned its socialist rhetoric and program almost a full decade prior to winning provincial office in 1944! [90] The theoretical usefulness of the term "agrarian socialism" is called profoundly into question.

C.B. Macpherson, in his study of Social Credit in Alberta, also recognized the roots of the movement in the earlier Populist formations that thrived in that province. [91] However, his initial focus is primarily on an analysis of the Albertan population's rejection of the traditional party system!

The political unorthodoxy of both movements [the UFA and the Social Credit] followed logically from the unorthodoxy of their social and economic ideas; experience had convinced their members that they could not get economic justice except by changing the system of government. The crucial political problem was to devise means to ensure that the will of the people should prevail. [92]

316

Of course such ideas were not unique to Alberta—they have always found expression in Populist formations in one form or another. However, Macpherson does locate the particular political developments in Alberta in the struggles of the agrarian petit-bourgeoisie for survival and prosperity against the inimical forces of "eastern financial domination and the party system." Yet the party system, in Macpherson's analysis, is always in the forefront of the grievances of the movement, whether UFA or Social Credit.[93] In the end, though, Macpherson does locate his analysis in the particular forms taken by the political class struggle of the agrarian petit-bourgeois in Alberta. In attempting to explain the oscillation between radicalism and conservatism of the movement he observes:

> The radicalism of both was that of a quasi-colonial society of independent producers, in rebellion against eastern imperialism but not against the property system. . . . It was not that the exigencies of government, as such, caused the leaders, on attaining office, to become orthodox both in their economic policies and in their practice of democracy. Rather, the exigencies of governing a society of independent producers, in revolt against outside domination but not against property, brought out the conservatism inherent in *petit-bourgeois* agrarian radicalism.[94]

Clearly we have here an echo of Lenin's analysis of Populism. Indeed, Macpherson essentially concludes his work by suggesting that his analysis of the Social Credit movement in Alberta basically confirms Lenin's account (although he never implicitly says so).[95] The closest Macpherson comes to suggesting a similarity between the Social Credit and CCF movements is when he admits that the CCF would be "the most likely contender" for power in Alberta should the Social Credit collapse as the leader of agrarian discontent.[96]

The fundamental problem with Macpherson's analysis is that he ends where he ought to have begun and places far too much emphasis on the party system as a source of the reform agitation. The critique of the party system was not unique to the UFA and Social Credit in Alberta—it was characteristic of the UFO, the UFM, and the Progressive party as well as the CCF. It is a familiar Populist echo

that can be found in the programs of the Populist movements of America as well as in the prepolitical programs of almost every organized farmer movement in North America. Perhaps it would have been more significant to have looked at Social Credit in Alberta as a particular political expression of the Populist phenomenon—of the protest against capitalism, and in this case regional domination, from the point of view of the agrarian small producer.

There are those who would disagree sharply. P.F. Sharp would see more of American Populism in Alberta due to the large number of American settlers who came there.[97] Certainly this has become almost a truism among scholars on Western Canadian Populism. For example, Walter Young, the closest there is to an official historian of the CCF-NDP, certainly, and somewhat too eagerly, agrees.[98] And so does Morton, the author of the classic on the Progressive party.[99]

A more recent attempt by Peter Sinclair to grapple with the emergence of apparently contradictory political protest movements in the similar agricultural environments of Saskatchewan and Alberta goes part of the way in applying the Populist schema.[100] Sinclair concedes that both the CCF and Social Credit were movements of Populist protest to defend the interests of the agrarian petit-bourgeoisie. He argues that although the CCF began as a socialist movement, it abandoned its socialism and became a progressive Populist party. On the other hand, the Social Credit in Alberta was an authoritarian Populist party resulting from the earlier collapse of an American-style agrarian Populism (the UFA). Again, the author makes too much of the apparent differences between the two movements, though he does take a fruitful step in asserting that the Populist schema is best for a complete analysis of both movements.

Other recent efforts to take this point of view have been made by Smart[101] and Naylor and Teeple.[102] Neither of these efforts goes far enough in substantiating the basic assertion that Populism, as a political movement in self-defense on the part of a threatened agrarian petit-bourgeoisie, is what fundamentally characterized the CCF and Social Credit. One can hope that the initial efforts of Sinclair, Smart, Naylor and Teeple reflect a new thrust in scholarship on the Canadian variant of Populism.

Although it is beyond the scope of this essay to complete the task it urges on Canadian scholarship, a few heuristic lessons may have been generated by this comparative review of the literature. We first concede that the facts are as stated in the major works on the CCF and Social Credit movements, and their predecessors. Indeed, the facts have been repeated with a regularity that has become tiresome.

The failure of Canadian scholarship, rather, has been its theoretical failure to seek a synthesis that could provide a deeper and more complete understanding of the most widely studied phenomena in Canadian social and political history. Is the Progressive phenomenon to be understood best as a sectional phenomenon? Are the Social Credit and the CCF to be best understood as *regional* rather than *class* reactions to the National Policy and its historic consequences for the prairie West? Such theoretical perspectives are commonplace and widely accepted among Canadian social scientists.

This essay hopes to have made the point that there are potentially deeper and more complete theoretical explanations of the commonly accepted facts of the cases regarding the CCF and the Social Credit parties and their predecessors. The basic theoretical question posed is this: Can these phenomena best be analyzed as the response of the Canadian agrarian petit-bourgeoisie to the structure and content of capitalist modernization as imposed by the National Policy? The answer lies in studies which reexamine the agitations, the policies, the government programs, and the eventual outcomes which characterized the Canadian agrarian petit-bourgeoisie's political offensive (an offensive which dominated Canadian history in the first part of this century) from such a theoretical orientation.

Canadian Journal of Political Science XI:1 (March/1978. *Author's note*: A revised and edited version of a paper presented to the meeting of the CSAA Quebec City, 1976. Editorial advice from the editors of the *Canadian Journal of Political Science* and its referrees is gratefully acknowledged.

NOTES

---

[1] The CCF affiliated with the Canadian Labour Congress in 1961 to become the New Democratic party, explicitly modelled on the social democratic parties of western Europe and the Labour parties of Britain and Australia. In so doing, there is a case for arguing that the CCF made a successful transition from a populist party to a social democratic party. Interestingly, the Saskatchewan branch put up some resistance to this move and only changed its official name to the NDP much later.

[2] The Social Credit party won provincial office in Alberta in 1935 and governed continuously until its defeat in 1971. The CCF won provincial office in Saskatchewan in the 1944 election and governed as the CCF until 1961, then as the CCF-NDP until 1964, when it lost power to the Liberals. In 1971 the party was swept back to power as the NDP and is still in office in that province at the time of publication. No work has provided a detailed and critical analysis of the records of the two governments. In 1952, the Social Credit party in British Columbia won provincial power, not losing to the NDP until 1972. Further, the CCF-NDP have remained major opposition parties in Manitoba (holding power there from 1969 to 1977) and Ontario. A curious variant of the Social Credit party has emerged as a significant opposition party in the province of Quebec. Of course, prior to the founding of either the CCF or Social Credit, their predeccessors as organized farm movements had won office in Ontario, Alberta, and Manitoba.

[3] Both the Social Credit and the CCF (now the NDP) have survived as permanent third parties federally, consistently winning a handful of seats in the federal House of Commons.

[4] Richard Hofstadter, *The Age of Reform: From Bryan to F.D.R.* (New York: Vintage Books, 1955), 12.

[5] See, for example, Irwin Unger, "Critique of Norman Pollack's Fear of Man," *Agricultural History* 39 (1965); and Daniel Bell (ed.), *The New American Right* (Garden City, N.Y.: Doubleday, 1955); updated and republished as *The Radical Right* (Garden City, N.Y.: Doubleday, 1963).

[6] L. W. Levy and A. Young, "Foreword," in N. Pollack (ed.), *The Populist Mind* (Indianapolis: Bobbs-Merrill, 1967), xxi-xxii.

[7] Ibid., vii.

[8]John D. Hicks, *The Populist Revolt: A History of the Farmers' Alliance and the People's Party* (Lincoln University of Nebraska Press, 1931), 422.

[9]Roscoe C. Martin, *The People's Party in Texas* (Austin: University of Texas Press. 1933).

[10]Norman Pollack, *The Populist Response to Industrial America* (New York: Norton, 1966). 6.

[11]Ibid., 11-12.

[12]Pollack (ed.). *The Populist Mind.*

[13]See Theodore Saloutos (ed.) *Populism: Reaction or Reform?* (New York: Holt, 1968), for an excellent effort to marshal systematically the evidence supporting both points of view.

[14]Clanton O. Gene, *Kansas Populism: Ideas and Men* (Lawrence: University of Kansas Press, 1969). Also, see an earlier work, Walter T. K. Nugent, *The Tolerant Populists: Kansas Populism and Nativism* (Chicago: University of Chicago Press, 1962); a good summary and analysis of the controversy appears on pp.3-32.

[15]Richard M. Abrams (ed.), *A Populist Reader: Selections from the Works of American Populist Leaders* (New York: Harper, 1966).

[16]George B. Tindall (ed.). *A Populist Reader: Selections from the Works of American Populist Leaders* (New York: Harper, 1966).

[17]Robert F. Durden, *The Climax of Populism: The Election of 1896* (Lexington: University of Kentucky Press, 1965). In his preface the author writes: "Mostly farmers, the Populists were not spokesmen for a static society, nor were they opposing and fleeing from the industrial future of the nation. They sought rather to capture federal power and use it both negatively to end economic abuses that had flourished since the Civil War and positively to improve the lot of the farmers and industrial workers of the land" (x).

[18]C. Vann Woodward, *Tom Watson: Agrarian Rebel* (New York: Oxford University Press, 1963).

[19]Durden, *Climax of Populism.*

[20]Albert D. Kirwan, *Revolt of the Rednecks: Mississipi Politics, 1876-1925* (New York: Harper, 1951).

[21]Ibid., 312-13.

[22]Thomas A. Clinch, *Urban Populism and Free Silver in Montana* (Missoula; University of Montana Press, 1970), 173.

[23]Ibid., 174.

[24]See John Chamberlain, *Farewell to Reform: The Rise, Life and Decay of the Progressive Mind in America* (Chicago: Quandrangle Paperbacks, 1965); and Gabriel Kolko, *The Triumph of Conservatism: A Reinterpretation of American History, 1900-1916* (Chicago: Quadrangle, 1963), 304.

[25]George McGovern's campaign in 1972 can partly be seen most properly as a modern-day irruption of hitherto quiescent populist sentiment among the American electorate. The fact that McGovern is a senator from a cradle of Populism–the Dakotas–goes far in explaining the anti-war, anti-corporate, and moralistic tone of his campaign.

[26]This phrase is a reworking of William Jennings Bryan's famous concluding statement in his speech at the Democratic Party National Convention in 1896 when he said: "You shall not press down upon the brow of labor this crown of thorns, you shall not crucify mankind upon a cross of gold." See W.J. Bryan, *The First Battle: The Story of the Campaign of 1896* (Chicago: Conkey Press, 1896), 199-206.

[27]Kenneth Minogue, "Populism as a Political Movement," in G. Ionescu and E. Gellner (eds.), *Populism: Its Meanings and National Characteristics* (London: Weidengeld and Nicolson, 1969), 197.

[28]All scholarly works on pre-revolutionary Russia make this point. See Part I of E. H. Carr, *The Bolshevik Revolution*, Vol. I (Harmondsworth: Penguin, 1950), especially 15-37; Leon Trotsky's *The History of the Russian Revolution*, trans. by Max Eastman (Ann Arbor: University of Michigan Press, 1932), especially Vol. I, 463; B. N. Ponomaryov et al., in the "official" (that is, Stalinist) *History of the Communist Party of the Soviet Union* (Moscow: Foreign Languages Publishing House, n.d.), 42-50; and finally, R. P. Palmer and Joel Colton, *A History of the Modern World* (New York: Knopf, 1965), the standard college history text, which agrees with the significance of the struggle between Marxism and Populism in pre-revolutionary Russia (706-11).

[29]The author finds the term "independent commodity producer" to be unnecessarily cumbersome. For the remainder of this work the term "agrarian petit-bourgeoisie" will be used. The reader will understand the term to be used in the classical Marxist sense–that is, the agrarian petit-bourgeoisie is that class which owns and controls some small capital (land, machinery, etc.) which, in combination with its own labour, is applied to the production of agricultural commodities for the market. It should be noted that the labour at the disposal of a particular petit-bourgeois includes not only his own but his family's unpaid labour, and only occasionally and/or marginally does he rely upon wage-labour.

[30]For this assertion and the analysis that follows see the following sources: E. P. Thompson, in *The Making of the English Working Class* (Harmondsworth: Penguin, 1963), puts it most cryptically when he says, "The process of industrialization must, in any conceivable social context, entail suffering and the destruction of older and valued ways of life" (223). Also see this theme's comparative development in Barrington Moore, Jr.'s, sweeping analysis of modernization in Europe, North America, and Asia in *Social Origins of Dictatorship and Democracy: Lord and Peasant in the Making of the Modern World* (Boston: Beacon, 1966). Another excellent study by a Marxist Scholar is Maurice Dobbs, *Studies in the Development of Capitalism* (New York: International, 1947), especially Chap. Six, "Growth of the Proletariat,"

221-54. Karl Marx's *Capital,* Vol. I (Moscow: Progress Publishers, 1966), parts VII and VIII, "The Accumulation of Capital," and "The So-called Primitive Accumulation," 564-774, remains the classic from which all others derive inspiration in an analysis of modernization, even when disagreeing. I would hasten to add the voices of Max Weber (*General Economic History* [New York: Collier, 1961]), and W. W. Rostow (*The Stages of Economic Growth: A Non-communist Manifesto* [Cambridge: Cambridge University Press, 1971]) to the chorus of support for this general analysis.

[31]The author accepts the classical Marxist definition of surplus value; it is the value extracted from a worker's labour by the capitalist and is equal to the exchange value of the products of the worker's labour less his wages and the costs of the means of production. See E. J. Hobsbawm, *The Age of Revolution, 1789-1848* (New York: Mentor, 1962), especially Chap. 11, "The Labouring Poor," for a discussion of the increasing exploitation of wage-labour as a source of capital accumulation.

[32]"Subsistence agriculture" is agricultural production which has as its main goal the subsistence of the immediate producer and his family and only incidentally the production of agricultural goods for sale on the market (and only then when there is a surplus over and above the immediate needs of the producer and his family). Of course, from the beginning, agriculture in the prairie West was commercially-oriented, but this fact did not prevent farm families from also producing for their own needs.

[33]Hobsdawm, *The Age of Revolution,* 48-49.

[34]Again, the author accepts the classical Marxist definition of the proletariat as that class which must sell its labour on the market for a wage in order to obtain the means of survival.

[35]Marx makes this point repeatedly throughout his analysis of capitalism. It is best expressed, though, in *Capital,* Vol, I, Chap. XV, "Machinery and Modern Industry," 371-507. At one point he says: "In the sphere of agriculture, modern industry has a more revolutionary effect than elsewhere, for this reason, that it annihilates the peasant, that bulwark of the old society, and replaces him by the wage-labourer" (505).

[36]A. Walicki, *The Controversy over Capitalism: Studies in the Social Philosophy of the Russian Populists* (Oxford: Clarendon Press, 1969), 6.

[37]V. I. Lenin, "The Economic Content of Narodism and the Critique of it in Mr. Struve's book," *Collected Works,* Vol. 1 (London: Lawrence and Wishart, 1963), 337. All references to Lenin are taken from this edition of his *Collected Works.*

[38]Ibid., 340-41.

[39]Ibid., 503.

[40]"A Characterisation of Economic Romanticism," ibid., Vol. 2, 178.

[41]Ibid., 200.

[42]Ibid., 208-20.

[43]Ibid., 243, 245.

[44]"The Heritage We Renounce," ibid., 516.

[45]Ibid., 524.

[46]"Letter to I. I. Skvortsov-Stepanov," ibid., Vol. 16, 119-20.

[47]"The Essence of the Agrarian Problem in Russia," ibid., Vol. 18, 73-77. See also "A Comparison of the Stolypin and the Narodnik Agrarian Programmes," ibid., 143-49.

[48]"The Land Question and the Rural Poor," ibid., Vol. 19, 376-78. See also "The Heritage We Renounce," ibid., Vol. 2, 461-534, and "There's a Trudovik for You!" ibid., Vol. 19, 432-35.

[49]Ibid., 377.

[50]Ibid., Vol. 2, 210.

[51]Ibid., 232.

[52]Ibid., 503.

[53]Ibid., Vol. 1, 503.

[54]Ibid., Vol. 2, 204, 212, 448. The "money power" is a phrase that recurs again and again in Populist movements everywhere.

[55]For confirmation of Lenin's characterizations see the following: Richard Kindersley, *The First Russian Revisionists: A Study of 'Legal' Marxism in Russia* (Oxford: Clarendon Press, 1962), especially Chap. I. Also see James H. Billington, *Mikhailovsky and Russian Populism* (Oxford: Clarendon Press, 1958), Richard Wartman, *The Crisis of Russion Populism* (Canbridge: Cambridge University Press, 1967); and, most definitively, Walicki, *The Controversy over Capitalism.*

[56]Lenin, "Gems of Narodnik Project Mongering," *Collected Works,* Vol. 2, 459-89.

[57]See Lenin, "The Handicraft Census of 1894-95 in Perm Gubernia and General Problems of 'Handicraft' Industry," ibid., 355-458, especially see pp. 445-58 for an excellent, critical summary of the Narodnik industrial program.

[58]Ibid., 446.

[59]Ibid., 448.

[60]Ibid., 456.

[61]Ibid., 236.

[62]Ibid., Vol. 16, 119-20.

[63]Ibid., Vol. 19, 430.

[64]Ibid., Vol. 1, 503.

[65]Ibid., Vol. 18, 358.

[66]Ibid., 359.

[67]Ibid., 524-25.

[68]Ibid., 556.

[69]Ibid., Vol. 2, 523.

[70]Ibid., Vol. 1, 366.

[71]Ibid., 380.

[72]Ibid., 384.

[73]Ibid., Vol. 2, 220.

[74]Ibid.,. 220-21.

[75]Our detailed inquiries in this regard should perhaps be limited to the early terms of each party in government. Both governed so long that any larger effort would be too massive to contemplate. Yet there are sounder reasons than merely convenience for such a limitation. First, we are more likely to find the fundamental orientation of the two movements during their first enthusiastic terms as governments. After the initial blush of success wore off, it is likely that expediency began more and more to determine the legislation of each. Further, there is no doubt that the two movements changed after a time in power. For example, the CCF over the years, made a successful transition from a rural-based Populist party to a social democratic party whose main constituency, nationally at least, became the working class, and, after 1961, with the founding of the NDP through affiliation with the CLC, the organized working class. The Social Credit in Alberta, even by their second (and most successful) leader's frank admission (see E. C. Manning, *Political Realignment: A Challenge to Thoughtful Canadians* [Toronto: McClelland and Stewart, 1967]), became a rather orthodox conservative parliamentary party. Yet there was a basic similarity in the origin of both movements in threatened agrarian petit-bourgeoisie.

[76]See L. A. Wood, *A History of Farmers' Movements in Canada* (Toronto: Ryerson, 1924), for the best and mose complete social history of these movements. For a rather overly sympathetic discussion of the movements of agrarian discontent in Ontario see R. Hann, "Some Historical Perspectives on Canadian Agrarian Political Movements," a pamphlet published by New Hogtown Press, Toronto, 1971.

[77]W. L. Morton, *The Progressive Party in Canada* (Toronto: University of Toronto Press, 1967), 85.

[78]W. L. Morton, *Manitoba: A History* (Toronto: University of Toronto Press, 1957), 211-12.

[79]B. McCutcheon, "The Patrons of Industry in Manitoba, 1890-1898," in D. Swanson (ed.), *Historical Essays on the Prairie Provinces* (Toronto: McClelland and Stewart, 1970).

[80]H. Moorehouse,e, *Deep Furrows* (Toronto: McLeod, 1918), 22-26.

[81]Morton, *Progressive Party*, 10-18.

[82]Ibid., 11.

[83]Ibid., 11-12.

[84]Ibid., Chap. Four, "The Progressive Movement and the General Election, 1920-21," 96-129; and C.B. Macpherson, *Democracy in Alberta* (Toronto: University of Toronto Press, 1953), Chap. Three, "The U.F.A.: Democracy in Practice," 62-92.

[85]*Progressive Party*, 283. Morton uses the phrase "western agrarianism" in almost the same way we are using the term "Populism." His term seems to suggest that the politics in question flow out of a region rather than a class. For Morton, Populism seems to mean simply the specific infuence of the various American movements on the Canadian farmer. This is a much too specific, and extremely theoretically confusing, use of the term.

[86]Ibid., 285. He says, for example: "Social Credit was a new departure, but it was also a lawful heir and successor to the U.F.A. and of the Progressive movement." There is a common assumption among many scholars on western Canada–the uniqueness and specificity of the CCF and Social Credit–almost as if these movements sprang into being without reference to what went before. This is clearly nonsense. Usually, like Morton, they concede a marginal impact from preexisting farmers' movements.

[87]S.M. Lipset, *Agrarian Socialism* (Berkeley: University of California Press, 1971), Chap. 1, "The Background of Agrarian Radicalism," 15-38.

[88]Ibid., Chap. 4, "The Farmers' Movement Goes Socialist," 99-117.

[89]Ibid., 161, 163. My emphasis.

[90]Ibid., Chap. 7, "Ideology and Program," 160-96.

[91]*Democracy in Alberta*, Chaps. II and III.

[92]Ibid., 3.

[93]Ibid., 216.

[94]Ibid., 220.

[95]Ibid., see Chap. VIII, "The Quasi-Party System," Subsection 2, "Political Implications of Independent Commodity Production," 221-30.

[96]Ibid., 236. It should also be noted that the precursor of Social Credit in Alberta, the UFA, affiliated with the CCF.

[97]See P. F. Sharp, *The Agrarian Revolt in Western Canada: A Survey Showing American Parallels* (Minneapolis: University of Minnesota, 1948), especially Chap. 1.

[98]Walter D. Young, *The Anatomy of a Party: The National C.C.F., 1932-61* (Toronto: University of Toronto Press, 1969), 15-16.

[99]Morton, *Progressive Party in Canada*, 14, 38-39.

[100]Peter R. Sinclair, "Populism in Alberta and Saskatchewan," unpublished Ph.D. dissertation, University of Edinburgh, 1972. See also, by the same author, "The Saskatchewan CCF: Ascent to Power and the Decline of Socialism," *Canadian Historical Review* 54 (1973), 419-33; and "Class Structure and Populist Protest in the Western Canadian Hinterland," a paper presented at the CSAA annual meeting, Toronto, August, 1974.

[101]John Smart, "Populist and Socialist Movements in Canadian History," in R.M. Laxer (ed.), *(Canada) Ltd.: The Political Economy of Dependency* (Toronto: McClelland and Stewart, 1973), 197-212.

[102]R.T. Naylor and G. Teeple, "Appendix: The Ideological Formations of Social Democracy and Social Credit," in Gary Teeple (ed.), *Capitalism and the National Question in Canada* (Toronto: University of Toronto Press, 1973(, 254-56.

ECONOMIC DEPENDENCE, POLITICAL SUBORDINATION AND NATIONAL OPPRESSION: QUEBEC, 1960-1977

Paul R. Bélanger and Céline Saint-Pierre translation David Toby Homel

The analyses of Quebec society's present situation alternate between two types of approaches. For some, Quebec's history was made through national struggles, and nationalism is the direct expression of this historical dynamic. But for others, this dynamic springs mainly from class struggles; the national question hardly surfaces in the discussion.

In the first case, class struggle is of no importance as a way of explaining things, and in the second case, national struggle suffers the same fate. In both approaches, national and class struggles are disassociated.

But we believe the problem has been formulated erroneously; the two factors must be linked if we are to explain the specificity of Quebec's historical development. In this article, then, we'd like to present an analysis—of a summary nature only, of course—that will try to depart from both these approaches. To do this, we will begin by introducing our subject through a short critique of the relations between national and class struggles such as Alain Touraine has presented them in his book *les Sociétés dépendantes*.

In the second and third sections of this text, we will try to stress the connection that exists between national struggle and class struggle, and we will end with a fourth section on the recent conjuncture in Quebec.

I. Social Movement or Class Struggle

In his essays on Latin America, Alain Touraine maintains that three analytic principles are necessary—social mobility, nationalism and class relations—to understand the complexity and dynamic of dependent societies. In dependent societies according to him, it is not really social classes that confront each other and take to the battle field of social struggle, but rather social development movements characterized by their multi-dimensionality. "The European experience has convinced us that a social movement was more important and central the more uni-dimensional it was; in other words, it more directly questioned class relations. In dependent societies, a movement dominated by class struggle, by the desire for national liberation or by an effort of social and economic modernization, is destined to be of little importance. . . Only the combination of these three dimensions—class struggle, national liberation, social modernization—clears the way for an important movement."[1]

This distinction permits Touraine to characterize the types of social movements (popular revolt, populism, national popular movements, etc.) according to the role given to one or the other of the elements by each of the movements.

At first, this formulation appears to be highly efficient, since it lets us identify the "most diverse aspects of national life,"[2] as it points to the type of links, through social movements, between the different stakes of social struggle. However, and without going into an epistemological critique of the place of the concept of social movement in Touraine's theory, it seems to us that this approach maintains the separation between national struggle and class relations.

Actually, in Touraine's thinking, the three themes of nationalism, social mobility and class conflict are associated with distinct analytic principles, with discourses that each represent one point of view for the analysis of the social and political problems of dependent societies. Because of this, the study can adopt only one analytic line and achieve interesting results. This eventuality is even a necessity in certain cases. "When we consider the most archaic situations, the more we take leave of the revolutionary path, the more the forces at work tend to oppose each other, or at least separate one from another, which leads us to consider separately the problems of mobility, nationalism and social classes."[3] The complexity of the situation demands a definition of social movements as a system of action, tying the three problems together, but these problems continue to reflect distinct analytic principles. In Touraine's way of formulating things, national and class struggles are juxtaposed one against the other, not integrated into a single conceptual system.

This absence of analytic connection between nation and class relations makes national liberation struggles appear like the opposition of one nation to foreign domination—as a relation between nations. Does this mean "nation" is to be defined as a community having homogeneous cultural traits, demanding its political autonomy? This community-based concept excludes the division of social classes within the nation. Moreover, it rules out considering the effects of dependence (or of oppression) on the structure of classes itself and on their relations.[4] It seems to us that national oppression should

really be defined as an aspect of the capitalist system of exploitation and domination, so that national struggle, while retaining its specificity, can be considered as one form of the class struggle. This way, nation and class relations no longer constitute juxtaposed analytic principles, but are integrated into the same formulation.

One of the difficulties of using this concept of social movement arises from a wavering between the two principle aspects of its definition—on one hand, normative orientations; on the other hand, social agents. Stress is most often placed on normative orientations as defined by the actors themselves; then the analysis pushes the concrete practice of the social forces at work into the background and runs the risk of disguising the complex alliances between classes and class components that are their principle agents. The temptation, then, is to distinguish a series of social movements according to the nature of their demands and their ideology.

For us, the sole use of the notion of social movement is to designate a Protean and undifferenciated grouping of classes or organizations whose unifying principle resides either in the identification of a problem (urban activists, etc.), or in certain characteristics of their members (student or women's movements, etc.).

An analysis of class relations is more useful for detecting, through struggles, both the *contradictory stakes and class interests* and the factions at work in order to identify the principle forms of organization of social relations, especially insofar as the national question is concerned. But first we must point out how national oppression constitutes a form of the capitalist system of exploitation and domination.

II. National Oppression and Class Relations

The central issue is to identify the many contradictions that run through Quebec, to point out their relations and to pick out those that are the object of mobilizing struggles—those that constitute a real stake. We'll study the effects of these structural elements on social classes, and then how social relations are organized in the conjuncture.

The *québécois* State, even if it has nearly all the characteristics of a State—a Parliament, a judicial system, bureaucracy, etc. – and even if it does contribute to the reproduction of social relations by its own means, is, in reality, only a segment, a unit of the Canadian State, because it does not have in its possession all the powers that have determined the specific forms of exploitation in Quebec. The principle mechanisms of economic intervention originate in the Canadian State: monetary and fiscal policy, tariffs and customs, banking and credit, foreign trade, etc. The provincial State of Quebec has predominant jurisdiction over the areas of education, language and culture, civil law and labour relations, and it shares jurisdiction with Ottawa over health, police, taxation, etc. In other words, the functions of capital accumulation and ideological legitimization are dominated respectively by federal and provincial forces; the functions of reproduction of the labour force (immigration, education, health), integration (labour laws, consulting bodies, "tripartism") and repression (army, police, penitentiaries) are shared by both levels of government. Quebec, by the mere existence of a provincial political State, must be analyzed as the coalescing of certain aspects only of class struggle, even if jurisdiction over labour relations and the presence of one part of the Anglo-Canadian bourgeoisie make many of the conflicts appear internal to Quebec.

This sharing of powers, realized in the middle of the last century under the direction of Anglo-British merchant and banking capital, whose interests were largely concentrated in commercial exchange and transportation,[5] is the result of the conditions of the formation of Confederation. By creating a sort of common market of English colonies, the federal regime gathered together economic interests that were already regionally diversified (independent producers in Ontario, bankers and industrialists in Montreal, the French-speaking petty bourgeoisie in Quebec, merchants in the Maritimes, etc.), and whose unity could be based only upon an increase of exchange and the central State's contribution to industrialization. With the development of more and more regional economies based on natural resources under provincial jurisdiction and tied to direct American investment, Canadian political unity remains fragile, since the new regionally dominant factions have a greater need to control and reinforce provincial States, which are growing more and more powerful in relation to Ottawa.[6]

In this way, the social forces that were present at the unification of the English colonies created a commercial economic space through the formation of the Canadian federal State. But the merchant and financial bourgeoisie, dominant in the middle of the last century, produced the very conditions of its own weakening, of its dependence and submission to American industrial capital, by hastening the entry of the mode of capitalist production into Canada. In effect, as far back as the end of the last century, the central State adopted a so-called national policy that consisted of a considerable increase in tariffs on imported manufactured goods. The principle behind this policy was to favour consumer products manufactured in Canada, and in fact it did permit considerable expansion of the textile, paper and tobacco industries, and maintain the importance of the leather and wood industries. Except for tobacco, all these sectors are still controlled by Canadian capitalists. But under the domination of the merchant bourgeoisie which was more interested in trade with England, Canadian industrial capital scarcely developed at all, so that the main effect of the tariff policy was the penetration of American industrial capital. American branch plants profited not only from local markets, but also from advantages agreed upon for exporting to the United States and England. As long ago as the end of the last century, half the mines in Quebec and Ontario were controlled by American interests. Today, this same capital controls about sixty per cent of the Canadian manufacturing industry. The thrust of American imperialism into Canada was achieved in large part (nearly ninety per cent, according to certain sources) with the aid of funds originating in Canada itself: undistributed branch plant profits and borrowing on the Canadian market. In short, governmental policies and the banking system contributed to American capital's stranglehold on the Canadian economy—a profitable stranglehold, since from 1960 to 1969, the United States took out $2.6 million more than it had invested in Canada.[7]

Three observations can be made from this historical overview:

1. Capitalist exploitation takes on a particular form to suit each region; the unequal penetration of capitalism into the different

branches of the economy is expressed by spatial concentrations of certain industrial sectors, Thus, the dissolution of old forms of small-scale or family-based agricultural production is more or less rapid, depending on the region. For example, entire branches of the economy where technology is less developed and labour more intensive—such as textiles or clothing—are concentrated in certain regions. In this case, large multinational monopolistic enterprises decentralize their activities and labour forces by dividing their production units into centrals and peripherals, and setting them up on different territories according to level of skill and labour costs. The fact that capitalist relations develop unequally in each region creates an objective basis for an opposition of interests between components of the bourgeoisie and the working class in the overall Canadian picture. At certain times, this can create an alliance between bourgeois and working class components on a regional level. For example, workers and management in the textile industry in Quebec favour tariffs and quotas on imports, whereas the Western "consumers" would prefer lower prices. Such is the case for gas and oil in the West, wood in British Columbia, etc.

2. Unequal development and regional fragmentation of the economy are accentuated by American imperialism which invests on one hand in the most productive economic sectors located in Ontario (automobiles, chemical products, electric tools, etc.), and on the other in industries linked to natural resources (Western oil, Quebec iron, etc.). Besides producing characteristic effects on regional specialization, American imperialism produces specific dominating effects on the Canadian economy: central units in the United States (head offices, research centres, finished products) and peripheral units in Canada (exploitation of natural resources, assembly plants), thereby transferring surplus value to the United States. Canada's economic development complements that of the United States, and is largely oriented directly by American multinationals.

3. Regionalization and economic dependence both explain Canada's decentralized political shape. American and Canadian economic interests are based on the competition between provincial States to benefit their own investments: mining concessions, electricity prices, direct grants, etc. But at the same time, the form of the State contributes to the maintenance—if not the increase—of regional disparities and economic dependence on the United States, because the provincial States are more concerned with their own particular interests than with national unity or economic independence. However, we must not forget the importance of those economic forces whose interest is to maintain or increase the central State's powers, but our current discussion is limited to locating the sources of tension and the stakes around which class struggle is built.

We're still left with the problem of the national oppression of French-speaking Quebeckers inside Canada. If what we've said is correct, then national oppression should present both specific and distinct signs of the unequal development that balkanizes the Canadian economy, the economic dependence on the United States and the central State. A brief examination of the national question in Canada will allow us to bring out another facet of the Canadian political configuration.

Here again, let's add a few brief historical notes that will spare us some long theoretical detours. We've said that Canadian Confederation marked the culmination of the commercial and financial bourgeoisie's efforts to create an autonomous economic domain for trade with England, distinct from the United States. This economic field included Quebec and its French-speaking population and turned it into a linguistic minority subject to commercial interests through the central State. Already the Union (1840-1867) had "done away with the major obstacle that Quebec nationalism represented to the economic growth of old Upper Canada."[8] The traditional petty bourgeoisie stood in opposition to the development of East-West communications and commercial capitalism, since its political power was linked to the upholding of agriculture predominance.[9] The presence of a French-speaking population (or what others have called Canada's bi-national character) accounts for Canada's decentralized political form, and in particular the provincial States' jurisdiction over the areas of culture, education and language. But at the same time, this power-sharing both consecrates and reproduces national oppression; it, too, can be defined as one particular form of exploitative capitalist relations, one specific form of class domination.[10] Actually, the formation of a nation-State from different linguistic groups already presupposes the existence of quite specific class relations—in particular, the hegemony of a bourgeois segment of one linguistic group. In this case it was the Anglo-Canadian merchant bourgeoisie, and later, the Anglo-Canadian industrial bourgeoisie, that maintained hegemony. It implies an assimilation process and the dissolving of all barriers that might impede the free movement of merchandise, capital and labour force. For the dominant bourgeoisie, language and culture represent obstacles to the homogenization of territory, communications and the dissemination of the national ideology. The existence of two languages in the same territory continually casts doubt on the legitimization of the nation-State, and also makes the unity of bourgeois components more difficult to realize.

National oppression is neither the domination of one nation over another, nor the co-existence of two class structures from different national backgrounds. National oppression is a form of class or social domination that is characterized by cultural and linguistic domination, just as "regional domination" is a particular connection of class relations and cannot be defined as a relation between regions. By crossing the boundaries of social class, cultural and linguistic domination introduces a particular dimension in class relations. Its concrete definition can be found in discriminatory cultural and linguistic practices, but its effects vary according to the position occupied in class relations.

Discriminatory practices don't effect social classes in the same way. For the working class, these practices show up in the form of specific limits to the exchange of its labour, its productive action and its reproduction. French-speaking workers suffer discrimination in the work force, the assigning of jobs, promotions, mobility, etc., a discrimination that takes the form of surplus exploitation and low salaries. Remember that French-speaking Quebeckers occupy the second-to-last spot in salary ranges of all the linguistic groups in Quebec.

For the bourgeoisie, discrimination effects the conditions of its development and capital accumulation, as well as its potential access to upper management positions. Arnaud Sales' recent thesis has shown that the French-speaking bourgeoisie's access to the financial resources of English-Canadian banks is difficult, and that there is a rather strict correspondence between the property's origin and that of its directors, and that French-speaking Quebeckers control only five per cent of the companies in the monopoly sector located in Quebec.[11]

Discrimination effects the petty bourgeoisie in a particular way, due to the position it occupies in the division of labour. The petty bourgeoisie is on the side of intellectual labour, and its knowledge of language, as well as its ability to communicate and express itself, are its privileged tools. In addition, the positions it occupies are often ideologically (e.g., information, education) or politically charged (e.g., civil service, personnel director in private enterprise), and they demand a certain adherence to the goals of the dominant classes. Herein lies part of the reason for the low ratio of French-speaking Quebeckers in the federal civil service and in the executive level of private enterprise.

If the forms of national oppression vary according to the class, so do the practices or struggles against this oppression. To struggle against surplus exploitation doesn't demand the same mobilization tactics and doesn't have the same implications as struggling to lift certain constraints on capital supply. Inversely, it would be interesting to track the rate of linguistic transfers according to class and class segment to appreciate more fully the forces of assimilation and the ability to resist, based on the position in social relations.

This way, the fundamental characteristics of Canadian social formation are linked one to the other; they form a whole and must be analyzed as a series of effects of a single social relationship. Economic dependence on American imperialism, national oppression and regional disparities are all concrete forms that the development of capitalist production relations in Canada has taken on, concrete forms that explain the tensions and conflicts between the central State and the provincial States—or more precisely, that explain the political subordination of the provincial States to the federal central State. In a rebound effect, this political subordination contributes to the maintenance and reproduction of the different forms of social relations. It is

326

important to stress this point, because the diverse explanations currently tend to confuse one or the other of these forms. For example, national struggles have often been understood as being the diverted expression of those demands whose real stake is the economic recovery of Quebec (cf. the thesis of the unequal development of Canada). Dominant classes use these reductions, since they reduce the exploitation of the working class to particular forms isolated one from the other: salary, working hours, skill levels, job security, etc.

In Quebec, these different forms of social relations cause a particular structuration of social classes and a specific organization of the struggles. The national question takes on even more importance, since the *québécois* State itself, in its limited power, assumes part of the overall function of the reproduction of class relations, including national oppression with the support of a coalition of both linguistic groups.

III. The Effects of National Oppression on the Class System in Quebec

Within the limits of this article, is impossible to explain the way social classes are effected by the different concrete forms through which exploitative relations manifest themselves. We'd have to point out the effects proper to unequal development, national oppression, etc. on the configuration of each of the classes and on class relations. A few examples of the effects of national oppression will show first that we're dealing with a type of domination distinct from that created by unequal development, and next that this oppression benefits a certain type of class alliance.

The New Petty Bourgeoisie

The development of monopoly capitalism (the concentration of capital and the complexified development of the forces of production) made the State's intervention in the economy necessary and increased its ideological and political role. These transformations brought about a modification of social class structure by considerably strengthening the limiting, supervisory and management functions, as much in production enterprises as in banking and commercial services and the State's ideological and political apparatuses. The extension of these functions created a material basis for the emergence of a neo-petty bourgeois class consisting of capital's intermediary agents. They don't fill positions of management in the total labour process and in production relations; they don't realize profit directly. Their surveillance jobs are delegations, or relay stations, of capitalist power at all levels: political, economic and ideological. If they do receive higher pay, it should be considered a premium for the political loyalty.

The interests of this class are therefore not tied to the direct appropriation of profit, as is the case of individual capitalists in the general process of capital accumulation. These executive overseers (engineers, technicians, labour managers, foremen, specialists in personnel selection and integration, directors of administrative or commercial services, heads of educational or research programs, etc.) depend more on the development of the forces of production and the extension of politico-ideological functions.

In Quebec, where the economy is largely controlled by American and Anglo-Canadian capitalists, where much of political power derives from the federal central State and where the working language in these sectors remains English, the French-speaking new petty bourgeoisie is limited in the number of positions it can occupy. It finds itself in unequal competition with English speakers whose career horizons are much broader.

The Report of the Royal Commission of Enquiry on Bilingualism and Biculturalism[12] had some very interesting things to say on this subject. It pointed out the effect of ethnicity on income disparities, as well as on career differences between English and French populations. For the whole of the working population in Canada, the Report emphasized the State's influence on regional development, professional structure and education level in its explanation of income disparities between these two groups. Adding age, industry and under-employment factors, there was still an unexplained difference evaluated by the authors of 38% or 24% in the Montreal area, according to their methods. They attributed it to ethnicity: "a clear influence of ethnic origin, all other factors remaining constant." (page 63). "In short, the factors mentioned above explain the majority of disparities we have found; we must consider elements linked to ethnicity as secondary, although appreciable." (page 78). In other words, to those factors linked to unequal development (under-employment, education level, structure of occupation), we must add national oppression (ethnicity) to explain the income disparities between French and English populations.

As far as the respective place of these two groups in technical and administrative professions in Quebec is concerned, the Commission clearly concludes discriminatory practices exist that orient the French-speaking population toward civil service in Quebec or independent private businesses. "Of all the areas of activity common to large enterprises, except for management, the French presence and the French language are most restricted in engineering, research and development. In our entire sample, only 22% of salaried employees working in these areas are French-speaking." (page 516). The same goes for French-speaking administrative or accounting experts who especially turn to private firms or government services (page 526). Lastly, "the participation of scientists in a host of industries whose qualifications come from French-speaking universities offers numerous analogies to the engineers' situation. In provincial government and municipal administration, 85% of scientists are French-speaking . . . Like French-speaking engineers, they are minimally represented in large mining and manufacturing enterprises (14%), as well as in building, transportation and communications (13%)." (page 527).

What explains these career and employment differences? According to the Commission, "it appears certain that some enterprises practice discrimination" (page 531), although it does add, without any facts to back up such a statement, that "in our time, rational selection has largely taken the place of subjective and empirical methods." (531).

More or less the same situation prevails in the federal public administration. While speakers of French represent 26% of the working population in Canada, they make up only 22% of civil servants, and *only 14.4% of the category of technicians and specialists* (engineers, scientists, jurists, doctors, sociologists, etc.). In addition, French-speaking civil servants receive salaries lower than their English-speaking colleagues with either the same education level or in the same professional category. It is significant to note that salary disparities are greatest among those with university degrees (page 224-231).

For the petty bourgeoisie, for whom language is the principle working tool, the effects of national oppression are all too clear. Observing regional disparities (unemployment rate, industrial structure, sectorial division of jobs, evolution of investments) accentuated by American imperialism would show the same effects: low salaries, few career openings in research positions, etc. Faced with these obstacles, the petty bourgeoisie resists by attempting to recover federal jurisdictions and their corresponding administrations, and creating State enterprises to compensate for the weakness of the French-speaking Quebec bourgeoisie. The repatriation of powers currently held by the central State will allow it, not only to increase the number of available jobs, but also to enlarge its sphere of influence on economic policies and unequal development. Economic dependence, political subordination and national oppression combine to furnish a material base for the creation of the new French-speaking petty bourgeoisie as an autonomous social force.

However, these objective conditions do not automatically lead to national struggles in the political arena. Besides, the different types of domination can contribute to the political fragmentation of the petty bourgeoisie, due to its extreme dependence on the bourgeoisie. Contradictions between capital factions can be reproduced in the different political allegiances within the petty bourgeoisie itself.

The Bourgeoisie

We've briefly covered the historical conditions that led to the marginalization of the French-speaking Quebec bourgeoisie by its Anglo-Canadian counterpart, and the penetration of American capitalism in both Canada and Quebec. The limited opportunity of the French-speaking Quebec bourgeoisie to own property and the movement of the economic centre from Montreal to Ontario are common facts, even if discussion continues on the importance of explanations such as technological change, concentration of capital, provincial and Canadian economic policies and the national question. Nevertheless, we're still convinced that national oppression produces effects of its own on the French-speaking Quebec bourgeoisie's possibilities to accumulate capital.

And in fact, Arnaud Sales' recent work has shown that the sources of capital supply open to Quebec enterprises when they go calling on banks are limited to say the least; the end result is that French firms turn to French banking capital. However, the French-speaking financial sector represents only 10% of Canadian banking. The same channelling effect exists in the case of recruiting high-level executives for business: "the national origin of the highest executives is for the most part determined by the ethnic or national origin of the principle share-holder or group that controls the enterprise."[13] French-speaking people's chances of reaching the top are quite slim, especially since we know that large companies (that is, those whose ownership and management are not provided by the same individual) controlled by the French-speaking bourgeoisie number only 4% to 5%.

We've seen that due to ethnicity, the French-speaking bourgeoisie runs up against certain obstacles to its expansion as a class. However, we shouldn't imagine that this fact makes it nationalist. On one hand, certain enterprises have been able to lessen–if not completely remove–the obstacles that stood in the way of its accumulation process, thereby occupying a more important place in big business. On the other hand, the French-speaking bourgeoisie in Quebec has found that its interests are fragmented according to the advantages it can derive from Confederation. Enterprises with Canadian markets–especially those that export finished products–depend much more on the central State's commercial tariff policies.[14] And finally, we should ask ourselves whether the P. Q.'s current brand of nationalism, supported especially by the petty bourgeoisie and seconded by the working class, isn't likely to frighten the bourgeoisie, given its method of managing social relations.

The Working Class

Little research has been done on the specific effects of national oppression on workers and employees. Therefore, we will limit ourselves to a few more general remarks.

One statement must be made at the start: capitalism's unequal development creates disparities of all sorts on the strictly economic level–between regions and industrial sectors and, within the latter, between the degree of the concentration of enterprises. These disparities, which are tied to different rates of exploitation and different rhythms of capital accumulation, are one of the main reasons for the lack of homogeneity in working class struggles. For example, some industrial sectors may be suffering while others are healthy, or working and salary conditions may vary from one enterprise or one sector to another, etc. Mobilization and struggles are, so to speak, staggered.

Add to that the divisions caused by dependence, subordination and oppression. First of all, the dual nature of political jurisdictions creates a divisive factor for the Canadian working class. Certain political struggles have been able to mobilize the whole of the working class, as was the case with the federal anti-inflation measures. But on the other hand, 'provincial' struggles are undertaken only if negotiations within public institutions concerned with health and education are involved, or the the repression brought on by the limitation of union rights or political activities is resisted.

Secondly, the positions of the English-Canadian working class toward the national question in Quebec are a source of tension within its French-speaking counterparts. Take the case of the Canadian Communist Party or the New Democratic Party, neither of which has ever recognized the legitimacy of Quebec's political autonomy. And thirdly, the Quebec working class itself has cultural and linguistic divisions of its own. "It would be accurate to say that the cultural and linguistic division between English- and French-speaking workers tends to reproduce the gulf between the 'workers' aristocracy–the highly skilled workers–and their less skilled counterparts. The fact is that French-speaking workers are relatively less skilled, and the growing tendency to eliminate unskilled workers in industrial labour effects them more than the largely English-speaking workers' aristocracy . . . The working class faces the national question in terms of the social division of labour within capitalist production relations."[15] We can hypothesize that the differences in the level of skilled workers are maintained by the political relations within English companies. Through selection, promotion and other advantages in salary or working conditions, English-speaking workers are constantly favoured over their French-

329

speaking counterparts. The latter suffer from linguistic and cultural discrimination by the English, and in addition, they are faced with the repression of their "popular" language and culture by the French-speaking bourgeoisie.

We'd like to sum up our arguments: a) national oppression is part and parcel of capitalist relations in Canada, because Canadian unity was fashioned under the hegemony of the Anglo-Canadian bourgeoisie; b) national oppression as the concrete form of these relations can be defined by linguistic and cultural discrimination, and can be distinguished from "regional domination," which is linked to unequal development; c) the effects of national oppression vary according to the position occupied in production relations, and in this way, they contribute to the shaping of class relations.

IV. Elements of the Socio-Economic and Political Conjuncture in Quebec

Before proceeding to an analysis of the current state of things in Quebec, we must first review the theoretical approaches that have characterized recent analyses of Quebec. On one hand, certain Marxist analysts who've turned their attention to Quebec have done nothing more than carry out a simplistic, idealistic transfer by applying the concept of social formation to Quebec society. Stating the problem this way only prolongs the nationalist path of Quebec analysis by granting a determining position to cultural characteristics (culture, language, lifestyle, specific ideologies) in the description of Quebec as a social formation. This way, they join traditional historiography for which Quebec's history is that of a nation oppressed by the Anglo-Saxons. This insistence on cultural characteristics has led to the reduction of the importance of political and economic characteristics, and to the neglect of all the explanatory factors linked to the development of Canadian capitalism and American imperialism, of which Quebec is an integral part. Opposed to this attempt to define Quebec society as a social formation is the hypothesis that defines Quebec as a region of Canada whose specificity stems from the unequal development of the Canadian economy. The national question then becomes subordinate to the economic one; it's no more or less than

one effect of Canada's economic structure. The national basis, the linguistic and cultural characteristics as well as the federal-provincial political structure are considered secondary, and for all intents and purposes do not appear in the analysis of the national question in Quebec. The dynamic of Quebec history is explained, according to this hypothesis, in terms of the American and Canadian economic situation, with internal national oppression referring back to the unequal development of the economy.

Faced with these two theoretical orientations, our opinion is that Quebec must be defined in terms of the specific connection between the national question and the class struggle.

In the present article, we will proceed to an analysis of social relations within Quebec, although we are aware it will have to be completed at a later date by a study of social relations in all of Canada.

In our analysis, we will be concentrating mostly on the period of 1960 to 1977. We will consider some of the aspects of this conjuncture that will enable us to go on to a discussion of political and sociological questions relative to Quebec's development. We will divide this period into three sub-periods to get a better idea of their characteristics: 1) 1960-1966, 2) 1966-1976, 3) 1976-1977.

The Quiet Revolution: 1960-1966

The sixties were characterized by a realignment of the different components of the bourgeoisie in Quebec. We will examine the relations that existed between the interests of each of these parts and the "nationalist" project of the Lesage government. The Anglo-Canadian bourgeoisie's struggle against traditional Quebec nationalism converged in the sixties with the struggles of the Quebec bourgeoisie and new petty bourgeoisie. The Liberal government that emerged from these struggles proceeded to modernize and extend the State apparatus and to install economic policies that would enable—at least on a short-term basis—the Anglo-Canadian bourgeoisie and the new petty bourgeoisie to identify their interests with them. As for the American bourgeoisie, its intervention in Quebec was not threatened by this new, apparently nationalist, policy. Consequently, there was no major rearrangement of the positions occupied by the different bourgeoisies during the "*révolution tranquille.*"

Let's review some element of the history of the Quiet Revolution and of the period that preceded it.

During the "Dark Ages" (the *grande noirceur*), from 1944 to 1960, when the clergy was at the helm of most health and education institutions, and when Premier Duplessis was maintaining control over Quebec's development under the banner of his autonomy policy, American investment poured into both Canada and Quebec. Prior to 1957, Liberal governments in Canada succeeded one another with the same objective: full employment. Ottawa undertook more and more centalization and allied itself directly with private enterprise as the source of employment. The policy of continentalism (USA-CANADA) had consequences the governments did not foresee until the 1960s. Federal economic development policies produced acute regional disparities that inspired a series of programs in the 1960s, notably in Quebec; they provided one of the bases of intervention by this "State of quiet revolution." Prior to 1960, the State hardly ventured into the economy. Quebec in particular experienced unequal regional development; between 1941 and 1960, agricultural labour decreased by half and tertiary sectors doubled their manpower. This swelling of the tertiary sector must not be interpreted as a sign of development, but rather attests to the under-development of secondary industries within Quebec; the USA buys our raw materials, imports them for processing and sells them back to us in the form of finished products. Herein lies a characteristic pattern of economic exploitation under American imperialism. During this same period, some industries linked to the processing of raw materials were developing; they also profited from the salary gaps between Quebec and the USA.

The Quebec conservative State and its ally the Catholic clergy kept the people in ideological and political dependence and submission. Only a few workers' conflicts let the working class see that its interests were incompatible with those of the State, church officials and industrial bourgeoisie. Elsewhere, intellectuals were denouncing repression, attacks on freedom, and were stating their demands within the framework of progress offered by the USA. We had to imitate the USA, they said, modernize society and get in step with the movement of economic progress. This was the framework of the Quiet Revolution of the 1960s that was set into motion by the Liberal Party's taking power in Quebec.

We'd like to make use of the definition of that period known as the Quiet Revolution provided by Jean-Marc Piotte in his preface to the book *les Travailleurs contre l'Etat bourgeois.*[16]

The Quiet Revoluion consisted neither of a quantitative nor of a qualitative transformation of Quebec's economic structure, even if it was based on a cyclic phase of the expansion of the capitalist system. The Quiet Revolution can be summed up essentially as a transformation of the ideological and political superstructures in order to adapt them to the economic stage capitalism had reached, that is, State monopoly capitalism—a transformation that bourgeois sociologists would call "catching up" or "modernization."

This transformation of superstructures was fundamentally carried out at the levels of the State's economic role, and of its role in the formation and maintenance of labour. On one hand, the State went from a conception of *laissez-faire*, inspired by an outmoded liberalism, to a will to rationalize and regularize the development of the capitalist system. All this was embellished and disguised by the trappings of nationalism (nationalization of electricity, launching of a series of economic organisms: S.G.F., S.O.Q.U.E.M., pension and investment funds), organisms whose true objective was to improve the workings of the capitalist system, and whose consequences were to consolidate the domination of American imperialism over Quebec.

On the other hand, to obtain a labour force that was in better health and better educated, the State completely reorganized the health apparatus (Hospitalization Insurance Bill, 1961, and Hospital Bill, 1962) and the education apparatus (creation of the Ministry of Education, 1964, and application of the principle recommendations of the Parent Report).

These responses by the education and health apparatuses took away the power the clergy was exercising over schools and hospitals and put it back in the hands of the State. As a result, the clergy's prestige dropped, technocratic ideology was substituted and apathy toward religion increased, especially in Montreal, where church attendance dropped from 60% to 30%.

At the same time, as we've already mentioned, the tertiary sector continued to develop and the public and para-public sectors built up their manpower. The employment index in these services went from 100 to 165 between 1961 and 1969. The unionization rate increased by 7 per cent from 1961 to 1967, a growth due to the unionizing of the trade and public and para-public sectors.

The extension of the State apparatus corresponds to the widening of the sectors open to State intervention. This leads to the formation of a new petty bourgeoisie and produces the platform upon which it will build its power; from that base, it will take its place in dominant social relations.

In Quebec, a new petty bourgeoisie, consisting mostly of laymen and technocrats, took over the management of the State administrative apparatuses and the ideological apparatuses (schools, health, recreation, culture, information . . .) by struggling against the traditional petty bourgeoisie, represented in the education apparatus by the clergy.

The first years of the Quiet Revolution were marked by the new petty bourgeoisie's struggle to occupy new positions in the State apparatus, and to reach a sharing of power with the hegemonic component of the dominant class, in this case the monopoly bourgeoisie. To this end, this new class attempted to appropriate certain areas of power for itself—the schools, for example.

This was one of the characteristics of the beginning period of the Quiet Revolution: while the agents of the new petty bourgeoisie were occupying management and organizational positions in State apparatuses such as health, schools and recreation, the American and Anglo-Canadian bourgeoisies were struggling to achieve hegemony in the control of economic development. For a very short period of time, we witnessed power-sharing between the bourgeoisies and the new petty bourgeoisie—or, at least, a phase during which the latter enjoyed relative autonomy in the State apparatuses mentioned previously.

During this period, we witnessed the participation of intermediary bodies through the development of certain institutions. This extension of the exercise of participatory democracy through consulting groups was to allow the new petty bourgeoisie, during the 1960-1966 period, to share power with the bourgeoisie, as well as political control in the arena of social and economic development in Quebec—all on a very fragile basis. The new petty bourgeoisie took up position in areas where it wouldn't be likely to encounter the bourgeoisie—at least for the time being.

We intend to analyze this period not only as a "moment" of adjustment of the State apparatus and rationalization of developmental objectives for the economy, but also as a "moment" of class struggle. Not only was the new petty bourgeoisie vying with the traditional petty bourgeoisie for control of the State apparatus, but also an alliance temporarily formed between the new petty bourgeoisie, the Anglo-Canadian bourgeoisie that had interests in Quebec and the French-speaking bourgeoisie.

The Quiet Revolution was a period during which the political alliance between the Anglo-Canadian and American bourgeoisies was fraught with instability.

To understand what the "Quiet Revolution" really was, we must turn to a complex analysis of the relations between the components of the bourgeois class and its allies. To the allies we've already mentioned, we should add that during this period, the union apparatus often took up the cause of both the new petty bourgeoisie and those components of the bourgeoisie (French-speaking and Anglo-Saxon) that had interests in Quebec. It did so by supporting the orientations of the development project centred on economic recovery and the modernizing of the Quebec State apparatus. This support can be explained by the fact that several reforms instituted by the Lesage government—such as the democratization of schools and health policies—could be considered as the partial culmination of what the workers had been demanding since the 1950s.

Although the roles held by the different bourgeoisies did not fundamentally change in the course of this period, we must still note that Quebec was a point of confrontation between them. For one group, it was a time for recapturing an important position in the economic field. This was the case of the Anglo-

Canadian bourgeoise against which Duplessis had mercilessly struggled for sixteen years. Other groups wanted to strengthen the position they already held, as was the case of the French-speaking and American bourgeoisies. And then new social groups organized under the new petty bourgeoisie were out to gain control of the positions created by the transformation of the State apparatus and, little by little, to dislodge the traditional petty bourgeoisie. There's good reason to recognize that the bourgeoisies intervened in political and economic domains on a national basis. However, the alliances varied according to the situation of the sub-periods during the years 1960-1977; only a close analysis of all the interests at stake will enable us to identify the causes of these variances. In this article we can only suggest the shape of an analytical grid, as the limits of our research keep us from going any further for the time being. For example, we believe it's important to analyze more closely how the growth of the State administrative apparatus–and the ideological apparatuses attached to it–allowed the building of a material basis for the political autonomization of the new petty bourgeoisie. In this connection, it would be worthwhile to collect and analyze additional data in order to describe the struggles between the bourgeoisies within each of these sectors: financial, industrial and commercial. This would allow us to work up a lay-out for the bourgeoisies and to watch the process of Canadian and American monopoly creation at work.

The End of the Quiet Revolution and Monopoly Capitalism's Political Stranglehold on Quebec: 1966-1976

The alliance didn't last long. As far back as 1963, the Anglo-Canadian bourgeoisie began attacking the gains made by the petty bourgeoisie to increase its own area of activity. From 1966 to 1970, it took the initiative and succeeded in 1970 in ousting the nationalist factions of the petty bourgeoisie and the Quebec bourgeoisie from the political management of the québécois State. This was the year when the Liberal Party under Robert Bourassa took power again, a power it had lost in 1966.

This period also showed that, in a capitalist State at the monopoly stage, it is impossible for power to be distributed or shared between the hegemonic faction represented by the monopolies, the reigning faction comprised of the French-speaking bourgeoisie and the new petty bourgeoisie, the latter two being anti-monopoly. After 1966, liberalization was followed by a repressive phase that coincided with the beginnings of recession. The State petty bourgeoisie had to submit and throw in its lot with the hegemonic management of the monopoly bourgeoisie. The new petty bourgeoisie was eliminated from the power block and the bourgeoisie as a whole was radicalized, a radicalization that brought about increased repression of the working class. The stakes shifted: after the economic recovery of the Quiet Revolution came a period when class struggle more directly pitted the working class against the bourgeoisie in the areas of exploitation and ideological and political domination.

On the economic level, inflation, which had been holding below 3 per cent until 1964, increased steadily from 1965, except for 1970, when it showed a decrease. From 1960 to 1966, unemployment dropped from 9.2 per cent to 4.7 per cent. But beginning in 1967, there were regular increases and the rate went from 5.3 per cent to 8.3 per cent in 1972, climbing to reach 11.3 per cent in 1977.

In this regard, a very large part of the labour force, about 2,500,000 workers, must now be retrained three times during their career. And of the 150,000 unemployed, 40 per cent are between 18 and 24 years of age, and their education level is higher than average. Besides the unemployed, there are 68,000 people on welfare who depend totally on the State for their economic survival.

In 1967, the capitalist system entered a crises period, due to the conjuncture of inflation and recession. Whereas during the Quiet Revolution, the Quebec parliamentary wing of the bourgeoisie took on reformist colours because of its alliance arrangements with the petty bourgeoisie and the support of a segment of the working class, during the recessionary phase it settled in at the controls of repression. This repression continued to increase and resulted in a hardening of State power, to the point where certain people commented that the political regime was becoming fascist. Four principal indications are useful to describe this process: 1) a decrease in State expenditures that are not directly profitable through direct or indirect aid to private enterprise; 2) a hardening in the bourgeoisie's position toward unions in private enterprise; 3) an increase in the bourgeoisie's control of the State's ideological apparatuses; 4) a reinforcement of the State's repression apparatus, notably the federal as well as provincial police.[17]

In 1967, the nationalist wing of the Liberal Party led by René Lévesque left and founded an *indépendantiste* political movement that became the *Parti québécois* a year later.

In the period known as the "Quiet Revolution," there were instances of collaboration and support for the Liberal government by workers' unions, student groups and the nationalist petty bourgeoisie. In 1966 and 1967, collaboration became struggle, and for the first time since 1960, the number of workers' conflicts was greater in Quebec than in Ontario (in the latter province, unionized labour has 200,000 more members than in Quebec). In 1967, 145,226 workers were involved in strikes and lock-outs, and 1,760,950 days lost. New categories of workers in the public and para-public sectors who had just obtained the right to strike were using it; they constituted 60 per cent of those who went on strike or were locked out between 1965 and 1971. Struggles in the public sector caused first the Liberal, then the *Union nationale* governments to harden their positions. The State used its legal apparatus against the employees of the public sector. After first giving them the right to strike, it attempted to deprive them of it, or rather to limit its utilization. The conflict between the State as legislator and the State as boss hit the unionized workers of the public sector hardest and led them to question the State's political function. Therein lies the path to the radicalization and politicization of the union centrals. Through negotiations, union members and their executives become aware that the State is tied to private enterprise interests that set the limits of its autonomy.

This radicalization of union organizations and of the workers' movement in general continued and took shape in the years after 1970. In 1960, common interests led to an alliance between the bourgeoisie and the petty bourgeoisie, but as far back as 1966 and 1967, the coalition was turning out to be a failure and drove an important section of the disappointed petty bourgeoisie to form its own party: the P.Q. In 1970 and after, the mo-

nopoly bourgeoisie asserted itelf on the political scene and attempted to impose its objectives of economic development and to subject the ideological apparatuses (such as schools and health) to the imperatives of economic rationality. One segment of the bourgeoisie found itself threatened and dispossessed by the development of monopolies in Quebec and Canada. This was the commercial and industrial component attached to the competition stage of capitalism, that had little capital and controlled a limited, if not local, market; it was incapable of following the rhythm of accumulation imposed by the development of capitalism in Canada. This segment of the bourgeoisie joined the nationalist movement. One part of it rallied to the ranks of the *Parti québécois*, while the other headed for the *Union nationale*. The passage from the competition to the monopoly stage transformed the conditions of development of the forces of production; the weaker commercial and industrial units had to submit to the stronger ones or disappear. At the competition stage, integration is carried out in such a way as to preserve the interests of small business owners by permitting the reconversion of capital in other sectors of activity. At the monopoly stage, the liquidation of small and medium businesses is one of the prerequisites of monopoly development. In Quebec, the disappearance of small farmers was a prelude to the liquidation of small and medium businesses.

The elections on November 15, 1976 took place within the context of this double movement: hardening of the Quebec State/radicalization of the union movement and of workers' struggles. The *Parti québécois* took power and seemed to be the party that had the solutions to the political and economic crisis.

The Parti québécois takes power: 1976-1977

The *Parti québécois* received electoral support not only from the nationalist petty bourgeoisie and bourgeoisie, but also from a high percentage of workers and employees in Montreal as well as in other parts of the province. The only opposition to speak of encountered by the P.Q. at the time of its election came from the federalist parties, while the P.Q. put forward its program of social and economic management. As for the vote, it was based on political motives that varied according to the social strata to which the voters belonged. For example, the workers supported the P.Q.'s economic program with its social-democratic orientation, believing it was most likely to solve the problems provoked by the crisis, rather than its political program. But the petty bourgeoisie was more interested in the question of political independence and less in strictly economic concerns.

Based on an examination of the P.Q.'s record since it's been in power, we feel free to state that, far from developing as the workers' party, the *Parti québécois*, under the cover of nationalism, is lining up on the side of the petty bourgeoisie and on that segment of the Quebec bourgeoisie whose economic interests are threatened by the development of Canadian monopoly capitalism. Nationalism is, then, the way these two social classes enter into the class struggle. That doesn't mean this non-monopolist bourgeoisie is ardently nationalist. It is so in the present scheme of things because the P.Q.'s economic project seems to present some economic proposals that agree with its own interests. Above all, what this bourgeoisie is looking for is the establishment and consolidation of a rhythm of production and a network of distribution that will not be hindered by monopoly expansion. Since nationalist politics can serve as a base for the achievement of their interests, businessmen and industrial entrepreneurs find themselves allies of the *Parti québécois*. However more than one member of that group has been seen to set up shop in Ontario to try to develop along the Quebec-Ontario axis.

It's not the same for the petty bourgeoisie intellectuals, for whom the P.Q.'s project is directly connected to what they themselves stand for—Quebec language and culture. As producers and reproducers of the *québécois* culture, the intellectual workers' *raison d'être*—including their material survival—is safeguarded in this linguistic and cultural specificity. A high percentage of them are among P.Q. militants; they wholeheartedly support Quebec's independence. The same goes for employees of the State bureaucracy and certain executives in private enterprise.

The union movement has remained ambivalent in the face of the *Parti québécois'* political project. Given the social-democratic feeling of the P.Q.'s program and the role given the national question in the pre-electoral period, the workers supported the *Parti québécois*. The economic crisis was worsening; inflation climbed at a dizzying rate from 1973-1974, and the weakened Liberal Party had no method in mind of shielding the workers from the repercussions of the crisis. With the P.Q.'s arrival on the electoral scene, the workers believed—or at least hoped—that the Party would be able to control the crisis and, through social laws and modifications to the Labour Code, improve their living conditions, as well as setting up power relations within labour conflicts that would be more beneficial to them.

The arrival of the *Parti québécois* on the political scene provoked fairly similar reactions from among union groups:

a) *La Centrale des syndicats démocratiques* resulted from a split with the *Centrale des syndicats nationaux* in 1972. The C.S.D. tried to establish a policy of collaboration with the Liberal Party under Robert Bourassa. Since the P.Q. took power, it hasn't formulated any clear position on the ruling party, and has stuck to supporting certain legal projects, such as Bill 45 concerning Labour Code reform.

b) *La Fédération des travailleurs du Québec* is affiliated with American "international" unions and includes the majority of unionized labour in Quebec. Within it is found strong pro-P.Q. sentiment, expressed openly by the United Steelworkers of America; other branches negotiate directly with the Ministry of Labour for closed shops on certain worksites, such as in construction. The F.T.Q.'s support of the P.Q. is a nod to the party whose worker relations policy is informed by trade unionism; the F.T.Q. also supports its program's economic policy which is likely to lead to an improvement of working conditions. The labour orientation of the struggles undertaken by the F.T.Q. is echoed in the P.Q. The government can turn this orientation into action through objectives such as consolidation of union members' rights, rationalization of economic development and establishment of social insurance procedures. These political programs involve the economic sector without altering the private ownership of capital. On the union's side, economic struggles focus mainly on salaries, but also concern certain elements of the work situation, such as job evaluation, job security, seniority and health conditions at the workplace. Therein lies the basis for the support the P.Q. receives from the F.T.Q. However, at the last congress of the Central in 1977, the F.T.Q. reiterated its support for the P.Q.–not without giving rise to stormy debates among the delegates and dissension between the unions.

c) *La Confédération des syndicats nationaux, la Centrale d'Enseignement du Québec* and some members of the F.T.Q. preach the formation of a workers' party. Moreover, the ideological discourse of the C.S.N., and especially that of the C.E.Q., whose members are largely white collar and intellectual workers, are surprisingly radical in tone. The published manifestos and mobilization slogans clearly show that the interests of the working class and the bourgeoisie are opposed. The C.S.N. and the C.E.Q. remain union centrals whose dominant orientation in the struggles undertaken by unionized members is trade unionist. However, for the last several years they have been undergoing a radical questioning of this orientation, and a revolutionary-type ideological struggle is ensuing. It can be characterized by the elaboration of an autonomous proletarian ideology whose goal is to combat the bourgeois ideology that is disseminated throughout the working class. The thrust of this practice is ideological. But in the absence of a working class party, there is a great risk of an over-ideologization that results in hesitation about the political task of constructing a party to take State power. On the economic level, these kinds of struggles aim at developing workers' consciousness about capitalist exploitation. On the political level, while breaking away from labour-management struggles, they attempt to uncover the State's class character. These practices most often bear the seal of the intellectual strata of high-level salaried employees. But the silence is almost total when it comes to discussing the right position to adapt on the national question and the *Parti québécois'* political project. The next general meetings of the union centrals will have to engage in some decisive debates on this question.

It is important to remember that if the union movement draws almost all the workers' political energies, it's not alone in this pursuit. Numerous popular organizations have sprung up to defend the interests of workers, the unemployed and those on welfare. Political organizations with Maoist and Trotskyist tendencies are on the upswing, while the Quebec Communist Party remains stagnant in its membership and practically absent from the political scene. Inter-union rivalry, the weakness of left-wing political organizations, the political opportunism of the *Parti québécois* and the important role played by counter-culture ideology among youth add up to a complex of explanatory factors when discussing the forms of politicization of the mass of workers and their *weak class consciousness*.

If the analysis we have just presented of the political conjuncture from 1960 to 1977 in Quebec seems focused mostly on the occupation of the political scene by the struggles undertaken by the monopoly and non-monopoly bourgeoisies and by the largely nationalist new petty bourgeoisie, *we must not assume the working class was absent in the class struggle*. Although historically it was ideologically and politically flanked by the petty bourgeoisie–which reduced its capacities for autonomous struggles within the class struggle–it is no less a complete class with its own organizations and specific struggles that, little by little, are moving toward a more and more severe confrontation with the State bourgeoisie.

The P.Q. Government's presentation of the first labour laws, such as the anti-scab measures, provoked strong reactions from among the unions. This was a key moment that influenced relations between the unions and the government, insofar as it let the workers establish the link between the national liberation project and the class character of the P.Q. government. But with the first projects proposed and approved by the Lévesque government, notably on the level of economic reforms, certain things became clear–namely, the limits within which the independence process of the *québécois* people is to be structured under the P.Q.'s direction. The proposed national liberation project is coloured by the class character of the P.Q. government, and it is increasingly shaped by the contradictions that rule class relations in Quebec. The development of these contradictions will be behind the contents of the independence project we will be seeing in the next few years. This project's proposals at the economic, political and cultural level will be the culmination of the power relations that have been established between the different classes in Quebec society.

Four principle issues at stake are currently orienting class struggles in Quebec:

1) National oppression, to which cultural and linguistic struggles correspond, which in turn are centred on the control of symbolic forms;

2) The unequal development of the Canadian economy which leads to regional struggles in an attempt to recover;

3) The economic exploitation of Quebec workers which provokes anti-capitalist struggles, especially by those blue- and white-collar workers effected in all aspects of their daily life by the rise of inflation;

4) The political subordination of the québécois State to the central State in Ottawa, which brings on autonomist struggles aiming at the decentralization of political powers. This final stake was put forward by the Duplessis regime, then picked up by Lesage. Later, it gave birth to a more radical movement that took shape with the Parti québécois.

To sum up the orientation of the struggles undertaken by the workers in the 1960-1977 period, we can say that ideological struggles remained at the fore. Militancy was focused first and foremost on the level of economic demands and, in a certain way, this form of militancy was exacerbated. Struggles at the political level that questioned State power were marginal.

We would like to add that each of the subperiods we've studied was distinguished by the dominance of one or the other of the four elements or stakes we've stressed to characterize the 1960-1977 conjuncture. Each period is distinguished by one or the other of these elements coming to the fore.

1960-1966: Unequal development is accentuated by struggles for economic recovery, modernization of the State apparatus and extension of State power.

1966-1976: The capitalist nature of economic development comes to the surface through strikes and anti-inflation struggles undertaken by a radicalized working class. The State as capitalist State is under attack from organized workers.

1976-1977: National oppression, political subordination and unequal development are more tied to one another, while still remaining confused. The centralization of powers in the federal government is perceived as a hindrance to Quebec's development.

One element is absent—or at least not clearly drawn out—in the definition of the stakes during the whole of this period: American imperialism. The relations that exist between national oppression, unequal development and capitalist exploitation, American imperialism and political subordination—relations that determine the specificity of Quebec society—have still not gained the necessary clarity in the québécois people's minds. These relations have yet to become the motivating element and the organizing principle in the complex of social struggles in Quebec. However, it's at this level that the history of the next decade will continue to be played out. We can foresee that workers' organizations will play a preponderant role, while the struggle for hegemony will be more lively than ever between the different bourgeoisies and the factions of which they are composed.

NOTES

[1]Touraine, Alain, les Sociétés dépendantes. Paris, Duculot, 1976. p.160.

[2]Ibid, p.161.

[3]Ibid, p.195.

[4]In the article quoted, Touraine refers to external foreign domination, while we're analyzing a situation of internal national domination within a social formation. But the argumentation is the same; that is, that dependence and oppression must not be analyzed as phenomena outside class relations.

[5]Naylor, Tom, "The History of Domestic and Foreign Capital in Canada," and Laxer, Jim, "Introduction to the Political Economy of Canada," in Canada, Ltd., Robert H. Laxer, ed. McClelland and Stewart, Toronto, 1973.

[6]Stevenson, Garth, "Federalism and the Political Economy of the Canadian State," in The Canadian

State, Political Economy and Political Power, Leo Panitch, ed. University of Toronto Press, Toronto, 1977. pp.71-100.

[7]*Ne comptons que sur nos propres moyens*, CSN document, 1972, and Kari Levitt, *la Capitulation tranquille*. L'Etincelle, 1972.

[8]Vallerand, Noël, "Histoire des faits économiques de la vallée du Saint-Laurent (1760-1866)," in *Economie québécoise*. Montreal, P.Q., 1969. p.68.

[9]Bourque, Gilles, and Frenette, Nicole, "La structure nationale québécoise," in *Socialisme québécois*. Numbers 21-22, 1971. pp.109-55.

[10]Cf. Carol Levasseur's text, "Mouvements nationalitaires et structure de domination nationale." Political Science Department, Université Laval, photocopy, autumn, 1977.

[11]Sales, Arnaud, "Capital, entreprises et bourgeoisie. La différenciation de la bourgeoisie industrielle au Québec." Doctoral thesis, Université de Paris VII, 1976.

[12]*Report of the Royal Commission of Enquiry on Bilingualism and Biculturalism*, Book III, *The World of Work*. Ottawa, Queen's Printer, 1969. pp.19-52 and 61-78.

[13]Sales, Arnaud, "La question linguistique et les directeurs d'entreprises," *le Devoir*, April 27, 1977. For a more complete view, see also Arnaud Sales, doctoral thesis, *op. cit.*

[14]Stevenson, Garth, *op. cit.*

[15]van Schendel, Michel, "Notes: dépendence et autonomies politiques de la classe ouvrière," in *Contradictions*. Number 3, January-June, 1973, pp.53-102 and 93-94.

[16]Piotte, Jean-Marc, *les Travailleurs contre l'Etat bourgeois*. L'Aurore, 1975, pp.19-20.

[17]Piotte, Jean-Marc, "La fascisation du régime," in *Chroniques*. Number 10, 1975.

"Dependence économique subordination politique et oppression nationale: le Québec 1960-1977," *Sociologie et Sociétés*, 10:2, Oct. *Author's note*: This text was written in the spring of 1976, then revised for publication in autumn, 1977. Therefore, our analysis of the conjuncture is dependent on the time of writing.

UNEQUAL CULTURAL EXCHANGE: A STUDY OF REGIONALISM AND CANADIAN WRITERS

J. Paul Grayson
L.M. Grayson

Introduction

The student of Canadian society and history cannot but be impressed by the historical and contemporary unequal distribution of wealth and power across the land. The disadvantaged economic position of the Maritimes and Newfoundland is now a virtual taken-for-granted way of Canadian life—at least for those living outside such areas. Equally accepted is the relative prosperity of Ontario and British Columbia. In recent years oil has also catapulted the province of Alberta into the top economic ranks. Along many dimensions, despite a wealth of natural resources, Quebec belongs with the Maritimes rather than with her rich sister to the west. And the provinces of Manitoba and Saskatchewan, while they have not always been the poorest

relatives, cannot be viewed as being as well off as Ontario.

A number of specific studies support these generalizations. In one case, it was shown that predominantly Ontario, and to a small degree Quebec, maintain trade surpluses with the other provinces. Such data confirm the fact "that interprovincial trade in manufactures favours central Canada."[1] It has also been demonstrated that so far as labour migration goes, particularly Ontario profits from the acquisition of talented people from other regions.[2] Figures on the economic elite reveal similar regional differences. By far the greatest percentage come from, and live in, Ontario.[3] Quebec runs a poor second in this regard. The historical record shows that that these contemporary patterns have roots deep in the past.[4]

What these and other studies indicate is a situation of internal colonialism with Ontario at the centre. Although it will not be discussed here, the explanation for this state of affairs can be found in the particular capitalistic form of production and exchange that characterizes Canada.[5] Equally important, from our point of view, is an examination of the degree to which similar imbalances are manifested in cultural matters. This type of concern has received less attention than it deserves.

When regionalism and culture are linked, it is usually in terms of what is found *embodied* in culture. For example, in speaking of literature during one period of our history, Patricia Marchak comments that: "the literatures of the different regions reflect . . . fundamental differences in economy and society."[6] Yet there is another way in which culture, and particularly literature, can be examined. Writers themselves can be treated as commodity producers having the product of their activities to sell, in the first instance, in an oligopolistic market place, the publishing companies.[7] One of the immediate questions that arises from defining authors in this way is: does their dependence on an oligopolistic publishing industry–centered by and large in Ontario–and the need for the great majority to derive their main incomes from other sources–chiefly in the media and schools/universities–lead to a regional distribution of authors that parallels the national movement of economic surplus and labour from peripheral regions to the centre?[8] The existence of parallelism would mean an outflow of writers from the Maritimes and the Prairies to Ontario. It is more difficult to hypothesize about British Columbia. Should such a trend be found, it would help account for the 'metropolitanization' of regional cultures.

Some general manifestations of metropolitanization can be found in under support in various media for indigenous regional cultures–for example, a disproportionate number of CBC programmes are produced in Toronto–approval of school texts best suited to other areas of the country or continent, and the unwarranted maintenance of beliefs that 'local' automatically means 'parochial'. The fact that, as S.N. Crean has pointed out, more than a fair share of Canada Council grants in the arts have been given to individuals located in Ontario and Quebec no doubt further weakens the potential of some areas for cultural expression. At the same time, the availability of state sponsored travelling art exhibits, dance companies, etc. are resulting in the neglect of local talent. Galleries and so on, that, because of a shortage of funds, were formerly patronizing indigenous artists, in many cases now spend their money on obtaining state subsidized forms of metropolitan culture. As a consequence, local culture is not given its due.[9] Ironically, then, some measures designed to culturally enrich the residents of certain regions are having the consequence of undermining their regional cultures.

At the international level, results of related developments have already been noted by students of Canadian culture. In analysing Canada's relationship to Britain, A.G. Bailey commented that the imperial tie "has . . . facilitated the flow of cultural traits from the imperial centre, to the partial exclusion of those from other centres . . . [and] has decreased the capacity of the outlying areas to profit, culturally, from the relationship."[10] Margaret Atwood and Robin Mathews, albeit from radically different perspectives, have extended the logic of this analysis to include the United States and its relation to Canada. Particularly in the twentieth century, they argue, cultural dominance of the U.S. has paralleled economic dependence and has led to a stifling of Canadian cultural efforts.[11]

Independent of the content of culture, if there is an internal flow of cultural producers from the periphery to the centre that parallels the flow of economic surplus and labour, it is unlikely that the periphery can withstand the resulting frontal assault of metropolitan culture. Obviously, a complete analysis of this phenomenon would require a more detailed study of literature and writers, the visual arts and artists, media institutions, and so on, than currently exists. It would also require further analyses of the ways in which connections to primarily Britain and the United States have affected internal cultural developments. Such an undertaking is beyond the scope of the current endeavour. However, it is possible to examine the consequences of historic imperial links for some of the Canadian literati. An examination can then be undertaken of the regional distribution and migration of writers.

339

The Writers

The writers we have chosen to deal with can be called elite writers—not in terms of orientation, but in terms of their being the best. How did we decide who was best? We left it up to experts in the field of Canadian literature.

A few years ago, Guy Sylvestre et al. compiled a biographical dictionary of Canadian authors. They included in it writers who "have produced a notable first or second book and have thereafter embarked upon a literary career with repeated publications of generally acknowledged merit."[12] A little more recently, Michael Gnarowski drew up a list based on a sense of "national limits with which the idea of the literature of English-speaking Canada would be satisfied."[13] Despite the slight difference in emphasis, these sources provide the names of 280 people who can be defined as elite writers.

Information on these individuals came from a number of sources including *Who's Who*, and other biographical dictionaries. Biographies, autobiographies, and newspaper and magazine accounts were also useful. For those of the 280 still alive, additional information was obtained by corresponding with them. In some cases, the Writers' Union of Canada, the League of Canadian Poets, and the Canadian Authors' Association were able to provide some assistance.

The Imperial Connection

Whatever the general cultural effects of the British and American connections, such as those revealed by Atwood and Mathews, they are not evident in writers' origins. From Table 1 it would appear that since 1835 the Canadian born have dominated the ranks of the best writers as defined in this study. The large number of British born Canadian writers who can be found in the pre-1835 period probably reflects British immigration of the time. Loyalist migrations no doubt account for the presence of some Americans born in this period. After 1835, however, the representation of the British-born varies little over the next century. The American-born, after a brief appearance in the early period, do not reappear until after 1900. The presence of those born in 'other' countries is not significant until the eighteen seventies. This latter

figure clearly reflects immigration patterns: it was not until the closing years of the last century that among the white population, substantial numbers of non-Anglo Saxons or non-French could be found in Canada.

Although reliable census data are unavailable for all periods under discussion, it is fair to say, on the basis of information available in the censuses of 1831, 1851, 1881, 1921 and 1951, that overall, the representation of the Canadian-born among the ranks of French-Canadian writers has been equal to the proportion of Canadian-born French-speaking individuals in the population. For the English-speaking, the situation is different. Although information for all years is unavailable, with the exception of the years 1870-99, Table 2 indicates that Canadian-born English-speaking individuals have been over represented among the best writers. British-born Canadian writers, have, over the past century, steadily declined in terms of the proportion of British-born Canadians in the population. It is also likely that English-speaking Canadians born in 'other' countries are also under represented among the best writers.

The information available suggests two things. First, in absolute terms, since 1835, the Canadian-born have been the largest single group among Canada's best writers. Second, among the best writers, the representation of French speaking natives has been roughly equal to their proportion of the population. English Canadian natives have been over represented among the best writers.

If, as suggested by John Porter, "National values and national purpose can probably [most] clearly be stated by those who have a sense of homeland derived from childhood experience and education within the society and its culture,"[14] we might expect that Canadian literature would reflect the values and purposes of the Canadian-born. However, despite the existence of some exceptional writers, there is no reason to believe that Canadian literature embodies 'national values and national purpose'. As Donald Creighton savagely puts it: "Imitation and plagiarism [have] become deep-seated Canadian instincts; economic and political dependence [have] grown into a settled way of life."[15] While the imperial connection has not necessarily resulted in a glut of foreign-born writers on Canadian shores, Creighton, and others like him, implicitly suggest, or explicitly argue, that it may have had consequences for the content of literature.

Unequal Origins of Writers

When figures dealing with region rather than country of origin are examined, it would appear, from Table 3, that the Atlantic colonies provided a plurality of the writers born prior to 1835. It is equally evident that in the years after 1835 the colonies produced decreasing numbers of the best Canadian writers. At first glance, we might relate this decline to the waning economic and political fortunes of the area.

Further initial support for this type of reasoning is provided by the Ontario experience. Although the pattern is not regular, from 1835 until the present Ontario has produced the greatest portion of the best English-Canadian writers—a feat consistent with the province's economic and political dominance. The pattern for English-speaking Quebec, from 1835 to 1935, was one of contributing approximately 15% of the best English-Canadian writers. Since 1935, however, the proportion has dwindled to zero. If hard pressed, one might make the argument that such a pattern reflects the waning dominance of an English Quebec in Canadian economic affairs.

Less easily dealt with, though, is the large number from the Prairie Provinces. Despite wheat booms in the early years of the century, short term windfalls hardly translated into long term prosperity and economic dominance. The Alberta oil boom, in turn, is a relatively recent phenomenon. The trends for British Columbia, on the other hand, might initially be understood in terms of the general prosperity of that province: material well being is consistent with the healthy crop of writers originating from B.C. However, despite the emergence of regional protest movements, none of these provinces can be thought of as politically dominant.

Overall, then, the trends found in Table 3 suggest weak support for any argument linking general economic and political dominance with the production of good writers. If nothing has been said of French-speaking Quebec, it is because, with one or two exceptions, the province has produced all of the best French-Canadian writers. It therefore does not make sense to examine the relative contribution of Quebec to the total compliment of French-Canadian authors.

If, contrary to the above procedure, we examine the numbers of writers coming from different regions in terms of the proportion that the English population of the area is of the total population of English Canada, the picture changes radically. We were able to make the comparisons on the basis of population figures provided by the censuses carried out in 1831, 1851, 1881, 1921, and 1951. Although not all censuses were carried out at the mid point of the intervals we are dealing with, they nonetheless provide a fairly clear indication of overall trends.

Perhaps one of the most striking observations to emerge from Table 4 is that the Atlantic colonies, despite some pre-Confederation prosperity, have always contributed fewer writers than the number of English-speaking individuals in the area would warrant. It was only in the 1900-34 period that the Maritimes produced a proportionate number of writers. Equally interesting is that in all periods, with the exception of 1835-69, Ontario has contributed less than its expected share of writers. By way of contrast, the English community of Quebec, in the years prior to 1935, always produced more writers than we might have expected. So have the Prairie Provinces and, currently, British Columbia. These findings should dispell any notions that the regional production of writers parallels economic and/or political dominance. Indeed, it is difficult to provide any explanation for the noted patterns.

Unequal Exchange of Writers

The inability to link the regional production of writers to more general centre-periphery dynamics changes when we examine regional residence. In Table 5 we have tabulated the place of origin and last known residence of authors born in the various periods. We have also calculated the net regional gain or loss of authors over the entire time span under study. The figures can be compared to similar data on the economic elite derived from a study carried out by Wallace Clement.[16]

The first observation that can be made from these data is that from time to time there have been fluctuations between the number of authors coming from an area and the numbers having residence in the same region. Between 1835 and 1869, for example, 28 per cent of Canadian writers were born in Ontario: 36 per cent lived there. In the following period, 27 per cent were born in Ontario, while only 18 per cent lived there. But despite these and other fluctuations, the most consistent trend is for the peripheral areas–leaving 'French Quebec' aside for a moment–to experience an overall loss of writers. Primarily for Ontario–the centre–the reverse is true.

The Maritimes, since 1835, have, in all periods, lost writers to other areas. Over all years, the net loss to the region has been 3 per cent of the total. The only loss sustained by Ontario, on the other hand, was in the 1870-99 period. Thereafter–and in the preceding periods–Ontario experienced a net gain. The total gain for Ontario over the long run has been 9 per cent of the total. This is the highest of any region.

If the French and English speaking populations of Quebec are treated separately, it is clear that with the exception of the 1835-69 period, 'English Quebec' has received slightly more authors than it produced. Most located in Montreal. The attraction of this centre resulted in a net gain of 4 per cent of the total over the study period. Equally important is the finding that in virtually all periods, 'French Quebec' has sustained a loss of authors. Unlike English authors who have experienced a great deal of inter-provincial migration, the movement of French Canadians has been to other countries. France and the United States have been the favourite choices of the French. The net consequence of such patterns has been a 4 per cent loss over the study period.

Given that western settlement has been relatively recent, the record for the Prairie Provinces and B.C. covers a shorter time span than other areas. Initially, and this was also true for older areas, the regions, for obvious reasons, attracted more writers than they produced. In the twentieth century, however, the Prairie Provinces have experienced a net loss. Despite nineteenth-century net gains, the twentieth-century pattern resulted in an overall 3 per cent loss of the total for the region. By way of contrast, for all periods, with the exception of the current one, B.C. has gained from regional migrations. The total consequence has been a 3 per cent gain.

Last of all, it should be noted that the United Kingdom has received fewer authors than it has sent to Canada. Conversely, between 1835 and 1934, the United States has had a net gain of Canadian writers. In the pre-1835 period, Canada experienced, as a consequence of Loyalist migrations, a slight gain from this source. In the current period, losses offset gains. It might also be noted that Canada has received a slight gain of writers from 'other' countries while it has lost a few to France.

By themselves, the figures mean little. When examined in the light of other developments, they take on significance. It has already been shown that particularly Ontario profits from inter-provincial flows of manufactured goods and labour. The final column in Table 5 also demonstrates a net gain for Ontario in terms of the proportion of the economic elite who reside there–5 per cent more live in Ontario than were born there. More interesting, though, is that the direction of the flow of the economic elite, for all regions, is the same as the direction of the flow for the literary elite. Granted, the data for the economic elite are only for some of its members born in this century, but, in view of other noted trends, the observed associations cannot simply be dismissed as coincidence. Thus, while there is no reason to believe that the regional production or origin of writers is related to general regional patterns of dominance and subordination, the regional distribution of writers does reflect relationships between the various parts of the country.

Conclusion

The main conclusion that can be drawn from this examination of elite writers is that the regional flows of authors tend to parallel the movement of economic surpluses and labour across the land. Despite the fact that Ontario has not produced as many writers as the size of the English-speaking population warrants, it has provided the largest single number of writers, and, more importantly, has experienced a net gain of writers, particularly from other regions of Canada. In this regard it is like B.C. and 'English Quebec' that have also had a net gain of writers. Their gains, however, are not as great as those for Ontario. They are nonetheless consistent with their relatively advantaged position within the country.

By way of contrast, the Prairie Provinces, despite an over supply of writers in terms of the English-speaking population, have undergone a net loss. The Prairie situation represents the clearest case of the centre drawing off the creative surplus of the periphery. The same process is evident for the Maritimes but with the exception of one period, they had a shortfall of writers to begin with. 'French Quebec' has also sustained a net loss of writers. In its case, however, the loss has been more to France and the U.S. than to other regions of Canada. Although we have not pursued the matter in this study, it can be hypothesized that such patterns would have had consequences for the maintenance and content of regional cultures.

A secondary conclusion is that despite the imperial connection of Canada to France, Britain and the U.S., its best writers have been Canadian-born. However, it does not seem warranted to argue that Canadian writing has therefore embodied Canadian ideals and purposes–whatever they are. The comments of those far more familiar with the content of literature than we are suggest that the imperial connection cannot be ignored. Its influence may go beyond what is measurable in this or any other study.

Table 1
Authors' Country of Origin By Ethnicity and Birthdate (in percent)

	to 1834			1835-69			1870-99			1900-34			1935 and on		
	E	F	O	E	F	O	E	F	O	E	F	O	E	F	O
Canada	33	100		87	100		79	96	25	80	98		86	100	
Britain	57			13		100	14	4	25	13		63			
U.S.	10									2	2	13			100
France									25						
Other							7		25	5		25	14		
Total %	100	100		100	100	100	100	100	100	100	100	100	100	100	100
Number	(21)	(1)		(23)	(9)	(1)	(28)	(23)	(4)	(83)	(46)	(8)	(14)	(5)	(1)

Legend: E = English Canadian; F = French Canadian; O = 'Other' Canadian

Table 2
Representation of Canadian and British Born Authors in Terms of Numbers of Canadian and British Born in General Population (in percent)

	to 1834	1835-69	1870-99	1900-34	1935 and on
Canadian Born		+7	—2	+10	+ 7
British Born			+3	— 3	—10

Table 3
Regional Origins of English Canadian Authors (in percent)

	to 1834	1835-69	1870-99	1900-34	1935 and on
Ontario	18	55	54	36	42
Quebec	33	15	14	17	0
Maritimes	50	30	23	18	8
Prairies			9	23	17
B.C.				6	33
Total %	101	100	100	100	100
Number	(6)	(20)	(22)	(66)	(12)

Table 4
Regional Representation of English Canadian Authors in Terms of
Proportion That English Canadian Population of Region is of Total English Canadian
Population (in percent)

	to 1834	1835-69	1870-99	1900-34	1935 and on
Ontario	−16	+ 1	− 1	− 9	− 4
Quebec	+18	+ 6	+ 5	+10	− 7
Maritimes	− 1	− 8	−11	0	−10
Prairies			+ 7	+ 1	0
B.C.				− 2	+22

Note: '0' indicates that the number of writers is proportionate to the number of English Canadians in the population of the region.

Table 5
Authors' Region of Birth and Residence (in percent)

	to 1834 B	to 1834 R	1835-69 B	1835-69 R	1870-99 B	1870-99 R	1900-34 B	1900-34 R	1935 and on B	1935 and on R	Net Gain Literary Elite	Net Gain Economic Elite
Ontario	5	23	28	36	27	18	19	32	31	53	+9	+5
Quebec												
English	5	18	8	4	5	9	10	11	0	11	+4	+5*
French	5	5	28	12	34	30	27	25	26	21	−4	**
Maritimes	13	23	20	4	11	7	9	8	5	0	−3	−5
Prairies			0	4	2	9	14	6	5	0	−3	−7
B.C.			0	4	0	9	2	6	21	5	+3	+2
Britain	59	23	16	12	11	2	11	4	0	0	−9	
U.S.	13	9	0	24	0	9	3	5	11	11	+5	
France					2	2	0	1	0	0	+2	
Other					7	5	5	3	0	0	−3	
Total %	100	100	100	100	100	100	100	100	100	100		
Number	(22)	(22)	(25)	(25)	(44)	(44)	(124)	(124)	(19)	(19)		

Legend: B = Birthplace;   R = Place of Residence
*Estimated on the basis of data presented by Wallace Clement in *Continental Corporate Power.*
**Clement's data reveal that French Canadians are virtually without representation in the economic elite when one considers the proportion they are of the general population.

NOTES

[1] Kenneth Campbell, "Regional Disparity and Interregional Exchange Imbalance," In Daniel Glenday et al. (eds.), *Modernization and the Canadian State*, Toronto: Macmillan, 1978, p.118.

[2] Carl J. Cuneo, "A Class Perspective on Regionalism," in Daniel Glenday et al.

[3] Wallace Clement, "A Political Economy of Regionalism," in Daniel Glenday et al.

[4] For examples, see W.A. Mackintosh, *The Economic Background of Dominion Provincial Relations*, Toronto: McClelland and Stewart, 1939/1964. R.T. Naylor, *The History of Canadian Business, 1867-1914*, Vols. 1 and 2, Toronto: Lorimer, 1975.

[5]An analysis of the relations between production and exchange can be found in H. Veltmeyer "Dependency and Underdevelopment: Some Questions and Problems," *Canadian Journal of Political and Social Theory*, Vol. 2, No. 2, 197.

[6]Patricia Marchak, "Given a Certain Latitude: A (Hinterland) Sociologist's View of Anglo-Canadian Literature," in Paul Cappon (ed.), *In Our Own House. Social Perspectives on Canadian Literature*, Toronto: McClelland and Stewart, 1978, p.192.

[7]In 1976, Statistics Canada reports that 'Canadian' publishing companies had sales of a quarter of a billion dollars. Although there are at least 167 publishing companies in Canada, 14 accounted for 59 per cent of total reported sales. So far as location is concerned, approximately 23 per cent of the total are in 'French Quebec'. Of those outside 'French Quebec', 60 per cent are found in Ontario (this figure includes most of the major companies). A further 17 per cent are located in B.C. The Prairies, the Maritimes and 'English Quebec' have 12 per cent, 4 per cent, and 8 per cent respectively. The attraction of Ontario to writers should be obvious.

[8]Information on writers' occupations can be obtained from J. Paul Grayson and L.M. Grayson, "The Canadian Literary Elite–A Socio-Historical Perspective," *Canadian Journal of Sociology*, Vol. 3, No. 3, August, 1978.

[9]S.N. Crean, *Who's Afraid of Canadian Culture*, Don Mills: General Publishing, 1976.

[10]A.G. Bailey, "Evidences of Culture Considered as Colonial," in A.G. Bailey, *Culture and Nationality*, Toronto: McClelland and Stewart, 1972, p.184.

[11]Margaret Atwood, *Survival*, Toronto: Anansi, 1972. Robin Mathews, *Canadian Literature: Surrender or Revolution*, Toronto: Steel Rail Publishing, 1978.

[12]Guy Sylvestre et al., *Canadian Writers: A Biographical Dictionary*, Toronto: Ryerson, 1966, p.v.

[13]Michael Gnarowski, *A Concise Bibliography of English Canadian Literature*, Toronto: McClelland and Stewart, 1973, p.5.

[14]John Porter, *The Vertical Mosaic*, Toronto: University of Toronto Press, 1965, p.498.

[15]Donald Creighton, *Canada's First Century*, Toronto: Macmillan, 1970, p.356.

[16]Wallace Clement, *Continental Corporate Power*, Toronto: McClelland and Stewart, 1977, Ch.8.

MARXISM AND CANADIAN POLITICAL ECONOMY

Introduction

Although its revelations were not particularly new to those concerned with the state of scholarship in Canada, the findings of the Symons' Commission, published in *To Know Ourselves*, (1975) bestowed a degree of legitimacy on the hitherto unheeded cries of cultural nationalists. For several years prior to the publication of the report, commissioned by the Association of Universities and Colleges of Canada, individuals such as Robin Mathews and James Steele had attempted to draw to public attention the harmful consequences of Americanization of the university (1969). At the same time, others were suggesting that the problem was not restricted to the university level. In 1968 Hodgetts revealed a scandalous inattention to Canadian materials in the schools. The lack of emphasis on Canadian history, literature, etc., referred to by Hodgetts, was reflected in a later study conducted by Hurtig (1975) on graduating highschool students. It was found, in this instance, that many senior highschool students were completely unfamiliar with the basics of Canadian geography, history, culture and economics. However, they had little difficulty in identifying things American–a characteristic demonstrated by their brothers and sisters in university. In 1980, it is not clear that this situation has changed drastically.

The class determination and class position of those concerned with findings such as the above has been succinctly analysed by Resnick (1977). In the Diefenbaker years, he maintains that the nationalism of the bourgeoisie was a function of the inability of Canadian capitalism to compete on a world scale. By the 1960s, the situation had changed. Corporations such as the Royal Bank were holding their own against all comers on the international scene. As a consequence, the most influential elements of the bourgeoisie were less concerned with American economic activities in Canada than they had been a decade earlier. Those who, in the late sixties and early seventies, were still interested in Canadian nationalism, were members of the new petty bourgeoisie and working class. The former, which includes teachers, professors, civil servants, etc., viewed the continued viability of their well being as contingent upon at least halting, if not reversing, the drift toward closer and closer ties with the United States. Some of these sentiments were shared by members of

347

the working class who were concerned with deindustrialization and the consequent loss of jobs for Canadians. The indictments of the Symons' Commission therefore had a receptive audience.

Some of the most scathing criticisms of the Symons' Commission related to the development of the social sciences in Canada. For example, the Commissioners found that "A number of leading Canadian sociologists expressed the view . . . that their profession was now so totally alienated from Canadian concerns and values that it was time to consider re-inventing sociology as a discipline at one or two selected universities in Canada" (1975:78). The situation in economics and political science, to name only two more disciplines, was not much better. In these disciplines, and others, it was felt that insufficient attention had been given to the study of Canadian matters from a perspective that recognized the particular historical and institutional characteristics of Canadian society. When Canadian materials were dealt with in various disciplines, analysis frequently consisted of little more than forcing Canadian examples into perspectives developed from the study of other societies, most noticably, the United States.

The orientation of sociology in Canada as revealed by the Commission is not hard to explain. Until the sixties, there were few Canadian sociologists (Clark, 1976). As a consequence, when, as a result of state policy, university enrollments increased dramatically in the 1960s, large numbers of American sociologists with little understanding of–and in many cases, little sympathy with–Canadian circumstances were given positions in Canadian universities. Largely as a consequence of the sheer number of American faculty members (Clark, 1976) and the belief that relevant developments in the discipline were taking place south of the border, recruitment practices tended to favour fellow Americans, even when qualified Canadians were available (Lamy, 1976). Not surprisingly, this situation was deplored by some Canadian scholars. In recent years, however, with a decline in university appointments, attention of those concerned with U.S. domination of sociology has tended to focus less on faculty citizenship and more on the development of a Canadian sociology (Hiller, 1979).

In his analysis, Lamy takes up some of these concerns as they relate to sociology. The important point of his article is that the "development of an American dominated sociology in Canada occurred within the context of, and can be viewed as part of, the process of growing structural and cultural dependence of Canada on the U.S. in the Post-War period." Such an analysis is consistent with other matters dealt with in this book. The economic, political and military dependency of Canada on outside powers–i.e. the United States–has resulted in a truncated development of, in this case, sociology. The sociology studied–at least in the period discussed by Lamy–is consistent with the status aspirations of its American practitioners and the demands of the American sociological community. While some would argue that by 1980 the situation has changed for the better in both schools and universities, others would maintain that any changes are more apparent than real.

Despite a comparable degree of Americanization of economics and political science, their situation is a little different. Unlike sociology, whose roots are most immediately American, prior to the Americanization of economics and political science in the fifties and sixties as outlined by the Symons' Commission and others, the peculiarities of Canadian development had given rise to a distinct and identifiable school of political economy centred on the 'staple thesis' as developed by H.A. Innis, W.A. Mackintosh, and others. In Mel Watkins' estimation, the staple thesis can be regarded as Canada's major contribution to economic theory (Watkins, 1967:49).

Starting with the premise that "staple exports are the leading sector of the economy and set the pace for economic growth" (Watkins, 1967:53) various Canadian political economists and historians have attempted to examine the impact of fish, fur, timber, wheat, mining, pulp and paper and oil and gas on the Canadian economy and polity (Innis, 1930/1956; 1936; 1940/1945; Lower, 1936; Fowke, 1957; Nelles, 1974; Pratt, 1976). Others have taken the assumptions of the staple theory for granted and have embarked upon an examination of the social relations that a particular staple-based economy has given rise to (Clark, 1968; Creighton, 1956/1970). Unfortunately, there have been too few of these latter attempts. As a consequence, the staple theory still remains primarily a theory of economic rather than social development.

Recently, there has been a resurgence of interest in studies of the political economy of Canada. More importantly, there have been a number of attempts, particularly on the part of young Canadian scholars, to combine the study of the political economy of Canada with Marxism. In the opinion of Clement et al (1978:iii) "The revival of both Marxism and political economy marks an invigoration of social science in Canada, an invigoration which combines an awareness of contemporary issues in Canadian society and a desire to do something about the Canadian condition." Some of the reasons for the renewed interest in this approach are analysed in the article by Parker.

In his article, Parker also attempts to show intellectual connections that link the works of Marx and Innis. He also attempts to demonstrate the way in which the works of both men complement one another. A combination of the orientations of both, he feels, holds the key to a better understanding of the nature of Canadian development. While many readers may disagree with Parker's argument, the mere fact that he and other historians, sociologists and political scientists are attempting to link Marx and Innis has enormous implications for the study of Canadian society. It means that after the dark ages of Canadian social science in the fifties and sixties, an interdisciplinary perspective that will permit a clear examination of Canadian development is in the making.

While this is primarily a book on Marxism, it should be clear that many of the authors of the enclosed articles appear to have one foot—or at least a few toes—in the Canadian political economy camp. As a consequence, their works can be viewed as planks in the bridge between Marxism and Canadian political economy.

As yet, however, there remains a great deal of research to be carried out before Canadian social scientists can feel assured that they are well along the road to displacing inappropriate modes of analysis. Some research that is proceeding in the right direction is described by Watkins in the final article in this section. Most important, perhaps, is his identification of two Marxist theories of Canadian capitalist development and his suggestion, after reviewing the pertinent literature, that the cornerstone of Canadian political economy, the staple thesis, can be given a clean bill of health.

THE GLOBALIZATION OF AMERICAN SOCIOLOGY: EXCELLENCE OR IMPERIALISM?

Paul Lamy

The domestic growth of American sociology and the growth in its international influence accompanied, and was facilitated by, the emergence of the American polity as a leading world power following World War II. As Birnbaum (1970:x) had observed:

> As the United States became a dominant world power, American sociology's international fortunes rose accordingly . . . (W)hat were once the great metropolitan centers of sociology fell under American influence.

It may, no doubt, be galling to some American sociologists if someone points out to them that the sway of American sociological paradigms was not due to their natural superiority in terms of the canons of a philosophy of science developed with the activities and paradigms of the physical sciences in mind, a philosophy of science which is itself the subject of considerable controversy (cf. Kuhn, 1962; Feyerabend, 1970), but due rather to the growth of the United States as a world power, and the economic, political, and cultural imperialism which accompanied it. Gouldner (1970:142) ties the growth of American sociology to the participation of American sociologists in the federal bureaucracy during World War II, a period in which sociologists became acquainted with the "power, prestige, and resources of the state apparatus," and to the growth of the welfare state in the post-war period which "with its massive financing and its emphasis on a broader *social* utilitarianism . . . provided the most favorable context for the institutionalization of sociology" (1970:161). Extensive funding on the part of federal agencies to institutions and individual scholars for research, publication, and travel at home and abroad contributed directly to the domestic and international expansion of American sociology. As Direnzo (1972:35-36) observes with regard to Italy:

> A major role in the early re-development of Italian sociology was played by the Italian-American Cultural Exchange program which brought, and continues to do so, but unfortunately in somewhat reduced numbers, Fulbright-Hays scholars as lectures [sic] and/or researchers, including some of the more distinguished names in American sociology to Italian universities. Significant assistance also was provided by several major Italian corporations, chief among them FIAT and Olivetti, which supported American sociologists, assisting and training Italian personnel in social research in the area of industrial sociology. Additionally, a great number of American sociologists worked independently in Italy on sabbatical leaves and/or research grants from various American foundations.

The events of the McCarthy era and the blacklisting of American scholars by federal funding agencies until quite recently indicate clearly that not all paradigms had equal freedom to flourish. The prevailing paradigm in American sociology in the post-war years—the structural-functionalism of Parsons and Merton—was particularly suited for both internal consumption and foreign export because of its congenial ideological connotations. As Gouldner (1970:148-149) notes of Parsons' brand of structural-functionalism, it "entailed a synthesis of Western European social theory within the framework of an American structure of sentiments, assumptions, and personal reality"; conveniently enough, the "internationalization of American Academic Sociology . . . began on a politically conservative, anti-Marxist basis." As such, this cultural product

351

qualified for export through the official propaganda agencies of the American state. Perhaps the most blatant instance is that of *American Sociology: Perspectives, Problems, and Methods* (Parsons, 1968), which presents in book form materials originally prepared by the elite of American mainstream sociology for the Voice of America.

The international expansion of American sociology has been remarkably successful, as Gouldner (1970:22) observes; throughout much of the world "sociology is practically synonomous with American sociology." Clark (1975:225) concludes with regard to Canada that "what has developed here is not a Canadian sociology but a sociology that is American." Allardt (1967:225) seems to claim the crown for Scandinavia: "Everywhere in the world sociologists are in debt to American sociology but hardly anywhere did this sociology find such fertile soil as in the Scandinavian countries." In the Netherlands, "the development of sociology . . . after World War II was accompanied by the reception of American structuralist-functionalist sociology" (Van Rossum, 1975:164). Hedley and Warburton (1973:309) report with regard to Britain that sociology there "is in some ways the most American discipline of all." Oromaner (1970), in comparing citations in the *American Sociological Review* (*ASR*) and *British Journal of Sociology* (*BJS*) at two time intervals to determine whether sociology was becoming more "internationalized," found a basic stability in the *ASR* citations, whereas in the *BJS*, references to British social anthropologists were displaced by references to contemporary American sociologists; he concludes (1970:327) that the "apparent internationalization of sociology in this case may in reality be an Americanization of British sociology." With regard to France and Germany, Shils (1970:791) maintains that "the point of reference . . . is . . . American research." Kassof (1965:120) remarks on the "rather embarrassing dependence on Western technique" among Soviet sociologists, and Parsons (1965) was impressed with their familiarity with American research. That sociology in Australia and New Zealand is heavily dependent on U.S. sociology, even in matters of staff and textbooks, will not come as a surprise to many (cf. Mol, 1968).

While there is a burgeoning literature originating from many points on the planet pertaining to the growth and dominance of the American social science community, as regards the Americanization of national sociologies the bulk of this literature is unsystematic, confused, often emotional and decidedly noncumulative in character.[1] Although Gouldner (1970) provides some useful insights, he does not concern himself with either the relationship of American sociology to other national sociologies or the imperialistic aspects of the international expansion of the sociology.

Shils on the Internationalization of American Sociology

Shils (1970:790) in attempting to account for the dominance of American sociology presents a viewpoint quite different from the one taken here:

> The far greater degree of institutionalization of sociology in the United States, the large scale of its output, the ascent of the United States to a condition of academic centrality (and the greater power and prominence of the United States outside the intellectual sphere), and the formation of an, to some extent, international sociological culture have all contributed to change the direction of the ecological process.

Shils, then, accords much more importance to the level of institutionalization, to the level of output, and to "academic centrality" in general, than to the power, wealth, and resources of nation states as predictors of the "academic centrality" of particular social science communities.[2] He argues that sociology became institutionalized earlier in the U.S. than anywhere else in the world, and that American social structure was much more supportive of such a development than those of European countries. Shils (1970:777) sees the level of institutionalization as a powerful determinant of "academic centrality" for the following reasons:

> Institutionalization serves . . . to make ideas more available to potential recipients, it renders possible concentration of effort on them, it fosters interaction about them, and it aids their communication.

He also argues (p.777) that "intellectual persuasiveness" of sets of ideas and their compatibility with prior dispositions and patterns of thought of potential recipients is of importance, but not of the same importance, it would seem, as the level of institutionalization and level of output. Increasing levels of institutionalization of sociology abroad is said to increase the dominance of American sociology in that this "increases receptive power between countries as well as within countries" (p.790).

Issue can be taken with Shils' argument on several grounds. (1) With regard to level of institutionalization as a predictor of academic centrality, one might be skeptical as to whether an increase in the institutionalization of sociology in Luxembourg to a level equal to that of sociology in the U.S. would be accompanied by a perceptible increase in its influence. Although Shils argues that sociology became institutionalized earlier in the U.S. than anywhere else, he himself notes that before World War I, Germany was the "academic center of the world," and that at that time, sociology in the U.S. "was either under the dominion of German-inspired ethnographers and *Volkskundler* . . . or it was conscientiously making its first contacts . . . with the urban masses" (1970:788). (2) Concerning level of output, even a miraculous increase in the output of Afrikaans-speaking sociologists is unlikely to increase the academic centrality of that social science community. As Shils (1970:797) says of some early authors and their ideas, both of which have been consigned to oblivion: "They might have been in the wrong countries and written in the wrong language." (3) The "intellectual persuasiveness" of sets of ideas cannot be abstracted from the prior dispositions and patterns of thought of potential recipients. Again, Shils (1970:788) himself mentions that before World War I, "Germany was really out of the question as a place for Durkheim to be influential." Why? Because "German scholars of that period . . . really did not regard foreign science or scholarship . . . as worthy of serious consideration . . . in addition to the deteriorating political relations between France and Germany at that time" (Shils 1970: 788-789). (4) In the light of the foregoing, it seems doubtful that an increase in either the level of institutionalization or of academic centrality is accompanied, as Shils maintains, by an increase in receptivity on the part of the dominant

social science community. Cairns (1975: 215-216) sees American political science as becoming more parochial *because of* the increase in its level of institutionalization and increased level of output. He attributes this increase in parochialism to the very size and power of that social science community which isolates it from other influence, to the high incidence of unilingualism of its members, and to the quality and number of its graduate schools which make education abroad less attractive. Oromaner (1970:329) has shown that at least in terms of citations in the *ASR*, "national influences on American sociology have not changed but have remained almost entirely American in origin." (5) What accounts for the level of institutionalization other than, as Shils (1970:779) puts it, "social structures which permitted it"?[3] He (p.778) notes that the level of institutionalization is affected by linkages with the environing institutional context, that is, by links within the universities, with foundations, government, business, and publishing concerns. Such structural support is obviously linked to national wealth and resources, and discrepancies in level of institutionalization can be expected to vary with these factors. And (6) overall academic centrality is not accounted for by Shils; and explanation of overall academic dominance could hardly fail to give considerable weight to differences in national power, wealth, and resources since these affect level of institutionalization, level of output, and receptivity on the part of other academic communities.

Shil's (1970) analysis has further shortcomings. He neglects the impact of the academic centrality of a particular social science community on what might be politely called the "less central" ones. Gouldner, despite his critical stance vis-à-vis mainstream American sociology, manifests a similar lack of sensitivity. He prophesies that a "major intellectual development in world sociology is impending" (1970:473). This event is said to be none other than the rapprochement of the sociologies of the U.S. and U.S.S.R. Rather than questioning the desirability of such a new hegemony, Gouldner (1970:473) warns that "any social change that contributes to peaceful cooperation between the United States and the Soviet Union has a claim upon the favor of all men of good will." The principal effects of the domination of American sociology in Western societies, and of its one-sided relationship with national sociologies of the Third World, have been to place other national sociologies in a position of cultural and/or structural dependence. The scenario envisaged by Gouldner would surely reinforce this situation.

On the Cultural and Structural Dependence of Social Science Communities

A national social science community is culturally dependent to the extent that definitions of what should be studied and how (theory and methods), and criteria of desirable scholarly activity (role models and standards of excellence) are those of another national social science community where these are not shared by social science communities in general. A national social science community is structurally dependent on another to the degree that (1) research and publication concerning the nation state to which that community corresponds are engaged in by members of another national social science community (relative to the output of its own members); (2) research activities are underwritten by the sources of support of another national social science community; (3) the media of another community are used to disseminate the results of research; (4) another social science community is involved in the training of its members; (5) it recruits new members from another social science community; and (6) it uses the products of the other national social science community in its own teaching and training activities.

It is being argued here that cultural and structural dependence on American sociology varies with the power, wealth, and resources of the national state within which national social science communities are located. Most of my remarks are, however, confined to nations at similar levels of development since among the principal structural conditions related to the institutionalization of sociology are (1) industrialization, to the point that it is self-sustaining, (2) the emergence of a technical and administrative elite, and (3) the emergence of sectorial autonomy (cf. Gouldner 1970:468). In the case of the U.S.S.R., there is a low level of cultural dependence on American sociology, but there is a complete absence of structural dependence. Among the "middle" powers—France, Great Britain, Japan, and West Germany—there ap-

pears to be a higher level of both cultural and structural dependence (though the level of cultural dependence is comparatively higher). In the case of the lesser industrialized nations–Australia, Canada, Israel, the Netherlands, New Zealand, and the Scandinavian countries–both cultural and structural dependence are relatively high. However, both cultural and structural dependence on American sociology appears higher in those countries which share a common language with the U.S., regardless of level of power, wealth, and resources–for instance, in Great Britain, Australia, Canada, and New Zealand. Another intervening variable is the extent to which the state, public opinion, the media, and other local institutions are hostile to the influence of the dominant social science community. Thus far I have assumed a situation of "laissez faire." While the cultural and structural dependence of Czechoslovakia, Hungary, Poland, and Yugoslavia is higher than in the case of the U.S.S.R., it is lower than in the other lesser industrial powers, which I have mentioned, in great part because of the active role of the state in limiting such dependence. Because of the slightly more tolerant attitude of the state, cultural and structural dependence on American sociology is higher in Poland and Yugoslavia than in Czechoslovakia or Hungary.

In what way does cultural dependence relate to structural dependence and vice versa? Using a rough working hypothesis, I would argue that the relationship is interactive and cumulative. However, it would appear that in France, Great Britain, Japan, and West Germany, for instance, cultural dependence is higher than the level of structural dependence on American sociology. In Australia, Canada, Israel, the Netherlands, New Zealand, and Scandinavia both cultural and structural dependence appear to be equally high. This might, of course, be related to the absolute size of these latter social science communities—perhaps a "critical mass" is needed before a particular community can achieve a high level of structural independence (and this "critical mass" might vary with the degree of specialization).

That structural dependence has an effect upon cultural dependence is a popularly held view. With regard to Canada, Clark (1975:225) attributes the Americanization of sociology in Canada to the recruitment of staff and the training of graduate students in the U.S. Latin American "radicals" argue that structural dependence on American sociology's sources of funding acts to increase cultural dependence. According to this argument, Latin American researchers become accustomed to styles of work which their own national resources cannot support. In their efforts to maintain this academic lifestyle, they become preoccupied with meeting the criteria of funding agencies and, eventually, at the institutional level

> . . . the original problem-oriented goals become gradually subordinated by the formal activities required for the preservation of the power-position of the institution. Means turn to ends, and, with this shift, the entire research enterprise becomes more surely controlled by U.S. sources than if the latter had dictated its activities in the first place (Ports, 1975:138).

The view that cultural dependence increases structural dependence is seldom voiced, for it has the consequence of shifting some of the responsibility for this structural dependence to the particular national sociological community.

What are the effects of cultural dependence? As Allardt (1967:225) reports concerning the Scandinavian countries:

> This eager adoption of American sociological thinking has had both functions and dysfunctions. On the positive side, we can say that Scandinavian sociology quickly became methodologically sophisticated. On the other hand, the dependence on American sociology has tended to hamper the flow of independent ideas as far as content is concerned.

What Allardt leaves unsaid is that the uncritical adoption of theoretical perspectives and methods which have arisen in responses to the conditions and problems in another society does not always help to generate relevant knowledge about your own. As Shils (1970:507) put it, sociologists are, after all, "citizens in their own societies . . . who . . . respond to the problems of their societies." Clark (1975:230-231) complains that the uncritical adoption of American theoretical perspectives and methods has not and cannot generate an understanding of how Canadian society came into being and survived. As

Stolzman and Gamberg (1975:98) put it: "a Canadian sociology cannot be built up by adopting putatively 'universal' models whose utilization is tantamount to filling American theoretical categories with Canadian information." Temu (1975:191) does not have a high opinion of the contribution of foreign scholarship to the understanding of African societies, and he voices a complaint quite similar in substance to Clark's (1975): "There is a need to study what internal forces hold the whole iceberg together, which forces are tending to pull it apart, and which determine the general direction in which it is drifting."[4] This, it seems to me, is what good sociology is all about, and one must develop a model that "fits" one's society, or at least work within a theoretical framework that shows promise of producing one that does.

The usefulness of the particular approach to the study of the internationalization of American sociology which has been discussed here can be ascertained only by means of a cross-national empirical study. In lieu of this, a case study of the Americanization of sociology in Canada will be substituted. The analysis which follows applies only to the English-speaking universe in Canada. French-Canadian sociology presents a problem in that it is influenced by American sociology in two ways: directly and indirectly through its cultural and structural dependence on French sociology.[5] The same difficulty emerges with regard to Indian sociology, for instance, which is influenced by American sociology directly and indirectly through its traditional dependence on British sociology.

The Americanization of Sociology in Canada

Prior to World War II, Canada, to all intents and purposes, was a colony of Great Britain. Sociologists were very few in number—fewer than ten in 1938 (Clark, 1975:231). The first department of sociology was established at McGill in the late thirties and, though several pioneering works were carried out there, it would be difficult to claim that sociology was established as a discipline in this period. In any event, the social sciences generally were culturally and structurally dependent on Great Britain, and the University of Chicago-dominated department at McGill flourished in solitary splendor. Following World War II, the colonial relationship of

Canada with Britain was rapidly replaced by the United States. As early as 1957, John Porter (1957:378) commented:

As American capital enters and exploits resources, and as American branch plants replace local firms, a feeling emerges that such developments are foreign economic occupation. The image is left of imperialism without war.

More than a decade and a half later, Page (1974:177) voices a growing complaint:

the relentless pressures of international technology and the steadily expanding influence of the American multinational corporations contribute to the process of cultural erosion.

Page (1974:176) mentions the flow of "foreign assumptions, images, and values . . . into every living room" and of "imported books and teaching guides" into the classrooms.

Paralleling the inroads of American multinational corporations into Canadian economic life were the inroads of American culture through the electronic and printed media and the subsequent Americanization of the educational system. In the 1960s, a rapidly expanding Canadian university system appointed a large number of non-Canadian academics to meet the spiralling demand for university teachers and researchers in the face of unprecedented and sustained annual increases in student enrollment of between 12-15% throughout the decade. The rationale behind this policy was that the hiring of foreign scholars would permit the building of good Canadian graduate schools which would eventually supply the Canadian university system with its own qualified personnel. However, this in itself is an indicator of the Americanization of Canadian values:

The minimal place accorded graduate work, and the less developed state of the social sciences in Britain, reduced the availability and attractivenesss of British models. The Canadian development of doctoral work was essentially modelled on American practice (Cairns, 1975:204).

By the time student enrollment levelled off in the early 1970s, more than one-third of full-time teaching staff at Canadian universities were non-Canadians, and the heaviest concentration of non-Canadians, mostly Americans, was in the social sciences. Sociology and anthropology had the highest proportion of American citizens. In 1970-71 only 40.3% of sociologists and anthropologists in Canadian universities were Canadian citizens, whereas 38.5% were Americans (Committee for an Independent Canada, 1974:199). If one takes into account that French-language universities in Canada hire very few Americans, it is apparent that in the English-language university system, American sociologists and anthropologists outnumbered their Canadian counterparts.

By the late 1960s, the negative effects of the presence of such large numbers of non-Canadian academics, especially the presence of so large a proportion of Americans concentrated in the social science faculties, began to make themselves felt. American-dominated departments had established an "old school tie" network which was used to hire new staff south of the border and to funnel back promising Canadian graduate students, the best quality research for publication, and some Canadian academics who turned out to be first-rate or better. In the Post-War era the Canadian social science community has been unable to retain the likes of Erving Goffman in sociology, David Easton in political science, and John Galbraith in economics. Finally, when Canadians began graduating from the new graduate schools, they found it difficult to obtain positions in their own system. Moreover, the proportion of foreign appointments was rising. Whereas foreign faculty comprised 36.2% of new appointments in the social sciences in 1962-63, this proportion had risen to 75.1% in 1971-72 (Committee for an Independent Canada, 1974:196). In the late sixties, what was to become known as the "Canadianization" movement emerged, which originated among young Canadian social scientists disgruntled with the undeveloped state of these disciplines in Canada, and among both graduate and undergraduate students seeking more Canadian content and relevance in their courses and training. The "Canadianization" movement in sociology and in the social sciences generally drew the attention of the national press at a time when public concern with American domination of the Canadian economy was becoming more vocal. Provincial governments, which are responsible for education in Canada, became concerned. The Alberta government set up the Moir Committee to investigate the situation in that province. The Moir Committee opposed the imposition of quotas and called for a greater effort to hire Canadians and for greater sensitivity to Canadian needs in course content. This was a very mild reaction in view of the fact that over two-thirds of the full-time staff of sociology and anthropology departments in Alberta universities and colleges were non-Canadians. The Select Committee on Economic and Cultural Nationalism of the Ontario Legislature tabled a report in late 1973 which recommended that "substantially higher percentages of new faculty appointments" should be made to Canadians and a similarly high proportion should have received most or all of their graduate training in Canadian universities.

The development of an American-dominated sociology in Canada occurred within the context of, and can be viewed as part of, the process of the growing structural and cultural dependence of Canada on the U.S. in the Post-War period. While the number of sociologists in Canada has increased spectacularly, the growth of an accompanying institutional framework has not been as impressive. Although there were fewer than ten sociologists in the country in 1938 (Clark, 1975), (Jones, 1974:1). In 1950, apart from the Department of Sociology at McGill, there was only the Department of Sociology and Anthropology at the University of British Columbia (Jones, 1975). By 1974, there were 46 departments of sociology, or of sociology and another discipline, of which twelve offered the Ph.D. programs (Jones, 1975). However, the *Canadian Review of Sociology and Anthropology* was not established until 1964. Prior to this time, sociologists in Canada either published in the *Canadian Journal of Economics and Political Science*, or as was more often the case, in American, British, and other foreign journals. The Canadian Sociology and Anthropology Association was not founded until 1966. The Canada Council, the major consistent source of domestic funding, did not provide significant input until the mid-1960s. Up until then, the Rockefeller, Carnegie, and Ford foundations were the major sources. Texts and other teaching materials have been mostly American. Overall, structural dependence on American sociology has been extremely high. In fact, it was only in 1973 that the members of the American Sociological Association (ASA) voted to grant Canadians the status of "international members" (ASA, 1973:8)–and this only after several previous requests to this effect by the Canadian Sociology and Anthropology Association had been rebuffed by the ASA executive.

Indeed, in attempting to develop a degree of structural and cultural independence, sociologists in Canada have been accused of racism and ethnocentrism. Writing in a British journal, Hedley and Warburton (1973:300) see nothing abnormal in that "students of sociology in Canada are presented with American examples and data far in excess of Canadian": in fact, to Hedley and Warburton (1973:314-315) recent efforts by the Canadian Sociology and Anthropology Association to and American dominance of the discipline in Canada are seen as "another somewhat alarming ethnocentric development" involving "nationalistic, primarily anti-American directives concerning hiring, graduate admissions, fellowships, fees and course content, and could have drastically far reaching effects on the practice and development of sociology in Canada."

These authors do not mention some of the major negative consequences of American domination of the discipline in Canada. Inglis (1973:8) paints a dismal but accurate picture:

> After twenty years of university expansion in Canada, our anthropology and sociology departments are still largely peripheral elements in a continental system, networks of communication within the country are poorly developed, and Canadians who dare to question the situation are castigated as backwards nationalists.

This is hardly surprising given the power and influence of American sociologists within Canada. Lambert and Curtis (1973:76) report that "American sociologists are more likely to be male, somewhat older, of higher rank . . . and better financially remunerated than Canadians." Their orientation is definitely American rather than Canadian, as evidenced by the significant proportion who manifests the following: "continuing exclusive membership in American professional associations, area knowledge, and citizenship status" (Lambert and Curtis, 1973:78). This situation has seriously hampered the growth and development of a Canadian sociology with its own communication network, research interests, and ideological commitments, from which might emerge theories and models which differ from those current in American sociology. There is resistance to such developments since they will tend to result in the replacement of the north-south network through which faculty, promising graduate students, research funds, publication opportunities, and professional prestige are funneled back and forth, by a predominantly east-west Canadian network and reward system.

A further aspect of the dominance of American sociologists in Canada is their influence in faculty-hiring committees. As Clark (1974:17) puts it, "[i]t is to a staffing committee American manned that the young Canadian sociologist must turn in seeking an appointment to a Canadian university." To many American sociologists, any attempt to change this is viewed as yet another manifestation of Canadian ethnocentrism. That the concept of "universalism" is operationalized in curious ways is indicated by the fact that "some departments are not making use of Canadian communication channels to find competent Canadians to fill available jobs" (Canadian Sociology and Anthropology Association, 1973:7). Despite the severe restrictions on the hiring of non-Americans in American universities, the main rhetoric of resistance to the preferential hiring of Canadian sociologists on the part of American sociologists in Canada is along the lines that "quotas" on the number of non-Canadian (i.e. American) academics is "racist" and "discriminatory," and that "universalistic" criteria should be applied in filling appointments. Leaving aside the consideration that American-dominated staffing committees apply nationally-biased criteria to Canadians in their own country, it turns out that publications in prestigious locations, degrees from prestigious universities, and the renown of one's supervisor and referees constitute the core criteria. Since the most prestigious sources of publication, the most prestigious universities, and the most renowned sociologists are located outside of Canada (especially from an American perspective), the outcome is already determined. But the implantation and perpetuation of such a reward system ensure the continued impoverishment of Canadian publications, communication networks, and Canadian sociology. It is the self-perpetuating nature of this reward system

which prevents the development of a sound Canadian sociological infrastructure.

Structural dependence on American sociology now appears to be on the wane; preference is being given to Canadian and Canadian trained sociologists by a growing number of departments; the number of Canadian sociology journals, monograph series, and other publication outlets has increased; non-Canadian academics are feeling pressure from their colleagues and students to make Canadian society, at least in part, the vehicle for their sociology; both graduate and undergraduate courses are changing in the direction of becoming more Canadian in content and relevance; the number of Canadian sociology texts and readers is growing rapidly. The emergence of the "Canadianization" movement in the late sixties contributed greatly to these changes. This movement emerged due to several factors; concern at the national level with American domination of the Canadian economy; the domestic crises in the U.S. the Viet Nam War, and other aspects of American foreign policy which both lowered U.S. prestige in the eyes of Canadians and accentuated the differences between the two societies. There was also the feeling among young Canadian faculty and students in the social sciences, that American domination of the Social science disciplines in Canada was part and parcel of Canada's colonial relationship to the U.S. Still other Canadian sociologists felt that prevailing paradigms, theories, and research in American sociology were irrelevant or inapplicable to Canadian society.

The next stage in the development of a Canadian sociology—the development of a communications network, research interests, and ideological commitments—seems to be underway. However, a mature Canadian sociology will emerge only with the development of theories and models of society which can be pitted against others in the arena of international sociology, their "universalism" lying in their capacity to persuade other sociologists to adopt them. Just as the "Canadianization" of sociology in Canada is being accomplished not only through the efforts of Canadian sociologists but through the pressure of student and public opinion and the subtle political intervention of provincial governments, the degree of acceptance of the future products of Canadian sociology will be no more divorced from the activities of the

Canadian state and from Canada's position in the world than has been the case with the products of American sociology.

Summary

Two of the most significant problems in the sociology of the social sciences appear to me to be that of accounting for the institutionalization of the various social sciences on the one hand, and, on the other, that of accounting for the emergence of dominant or, if you prefer, "academically central" social science communities, and the consequent cultural and structural dependence of other national social science communities. With regard to the first problem, Gouldner (1970) calls attention to such variables as level of industrialization, the emergence of a technical and administrative elite, and development of sectorial autonomy; and Shils (1970) focuses on intra national factors facilitating institutionalization. With regard to the second problem, Shils (1970) attributes the dominance of American sociology primarily to its level of institutionalization, level of output, and to the persuasiveness of the ideas generated by this community. It has been pointed out here that it is the power, wealth, and resources of the nation-states within which specific social science communities are located which best predict their dominance or dependence, level of institutionalization, level of output, and the persuasiveness of their ideas. Language factors, the absolute size of the national social science community, the degree of specialization, and the attitude of the state and other domestic institutions were seen as important intervening variables. A distinction was made between cultural and structural dependence, and an attempt was made to provide definitions conducive of operationalization. It is argued that the relationship between cultural and structural dependence tends to be cumulative and interactive and that excessive cultural dependence on other social science communities is detrimental in that particular national social science communities may find themselves functioning as "branch plants" of another social science community. "Sociology," in such instances, may amount to little more than the filling of imported theoretical categories with local information.

NOTES

[1] The emergence of this spate of literature seems related to the military, political, economic setbacks experienced by the U.S. in recent years and to its civic crises. American sociology appears to have declined in prestige for other reasons as well. The collaboration of many eminent American sociologists in Project Camelot, in the Voice of America series, and in other politically suspect government-sponsored activities did not do much good for the "value-free" image. Moreover, during the affluent sixties academic standards appeared to decline. Portes (1975:131) reports that a negative impression was created in Latin American countries by "lower quality of personnel associated with increased number," and that as the numbers of specialists increased, "their familiarity with the language, history, and culture of the countries in the region decreased." It is interesting to note that in this period, the time taken to complete the Ph.D. in the U.S. declined (Janes and Seeman, 1975). There appears to have been an increase in the grinding out of what Davis (1964:233) has called "academic development housing."

[2] Shils (1970:763) defines "institutionalization" as follows: "By the institutionalization of an intellectual activity I mean the relatively dense interaction of persons who perform that activity. The interaction has a structure; the more intense the interaction, the more its structure makes place for authority, which makes decisions regarding assessment, admission, promotion, allocation."

[3] Morgan (1970) provides an interesting supplement to Shils in that he deals more extensively with the institutionalization of sociology in the U.S. prior to World War I.

[4] Temu (1975:193) appears to have a legitimate complaint: " . . . many social scientists working in Africa, or on Africa, are foreigners. Most of them are short-term visitors. . . . On successful completion of their stay, these budding Africanists publish their findings . . . often confirming with slight modification the hypotheses which are already in vogue and cherished by their academic supervisors. And so the literature grows, the Africana sections get bigger, Africanists multipy –but alas African problems remain."

[5] While French-Canadian sociologists often work hard at disassociating themselves and their tradition from their English-speaking counterparts, they are more dependent on the same sources than they would ever care to admit. Rocher (1974:10) maintains that American sociology has profoundly influenced French-Canadian sociology. This influence is seen not only in research methods used but also in the perspectives French-Canadian sociologists have adopted. Degree programs are based on the American model.

REFERENCES

Allardt, Erik. "Scandinavian Sociology." In *Social Science Information 6* (August): 223-246, 1967.

American Sociological Association. "Nominations Opened and Canadians Internationalized." *ASA Footnotes* (December):8, 1973.

Birnbaum, Norman. Foreword. In *A Sociology of Sociology* by Robert W. Friedrichs, pp. ix xvii. New York: Free Press, 1970.

Cairns, A.C. "Political Science in Canada and the Americanization Issue." In *Canadian Journal of Political Science* 8 (June):191-234, 1975.

Canadian Sociology and Anthropology Association. "Canadianization." In *Canadian Sociology and Anthropology Association Bulletin* (April):7, 1973.

Clark, S.D. "The American Take-over of Canadian Sociology:Myth or Reality?" In *University Affairs* (September):16-17, 1974.

Clark, S.D. "Sociology in Canada: An Historical Overview." In *Canadian Journal of Sociology* I (Summer):225-234, 1975.

Committee for an Independent Canada (Research and Policy Staff). "Faculty Citizenship in Canadian Universities." In *Getting It Back: A Program for Canadian Independence*, edited by Abraham Rotstein and Gary Lax, pp. 192-200. Toronto: Clarke, Irwin, 1974.

Davis, J.A. "Great Books and Small Groups: An Informal History of a National Survey." In *Sociologists at Work: Essays on the Craft of Social Research*, edited by Philip E. Hammond, pp. 212-234. New York: Basic Books, 1964.

Direnzo, D.J. "Sociology in Italy Today." In *International Review of Modern Sociology 2* (March):33-58, 1972.

Feyerabend, Paul K. "Against Method: Outline of an Anarchistic Theory of Knowledge." In *Minnesota Studies in the Philosophy of Science*, 4, edited by Michael Radner and Stephen Winokur, pp. 17-130. Minneapolis: University of Minnesota Press, 1970.

Gouldner, Alvin W. *The Coming Crisis of Western Sociology*. New York: Basic Books, 1970.

Hedley, R. Alan and T. Rennie Warburton. "The Role of National Courses in the Teaching and Development of Sociology: The Canadian Case." In *Sociological Review* 21 (July):299-319, 1973.

Inglis, Gordon. "Communication." In *Canadian Sociology and Anthropology Association Bulletin* (October) 1973:8, 1973.

Janes, R.W. and C.M. Seeman. "Factors Associated with Trends in Time Spent to Acquire the Sociology Doctorate." In *The American Sociologist* 10 (May): 118-122, 1975.

Jones, F.E. "Current Sociological Research in Canada." In Paper presented at the Eighth World Congress of Sociology, Toronto (August), 1974.

Kassof, A. "American Sociology Through Soviet Eyes." In *American Sociological Review* 30 (February): 114-121, 1965.

Kuhn, T.S. *The Structure of Scientific Revolutions*. Chicago: University of Chicago Press, 1962.

Lambert, Ronald D. and James Curtis. "Nationality and Professional Activity Correlates Among Social Scientists." In *Canadian Review of Sociology and Anthropology* 10 (February): 62-80, 1973.

Mol, Hans. "Sociology in Australia and New Zealand." In *The American Sociologist* 3 (May): 146-147, 1968.

Morgan, J.G. "Contextual Factors in the Rise of Academic Sociology in the United States." In *Canadian Review of Sociology and Anthropology* 7 (August): 159-171, 1970.

Oromaner, M.J. "Comparison of Influentials in Contemporary American and British Sociology: A Study in the Internationalization of Sociology." In *British Journal of Sociology* 21 (September): 324-332, 1970.

Page, Robert. "Canadian Studies: The Current Dilemma." In *Getting It Back: A Program for Canadian Independence*, edited by Abraham Rotstein and Gary Lax, pp. 175-190. Toronto: Clarke, Irwin, 1974.

Parsons, Talcott. "An American Impression of Sociology in the Societ Union." In *American Sociological Review* 30 (February): 121-125, 1965.

Parsons, Talcott, ed. *American Sociology: Perspectives, Problems, Methods*. New York: Basic Books, 1968.

Porter, John. "The Economic Elite and the Social Structure in Canada." In *Canadian Journal of Economics and Political Science* 23 (August): 376-394, 1957.

Portes, Alejandro. "Trends in International Research Cooperation: The Latin American Case." In *The American Sociologist* 10 (August): 131-140, 1975.

Rocher, Guy. "La Sociologie Canadienne et Quebecoise." In Paper presented at the Eighth World Congress of Sociology, Toronto (August), 1974.

Shils, Edward. "Tradition, Ecology and Institution in the History of Sociology." In *Daedalus* 99 (Fall): 760-825, 1970.

Stolzman, James and Herbert Gamberg. "The National Question and Canadian Sociology." In *Canadian Journal of Sociology* 1 (Spring): 91-106, 1975.

Temu, P.E. "Reflections on the Role of Social Scientists in Africa." In *International Journal of Social Science* 27 (Spring): 190-194, 1975.

Van Rossum, Wouter. "The Problem of Cognitive Institutionalization in the Social Sciences: The Case of Dutch Sociology." In *Social Science Information* 14 (April): 155-172, 1975.

360

HAROLD INNIS, KARL MARX AND CANADIAN POLITICAL ECONOMY

Ian Parker

Canadian Political Economy is on the verge of a renaissance. Following the Second World War, the Political Economy tradition in Canadian social science entered a period of relative (and in some centers, absolute) decline. As an integrated field of study, the discipline responded to centrifugal pressures promoting the extension of disciplinary specialization, and gave way to the now conventional sub-disciplines of economics and political science. This fragmentation manifested itself in the increasing distance between economists and political scientists which emerged in most Canadian universities, and in the development of two journals (the *Canadian Journal of Economics* and the *Canadian Journal of Political Science*) from the original *Canadian Journal of Economics and Political Science*.

During this period, problems of communication increased not only *between* social science disciplines but also *within* social science disciplines. Within economics, for example, the gap between mainstream economic theory and economic history widened, despite Innis' argument that "Any substantial progress in economic theory must come from a closer synthesis between economic history and economic theory," and despite (and on occasion because of) recent attempts to apply simple neoclassical "cliometric" models directly to the explanation of complex historical situations. Similarly, specialists in various subfields of applied economics encountered increasing difficulty in communicating among themselves across the linguistic barriers posed by the specialized vocabularies which developed within each subfield, despite the manifest interdependence of the phenomena which constitute their primary concerns. Pressures promoting such specialization have increased since 1945, because of the rapid increase in the volume of research in most subfields, accompanied by the dramatic expansion in the overall size of the economics profession.

Difficulties of communication within economics have become more complex as a result of the increased importation of mathematics since the end of World War II. Innis' remark on the introduction of the phonetic alphabet into Greece between the ninth and seventh centuries BC is relevant to an appraisal of the impact of mathematics on economics. The scientific prestige of mathematics as a mode of economic communication (to be distinguished from its role in certain contexts as a necessary mode of economic analysis) has similarly produced in recent years a number of certified "economists" who are at best moderately competent applied mathematicians, limited both in their understanding of the mathematical foundations of certain types of economic analysis and in their sensitivity to the types of economic phenomena which can legitimately be represented in mathematical form.

These changes in the structure of production of economic knowledge have been accompanied by two distinct developments, one at the center and one at the margin of contemporary mainstream economics. At the center, these centrifugal strains have tended to promote the development and to legitimate the hegemony of that body of economic theorems which Samuelson has described as the "neo-neoclassical synthesis," insofar as this "synthesis" provides a common paradigm or universe of discourse among specialists in different economic subfields.

At the margin of mainstream economics, however, the contradictions inherent in the fragmentation of economic knowledge, and accentuated by developments in the North American and global political economics, particularly since the early 1960s, have led to a rebirth of interest and activity in political economy as an integrated social scientific discipline. Consciousness of the need for a more comprehensive analytical perspective has increased in relation to recognition of the interpenetration of political and economic elements in phenomena such as the US military involvement in Southeast Asia; the manifestation of Russian "social imperialism," as in the 1968 invasion of Czechoslovakia; the successful liberation struggles in southern Africa; the emergence of the Organization of Petroleum Exporting Countries (OPEC) as catalyzed by the global inflation fueled by the massive outflow of US dollars incidental to US prosecution of the Vietnam War; the existence of racism, sexism, and religious, cultural and linguistic prejudice and discrimination; and the increase in foreign (particularly US-based) proprietary control of Canadian industry and natural resources.

At the same time, recognition of the significance of such historical phenomena has heightened awareness of the limitations of mainstream economic theory, and of its narrow preoccupation with phenomena which presuppose (and are dependent for their interpretation on) the existence of a well-developed *price system*, as a given rather than as an analytical *problem*. The re-emergence of Canadian political economy can thus be traced both to the intensification of internal contradictions in mainstream economics and social science as a result of the postwar increase in disciplinary and intra-disciplinary specialization, and to the increased awareness of historical contradictions in the global political economy.

It is now a quarter of a century since Innis' death in 1952, and close to a century since the death of Marx in 1883; yet their analyses have justifiably been considered as together constituting the theoretical or logical-historical basis for the resurgence and future development of Canadian political economy. The linking of the names of Innis and Marx in this fashion, however, raises important methodological and theoretical problems, because of their apparently divergent and antagonistic theoretical frameworks. There is need for a coherent understanding of the relations between their thought if Canadian political economy is not to degenerate into a undisciplined, undiscriminating eclecticism. The problems in comprehending the relations between Innis and Marx are not, however, purely theoretical.

Some Canadian Marxists and political economists have suggested that Innis' theoretical framework is nothing more than that of a renegade "bourgeois" social scientist,

albeit one who provides certain insights into Canadian history. Frank Underhill, for example, described Innis as one of the "garage mechanics" of Canadian capitalism. On the other hand, some students of Innis have criticized Marxian analysis with an equally opaque understanding. In his study of Innis, for example, Robin Neill argues that "Like its bourgeois counterpart, the Marxian analysis reduces to a set of theoretical categories in terms of which the growth process can be described without an elaboration of the actual cause and effect relations involved." The present study, however, is based on the inductively grounded assumption that there are important affinities between Innis and Marx which warrant closer attention. Its purpose is to outline certain basic theses regarding the significance of the work of Innis and Marx for the future development of Canadian political economy; to indicate the relationships which exist between their modes of analysis; and to outline the ways in which each can contribute to the clarification and development of the thought of the other.

My argument may be summarized in five propositions, each of which requires the documentation of the remainder of this study to establish its plausibility. The first is that Innis and Marx are the two most important social scientists (as theorists and as historians) for the future development of Canadian political economy and social science. The second is that the affinities between their thought deserve more careful and detailed consideration than they have so far received, at least in printed form. The third is that Innis' work, taken as a whole in its historical trajectory from 1920 to 1952, can best be understood as that of a historical materialist, and a developing dialectical materialist, notwithstanding certain contradictions when his thought is viewed in these terms. The fourth is that the dialectical materialist character of Innis' thought became most evident in the period including and following the preparation of *The Cod Fisheries: The History of an International Economy*, first published in 1940, the period which includes the publication of *Political Economy in the Modern State* (1946), *Empire and Communications* (1950, 1972), *The Bias of Communication* (1951, 1964), and the posthumous *Changing Concepts of Time* (1952), as well as the unpublished "History of Communications" (available in microfilm at the University of Toronto). Hence, just as Marx's so-called "mature" analysis (in the period from, say, 1857 to his death) not only *builds on* but also *advances beyond* the analyses of *The German Ideology* (1845-46) and *The Poverty of Philosophy* (1846-47), so the later work of Innis constitutes a significant methodological advance over his earlier works, such as the *History of the Canadian Pacific Railway* (1923) and *The Fur Trade in Canada* (1930).

Finally, just as Marx's works provide historical insights and a methodological approach which can assist in the reformulation and extension of Innis' concept of Canadian and of Western political-economic development, so Innis' analysis of the political economy of communication provides a means of dealing in dialectical materialist terms with several crucial lacunae in Marx's analysis: those of the dialectic between the forces and relations of production and between the economic base and the superstructure; and at a more concrete level, those of the theory of the State and of the international economy that were to have occupied the unwritten fifth and sixth volumes of *Capital*.

A materialist epistemological perspective involves the presupposition that human experience ultimately determines human consciousness, rather than that human consciousness is the ultimate determinant of human experience. The ground of human experience is the process of production of human existence, or the process of production of the means of reproduction of human experience. Marx and Engels expressed this presupposition as follows: "As individuals express their life, so they are. What they are, therefore, coincides with their production, both with *what* they produce and with *how* they produce. The nature of individuals thus depends on the material conditions determining their production." Even "consciousness" itself arises through the fundamental material medium of human social communication, language: "Language is as old as consciousness, language *is* practical consciousness that exists also for other men, and for that reason alone it really exists for me personally as well; language, like consciousness, only arises from the need, the necessity, of intercourse with other men. . . . Consciousness is, therefore, from the very be-

ginning a social product, and remains so as long as men exist at all."

As the latter passage suggests, a second presupposition of historical materialism is that all human activity, including that of an "isolated" individual such as Robinson Crusoe, is social activity, as is evidenced by one of Crusoe's first activities once he is stranded: taking an inventory, in true bourgeois fashion, of the usable resources from the wrecked ship of which he is a castaway.

A third materialist presupposition is that the process of production is fundamentally a process of reproduction: that "the economic problem" is not simply a matter of allocating given scarce resources among given and competing alternative uses, but is fundamentally a process in space and time involving the survival, the simple or expanded reproduction, and the potential transformation of a social-economic *system*.

Finally, the materialist standpoint assumes that the analytical categories and laws of motion appropriate to a particular historical epoch are peculiar to the mode of production that characterizes that epoch, and cannot necessarily be readily translated in the description of other modes of production. As Marx commented, "there are categories which are common to all stages of production and are established by reasoning as general categories; the so-called *general conditions* of all and any production, however, are nothing but abstract conditions which do not define any of the actual historical stages of production."

Dialectical method similarly involves certain presuppositions which distinguish it from non-dialectical modes of thought. Hegel's concept of the "Master-Slave" (or "Lordship and Bondage") relation is a *locus classicus* of dialectical reasoning in the social-scientific sphere. The roots of the Hegelian dialectic, however, can be traced through Luther's translation of the Bible to Pauline and Mosaic theology, within the Western Tradition, and to the yin-yang dialectic of Eastern philosophy.

Dialectical thought in all of these manifestations involves a rejection of the Aristotelean "axiom of the excluded middle," which asserts that a phenomenon is either A or not-A. In dialectical thought, a phenomenon is both A and not-A, insofar as all phenomena are assumed to be defined relationally, so that a phenomenon cannot be defined independently of its negation, which both establishes the boundaries of the phenomenon and is incorporated in its self-definition. The "interpenetration of opposites" assumed in dialectical reasoning is not, however, in any way mystical. It simply expresses the necessarily logical-historical character of all categories utilized in social-scientific investigation and discourse. Moreover, it is precisely in the contradictory character of social phenomena that the origins of change or transformation are situated: in Blake's words, "Without contraries, there is no progression."

In related fashion, dialectical reasoning does not assume the applicability to the "axiom of reflexivity": that phenomenon X stands in a certain relation (R) to phenomenon Y (XRY) does not necessarily imply that YRX. Just as Hegel recognized that there was an asymmetry in the Master-Slave relation, for example, so Marx recognized that there exists an asymmetry in the exchange of commodities (so that the "relative form" of value is not identical to the "equivalent form" of value), an asymmetry which historically underlies the emergence of money and of the price system which precedes the full-scale development of capitalism.

A third presupposition of dialectical reasoning relates to its treatment of time. There is a difference between *open*, dialectical, and *closed*, nondialectical systems. Epistemologically, a closed system is ahistorical and tautological: this is the world of the mathematical theorem, and of neoclassical economics. An *open* economic system is open to time; it involves necessarily unpredictable change, and implies the bounded usefulness of purely tautological modes of analysis. Since all historical economic systems are open economic systems, however, non-dialectical modes of political-economic analysis are temporally bounded in their referential range, and moreover cannot provide in theoretical terms an indication of their temporal bounds; whereas dialectical analysis presupposes this irreducible uncertainty, and its consequences for social-economic behavior.

Finally, dialectical thought assumes the interdependence of quantitative and qualitative change. In essence, this aspect of the articulation of the dialectic expresses nothing more than the fact that *quantitative* changes in an economic system (the classic example in Marx is the increase of population) produce *qualitative* or structural changes in that system: that is, significant mediated alterations in political-economic behaviour, or changed social behavior incidental to the change in the mediational or media structure which necessarily accompanies quantitative economic change. Such qualitative changes in the media-structure of an economic system in turn generate quantitative changes in the elements which constitute the system.

In this context, it is possible to ground the four approaches logically produced by these two polarities, and to suggest that Marx's thought is that of a dialectical materialist, while Hegel's thought is that of a dialectical idealist. In related fashion, many of the writings which have emerged from the "institutionalist" thought of the German stage-theorists, and of John R. Commons, Thorstein Veblen and Karl Polanyi can be described as forms of non-dialectical materialism, while neo-neoclassical economic theory may properly be described as a form of non-dialectical idealism.

If it is postulated, however, that the explanatory value of a mode of social analysis depends directly on the degree of correspondence between its logical or theoretical constructs and their historical or empirical referents, it is reasonable to conclude that dialectical materialism constitutes a mode of analysis with greater heuristic and explanatory value than alternative modes—insofar as non-dialectical modes are tautological, atemporal and ahistorical; and insofar as idealist modes neglect the ultimate dependence of epistemic factors on economic forces, given that economic forces are a principal historical determinant of processes of epistemological reproduction and transformation.

To establish the plausibility of the five basic propositions of the study, it remains to document the significant affinities which exist between Innis and Marx; the sense in which Innis' later work is that of a developing dialectical materialist; and the ways in which Marx's work illuminates that of Innis, while Innis' work in turn illuminates that of Marx.

The affinities between Innis and Marx may be identified in two ways: by reference to the historical relations between their thought; and by reference to common elements in their theoretical/historical methods and analyses.

With regard to the historical relations between Marx and Innis as social theorists, four major channels of influence are noteworthy: the direct impact of Marx's writings on Innis; the mediated impact of Marx through Veblen on Innis; the impact of Hegel on both (which was much more direct, pervasive and strong for Marx than for Innis, but influential in the mature thought of both); and the influence of Adam Smith (directly in the case of Innis, principally as mediated by Ricardo in the case of Marx).

The direct impact of Marx's writings on Innis, from all appearances, was negligible. In fact, Innis' own references to Marx provide one of the most telling arguments against any significant association between their thought. Innis, for example, cited Keynes's misguided comment on "the final *reductio ad absurdum* of Benthamism known as Marxism," and Kohn's equally misguided interpretation of Marx's view of time as involving "formless inevitability." He also suggested in 1948, with regard to his own analysis of the "structural and moral changes produced in modern society by scientific and technological advances," that "much of this will smack of Marxian interpretation but I have tried to use the Marxian interpretation to interpret Marx. There has been no systematic pushing of the Marxian conclusion to its ultimate limit, and in pushing it to its limit, showing its limitations."

In this last remark, however, Innis demonstrates, if not a familiarity with Marx, at least an awareness of the significance of Marx's interpretation of history for his own work. Moreover, he had observed, as early as 1936, that "Marx contributed much in building the ladder to escape from his enemies, his followers, and himself." The ladder Innis had in mind was the materialist interpretation of history. Finally, in a letter to Arthur Lower, Innis made the following self-referential observation: "Our differences probably go back to religion—the Methodists are always anxious to control things—the Baptists are always suspicious of control. . . . The Marxist interpretation probably also applies—the background of farm life plus a training in economics leaves me very sceptical about methods of control—heretofore, they have been largely new methods of exploitation.

In short, Innis' *direct* relationship to Marx clearly involved ignorance, and a reductionistic interpretation, of Marx's analysis. It is perhaps useful, however, to note the recurrent implicit expressions of sympathy with the basic thrust of Marx's analysis by Innis, amidst his general expressions of scepticism regarding the dogmatism of Marxists.

Moreover, Innis' observations that "Perhaps in a very real sense, a great institution is the tomb of the founder," and that "To the founder of a school, everything may be forgiven, except his school," not only invoke the necessary distinction between Keynes and the Keynesians, between Innis and the Innisians, and between Marx and the Marxists, but also recall Marx's comment, "Thank God, I at least am not a Marxist," and Blake's earlier "I must create my own system or be enslaved by another man's." A first link between Marx and Innis thus lies in their mutual strong anti-dogmatic biases, a link which exists partly despite, and partly because of Innis' *ignorance* of Marx's works, many of which were not translated until after Innis' death.

Innis' analysis, however, is historically related in *mediated* fashion to Marx's, in at least three ways. First, there is the channel through Veblen, with whose work Innis was very familiar, whose study of Marx's analysis noted the influence of Hegel on Marx, and whose own iconoclastic interpretation of capitalism owes more than is immediately apparent to Marx. Innis' work is most evidently dependent on Veblen in *The Fur Trade in Canada* (1930), one of his least explicitly dialectical works.[1] In his later studies, Innis moved increasingly away from Veblen's form of institutionalism, in response to a developing deeper awareness of the *dialectical* character of the historical process. In so doing, he implicitly moved closer to Marx's mode of analysis, albeit through *historical* analysis, or through the utilization of *materialist method.*

Moreover, Innis' later studies involved an increasingly self-conscious exploration of the philosophy of history, in which Hegel's work was acknowledged and transformed. Hegel's comment on "Minerva's Owl" in the *Philosophy of Right,* for example, served as the title of Innis 1947 Presidential Address to the Royal Society of Canada. Similarly, Hegel's position that "Reason advances by bending to its will men's thoughts . . . and their passions: 'the one the warp, the other the woof of the vast arras-web of Universal History'," was transmuted by Innis into his own materialist version of the fabric of history: "It is assumed that history is not a seamless web but rather a web of which the warp and woof are space and time, woven in a very uneven fashion and producing distorted patterns."

It is unnecessary to trace Hegel's influence on Marx: Marx's admiration for Hegel's logic, historical sense and erudition, as well as his critique of Hegel's idealism, are well known. What is significant for the present study is that Innis and Marx both reached positions in relation to Hegel which involved a materialist reformulation of Hegel's idealist understanding of the dialectic of history. It is of secondary importance that Innis arrived at his reformulation of Hegel principally through direct reflection on his own *concrete historical* studies, while Marx's reformulation initially arose from his *philosophical* struggle with Hegel and the "Young Hegelians."

The impact of the work of Adam Smith on Innis differed from that on Marx in several respects which are of importance in assessing the relationships between Innis' and Marx's analyses. The primary impact of Smith on Innis was direct, and was reflected particularly in Innis' analysis of the "penetrative powers of the price-system" (which also drew on Veblen) and in Innis' extension of Smith's "vent-for-surplus" analysis of the origins of trade, which provided a principal underpinning for Innis' so-called "staples thesis" regarding the sources and character of Canadian economic development.

Smith's impact on Marx was also significant, but it manifested itself more in Marx's analysis of the sphere of production than (as in the case of Innis) of the sphere of circulation,[2] particularly in Marx's extension of Smith's analysis of the "division of labour" in the chapter on "Cooperation" in Volume I of *Capital*. Moreover, Ricardo's mediation, and his critique of Smith's theory of value, figured much more in the development of Marx's theoretical system than it did in Innis', since Innis (despite his references at various points to the process of "exploitation") did not explicitly make the extraction of surplus value central to his analysis of capitalist development, as Marx had.

While an analysis of the historical relations between the thought of Innis and Marx may be illuminating, however, any appraisal of the relations between them which relies solely on an analysis of the direct and mediated historical links between their theories is ultimately an inadequate means of establishing the relations between their approaches. The remainder of my study therefore analyses (*a*) the parallels between Marx's and Innis' work, and (*b*) the differences between their analytical emphases and the complementarity of their approaches. Three aspects of their thought appear to be of particular interest in an outline of their relationship: the dialectical bases of their thought; their common ecological approach to the historical process; and their common awareness of the political-economic significance of communications phenomena.

Perhaps the most basic analogue between Innis' and Marx's work emerges in their respective versions of the Hegelian Master-Slave dialectic. In Marx, the Master-Slave dialectic is present in the dialectic between the *money-form* of the commodity and *the commodity*, as manifested in the circuit of capital; between *capital* and *labor*; and between the *market* and the *individual producer*. As Marx noted regarding the third of these dialectical relations:

> To the degree that production is shaped in such a way that every producer becomes dependent on the exchange value of his commodity, . . . to the same degree must *money relations* develop, together with the contradictions in the *money relation*, in the relation of the product to itself as money. . . . [T]he exchange relation establishes itself as a power external to and independent of the producers. . . . As the producers become more dependent on exchange, exchange appears to become more independent of them, and the gap between the product as product and the product as exchange value appears to widen.

What is particularly significant in Marx, apart from the interdependence between the market-producer, money-commodity and capital-labor relations, is that the emergence of these relations is not purely a *logical*, but also an *historical* process.

The analogue in Innis to Hegel's Master-Slave dialectic is the *center-margin* dialectic, which drew on Veblen's concepts of "marginality," N.S.B. Gras's "metropolitan-hinterland" schema, and later on Burckhardt and Hume. At the outset of Innis' studies, the center-margin framework was not explicitly dialectical in character. The underlying theme of Innis' *History of the CPR*, for example, was "the spread of Western civilization over the northern half of North America." His study of *The Fur Trade in Canada* concluded with the observation that

> The economic history of Canada has been dominated by the discrepancy between the center and the margin of Western civilization. Energy has been directed towards the exploitation of staple products and the tendency has been cumulative. . . . The history of the fur trade is the history of contact between two civilizations, the European and the North American. . . . The limited cultural background of the North American hunting peoples provided an insatiable demand for the products of the more elaborate cultural development of Europeans.

As late as 1938, although his powerful study of "The Penetrative Powers of the Price System" contained much sophisticated dialectical analysis, that analysis transcended the non-dialectical bias implicit in the title. (The term "discrepancy" is not analytically equivalent to "contradiction.")

By this point, however, Innis had generalized and tranformed the center-margin framework so that it was genuinely a tool of dialectical historical analysis. From the late 1930s until his death in 1952, he extended his exploration of the center-margin dialectic in a number of important directions which both brought his analysis closer to Marx's and provided means of overcoming theoretical difficulties which had been confronted, but only incompletely dealt with, by Marx in the *Grundrisse* and the *Theories of Surplus-Value*, and which had been downplayed in the first three volumes of *Capital*.[3]

In this period, which saw the publication of his major writings on the economics of communication, Innis made three principal theoretical advances. First, he began to analyze explicitly patterns of political-economic competition among centers and margins not only *between* but also *within* open economic systems, and to exphasize not only the historical mechanisms by which control of space and time has been maintained, but also the nature of the contradictions which have historically resulted in the breakdown of such control.

Second, he recognized that forms of social-economic control were not uni-dimensional: that there were typically multiple centers and margins even within a single open economic system, and that monopolies of knowledge and monopolies of organized force were often situated in complementary and competitive (but nonetheless potentially distinct) centers within any given system. In historically documenting these distinguishable dimensions of political-economic hegemony, he provided that basis for a more articulated concept of class relations than is possible on the basis of the criterion of "ownership or control of the means of production (narrowly defined)" alone.

Moreover, he began to develop an analysis of center-margin interaction which accounted for the extended maintenance of relations of dominance and subordination within and between systems in some historial contexts, and for the transformation, transcendence or evasion of those relations in others: " . . . the rich development of Greek culture checked that of Rome and compelled the latter to concentrate on its own capacities notably in law"; "the expansion of literary activity in Great Britain, which had served as an outlet to political repression, overwhelmed the colonies and compelled concentration on newspapers"; "The cultural life of English-speaking Canadians subjected to constant hammering from American commercialism is increasingly separated from the cultural life of French-speaking Canadians. American influence on the latter is checked by the barrier of the French language but is much less hampered by visual media."

In addition to these examples of central restriction of marginal activity, however, Innis also documented some of the preconditions of dynamic marginal activity and of marginal resistance to domination by an external center. "The blotting-out of the learning of Spain by the Mohammedans and restricted interest in learning in Europe [in the early ninth century] meant that the most distant area of Europe, namely Ireland, alone remained enthusiastic for knowledge and from here an interest in learning spread backwards to Scotland and England and to Europe." "The cultural tenacity of language was shown in the conquest of the conquered, the adoption of the French language in Normandy and eventually of the English language by the Normans." Similarly, the marginal position of Genoa and Venice in relation to Roman and Byzantine influence facilitated the rise of commerce in the medieval period which laid the foundation for the subsequent emergence of capitalism. Analogously, the diversified economic capacities of New England, which paralleled those of England itself, in combination with maritime spatial advantages and the decline in external insecurity incidental to the British conquest of New France, were instrumental in establishing the origins and the preconditions for success of the American Revolution.

A final aspect of Innis' center-margin dialectic was that it increasingly incorporated a recognition that the course of development of open economic systems is determined by the articulation of internal and external contradictions resulting from the "rigidities" or "biases" of the spatial-temporal structure of production, communication and reproduction of such systems; and that system development frequently involves intense competition and violence:

> We seem destined in economics to follow the meteorologist in modifying equilibrium analysis and turning to what he has called the polar front theory in which the meeting of economic masses becomes important rather than trade between nations. There are serious weaknesses in the analogy of flowing from high to low pressure areas, and great advantages in discussing pressure groups.
> Von Eicken's thesis that the master key to history lies in the conclusion that human movements provoke violent reactions has much to support it. . . . The bias of communication in space or in time involves a sponge theory of the distribution of wealth which assumes violence.

The second important parallel between Innis and Marx lies in their common adoption of an ecological and holistic perspective on political-economic systems. For Marx, as for Innis, human activity is that of the social individual responding to, acting on, and transforming the natural environment.

Reflection on and acceptance of the natural environment (including other individuals and systems as part of nature) constitutes one moment of the human relation to nature, which is manifested in social *mythology* (including science, as a hypothetical system of belief or basis for action). The drive for control and transformation of nature constitutes the other moment, which is principally mani-fested in the development of *technology*. Moreover, insofar as individuals consciously or mythologically view others and themselves as a part of nature, the same impulse underlies the articulation of modes of social organization and of self-control. "Technology" in Innis' and Marx's analyses refers to both communication technology (including transportation and information transmission technology) and production technology (including industrial productive and military technology).[4] What is characteristic of both of their approaches, in these terms, is that their analyses assume the existance of continuous dialectical interaction between these elements of open economic systems. Central to Marx's approach is the concept of the mode of production, which is constituted by the "forces of production" (including natural forces, technologies of production and communication, and humans in society); and by the social "relations of production," which develop over time with the forces of production, communication technology, and social mythology.

Similarly, from the outset of his studies Innis adopted an ecological framework in which the interaction of geographical, technical, political-economic, and cultural or mythological factors was assumed to be central to the process of social-economic development. The introductory chapters to his studies of the fur trade and of the cod fisheries, for example, are composed of detailed ecological discussions of the life and mating habits of the beaver and of the cod as an essential prerequisite for understanding the influence of the former in Canada in producing a centralized constitutional system in relation to extensive spatial development involving a capital-intensive defense and supply network constructed along lines determined by the east-west orientation of a continental river system penetrable by the St Lawrence; and of the latter in promoting a decentralized constitutional pattern related to the small scale and low capital requirements of a maritime enterprise conducted along an extensive, principally north-south coastline and based on an abundant and localized staple produced for final consumption in a wide range of markets accessible by low cost maritime transport fostering commercial enterprise.

The ecological character of Innis' mode of analysis is rarely so apparent as in his observation that "The timber trade, based on [Imperial] preferences and the specific gravity of white pine, hastened settlement in Upper Canada." Just as the Zen Buddhist suggests that we can recreate or reconstruct the universe by *fully* understanding a single leaf, so we can understand much of Innis' analysis (and much of Canadian history) by fully comprehending the relationships implicit in this epigram.

Both Marx and Innis have been accused of technological (and, in the case of Innis, geographical) determinism. There are passages, particularly the epigrammatic ones, in the writings of both which would appear to lend credence to this view. Marx's formula, "The hand-mill gives you society with the feudal lord; the steam-mill, society with the industrial capitalist," has been a favorite target of unsympathetic critics. The same can be said of the following passage from the first volume of *Capital*: "My standpoint, from which the evolution of the economic formation of society is viewed as a process of natural history, can less than any other make the individual responsible for relations whose creature he socially remains, however much he may subjectively raise himself above them." In related fashion, passages of Innis' such as the following extended metaphor appear to warrant a charge of "determinism":

> Into the moulds of the commercial period, set by successive heavier and cheaper commodities, and determined by geographic factors, such as the St Lawrence River and the Precambrian formation; by cultural considerations, such as the English and French languages; by technology, such as the canoe and the raft; by business organization, such as the Northwest Company and Liverpool timber firms; and by political institutions peculiar to France and England, were poured the rivers of iron and steel in the form of steamships and railways which hardened into modern capitalism.

Yet even in these passages, where the deterministic element is apparently most obvious, it is clear that neither Marx nor Innis is concerned to establish a narrowly deterministic monocausality; rather, both intend to establish the natural-historical forces which *determine*, or establish bounds on the feasible range of, human social-economic activity. In fact, these passages, interpreted sensitively in the context of the overall *corpus* of each writer, constitute prime examples of the materialist ecological orientation of both.

The third principal affinity between their work is of particular significance for the future development of Canadian political economy. Both Innis and Marx were preoccupied with the role of communications, including media of transportation and of information-transmission, in the development of open economic systems. In the case of Innis, this preoccupation is readily apparent. His first major study was an analysis of the Canadian Pacific Railway; his subsequent historical studies of major staple exports in the development of the Canadian political economy involved a continuing concern with the interaction between geographical factors, communications media, cultural factors, and the ecological characteristics of particular staples; his theory of rigidities or biases as determinants of the course of system development depended on the systematic character of communications processes, and on the phenomena of overhead costs, excess capacity and increasing returns to scale implied by the nature of communication activities; and his principal works after 1940 were directly concerned with the interaction between the development of communications and the political-economic development of Western civilization.

Marx's preoccupation with communication is perhaps less immediately evident, but is nonetheless equally pervasive. The second volume of *Capital* (which deals with the process of circulation of capital), for example, is a major study in the political economy of communication under capitalism. Moreover, Marx's analysis of the Commodity at the outset of Volume I of *Capital* is from one standpoint a brilliant logical-historical analysis of the semiology of money. Innis commented on the limitations of the price-system as a medium of communication as follows:

> It has been dependent on a widespread diffusion of mathematics, i.e. in the ability to make change, and on an intensive study of its mathematical character. The compilation and dissemination of information as to prices has been dependent on the effectiveness of communication in the newspaper, the radio, and other media. It operates more intensively in areas where

information can be quickly disseminated—in urban rather than rural areas. It is more effective in allocating resources at some times than others. It requires constant attention on the part of accountants, lawyers and other professional groups.

Similarly, Marx noted that

> Since . . . the autonomization of the world market . . . increases with the development of monetary relations (exchange value) and vice versa, since the general bond and all-round interdependence in production and consumption increase together with the independence and indifference of the consumers and producers to one another; since this contradiction leads to crises, etc. . . . efforts are made to overcome it: institutions emerge whereby each individual can acquire information about the activity of all others and attempt to adjust his own accordingly, e.g., lists of current prices, rates of exchange, interconnections between those active in commerce through the mails, telegrpahs, etc. (the means of communication of course grow at the same time). (This means that, although the total supply and demand are independent of the actions of each individual, everyone attempts to inform himself about them, and this knowledge then reacts back in practice on the total supply and demand. . . .)

In related fashion, Marx observed in a paradoxical but typically brilliant passage that "A relatively thinly populated country, with well-developed means of communication, has a denser population than a more numerously populated country, with badly-developed means of communication; and in this sense the Northern States of the American Union, for instance, are more thickly populated than India."

Marx's concern with communication, moreover, was not confined to media of transportation alone. As he remarked in an apparently esoteric comment on renaissance English, which in fact illuminates the medieval class-structure of England: "In English writers of the seventeenth century we frequently find 'worth' in the sense of value in use, and 'value' in the sense of exchange-value. This is quite in accordance with the spirit of a language that likes to use a Teu-

tonic word for the actual thing, and a Romance word for its reflection." Elsewhere, Marx explored the relation of artistic creation to the historical development of the forces of production and communication in terms which would have been congenial to Innis:

> Let us take, for example, the relation of Greek art, and that of Shakespeare, to the present time. . . . Is the conception of nature and of social relations which underlies Greek imagination and therefore Greek [art] possible when there are self-acting mules, railways, locomotives and electric telegraphs? What is a Vulcan compared with Roberts and Co., Jupiter compared with the lightning conductor, and Hermes compared with the *Credit mobilier*? . . . What becomes of Fama side by side with Printing House Square? . . .
>
> Regarded from another aspect: is Achilles possible when powder and shot have been invented? And is the *Iliad* possible at all when the printing press and even printing machines exist? Is it not inevitable that with the emergence of the press bar the singing and the telling and the muse cease, that is the conditions necessary for epic poetry disappear?

The importance of Innis' and Marx's mutual concern with the role of communications processes for Canadian political economy is twofold. First, communications, in the technological, organizational and cultural aspects, were seen by both theorists as central determinants of what Innis would have described as "the structure of spatial-temporal relations," or "the capacity to maintain control over space and time (spatial extent and temporal duration)," within economic systems; and of what Marx would have described as "the preconditions of reproduction" of economic systems. Second, both regarded the sphere of communications as constituting a strategic link between what Marx referred to as the forces and relations of production, and between the economic base and the superstructure. Insofar as communications activities in advanced capitalist economies constitute roughly half of GNP as conventionally measured, and insofar as neoclassical economic theory is singularly ill-equipped to analyze the sphere of communications, the analyses of communication of Innis and Marx are of considerable practical importance for Canadian political economy.

The tenor of the argument to this point may have given the impression of an attempt to conflate the analyses of Innis and Marx, and to suggest that there are no differences or incompatibilities between their approaches. Such an impression would be incorrect. There are significant differences between their approaches, and the resolution of those differences is an important task, although one which is beyond the scope of the present study. In concluding, however, it is perhaps worth suggesting some of the principal differences between Innis and Marx, and some of the ways in which each of their approaches illuminates and extends that of the other.

At the outset, it is important to recall that Innis' political stance was that of a radical conservative, whereas Marx's was that of a radical revolutionary. Hence, even when their analyses (allowing for the spatial and temporal distance which separated them) led them to similar conclusions, their attitudes towards those conclusions often differed. The phenomena analyzed in the conclusion of Innis' "Plea for Time," which was a plea simultaneously for historical consciousness, the oral dialectic, and the university tradition, in response to the increasing mechanization and commercialization of thought, for example, would likely have been regarded by Marx as a necessary concomitant of the expansion of capital and of the extension of capitalist relations of production, while at the same time Marx would likely have acknowledged their significance as manifestations of the contradictions of advanced monopoly capitalism.

A second point of significance is that the level of analysis of most of Innis' major writings differed from that adopted by Marx in, for instance, *Capital*. Innis' writings were principally and explicitly historical in character, and at many points the theoretical basis of an analysis is only implicit; on the other hand, *Capital*, despite its wealth of historical detail, is principally a theoretical work. It would be more appropriate to compare many of Innis' writings with Marx's *Eighteenth Brumaire or his writings on the US Civil War than with Capital* itself.

Given these qualifications, however, it can be suggested that Marx's principal contributions to the reformulation and extension of Innis' approach will be found in the central role Marx ascribed to class antagonisms and class struggle in the development of economic systems; in his analysis of the "laws of motion" of capitalism as a mode of production; and in the conceptual tools (such as the concepts of "exploitation" and of "surplus value," and the notion of capital as "self-expanding value," and as neither a *fund* nor a *stock of means of production*, but rather *at base* as a *social relation* presupposing free wage-labor) which he developed to ground his analysis. These aspects of political-economic development were not fully dealt with by Innis, although they implicitly have a significant place in Innis' studies from *The Cod Fisheries* onward.

On the other hand, Innis' theoretical framework is more important for the extension of Marx's analysis than has perhaps so far been appreciated. For Canadian political economists, the fact that most of Innis' historical studies were focused directly on Canada, a marginal "country of new settlement," rather than on a metropolitan center such as the England of Marx's time, is of obvious significance, particularly insofar as this focus led Innis to analyze more deeply than Marx had the forms of dependency which characterize colonial relations, from the standpoint of colonial margins.

Yet in the longer view, this element is possibly less important than the specific theoretical advances made by Innis, which contribute to the resolution of crucial lacunae in Marxist theory. In particular, Innis' analysis of the role of fixed capital, indivisibilities, overhead costs and excess capacity in economic development is basic to an understanding of Marx's "realization problem" and to the interpretation of his concept of the "organic composition of capital" and of the time-structure of production, and (through both) to the theory of the interrelations between the development of capitalism and the emergence of the nation state.

In addition, Innis' analysis of communications in economic history, which was conducted more systematically and on a broader scale than Marx's, offers basic insights into the dialectic between the forces and relations of production which were not captured by Marx. Innis' emphasis on the mode of ideological production and reproduction, and his focus on the character of media, or on the forces of ideological production, and on the classes which sustained and were sustained by them, however provide the core of a materialist interpretation of the relations between the economic base of a society and its superstructure which complements Marx's analysis in several vital respects.

A full incorporation of Innis' analysis into contemporary Marxist thought would require a recognition that the "forces of production" of any historical political-economic system comprehend not only the population, the means of material production, and the resource base, but also the communications media or networks which sustain and are sustained by that system: the forces of ideological reproduction, and the transport media which are conditioned by and determine the structure of spatial-temporal relations between individuals and classes within the system. Innis' analysis of communication makes possible an extension of Marx's materialist concept of economic history by producing not a naive form of economic or technological determinism, but rather a broader and more sophisticated concept of the material bases of class formation, antagonisms, and realignments over time.

This extension is of considerable importance for Marxist analysis in numerous ways. First, it enhances considerably the analysis of class formation and of class hegemony, particularly in pre-capitalist economic formations, where, for example, the hegemonic role of priestly (including monastic) orders or classes has been more significant than under capitalism. Second, it permits a readier recognition and incorporation of the role of communications media, in relation to their systemic or indivisible character, in necessitating concerted support, from the Imperial Roman road network, through the English Navy, the *Pax Britannica* and the continental extension of North American railroads, to the present support of the Penn Central system and Lockheed by the US State. In this extended temporal framework, the historical economic role of the State, particularly in the development of communication networks essential for imperial control, as abundantly documented by Innis, may also be seen as an integral element in the development of finance-capitalism and of monopoly capitalism.

Finally, and perhaps most significantly, Innis' theoretical framework (since it is concerned, as has been indicated above, with a less abstract and more historically-oriented level of analysis than characterizes Marx's major works) provides one with tools—such as the dialectically related concepts of "monopolies of knowledge and monopolies of force" and of "control over space and control over time"—which are not closed in character, but rather serve to direct historical categorical articulation.

On the basis of the foregoing discussion, it can be proposed that the work of neither Marx nor Innis is sufficient in itself to provide an adequate analytical basis for the future development of Canadian political economy, and that the work of both must be taken into account. The relations between Innis and Marx considered above are at best an introduction to the problems posed in the form of the five theses put forward at the outset of the study. The evidence adduced in support of those propositions, however, suggests that Canadian political economists can ill afford to overlook these crucial intellectual ties in future studies.[5]

NOTES

[1]Veblen's emphasis on the significance of "marginality," which was developed particularly clearly at the social level in Chapter II of *Imperial Germany and the Industrial Revolution* and at the individual level in the projected autobiography of "The Intellectual Pre-eminence of Jews in Modern Europe," was a significant influence in Innis' subsequent articulation of the center-margin dialectic in terms which took him away from Veblen toward the dialectical analysis of Marx and Hegel.

[2]In one sense, it is not surprising that Innis' debts to Smith relate more to the sphere of circulation than to the sphere of production, since his first two major studies on the Canadian Pacific Railway and the fur trade in Canada were for obvious reasons grounded in the sphere of commodity circulation; the history of the cod fisheries is integrally linked to the development of communications and export markets; and both gold-mining and the pulp and paper industry occupy peculiar and strategic positions within the system of commodity exchange.

[3]In particular, the implications of the time-structure of production, fixed capital, indivisibilities, overhead costs and excess capacity for the development of rigidities, innovation, monopolies, and the State are developed systematically by Innis with a degree of logical-historical detail which far exceeds that accomplished by Marx before his death.

[4]There are certain heuristic advantages in distinguishing between "production" and "communication" technology at this level of abstraction, insofar as the distinction relates to Marx's analytical distinction between the spheres of production and of circulation and to Innis' emphasis on communication as a principal determinant of the spatial and temporal structure of open economic systems. Clearly, however, the two forms of technology interpenetrate, and must be interrelated in any historical analysis.

[5]I want to thank Leo Casey, David Mole, Abraham Rotstein, Tom Walkom, and Andrew Watson for analyses, discussions, comments and questions which forced me to rethink my own understanding of the relationships between Innis an Marx. My debt to W. T. Easterbrook is that of any student to an inspiring teacher, but in the present case it is also much more. With any luck at all, the above-named colleagues would be among the first to establish a distance between themselves and the conclusion of the present study, at least on first reading.

THE STAPLE THEORY REVISITED
Mel Watkins

The substantial contribution of Canadian economic historians, and others, to the study of Canadian economic history is the staples approach. Indeed, it is Canada's most, if not only, distinctive contribution to political economy, and the occasion of the formal recognition of the existence of the latter by the Canadian Political Science Association is an appropriate time to re-examine the staples approach.

Let me begin by reference to a previous paper on this topic published in 1963.[1] That paper attempted to pull out of more diffuse historical writings, notably by Innis, an explicit theory of economic growth appropriate to Canada and other "new" countries. At least in retrospect, its contribution was to give legitimacy to the staples approach–by showing that it was respectable within orthodox economics–but this was bought at the high price of constraining the theory to the very limiting paradigm of orthodox economics in general and the theory of international trade in particular.

In revisiting the theory,[2] it seems appropriate to review in particular the literature that has appeared since 1963 that is of *analytical* interest.[3] That literature can be conveniently classified under four heads: (1) quantitative testing of the staple theory under the influence of the new economic history; (2) studies on the closely related topics of foreign ownership and the structure of Canadian industry, to the extent that they are concerned with the evident bias toward staple export, on the one hand, and a retarded industrial structure on the other hand; (3) historical and contemporary analysis of resource policy, with particular respect to the further processing of staples, the appropriation of economic rents from staple production, and the North; (4) work based on the Marxist paradigm.

The bias of the paper is toward the Marxist paradigm. This reflects the straightforward fact that, in quantitative terms and, in my opinion, in qualitative terms as well, it is scholars working out of the Marxist paradigm who are now predominant in the literature on the staples approach. This presumably is the result of a general resurgence of scholarly interest in Marxism that is, of course, not confined to Canada.

That Marxists should be attracted specifically to the staple approach is wholly understandable and should give no offense.[4] While its leading proponents were certainly liberals, at least in the beginning it was clearly political economy and at least in the hands of Innis it was about dependence–and these latter two characteristics are, of course, central to Marxists. Innis in particular was a liberal with a difference, who saw the dark underside and the gross contradictions and this makes him susceptible to an approach that specializes in such matters.[5]

* * *

Beginning in the late '50s and thereafter, the postwar quantitative bias of American scholarship spread from economics into economic history, and the resulting new economic history penetrated the study of Canadian economic history in some part through the work done by American scholars and Canadian-born scholars resident in the U.S. The latter is indicative of the difficulties of transplanting the new phenomenon to Canada and suggests that its contribution is likely to be second-order. Nonetheless, worthwhile contributions have been made, directly by Bertram[6] and Caves,[7] and indirectly by Chambers and Gordon[8] in a joint article so scandalous as to compel reasoned defense of the staples approach.[9]

Bertram's first article, appearing simultaneously with my own in 1963, demonstrates the gradual but steady filling in of the manufacturing sector around the impetus generated by staple exports. The two articles have much in common in terms of giving not only the staples approach but the Canadian staples-oriented economy a relatively clean bill of health, but Bertram goes further in the second respect. Drache has recently suggested[10] that there are not one but two (non-Marxist) theories of capitalist development based on the staple theory, the steady-progress view of Mackintosh and the dependency view of Innis. Bertram, and the other writers in the new economic history, opt wholeheartedly for the more laundered Mackintosh approach.[11] MacDonald in his critique of Naylor[12] (of which more below) makes an analogous distinction between two branches of the staples approach: first, metropolitanism, or the commercial penetration of the hinterland positively viewed, as evidenced by (the early) Creighton and Ouellet; and, second, the entirely different principle that a dominant trade might organize an economy inexorably around itself and lead to stagnation. MacDonald puts my 1963 article in the second category—as well as the writings of Fowke, Pentland, Dubuc and Ryerson.

Caves' first article enhanced the legitimacy of the staple model for orthodox economists by showing its formal similarity with the unlimited-supply-of-labour model in the literature on economic development, that is, both were "vent for surplus" models of trade and growth rather than models based on growth through more efficient allocation of an existing stock of employed factors of production. Caves focusses narrowly on the linkages of the staple sector to other sectors, while urbanely noting in passing that there was "of course, the whole field of possible influences of the pattern of industry upon social and political development" (112). He sensibly concludes that the staple model, at least in its simple form, "probably yields no normative conclusions" (113) and that both vent-for-surplus models "received their respective laurels and brickbats as a source of guidance for policy on the basis of what the linkages have or have not done in a particular case" (114).

But he is very much of the Mackintosh cast of mind. As well as staple-induced growth, there will be "an underlying steady swell of neoclassical growth" such that "export-based growth may explain a large part of the *variation* in the aggregate rate of growth . . . whether or not it explains a large part of the average level of that growth rate" (102). Following Baldwin,[13] he recognizes the possibility of staple production having unfavourable effects on the character of factor supplies and the resulting distribution of income and hence on the composition of final demand, but dismisses it as improbable: "The staple version includes no . . . likely appearance of a mal-distribution of income, especially if the rents accruing to natural resources (in the staples region) are allotted somewhat randomly among the erstwhile workers and capitalist elements of the population . . . [A] happy partnership of immigrant labor and capital is further cemented by windfall gains to the fortunate finders of natural resources" (115). While Caves is basically correct with respect to the overall distribution of income, his facile comments on rents—in both this, and to a lesser extent, his second paper—denied him an important insight that others have shown can be derived from the liberal paradigm, and that has less happy implications for generating sustained growth (see below).

In the best—or worst—tradition of the new economic history, Robert Fogel having allegedly demonstrated the limited contribution of railroads to American economic growth, Chambers and Gordon set out to demonstrate that the opening of the Canadian West, or the wheat boom, had likewise made a limited contribution to Canadian economic growth. Had they succeeded, the staple approach would indeed be in disarray, but, in fact, they failed miserably. They asked the wrong, or at best distinctly second order, question, that is, what contribution did the export of wheat make to the growth of income *per capita* rather than what contribution did it make to the growth of aggregate national income. Insofar as the staple theory has always been about understanding the successive opening up of the country, or increasing the stock of land, with resultant inflows of labour and capital, or, increases in *their* stocks, rather than about re-allocating fixed endowments of factors, Chambers and Gordon, whatever they were doing, were hardly testing any known version of the staple theory. (This makes it all the more unfortunate that the Canadian edition of Samuelson's *Economics*–though Canadianized by Scott, a specialist in resource economics–insists on taking Chambers and Gordon seriously.[14])

To compound their problems, Chambers and Gordon appear not only to have misspecified the model, but to have handled the data badly. Both Bertram and Caves make new quantitative estimates which show wheat to have, in fact, made a major contribution to Canadian economic growth. Bertram confines himself narrowly to quantitative testing, but Caves shows that the staple theory, depending on the staple, does not necessarily yield easy growth. If, because of scale economies in staple production, there are large capital requirements for staple enterprises, there will be "extraregional or foreign borrowing (with no incentive for local saving), absentee ownership and no contribution to the supply of local entrepreneurial talent or profit available for local reinvestment" (433-34). On a closely related point, he notes that the drawing in of undiscovered resources vents a surplus and creates a rent (408), and that "where natural-resource rents accrue as profits to foreign entrepreneurs, the critical question for national welfare is the extent to which they are recaptured in taxation" (436). Nevertheless, he makes the curious observation in a footnote that "The extent to which export-led growth possesses any special virtues in furthering sustainable growth remains to be demonstrated, but any that it possesses seems un-

likely to derive from the creation of rents" (409).

In sum, then, the new economic history, which has been a central obsession of economic historians in recent years, to the extent it poses real questions has upheld the validity of the staples approach–though making little or no contribution to our theoretical understanding. The staple theory has survived the worse onslaughts of Americanization and for that reason alone must be seen as hardy and genuinely Canadian.

* * *

In the postwar period, and notably in the past two decades, a very substantial literature has emerged on the structure of Canadian industry and on the closely related topic of foreign ownership. The concern of this literature has not been with the staple theory *per se*– and therefore there will be no exhaustive review of it here–but it is necessary to enquire to what extent that literature sheds light on the viability of the staple theory, and to what extent the staple theory might shed some light on the topics of industrial structure and foreign ownership.

The historic tendency for staple production to take place under the aegis of foreign capital has persisted, indeed accelerated. In the first substantive study of foreign ownership in the postwar period, Hugh G.J. Aitken's *American Capital and Canadian Resources* in 1961, that simple fact was the central theme. Unfortunately, it has tended to be obscured in most subsequent studies–Safarian,[15] the Watkins Report,[16] the Gray Report[17]–but it does figure prominently in Levitt.[18] The most straightforward explanation, which requires no stepping outside the liberal paradigm, is the high American demand for Canadian staples and the high capital-intensity of the new staples which create an advantage for the typically large established American company over a potential Canadian company. Put differently, the staples approach enables us to "explain" the continuing and rising level of foreign ownership of staple production.

But that begs the question of why there is *so much* foreign ownership, not only in the staple sector but in the rest of the economy too, and particularly in manufacturing proper. Putting aside the tendency of Canadian economists to claim it does not really matter, and therefore presumably needs no explanation, those who have wished to explain it have ultimately fallen back for the most part on a Schumpeterian-like argument about the inadequacies of Canadian entrepreneurship; this is true even of as perceptive a writer as Levitt. This, of course, is something less than a satisfactory answer, since it merely poses the question of the cause of the deficiency of Canadian entrepreneurship. As we shall see shortly, the first serious answer is offered by Naylor,[19] but from the Marxist paradigm.

The more conventional staples approach nevertheless contains some insights, having primarily to do with the tendency toward an excessive preoccupation with staple production that inheres in staple production itself, e.g., the sucking of domestic capital into the staple sector, notwithstanding the predominance of foreign capital, and the propensity of government to see staple production as a panacea for economic growth and neglect the working out of a proper industrial strategy. We are unlikely to be able to improve on Innis' cryptic formulation:

> Energy has been directed toward the exploitation of staple products and the tendency has been cumulative . . . Energy in the colony was drawn into the production of the staple commodity both directly and indirectly in the production facilities promoting production. Agriculture, industry, transportation, trade, finance, and governmental activities tend to become subordinate to the production of the staple for a more highly specialized manufacturing community.[20]

Work on the structure of industry proper, notwithstanding many useful insights about the miniature replica effect, has concerned itself *ad nauseum* with the Canadian tariff as *the* source of the problem. This begs the question as to the "source" of the tariff and the answer has tended, as before, quickly to degenerate into an appeal to the inadequacies of Canadian businessmen. With respect to the narrower mechanisms of the staple theory, Naylor reminds us of one that was once well-known in the literature, namely, that the National Policy, protectionist though it was, generated a flood of government revenue that

greatly facilitated the building, and over-building, of infrastructure for staple production.[21]

The failure of a resource base developed to meet the exigencies of staple export to lead to an industrial complex—which is, after all, the heart of the matter—has been ably described by a non-economist, Pierre L. Bourgault, in a study not for the Economic Council but the Science Council:

> We are the world's largest producer of nickel, but we are net importers of stainless steel and manufactured nickel products . . . ; we are the world's second largest producer of aluminum, but we import it in its more sophisticated forms such as . . . precision aluminum parts for use in aircraft; we are the world's largest exporters of pulp and paper, but we import much of our fine paper and virtually all of the highly sophisticated paper, such as backing for photographic film; we are one of the principle sources of platinum, but it is all exported for refining and processing and reimported in finished forms; we are large exporters of natural gas and petroleum, but we are net importers of petrochemicals; and although we are the world's foremost exporter of raw asbestos fibres, we are net importers of manufactured asbestos products.[22]

Neither orthodox studies of industrial structure nor a staple theory focused microscopically on linkages seems quite to come to terms with this matter; we must either retreat to Innis or move forward to Naylor.

* * *

In the area of resource policy proper, two names stand out, Kierans and Nelles. A long-neglected theme in the economic analysis of staple production, but one that grows logically out of the liberal paradigm, is that intramarginal "land" commands its own reward, or economic rent. The relevant questions are: What is the size of the rents? Who gets them? What difference does their distribution make to sustained economic growth? Kierans' pioneering study on the metal-mining industry in Manitoba[23] shows that the rents are large relative to the wage-bill, and that they disproportionately accrue to capital which is frequently foreign. Clearly, the conventional focus on linkages has obscured an important point, that is, that the prospects for sustained and more diversified development in the wake of non-renewable resource exploitation are decreased to the extent that rents, or "superprofits," are appropriated by the resource-capitalists, and particularly if they are foreign capitalists.

Without respect to the nationality of capital, the rents, to the extent to which they are retained by the corporations, tend to remain locked into resource exploitation and eventually leave the region that had the resources. This is so because resource companies are generally not diversified outside the resource sector and are increasingly large multinationals prepared to exploit resources anywhere in the world. To the extent that the rents accrue, immediately or ultimately, to shareholders as dividends or capital gains on shares, the staple-producing country benefit –specifically, that small portion of its population that owns most of the shares–when the capital is domestic but not when it is foreign. To the extent governments in the staple-producing country appropriate the rents through taxation or public ownership, the country benefits–though the nature of the benefit depends on how governments spend the additional revenue and/or reduce other forms of taxation. Finally, regionally, or locally, the major consequence of losing the rents from non-renewable resources is the well-known Canadian phenomenon of the ghost town.[24]

The addition of an analysis of economic rent to orthodox staple theory has the important result of showing how staple production can create a "blockage" to diversified development, that is, by denying the potential, create "underdevelopment."[25] In effect, the liberal paradigm can be made to yield a version of the staple approach that explains phenomena strikingly similar to what is yielded by the Marxist paradigm in which the analogous mechanism is the outward drain of surplus.

Nelles' massive study of Ontario government policy in the new staple industries of forest products, mining and hydro-electricity over almost a century[26] is the most important descriptive work done within the context of the staple approach since Rich's monumental study of the Hudson's Bay Company.[27] He eschews economic theory, but his central concern with "the manufacturing condition" as Ontario's "little National Policy" is evidence of how staple production, at its best, leads to more of the same–in the sense of more value added within the resource sector–rather than causing a quantum leap into a diversified industrial economy under domestic control.

The Canadian North, as the new and last "frontier," is also attracting increasing attention from historians working basically around the theme of resource policy. The major writings of Zaslow[28] and Rea[29] are mostly valuable for their great detail. Rea uses a simple staple model that focuses on linkages and ignores rent. Neither shows any real grasp of the economy of the native people, and both fall prey–and Rea explicitly so[30]–to the dual economy thesis, thereby missing the point that non-renewable resource exploitation sets up mechanisms which create underdevelopment for native people. Fumoleau on the history of the Treaties[31] and Asch on the economic history of the Slavey people[32] correct the bias, as does research sponsored by the Indian Brotherhood of the N.W.T., which is articulated around the theme of the right to alternative community-based development.[33]

* * *

In the last decade, a mere handful of Marxist writers in Canada has suddenly been joined by a small army of younger scholars.[34] At least from the perspective of the analytics of the staple approach, by far the most important contribution is Naylor's two-volume *History of Canadian Business* in the critical period from Confederation to World War 1. Indeed, his work is, in my opinion, the most important historical writing on Canada since the early Innis and the early Creighton–and I am aware of what high praise that constitutes.

As we have already seen, liberal scholarship, in attempting to explain the dependent and structurally underdeveloped nature of the Canadian economy has been able to do no better than appeal to the deficiencies of Canadian entrepreneurship. Naylor saves us from this theoretical quagmire by centering our attention on the nature of capital, and specifically on the distinction between merchant capital and industrial capital and the difficulty of transforming an economy dominated by the first into an economy dominated by the second. From a contemporary perspective, his concern is with "the overexpansion of resource industries relative to manufacturing, and the drainage of surplus income as service payments for foreign investment instead of its being used to generate new capital formation within Canada" (I, xix).

The ties to the staple approach are obvious. Naylor writes:

Two fundamental structural attributes of the Canadian economy in the period from 1867 to 1914 must be made central to analysis. First, it was a colony, politically and economically. In terms of commercial patterns it was a staple-extracting hinterland oriented toward serving metropolitan markets from which, in turn, it received finished goods. In such a structure, any economic advance in the hinterland accrues to the benefit of the metropole and perpetuates the established division of labour . . . Canada's commercial and financial system grew up geared to the international movement of staples, rather than to abetting secondary processing for domestic markets. . . . Canada's social structure and therefore the proclivities of its entrepreneurial class, reflected and reinforced its innate colonialism. The political and economic elite were men associated with the staple trades, with the international flow of commodities and of the capital that complemented the commodity movements. . . . A second trait of the economy of the period, in part derivative from the first, was that it had only begun to make the difficult transition from a mercantile agrarian base to an industrial one. Wealth was accumulated in commercial activities and tended to remain locked up in commerce. Commercial capital resisted the transformation into industrial capital except under specific conditions in certain industries, in favour of remaining invested in traditional staple-oriented activities [I, 3-4].

In short, the necessary origins of Canada as a staple-producer are perpetuated because of the nature of the capitalist class that emerges, and re-emerges, out of the staple trades that spring into being to serve the needs of the metropole.

Naylor, like Innis before him, provides a wealth of detail to support his very original contribution to Canadian historiography. Suffice it here to note some of the more important specific mechanisms which Naylor cites as to how staple production leads to the over-development of the staple industries and the underdevelopment of manufacturing. The capital requirements for infrastructure to service the staple trades absorbed domestic as well as foreign capital and retarded industrial capital formation (I, 15). Regionally, the Maritime Provinces were drained of surplus to finance Central Canada's development objectives in the West, thereby retarding their indigenous industrial development,[35] while Québécois industrial entrepreneurship was submerged under a wave of anglophone-controlled mergers (I, 15). The Canadian banking system, and Canadian financial institutions in general, grew out of merchants' capital involved in the staple trades (I, 110) and took a form appropriate to facilitating the movement of staples from Canada to external markets rather than promoting secondary industries (I, 67). The National Policy was a policy of industrialization-by-invitation and attracted foreign capital, and thus foreign ownership under the aegis of the multinational corporation, rather than encouraging domestic capital, which would have strengthened industrial capital relative to merchant capital within Canada and thereby facilitated a transformation out of a staples structure. Railways were built to facilitate staple-production and only incidentally to create industrialization, and their operation favoured international trade over inter-regional trade. And so on.

For Naylor, the consequence was that by the end of his period, the Canadian economy was locked into "the staple trap" (II, 283). His model, then, is a Marxist version of the Innisian version.

It might be thought that the Marxist paradigm necessarily yields a dependency version of the staple model, but that is apparently not certain. There are hints in the scholarly literature—not to mention vast amounts of diatribe in the sectarian literature—that there is a steady-progress version, in this case toward the creation of a viable national capitalist class that has come to rule Canada. Ryerson, writing pre-Naylor, emphasizes the slow but steady growth of industrial capital out of merchant capital in the nineteenth century.[36] MacDonald, in his critique of Naylor, insists that "a close look at the evidence . . . shows that mercantile and industrial capital were inseparable . . . " (266), but he wrote without benefit of the much closer look of Naylor's two volumes and hence he, and those who rely on the *Canadian Historical Review* for their knowledge of Canadian economic history, risk being the victims of instant obsolescence. It is not at all clear what MacDonald intends us to believe about the nature of the Canadian capitalist class, so it may be that he is of the dependency school and rejects Naylor's explanation without choosing to give us any indication of what he would put in its place. But from what he does tell us, he seriously underestimates the extent of American control of the Canadian economy by 1914,[37] and profoundly misunderstands the nature of the multinational corporation.[38] A reasonable inference therefore is that he is biased against the dependency version of the staple model.

On this murky, but important, question mention must also be made of the work of Wallace Clement.[39] He understands that Canada is a staple economy and accepts Naylor's argument on the distinction between merchant capital and industrial capital and the tendency for the former to be Canadian and the latter foreign. Nevertheless, he concludes that "the Canadian economy remains controlled in large part by a set of families who have been in the past and still remain at the core of the Canadian economy" (150), and that the split between the commercial and industrial capitalist classes "does not mean the total [Canadian] bourgeoisie is not powerful—indeed, it may be more powerful because of the continental context" (335). On the basis of the evidence presented in his book, and so much other published evidence to the contrary, Clement's views are unconvincing.[40]

We can look forward to further controversy around Naylor's seminal arguments, in the hope that it will illuminate whether there is one or two Marxist versions of the staple theory. For the moment, it seems to me that the dependency-version will, in any event, win hands down.

So much for the capitalists themselves;

what of the nature of the state that emerges out of staple production? And what is the likelihood of it showing the way out of the staple trap? Now, to transcend staple production, that is, to escape subservience to the rising American empire, would surely have required a state prepared to go well beyond the limitations of the actual National Policy.[41] But the state itself is almost a by-product of the exigencies of staple production, an argument central to Innis' analysis and now to Naylor's.

For Innis, both the Act of Union and Confederation were essentially dictated by the need to raise capital, first for canals and then railways, to facilitate the movement of staples. Creighton's *British North America at Confederation* brilliantly demonstrated the latter, and the implications for the post-Confederation period have been skillfully outlined by Dubuc.[42] For Naylor, Confederation and the National Policy reflects a state and a state-policy created by the merchant capitalist class in its own image. If anything of analytic substance remains to be said on this matter, it may be that more attention should be devoted to the process by which the Canadian state successively suppressed re-emerging domestic capital within the staple sector itself, and within the manufacturing sector, in the interest of foreign capital.[43]

While none of the other new Marxist writers have matched Naylor in depth and breadth, some significant analytical gains have been made in fleshing out a Marxist version of the staple theory. The latter would require the recasting of the staple theory as a theory of class formation; this paper is only a tentative first step in that direction.

If we are to begin at the beginning, we must enquire as to the fate of the aboriginal population. How, in the most fundamental sense, do they fit into the staple theory? Innis makes the essential point, at least implicitly, when he writes "Fundamentally the civilization of North America is the civilization of Europe . . . " and again, "Canada has remained fundamentally a product of Europe."[44] The Indian way-of-life, indeed the Indian himself, was swept aside. Only in the era of the fur-trade was the Indian functional to the Euro-Canadian, and everywhere in the long-run the fur trade retreated in the face of settlement and was ultimately obliterated by it. The Indian was made irrelevant. This functional irrelevancy is dramatically demonstrated in the very terminology that is used to characterize Canada—and other like cases such as the United States, Australia and New Zealand. Their aboriginal populations notwithstanding, they are called "new countries" or "empty lands" or "areas of recent settlement" or "undeveloped areas"—or simply "the frontier."

The analytical significance of this point can be appreciated if we imagine a very opposite situation, namely, that the aboriginal population, which we would have to assume was much larger, had not been easily pushed to the margins of society, geographically and socially. Rather than being a "colony of settlement" Canada might have been a "colony of conquest" analogous to those of Asia and Africa. Or it might have been a "white settler colony" proper, like the Union of South Africa or Rhodesia. Or it might have been a mixed case as abound in Central and South America. In any event, Canadian development would have been different and much more difficult. A pre-capitalist indigenous population that could not be ignored would be reduced to under-development, and either slowly converted to the capitalist mode of production or contained by massive repression and discrimination. We would not have our very high *average* standard of living; though the European stock—if it had not yet been turfed out—might be doing very well. Methodologically, there would be no special case amenable to the literal staple theory.

The aboriginal populations by being separated from the means of production have been reduced to the status of an underclass or lumpenproletariat. The historic process is outlined by Elias;[45] Brody shows the process at work today with respect to the Inuit.[46]

The aboriginal people were pushed aside; settlers poured in from the Old World; a class of capitalists emerged in the staples-region; it created a state structure and a "national policy" in its own image. What remains? Depending on the staple, the creation either of a class of commodity producers or a class of wage-earners. The distinction hinges on whether the staple activity is a trade or an industry. The great staple *trades* of cod, fur and wheat have been extensively researched, and wheat has been explicitly analyzed in Marxist terms in C.B. Macpherson's classic *Democracy in Alberta*.

The independent commodity producer is a capitalist, because he uses capital; he is not a wage-earner and does not himself employ wage labour. The important question is not whether independent commodity production exists as a mode of production, but whether it is a dominant or subordinate mode. As a mode of production, it coexists with merchant capital and increases its sway. Hence, both in its own right but, more importantly, because it reinforces merchant capital, independent commodity production tends to retard the development of mature industrial capitalism.[47] In the case of the wheat economy, the prairie farmer was interested solely in costs of inputs to the wheat economy and hence disinterested in whether a viable industrial structure was created within Canada.

But timber and lumber were to some extent industries; the old staples created industrialization in their wake; and the new mineral staples are explicitly industries. Commodity producers are a declining class.[48] We must enquire as to the formation of the working class.

This is a critical matter neglected by Innis and thus far by Naylor. In spite of a considerable and growing literature on the history of labour, the analytical relationship between the evolution of the working class and the imperatives of staple production has yet to be definitively worked out—and this paper is not the place to attempt it.

The basic characteristics of the process were set out by Pentland some time ago:[49]

> The production for export of staples drawn from an extensive area, usually a seasonal activity in Canada, and one subject to abrupt changes in prices and profitability, is quite unfavourable to the formation of a capitalistic labour market. It is the integration of an economy—the growth of manufactures, of cities, of a home market—that provides the concentration and balance of demand for it. Construction of the transportation facilities that integrated the Canadian economy produced transitional conditions, in the direction of a domestic product market and a socialized labour market. . . . When completed, the transport systems fostered centralization of production and the growth of cities by welding the country into an economic unit. The railways promoted the growth of particular cities, through the

employment of hundreds and thousands of permanent skilled workers in their extensive shops. . . . Much the same places (Montreal, Toronto, Hamilton and London) benefited from the growth of manufactures, now supported by a coherent domestic market, fostered by a new technical *milieu* and encouraged by some explicit protection after 1858. Early manufactures depended heavily on craftsmanship, but factory production based on machinery and unskilled labour and mass demand was a feature of the 1860s [456-57].

Pentland argues as well that the raw material of the labour market came via the immigrant stream, and that this was the case both for the unskilled and the skilled.

Many of the immigrants, moreover, were highly responsive to market incentives. But this fact produced a new hazard. The more capitalist-minded the immigrants, the more determined they were to be farm proprietors rather than wage-earners. . . . It was just such a rejection of wage employment that inspired Edward Gibbon Wakefield, in the interest of capitalist development to demand new barriers to the ownership of land.

Teeple has subsequently argued[50] that, in fact, a glut of landless labour existed in British North America by 1820, a situation he attributes not only to monopolizing land policies —an historically well-recognized phenomenon—but also, following Naylor to "the lack of industrial growth due to the presence of a mercantile ruling class" (45).

In general, Pentland, from our present perspective, veered more to a Ryersonian than Naylorian view of industrialization, so we need to be on our guard. And beyond the question of class structure lies the complex matter of the nature of the labour movement, and of not only its class consciousness but also its national consciousness. Canada's dependent trade unionism has been much discussed in the literature, and the rationale and consequences have been ably stated by Robert H. Babcock in particular.[51]

American craft unions first invaded British North America during the middle of the nineteenth century. Older, larger, and richer than their Canadian counterparts, they were welcomed by Canadian workers who sought strike support and insurance benefits of a kind unavailable to them elsewhere. American unions willingly lent such help in order to organize the Canadian segment of a new continental product and labour market which developed at mid-century. The unions wanted to protect generally superior American wage levels and working conditions from the deteriorating effects of cheaper labour.

. . . The international craft unions brought to Canada structural characteristics and policy predilections that were products of the American environment. Craft-union organization, short-term economic goals, apolitical unionism, and the pursuit of monopoly developed within the AFL. . . . [A] new impulse soon changed the rationale if not the direction of AFL policy. . . . American businessmen, seeking new markets and raw materials, turned their attention to Canada. American capital and technology began to flow northward on an unprecedented scale. . . . American branch plants flourished. . . . All these new developments seemed to demand a comparable expansion by the America labour movement into Canada. Gompers and his colleagues decided that it had become absolutely essential for them to organize Canadian workers in order to protect the North American labour and product market. . . . The structure and policies of the American Federation of Labour exerted a powerful influence upon the Canadian labour movement. . . . [T]he AFL operated as a divisive force when the Trades and Labour Congress was transformed from a body unifying Canadian unionists into an arm of the international crafts. In a country wracked if not wrecked by regionalism, the loss of a truly national labour institution was doubtless unfortunate. The evidence suggests that Gompers and Morrison [AFL secretary] retarded the growth of a movement linking trade unions with moderate socialist policies. . . . Still, wages and working conditions might well be less satisfactory in Canada had not the international unions exerted a constant pressure upon Canadian industry to match American standards [210-16].

The full analytical relationship between dependent trade unionism and staple production needs to be pulled together from the literature. A critical aspect of this is the tendency of international unionism, directly in its own right and indirectly through its control of the New Democratic Party, to constrain Canadian nationalism and hence the potential for restructuring the Canadian economy away from its staple bias.[52]

Finally, in the process of doing all this, it would become apparent that staple production in Canada has not only generated economic growth—as emphasized by mainstream writers—but has also generated social disturbances (such as protest movements) and social rigidities (regional disparities and the social costs of regional underdevelopment).

* * *

In conclusion, then, there are clearly two liberal versions of the staple theory and one certainly, and perhaps two, Marxist versions. The continuing viability of the two dependent versions, one liberal and one Marxist and both owing much to Innis, augurs well for future work. In his one truly perceptive observation, MacDonald writes that Naylor has "synthesized, in an unprecedented way, radical and nationalist themes in Canadian economic thought" (265), but he errs in his grasp of the analytical, or methodological, respectability of that "thought"—as I hope this paper has demostrated.

Finally, here are some suggestions as to the directions in which future research might go. There is always a need for serious theoretical work; specifically, Naylor's thesis might be re-examined in conjunction with Kay's masterful treatise,[53] where the dichotomy between merchant and industrial capital, and the consequences, in his case, for the nature of Third World underdevelopment, also figures so prominently. There can, of course, be no substitute for the detailed historical writing needed to expose the pervasive and peculiar impact of each particular staple; notwithstanding Innis' *Settlement and the Mining Frontier*, some of Aitken's writings, and now Nelles' very important contribution, the new staples, of mining and oil and gas, still await definitive analysis. As previously suggested, the impact of staple production on the working class, both in terms of its existence as a class and its consciousness of its existence, is in need of sustained analysis. Finally, the staple theory is so specifically Canadian in origin and development, and yet so apparently applicable to other new countries, as to make it highly probable that its application elsewhere in a comparative context would be beneficial to its continuing utility in Canadian studies.

* This is a revised version of a paper presented to the Annual meeting of the Canadian Political Science Association, Quebec City, May 30, 1976; I am indebted to A. Rotstein, R.T. Naylor and D. Drache for helpful comments on earlier drafts. I have also benefitted from reading Roy T. Bowles, "The Staples School of Canadian History and the Sociological Analysis of Canadian Society," paper presented to the Canadian Sociology and Anthropology Association, Annual Meeting, Quebec City, 1976.

NOTES

[1]M.H. Watkins, "A Staple Theory of Economic Growth," *Canadian Journal of Economics and Political Science*, XXIX (May, 1963), 141-58; reprinted in W.T. Easterbrook and M.H. Watkins (eds.), *Approaches to Canadian Economic History* (Toronto, 1967), 49-73.

[2]I have previously revisited the theory, albeit less explicitly and analytically, in "Resources and Underdevelopment" in Robert Laxer (ed.), *(Canada) Ltd: The Political Economy of Dependency* (Toronto, 1973); and "Economic Development in Canada" in Immanuel Wallerstein (ed.), *World Inequality: Origins and Perspectives on the World System* (Montreal, 1976).

[3]Beyond that considerable constraint, I have further defined analytical interest in such a way as to exclude writings which are explicitly analytical but use what might be called an institutional approach; with respect to the latter I have in mind the important, albeit different, institutional writings of W.T. Easterbrook and Abraham Rotstein.

[4]One response to my 1963 paper by Innisians was that it emasculated Innis. Such people may object even more strenuously to the suggestion that Innis should now be translated explicitly into the Marxist paradigm. But there are only two paradigms, and translating into both is in order.

[5]See Daniel Drache, "Harold Innis: A Canadian Nationalist," *Journal of Canadian Studies*, IV (May, 1969), 7-12. Only last year at these meetings Drache gave an overview of the literature around the staples approach, and he cast his net much wider than mine; see his "Rediscovering Canadian Political Economy," *Journal of Canadian Studies*, XI (August, 1976), 3-18. On the narrower analytical front, see his "Canadian Capitalism: Sticking with Staples," *This Magazine* (July-August, 1975). In general, *This Magazine* has emerged as the most important forum for discussions of Canadian political economy around the theme of the staples approach.

[6]Gordon W. Bertram, "Economic Growth and Canadian Industry, 1870-1915: The Staple Model and the 'Take-Off Hypothesis,' " *CJEPS*, XXIX (May, 1963), 162-84, reprinted as "Economic Growth in Canadian Industry, 1870-1915: The Staple Model" in *Approaches to Canadian Economic History*; "The Relevance of the Wheat Boom in Canadian Economic Growth," *Canadian Journal of Economics*, VI (November, 1973).

[7]Richard E. Caves, " 'Vent for Surplus' Models of Trade and Growth" in *Trade, Growth and the Balance of Payments: Essays in Honour of Gottfried Haberler (Chicago, 1965)*; "Export-Led Growth and the New Economic History" in Jagdish N. Bhagwati et. al. (eds.), *Trade, Balance of Payments and Growth: Papers in International Economics in Honor of Charles P. Kindleberger* (Amsterdam, 1971).

[8]E.J. Chambers and D.F. Gordon, "Primary Products and Economic Growth: An Empirical Measurement," *Journal of Political Economy*, LXXIV (1966), 315-32.

[9]The second articles of both Bertram and Caves are responses thereto; see also J.H. Dales, J.C. McManus and M.H. Watkins, "Primary Products and Economic Growth: A Comment," *JPE* (December, 1967), and Edward Vickery, "Exports and North American Economic Growth: 'Structuralist' and 'Staple' models in historical Perspective," *CJE*, VII (February, 1974).

[10]"Rediscovering Canadian Political Economy."

[11]So too do some prominent Canadian historians. The sub-title of Craig Brown and Ramsay Cooks' *Canada 1896-1921* is *A Nation Transformed*, thereby begging two questions. Certainly Innis and Creighton raise doubts as to the extent of nationhood from anything but a narrow juridical perspective, and Caves and Holton demonstrated very effectively some time ago that there was no discontinuity in this period that would justify the use of the word "transformed": see Richard E. Caves and Richard H. Holton, *The Canadian Economy: Prospect and Retrospect* (Cambridge, Mass., 1959). Yet Margaret Prang says that the sub-title of the book "could scarcely be more aptly chosen" (*Canadian Forum*, October, 1974).

[12]L.R. MacDonald, "Merchants against Industry: An Idea and its Origins," *Canadian Historical Review*, LVI (September, 1975), which is a critique of R.T. Naylor, "The Rise and Fall of the Third Commercial Empire of the St. Lawrence" in Gary Teeple (ed.), *Capitalism and the National Question in Canada* (Toronto, 1972), 1-41.

[13]R.E. Baldwin, "Patterns of Development in Newly Settled Regions," *Manchester School of Economic and Social Studies* (May, 1956), which was central to the analysis of my 1963 paper; see also his "Export Technology and Development from a Subsistence Level," *Economic Journal* (March, 1963).

[14]Paul A. Samuelson and Anthony Scott, *Economics*, Fourth Canadian Edition (1975), 679.

[15]A.E. Safarian, *Foreign Ownership of Canadian Industry* (Toronto, 1966).

[16]Canada, Privy Council, *Foreign Ownership and the Structure of Canadian Industry* (Ottawa, 1968).

[17]Canada, *Foreign Direct Investment in Canada* (Ottawa, 1972).

[18]Kari Levitt, *Silent Surrender: The Multinational Corporation in Canada* (Toronto, 1970).

[19]R.T. Naylor, *The History of Canadian Business 1867-1914*, Vols. I & II (Toronto, 1975).

[20]H.A. Innis, *The Fur Trade in Canada: An Introduction to Canadian Economic History* (Toronto, 1930: 2nd. ed, 1956), 385.

[21]*The History of Canadian Business*, I, 56-7.

[22]Pierre L. Bourgault, *Innovation and the Structure of Canadian Industry*, Science Council of Canada, Special Study No. 23 (Ottawa, 1972).

[23]Eric Kierans, *Report on Natural Resources Policy in Manitoba* (Manitoba, 1973).

[24]Northrop Frye observed in his Images of Canada television special (CBC 1976) that "Canada is full of ghost towns: visible ruins unparalleled in Europe." Bourgault goes so far as to suggest that this could happen to the whole country; he observes that Canada is becoming increasingly reliant on staple exports and that if we keep on this path "Before the children of today could reach middle age most of the resources would be gone, leaving Canada with a resource-based economy and no resources" (126).

[25]See Russ Rothney and Steve Watson, "A Brief Economic History of Northern Manitoba" (mimeo, July, 1975). They define underdevelopment as "Blockage of potential, sustained economic and social development geared to local human needs. In other words, the process by which economical and cultural leverage is taken or kept from the people of a region" (iii). They insist on the need to pay attention to "restrictions on local social and economic development generated by institutional processes of surplus extraction in the region. These processes hinge upon specific relations between social-economic classes and between commercial metropoles and their economic hinterlands."

[26]H.V. Nelles, *The Politics of Development: Forest, Mines and Hydro-electric Power in Ontario, 1849-1941* (Toronto, 1974).

[27]E.E. Rich, *Hudson's Bay Company, 1670-1870*, 2 vols. (London, 1958-1959).

[28]Morris Zaslow, *The Opening of the Canadian North 1870-1914* (Toronto, 1971).

[29]K.J. Rea, *The Political Economy of the Canadian North* (Toronto, 1968) and *The Political Economy of Northern Development*, Science Council of Canada Background Study No. 36 (Ottawa, 1976).

[30]*The Political Economy of Northern Development*, 39.

[31]Rene Fumoleau, OMI, *As Long as this Land Shall Last, A History of Treaty 8 and Treaty 11, 1870-1939* (Toronto, 1975). Fumoleau shows how the gold rush into the Klondike led to the signing of Treaty 8 in 1899 while Imperial Oil's discovery of oil near Fort Norman led to the signing of Treaty 11 in 1921; it would be difficult to find a clearer case of Government policy as a response to the needs of staple producers.

[32]Michael Asch, "Past and Present Land-Use by Slavery Indians of the Mackenzie District," Evidence before the Mackenzie Valley Pipeline Inquiry (April 1976).

[33]Arvin Jelliss h as done detailed rent calculations for the producing mines of the Mackenzie District, the Imperial Oil Refinery at Norman Wells and the Pointed Mountain gas development; see in particular his "Natural Resources Projects, Economic Rents, and Problems of Native Peoples' Development in the Mackenzie District," *ibid*, (June, 1976). See also my "Resource Exploitation and Economic Underdevelopment on Dene Land," *ibid.* (June 1976) and Peter Puxley "Colonialism or Development?: The Meaning of Development," *ibid.* (June 1976).

[34]It is not my intention to classify people in a manner that may in any way be unacceptable to them. Whether or not availing oneself of the Marxist paradigm makes one a Marxist in any other sense is not relevant to scholarship. We now have it on the authority of Paul Samuelson that we all have something to gain from the use of Marxis analysis; see the most recent edition of *Economics*.

[35]See also Bruce Archibald, "Atlantic Regional Under-Development and Socialism" in Laurier LaPierre *et. al.* (eds.), *Essays on the Left* (Toronto, 1971).

[36]Stanley Ryerson, *Unequal Union* (Toronto, 1968).

[37]For evidence on the significant level of American Control of the Canadian Economy by World War I, see Glen Williams, "Canadian Industrialization: We Ain't Growin' Nowhere," *This Magazine* (March-April 1975), and Tom Naylor "Commentary" on Simon Rosenblum, "Economic Nationalism and the English-Canadian Socialist Movement," *Our Generation*, 11 (Fall 1975), 20-1.

[38]MacDonald writes "Possibly the origin of the branch plant should be sought not in industry but in trade: from a management standpoint it was the application to manufacturing of the organizational principles of a commercial branch of a trading company" (269). It is difficult to say other than that this flies in the face of virtually all known literature on the multinational corporation; see particularly the writings of the late Stephen Hymer, who made signal contributions successively to both the liberal and Marxist analysis of foreign ownership.

[39]Wallace Clement, *The Canadian Corporate Elite: An Analysis of Economic Power* (Toronto, 1975).

[40]At the same CPSA session at which this paper was presented, Clement reported on his further researches based on his recently-completed doctoral thesis. Clement appears now to be closer to Naylor; in any event, his important work needs much more extensive consideration than is possible here.

[41]See my "The 'American System' and Canada's National Policy," *Bulletin of the Canadian Association of American Studies* (Winter 1967).

[42]Alfred Dubuc, "The Decline of Confederation and the New Nationalism" in Peter Russell (ed.), *Nationalism in Canada* (Toronto, 1966).

[43]This is a point that became very evident to this writer on reading the chapters in Nelles on the nickel industry; see my "Economic Development in Canada." On the subsidies to capital formation under foreign control in the period 1945-1957, and their apparent success in leading to a quantum leap in American ownership of the Canadian economy, see David Wolfe, *Political Culture, Economic Policy and the Growth of Foreign Involvement in Canada, 1945 to 1957,* M.A. Thesis, Carleton University (1973).

[44]*The Fur Trade in Canada* (1956), 383, 401.

[45]Peter Douglas Elias, *Metropolis and Hinterland in Northern Manitoba* (Manitoba, 1975), 2. Elias characterizes native people as "a totally pauperized class," "permanent state-supported class" and as being "at the absolute fringe of industrial capitalist society" (8).

[46]Hugh Brody, *The People's Land: Eskimos and Whites in the Eastern Arctic* (London, 1975), 229. On tendencies toward the emergence of a class structure along ethnic lines in the more "impacted" Western Arctic, see the writings of Peter Usher, in particular "Geographers and Northern Development: Some Social and Political Considerations," *Alternatives* (Autumn 1974) and "The Class System, Metropolitan Dominance and Northern Development," paper presented to the Canadian Association of Geographers, Vancouver, 1975.

[47]See *Monthly Review* (May 1976) for an exchange between Robert Sherry and James O'Connor on independent commodity production in early America.

[48]This is a major theme of Leo A. Johnson, "The development of class in Canada in the twentieth century" in *Capitalism and the National Question in Canada*. On the nature of Canada's capitalist class and the general issues of Canadian dependency, however, Johnson's views are confused and unreliable. At best, there is an apparent tendency to agree with everyone. At worst, there is a willingness to endorse utterly useless sectarian scribbling; on the latter, see his effusive "Introduction" to Steve Moore and Debi Wells, *Imperialism and the National Question in Canada* (Toronto, 1975) and compare with the devas-

tating critiques of the book by Ian lumsden in *This Magazine* (Nov.-Dec. 1975) and Jack Warnick in *Canadian Dimension* (March, 1976).

[49]H.C. Pentland, "The Development of a Capitalistic Labour Market in Canada," *CJEPS*, 25 (November 1959), 450-61; for a fuller statement see his *Labour and the Development of Industrial Capitalism in Canada*, Ph. D. Thesis, University of Toronto (1960) which is still–incredibly–unpublished. Pentland deserves great credit for working within the Marxist paradigm when it was distinctly unusual to do so, and the tendency for his work to be ignored by the mainstream of Canadian economic historians–including myself in the 1963 article–tells us much about the limitations of orthodox economics as it impinges on economic history.

[50]Gary Teeple, "Land, labour and capital in pre-Confederation Canada," in *Capitalism and the National Question in Canada.*

[51]Robert H. Babcock, *Gompers in Canada: A Study in American Continentalism Before the First World War* (Toronto, 1974). See also Charles Lipton, *The Trade Union Movement in Canada 1827-1959* (Montreal, 1967); I.M. Abella, *Nationalism, Communism and Canadian Labour: The CIO, the Communist party and the Canadian Congress of Labour 1935-1956* (Toronto, 1973); and the essays by Roger Howard and Jack Scott, R.B. Morris, and Lipton in *Capitalism and the National Question in Canada.*

[52]James Laxer's "Introduction to the Political Economy of Canada," *(Canada) Ltd.*, 37-40, is particularly suggestive.

[53]Geoffrey Kay, *Development and Underdevelopment: A Marxist Analysis* (London, 1975).

POSTSCRIPT

It was stated in the General Introduction that this volume was put together to provide undergraduate students and their instructors materials on Canada written from a Marxist perspective. It was also stated that while there are a number of current debates taking place among Marxist scholars, these would not be emphasized. After covering the material presented in this book, however, the reader may now be ready to examine more works on Canada written from a Marxist perspective.

A good way in which to begin this inquiry is to obtain a copy of Wallace Clement et al. (eds.), *A Practical Guide to Canadian Political Economy*, Toronto: James Lorimer and Company, 1978. This bibliography includes 1500 items organized topically germane to the study of Canadian political economy. A number of these works are written from a Marxist perspective. To those who are interested in some of the ongoing debates in which Canadian Marxists have been involved, a book edited by Daniel Drache entitled, *Debates and Controversies from This Magazine*, Toronto: McClelland and Stewart, 1979, might prove useful as a starting point.

REFERENCES TO SECTION INTRODUCTIONS

GENERAL INTRODUCTION

Althusser, Louis. *Reading Capital.* New York: Panthenon Books. 1971a.
_____. *Lenin and Philosophy and Other Essays.* London: NLB. 1971b.
Bergeron, Léandre. *The History of Quebec.* Toronto: New Press. 1971.
Brym, R. and R.J. Sacouman (eds.). *Underdevelopment and Social Movements in Atlantic Canada.* Toronto: New Hogtown Press. 1979.
Clement, Wallace. *The Canadian Corporate Elite.* Toronto: McClelland and Stewart. 1975.
_____. *Continental Corporate Power.* Toronto: McClelland and Stewart. 1977.
Foster-Carter, Aidan. "The Modes of Production Controversy," *New Left Review.* 107. 1978.
Fournier, Pierre. *The Quebec Establishment.* Montreal: Black Rose Books. 1976.
Gold, David A. et al. "Recent Developments in Marxist Theories of the Capitalist State," *Monthly Review* 27:5. 1975.
Jalée, Pierre. *How Capitalism Works.* New York: Monthly Review Press. 1977.
Laclau, Ernesto. *Politics and Ideology in Marxist Theory* London: NLB. 1977.
Lumsden, Ian (ed.). *Close the 49th Parallel.* Toronto: University of Toronto Press. 1970.
Macpherson, C.B. *Democracy in Alberta.* Toronto: University of Toronto Press. 1953.
Mandel, Ernest. *Capitalism and Regional Disparities.* Toronto: New Hogtown Press. 1973.
_____. *An Introduction to Marxist Economic Theory.* New York: Pathfinder Press. 1976.
Marx, Karl. *A Contribution to the Critique of Political Economy.* Quoted in T.B. Bottomore (ed.), *Karl Marx.* Toronto: McGraw Hill. 1858/1964.
Miliband, Ralph. *The State in Capitalist Society.* London: Weidenfeld and Nicholson. 1969.
_____. *Marxism and Politics.* Oxford: Oxford University Press. 1977.
Naylor, R.T. *The History of Canadian Business, 1867-1914,* Vols. 1&2. Toronto: Lorimer. 1975.
Newman, Peter. *The Canadian Establishment.* Toronto: McClelland and Stewart. 1975.
O'Connor, James. *The Fiscal Crisis of the State.* New York: St. Martin's Press. 1973.
Olsen, Denis. "The State Elites," in Leo Panitch (ed.), *The Canadian State.* Toronto: University of Toronto Press. 1977.
Panitch, Leo (ed.). *The Canadian State: Political Economy and Political Power.* Toronto: University of Toronto Press. 1977.
Pentland, H.C. "The Development of a Capitalistic Labour Market in Canada," *Canadian Journal of Economics and Political Science.* 12:4. 1959.
Porter, John. *The Vertical Mosaic.* Toronto: University of Toronto Press. 1965.
Poulantzas, Nicos. *Classes in Contemporary Capitalism.* London: Verso. 1978.
Pratt, Larry. *The Tar Sands.* Edmonton: Hurtig. 1976.
Resnick, Philip. *The Land of Cain.* Vancouver: New Star Books. 1977.
Rioux, Marcel. *Quebec in Question.* Toronto: James, Lewis and Samuel. 1971.
Ryerson, Stanley. *Unequal Union.* Toronto: Progress Books. 1968.
Teeple, G. (ed). *Capitalism and the National Question in Canada.* Toronto: University of Toronto Press. 1972.
Williams, Raymond. *Marxism and Literature.* Oxford: Oxford University Press. 1977.

CLASS

Bercuson, David J. *Fools and Wise Men*. Toronto: McGraw-Hill Ryerson. 1978.

Bliss, Michael "Review of R.T. Naylor,"*The History of Canadian Business, 1867-1914*, Vols. 1 and 2. *Social History*, 9:1. 1976.

Clark, S.D. *Church and Sect in Canada*. Toronto: University of Toronto Press. 1948.

Clement, Wallace *Continental Corporate Power*. Toronto: McClelland and Stewart. 1977.

Conway, J.F. "Populism in the United States, Russia and Canada: Explaining the Roots of Canada's Third Parties," *Canadian Journal of Political Science*, 11:1. 1978.

Drache, D. "Rediscovering Canadian Political Economy," in Wallace Clement et al. (eds.), *A Pratical Guide to Canadian Political Economy*. Toronto: Lorimer. 1978.

Drummond, I. "Review of R.T. Naylor,"*The History of Canadian Business, 1867-1914*, Vols. 1 and 2," *Canadian Historical Review*, 59:1. 1978.

Hedley, Max J. "Independent Commodity Production and the Dynamics of Tradition," *Canadian Review of Sociology and Anthropology*, 13:4. 1976.

Johnson, Leo "The Development of Class in the Twentieth Century," in G. Teeple (ed.), *Capitalism and the National Question in Canada*. Toronto: University of Toronto Press. 1972.

MacDonald, Larry "Merchants Against Industry," *Canadian Historical Review*, 56:3. 1975.

MacPherson, C.B. *Democracy in Alberta*. Toronto: University of Toronto Press. 1953.

Naylor, R.T. *The History of Canadian Business, 1867-1914*, Vols. 1 and 2. Toronto: Lorimer. 1975.

Pentland, H.C. "The Development of a Capitalistic Labour Market in Canada," *Canadian Journal of Economics and Political Science*, 25:4. 1959.

Resnick, Philip *The Land of Cain*. Vancouver: New Star Books. 1977.

Statistics Canada *Perpectives Canada*. 1974.

STATE

Aitken, Hugh. "Defensive Expansionism: The State and Economic Growth in Canada," in W.T. Easterbrook et al. (eds.), *Approaches to Canadian Economic History*. Toronto: McClelland and Stewart. 1967.

Ames, H.B. *The City Below the Hill*. Toronto: University of Toronto Press. 1972.

Armstrong, C. and Nelles, V. "Private Property in Peril: Ontario Businessmen and the Federal System," in G. Porter et al. (eds.), *Enterprise and National Development*. Toronto: Hakkert. 1973.

Berry, G.R. "The Oil Lobby and the Energy Crisis," in K.J. Rea et al. (eds.), *Business and Government in Canada*. Toronto: Methuen. 1976.

Berton, Pierre. *The National Dream*. Toronto: McClelland and Stewart. 1970.

Clark, S.D. "The Post Second World War Canadian Society," *Canadian Review of Sociology and Anthropology*, 12:1. 1975.

Kilbourn, W. *Pipeline*. Toronto: Clarke Irwin. 1970.

Litvak, I.A. and Maule, J. "Interest Group Tactics and the Politics of Foreign Investment: The Time Reader's Digest Case Study," *Canadian Journal of Political Science*, 7:4. 1974.

Naylor, R.T. *The History of Canadian Business, 1867-1914*, Vols. 1 and 2. Toronto: Lorimer. 1975.

Nelles, V. *The Politics of Development*. Toronto: Macmillan. 1974.

Pratt, Larry. *The Tar Sands*. Edmonton: Hurtig. 1976.

Resnick, Philip. *The Land of Cain*. Vancouver: New Star Books. 1977.

Stevenson, Garth. "Federalism and the Political Economy of the Canadian State," in Leo Panitch (ed.), *The Canadian State*. Toronto: University of Toronto Press. 1977.

Woodsworth, J.S. *My Neighbour*. Toronto: University of Toronto Press. 1972.

IDEOLOGY

Aitken, Hugh."Defensive Expansionism: The State and Economic Growth in Canada," in W.T. Easter-brook et al. (eds.), *Approaches to Canadian Economic History*. Toronto: McClelland and Stewart. 1967.

Clark, S.D. *Movements of Political Protest in Canada*. Toronto: University of Toronto Press. 1959.

Creighton, Donald. *The Empire of the St. Lawrence*. Toronto: Macmillan. 1956.

Hartz, Louis.*The Founding of New Societies*. New York: Harcourt, Brace and World. 1964.

Horowitz, Gad."Conservatism, Liberalism and Socialism in Canada," *Canadian Journal of Economics and Political Science*, 32. 1966.

_____. *Canadian Labour in Politics*. Toronto: University of Toronto Press. 1968.

Irving, John.*The Social Credit Movement in Alberta*. Toronto: University of Toronto Press. 1959.

Lipset, S.M. *Agrarian Socialism*. Berkeley: University of California Press. 1950.

_____.*Revolution and Counter-Revolution*. Garden City: Doubleday. 1970.

Lord, Barry. *The History of Painting in Canada: Toward a People's Art*. Toronto: NC Press. 1974.

Macpherson, C.B. *Democracy in Alberta*. Toronto: University of Toronto Press. 1953.

Morton, W.L. *The Progressive Party in Canada*. Toronto: University of Toronto Press. 1950.

Ryerson, Stanley.*Unequal Union*. Toronto: Progress Books. 1968.

Sharp, Paul.*The Agrarian Revolt in Western Canada*. Minneapolis: University of Minnesota Press. 1948.

Truman, Tom."A Critique of S.M. Lipset's Article, 'Value Differences, Absolute or Relative: The English Speaking Democracies,' " *Canadian Journal of Political Science*, 4:4. 1971.

Watt, F.W. *Radicalism in English Canadian Literature Since Confederation*. Ph.D. thesis, University of Toronto. 1957.

Wood, L.A. *A History of Farmers' Movements in Canada*. Toronto: University of Toronto Press. 1975.

Young, Walter. *The Anatomy of a Party*. Toronto: University of Toronto Press. 1969.

CHANGE

Forbes, E.R. "The Origins of the Maritime Rights Movement," *Acadiensis*, 5:1. 1975.

MARXISM AND CANADIAN POLITICAL ECONOMY

Clark, S.D. *The Developing Canadian Community*. Toronto: University of Toronto Press. 1968.

_____.*Canadian Society in Historical Perspective*, Toronto: McGraw-Hill Ryerson. 1976.

Clement, Wallace, and Drache, Daniel. *A Practical Guide to Canadian Political Economy*, Toronto: Lorimer. 1978.

Creighton, Donald.*The Empire of the St. Lawrence*. Toronto: Macmillan. 1970.

Fowke, V.C. *The National Policy and the Wheat Economy*, Toronto: University of Toronto Press. 1957.

Hiller, H. "The Canadian Sociology Movement: Analysis and Assessment," *Canadian Journal of Sociology*, 4:2. 1979.

Hodgetts, A.B. *What Culture? What Heritage?* Toronto: OISE. 1968.

Hurtig, Mel.*Never Heard of Them . . . They Must be Canadian*. Toronto: Canadabooks. 1975.

Innis, H.A. *Fur Trade in Canada: An Introduction to Canadian Economic History*. Toronto: University of Toronto Press. 1956.

_____.*Settlement and the Mining Frontier*. Toronto: Macmillan. 1936.

_____. *The Cod Fisheries*. (rev. ed.) Toronto: University of Toronto Press. 1954.

Lamy, Paul."The Globalization of American Sociology: Excellence or Imperialism," *The American Sociologist*, 2. 1976.

Lower, A.R.M. *Settlement of the Forest Frontier in Eastern Canada*. Toronto: Macmillan. 1936.

Mathews, Robin and Steele, James.*The Struggle for Canadian Universities*. Toronto: New Press. 1969.

Nelles, V. *The Politics of Development*. Toronto: Macmillan. 1974.

Pratt, Larry.*The Tar Sands*. Edmonton: Hurtig. 1976.

Resnick, Philip.*The Land of Cain*. Vancouver: New Star Books. 1977.

Symons, T.B.H. *To Know Ourselves*. Ottawa: AUCC. 1975.

Watkins, Mel."A Staple Theory of Economic Growth," In W.T. Easterbrook et al. (eds.), *Approaches to Canadian Economic History*. Toronto: McClelland and Stewart. 1967.